THE WORKS OF
GEORGE FARQUHAR

George Farquhar was the most popular and perhaps the best playwright to grace the stage at the turn of the eighteenth century, and he dominated the repertory for the next fifty years. The Irish-born actor and military officer arrived in London before he was twenty, captivated audiences with his lively, good-natured comedy, philandered with the leading actresses and female playwrights, married a widow with children, and wrote, besides the eight plays, many poems, letters, prologues, and epilogues, an epic, and a miscellany—all before his untimely death in 1707, when he had not yet turned thirty.

Shirley Strum Kenny has provided the first scholarly edition of the works since Stonehill's edition of 1930, in a reliable old-spelling text. She has added to the canon materials not printed since the beginning of the eighteenth century, some of which have never before been identified as Farquhar's.

Each play has an introduction describing its sources and composition, theatrical and publication history, influence, and textual problems. The introductions of the non-dramatic works contain similar information and relate the works to the contemporary events which occasioned them. Questions of authorship for newly identified works and possible or doubtful attributions are carefully considered.

Professor Kenny is President of Queen's College, Flushing, New York, and editor of *The Plays of Richard Steele*, among other books.

Tantum de medio Sumptis accedit honoris.

Ben Jonson presenting George Farquhar to Apollo. Frontispiece, *The Comedies of George Farquhar*, [1711]. By permission of the Folger Shakespeare Library.

THE WORKS OF GEORGE FARQUHAR

EDITED IN TWO VOLUMES BY
SHIRLEY STRUM KENNY

VOLUME I

CLARENDON PRESS · OXFORD
1988

Oxford University Press, Walton Street, Oxford OX2 6DP

Oxford New York Toronto
Delhi Bombay Calcutta Madras Karachi
Petaling Jaya Singapore Hong Kong Tokyo
Nairobi Dar es Salaam Cape Town
Melbourne Auckland
and associated companies in
Berlin Ibadan

Oxford is a trade mark of Oxford University Press

Published in the United States
by Oxford University Press, New York

© Oxford University Press, 1988

British Library Cataloguing in Publication Data
Farquhar, George
The works of George Farquhar.
I. Title.   II. Kenny, Shirley Strum
822'.4 PR3435
ISBN 0–19–811858–9 v.1
ISBN 0–19–812342–6 v.2

Library of Congress Cataloging in Publication Data
Farquhar, George, 1677?–1707.
The works of George Farquhar.
Includes indexes.
1. Kenny, Shirley Strum. II. Title.
PR3435.A5K44 1986 822'.4 85–25942
ISBN 0–19–811858–9 (v. 1)
ISBN 0–19–812342–6 (v. 2)

Set by Hope Services, Abingdon
Printed in Great Britain
at the University Printing House, Oxford
by David Stanford
Printer to the University

For my husband,
    ROBERT W. KENNY
and for our children,
    DAVID,
        JOEL,
            DANNY,
                JONATHAN,
                    and
                    SARAH

. . . Mr. *Farquhar* had a Genius for Comedy, of which one may say, that it was rather above Rules than below them. His *Conduct*, tho not *Artful*, was *surprizing*: his *Characters*, tho not Great, were Just: His Humour, tho *low, diverting*: His *Dialogue*, tho *loose* and *incorrect, gay* and *agreeable*; and his *Wit*, tho not *super-abundant, pleasant*. In a word, his Plays have in the *toute ensemble*, as the Painters phrase it, a certain Air of *Novelty* and *Mirth*, which pleas'd the Audience every time they were represented. . . .

Muses Mercury, May 1707

. . . a man whose writings have considerable merit. . . .

Samuel Johnson, as quoted by James Boswell

Of the four dramatists [Wycherley, Congreve, Vanbrugh, Farquhar]. . . . Farquhar had the highest animal spirits, with fits of the deepest sympathy, the greatest wish to please rather than to strike, the most agreeable diversity of character, the best instinct in avoiding revolting extravagances of the time, and the happiest invention in plot and situation; and, therefore, is to be pronounced, upon the whole, the truest dramatic genius, and the most likely to be of lasting popularity. . . .

Leigh Hunt

ACKNOWLEDGEMENTS

THE years during which I prepared *The Works of George Farquhar* have produced a rich harvest of scholarship on the theatre of the Restoration and eighteenth century. I am indebted to many scholars for their published work and especially grateful to some for their generous and knowledgeable personal assistance. Arthur Friedman, Fredson T. Bowers, and Donald F. Bond, my teachers in times past and my admired colleagues, provide models to all who aspire to edit; they also provided me particularly with help on problems in the edition of Farquhar. My colleagues in the field of Restoration and eighteenth-century theatre were, as always, incredibly knowledgeable and exceedingly generous in their assistance. Philip H. Highfill, Jr., Kalman A. Burnim, and Edward A. Langhans provided early access to the files and manuscript of the *Biographical Dictionary of Actors, Actresses, Musicians, Dancers, Managers and Other Stage Personnel in London, 1600–1800*. Calhoun Winton, Robert D. Hume, David Mann, Leo Hughes, Giles E. Dawson, Gwin J. Kolb, Cecil Price, Curtis A. Price, Joseph Donohue, Charles C. Mish, Judith Milhous, Steve Ackerman, E. Eugene Helm, Robert J. Rowland, and Albert Wertheim have all afforded me special insights and assistance. To have the double pleasure of working on a playwright as enjoyable as Farquhar and working with colleagues of such remarkable knowledge and collegiality has made this undertaking particularly gratifying.

Four research assistants have performed excellent work. James May checked my collations of the texts carefully and well. Barbara Graves found many military records concerning the battle of Barcelona. Linda Merians, who, by the end of the project, was as engulfed in it as I, did impressive and intensive detective work and unearthed some seemingly inaccessible information for the commentaries. Michael Selmon helped in the final stages.

The typing of such a lengthy manuscript was no ordinary task. I wish to thank Molly Emler, Dorothy Zachman, Eileen

Moye, Adele DiDio, Joan Bishop, Joan Wood, Joan Vincent, and especially Erlinda Gatbonton for their roles in preparation of the manuscript.

A Guggenheim Fellowship greatly aided me in the completion of my work, and grants from the Graduate Research Board of the University of Maryland gave me additional support to pursue the project. Librarians at the Folger Shakespeare Library, the British Library, the Bodleian, Huntington, Clark, University of Texas, University of Pennsylvania, Harvard, and many other institutions have been gracious in allowing me access to their collections. In particular I am grateful to the librarians at the Folger, Sandy Powers and many others, for their patience with my gargantuan appetite for eighteenth-century books.

Finally I want to thank my family for their help. My husband, Robert W. Kenny, as always, shared his knowledge of the history of the period and criticized portions of the manuscript. My mother, Florence Strum, helped with the acquisition of data on theatrical history. My father, Marcus L. Strum, cheered us all. My children, David, Joel, Danny, Jonathan, and Sarah, gave me patient—or perhaps tolerant— understanding.

Queen's College   SHIRLEY STRUM KENNY

CONTENTS

VOLUME I

VOLUME II

LIST OF ILLUSTRATIONS

VOLUME I

VOLUME II

ABBREVIATIONS FOR
FREQUENTLY QUOTED SOURCES

Archer | William Archer, ed. *George Farquhar*. Mermaid Series. Rept. London, 1959.

Biographia | *Biographia Dramatica; or a Companion to the*
Dramatica | *Playhouse*, David Erskine Baker (to 1764) and Isaac Reed (to 1782) and Stephen Jones (to 1811). 3 vols., London, 1812.

Biographical Dictionary | Philip H. Highfill, Jr., Kalman A. Burnim, and Edward A. Langhans. *A Biographical Dictionary of Actors, Actresses, Musicians, Dancers, Managers, and Other Stage Personnel in London, 1600–1800*. Carbondale, 1973– .

Churchill | Winston S. Churchill. *Marlborough His Life and Times.* 6 vols. London and New York, 1933–8.

Cibber | Colley Cibber. *An Apology for the Life of Colley Cibber*, ed. B. R. S. Fone. Ann Arbor, 1968.

Cunnington, | C. Willett and Phillis Cunnington, *Handbook*
Eighteenth | *of English Costume in the Eighteenth Century.* London, 1957.

Cunnington, | C. Willett and Phillis Cunnington, *Handbook*
Seventeenth | *of English Costume in the Seventeenth Century.* London, 1955.

Genest | John Genest. *Some Account of the English Stage.* 10 vols. Bath, 1832.

Hume | Robert D. Hume. *The Development of English Drama in the Late Seventeenth Century.* Oxford, 1976.

Hunt | Leigh Hunt, ed. *The Dramatic Works of Wycherley, Congreve, Vanbrugh, and Farquhar.* London, 1840.

James | Eugene Nelson James. *The Development of George Farquhar as a Comic Dramatist.* The Hague, 1972.

Jordan — Robert John Jordan. 'George Farquhar's Military Career', *Huntington Library Quarterly*, 37 (1973–4), 251–64.

Lawrence — W. J. Lawrence, 'The Mystery of "The Stage Coach"', *Modern Language Review*, 27 (1932), 392–7.

London Stage — *The London Stage 1660–1800*, ed. William Van Lennep, Emmett L. Avery, Arthur H. Scouten, G. W. Stone, Jr., and Charles Beecher Hogan, 5 Parts in 11 vols., Carbondale, Ill., 1960–8.

Military Dictionary — *A Military Dictionary Explaining All Difficult Terms in Martial Discipline, Fortification, and Gunnery*. 3rd edn., London, 1708.

Misson — *M. Misson's Memoirs and Observations in his Travels over England*. London, 1719.

NDCC — B. E. Gent. *A New Dictionary of the Terms Ancient and Modern of the Canting Crew*. London, [1690].

N&Q — *Notes and Queries*.

OED — *Oxford English Dictionary*.

Price — Curtis A. Price. *Music in the Restoration Theatre*. Ann Arbor, 1979.

Rothstein — Eric Rothstein. *George Farquhar*. Twayne English Authors Series. New York, 1967.

Scouller — R. E. Scouller. *The Armies of Queen Anne*. Oxford, 1966.

Spectator — *The Spectator*, ed. Donald F. Bond. 5 vols. Oxford, 1965.

Stonehill — Charles Stonehill, ed. *The Complete Works of George Farquhar*. 2 vols. 1930, rept. New York, 1967.

TLS — *Times Literary Supplement*.

Wheatley — Henry B. Wheatley. *London, Past and Present: Its History, Associations, and Traditions*. 3 vols. London, 1891.

Wilkes — *The Works of George Farquhar*. Dublin, 1775.

CHRONOLOGY

1677 (?)		Farquhar born.
1694	17 July	Farquhar matriculated, Trinity College, Dublin, at age 17.
1696–8		Farquhar performed at Smock Alley Theatre.
1698		Farquhar arrived in London (?).
	December (?)	*Love and a Bottle* opened at Drury Lane.
	15 (?) December	*The Adventures of Covent-Garden* published.
	29 December	*Love and a Bottle* published.
1699	Autumn (?)	'An Epilogue, spoken by Mr. Wilks at his first Appearance upon the English Stage' spoken at Drury Lane.
	28 November	First known performance of *The Constant Couple* at Drury Lane.
	11 December	*The Constant Couple* published.
1700	1 February	Second edition of *The Constant Couple* published.
	On or before 19 February	Epilogue to Oldmixon's *The Grove* spoken at Drury Lane.
	11 May	*Familiar and Courtly Letters* published.
	9 July	Prologue to Crauford's *Courtship A-la-Mode* spoken at Drury Lane.
1700	13 July	The New Prologue to *The Constant Couple* spoken at Drury Lane.
	7 August	Farquhar left England for the Netherlands.
	20 August	Third edition of *The Constant Couple* published.
	After 23 October	Farquhar returned to England.
1701	April (?)	*Sir Harry Wildair* opened at Drury Lane.

1701	3 May	Second volume of *Familiar and Courtly Letters* published.
	13 May	*Sir Harry Wildair* published.
	24 July	*Letters of Wit, Politicks and Morality* published.
	?	'A Prologue on the propos'd Union of the Two Houses' spoken.
	22 November	*Love and Business* published.
1701–2	Winter 1701– February 1702	*The Stage-Coach* opened at Lincoln's Inn Fields.
1702	February (?)	*The Inconstant* opened at Drury Lane.
	28 February	Second issue of *Love and Business* published.
	11 March	*The Inconstant* published.
	October–November	Prologue to Manning's *All for the Better* spoken at Drury Lane.
	November–December	Epilogue to Gildon's *The Patriot* spoken at Drury Lane.
	14 December	*The Twin-Rivals* opened at Drury Lane.
	22 December	Lintott bought copyright to it.
	29 December	*The Twin-Rivals* published.
1703 (?)		Farquhar married Margaret Pemell.
1704		Fourth edition of *The Constant Couple* published. *The Stage-Coach* published in Dublin.
	March (?)	Farquhar became a recruiting officer.
	14 June– 20 October (?)	Farquhar served on recruiting duty, perhaps in Shrewsbury.
1704–5	October 1704– July 1705	Farquhar continued military service in Ireland.
	Between 15 November and 10 April (probably in March)	Benefit performance of *The Constant Couple* given in Dublin, with Farquhar as Sir Harry Wildair.
1705	3 or 4 May	*The Stage-Coach* published in London.

1705	12 June–10 July	Farquhar's regiment at encampment at the Curragh of Kildare.
	27 July	Farquhar sat in judgment at court martial in Dublin Castle.
	After August–before November	Farquhar departed Dublin, perhaps recruited in Lichfield.
1706	12 February	Lintott bought copyright to *The Recruiting Officer*.
	Before 1 March	Farquhar left his regiment.
	8 April	*The Recruiting Officer* opened at the Queen's Theatre in the Haymarket.
	25 April (or shortly before)	*The Recruiting Officer* published.
	15 October	'The Prologue Spoken by Mr. Wilks, At the Opening of the Theatre in the Hay Market' spoken.
	26 October	Second edition of *The Recuiting Officer* published.
	25 November	Prologue to Centlivre's *The Platonick Lady* spoken at the Queen's Theatre in the Haymarket.
	6 December	Third edition of *The Recruiting Officer* published.
1707	27 January	Lintott bought copyright to *The Beaux Stratagem*.
	8 March	*The Beaux Stratagem* opened at the Queen's Theatre in the Haymarket.
	27 March	*The Beaux Stratagem* published.
	23 May	Farquhar buried at St. Martin's-in-the-Fields.
	4 December	Lintott bought half rights to *Love and a Bottle* from Francis Coggen.
1708	27 March	First edition of *The Comedies* published.
1710		*Barcellona* published.
1711	18 January	'Second edition' of *Works* published.

INTRODUCTION

GEORGE FARQUHAR'S entire theatrical and literary career
spanned a mere eight and a half years. Everything—eight
plays, a miscellany, a novella, a discourse on comedy, poems,
songs, prologues and epilogues, not to mention a military
career—was accomplished within those few years. He came to
London from Ireland at twenty-one; he succeeded beyond any
of his contemporaries or indeed any later eighteenth-century
playwrights in creating popular plays; he took mistresses and
a wife; he served his queen; and then he died before he turned
thirty.

His theatrical career, meteoric and spectacular at beginning
and end and yet financially and probably personally disappointing in its mid years, made a lasting impression on the
sensibilities of Englishmen. After *Love and a Bottle*, a first
comedy lacking in striking originality, he triumphed in *The
Constant Couple*, a brilliantly developed combination of the old
and new that brought the English stage two great favourites,
Sir Harry Wildair and Jubilee Dicky; Sir Harry was to shape
future comic heroes for many years. The middle years showed
various kinds of experimentation: the sequel *Sir Harry Wildair*,
in which he attempted to blend the same characters into a
marriage comedy; the slight but extravagantly successful farce
called *The Stage-Coach*, an adaptation from the French; another
adaptation, this time from Fletcher, in *The Inconstant*; a
melodramatic comedy of good and evil in *The Twin-Rivals*.
Although he expressed disappointment in the initial reception
of some of the middle plays, only *Sir Harry Wildair* failed to
become a staple of the repertory. He next sought his fortune as
a lieutenant on a recruiting mission, an enterprise that proved
so financially debilitating that he sold his commission and
returned to London. *The Recruiting Officer*, inspired by his
military adventures in the countryside, re-established him as a
leading playwright, really the leading playwright, since his
contemporaries, Congreve, Cibber, Steele, and Vanbrugh had
either mostly or altogether retired from stage-writing. In *The*

Recruiting Officer he returned to the kind of good humour, amiable characterizations, and rumbustious plot that had made *The Constant Couple* a success. Finally, in his last play, written from his death-bed, his remarkable creative talents came to flower; *The Beaux Stratagem* combines *joie de vivre* with the bittersweet melancholy of life as it really is; good humour with bad fortune; the frivolous love-making that social conventions demand with the genuine emotion, even passion, that one's heart urges; intellectual meat with the heady wine of highly adventurous plots and counterplots.

Farquhar's popularity on stage was phenomenal. He was not, like Cibber or, to a lesser extent, Steele, involved in theatrical management and so could have done little to promote his own plays. The comedies simply sold themselves. *The Constant Couple* is said to have played fifty-three nights in its first season. Although his other plays could not boast such runs (most opened in the spring so that such runs were impossible), they continued on stage for generations of playgoers. In the season of 1730–1, his plays ran sixty-one times in London; ten years later, fifty performances were given, and five years after that, in 1745–6, fifty-one. Year after year, between thirty-five and fifty theatrical evenings featured Farquhar; sometimes more than one house ran his plays on a single night. Although the demand for Farquhar's plays receded in the later years of the century, it never disappeared; they were still popular in the nineteenth century and the last two continue to be produced more than most plays of the period.

Moreover, editions of his works were published throughout the century. Not only individual comedies but also collected editions of the plays and the works remained popular. *The Recruiting Officer* and *The Beaux Stratagem* were each published more than fifty times in the eighteenth century. Three octavo editions of the *Comedies* were printed in 1708, 1711, and 1714; copies were combined with copies of *Love and Business* as the *Works*.[1] Two-volume duodecimo editions followed in rapid succession: in 1718, 1721, 1728, 1736, 1742, 1760, and 1772 in London. Editions of the *Works* and the individual plays also appeared frequently in Dublin.

Farquhar, like other dramatists of his day, was not anxious

about revision of his printed texts, although he did revise *The Constant Couple* and *The Recruiting Officer*. But remarkably enough, at least some of the later editions, long after his death, particularly the 1728 edition of the *Works*, provide theatre-based revisions. Therefore, Farquhar's canon provides an unusually rich corpus for investigating theatrical and publishing practices in the eighteenth century.

Although Farquhar's works have often been reprinted, they have seldom been treated with intellectual rigour. Early editors and twentieth-century editors including Stonehill have reproduced errors from one text to the next without serious attempts at accuracy. Only within the last few decades has Farquhar begun to get the scholarly attention he requires.

The present text includes some additions to Farquhar's canon, including three songs performed during the first run of *Love and a Bottle*, three prologues, and a poem never before printed with his works. I have also been able to provide new textual information and, I hope, solve some of the cruces concerning his authorship of minor works.

The wealth of material on theatrical history published within the last two decades has enabled me to include new information concerning the theatrical history of the plays. Textual problems are complicated, unusual, in some cases seemingly unique; I have introduced new bibliographical evidence for each of the texts.

I have tried to make Farquhar's works readily and reliably available to modern readers in an old-spelling text. The text includes revisions which are demonstrably Farquhar's and corrections of obvious errors, some caught by eighteenth-century printing-house employees, some by me. Corrections arising from the performance texts are noted and occasionally included in this edition. Although routine emendations in early editions have no authorial basis, I have accepted them if they satisfactorily correct errors; if they do not, I have followed copy-text or substituted more appropriate emendations.

For simplicity in reading, I have regularly standardized characters' names when more than one name or spelling occurs in the speech prefixes and stage directions, following Farquhar's intentions when they can be determined and arbitrarily choosing a single form when they can not. I have also added necessary stage directions, recording those from early editions in the footnotes and identifying those new to this edition by square brackets. With these few exceptions, the edition adheres as closely as possible to the copy-text.

Accidentals as well as substantives follow the copy-text very closely. My criterion is spelling and punctuation which is neither confusing nor misleading to readers familiar with eighteenth-century texts. Therefore pointing acceptable in Farquhar's time but not now (for example, a question mark used for a mild exclamation) stands. But since I do not consider compositorial foibles sacrosanct, I have freely changed obvious errors, such as a lower-case initial beginning a speech or the omission of punctuation at the end of one.

Typography and some accidentals are silently regularized. The edition neither reproduces nor notes initials, factotums, display capitals, swash letters, long *s*s, ligatures, *v* used for *u*, *vv* used for *w*, wrong-fount letters and italics used in shortages, turned letters except *u* and *n*, lost letters, or words jammed together in tight lines. Regardless of the copy-text, rhymed poetry, quotations, and letters are indented and italicized. Also italicized are characters' names in roman passages, but not accompanying titles such as 'Sir' or 'Mr.' unless they are part of a speech prefix. Characters' names in italic passages and stage directions appear in roman type. Proper nouns are regularly italicized in roman passages, and romanized in italic passages. Speech prefixes and stage directions, consistently italicized, begin with capitals, end with periods or dashes, and contain corrections of obvious misspellings. Entrances are centred, exits set full right, major stage directions between speeches centred, those within speeches closed in parentheses, and those incorrectly placed in the text positioned properly. The changes of typography and accidentals in speech prefixes and stage directions do not affect the lines written for the stage, but simplify the mechanical elements of the texts for which compositors were responsible. Lineation takes note of speech only; stage directions are not included in it.

The introduction to each play briefly treats the composition, sources, first production, theatrical history, critical reception, influence, textual problems, and history of publication.

Farquhar well knew the traditions of English comedy, but few direct debts can be proved. I also hesitate to claim specific influences on later works, unless there is strong evidence of a specific relationship. The bibliographical section of each introduction describes the printing of the first edition and other significant ones to explain textual cruces. It develops the rationale for editorial decisions in each case. Textual notes record all substantive emendations of the copy-text and any debatable refusals to emend. Explanations provide information on textual decisions about which questions can reasonably arise. In *The Recruiting Officer* and *The Beaux Stratagem* in particular, I have also listed important theatrical revisions not included in the present text. Emendations of accidentals list all changes from copy-text in punctuation and spelling, except silent alterations; to prevent misunderstanding of the original accidentals, I include hyphenations of compound words at the ends of lines in both the copy-text and the present edition unless the second part of the compound is capitalized. The abbreviation 'ed.' stands for 'editor', and 'om.' for 'omitted'. If an emendation is chosen from an early edition which contains different accidentals, the exact variant reading is indicated in square brackets following the siglum, as in 'fellow] Q2 [Fellow]; follow'. The commentary provides the reader with the necessary background of topical and literary allusions, sources, and occasionally relations to works by Farquhar or others.

The treatment of the non-dramatic works differs only in a few details. Introductions treat when possible the composition and sources, critical reception, influence, textual problems, and publication history; however, information is sparse for some minor works. Spelling of proper nouns is not regularized. For works published in a single edition, textual notes and emendations of accidentals do not include a siglum since they are invariably editorial corrections.

NOTE

1. I have not seen a copy of a first edition of the *Works* in 1708 or advertisements for it. Charles A. Stonehill claimed that such a volume existed. If so, it probably was a result of binding together the *Comedies* and *Love and Business*. See my letter 'George Farquhar' in *TLS*, 21 Sept. 1971, p. 1119.

THE PLAYS

LOVE AND A BOTTLE

INTRODUCTION

SOURCES AND COMPOSITION

GEORGE FARQUHAR'S life is shrouded in obscurity. Although there were four biographies published in eighteenth-century editions of his works,[1] none can be proved authoritative. Modern scholars have been able to add little to our record of his life.[2] No manuscripts have been discovered; only one contemporary picture of him is known, the frontispiece of his collected *Comedies* (1708), which shows him being presented to Apollo. The tendency, therefore, has been to extrapolate from his plays and letters if not a life at least a character for the young Irishman who proved inordinately successful in the London theatre. Of all the plays, *Love and a Bottle* seems the most audaciously autobiographical.

Farquhar, who was born probably in 1677, perhaps 1678,[3] left a chequered college career in 1696 to join the Smock Alley Company in Dublin for two seasons.[4] After a serious accident in which, as Guyomar in Dryden's *The Indian Emperor*, he forgot to exchange his sword for a foil and as a result actually wounded the actor who represented Vasquez,[5] he left the stage and headed for London. Biographers disagree on whether he arrived in London in 1697 or 1698,[6] and nothing is known of the journey, although one is tempted to speculate on whether he fell ill: Roebuck, his protagonist, irrelevantly remarks that he was detained a month at Coventry by a 'violent Fit of Sickness' that exhausted his health and money, and the preface to *The Adventures of Covent Garden* also speaks of the author's being very young and 'Recovering from a fit of sickness'.

Biographers are divided on whether Farquhar arrived in London with his manuscript in hand. Thomas Wilkes gives the following account:

Long before this accident [i.e. the wounding of Vasquez], Mr. Wilkes [Robert Wilks, the actor, then at Smock Alley], who was well

acquainted with the abilities of our author, recommended to him to
quit the Stage, and write a Comedy; for that he was considered by
all his acquaintance in a much brighter light than he had shewn
himself in; and that he was much better calculated to furnish
compositions for the Stage, than to echo those of other Poets on it;
and recommended to him to set out for London as soon as possible.
Our author acquainted him with his unhappy circumstances, that
he was not master of a shilling; Mr. Wilkes gave him ten guineas,
and applied to Mr. Ashbury, who in about a month after gave him a
free Benefit; by this time he had drawn up the Drama of Love and a
Bottle which he shewed to Mr. Wilkes, who approving of it, he set
out for London the next day.[7]

The account is pat and completely unsubstantiated, except by
an earlier, equally unreliable account in Daniel O'Bryan's
*Authentic Memoirs . . . Of that most Celebrated Comedian, Mr. Robert
Wilks*. Wilks, O'Bryan says, advised Farquhar to leave acting
for playwriting:

. . . he told him at the same time that he would not meet with
Encouragement in *Ireland*, adequate to his Merit, and therefore
counselled him to go to *London*. . . . By this time Mr. *Farquhar* had
prepared the Drama of his Comedy, call'd *Love and a Bottle*, which he
shewed to Mr. *Wilks*, who approving of it, advised him to set out for
London before the Tide was too far spent, meaning while he had any
Money left to support him; he took his Counsel, and bid him adieu,
and the next Day went on board a Ship bound for *West-Chester*.[8]

Later scholars have tended to agree that Farquhar 'set off
from London with the rough copy of *Love and a Bottle*'.[9] Ewald
incorrectly believes Wilks came to London with Farquhar and
interceded with Christopher Rich for its performance.[10]
Schmid believes he left Ireland before 1697, carrying his
manuscript.[11] Clark believes Farquhar left for London 'about
1698',[12] but offers no speculation about when and where he
wrote the comedy. Stonehill, who says he departed in 1697,
theorizes that Farquhar would have needed intimate knowledge of the town and its resorts and amusements; the play
'could only have been written by one already familiar with
London'.[13]

Internal evidence offers little support for Stonehill's assertion.
There are references to fashions (topknots, campaign wits,
fencing and dancing lessons for beaux), places (Moorfields,

Will's, Bedlam, the booksellers' stalls around St. Paul's), and fashionable talk ('Zauns' not 'Zoons', 'Dem me', etc.). But residence was scarcely a requirement to mention these details of London life. Most of the literary allusions come from established writers—Shakespeare, Dryden, Lee, Banks. The only contemporary one refers to 'the last Miscellanies', probably *Miscellanies over Claret*, published in 1698 and perhaps seen by Farquhar in London. But these 'London' references, regardless of the date or place of their inclusion in the manuscript, give no indication of whether Farquhar came to town with a rough draft in hand or for that matter even a finished text.

One glances hesitantly at the quicksand of seeming biographical details in the play itself. One cannot but wonder if Farquhar wrote a play about a young Irishman's arrival in London because he was either planning to go there or newly arrived. Why should he refer to Roebuck's illness at Coventry unless the reference was autobiographical and thereby intrinsically interesting to the nineteen- or twenty-year-old author? If the line was indeed autobiographical, it had to be written after the journey from Ireland. It is not a line for which an author would revise a passage but rather a line that was never expunged:

Thy profession of kindness is so great, that I cou'd almost suspect it of design.—But come, Friend, I am heartily tir'd with the fatigue of my Journey, besides a violent Fit of Sickness, which detain'd me a Month at *Coventry*, to the exhausting my Health and Money. Let me only recruit by a relish of the Town in Love and a Bottle, and then—

The information about his 'violent Fit of Sickness' interrupts his misanthropy in the first sentence and jostles oddly with his appetites in the last one. Further, his rampant lust scarcely bespeaks a recent serious illness—rather than building Roebuck's characterization, the illness jars the image. Therefore, autobiographical event rather than character development furnishes the likely motive for the line. One cannot but believe the passage was written in London.

Whether Farquhar wrote in Dublin, in London, during a feverish month in Coventry, or in more than one location, his sources were clearly those with which he was endowed by

experience and education rather than the raw materials of
London life; that is, his play bears the stamp of autobiographical characterization plus the literary bequests of favourite
playwrights whose works Farquhar had read, seen, and
perhaps acted.

There are many similarities between George Farquhar and
George Roebuck, few provable. The poet Lyrick in Act IV,
Scene ii, a satirist in his own right, says that the hero of
comedy 'is always the Poet's Character', a remark interpreted
by generations of critics as Farquhar's admission that
Roebuck represents his creator. The claim was made during
Farquhar's lifetime by the author of the *Memoirs Relating to the
late Famous Mr. Tho. Brown*, who asserted that Farquhar 'knew
how necessary Lewdness was to establish his Reputation,
when he expos'd *Roebuck* in the first Play he writ for his own
Character'.[14] Most later critics have agreed there is 'a spice of
autobiography'[15] in Roebuck. There are many obvious
similarities between author and character: both Georges are
newly arrived from Ireland, probably both impecunious. Both
are rakish and devilishly successful with the ladies.

Love and a Bottle is the most literary of Farquhar's plays; that
is, through imitation and even quotation, it reflects knowledge
of earlier English drama more relentlessly than he later found
desirable. The plot of the young Irishman coming to London
is original, but other plot devices and characterizations are
clearly derivative. Farquhar, however, seems primarily to
have imitated elements of comedy rather than specific
characters and plot devices. That *modus operandi* perhaps
explains why critics have attributed his characters to such a
wide variety of antecedents.

One source generally acknowledged by critics is Molière's
Le Bourgeois Gentilhomme.[16] Mockmode is a university fool
rather than a *bourgeois gentilhomme* like Monsieur Jourdain. He
deals with a dancing-master and a fencing-master but not a
music master, teacher of philosophy, or tailor. There is no
direct translation in the scene, but there are certainly
similarities between Mockmode's and Jourdain's sessions
with the hired beau-makers. Peter Kavanagh says the fencing
and dancing scenes are obvious imitations of Molière's play,
but John Wilcox believes Mockmode's similarity to Jourdain

'lies merely in the fact that both had tutors'.[17] Dudley H. Miles, however, sees the character Mockmode as related to both Jourdain and M. de Pourceaugnac.[18]

Shakespeare too has been cited as a source, particularly for Leanthe disguising herself as a page to follow her love as Viola does in *Twelfth Night*; however, Wycherley's Fidelia in *The Plain Dealer* as well as Aphra Behn's Olivia in *The Younger Brother* and Helena in *The Rover* have all been suggested as source or analogue.[19] There are verbal echoes from Shakespeare in the bawdy wit and in the quibbles, particularly those of Brush and Lovewell (Act I). Further, there are specific echoes: 'A hit, a very palpable hit' becomes, in a parodic fencing scene, 'a palpable crack. A very palpable crack truly'. The bawdy punning on an 'Irish quagmire' brings to mind the 'Irish bog' in the geographical description of Nell in *The Comedy of Errors* (III. ii. 121). The verbal luxuriance and pyrotechnical word play in such scenes as those in which Lucinda displays her sophisticated wit are also reminiscent of Shakespeare's comedies.

The young Farquhar alluded to Restoration plays with Lyrick's parody of Nathaniel Lee's lines in *Sophonisba* and quotations from John Banks's *Unhappy Favourite* and John Dryden's *Conquest of Granada*. In characterization he was heavily dependent on English tradition, but he did not rely on specific characters and plots. His Roebuck has been associated with Behn's Rover; Lovewell has called to mind Vanbrugh's Constant and Worthy.[20] Eric Rothstein also evokes a contemporary, Colley Cibber, as a source for moral equivocation in the 'secret salacious consummation' at the end.[21] But despite specific predecessors mentioned by various critics, one is struck primarily by Farquhar's use of stage types, stock characters whom he must have seen portrayed by fellow actors at Smock Alley: the two sets of contrasting lovers and the myriad minor characters such as the university beau come to town, the witty servant and the slow servant, the bawdy serving girl, the cast mistress, a poet and a bookseller, a dancing-master and a fencing-master. Plot devices were equally well worn—mistaken identity, multiple disguises, and two tricked marriages, one binding and one not binding. But there are obvious awkwardnesses in the new blend of old playwrights' tricks. Why, for example, in the middle of his blissful wedding night, does Roebuck wander on stage to exude his ecstasy in blank verse rather than staying with his bride?

Love and a Bottle also contains phrasing found in Farquhar's own *Adventures of Covent Garden*. Two lines of a poem, later reprinted in *Love and Business*, occur in both works with slight revisions. The *Adventures* reads:

> He thought her Naked, soft, and yielding Waste,
> Within his pressing Arms was folded fast,

whereas Roebuck says:

> When her soft, melting white, and yielding Waste,
> Within my pressing Arms was folded fast,

We cannot know which work borrowed from the other; the play opened probably in early December, the novella appeared around 15 December, and the play was published on 29 December. All we can know is that the lines served double duty.

Farquhar's lack of ability to weld his theatrical materials successfully is somewhat ameliorated by the exuberance of his language and the energy of his action. This is the play of a young man recently dropped out of college, just turning twenty. He has gathered to him all the theatre he knows and stirred the borrowed ingredients into a new olio. Even his language is somewhat derivative—he uses proverbial expressions with notable frequency and borrows bawdy *double entendre*s from his forebears. But he also creates new *double entendre*s, perhaps too thickly strewn, sometimes strained, but original. In many ways, *Love and a Bottle* was the product of Farquhar's apprenticeship as a playwright.

STAGE HISTORY

Love and a Bottle opened at Drury Lane Theatre probably in December 1698. No one knows how the young Irishman made his contact with Christopher Rich when he brought the play or, for that matter, what the terms of the agreement were. The Drury Lane and Lincoln's Inn Fields theatres were desperately seeking audiences in the years following the dissolution of the United Company in 1695. A plethora of new plays, mostly unsuccessful, found their way to the stage. Twenty-five new plays opened in the season of 1695–6, twenty more in 1696–7, and nineteen in 1697–8.[22] But by 1698–9, either the supply of decent plays had run low or the supply of energy to mount them had waned. Only ten *premières* occurred that year, and only four of those at Drury Lane. When *Love and a Bottle* opened, the only other two *premières* had been the rival operas of November, *The Island Princess* at Drury Lane and *Rinaldo and Armida* at Lincoln's Inn Fields. Drury Lane had no other new plays after *Love and a Bottle* until a comedy, *Love Without Interest*, appeared, probably in mid April, and Lincoln's Inn Fields offered only Cibber's tragedy *Xerxes* and Joseph Harris's comedy *Love's a Lottery* in March or April. The pace at the theatres, then, had slackened strikingly from the previous three years.

Thomas Wilkes claimed the role of Roebuck was intended for Robert Wilks who stayed at Smock Alley[23] for the season. Joseph Williams, however, played the role. The production relied heavily on the broad comedians of the company, William Bullock as Mockmode, Joseph Haines doubling as Pamphlet and Rigadoon, and Will Pinkethman as Club. The other parts were predictable—John Mills as the serious suitor Lovewell, Jane Rogers as Lucinda, and Maria Allison as Leanthe.

The company was anxious, it would appear, to ensure the success of the new comedy. The programme was embellished with both prologue and epilogue by Joseph Haines, the former spoken drunkenly by George Powell, the latter bawdily by Haines himself incongruously dressed in mourning for the demise of Drury Lane.

Furthermore, songs and dances enlivened the performance. The song in Act III, 'How Blessed Are Lovers in Disguise', was set by Vaughan Richardson, organist at Winchester Cathedral and composer in 1697 of music to celebrate the Peace of Ryswick, performed at York Buildings. 'France Ne're Will Comply', a drinking-song sung by Joseph Williams as Roebuck, was printed in III. ii, but no setting for it has been located. Furthermore, the text indicates other points at which actors burst into song, Rigadoon sings at one point (II. ii), Roebuck sings yet again (III. i). The printed version of the play does not include three additional songs set by Richard Leveridge, then a member of the Drury Lane Company: 'When Cupid from his Mother Fled', sung by Maria Allison in the role of Leanthe (III. i); 'On Sunday after Mass', a bawdy Irish song, by Mrs Mills, who played Trudge (IV. ii); and 'Early in the Dawning of a Winter's Morn', by William Pinkethman as Club (II. ii). The fact that the songs, issued as half-sheet broadsides, were not printed within the play text suggests that they were added at the last moment or perhaps after the run had begun. They were unquestionably played during the comedy's first season, for that was the only season in which all three actors performed at Drury Lane, and Leveridge himself spent the following season at Smock Alley. There is no way to know whether Farquhar wrote the lyrics. Leveridge, who earned extra money by songwriting, sometimes wrote only the music, sometimes both words and music, but the engravings for these songs merely say 'Set by Mr. Leveridge'. Nor is there any incontrovertible evidence as to the placement of the songs in the text or between the acts, but the songs are entirely appropriate to the characters portrayed by the singers and to the action of the play. Leanthe's song links with her opening speech in Act III, which begins 'Methinks this Livery suits ill my Birth'. Both song and speech concern her disguise to follow her love. Trudge's song fits into Act IV, Scene ii, in which Mockmode asks her to sing; Club's song fits in the witty drinking scene at the end of Act II.

It is, of course, possible that the songs were sung *entr'acte*. Act tunes ordinarily covered the transitions between acts in this period. Before 1700 *entr'acte* songs were rarely substituted for instrumental tunes; however, a few examples exist.[24] No set of act tunes is extant for *Love and a Bottle*; consequently there is no way to know if a full set of nine existed or if possibly the three songs replaced three of them.

As an *entr'acte* song, 'When Cupid from his Mother Fled' would have been sung between Acts II and III, for Leanthe's opening speech in Act III clearly preceded or followed it; the speech and song are closely interrelated. The two bawdy songs would probably have appeared after Acts I and III, but there is little clear evidence for placement. *Entr'acte* songs were often irrelevant to the scenes that preceded and followed them;[25] arguments can be made for both placements. Although no incontrovertible evidence exists for placement either within or between acts, the appropriateness within the scenes is notable.

There is some dancing too, not only Rigadoon's performance with and without Mockmode but also an '*Irish* Entertainment of three Men and three Women, dress'd after the *Fingallion* fashion'. Here the stage directions become so precise that one suspects Farquhar is describing exactly what appeared on stage, a fact which makes the omission of the Leveridge songs seem even more surprising. In the 1720s a Fingalian dance by Newhouse and Mrs Ogden was traditionally performed with the play, and in the 1730s an 'Irish Trot' was included, but these performances were apparently reduced from six dancers to two.

Whether the lily was further gilded remains unknown. Act tunes and *entr'acte* dances or songs were often added to a programme. At any rate, the thorough-going musicalization of the play plus the prologue and epilogue by Haines, which would have cost the theatre a few pounds, suggest that the management invested enthusiastically in audience-pleasers to promote *Love and a Bottle*. The treatment must have worked, for the play reached at least its third night: Farquhar gratefully mentioned in a letter to playwright Catharine Trotter her appearance at his benefit.[26] Other accounts would suggest a successful run, but whether three nights or nine remains unclear. Joseph Addison, in the poem 'The Play-House. A Satyr', published some time between December 1698 and April 1699 according to Frank H. Ellis, suggests the play's popularity:

> The Comick Tone, inspir'd by *Farquhar*, draws
> At every Word, loud Laughter and Applause:[27]

An early biographer of Farquhar claimed the success of *Love and a Bottle* 'far exceeded his Expectations, as indeed did most of his other pieces'.[28] Theophilus Cibber said that 'for its sprightly dialogue, and busy scenes [it] was well received by

the audience'.[29] Robert Hitchcock says it was brought out
'with great success'.[30] Thomas Wilkes claims that the play ran
for nine nights 'with applause'.[31] Farquhar's success cannot
now be measured. The play was, however, 'scandalously
aspersed for affronting the ladies'.[32] Despite the playwright's
protestations of innocence, one cannot be surprised that
nerves rubbed raw by Jeremy Collier's attack on the theatres
would have experienced pain at the bawdry of this play.

   After the first season, the next known performance occurred
in 1712. Williams had left for Lincoln's Inn Fields in
1699–1700, and it seems likely that the play was 'laid up in
lavendar', as Farquhar would say, with the disappearance of
its Roebuck. Performance records are exceedingly sketchy
until 1703; the play may have been staged during that time.
But it was advertised 22 July 1712 as 'Not Acted these Twelve
Years'. Such disclaimers are not always accurate, but in this
case one suspects that the play indeed had not been performed
for more than a decade. Mills, the original Lovewell, played
Roebuck for two performances in the summer of 1712 at
Drury Lane. Wilks never assumed the role; had he done so,
the play might have been revived regularly at Drury Lane, but
in fact it never played there again.

   After a single performance at the New Haymarket in
February 1724, a 'Carefully revis'd' version was offered
during the summer season at Lincoln's Inn Fields and ran five
nights. An Irish dance 'in Fingalian Habits' was included, as
it had been in the original. The comedy played three more
times in 1724–5, once in 1725–6, and twice in 1727–8.
Thomas Walker played Roebuck in all the performances at
Lincoln's Inn Fields. The play ran at least six more times
between 1733 and 1740, playing twice at Covent Garden,
twice at the Haymarket, and twice at Goodman's Fields. Most
of the time Walker continued to play Roebuck, although once
the role was assumed 'By a Friend to the Distress'd, and a
Citizen of London'. Twice during this time it was performed
at the particular desire of several Freemasons, a group
asserting an increasing influence on the theatre.[33] After 1740
the comedy disappeared from the stage until 26 March 1781,
when it was advertised as 'Not acted these 80 years', produced
'with alterations', and supplemented with an afterpiece,

dancing, catches, and glees. The performance had some appeal: the theatre advertised, 'A great demand being made for places, Ladies and Gentlemen are requested to send their Servants by Five O'Clock'. But apparently one performance was enough to satisfy the demand. Except for *Sir Harry Wildair*, *Love and a Bottle* was Farquhar's least often performed comedy.

REPUTATION AND INFLUENCE

Had Farquhar not succeeded in almost all his later plays and become one of the most frequently performed British play-wrights of his century, *Love and a Bottle* might well have flickered into obscurity, but every time Farquhar's *Comedies*, *Dramatick Works*, or *Works* were reprinted, *Love and a Bottle* again appeared. It was accessible, hence read and commented upon by critics of Farquhar. Even so, one must conclude that its influence on later works was minimal.

THE TEXT

Love and a Bottle was published by Richard Standfast and Francis Coggen on 29 December 1698.[34] In the advertisement in the *Post Man*, Farquhar was misspelled 'Farghner'; on 28–31 January 1699 the comedy was advertised again, with the misspelling 'Farynhens'—obviously Farquhar's name was not yet a readily recognizable one. There is no record of the money Farquhar received for the copyright but, judging from his later agreements with Lintott, one suspects he was not a good businessman. Standfast had issued *The Adventures of Covent-Garden* only days before: perhaps there was an agree-ment for both works.[35]

The first edition was carelessly printed. The only stop-press correction was the addition of the catch-word '*Love.*' on p. 5. Egregious misspellings and incorrect speech prefixes were never corrected.

The entire play was imposed on two formes, judging from running-title evidence. About midway through the text, the pattern of imposition becomes less regular.

On 4 December 1707, almost six months after Farquhar's

death, Bernard Lintott bought half the rights to *Love and a Bottle* from Francis Coggen for £2. 3s.[36] Lintott had by then published four other of Farquhar's works, *Love and Business*, *The Twin Rivals*, *The Recruiting Officer*, and *The Beaux Stratagem*, and he had acquired rights to three others, for he had advertised *The Constant Couple*, *Sir Harry Wildair*, and *The Inconstant* as well; only the farce *The Stage-Coach* and the anonymous *Adventures of Covent Garden* remain outside his copyright.[37] Lintott published the undated second edition of *Love and a Bottle*, another quarto, probably between 4 December 1707, when he acquired the copyright, and 27 March 1708, when he published the first edition of the *Comedies*. The compositors corrected misspellings and other obvious errors, changing 'bush' to 'blush' and 'squalawling' to 'squawling', for example, but more serious errors such as incorrect speech prefixes were ignored. Farquhar, who died in May 1707, had made no revisions for the press.

The third edition of the play appeared in the first collected *Comedies* published by Lintott in 1708. Oddly enough, the copy-text for this edition was, once again, the original quarto, not the second edition, which Lintott himself had published. Thereafter the play was issued regularly with editions of the *Comedies* and the *Works*, sometimes with a separate title-page. An edition appeared in Dublin (copy at Princeton) in 1727 and another in Glasgow in 1759 (copies at Yale and the University of Illinois).

The three songs by Leveridge were never printed with the play, although they were engraved and issued separately. 'When Cupid from his Mother Fled' and 'On Sunday after Mass' both appeared in two early engravings, one by Thomas Cross, one which resembles other engravings by John Walsh, both presumably shortly after the play opened. A third appeared in 1710. 'Early in the Dawning of a Winter's Morn' appeared with the other two in the early engravings presumably by Walsh. All were issued as half-sheet broadsides; the three engravings attributed to Walsh were apparently issued together, for only 'When Cupid from his Mother Fled' has a title, which is 'Songs in the new Comedy call'd Love & a Bottle. Sung by Mrs. Allinson'. The other two are headed merely 'Sung by Mrs. Mills' and 'Sung by Mr. Penkethman'.

The Cross engraving (Chetham Library, H. Phillips, No. 1908) is labelled 'A Song in the Comedy call'd Love and a Bottle Set by Mr. Leveridge Sung by Mrs. Allinson and exactly engrav'd by Tho. Cross'. The misspelling 'Allinson', which occurs in both, and the close similarities between the two suggest that one derived from the other.

Haines's epilogue was also frequently reprinted, probably because it was a favourite epilogue, which was 'many times spoken with Universal Applause, not only to *This*, but several other Plays, as a just Rebuke of the vitiated *Taste* of the Town'.[38] In 1793 it appeared in D'Urfey's *Apollo's Feast: or, Wits Entertainment*. It was reprinted in Curll's *Memoirs of Wilks* and Betterton's *History of the English Stage*, another work usually attributed to Curll; the text in the latter was derived from the *Wilks* text.

I have used the first edition of *Love and a Bottle* as copy-text. Since the text is poorly printed and not significantly corrected during the press run, I have felt no hesitation to correct spelling and clarify confusing or incorrect punctuation, although I have not made more corrections than necessary for easy reading. When possible, I have chosen the corrections of the second quarto, although they bear no authorial authority, because they represent normal spellings and punctuation of the period.

The Leveridge songs are reprinted for the first time. Although there is no incontrovertible evidence that they were sung within rather than between the acts, the obvious openings for them in the scenes make placement within the text seem most likely.[39] I have marked them with square brackets.

I have collated the following copies of *Love and a Bottle*: first edition at the Folger, Bodleian, Library of Congress, Harvard, University of Pennsylvania; second edition, Bodleian, University of Pennsylvania; *Comedies* (first edition) William Clark Library, UCLA.

The text of the epilogue has been collated not only in the editions of the play but in the additional printings in *Apollo's Feast*, *Memoirs of Wilks*, and *History of the English Stage*.

NOTES

1. One biography, first printed in Curll's edition of *The Stage-Coach* in 1718, begins 'Mr. George Farquhar was a Gentleman by Birth . . .'. It reappears in the Dublin editions of that play in 1719 and 1728. A second biography 'Some Memoirs of Mr. *George Farquhar*', which begins ' 'Tis observ'd that the World is naturally apt to enquire into the Life . . .', was printed in the sixth, seventh, eighth, and ninth London editions of *The Stage-Coach* (1728, 1735, 1742, 1760) as well as the sixth Dublin edition of the *Poems, Letters, and Essays*. This memoir was probably written by W. R. Chetwood, who claimed his short account of Farquhar in *A General History of the Stage* (1749) was taken from the life 'that I collected several Years past, to prefix to his Works. The Materials I received from Mr. *Wilks* [i.e. Farquhar's good friend, the actor Robert Wilks], who approved of them before they went to the Publisher.' In the *History* Chetwood quotes a poem from the seventh edition of Farquhar's works, and the account is based on the same facts. The third biography begins 'Mr. Farquhar, an ingenious Comic Writer and Poet . . .'; it appeared in the Lowndes edition of *The Stage-Coach* in 1766, the 'Tenth Edition' in 1772, and the Oxlade edition in 1775. A fourth biography, by Thomas Wilkes of Dublin, heads the 1775 Dublin edition of the *Works*. Chetwood's account and that of Theophilus Cibber in *The Lives of the Poets of Great Britain and Ireland* (1753) are two more early biographies. Details from the earliest accounts gained currency and were repeated in later memoirs.

2. Biographical sketches include David Erskine Baker, Isaac Reed, and Stephen Jones, *Biographica Dramatica* (3 vols. London, 1812); Leigh Hunt, *The Dramatic Works of Wycherley, Congreve, Vanbrugh, and Farquhar* (London, 1840); Willard Connely, *Young George Farquhar* (London, 1949); Eric Rothstein, *George Farquhar* (New York, 1967); Charles A. Stonehill, *The Complete Works of George Farquhar* (2 vols., London, 1930; rept. New York, 1967). Research on particular aspects of Farquhar's life has been completed, most notably Robert John Jordan, 'George Farquhar's Military Career', *Huntington Library Quarterly*, 37 (1973–4), 251–64.

3. Hunt lists 1678; Stonehill between May and July 1677; Rothstein 1677 or 1678. *Alumni Dublinenses* says he matriculated in July 1694 at age 17.

4. William Smith Clark, *The Early Irish Stage* (Oxford, 1955), p. 104.

5. Chetwood, pp. 149–50.

6. Clark, p. 104; Stonehill, I. p. xiv; La Tourette Stockwell in *Dublin Theatres and Theatre Customs (1637–1820)* (Kingsport, Tenn., 1938), p. 316 n. 103, concurs with Thomas Wilkes that Farquhar left Dublin in 1696 or more probably 1697.

7. Thomas Wilkes, 'The Life of George Farquhar', in *The Works of George Farquhar* (3 vols., Dublin, 1775), I. p. v.

8. Daniel O'Bryan, *Authentic Memoirs . . . Of That Most Celebrated Comedian, Mr. Robert Wilks* (London, 1732), pp. 13–14, quoted in Rothstein, p. 17.

9. Robert Hitchcock, *An Historical View of the Irish Stage from the Earliest Period Down to the Close of the Season 1788* (2 vols., Dublin, 1788–94), I. 315; Stockwell, p. 316 n. 102; Connely, p. 48; Rothstein, p. 17.

10. A. C. Ewald, Preface, *The Dramatic Works of George Farquhar* (2 vols., London, 1892), I. p. vii.

11. D. Schmid, *George Farquhar, Sein Leben und Seine Original-Dramen* (Leipzig, 1904), p. 20.

12. Clark, p. 104.

13. Stonehill, I. pp. xiv–xv.

14. *Memoirs Relating to the late Famous Mr. Tho. Brown* (London, 1704), pp. 1–2.

15. Malcolm Elwin, *The Playgoer's Handbook to Restoration Drama* (London, 1928), p. 186.

16. Louis A. Strauss, ed., *A Discourse upon Comedy, The Recruiting Officer, and the Beaux Stratagem* (Boston and London, 1914), p. xxxvi; Stonehill, I. 3.

17. Peter Kavanagh, *The Irish Theatre* (Tralee, 1946), p. 205; John Wilcox, *The Relation of Molière to Restoration Comedy* (New York, 1938), p. 176.

18. Dudley H. Miles, *The Influence of Molière on Restoration Comedy* (1910; rept. New York, 1971), p. 232.

19. Schmid, p. 43; Stonehill, I. pp. xv–xvi; Elwin, p. 187; Eugene Nelson James, *The Development of George Farquhar as a Comic Dramatist* (The Hague, 1972), pp. 71–2.

20. Ashley H. Thorndike, *English Comedy* (New York, 1929), p. 335.

21. Rothstein, p. 32.

22. Shirley Strum Kenny, 'Theatrical Warfare, 1695–1710', in *Theatre Notebook*, 27 (1973), 134.

23. Clark, p. 106. The authors of the *Biographical Dictionary* find no evidence that Wilks returned to London before 1699. His first London performance for which there is evidence was *The Constant Couple* on 28 Nov. 1699, but he had appeared earlier, notably in the performance for which Farquhar wrote the prologue. (I am indebted to Edward A. Langhans for pre-publication access to the Wilks biography.)

24. Curtis A. Price, *Music in the Restoration Theatre* (Ann Arbor, 1979), p. 61.

25. Price, pp. 61–5.

26. *The Works of Mrs. Catharine Cockburn . . . With an Account of the Life of the Author*, by Thomas Birch (2 vols., London, 1751), I. p. vii.

27. *Poems on Affairs of State, Augustan Satirical Verse, 1660–1714*, ed. Frank H. Ellis (New Haven and London, 1970), Vi. 32.

28. 'Some Memoirs of Mr. *George Farquhar*', in *The Stage-Coach* (1735), p. viii.

29. Theophilus Cibber, p. 127.

30. Hitchcock, p. 30.

31. Wilkes, p. v.

32. Cockburn, I, p. viii.

33. See Harry William Pedicord, 'White Gloves at Five: Fraternal Patronage of London Theatres in the Eighteenth Century', *Philological Quarterly*, 45 (1966), 270–88; Harry William Pedicord, 'George Lillo and "Speculative Masonry"', *Philological Qurterly*, 53 (1974), 401–12.

34. Advertisement, *The Post Man*, 27–9 Dec. 1698.

35. Plomer lists Standfast as a London printer 1711–25. (Henry R. Plomer, *A Dictionary of the Printers and Booksellers . . . in England, Scotland and Ireland from 1668 to 1725* [Oxford, 1922], p. 280.)

36. John Nichols, *Literary Anecdotes of the Eighteenth Century* (9 vols., London, 1812–15), Viii. 295.

37. Shirley Strum Kenny, 'The Publication of Plays', in Robert D. Hume, ed., *The London Theatre World, 1660–1800* (Carbondale, Ill., 1980), p. 330.

38. [Edmund Curll], *The Life of that Eminent Comedian, Robert Wilks, Esq.* (London, 1733), p. 11.

39. I am indebted to Curtis A. Price for his advice on whether the songs should be placed within the text.

Songs in the new Comedy call'd Love & a Bottle.
Sung by Mr Allinson. 1699

When Cupid from his Mother fled, he Changing his Shape thus made his es=

=cape, his Mother thought him Dead, Som did him a kindness, & Cur'd him of

blindness, and thus disguis'd like me, thus disguis'd, thus disguis'd thus dis=

=guis'd like me, the little God, the little God, the little God cou'd see.

Set by Mr Leveridge

2.
He enters into Hearts of Men,
And there dos spy,
(Iust so do I)
That falshood lurks within,
That sighing and dying,
Is swearing and lyeing,
All this disguis'd like me,
The little God, ye little God coud see.

For the Flute

'When Cupid from his Mother fled', from *Love and a Bottle*. Set by
Richard Leveridge, engraved by John Walsh, 1699. By permission of the
Folger Shakespeare Library.

LOVE AND A BOTTLE

A Comedy

Vade sed incultus, qualem decet exulis esse.
                    Ovid, *Tristia*, El. I.

ABBREVIATIONS USED IN THE NOTES

Q   First edition. London: Standfast & Coggen, 1699.

Q2   Second edition. London: Lintott [late 1707 or early 1708].

O1   *Comedies*. First edition. London: Knapton, Smith, Strahan, and Lintott [1708].

1728   *Works*. Sixth edition. London: J. and J. Knapton, Lintott, Strahan, and Clark, 1728.

To the Right Honourable,
PEREGRINE,
Lord Marquiss of *Carmarthen*, &c.

My Lord,
Being equally a stranger to your Lordship, and the whole
Nobility of this Kingdom, something of a natural impulse and
aspiring motion in my inclinations, has prompted me, tho I
hazzard a presumption, to declare my Respect. And be the
Success how it will, I am vain of nothing in this piece, but the
choice of my Patron; I shall be so far thought a judicious
Author, whose principal business is to design his Works an
offering to the greatest Honour and Merit.

I cannot here, my Lord, stand accused of any sort of 10
Adulation, but to my self, because Compliments due to Merit
return upon the giver, and the only flattery is to my self, whilst
I attempt your Lordships praise. I dare make no essay on your
Lordships youthful Bravery and Courage, because such is
always guarded with Modesty, but shall venture to present
you some lines on this Subject, which the world will
undoubtedly apply to your Lordship.

Courage, the highest gift, that scorns to bend
To mean devices for a sordid end.
Courage—an independent spark from Heaven's bright
Throne,   20
By which the Soul stands rais'd, triumphant, high,
alone.
Great in it self, not praises of the crowd,
Above all vice, it stoops not to be proud.
Courage, the mighty attribute of powers above,
By which those great in War, are great in Love.
The spring of all brave Acts is seated here,
As falshoods draw their sordid birth from fear.

The best and noblest part of mankind pay homage to
Royalty, what veneration then is due to those Vertues and

30 Endowments which even engag'd the respect of Royalty it self, in the person of one of the greatest Emperours in the World, who chose your Lordship not only as a Companion, but a Conductor.

He wanted the Fire of such a *Britton* to animate his cold *Russians*, and wou'd therefore choose you his Leader in War, as in Travel: he knew the Fury of the *Turk* cou'd be only stopt by an *English* Nobleman, as the Power of *France* was by an *English* King. A sense of this greatness which might deter others, animates me to Address your Lordship; resolv'd that
40 my first Muse shou'd take an high and daring flight, I aspir'd to your Lordships Protection for this trifle, which I must own my self now proud of, affording me this opportunity of Humbly declaring my self,

> My Lord,
> Your Lordships
> most devoted Servant,
> *G. Farquhar.*

PROLOGUE:

By *J. H.* spoken by Mr. *Powell*, a Servant
attending with a Bottle of Wine.

As stubborn Atheists, who disdain'd to pray,
Repent, tho late, upon their dying day,
So in their pangs, most Author's rack'd with fears,
Implore your mercy in our suppliant pray'rs.
But our new Author has no Cause maintained,
Let him not lose what he has never gained.
Love and a Bottle *are his peaceful arms:*
Ladies, and Gallants, have not these some Charms?
For Love, all mankind to the Fair must sue,
And Sirs, the Bottle, he presents to you.   10
Health to the Play, (Drinks.) *e'en let it fairly pass,*
Sure none sit here that will refuse their glass.
O there's a damning Soldier—let me think—
He looks as he were sworn—to what!—to drink. (Drinks.)
Come on then; foot to foot be boldly set,
And our young Author's new Commission wet.
He and his Bottle here attend their doom,
From you the Poets Hellicon *must come;*
If he has any foes, to make amends,
He gives his service (Drinks.) *sure you now are friends.*   20
No Critick here will he provoke to fight,
The day be theirs, he only begs his Night;
Pray pledge him now, secur'd from all abuse, ⎫
Then name the health you love, let none refuse, ⎬
But each man's Mistress be the Poet's Muse. ⎭

Dramatis Personæ.

[MEN.]

Roebuck.	An *Irish* Gentleman, of a wild roving temper; newly come to *London*.	Mr. *Williams*.
Lovewell.	His Friend sober and modest, in love with *Lucinda*.	Mr. *Mills*.
Mockmode.	A young Squire, come newly from the University, and setting up for a Beau.	Mr. *Bullock*.
Lyrick.	A Poet.	Mr. *Johnson*.
Pamphlet.	A Bookseller.	Mr. *Haynes*.
Rigadoon.	A Dancing-Master.	Mr. *Haynes*.
Nimblewrist.	A Fencing-Master.	Mr. *Ashton*.
Club.	Servant to *Mockmode*.	Mr. *Pinkethman*.
Brush.	Servant to *Lovewell*.	Mr. *Fairbank*.

WOMEN.

Lucinda.	A Lady of considerable Fortune.	Mrs. *Rogers*.
Leanthe.	Sister to *Lovewell*, in love with *Roebuck*, and disguised as *Lucinda*'s Page.	Mrs. *Maria Alison*.
Trudge.	Whore to *Roebuck*.	Mrs. *Mills*.
Bullfinch.	Landlady to *Mockmode*, *Lyrick*, and *Trudge*.	Mrs. *Powell*.
Pindress.	Attendant and Confident to *Lucinda*.	Mrs. *Moor*.

Bailiffs, Cripple, Porter, Masques, and Attendants.

SCENE *LONDON*.

Love and a Bottle.

ACT I.

SCENE *Lincolns-Inn-Fields.*

Enter Roebuck *in Riding habit* Solus, *repeating the following Line.*

Roebuck. Thus far our Arms have with Success been Crown'd.—
Heroically spoken, faith, of a fellow that has not one farthing
in his Pocket. If I have one Penny to buy a Halter withal in my
present necessity, may I be hang'd; tho I'm reduc'd to a fair
way of obtaining one methodically very soon, if Robbery or
Theft will purchase the Gallows. But hold—Can't I rob
honourably, by turning Soldier?

Enter a Cripple *begging.*

Cripple. One farthing to the poor old Soldier, for the Lord's
sake.

Roebuck. Ha!—a glimpse of Damnation just as a Man is 10
entering into sin, is no great policy of the Devil.—But how
long did you bear Arms, friend?

Cripple. Five years, an't please you Sir.

Roebuck. And how long has that honourable Crutch born
you?

Cripple. Fifteen, Sir.

Roebuck. Very pretty! Five year a Soldier, and Fifteen a
Beggar!—This is Hell right! an age of Damnation for a
momentary offence. Thy condition fellow, is preferable to
mine; the merciful Bullet, more kind than thy ungrateful 20
Country, has given thee a Debenter in thy broken Leg, from
which thou canst draw a more plentiful maintenance than I
from all my Limbs in perfection. Prethee friend, why wouldst
thou beg of me? Dost think I'm rich?

Cripple. No, Sir, and therefore I believe you charitable.
Your warm fellows are so far above the sense of our Misery,

I. 1 *Roebuck*] ed.; [om.]

that they can't pitty us; and I have always found it, by sad experience, as needless to beg of a rich Man as a Clergyman. Our greatest Benefactors, the brave Officers are all disbanded,
30 and must now turn Beggars like my self; and so, Times are very hard, Sir.

Roebuck. What, are the Soldiers more charitable than the Clergy.

Cripple. Ay, Sir, A Captain will say Dam'me, and give me Six-pence; and a Parson shall whine out God bless me, and give me not a farthing: Now I think the Officers Blessing much the best.

Roebuck. Are the Beau's never compassionate?

Cripple. The great full Wigs they wear, stop their Ears so
40 close, that they can't hear us; and if they shou'd, they never have any farthings about 'em.

Roebuck. Then I am a Beau, friend; therefore pray leave me. Begging from a generous Soul that has not to bestow, is more tormenting than Robbery to a Miser in his abundance. Prethee friend, be thou charitable for once; I beg only the favour which rich friends bestow, a little Advice. I am as poor as thou art, and am designing to turn Soldier.

Cripple. No, no, Sir. See what an honourable Post I am forc'd to stand to, My Rags are scarecrows sufficient to
50 frighten any one from the Field; rather turn bird of prey at home. (*Shewing his Crutch.*)

Roebuck. Grammercy, old Devil. I find Hell has its Pimps of the poorer sort, as well as of the wealthy. I fancy, friend, thou hast got a Cloven-foot instead of a broken Leg. 'Tis a hard Case, that a Man must never expect to go nearer Heav'n than some steps of a Ladder. But 'tis unavoidable: I have my wants to lead, and the Devil to drive; and if I cann't meet my friend *Lovewell,* (which I think impossible, being so great a stranger in Town) Fortune thou hast done thy worst; I proclaim open
60 War against thee.

> *I'll stab thy next rich Darling that I see;*
> *And killing him, be thus reveng'd on thee.*

Goes to the back part of the Stage, as into the Walks,
making some turns cross the Stage in disorder, while
the next speak.

Exit Cripple.

Enter Lucinda *and* Pindress.

Lucinda. Oh these Summer mornings are so delicately fine, *Pindress*, it does me good to be abroad.

Pindress. Ay, Madam, these Summer mornings are as pleasant to young folks, as the Winter nights to marri'd people, or as your morning of Beauty to Mr. *Lovewell*.

Lucinda. I'm violently afraid the Evening of my Beauty will fall to his share very soon; for I'm inclinable to marry him. I shall soon lie under an Eclipse, *Pindress*.   70

Pindress. Then it must be full Moon with your Ladyship. But why wou'd you choose to marry in Summer, Madam?

Lucinda. I know no cause, but that people are aptest to run mad in hot weather, unless you take a Womans reason.

Pindress. What's that, Madam?

Lucinda. Why, I am weary of lying alone.

Pindress. Oh dear Madam! lying alone is very dangerous; 'tis apt to breed strange Dreams.

Lucinda. I had the oddest Dream last night of my Courtier that is to be, 'Squire *Mockmode*. He appear'd crowded about 80 with a Dancing-Master, Pushing-Master, Musick-Master, and all the throng of Beau-makers; and methought he mimick'd Foppery so awkwardly, that his imitation was down-right burlesquing it. I burst out a laughing so heartily, that I waken'd my self.

Pindress. But Dreams go by contraries, Madam. Have not you seen him yet.

Lucinda. No; but my Unkles Letter gives account that he's newly come to Town from the University, where his Education could reach no farther than to guzzle fat Ale, smoak Tobacco, 90 and chop Logick.—Faugh—it makes me Sick.

Pindress. But he's very rich, Madam; his Concerns joyn to yours in the Country.

Lucinda. Ay, but his Concerns shall never joyn to mine in the City: For since I have the disposal of my own Fortune, *Lovewell*'s the Man for my Money.

Pindress. Ay, and for my Money; for I've had above twenty

Pieces from him since his Courtship began. He's the prettiest sober Gentleman; I have so strong an opinion of his modesty, that I'm afraid, Madam, your first Child will be a Fool.

Lucinda. Of God forbid! I hope a Lawyer understands bus'ness better than to beget any thing *non compos.*—The Walks fill a pace; the Enemy approaches, we must set out our false Colours. (*Put on their Masks.*)

Pindress. We Masks are the purest Privateers! Madam, how would you like to Cruise about a little?

Lucinda. Well enough, had we no Enemies but our Fops and Cits: But I dread these blustring Men of War, the Officers, who after a Broad-side of Dam'me's and Sinkme's, are for boarding all Masks they meet, as lawful Prize.

Pindress. In truth Madam, and the most of 'em are lawful Prize, for they generally have *French* Ware under Hatches.

Lucinda. Oh hidious! O' my Conscience Girl thou'rt quite spoild. An Actres upon the Stage would blush at such expressions.

Pindress. Ay Madam, and your Ladyship wou'd seem to blush in the Box, when the redness of your face proceeded from nothing but the constraint of holding your Laughter. Did you chide me for not putting a stronger Lace in your Stays, when you had broke one as strong as a Hempen Cord, with containing a violent Tihee at a smutty Jest in the last Play.

Lucinda. Go, go, thou'rt a naughty Girl; thy impertinent Chat has diverted us from our bus'ness. I'm afraid *Lovewell* has miss'd us for want of the Sign.—But whom have we here? an odd figure! some Gentleman in disguise, I believe.

Pindress. Had he a finer Suit on, I shou'd believe him in disguise; for I fancy his friends have only known him by that this Twelve-month.

Lucinda. His Mien and Air shew him a Gentleman, and his Cloaths demonstrate him a Wit. He may afford us some sport. I have a Female inclination to talk to him.

Pindress. Hold, Madam, he looks as like one of those dangerous Men of War you just now mention'd as can be; you had best sent out your Pinnace before to discover the Enemy.

Lucinda. No, I'll hale him my self. (*Moves toward him.*) What, Sir, dreaming? (*Slaps him o'th' Shoulder with her Fan.*)

Roebuck. Yes, Madam. (*Sullenly.*)

Lucinda. Of what?

Roebuck. Of the Devil, and now my Dream's out.

Lucinda. What! Do you Dream standing? 140

Roebuck. Yes faith, Lady, very often when my sleep's haunted by such pretty Goblins as you. You are a sort of Dream I wou'd fain be reading: I'm a very good interpreter Indeed, Madam.

Lucinda. Are you then one of the Wise Men of the East?

Roebuck. No, Madam; but one of the Fools of the West.

Lucinda. Pray what do you mean by that?

Roebuck. An *Irish*-man, Madam, at your Service.

Lucinda. Oh horrible! an *Irish*-man! a meer Wolf-Dog, I protest. 150

Roebuck. Ben't surpriz'd Child; the Wolf-Dog is as well natur'd an Annimal as any of your Country Bull-Dogs, and a much more fawning Creature, let me tell ye. (*Lays hold on her.*)

Lucinda. Pray good *Caesar*, keep off your Paws; no scraping acquaintance, for Heaven's sake. Tell us some news of your Country; I have heard the strangest Stories,—that the people wear Horns and Hoofs.

Roebuck. Yes, faith, a great many wear Horns: but we had that among other laudable fashions, from *London*. I think it came over with your mode of wearing high Topknots; for ever 160 since, the men and Wives bear their heads exalted alike. They were both fashions that took wonderfully.

Lucinda. Then you have Ladies among you?

Roebuck. Yes, yes, we have Ladies, and Whores; Colleges, and Playhouses; Churches, and Taverns; fine Houses, and Bawdy-houses; in short, every thing that you can boast of, but Fops, Poets, Toads and Adders.

Lucinda. But have you no Beau's at all?

Roebuck. Yes, they come over, like the Woodcoks, once a year. 170

Lucinda. And have your Ladies no Springes to catch 'em in?

Roebuck. No, Madam; our own Country affords us much better Wild-fowl. But they are generally stripp'd of their feathers by the Playhouse and Taverns; in both which they pretend to be Criticks; and our ignorant Nation imagines a full Wig as infallible a token of a Wit as the Lawrel.

154 scraping] Q2; scarping

Lucinda. Oh Lard! and here 'tis the certain sign of a Blockhead. But why no Poets in *Ireland*, Sir!

Roebuck. Faith, Madam, I know not, unless St. *Patrick* sent
180 them a packing with other venomous Creatures out of *Ireland*. Nothing that carries a Sting in its Tongue can live there. But since I have described my Country, let me know a little of *England*, by sight of your Face.

Lucinda. Come you to particulars first. Pray, Sir, unmasque, by telling who you are; and then I'll unmasque, and shew who I am.

Roebuck. You must dismiss your attendant then, Madam; for the distinguishing particular of me is a Secret.

Pindress. Sir, I can keep a Secret as well as my Mistress; and
190 the greater the secrets are, I love 'em the better.

Lucinda. Can't they be whisper'd, Sir?

Roebuck. Oh yes, Madam, I can give you a hint, by which you may understand 'em—(*Pretends to whisper, and kisses her.*)

Lucinda. Sir, you're Impudent—

Roebuck. Nay, Madam, since you're so good at minding folks, have with you. (*Catches her fast, carrying her off.*)

Lucinda. }
Pindress. } Help! help! help!

Enter Lovewell [*and* Brush].

Lovewell. Villain, unhand the Lady, and defend thy self. (*Draws.*)

Roebuck. What! Knight-Errants in this Country! Now has
200 the Devil very opportunely sent me a Throat to cut; Pray Heaven his Pockets be well lin'd.—

Quits 'em, they go off.
Have at thee—St. *George* for *England.*—(*They fight, after some passes,* Roebuck *starts back and pauses.*) My Friend *Lovewell?*

Lovewell. My dear *Roebuck!* (*Fling down their Swords and embrace.*) Shall I believe my eyes?

Roebuck. You may believe your ears; 'Tis I be gad.

Lovewell. Why thy being in *London* is such a mystery, that I must have the evidence of more senses than one to confirm me of its truth.—But pray unfold the Riddle.

210 *Roebuck.* Why Faith 'tis a Riddle. You wonder at it before the Explanation, then wonder more at your self for not

guessing it.—What is the Universal cause of the continued Evils of mankind?

Lovewell. The Universal cause of our continu'd evil is the Devil sure.

Roebuck. No, 'tis the Flesh, *Ned.*—That very Woman that drove us all out of Paradise, has sent me a packing out of *Ireland.*

Lovewell. How so?

Roebuck. Only tasting the forbidden Fruit: that was all.   220

Lovewell. Is simple Fornication become so great a Crime there, as to be punishable by no less than Banishment?

Roebuck. I gad, mine was double Fornication, *Ned*—The Jade was so pregnant to bear Twins; the fruit grew in Clusters; and my unconscionable Father, because I was a Rogue in Debauching her, wou'd make me a fool by Wedding her: But I wou'd not marry a Whore, and he would not own a disobedient Son, and so—

Lovewell. But was she a Gentlewoman?

Roebuck. Pshaw! No, she had no Fortune. She wore indeed a   230 Silk Manteau and High-Head; but these are grown as little signs of Gentility now a-days, as that is of Chastity.

Lovewell. But what necessity forc'd you to leave the Kingdom?

Roebuck. I'll tell you.—To shun th' insulting Authority of an incens'd Father, the dull and often-repeated advice of impertinent Relations, the continual clamours of a furious Woman, and the shrill bawling of an ill natur'd Bastard.—From all which, Good Lord deliver me.

Lovewell. And so you left them to Grand Dada! —Ha, ha, ha.   240

Roebuck. Heaven was pleased to lessen my affliction, by taking away the she Brat; but the t'other is, I hope, well, because a brave Boy, whom I christen'd *Edward*, after thee, *Lovewell*; I made bold to make my man stand for you, and your Sister sent her Maid to give her name to my Daughter.

Lovewell. Now you talk of my Sister, pray how does she?

Roebuck. Dear *Lovewell*, a very Miracle of Beauty and Goodness.—But I don't like her.

Lovewell. Why?

Roebuck. She's Virtuous;—and I think Beauty and Virtue   250 are as ill joyned as Lewdness and Ugliness.

Lovewell. But I hope your Arguments could not make her a Proselyte to this Profession.

Roebuck. Faith I endeavour'd it; but that Plaguy Honour— Damn it for a whim—Were it as honourable for Women to be Whores, as men to be Whore-masters, we shou'd have Lewdness as great a Mark of Quality among the Ladies, as 'tis now among the Lords.

Lovewell. What! do you hold no innate Principle of Vertue 260 in Women?

Roebuck. I hold an innate principle of Love in them: Their Passions are as great as ours, their Reason weaker. We admire them and consequently they must us. And I tell thee once more, That had Women no safe guard but your innate Principle of Vertue, honest *George Roebuck* wou'd have lain with your Sister, *Ned,* and shou'd enjoy a Countess before night.

Lovewell. But methinks, *George,* 'twas not fair to tempt my Sister.

270 *Roebuck.* Methinks 'twas not fair of thy Sister, *Ned,* to tempt me. As she was thy Sister, I had no design upon her: but as she's a pretty Woman, I could scarcely forbear her, were she my own.

Lovewell. But, upon serious reflection, Cou'd not you have liv'd better at home, by turning thy Whore into a Wife, than hear by turning other Mens Wives into Whores? There are Merchants Ladies in *London,* and you must trade with them, for ought I see.

Roebuck. Ay, but is the Trade open? Is the Manufacture 280 incourag'd, old Boy?

Lovewell. Oh, wonderfully!—a great many poor people live by't. Tho the Husbands are for engrossing the Trade, the Wives are altogether for encouraging Interlopers. But I hope you have brought some small Stock to set up with.

Roebuck. The greatness of my wants, which wou'd force me to discover 'em, makes me blush to own 'em. (*Aside.*) Why faith, *Ned,* I had a great Journey from *Ireland* hither, and wou'd burden my self with no more than just necessary Charges.

290 *Lovewell.* Oh, then you have brought Bills?

Roebuck. No, faith. Exchange of Money from *Dublin* hither is so unreasonable high, that—

Lovewell. What?

Roebuck. That—Zoons I have not one farthing.—Now you understand me?

Lovewell. No faith, I never understand one that comes in *formâ pauperis*; I han't study'd the Law so long for nothing.— But what prospect can you propose of a supply?

Roebuck. I'll tell you. When you appear'd, I was just thanking my Stars for sending me a Throat to cut, and 300 consequently a Purse: But my knowledge of you prevented me of that way, and therefore I think you're oblig'd in return to assist me by some better means. You were once an honest Fellow; but so long study in the Inns may alter a Man strangely, as you say.

Lovewell. No, dear *Roebuck*, I'm still a friend to thy Vertues, and esteem thy Follies as Foils only to set them off. I did but rally you; and to convince you, here are some Pieces, share of what I have about me; Take them as earnest of my farther supply; you know my Estate sufficient to maintain us both, if 310 you will either restrain your Extravagancies, or I retrench my Necessaries.

Roebuck. Thy profession of kindness is so great, that I cou'd almost suspect it of design.—But come, Friend, I am heartily tir'd with the fatigue of my Journey, besides a violent Fit of Sickness, which detain'd me a Month at *Coventry*, to the exhausting my Health and Money. Let me only recruit by a relish of the Town in Love and a Bottle, and then—(*As they are going off,* Roebuck *starts back surpriz'd.*)

Oh Heav'ns! and Earth!

Lovewell. What's the matter, Man?   320

Roebuck. Why! Death and the Devil; or, what's worse, a Woman and a Child.—Oons! don't you see Mrs. *Trudge* with my Bastard in her Arms crossing the field towards us?—Oh the indefatigable Whore to follow me all the way to *London*!

Lovewell. Mrs. *Trudge*! my old acquaintance!

Roebuck. Ay, ay, the very same; your old acquaintance; and for ought I know, you might have clubb'd about getting the Brats.

Lovewell. 'Tis but reasonable then I shou'd pay share at the Reckoning. I'll help to provide for her; in the mean time, you 330 had best retire.—*Brush*, conduct this Gentleman to my Lodgings, and run from thence to Widow *Bullfinch*'s, and provide a Lodging with her for a Friend of mine.—Fly, and come back presently.—

Exeunt Roebuck *and* Brush.

—So; my Friend comes to Town like the Great *Turk* to the Field, attended by his Concubines and Children; and I'm afraid these are but parts of his Retinue.—But hold—I shan't be able to sustain the shock of this Womans Fury. I'll withdraw till she has discharged her first Volley, then surprize 340 her.

Enter Trudge, *with a Child crying.*

Trudge. Hush, hush, hush.—And indeed it was a young Traveller.—And what wou'd it say? It says that Daddy is a false Man, a cruel Man, and an ungrateful Man.—In troth so he is, my dear Child.—What shall I do with it, poor Creature?—Hush, hush, hush.—Was ever poor Woman in such a lamentable condition? immediately after the pains of one Travel to undergo the fatigues of another?—But I'm sure he can never do well; for tho I can't find him, my curses, and the misery of this Babe, will certainly reach him.

350 *Lovewell.* Methinks I shou'd know that voice.—(*Moving forward.*) What! Mrs. *Trudge*! and in *London*! whose brave Boy hast thou got there?

Trudge. Oh Lord! Mr. *Lovewell*! I'm very glad to see you,—and yet am asham'd to see you. But indeed he promis'd to marry me, (*Crying.*) and you know, Mr. *Lovewell*, that he's such a handsome Man, and has so many ways of insinuating, that the frailty of Woman's Nature could not resist him.

Lovewell. What's all this?—A handsome Man? Ways of insinuating? Frailty of Nature?—I don't understand these 360 ambiguous terms.

Trudge. Ah, Mr. *Lovewell*! I'm sure you have seen Mr. *Roebuck*, and I'm sure 'twou'd be the first thing he wou'd tell you. I refer it to you, Mr. *Lovewell*, if he is not an ungrateful man, to deal so barbarously with any Woman that had us'd him so civily. I was kinder to him than I would have been to my own born Brother.

Lovewell. Oh then I find kissing goes by favour, Mrs. *Trudge.*

Trudge. Faith you're all alike, you men are alike.—Poor Child! he's as like his own Dadda, as if he were spit out of his mouth. See, Mr. *Lovewell*, if he has not Mr. *Roebuck*'s Nose to a 370 hair; and you know he has a very good Nose;—and the little Pigsnye has Mamma's Mouth.—Oh the little Lips!—and 'tis the best natur'd little dear—(*Smuggles and kisses it.*)—And wou'd it ask its God-Father Blessing?—Indeed, Mr. *Lovewell*, I believe the Child knows you.

Lovewell. Ha, ha, ha! Well, I will give it my Blessing. (*Gives it Gold.*)

> As he gives her the Gold, enter Lucinda *and*
> Pindress, *who seeing them stand, abscond.*

Come, Madam, I'll first settle you in a Lodging and then find the false Man, as you call him.—

> *Exeunt* Lovewell [*and* Trudge.]
> Lucinda *and* Pindress *come forward.*

Lucinda. The false man is found already.—Was there ever such a lucky discovery?—My care for his preservation 380 brought me back, and now behold how my kindness is return'd!—Their Fighting was a downright trick to frighten me from the place, thereby to afford him opportunity of entertaining his Whore and Brat.

Pindress. Your conjecture, Madam, bears a colour; for looking back, I could perceive 'em talking very familiarly; so that they cou'd not be strangers as their pretended Quarrel would intimate.

Lucinda. 'Tis all true as he is false.—What! slighted! despis'd! my honourable Love truck'd for a Whore! Oh 390 Villain! Epitome of thy Sex!—But I'll be reveng'd. I'll marry the first man that asks me the Question; nay, though he be a disbanded Soldier, or a poor Poet, or a senseless Fop;—Nay, tho' Impotent I'll Marry him.

Pindress. Oh Madam! that's to be reveng'd on your self.

Lucinda. I care not, Fool! I deserve punishment for my Credulity, as much as he for his Falshood—And you deserve it too, Minx; your perswasions drew me to this Assignation: I never lov'd the false man.

Pindress. That's false, I'm sure. (*Aside.*)   400

Lucinda. But you thought to get another piece of Gold. We

shall have him giving you Money on the same score he was so
liberal to his Whore just now. (*Walks about in Passion.*)

Enter Lovewell [*and* Brush].

Lovewell. So much for Friendship—now for my Love.—I
han't transgressed much.—Oh, there she is.—Oh my Angel!
(*Runs to her.*)

Lucinda. Oh thou Devil!— (*Starts back.*)

Lovewell. Not unless you damn me, Madam.

Lucinda. You're damn'd already; you're a Man.

Exit pushing Pindress.

Lovewell. You're a Woman, I'll be sworn.—Hey day! what
410 giddy Female Planet rules now! By the Lord, these Women
are like their Maidenheads, no sooner found than lost.—Here,
Brush, run after *Pindress,* and know the occasion of this.—(Brush
runs.)—Stay, come back—Zoons, I'm a fool.

Brush. That's the first wise word you have spoke these two
months.   ·

Lovewell. Trouble me with your untimely Jests, Sirrah, and
I'll—

Brush. Your Pardon, Sir; I'm in down-right earnest.—'Tis
less Slavery to be Apprentice to a famous Clap-Surgeon, than
420 to a Lover. He falls out with me, because he can't fall in with
his Mistress. I can bear it no longer.

Lovewell. Sirrah, what are you mumbling?

Brush. A short Prayer before I depart, Sir.—I have been
these three years your Servant, but now, Sir, I'm your humble
Servant. (*Bows as going.*)

Lovewell. Hold, you shan't leave me.

Brush. Sir, you can't be my Master.

Lovewell. Why so?

Brush. Because you're not your own Master; yet one would
430 think you might, for you have lost your Mistress. Oons, Sir, let
her go, and a fair riddance. Who throws away a Tester and a
Mistress, loses six-pence. That little Pimping *Cupid* is a blind
Gunner. Had he shot as many Darts as I have carry'd *Billets
deux,* he wou'd have laid her kicking with her heels up e're
now. In short, Sir, my Patience is worn to the stumps with
attending; my Shoes and Stockings are upon their last Legs
with trudging between you. I have sweat out all my moisture

of my hand with palming your clammy Letters upon her. I
have—

Lovewell. Hold, Sir, your trouble is now at an end, for I 440
design to marry her.

Brush. And have you courted her these three years for
nothing but a Wife?

Lovewell. Do you think, Raskal, I wou'd have taken so much
pains to make her a Miss?

Brush. No, Sir; the tenth part on't wou'd ha' done.—But if
you are resolv'd to marry, God b'w'ye.

Lovewell. What's the matter now, Sirrah!

Brush. Why, the matter will be, that I must then Pimp for
her.—Hark ye, Sir, what have you been doing all this while, 450
but teaching her the way to Cuckold ye?—Take care, Sir; look
before you leap. You have a ticklish point to manage.—Can
you tell, Sir, what's her quarel to you now?

Lovewell. I can't imagine. I don't remember that ever I
offended her.

Brush. That's it Sir. She resolves to put your easiness to the
Test now, that she may with more security rely upon't
hereafter.—Always suspect those Women of Designs that are
for searching into the humours of their Courtiers; for they
certainly intend to try them when they're marry'd.   460

Lovewell. How cam'st thou such an Engineer in Love?

Brush. I have sprung some Mines in my time, Sir; and since
I have trudg'd so long about your amorous Messages, I have
more Intrigue in the sole of my feet, than some Blockheades in
their whole Body.

Lovewell. Sirrah, have you ever discover'd any behaviour in
this Lady, to occasion this suspicious discourse?

Brush. Sir, has this Lady ever discover'd any behaviour of
yours to occasion this suspicious quarrel? I believe the Lady
has as much of the innate Principle of Vertue (as the 470
Gentleman said) as any Woman: But that Baggage her
Attendant is about ravishing her Ladies Page every hour. 'Tis
an old saying, like Master, like Man; why not as well, like
Mistress, like Maid?

Lovewell. Since thou art for trying humours, have with you
Madam *Lucinda.* Besides, so fair an opportunity offers, that

Fate seem'd to design it.—Have you left the Gentleman at my Lodgings?

Brush. Yes, Sir, and sent a Porter to his Inn to bring his
480 things thither.

Lovewell. That's right—Love like other Diseases, must sometimes have a desperate Cure. The School of *Venus* imposes the strict Discipline; And awful *Cupid* is a chastning God; He whips severely.

Brush. No, not if we kiss the Rod.

                                                 Exeunt.

The End of the First Act.

ACT II. [Scene i.]

SCENE Lovewell's *Lodgings.*

Enter Lovewell, Roebuck *dress'd, and* Brush.

Lovewell. O' my Conscience the fawning Creature loves you.

Roebuck. Ay, the constant effects of debauching a Woman are, that she infallibly loves the Man for doing the business, and he certainly hates her.—But what Company is she like to have at this same Widows, *Brush?*

Brush. Oh the best of Company, Sir; a Poet lives there, Sir.

Roebuck. They're the worst Company, for they're ill natur'd.

Brush. Ay, Sir, but it does no body any harm; for these
10 fellows that get Bread by their Wits, are always forc'd to eat their words. They must be good natur'd, 'spight of their Teeth, Sir. 'Tis said he pays his Lodging by cracking some smutty Jests with his Landlady over-night; for she's very well pleas'd with his natural parts. (*While* Roebuck *and* Brush *talk,* Lovewell *seems to project something by himself.*)

Roebuck. What other Lodgers are there?

Brush. One newly entr'd, a young Squire, just come from the University.

Roebuck. A meer Peripatetick I warrant him.—A very pretty Family A Heathen Philosopher, an *English* Poet, and an *Irish*
20 Whore. Had the Landlady but a *Highland* Piper to joyn with

'em, she might set up for a Collection of Monsters.—Any body within. (*Slaps* Lovewell *on the Sholder.*)

Lovewell. Yes, you are, my Friend. All my thoughts were employ'd about you. In short, I have one request to make, That you would renounce your loose wild Courses, and lead a sober life, as I do.

Roebuck. That I will, if you'll grant me a Boon.

Lovewell. You shall have it, be't what it will.

Roebuck. That you wou'd relinquish your precise sober behaviour, and live like a Gentleman as I do.   30

Lovewell. That I can't grant.

Roebuck. Then we're off; Tho shou'd your Women prove no better than your Wine, my Debaucheries will fall of themselves, for want of Temptation.

Lovewell. Our Women are worse than our Wine; our Claret has but little of the *French* in't, but our Wenches have the Devil and all: They are both adulterated, To prevent the inconveniencies of which, I'll provide you an honourable Mistress.

Roebuck. An honourable Mistress! what's that?   40

Lovewell. A vertuous Lady, whom you must Love and Court; the surest method of reclaiming you.—As thus.—Those superfluous Pieces you throw away in Wine may be laid out.—

Roebuck. To the Poor?

Lovewell. No, no. In Sweet Powder, Cravats, Garters, Snuff-boxes, Ribbons, Coach-hire, and Chair-hire. Those idle hours which you mispend with lewd sophisticated Wenches, must be dedicated—

Roebuck. To the Church?   50

Lovewell. No, To the innocent and charming Conversation of your vertuous Mistress; by which means, the two most exorbitant Debaucheries, Drinking and Whoring will be retrench'd.

Roebuck. A very fine Retrenchment truly! I must first despise the honest jolly Conversation at the Tavern, for the foppish, affected, dull, insipid Entertainment at the Chocolate-house; must quit my freedom with ingenious Company, to harness my self to Foppery among the fluttering Crowd of

60 *Cupid*'s Livery-boys.—The second Article is, That I must
resign the Company of lewd Women for that of my Innocent
Mistress; That is, I must change my easie natural sin of
Wenching, to that constrain'd Debauchery of Lying and
Swearing.—The many Lyes and Oaths that I made to thy
Sister, will go nearer to damn me, than if I had enjoy'd her a
hundred times over.

Lovewell. Oh *Roebuck*! your Reason will maintain the contrary, when you're in Love.

Roebuck. That is, when I have lost my Reason, Come, come,
70 a Wench a Wench! a soft, white, easy, consenting Creature!—
Prithee *Ned* leave Musteness, and shew me the Varieties of
the Town.

Lovewell. A Wench is the least Variety—Look out—See
what a numerous Train trip along the street there—(*Pointing
outwards.*)

Roebuck. Oh *Venus*! all these fine stately Creatures! Fair you
well, *Ned*.—(*Runs out; Lovewell catches him, and pulls him back.*)
Prithee let me go: 'Tis a deed of Charity; I'm quite starv'd. I'll
just take a snap, and be with you in the twinkling.—As you're
my friend.—I must go.

80 *Lovewell.* Then we must break for altogether?—(*Quits him.*)
—He that will leave his friend for a Whore, I reckon a
Commoner in Friendship as in Love.

Roebuck. If you saw how ill that serious face becomes a
Fellow of your years, you wou'd never wear it again. Youth is
taking in any Masqurade but Gravity.

Lovewell. Tho Lewdness suits much worse with your Circumstances, Sir.

Roebuck. Ay these Circumstances. Damn these Circumstances.—There he has Hamstring'd me. This Poverty! how it
90 makes a Man sneak! [*Aside.*]—Well prithee let's know this
Devilish Vertuous Lady. By the Circumstances of my Body I
shall soon be off or on with her.

Lovewell. Know then, for thy utter Condemnation, that
she's a Lady of Eighteen, Beautiful, Witty, and nicely
Vertuous.

Roebuck. A Lady of Eighteen! Good.—Beautiful! Better.—
Witty!—Best of all—Now with these three Qualifications, if
she be nicely Vertuous, then I'll henceforth adore every thing

that wears a Petycoat.—Witty and Vertuous! ha, ha, ha.
Why, 'tis as inconsistant in Ladies as Gentlemen; And were I   100
to debauch one for a Wager, her Wit shou'd be my
Bawd.—Come, come; the forbidden Fruit was pluck'd from
the Tree of Knowledge, Boy.
   Lovewell. Right.—But there was a cunninger Devil than
you, to tempt.—I'll assure you *George*, your Rhetorick wou'd
fail you here; she wou'd worst you at your own Weapons.
   Roebuck. Ay, or any Man in *England*, if she be Eighteen as
you say.
   Lovewell. Have a care, friend, this Satyr will get you torn in
pieces by the Females; you'll fall into *Orpheus*'s fate.   110
   Roebuck. Orpheus was a blockhead, and deserv'd his fate.
   Lovewell. Why?
   Roebuck. Because he went to Hell for a Wife.
   Lovewell. This happens right.—(*Aside.*)—But you shall go
to Heav'n for a Mistress, you shall Court this Divine
Creature.—I don't desire you to fall in Love with her; I don't
intend you shou'd marry her nither: but you must be
convinc'd of the Chastity of the Sex; Tho, if you shou'd
conquer her, the Spoil, you Rogue, will be glorious, and
infinitely worth the pains in attaining.   120
   Roebuck. Ay, but *Ned*, my Circumstances, my Circum-
stances.—
   Lovewell. Come, you shan't want Money.
   Roebuck. Then I dare attempt it. Money is the Sinews of
Love, as of War. Gad friend, thou't the bravest Pimp I ever
heard of.—Well, give me directions to sail by, the name of
my Port, laden my Pockets, and then for the Cape of Good
Hope.
   Lovewell. You need no directions as to the manner of
Courtship.   130
   Roebuck. No; I have seen some few Principles, on which my
Courtship's founded, which seldom fail. To let a Lady rely
upon my modesty, but to depend my self altogether upon my
Impudence; To use a Mistress like a Deity in publick, but like
a Woman in private: To be as cautious then of asking an
Impertinent question, as afterwards of telling a story; re-
membring, that the Tongue is the only Member that can hurt
a Ladies Honour, tho touch'd in the tender'st part.

Lovewell. Oh, but to a Friend, *George*; you'll tell a Friend
140 your success?

Roebuck. No, not to her very self; it must be as private as
Devotion.—No blabbing, unless a squawling Brat peeps out
to tell Tales.—But where lies my Course?

Lovewell. *Brush* shall shew you the house; the Ladies name is
Lucinda; her Father and Mother dead; she's Heiress to Twelve
hundred a year: But above all, observe this: She has a Page
which you must get on your side; 'Tis a very pretty Boy; I
presented him to the Lady about a fortnight ago; he's your
Country-man too; he brought me a Letter from my Sister,
150 which I have about me.—Here you may read it.

Roebuck. Ay, 'tis her hand; I know it well; and I almost
blush to see it. (*Aside.*) (*Reads.*)

Dear Brother,
*A Lady of my acquaintance lately dying, begg'd me, as her last
request, to provide for this Boy, who was her Page. I hope I have
obeyed my Friend's last Command, and oblig'd a Brother, by
sending him to you. Pray dispose of him as much as you can for his
advantage. All friends are well, and I am*
                              Your affectionate Sister, *Leanthe.*

(*While he reads,* Lovewell *talks to* Brush, *and gives
him some directions seemingly.*)
160   All friends are well? Is that all? not a word of poor
Roebuck.—I wonder she mention'd nothing of my misfortunes
to her Brother. But she has forgot me already. True Woman
still.—Well, I may excuse her, for I'm making all the haste I
can to forget her. [*Aside.*]

Lovewell. Be sure you have an eye upon him, and come to
me presently at Widow *Bullfinch*'s—(*To* Brush.)—Well, *George*,
you won't communicate your success?

Roebuck. You may guess what you please.—I'm as merry
after a Mistress as after a Bottle.—All Air; brimfull of Joy, like
170 a Bumper of Claret, smiling and sparkling.

Lovewell. Then you'll certainly run over.

Roebuck. No, no; nor shall I drink to any body.—

                                        Exeunt severally.

[ACT II. Scene ii.]

SCENE changes to a Dining Room in Widow
Bullfinch's *house, A Flute, a Musick-book on the*
Table; a Case of Toyes hanging up.—

Enter Rigadoon *the Dancing-Master, leading in*
Mockmode *by both hands, as teaching him the Minuet;*
he sings, and Mockmode *dances awkwardly;* Club *follows.*

Rigadoon. Tal—dal—deral—One—Two.—Tal—dal—
deral—Coupé—Tal—dal—deral—Very well—Tal—dal—
deral—Wrong.—Tal—dal—deral—Toes out—Tal—dal—
deral—Observe Time:—Very well indeed, Sir; you shall
dance as well as any Man in *England*; you have an excellent
disposition in your Limbs, Sir—Observe me, Sir. (*Here the*
Master dances a new Minuet; and at every Cut Club *makes an*
awkward imitation, by leaping up.) And so forth, Sir.
Mockmode. I'm afraid we shall disturb my Landlady.
Rigadoon. Landlady! you must have a care of that; she'll
never pardon you.—Landlady!—Every Woman, from a 10
Countess to a Kitchen-Wench, is *Madam*; and every Man,
from a Lord to a Lacquey, *Sir.*
Mockmode. Must I then lose my Title of 'Squire, 'Squire
Mockmode?
Rigadoon. By all means, Sir; 'Squire and Fool are the same
thing here.
Mockmode. That's very Comical, faith!—But is there an Act
of Parliament for that, Mr. *Rigadoon?*—Well, since I can't be a
'Squire, I'll do as well: I have a great Estate, and want only to
be a great Beau, to qualifie me either for a Knight or a Lord. 20
By the Universe, I have a great mind to bind my self 'Prentice
to a Beau.—Cou'd I but dance well, push well, play upon the
Flute, and swear the most modish Oaths, I wou'd set up for
Quality with e're a young Nobleman of 'em all.—Pray what
are the most fashionable Oaths in Town? *Zoons*, I take it, is a
very becoming one.
Rigadoon. Zoons is only us'd by the disbanded Officers and
Bullies: but Zauns is the Beaux pronunciation.
Mockmode. Zauns—

30 *Club.* Zauns—
    Rigadoon. Yes, Sir, we swear as we Dance; smooth, and with
    a Cadence.—Zauns!—'Tis harmonious, and pleases the Ladies,
    because 'tis soft.—Zauns, Madam.—is the only Compliment
    our great Beaux pass on a Lady.
        Mockmode. But suppose a Lady speaks to me? what must I
    say?
        Rigadoon. Nothing, Sir.—you must take Snush, Grin, and
    make her an humble Cringe—Thus:
        He bows Foppishly, and takes Snush; Mockmode *imitates him*
            awkwardly; and taking Snush, sneezes.
        Rigadoon. O Lard, Sir, you must never sneeze; 'tis as
40 unbecoming after *Orangere*, as Grace after meat.
        Mockmode. I thought People took it to clear the Brain.
        Rigadoon. The Beaux have no Brains at all, Sir; their Skull is
    a perfect Snush-box; and I heard a Physician swear, who
    open'd one of 'em, that the three divisions of his head were
    filled with *Orangere, Bourgamot,* and Plain-*Spanish.*
        Mockmode. Zauns I must sneeze—(*Sneezes.*)—Bless me.
        Rigadoon. O fie, Mr. *Mockmode!* what a rustical expression
    that is.—Bless me!—you shou'd upon all such occasions cry,
    Dem me. You wou'd be as nauseous to the Ladies, as one of
50 the old Patriarks, if you us'd that obsolete expression.
        Club. I find that going to the Devil is very modish in this
    Town—Pray, Master, Dancing-Master, what Religion may
    these Beaux be of?
        Rigadoon. A sort of *Indians* in their Religion, They worship
    the first thing they see in the Morning.
        Mockmode. What's that Sir?
        Rigadoon. Their own shadows in the Glass; and some of 'em
    such hellish Faces, that may frighten 'em into Devotion.
        Mockmode. Then they are *Indians* right, for they worship the
60 Devil.
        Rigadoon. Then you shall be as great a Beau as any of 'em.
    But you must be sure to mind your Dancing.
        Mockmode. Is not Musick very convenient too?—I can play
    the *Bells* and *Maiden Fair* already. *Alamire, Bifabemi, Cesolfa,*
    Delasol, Ela, Effaut, Gesolreut. I have 'em all by heart already.
    But I have been plaguily puzzl'd about the Etymology of these
    Notes; and cerainly a Man cannot arrive at any perfection,

unless he understands the derivation of the Terms.
Rigadoon. O Lard, Sir! That's easie. *Effaut* and *Gesolreut*
were two famous *German* Musicians, and the rest were *Italians.* 70
Mockmode. But why are they only Seven?
Rigadoon. From a prodigious great Bass-Viol with seven
Strings, that play'd a Jig call'd the *Musick of the Spheres*: The
seven Planets were nothing but Fiddle-strings.
Mockmode. Then your Stars have made you a Dancing-
master?
Rigadoon. O Lard, Sir! *Pythagoras* was a Dancing-master; he
shews the Creation to be a Country-Dance, where after some
antick Changes, all the parts fell into their places, and there
they stand ready, till the next squeak of a Philosopher's Fiddle 80
sets 'em a Dancing again.
Club. Sir, here comes the pushing Master.
Rigadoon. Then I'll be gone. But you must have a care of
Pushing, 'twill spoil the niceness of your steps. Learn a
flourish or two; and that's all a Beau can have occasion for.

Enter Nimblewrist.

Mockmode. Oh, Mr. *Nimblewrist,* I crave you ten thousand
pardons, by the Universe.
Nimblewrist. That was a home thrust. Good Sir. I hope ya're
for a breathing this Morning. (*Takes down a Foyl.*)—I'll assure
you, Mr. *Mockmode*, you will make an excellent Swords Man; 90
y're as well shap'd for Fencing as any Man in *Europe.* The
Duke of *Burgundy* is just of your Make; he pushes the finest of
any Man in *France.*—Sa, sa—like Lightning.
Mockmode. I'm much in Love with Fencing: But I think
Back-Sword is the best play.
Nimblewrist. Oh Lard Sir!—Have you ever been in *France*,
Sir?
Mockmode. No, Sir; but I understand the Geography of
it.—*France* is bounded on the North with the *Rhine.*
Nimblewrist. No, Sir, a *Frenchman* is bounded on the North 100
with *Quart*, on the South with *Tierce*, and so forth. 'Tis a Noble
Art, Sir; and every one that wears a Sword is oblig'd by his
Tenure to learn. The Rules of Honour are engrav'd on my
Hilt, and my Blade must maintain 'em. My Sword's my
Herauld, and the bloody Hand my Coat of Arms.

Mockmode. And how long have you profess'd this Noble Art, Sir?

Nimblewrist. Truly, Sir, I serv'd an Apprenticeship to this Trade, Sir.

110 *Mockmode.* What are ye a Corporation then?

Nimblewrist. Yes, Sir; the Surgeons have taken us into their's, because we make so much work for 'em.—But, as I was telling you, Sir, I profess'd this Science till the Wars broke out: But then, when every body got Commissions, I put in for one, serv'd the Campaigns in *Flanders*; and when the Peace broke out, was disbanded; so among a great many other poor Rogues, am forc'd to betake to my old Trade. Now the publick Quarrel's ended, I live by private Ones. I live still by dying, as the song goes, Sir. While we have *English* Courages, *French* 120 Honour, and *Spanish* Blades among us, I shall live, Sir.

Mockmode. Surely your sword and skill did the King great service a broad.

Nimblewrist. Yes, Sir, I kill'd above fifteen of our own Officers by Private Duels in the Camp, Sir; kill'd 'em fairly; kill'd 'em thus, Sir.—Sa, sa, sa, sa. Parry, parry, parry,—

He pushes Mockmode *on the ribs; he strikes* Nimblewrist *over the head, and breaks the Foil.*

Club. What's the name of that Thrust, pray, Sir?

Nimblewrist. Oh Lard, Sir, he did not touch me; not in the least, Sir. The Foyl was crack'd, a palpable crack. (*Blood runs down his Face.*)

Club. A very palpable crack truly. Your Skull is only 130 crack'd, palpably crack'd, that's all.

Mockmode. Well, Sir, if you please to teach me my Honours —My Dancing-Master has forbid me any more, lest I should discompose my steps.

Nimblewrist. Your Dancing-Master is a Blockhead, Sir.

Enter Rigadoon.

Rigadoon. I forgot my Gloves, and so—

Mockmode. Oh Sir, he calls you Blockhead, by the Universe.

Rigadoon. Zauns, Sir— (*Foppishly.*)

Nimblewrist. Zoons, Sir. (*Bluffishly.*)

Rigadoon. I have more Wit in the sole of my foot then you 140 have in your whole body.

Nimblewrist. Ay, Sir, you Caperers daunce all your Brains

into your heels, which makes you carry such empty Noddles.
Your Rational's revers'd, carrying your understandings in
your Legs. Your Wit is the perfect *Antipodes* to other Mens.
Rigadoon. And what are you good Monsieur, sa, sa? Stand
upon your Guard Mr *Mockmode*, he's the greatest falsify in his
Art; he'll fill your head so full of *French* Principles of Honour,
that you won't have one of Honesty left. His Breast-plate there
he calls the But of Honour, at which all the Fools in the
Kingdom shoot, and not one can hit the Mark.   150
Nimblewrist. You talk of *Robin Hood*, who never shot in his
Bow, Sir.—You Dancers are the Battledoors of the Nation,
that toss the light Foppish Shuttlecocks to and agen, to get
your selves in heat.—Have a care, Mr. *Mockmode*, this Fellow
will make a meer Grashopper of you. Sir, you're the grand
Pimp to Foppery and Lewdness; and the Devil and a
Dancing-Master, Dance a Corante over the whole Kingdom.
Rigadoon. A Pimp, Sir! what then, Sir? I engage Couples
into the Bed of Love, but you match 'em in the Bed of Honour.
We only juggle People out of their Chastity, but you cheat 'em   160
out of their Lives. We shall have you, Mr. *Mockmode*, grinning
in the Bed of Honour, as if you laugh'd at the Fool who must
be hang'd for you.—Which is best, Mr. *Nimblewrist*, an easie
Minuet, or a *Tyburn* Jig?
Nimblewrist. Don't provoke my sword, Sir, least that Art
you so revile shou'd revenge it self; for every one of you that
live by Dancing should die by Pushing, Sir.
Rigadoon. And every Man that lives by Pushing, shou'd die
Dancing, I take it.
Nimblewrist. Zoons, Sir! what d'ye mean?   170
Rigadoon. Nothing,   Sir;—Tal—dal—deral.—(*Daunces.*)—
This takes the Ladies, Mr. *Mockmode*; this runs away with all
the great Fortunes in Town. Tho' you be a Fool, a Fop, a
Coward, Dance well, and you Captivate the Ladies. The
moving a man's Limbs pliantly, does the business. If you want
a Fortune, come to me—Tal—dal—deral—(*Daunces.*)
Nimblewrist. No, no, to me, Sir.—sa, sa,—does your business
soonest with a Woman. A clean and manly extension of all
your parts—Ha—Carrying a true point, is the matter.—Sa,
sa, sa, sa.—Defend your self.   180

Pushes at Rigadoon, *who Dances, and Sings, retiring*
off the Stage.
Enter Bullfinch.

Bullfinch. Oh goodness! what a Room's here! Cou'd not
these fellows wipe their feet before they came up. And here's
such a tripping and such a stamping, that they have broke
down all the Cieling. You Dancing and Fencing-Masters have
been the downfal of many Houses. Get out of my Doors; my
house was never in such a pickle.—You Country Gentlemen,
newly come to *London,* like your own Spaniels out of a Pond,
must be shaking the Water off, and bespatter every body
about you.— (Mockmode *having taken snush, offering to sneeze,*
sneezes in her face.)

190 *Mockmode.* Zauns, Madam—(*Sneezes.*)—Bless me!—Dem
me, I mean.

Bullfinch. He's tainted. These cursed Flies have blown upon
him already.

Mockmode. Sa, sa—Defend Flankonade, Madam.

Bullfinch. Ah, Mr. *Mockmode,* my Pushing and Dancing days
are done, But I had a Son, Mr. *Mockmode,* that wou'd match
you—Ah my poor *Robin!*—he dy'd of an Apoplexy; he was as
pretty a young man as ever stept in a Black-Leather Shoe: he
was as like you, Mr. *Mockmode;* as one Egg is like another; he
200 dy'd like an Angel—But I am sure he might have recover'd
but for the Physicians—oh thee Doctor's! these Doctors!

Mockmode. Bless the Doctors, I say; for I believe they kill'd
my honest old Father.

Bullfinch. Ay, that's true. If my *Robin* had left me an Estate,
I shou'd have said so too.—(*Cries.*)

Mockmode. Zauns, Madam, you must not be melancholy,
Madam.

Bullfinch. Well, Sir, I hope you'll give us the Beverage of
your fine Cloaths. I'll assure you, Sir, they fit you very well,
210 and I like your fancy mightily.

Mockmode. Ay, ay, Madam. But what's most modish for
Beverage? for I suppose the fashion of that alters always with
the Cloaths.

Bullfinch. The Taylors are the best Judges of that—But
Champaigne, I suppose.

II. ii 185 downfal] Q2; downful

Mockmode. Is Champaigne a Taylor? Now methinks that were a fitter name for a Wig-maker.—I think they call my Wig a Campaigne.

Bullfinch. You're clear out, Sir, clear out. Champaigne is a fine Liquor, which all you great Beaux drink to make 'em 220 witty.

Mockmode. Witty! Oh by the Universe I must be witty. I'll drink nothing else; I never was witty in all my life. I love Jokes dearly.—Here, *Club*, bring us a Bottle of what d'ye call it? the witty Liquor.

Exit Club.

Bullfinch. But I thought all you that were bred at the University shou'd be Wits naturally.

Mockmode. The quite contrary, Madam, there's no such thing there. We dare not have Wit there, for fear of being counted Rakes. Your solid Philosophy is all read there, which 230 is clear another thing. But now I will be a Wit by the Universe. I must get acquainted with the great Poets. Landlady, you must introduce me.

Bullfinch. Oh dear me, Sir! wou'd you ruin me? I introduce you! no Widow dare be seen with a Poet, for fear she shou'd be thought to keep him.

Mockmode. Keep him! what's that? They keep nothing but Sheep in the Country; I hope they don't fleece the Wits.

Bullfinch. Alas, Sir, they have no Fleeces; there's a great cry, but little Wooll. However, if you wou'd be acquainted with 240 the Poets, I can prevail with a Gentleman of my acquaintance to introduce you; 'Tis one *Lovewell*, a fine Gentleman, that comes here sometimes.

Mockmode. Lovewell! By the Universe my Rival; I heard of him in the Country. This puts me in mind of my Mistress.— Zauns I'm certainly become a Beau already; for I was so in love with my self, I quite forgot her.—I have a Note in my Pocket-book to find her out by.—(*Pulls out a large Pocket-book, turning over the leaves, reads to himself.*)

Six-pence for Washing.—Two pence to the Maid.—Six- pence for Snush—One Shilling for Butter'd Ale—By the 250 Universe I have lost the Directions.—Hark ye, Madam; Does this same *Lovewell* come often here, say you?

Bullfinch. Yes, Sir, very often.—There's a Lady of his

acquaintance, a Lodger in the house just now.

Mockmode. A Lady of his acquaintance a Lodger in the house just now? of his acquaintance, do you say?

Bullfinch. Yes, and a pretty Lady too.

Mockmode. And he comes often here, you say? By the Universe! shou'd I happen to lodge in the same house with my
260 Mistress? I gad it must be the same. Can you tell the Woman's Name?—Stay—Is her Name *Lucinda*?

Bullfinch. Perhaps it may, Sir; but I believe she's a Widdow, for she has a young Son, & I'm sure 'tis legitimately begotten, for 'tis the bravest Child you shall see in a Summers-day; 'Tis not like one of our puling Brats o'th' Town here, born with the Diseases of half a dozen Fathers about it.

Mockmode. By the Universe I don't remember whether my Mistress is Maid or Widow: But a Widow, so much the Better; for all your *London* widows are devilish rich they say. She came
270 in a Coach, did she not, Madam?

Bullfinch. Yes, Sir, yes.

Mockmode. Then 'tis infallibly she.—Does she not always go out in her Coach?

Bullfinch. She has not stirr'd abroad since she came, Sir.

Mockmode. Oh, I was told she was very reserv'd, tho 'tis very much of a Widow. I have often heard my Mother say, that sitting at home and silence were very becoming in a Maid; and she has often chid my Sister *Dorothy* for gadding out to the Meadows, and tumbling among the Cocks with the
280 Haymakers. I gad I'm the most lucky Son of a Whore; I was wrapt in the Tail of my Mothers Smock, Landlady.

Enter Servant.

Bullfinch. Oh but this Lady, Sir.—

Servant. Madam here's a Gentleman below wants to speak with you instantly.

Bullfinch. With me, Child? I'll wait on you in a minut.

Exit with Servant.

Enter Club *with Wine and Glasses.*

Mockmode. Is that the Witty Liquor? Come, fill the Glasses. Now that I have found my Mistress, I must next find my Wits.

Club. So you had need, Master; for those that find a
290 Mistress, are generally out of their Wits.—(*Gives him a Glass.*)

Mockmode. Come, fill for your self. (*They jingle and drink.*) But
where's the Wit now *Club?* have you found it?
Club. I gad Master I think 'tis a very good Jest.
Mockmode. What?
Club. What! why, Drinking. You'll find, Master, that this
same Gentleman in the Straw Doublet, this same Will
i'th'Wisp, is a Wit at the bottom.—(*Fills.*)—Here, here,
Master; how it puns and quibbles in the Glass!

[SONG: Set by Mr *Leveridge*. Sung by Mr *Pinkethman*.

> *Early in the Dawning of a Winters Morn,*
> *Brother Dick, & I went forth into the Bearn;*   300
>   *To get our Selves a heat,*
>   *By Threshing of the Wheat*
> *From the Stack, from the Stack, from the Stack, the Stack;*
>   *The Straw's they flew about*
>   *And the Flailes they kept a rout,*
> *With a Thwack, Thwack, Thwack, Thwack, Thwack.*

2.

> *Margery came in then with an Earthen Pot,*
> *Full of a Pudding that was pipeing hot,*
>   *I caught her by the Neck fast,*
>   *And thank'd her for my breakfast,*   310
> *With a Smack, &c.*
>   *Up went her tail,*
>   *And down went the flail,*
> *With a Thwack, thwack, thwack, thwack.*

3.

> *Dick Threshing on Cry'd out fie for shame,*
> *Must I beat the bush while you catch the Game.*
>   *Sow your wild oates,*
>   *And mind not her wild notes,*

298.1–330 [Song] The text derives from the half-sheet broadside attributed to
Walsh; a few accidentals have been emended for printing in verse form. The
placement of this song is less certain than that of the other two by Leveridge. The talk
of puns, however, provides a likely frame for the song.

> *Of Alack, &c.*
320 > *Faith I did the Job*
> *Whilst the flail bore a bob*
> *With a Thwack &c.*

4.

> *She Shook of the straws & did nothing aile*
> *Swearing there was no defence against a flail*
> *But quietly lay still*
> *And bid me fill fill fill*
> *Her Sack &c.*
> *But twas all in Vaine*
> *For I had spilt my Graine*
330 > *With a Thwack, &c.*

Mockmode. By the Universe now I have it; The Wit lies in
the Jingling: All Wit consists most in Jingling. Hear how the
Glasses rhime to one another.

Club. What, Master, are these Wits so apt to clash? (*Jingle
the Glasses.*)

Mockmode. Oh by the Universe, by the Universe this is Wit.
(*Break 'em.*) My Landlady is in the right.—I have often heard
there was Wit in breaking Glasses. It would be a very good
Joke to break the Flask now?

Club. I find then that this same Wit is very britle
340 Ware.—But I think, Sir, 'twere no Joke to spill the Wine.

Mockmode. Why there's the Jest, Sirrah; all Wit consists in
losing; there was never any thing got by't. I fancy this same
wine is all sold at *Will*'s Coffee-house. Do you know the way
thither Sirrah? I long to see Mr. *Comick* and Mr. *Tagrhime*,
with the rest of 'em. I wonder how they look! Certainly these
Poets must have something extraordinary in their faces. Of all
the Rarities of the Town, I long to see nothing more than the
Poets and *Bedlam.*—Come in, *Club*; I must go practice my
Honours.—Tal—dal—deral.—

Exit dancing, and Club *topeing.*
Enter Lovewell *and* Bullfinch.

350 *Bullfinch.* Oh Mr. *Lovewell!* you come just in the nick; I was
ready to spoil all, by telling him that she was a Stranger, and
just now come.

Lovewell. Well, dear Madam, be cautious for the future; 'tis the most fortunate chance that ever befell me. 'Twere convenient we had the other lodgers of our side.

Bullfinch. There's no body but Mr. *Lyrick*; and you had as safely tell a secret over a Groaning Cheese, as to him.

Lovewell. How so?

Bullfinch. Why you must know that he has been Lying-in these four months of a Play; and he has got all the Muses 360 about him; a parcel of the most tattling Gossips.

Lovewell. Come, come; no more words; but to our business. I will certainly reward you. But have you any good hopes of its succeeding?

Bullfinch. Very well of the 'Squire's side. But I'm afraid your Widow will never play her part, she's so awkward, and so sullen.

Lovewell. Go you and instruct her, while I manage Affairs abroad.

Bullfinch. She's always raving of one *Roebuck*. Prithee who is 370 this same *Roebuck*?—Ah, Mr. *Lovewell*, I'm afraid this Widow of yours is something else at the bottom; I'm afraid there has been a Dog in the Well.

Exit.

Enter Brush.

Lovewell. So, Sirrah! where have you left the Gentleman?

Brush. In a friend's house, Sir.

Lovewell. What friend?

Brush. Why, a Tavern.

Lovewell. What took him there?

Brush. A Coach, Sir.

Lovewell. How d'ye mean?   380

Brush. A Coach and Six, Sir, no less, I'll assure you, Sir.

Lovewell. A Coach and Six!

Brush. Yes, Sir, six Whores and a Carted Bawd. He pick'd 'em all up in the street, and is gone with this splendid Retinue into the *Sun* by *Covent-Garden*. I ask'd him what he meant? he told me, That he only wanted to Whet, when the very sight of 'em turn'd my Stomach.

Lovewell. The fellow will have his swing, tho he hang for't. However, run to him, and bid him take the name of *Mockmode*; call himself *Mockmode* upon all occasions; and tell him that he 390

shall find me here about Four in the afternoon,—Ask no
questions, but fly.

Exit Brush.

—So.—His usurping that name gives him a Title to Court
Lucinda, by which I shall discover her Inclinations to this
Mockmode, whose coming to Town has certainly occasion'd her
quarrel with me; while I set the Hound himself upon a wrong
scent, and ten to one provide for Mistress *Trudge* by the
bargain. 'Tis said, one can't be a Friend and a Lover.
But opposite to that, this Plot shall prove;
400 *I'll serve my Friend by what assists my Love.*

Exit.

The End of the Second Act.

ACT III. [Scene i.]

scene, Lucinda *'s House.*

Enter Leanthe Sola, *dress'd like a Page.*

Leanthe. Methinks this Livery suits ill my Birth: but slave to
Love, I must not disobey; his service is the hardest Vassalage,
forcing the Powers Divine to lay their Godships down, to be
more Gods, more happy here below.—

[SONG: Set by Mr. *Leveridge.* Sung by Mrs. *Allison.*

When Cupid from his Mother fled,
He Changing his Shape
Thus made his escape
His Mother thaught him Dead.
Som did him a kindness
10   *And Cur'd him of blindness,*

<hr>

III. i 1 *Leanthe*] ed.; [om.]   4.1–21 [Song] The text derives from the half-sheet
broadside attributed to Walsh; a few accidentals have been emended for printing in
verse form.

*And disguis'd like me, thus disguis'd, thus disguis'd thus
     disguis'd like me,*
The little God, the little God, the little God cou'd see.

2.

He enters into Hearts of Men,
   And there dos spy
   (Just so do I)
That falshood lurks within,
   That sighing and dying
   Is swearing and lyeing,
All this disguis'd like me,
The little God, the little God coud see.]   20

Thus I, poor Wanderer, have left my Country, disguis'd my self so much, I hardly know whether this Habit or my Love be blindest; to follow one, perhaps that loves me not, tho every breath of his soft words was Passion, and every accent Love. Oh *Roebuck!* (*Weeps.*)

              Enter Roebuck.

Roebuck. This is the Page, Love's Link-boy, that must light me the way.—How now, pretty Boy? Has your Lady beaten you? ha?—This Lady must be a *Venus*, for she has got a *Cupid* in her Family. 'Tis a wondrous pretty Boy, (Leanthe *starts, and stares at him.*) but a very Comical Boy.—What the Devil does 30
he stare at?

Leanthe. Oh Heav'n's! is the Object real, or are my eyes false? Is that *Roebuck*, or am I *Leanthe*? I am afraid he's not the same; and too sure I'm not my self.—[*Aside.*] (*Weeps.*)

Roebuck. What offence cou'd such pretty Innocence commit, to deserve a punishment to make you cry?

Leanthe. Oh Sir! a wondrous offence.

Roebuck. What was it, my Child?

Leanthe. I prick'd my Finger with a Pin, till I made it bleed.   40

Roebuck. Such little Boys as you, shou'd have a care of sharp things.

Leanthe. Indeed, Sir, we ought; for it prick'd me so deep that the sore went to my very heart.

Roebuck. Poor Boy!—here's a plaister for your sore Finger— (*Gives him Gold.*)

Leanthe. Sir, you had best keep it for a sore Finger. (*Returns it.*)

Roebuck. O' my Conscience the Boy's witty, but not very wise in returning Gold.—Come, come, you shall take it. (*Forces it upon him, and kisses him.*)

50 *Leanthe.* That's the fitter cure for my sore Finger.—The same dear Lips still. Oh that the Tongue within them were as true! (*Aside.*)

Roebuck. By Heavens this Boy has the softest pair of Lips I ever tasted. I ne're found before that Ladys kiss'd their Pages; but now if this Rogue were not too young, I shou'd suspect he were before-hand with me. I gad, I must kiss him again. [*Aside.*]—Come, you shall take the Money. (*Kisses.*)

Leanthe. Oh how he bribes me into Bribery; [*Aside.*]—But what must I do with this Money, Sir?

60 *Roebuck.* You must get a little mistress, and treat her with it.

Leanthe. Sir, I have one Mistress already; and they say no man can serve two Masters, much less two Mistresses. How many Mistresses have you, pray?

Roebuck. Umh!—I gad the Boy has pos'd me. [*Aside.*]—How many, Child?—Why, let me see.—There was Mrs. *Mary*, Mrs. *Margaret*, Mrs. *Lucy*, Mrs. *Susan*, Mrs. *Judy*, and so forth; to the number of five and twenty, or thereabouts.

Leanthe. Oh ye Powers! and did you love 'em all?

Roebuck. Yes, desperately.—I wou'd have drank and fought 70 for any one of 'em. I have sworn and ly'd to every one of 'em, and have lain with 'em all: That's for your Encouragement, Boy. Learn betimes, Youth; young Plants shou'd be water'd. Your Smock face was made for a Chamber Utensil.

Leanthe. And did not one escape ye?

Roebuck. Yes, one did,—the Devil take her.

Leanthe. What, don't you love her then?

Roebuck. No, faith; but I bear her an amorous grudge still; something between Love and spight.—I cou'd kill her with kindness.

80 *Leanthe.* I don't believe it, Sir; you cou'd not be so hard-hearted sure: Her honourable Passion, I think, shou'd please you best.

Roebuck. O Child! Boys of your age are continually reading Romances, filling your Heads with that old bombast of Love

and Honour: But when you come to my years, you'll
understand better things.

Leanthe. And must I be a false treacherous Villain, when I
come to your years, Sir? Is Falshood and Perjury essential to
the perfect state of manhood?

Roebuck. Pshaw, Children and old men always talk thus 90
foolishly.—you understand nothing, Boy.

Leanthe. Yes, Sir, I have been in Love and much more than
you, I perceive.

Roebuck. It appears then, that there's no service in the
World so educating to a Boy, as a Ladies.—By *Jove*, this
Spark may be older than I imagin. Hark ye, Sir; do you never
pull off your Ladies Shoes and Stockins? Do you never
reach her the—Pincushion? Do you never sit on her bed-side,
and sing to her? ha!—Come, tell me, that's my good
Boy.—(*Makes much of him.*)   100

Leanthe. Yes, I do sing her asleep sometimes.

Roebuck. But do you never waken her again?

Leanthe. No, but I constantly wake my self; my rest's always
disturbed by Visions of the Devil.

Roebuck. Who wou'd imagin now that this young shaver
cou'd dream of a Woman so soon?—But what Songs does your
Lady delight in most?

Leanthe. Passionate ones, Sir; I'll sing you one of 'em, if
you'll stay.

Roebuck. With all my heart, my little Cherubim. The Rogue 110
is fond of shewing his parts. [*Aside.*]—Come, begin.

A SONG: Set by Mr. *Richardson.*

> *How bless'd are Lovers in disguise!*
>   *Like Gods, they see,*
>   *As I do thee,*
> *Unseen by human Eyes.*
>   *Expos'd to view.*
> *I'm hid from you;*
> *I'm alter'd, yet the same:*
>   *The dark conceals me,*
>   *Love reveals me;*   120
> *Love, which lights me by its Flame.*

97 off] Q2; of

2.

Were you not false, you me wou'd know;
For tho' your Eyes
Cou'd not devise,
Your heart had told you so.
Your heart wou'd beat
With eager heat,
And me by Sympathy wou'd find:
True Love might see
130   *One chang'd like me,*
False Love is only blind.

Roebuck. Oh my little Angel in voice and shape—(*Kisses her.*) I cou'd wish my self a Female for thy sake.

Leanthe. You're much better as you are for my sake.—(*Aside.*)

Roebuck. Or if thou wert a Woman, I wou'd—

Leanthe. What wou'd you? Marry me? wou'd you marry me?

Roebuck. Marry you, Child? No, no; I love you too well for that, you shou'd not have my hand, but all my Body at
140 once.—But to our business. Is your Lady at home?

Leanthe. My Lady! What bus'ness have you with my Lady, pray Sir?

Roebuck. Don't ask Questions. You know Mr. *Lovewell?*

Leanthe. Yes, very well. He's my great Friend, and one I wou'd serve above all the World—but his Sister.

Roebuck. His Sister!—Ha! that gives me a twinge for my Sin. [*Aside.*]—Pray, Mr. Page, was *Leanthe* well when you left her?

Leanthe. No, Sir; but wondrous melancholy, by the departure of a dear Friend of hers to another World.

150   *Roebuck.* Oh that was the person mention'd in her Letter, whose departure occasion'd your departure for *England.*

Leanthe. That was the occasion of my coming, too sure, Sir.—Oh, 'twas a dear Friend to me! the loss makes me weep.

Roebuck. Poor tender-hearted Creature!—But I still find there was not a word of me.—Pray, good Boy, let your Mistress know here's one to wait on her.

Leanthe. Your business is from Mr. *Lovewell,* I suppose, Sir?

Roebuck. Yes, yes.

Leanthe. Then I'll go.

Exit.

Roebuck. I've thrown my cast, and am fairly in for't. But 160
an't I an impudent Dog? Had I as much Gold in my Breeches,
as Brass in my Face, I durst attempt a whole Nunnery. This
Lady is a reputed Vertue, of Good Fortune and Quality; I am
a Rakehelly Rascal not worth a Groat; and without any
further Ceremony, am going to Debauch her.—But hold.—
She does not know that I'm this Rakehelly Rascal, and I know
that she's a Woman, one of eighteen too; Beautiful, Witty.—O'
my Conscience upon second thoughts, I am not so very
Impudent neither.—Now as to my management, I'll first try
the whining Addresses, and see if she'll bleed in the soft Vein. 170

Enter Lucinda.

Lucinda. Have you any business with me, Sir?

Roebuck. Thus look'd the forbidden Fruit, luscious and
tempting. 'Tis ripe, and will soon fall, if one will shake the
Tree. (*Aside.*)

Lucinda. Have you any bus'ness with me, Sir?—(*Comes
nearer.*)

Roebuck. Yes, Madam, the bus'ness of mankind; To adore
you.—My Love, like my Blood, circulates thro' my Veins, and
at every pulse of my heart animates me with a fresh
Passion.—Wonder not, Madam, at the power of your Eyes,
whose pointed Darts have struck on a young and tender heart 180
which they easily pierced, and which unacustom'd to such
wounds finds the smart more painful.

Leanthe. (*Peeps.*) Oh Traytor! Just such words he spoke to
me. [*Aside.*]

Lucinda. Hey day. I was never so attack'd in all my Life.
[*Aside.*] In love with me, Sir! Did you ever see me before?

Roebuck. Never, by *Jove.*—(*Aside.*)—Oh, ten thousand times,
Madam. Your lovely Idea is always in my view, either asleep
or awake, eating or drinking, walking, sitting or standing;
alone, or in Company, my fancy wholly feeds upon your dear 190
Image, and every thought is you.—Now have I told about
fifteen lies in a Breath. (*Aside.*)

Lucinda. I suppose, Sir, you are some conceited young

180 pointed] Q2; painted

Scribler, who has got the benefits of a first Play in your Pocket, and are now going a Fortune hunting.

Roebuck. But why a Scribler, Madam? Are my Cloaths so course, as if they were spun by those lazy Spinsters the Muses? Does the parting of my Fore-top shew so thin, as if it resembled the two wither'd tops of *Parnassus?* Do you see any
200 thing peculiarly Whimsical or ill-natur'd in my Face? Is my Countenance strain'd, as if my head were distorted by a Stranguary of Thought? Is there any thing proudly, slovenly, or affectedly careless in my Dress? Do my hands look like Paper moths? I think, Madam, I have nothing Poetical about me.

Lucinda. Yes, Sir, you have Wit enough to talk like a Fool; and are Fool enough to talk like a Wit.

Roebuck. You call'd me Poet, Madam, and I know no better way of Revenge, than to convince you that I am one by my
210 Impudence.—(*Offers to kiss her hand.*)

Lucinda. Then make me a Copy of Verses upon that, Sir.

Hits him on the ear, and Exit.

Leanthe *Entring.*

Leanthe. How d'ye like the Subject, Sir?

Roebuck. 'Tis a very copious one. (*Spitting.*)—It has made my Jolls rhime in my Head. This it is to be thought a Poet; every Minx must be casting his Profession in his Teeth.— What: Gone!

Leanthe. Ay, she knows that making Verses requires Solitude and Retirement.

Roebuck. She certainly was afraid I intended to beg leave to
220 dedicate something.—If ever I make Love like a Poetical fool again, may I never receive any favour but a Subject for a Copy of Verses.

Re-enter Lucinda.

Lucinda. I won't dismiss him thus, for fear he Lampoon me. [*Aside.*]—Well, Sir, have you done them?

Roebuck. Yes, Madam, will you please to read. (*Catches her and kisses her three or four times.*)

Leanthe. Oh Heav'n I can never bear it. I must devise some means to part 'em. [*Aside.*]

Exit.

212 *Leanthe*] Q2 [*Lean.*]; [om.]

Lucinda. Sir, your Verses are too rough and constrain'd.
However, because I gave the occasion, I'll pardon what's
past.   230
Roebuck. By the Lord, she was angry only because I did not
make the first offer to her Lips. (*Aside.*)—Then, Madam, the
Peace is concluded?
Lucinda. Yes, and therefore both parties should draw out of
the Field. (*Going.*)
Roebuck. Not 'till we make Reprizals. I make Peace with
Sword in hand, Madam, and till you return my heart, which
you have taken, or your own in exchange, I will not put up.
And so, Madam, I proclaim open War again.—(*Catches her.*)
                    Enter Leanthe.
Leanthe. Oh, Madam! yonder's poor little *Crab*, your Lap- 240
Dog, has got his head between two of the Window-bars, and is
like to be strangl'd.
          The Dog howls behind the Scenes.
Lucinda. Oh Lard, my poor *Crabby*! I must run to the rescue
of my poor Dog; I'll wait on you instantly.—Come, come,
Page.—Poor *Crabby*!—
                                        Exit with Leanthe.
Roebuck. Oh the Devil chock *Crabby*!—Well, I find there's
much more Rhetorick in the Lips than in the Tongue.—Had
Buss been the first word of my Courtship, I might have gain'd
the Outworks by this. Impudence in Love, is like Courage in
War; tho Both blind Chances, because Women and Fortune 250
rule them.
                    Re-enter Leanthe.
Leanthe. Sir, my Lady begs your pardon; there's something
extraordinary happen'd, which prevents her waiting on you,
as she promis'd.
Roebuck. What has Monsieur *Crabby* rubb'd some of the
hairs off his Neck? Has he disorder'd his pretty ears? she won't
come again then?
Leanthe. No, Sir; you must excuse her.
Roebuck. Then I'll go be Drunk. Harkye, Sirrah; I have half
a dozen delicious Creatures waiting for me at the *Sun*; you 260
shall along with me, and have your Choice. I'll enter you into
the School of *Venus* Child. 'Tis time you had lost your Maidenhead, you're too old for Play-things.

Leanthe. Oh Heavens! I had rather he shou'd stay then go
there. (*Aside.*) But why will you keep such Company, Sir?
Roebuck. Nay, if y're for Advice, farewell:
   Men of ripe understanding shou'd always despise
   What Babes only practise, and Dotards advise.
                                              Exit singing.
   Leanthe. Wild as Winds, and unconfin'd as Air.—Yet I
270 may reclaim him. His follies are weakly founded, upon the
Principles of Honour, where the very Foundation helps to
undermine the Structure. How charming wou'd Vertue look
in him, whose behaviour can add a Grace to the unseemliness
of Vice!
                         Enter Lucinda.
Lucinda. What is the Gentleman gone?
Leanthe. Yes, Madam. He was instantly taken ill with a
violent pain in his Stomach, and was forc'd to hurry away in a
Chair to his Lodging.
Lucinda. Oh poor Gentleman! He's one of those conceited
280 fools that think no Female can resist their Temptations.
Blockheads, that imagin all Wit to consist in blaspheming
Heav'n and Women.—I'll feed his Vanity, but starve his
Love.
   And may all Coxcombs meet no better Fate,
   Who doubt our Sexes Virtue, or dare prompt our hate.
                                                    Exeunt.

                    [ACT III. Scene ii.]

   SCENE Lyrick*'s Chamber in Widow* Bullfinch*'s*
   house; Papers scatter'd about the Table, himself
      sitting writing in a Night-Gown and Cap.

Lyrick. Two as good Lines as ever were written.—(*Rising.*) I
gad I shall maull these topping fellows.—Says Mr. *Lee,*
   Let there be not one Glimps, one Starry spark,
   But God's meet Gods, and justle in the Dark.
Says little *Lyrick,*
   Let all the Lights be burnt out to a Snuff,
   And Gods meet Gods, and play at Blind-man's buff.

                285.1 *Exeunt*] ed.; *Exit*

Very well!

Let Gods meet Gods, and so—fall out and cuff.

That's much mended. They're as noble Lines as ever were 10
penn'd. Oh, here comes my damn'd Muse; I'm always in the
Humour of writing Elegy after a little of her Inspiration.

Enter Bullfinch.

Bullfinch. Mr. *Lyrick*, what do you mean by all this? Here
you have lodg'd two years in my house, promised me
Eighteen-pence a week for your Lodging, and I have ne're
receiv'd eighteen farthings, not the value of that, Mr *Lyrick*
(*Snaps with her fingers.*) you always put me off with telling me of
your Play, your Play.—Sir, you shall play no more with me,
I'm in earnest.

Lyrick. This living on Love is the dearest Lodging—a 20
Man's eternally dunn'd, tho perhaps he have less of one ready
Coin than t'other.—There's more trouble in a Play than you
imagin, Madam.

Bullfinch. There's more trouble with a Lodger than you
think, Mr. *Lyrick*.

Lyrick. First there's the decorum of Time.

Bullfinch. Which you never observe, for you keep the worst
hours of any Lodger in Town.

Lyrick. Then there's the exactness of Characters.—

Bullfinch. And you have the most scandalous one I ever 30
heard.

Lyrick. Then there's laying the Drama.—

Bullfinch. Then you foul my Napkins and Towels.

Lyrick. Then there are preparations of Incidents, working
the Passions, Beauty of Expression, Closeness of Plot, Justness
of Place, Turn of Language, Opening the Catastrophe.—

Bullfinch. Then you wear out my Sheets, burn my Fire and
Candle, dirty my House, eat my Meat, destroy my Drink,
wear out my Furniture—I have lent you Money out of my
Pocket.   40

Lyrick. Was ever poor Rogue so ridden? If ever the Muses
had a Horse, I am he.—Faith Madam, poor *Pegasus* is Jaded.

Bullfinch. Come, come, Sir, he shan't slip his Neck out of the
Collar for all that. Money I will have, and Money I must
have; let your Play and you both be damn'd.

Lyrick. Well, Madam, my Bookseller is to bring me some

twenty Guinea's for a few Sheets of mine presently, which I
hope will free me from your Sheets.
  Bullfinch. My Sheets, Mr. *Lyrick*! Pray what d'ye mean? I'll
50 assure you, Sir, my Sheets are finer than any of your Muses
spinning.—Marry come up.
  Lyrick. Faith you have spun me so fine, that you have
almost crack'd my Thread of Life, as may appear by my
Spindle-shanks.
  Bullfinch. Why sure—Where was your *Thalia*, and your
Melpomene, when the Tayler wou'd have stripp'd you of your
Silk Wastcoat, and have clapt you on a Stone-doublet? Wou'd
all your Golden Verse have paid the Serjeants Fees?
  Lyrick. Truly, you freed me from Gaol, to confine me in a
60 Dungeon; you did not ransom me, but bought me as a slave;
So, Madam, I'll purchase my freedom as soon as possible.
Flesh and Blood can't bear it.
  Bullfinch. Take your course, Sir.—There were a couple of
Gentlemen just now to enquire for you; and if they come
again, they shan't be put off with the old story of your being
abroad, I'll promise you that, Sir.

Exit.

  Lyrick. Zoons! if this Bookseller does not bring me Money—
Enter Pamphlet.
Oh, Mr. *Pamphlet*, your Servant. Have you perus'd my Poems?
  Pamphlet. Yes, Sir, and there are some things very well,
70 extraordinary well, Mr. *Lyrick*: but I don't think 'em for my
purpose.—Poetry's a meer Drug, Sir.
  Lyrick. Is that because I take Physick when I write? Damn
this costive fellow, now he does not apprehend the Joke.
[*Aside.*]
  Pamphlet. No, Sir; but your name does not recommend 'em.
One must write himself into a Consumption before he gain
Reputation.
  Lyrick. That's the way to lye abed when his Name's up.
Now I lye abed before I can gain Reputation.
  Pamphlet. Why so, Sir?
80 *Lyrick.* Because I have scarcely any Cloaths to put on.—If
ever man did Penance in a White Sheet—
  Pamphlet. You stand only sometimes in a White Sheet for
your offences with your Landlady. Faith, I have often

wonder'd how your Muse cou'd take such flights, yoak'd to
such a Cartload as she is.

Lyrick. Oh, they are like the *Irish* Horses, they draw best by
the Tail—Have you ever seen any of my Burlesque, Mr.
Pamphlet? I have a Project of turning three or four of our most
topping fellows into Doggrel. As for Example;—(*Reads.*)

   Conquest with Lawrels has our Arms adorn'd,   90
   And Rome *in tears of Blood our anger mourn'd.*
Now, *Butchers with Rosemary have our Beef adorn'd.*
   Which has in Gravy Tears our Hunger mourn'd.

How d'ye like it, Mr *Pamphlet*, ha?—Well—

   Like Gods, we pass'd the rugged Alpine *Hills;* ⎫
   Melted our way, and drove our hissing Wheels; ⎬
   Thro cloudy Deluges, Eternal Rills. ⎭

Now observe, Mr. *Pamphlet*; pray observe.

   Like Razors keen, our Knives cut passage clean
   Through Rills of Fat, and Deluges of Lean.   100

Pamphlet. Very well, upon my Soul.

Lyrick. *Hurl'd dreadful Fire and Vinegar infus'd.*

Pamphlet. Ay, Sir, Vinegar! how patly that comes in for the
Beef, Mr. *Lyrick!* 'Tis all wondrous fine indeed.

Lyrick. This is the most ingenious fellow of his Trade that I
have seen; he understands a good thing.—(*Aside.*)—But as to
our bus'ness.—What are you willing to give for these Poems?
Prithee say something. There are about three thousand
lines.—Here, take 'em for a couple of Guinea's.

Pamphlet. No, Sir; Paper is so excessive dear that I dare not 110
venture upon 'em.

Lyrick. Well, because you're a Friend, I'll bestow 'em upon
you.—Here, take 'em all.—There's the hopes of a Dedication
still. (*Aside.*)

Pamphlet. I give you a thousand thanks, Sir; but I dare not
venture the hazard; they'll ne're quit cost indeed, Sir.

Lyrick. This fellow is one of the greatest Blockheads that
ever was Member of a Corporation.—How shall I be
reveng'd? [*Aside.*]

      Enter Boy.

Boy. Sir, there are two Men below desire to have the 120
Honour of kissing your hand.

Lyrick. They must be Knaves or Fools, By their fulsome

Complement. Hark ye—(*Whispers the* Boy.)—Bid 'em walk up.

Pamphlet. Since you have got Company, Sir, I'll take my leave.

Lyrick. No, no, Mr. *Pamphlet,* by no means! we must drink before we part. Boy, a Pint of Sack and a Toast. These are two Gentlemen out of the Country, who will be for all the new things lately published; they'll be good Customers.—Come,
130 sit down.—You have not seen my Play yet?—Here, take the Pen, and if you see any thing amiss, correct it; I'll go bring 'em up.—Stay, lend me your Hat and Wig, or I shall take cold going down Stairs. (*He takes* Pamphlet*'s Hat and Wig, and puts his Cap on* Pamphlet*'s Head.*) [*Exit.*]

Pamphlet. (*Solus.*) This is a right Poetical Cap; 'tis Bays the outside, and the Lining Fustian.—(*Reading.*)—This is all stuff, worse than his Poems.

Enter two Bailiffs *behind him, and clap him on the shoulder.*

1 Baliff. Sir, you're the King's Prisoner.

Pamphlet. That's a good Fancy enough, Mr. *Lyrick.* But pray don't interrupt me, I'm in the best Scene.—I gad the Drama
140 is very well laid.

2 Bailiff. Come, Sir.

Pamphlet. Well, well, Sir, I'll pledge ye. Prithee now good Mr. *Lyrick* do'nt disturb me.—

And furious Lightnings brandish'd in her Eyes.

That's true Spirit of Poetry.

1 Bailiff. Zoons, Sir, d'ye banter us? (*Takes him under each arm, and hauls him up.*)

Pamphlet. Gentlemen—I beg your pardon. How d'ye like the City Gentlemen? If you have any occasion for Books to carry into the Country, I can furnish you as well as any man
150 about *Pauls.* Where's Mr. *Lyrick.*

1 Bailiff. These Wits are damnable Cunning. I always have double Fees for Arresting one of you Wits. All your Evasions won't do; we understand trap, Sir; you must not think to catch old Birds with Chaff, Sir.

Pamphlet. Zoons, Gentlemen, I'm not the Person; I'm a Freeman of the City; I have good Effects, Gentlemen, good Effects. D'ye think to make a Fool of me I'm a Bookseller, no Poet.

III. ii. 147 your] Q2; you

2 Bailiff. Ay, Sir, we know what you are by your Fools Cap there.   160

1 Bailiff. Yes, one of you Wits wou'd have pass'd upon us for a Corn-cutter yesterday; and was so like one, we had almost believed him. (*Hauls him.*)

Pamphlet. Why Gentlemen, Gentlemen, Officers, have a little Patience, and Mr. *Lyrick* will come up Stairs.

1 Bailiff. No, no; Mr. *Lyrick* shall go down Stairs. He wou'd have us wait till some Friends come in to rescue him. Ah these Wits are Devilish Cunning.—

Exeunt hauling Pamphlet.

Enter Lyrick, Mockmode, *and* Club; Lyrick *dress'd.*

Lyrick. Ha, ha, ha. Very Poetical Faith; a good Plot for a Play, Mr. *Mockmode*; a Bookseller bound in Calves-Leather.— 170 Ha, ha, ha.—How they walk'd along like the three Volumes of the *English Rogue* squeez'd together on a shelf.

Mockmode. What was it, what was it, Mr. *Lyrick?*

Lyrick. Why, I am a States-man, Sir.—I can't but laugh, to think how they'll spunge the sheet before the Errata be blotted out; and then how he'll hamper the Dogs for false Imprisonment.

Mockmode. But pray what was the matter, Mr. *Lyrick!*

Lyrick. Nothing, Sir, but a Shurking Bookseller that ow'd me about Forty Guinea's for a few lines. He wou'd have put 180 me off, so I sent for a couple of Bull-Dogs, and Arrested him.

Mockmode. Oh Lord, Mr. *Lyrick*, Honesty's quite out of doors; 'tis a rare thing to find a man that's a true Friend, a true Friend is a rare thing indeed!—Mr. *Lyrick*, will you be my Friend? I only want that Accomplishment. I have got a Mistress, a Dancing and Fencing-Master; and now I want only a Friend, to be a fine Gentleman.

Lyrick. Have you never had a Friend, Sir?

Mockmode. Yes, a very honest fellow; our Friendship commenc'd in the College-Cellar, and we lov'd one another like 190 two Brothers, till we unluckily fell out afterwards at a Game at Tables.

Lyrick. I find then that neither of ye lost by the set. (*Aside.*) But my short acquaintance can't recommend me to such a Trust.

167 in to] Q2; into   168.1 Exeunt] 1728; *Exit*

Mockmode. Pshaw! Acquaintance?—You must be a man of Honour, as you're a Poet, Sir.

Lyrick. But what use wou'd you make of a Friend, Sir?

Mockmode. Only to tell my Secrets too, and be my Second.

200 —Now, Sir, a Wit must be best to keep a Secret, because what you say to one's prejudice will be thought malice. Then you must have a Devilish deal of Courage by your Heroick Writing.—

> *But know, that I alone am King of Me.*

Heav'ns! sure the Author of that Line must be a plaguy stout fellow; it makes me Valiant as *Hector* when I read it.

Lyrick. Sir, we stick to what we write as little as Divines to what they preach.—Besides, Sir, there are other qualifications requisite in a Friend, he must lend you Money. Now, Sir, I

210 can't be that Friend, for I want forty Guinea's.

Mockmode. Sir, I can lend you fifty upon good security.— 'Twas the last word my Father spoke on his Death-bed, that I shou'd never lend Money without security.

Lyrick. Fie, Sir! Security from a Friend, and a Man of Honour by his Profession too!

Mockmode. By the Universe, that's true, you are my Friend. Then I'll tell you a Secret—(*They whisper.*)

Club. Now will this plaguy Wit turn my Nose out of Joynt—I was my Master's Friend before, tho' I never found

220 the knack of borowing Money; tho' I have receiv'd some marks of his Friendship, some sound drubs about the Head and Shoulders, or so. I have been bound for him too, in the Stocks, for his breaking Windows very often. [*Aside.*]

Lyrick. Mr. *Mockmode*, you may be impos'd upon. I wou'd see this Lady you court. I know Mr. *Lovewell* has a Mistress nam'd *Lucinda*; but that she lodges in this house, I much doubt.

Mockmode. Impos'd upon. That's very Comical.—Ha, ha, ha! you shall see, Sir; come.—Pray Sir, you're my Friend.

230 *Lyrick.* Nay, pray; Indeed, Sir, I beg your (*They Complement for the door.*) Pardon; you're a 'Squire, Sir.

Mockmode. Zauns, Sir, you lie, I'm not a Fool; I'll take an affront from no man.—Draw, Sir. (*Draws.*)

Club. Draw, Sir.—I gad I'll put his Nose out of joynt now.

Lyrick. Unequal numbers, Gentlemen.

Club. I'm only my Master's Friend, his Second, or so, Sir.
Lyrick. What's the matter, noble 'Squire?
Mockmode. You lie again, Sir. Zauns, draw.—(*Strikes him with his sword.*)
Lyrick. Ha!—a blow!—*Essex*, a blow—yet I will be calm.
Club. Zoons, draw, Sir. (*Strikes him.*)   240
Lyrick. Oh patience Heaven!—Thou art my Friend still.
Mockmode. You lie, Sir.
Lyrick. Then thou art a Traytor, Tyrant, Monster.
Mockmode. Zauns, Sir, you're a Son of a Whore, and a Rascal.
Club. A Scribler.
Lyrick. Ah, ah,—That stings home.—Scribler!
Mockmode. Ay, Scribler, Ballad-maker.
Lyrick., Nay then—I and the Gods will fight it with ye all. (*Draws.*)

           Enter Roebuck *drunk, and singing.*
      France *ne're will comply*   250
      Till her Claret run dry;
      Then let's pull away, to defeat her:
      He hinders the Peace,
      Who refuses this Glass,
      And deserves to be hang'd for a Traytor.
Now, my *Mirmydons* fall on; I have taken off the odds.
      Dub a dub, dub a dub, to the Battle. (*Sings.*)
Zoons Gentlemen, why don't ye fight?—Blood fight. Oblige
me so far to fight a little; I long to see a little sport.
Lyrick. Sir, I scorn to shew sport to any man. (*Puts up.*)   260
Mockmode. And so do I, by the Universe.
Club. And I, by the Universe.
Lyrick. I shall take another time.

                            Exit.
Roebuck. Here Rascal, take your Chopping-knife,—(*Gives*
Club *his Sword.*) and bring me a Joynt of that Coward's flesh
for your Master's Supper.—Fly, Dog.—(*Takes him by the Nose.*)
Club. Auh!—This fellow's likeliest to put my Nose out of joint.
Roebuck. Now, Sir, tell me, how you durst be a Coward?
Mockmode. Coward, Sir? I'm a Man of a great Estate, Sir; I   270
have five thousand Acres of as good fighting ground as any in

England, good *Terrafirma*, Sir, Coward, Sir! Have a care what you say, Sir.—My Father was a Parliament Man, Sir, and I was bred at the College, Sir.

Roebuck. Oh then I know your Genealogy; your Father was a Senior-Fellow, and your Mother was an Air-pump. You were suckl'd by Platonick Idea's, and you have some of your Mothers Milk in your Nose yet.

Mockmode. Form the Proposition by Mode and Figure, Sir.

280   *Roebuck.* I told you so.—Blow your Nose Child, and have a care of dirting your Philosophical slabbering-bib.

Mockmode. What d'ye mean, Sir?

Roebuck. Your starch'd Band, set by Mode and Figure, Sir.

Mockmode. Band Sir?—This fellow's blind, Drunk. I wear a Cravat, Sir?

Roebuck. Then set a good face upon the matter. Throw off Childishness and Folly with your hanging-sleeves. Now you have left the University, learn, learn.

Mockmode. This fellow's an Atheist, by the Universe; I'll
290   take notice of him, and inform against him for being Drunk. [*Aside.*]—Pray, Sir, what's your Name?

Roebuck. My name? by the Lord I have forgot.—Stay, I shall think on't by and by.

Mockmode. Zauns, forget your own Name! your memory must be very short, Sir.

Roebuck. Ay, so it seems, for I was but Christen'd this morning, and I have forgot it already.

Mockmode. Was your Worship then *Turk* or *Jew* before?—I knew he was some damn'd bloody Dog.—(*Aside.*)

300   *Roebuck.* Sir, I have been *Turk*, or *Jew* rather, since; for I have got a plaguy heathenish Name.—Pox on't.—Oh! now I have it.—*Mo—Mock—mo—Mockmode.*

Mockmode. Mockmode! Mockmode, Sir, Pray how do you spell it?

Roebuck. Go you to your A, B, C, you came last from the University.

Mockmode. Sir, I'm call'd *Mockmode.*—What Family are you of, Sir?

Roebuck. What Family are you of, Sir?

310   *Mockmode.* Of *Mockmode-Hall* in *Shropshire.*

Roebuck. Then I'm of the same, I believe.—I fancy, Sir, that you and I are near Relations.

Mockmode. Relations. Sir! There are but two Families; my Fathers, who is now dead, and his Brothers, Colonel *Peaceable Mockmode.*

Roebuck. Ay, ay, the very same Colonel *Peaceable.*—Is not he Colonel of Militia?

Mockmode. Yes, Sir.

Roebuck. And was not he High-Sheriff of the County last year?   320

Mockmode. The very same, Sir.

Roebuck. The very same; I'm of that Family.—And your Father dy'd about—let me see—

Mockmode. About half a year ago.

Roebuck. Exactly. By the same token you got drunk at a Hunting-match that very day seven-night he was buri'd.

Mockmode. This fellow's a Witch. [*Aside.*]—But it looks very strange that you shou'd be Christen'd this morning. I'm sure your Godfathers had a plaguy deal to answer for.

Roebuck. Oh, Sir, I'm of age to answer for my self.   330

Mockmode. One wou'd not think so, y're so forgetful. 'Tis two and twenty years since I was Christen'd, and I can remember my name still.

Roebuck. Come, we'll take a Glass of Wine, and that will clear our understanding. We'll remember our friends.

Mockmode. You must excuse me, Sir.—This is some Sharper. (*Aside.*)

Roebuck. Nay, prithee Cousin, good Cousin *Mockmode,* one Glass. I know you are an honest fellow. We must remember our Relations in the Country indeed, Sir.

Mockmode. Oh, Sir, you're so short of memory, you can 340 never call 'em to mind. You have forgot your self, Sir. *Mockmode* is a Heathenish Name, Sir, and all that, Sir. And so I beg your pardon, Sir.—

                                                              Exit.

Roebuck. Now were I Lawyer enough, by that little enquiry into that fellow's Concerns, I cou'd bring in a false Deed to cheat him of his Estate.

                         Enter Brush.

Where the Devil is thy Master? You said I shou'd find him here.

Brush. 'Tis impossible for you, or me, or any body, to find
350 him.
Roebuck. Why?
Brush. Because he has lost himself. The Devil has made a
Juglers Ball of him I believe. He's here now; then Presto, pass
in an instant. He has got some damn'd bus'ness to day in
hand.
Roebuck. Ay, so it seems.—I must be Squire *Mockmode*, and
court an honourable Mistress in the Devils name! Well, let my
sober thinking Friend plot on, and lay Traps to catch
Futurity; I'm for holding fast the present.—I have got about
360 twenty Guinea's in my Pocket; and whilst they last, the Devil
take *George* if he thinks of Futurity. I'll go hand in hand with
Fortune.
She is an honest, giddy, reeling Punk;
My Head, her Wheel, turn round, and so we both are drunk.
                                        Exit reeling.

            The End of the Third Act.

            ACT IV. [Scene i.]

            SCENE Lucinda's *House.*

    Enter Leanthe, *and* Pindress *following with Paper of*
                Sweetmeats in her hand.

Pindress. Here, here, Page; your Lady has sent you some
Sweetmeats; but indeed you shan't have 'em till you hire me.
Leanthe. She sent sower Sauce, when she made you the
Bearer. (*Aside.*)
Pindress. Prithee now what makes you constantly so melan-
choly? Come you must be merry, and shall be merry, I'll get
you some Play-things.
Leanthe. I believe you want Play-things more than I.—But I
wou'd be private *Pindress.*
10 *Pindress.* Well, my Child, I'll be private with you; Boys and
Girls shou'd still be private together; and we may be as retir'd
as we please; for my Mistress is reading in her Closet, and all

the Servants are below.—But what Concerns have you? I'm
sure such a little Boy can have no great bus'ness in private.
   Leanthe. I will try thee for once (*Aside.*)—Yes, Mrs. *Pindress*,
I have great inclination.—
   Pindress. To what? To do what, Sir?—Don't name it:—'Tis
all in vain;—you shan't do it, you need not ask it.
   Leanthe. Only to kiss you.— (*Kisses her.*)
   Pindress. Oh fie, Sir! Indeed I'll none of your kisses. Take it 20
back again. (*Kisses him.*) Is not the taste of the Sweet-meats
very pretty about my Lips?
   Leanthe. Oh hang your liquorish Chaps; you'd fain be
licking your Lips, I find that.
   Pindress. Indeed, Mr. Page, I won't pay you the Kisses you
won from me last night at Cross-purposes;—and you shan't
think to keep my Pawn neither.—Pray give me my *Hungary-*
bottle.—As I hope to be sav'd I will have my *Hungary-*
bottle—(*Rummaging him.*)—I'm stronger than you.—I'll carry
you in, and throw you upon the bed, and take it from 30
you.—(*Takes him up in her Arms.*)
   Leanthe. Help! help! I shall be ravish'd! Help! help!
                    Enter Lucinda.
   Lucinda. What's the matter?—Oh bless me!
   Pindress. Oh dear Madam, this unlucky Boy had almost
spoil'd me. Did not your Ladiship hear me cry I shou'd be
ravish'd? I was so weak, I cou'd not resist the little strong
Rogue; he whipt me up in his arms, like a Baby, and had not
your Ladiship come in—
   Lucinda. What, Sirrah, wou'd you debauch my Maid? you
little Cock-Sparrow, must you be Billing too? I have a great 40
mind to make her whip you Sirrah.
   Pindress. Oh dear, Madam, let me do't. I'll take him into
the Room and I will so chastise him.—
   Lucinda. But do you think you'll be able, *Pindress*? I'll send
one of the Men to help you.
   Pindress. No, no, Madam; I cou'd manage him with one
hand.—See here Madam. (*Takes him in her arms, and is running
away.*)
   Lucinda. Hold, hold—Is this you that the little strong Rogue

had almost Ravish'd? He snatch'd you up in his arms like a
50 Baby.—Ah, *Pindress, Pindress*! I see y'are very weak indeed.—
Are not you asham'd, Girl, to debauch my little Boy?

Pindress. Your Ladyship gave me orders to make him
merry, and divert his melancholy, and I know no better way
than to teize him a little. I'm afraid the Boy is troubl'd with
the Rickets, and a little shaking, Madam, wou'd do him some
good.

Leanthe. I'm tir'd with impertinence, and have other bus'ness
to mind. (*Aside.*)

Exit.

Pindress. I hope your Ladyship entertains no ill opinion of
60 my Virtue.

Lucinda. Truly I don't know what to think on't: but I've so
good an opinion of your sense, as to believe you wou'd not
play the fool with a Child.

Pindress. W'ere all subject to playing the fool, if you
continue your Resolution in marrying of the first man that
asks you the Question.

Lucinda. No, my mind's chang'd; I'll never marry any Man.

Pindress. I dare swear that resolution breaks sooner, than
the former. (*Aside.*) Ah Madam, Madam! if you never believe
70 Man again, you must never be Woman again; for tho' we are
as cunning as Serpents, we are naturally as flexible too. Speak
ingenuously, Madam; if Mr. *Lovewell* shou'd with an amorous
whine and suppliant cringe tell you a formal story, contrary to
what we suspect, wou'd you not believe him?

Lucinda. What, believe his vain assertations, before the
demonstration of my senses? No, no; my Love's not so blind.
Did I not see his Miss and his Child? did I not behold him
giving her Money? did I not hear him declare he wou'd settle
her in a Lodging?

80 *Pindress.* But, Madam, upon serious reflection, where's the
great harm in all this? Most Ladies wou'd be over joy'd at
such a discovery of their Lovers ability. The Child seem'd a
lusty chopping Boy; and let me tell you, Madam, it must be a
lusty chopping Boy that got it.

Lucinda. Urge no farther in his defence; he's a Villain, and

70 Woman] Q2; Women   72 ingenuously] Q2; ingeniously

of all Villains that I hate most, an hypocritical one. The
Ladies give him the Epithet of modest, and the Gentlemen
that of sober *Lovewell*. Now methinks such a piece of
Debauchery sits so awkwardly on a person of his Character,
that it adds an unseemliness to the natural vileness of the   90
Vice; and he that dares be a Hypocrite in Religion, will
certainly be one in Love.—Stay, is not that he? (*Pointing
outwards.*)

Pindress. Yes, Madam; I believe he's going to the Park.

Lucinda. Call a couple of Chairs quickly; we'll thither
Masqu'd. This day's adventures argue some intended Plot
upon me, which I may countermine by only setting a Face
upon the matter. (*Puts her Masque on.*)

> For as Hypocrisie in men can move,
> Here's the best Hypocrite in Female Love.
> On even scores designing Heaven took care;   100
> Since Men false Hearts, that we false Faces wear.

                                                    Exit.

[ACT IV. Scene ii.]

SCENE *the Park.*

Enter Lovewell *and* Lyrick *meeting*; Lyrick *reading.*

Lyrick. I'll rack thy Reputation, blast thy Fame,
      And in strong grinding Satyr Gibbet up thy Name.

Lovewell. What, in a Rapture, Mr. *Lyrick*?

Lyrick. A little Poetical fury, that's all.—I'll 'Squire him;
I'll draw his Character for the Buffoon of a Farce; he shall be
as famous in Ballad as *Robin Hood*, or Little *John*; my Muses
shall haunt him like Demons; they shall make him more
ridiculous than *Don Quixote.*

Lovewell. Because he encounter'd your Windmill-Pate.—
Ha, ha, ha.—Come, come, Mr. *Lyrick*, you must be pacify'd.   10

Lyrick. Pacify'd, Sir! Zoons, Sir, he's a Fool, has not a grain
of sense. Were he an ingenious Fellow, or a Man of Parts, I

IV. ii 1 *Lyrick.*] ed.; [om.]

cou'd bear a kicking from him: But an abuse from a
Blockhead! I can never suffer it.
      Pert Blockhead, who has purchas'd by the School
      Just sense enough to make a noted Fool.
That stings, Mr. *Lovewell*.
      Lovewell. Pray, Sir, let me see it.
      Lyrick. This is imperfect, Sir: But if you please to give your
20 Judgment of this Piece.—(*Gives him a Paper.*) 'Tis a Piece of
Burlesque on some of our late Writings.
      Lovewell. Ay, you Poets mount first on the Shoulders of your
Predecessors, to see farther in making Discoveries; and having
once got the upper-hand, you spurn them under-foot. I think
you shou'd bear a Veneration to their very Ashes.
      Lyrick. Ay, if most of their Writings had been burnt. I
declare, Mr. *Lovewell,* their Fame has only made them the
more remarkably faulty: Their great Beauties only illustrate
their greater Errors.
30   *Lovewell.* Well, you saw the new Tragedy last night; how
did it please ye?
      Lyrick. Very well; it made me laugh heartily.
      Lovewell. What, laugh at a Tragedy!
      Lyrick. I laugh to see the Ladies cry. To see so many weep
at the Death of the fabulous Hero, who would but laugh if the
Poet that made 'em were hang'd? On my Conscience, these
Tragedies make the Ladies vent all their Love and Honour at
their Eyes, when the same white Hankerchief that blows their
Noses, must be a Winding-Sheet to the deceased Hero.
40   *Lovewell.* Then there's something in the Handkerchief to
embalm him, Mr. *Lyrick*, Ha, ha, ha.—But what relish have
you of Comedy?
      Lyrick. No satisfactory one—My curiosity is fore-stall'd by
a fore-knowledge of what shall happen. For as the Hero in
Tragedy is either a whining cringing Fool that's always a
stabbing himself, or a ranting hectoring Bully that's for killing
every-body else: so the Hero in Comedy is always the Poet's
Character.
      Lovewell. What's that?
50   *Lyrick.* A Compound of practical Rake, and speculative

29 greater] O1; greating

Gentleman, who always bears off the great Fortune in the Play, and Shams the Beau and 'Squire with a Whore or Chambermaid; and as the Catastrophe of all Tragedies is Death, so the end of Comedies is Marriage.

Lovewell. And some think that the most Tragical conclusion of the two.

Lyrick. And therefore my eyes are diverted by a better Comedy in the Audience than that upon the Stage.—I have often wonder'd why Men shou'd be fond of seeing Fools ill represented, when at the same time and place they may behold the mighty Originals acting their Parts to the Life in the Boxes.— 60

Lovewell. Oh be favourable to the Ladies, Mr. *Lyrick*, 'tis your Interest. Beauty is the Deity of Poetry; and if you rebel, you'll certainly run the Fate of your first Parent, the Devil.

Lyrick. You're out, Sir. Beauty is a merciful Deity, and allows us sometimes to be a little Atheistical; and 'tis so indulgent to Wit, that it is pleas'd with it, tho' in the worst habit, that of Satyr. Besides, there can appear no greater Argument of our Esteem, than Raillery, because 'tis still 70 founded upon Jealousie; occasion'd by their preferring sense-less Fops and Wealthy Fools to Men of Wit and Merit, the great Upholders of the Empire.

Lovewell. Now I think these Favourites of the Ladies are more Witty than you.

Lyrick. How so, pray, Sir?

Lovewell. Because they play the Fool, conscious that it will please; and you're a Wit, when sensible that Coxcombs only are encourag'd. I wonder, Mr. *Lyrick*, that a man of your sense should turn Poet; you'll hardly ever find a Man that is capable 80 of the Imployment will undertake it.

Lyrick. The reason of that is, every one that knows not a tittle of the matter pretends to be a judge of it.—By the Lard, Mr. *Lovewell*, I put the Criticks next to Plague, Pestilence and Famine in my Litany.—Had you seen 'em last night in the Pit, with such demure supercilious Faces—their contemplative Wigs thrust judiciously backwards; their hands rubbing their Temples to chaff ill nature; and with a hissing venomous

59 fond] Q2; found   66 *Lyrick*] Q2; *Luc.*

Tongue pronouncing Pish! Stuff! Intollerable! Damn him!—
90 Lord have mercy upon us.

Lovewell. Ay, and you shall have others as foolish as they
are ill-natur'd; fond of being thought Wits, who shall laugh
outragiously at every smutty Jest; cry, Very well, by Gad;
that's fine, by Heavens; and if a Dystich of Rhime happens,
they clap so damnably loud, that they drown the Jest.

Lyrick. That's the Jest. The Wit lies in their hands; and if
you would tell a Poet his Fortune, you must gather it from the
Palmistry of the Audience; for as nothing's ill said, but what's
ill taken; so nothing's well said, but what's well taken. And
100 between you and I, Mr. *Lovewell*, Poetry without these
laughing Fools, were a Bell without a Clapper; an empty
sounding bus'ness, good for nothing; and all we Professors
might go hang our selves in the Bell-ropes.

Lovewell. Ha, ha, ha.—But I thought Poetry was instructive.

Lyrick. Oh Gad forgive me, that's true; To Ladies it is
morally beneficial; For you must know they are too nice to
read Sermons; such Instructions are too gross for their refin'd
apprehensions: but any Precepts that may be instill'd by easie
Numbers, such as of *Rochester*, and others, make great
110 Converts. Then they hate to hear a fellow in Church preach
methodical Nonsense, with a *Firstly*, *Secondly*, and *Thirdly*: but
they take up with some of our modern Plays in their Closet,
where the Morallity must be Devilish Instructive.—But I
must be gone; here comes the 'Squire. What in the name of
wonder has he got with him?

Lovewell. That which shall afford you a more plentiful
Revenge than your Lampoon, if you joyn with me in the Plot.
To the better effecting of which, you must be seemingly
reconcil'd to him.—Let's step aside, and observe 'em while I
120 give you a hint of the matter.

> *Exeunt between the Scenes, and seem to confer and hearken.*
> *Enter* Mockmode, *leading* Trudge *dress'd like a Widow.*

Mockmode. This is very fine Weather, blessed Weather
indeed, Madam; 'twill do abundance of good to the Grass and
Corn.

Trudge. Ay, Sir, the Days are grown a great length; and I
think the Weather much better here than in *Ireland*.

Mockmode. Why, Madam, were you ever there?

Trudge. Oh no, not I indeed, Sir; but I have heard my first Husband (Rest his Soul) say so; he was an *Irish* Gentleman.

Mockmode. I find, Madam, you have lov'd your first Husband mightily, for you affect his tone in discourse.—Pray, 130 Madam, what did that Mourning cost a Yard?

Trudge. Oh Lard, what shall I say now? 'tis none of mine. (*Aside.*) It cost, Sir; let me see—it cost about—but it was my Steward bought it for me, I never buy such small things.

Mockmode. By the Universe she must be plaguy Rich; I will be brisk. (*Aside.*) Pray, Madam—I—I pray Madam, will you give us a Song?

Trudge. A Song! Indeed then I had a good voice, before Mr. *Roebuck* spoil'd it.

Mockmode. Mr. *Roebuck*? was that your first Husband's 140 Name, Madam?

Lovewell. (*Behind.*) She'll spoil all.

Trudge. No, Sir; *Roebuck* was a Doctor, that let me blood under the Tongue for the Quinsey, and made me hoarse ever since.

[SONG.

Sung by Mrs. *Mills*.

On Sunday after Mass,
Dormett and his Lass,
To the Green wood did pass, all alone, all alone, all alone,
    all alone:
He ask'd for a pouge,
She call'd him a Rogue, 150
And Struck him with her brouge, Oh hone, Oh hone, Oh
    hone.

2

Said he my dear Joy,
Why will you be Coy,

---

128 Gentleman] Q2; Gentlemen
145.1–66 [Song] The text derives from the half-sheet broadside attributed to Walsh; a few accidentals have been emended for printing in verse form. The song must be placed after Mockmode's original request for Trudge to sing and her exclamation 'A Song!' (l. 138) or after the short subsequent dialogue. I have chosen the latter placement as the more likely since her melodious *double entendre* convinces him she is a widow and leads him to 'be a little brisk'.

> *Let us play lett us toy, all alone, all alone, all alone.*
> *If I were too mild,*
> *You are so very wild,*
> *You wou'd gett me with Shild, o hone, o hone, o hone.*

3

> *He brib'd her with Sloes,*
> *And brib'd her with Nutts,*
> *Then a thorn prickt her foots, halla lu, halla lu,*
> 160   *halla lu,*
> *Let me pull it out,*
> *You'l hurt me I doubt*
> *And make me to Shout, halla lu, halla lu, halla lu.*]

Mockmode. By the Universe she's a Widow, and I will be a little brisk. Madam, will you grant me a small favour, and I will bend upon my knees to receive it.—(*Kneels.*)

Trudge. What is't, pray?

Mockmode. Only to take off your Garter.

Lovewell *Enters.*

Lovewell. Zoons, her thick Leg will discover all. [*Aside.*]—By 170 your leave, Sir, have you any pretensions to this Lady? (*Pushes* Mockmode *down.*)

Mockmode. I don't know whether this be an affront or not.—(*Aside.*)—Pretensions, Sir? I have so great a Veneration for the Lady, that I honour any man that has pretensions to her.—Dem me, Sir, may I crave the honour of your Acquaintance?

Lovewell. No, Sir.

Mockmode. No, Sir! I gad that must be Wit, for it can't be good Manners.—Sir, I respect all men of sense, and wou'd therefore beg to know your Name.

180   *Lovewell.* No matter, Sir; I know your Name's *Mockmode.*

Mockmode. By the Universe, that's very Comical! that a fellow shou'd pretend to tell me my own Name!—Another Question, if you please, Sir.

Lovewell. What is it, Sir?

Mockmode. Pray Sir, what's my Christen'd Name?

Lovewell. Sir, you don't know.

169 *Lovewell.*] Q2; [om.]

Mockmode. Zauns, Sir, wou'd you perswade me out of my
Christen'd Name? I'll lay you a Guinea that I do know, by the
Universe.—(*Pulls a handful of Money out.*) Here's Silver, Sir,
here's Silver, Sir; I can command as much Money as another, 190
Sir; I am at Age, Sir, and I won't be bantered, Sir.

Lovewell. Sir, you must know, that I baptize you Rival; for
your Love to this Lady, is the only sign of Christianity you can
boast of.—And now Sir, my name's *Lovewell.*

Mockmode. Then I say, Sir, that your Love to that Lady is
the only sign of a *Turk* you can brag of.—I wish *Club* were
come. (*Aside.*)

Lovewell. Sir, I shall certainly Circumcise you, if you make
any farther pretensions to Madam *Lucinda* here.

Mockmode. Circumcise me! Circumcise a Puddings end, 200
Sir.—Zauns, Sir, I'll be judg'd by the Lady who merits
Circumcission most, you or I, Sir. These *London*-Blades are all
stark mad;—

> Lucinda *enters, and observes* Lovewell *courting* Trudge
> *in dum signs.*

I met one about two hours ago, that had forgot his Name, and
this fellow wou'd perswade me now that I had forgot mine. Mr.
Lyrick is the only man that speaks plain to me. I must be
Friends with him, because I find I may have occasion for such
a Friend; I'll find him out strait.

> *Exit.*

Lovewell. Madam, will you walk.—

> *Exit with* Trudge.
> Lucinda *and* Pindress *come forward.*

Lucinda. Now my doubts are remov'd.   210

Pindress. Mine are more puzzling. There must be something
in this, more than we imagine. You had best talk to him.

Lucinda. Yes, if my Tongue bore Poyson in it, and that I
could spit Death in his face.

Pindress. If he is lost, your hard usage this morning has
occasion'd it.

Lucinda. I'm glad on't; I've gain'd by the loss, I despise him
more now than e're I lov'd him. That Passion which can stoop
so low as that Blowze, is an Object too mean for anything but
my scorn to level at.   220

Pindress. This were a critical minute for your new Lover the 'Squire I fancy; Mr. *Lovewell's* disgrace wou'd bring him into favour presently.

Lucinda. It certainly shall, if he be not as great a Fool as t'other's false.

Pindress. You may be mistaken in your opinion of him, as much as you have been in Mr. *Lovewell.*

Lucinda. No, *Pindress*, I shall find what I read in the last Miscellanies very true.

230   *But two distinctions their whole Sex does part;*
All Fools by Nature, or all Rogues by Art.

[*Exeunt.*]

[ACT IV. Scene iii.]

SCENE *continues.*

Enter several Masques *crossing the Stage, and*
Roebuck *following.*

Roebuck. 'Sdeath! what a Coney-burrough's here! The Trade goes swimingly on. This is the great Empory of Lewdness, as the Change is of Knavery.—The Merchants cheat the World there, and their Wives gull them here.—I begin to think Whoring Scandalous, 'tis grown so Mechanical. —My modesty will do me no good, I fear.—Madam, are you a Whore? (*Catches a* Masque.)

1 Masque. Yes, Sir.

Roebuck. Short and pithy.—If ever Woman spoke truth, I
10 believe thou hast. (*Second* Masque *pulls him by the Elbow.*) Have you any bus'ness with me, Madam?

2 Masque. Pray, Sir be civil; you're mistaken, Sir.—I have had an Eye upon this fellow all this afternoon. (*Aside.*) You're mistaken, Sir.

Roebuck. Very likely, Madam; for I imagin'd you modest.

2 Masque. So I am, for I'm marry'd.

Roebuck. And marry'd to your sorrow, I warrant you!

2 Masque. Yes, upon my Honour, Sir.

224 *Lucinda*] Q2; *Lov.*

Roebuck. I knew it. I have met above a dozen this Evening, all marry'd to their Sorrow.—Then I suppose you're a 20 Citizen's Wife; and by the broadness of your bottom, I shou'd guess you sat very much behind a Counter.

2 Masque. My Husband's no Mercer, he's a Judge.

Roebuck. Zoons! A Judge! I shall be arraign'd at the Bar for keeping on my Hat so long.—'Tis very hard, Madam, he shou'd not do you Justice: Has not he an Estate in Tail, Madam?

2 Masque. I seldom examine his Papers; They are a parcel of old dry shrivel'd Parchments; and this Court-hand is so devilish crabbed, I can't endure it.   30

Roebuck. Umph!—then I suppose, Madam, you want a young Lawyer to put your Case to. But faith, Madam, I'm a Judge too.

2 Masque. Oh Heav'ns forbid! such a young Man?

Roebuck. That's, I'll do nothing without a Bribe.—Pray, Madam, how does that Watch strike?

2 Masque. It never strikes, it only points to the business, as you must do, without telling Tales. Dare you meet me two hours hence?

Roebuck. Ay, Madam, but I shall never hit the time exactly 40 without a Watch.

2 Masque. Well, take it.—At Ten exactly, at the Fountain in the *Middle Temple*. *Cook upon Littleton* be the word.

Exit.

Roebuck. So—If the Law be all such Volumes as thou, Mercy on the poor Students. From *Cook upon Littleton* in Sheets deliver me.

Enter Lovewell.

Lovewell. What! engag'd *Mirmydon*! I find you'll never quit the Battle till you have crack'd a Pike in the Service.

Roebuck. Oh dear friend! thou'rt critically come to my Relief; for faith I'm almost tir'd.   50

Lovewell. What a miserable Creature is a Whore! whom every Fool dares pretend to love, and every Wise Man hates.

Roebuck. What, morallizing again! Oh I'll tell thee News, Man; I'm enter'd in the Inns, by the Lard.

Lovewell. Pshaw!

Roebuck. Nay, if you won't believe me, see my Note of

admission. (*Shews the Watch.*)

Lovewell. A Gold Watch, boy?

Roebuck. Ay, a Gold Watch, boy.

60 *Lovewell.* Whence had you money to buy it?

Roebuck. I took it upon tick, and I design to pay honestly.

Lovewell. I don't like this running o'th'Score.—But what news from *Lucinda*, boy? Is she kind? ha?

Enter a Masque *crossing the Stage.*

Roebuck. Ha! there's a stately Cruiser; I must give her one chase.—I'll tell you when I return.

Exit running.

Lovewell. I find he has been at a loss there, which occasions his eagerness for the Game here. I begin to repent me of my suspicion; I believe her Vertue so sacred that 'tis a piece of Atheism to distrust its Existence. But jealousie in Love, like 70 the Devil in Religion, is still raising doubts which without a firm Faith in what we adore, will certainly damn us.

Enter a Porter.

Porter. Is your name Mr. *Roebuck*, Sir?

Lovewell. What wou'd you have with Mr. *Roebuck*, Sir?

Porter. I have a small Note for him, Sir.

Lovewell. Let me see't.

Porter. Ay, Sir, if your name be Mr. *Roebuck*, Sir.

Lovewell. My Name is *Roebuck*, Blockhead.

Porter. God bless you, master.

Gives him a Letter, and Exit.

Lovewell. This is some tawdry Billet, with a scrawling Adieu 80 at the end on't. These strolling Jades know a young wholesome fellow newly come to Town, as well as a Parsons Wife does a fat Goose. 'Tis certainly some secret, and therefore shall be known. (*Opens the Letter.*)

Tuesday three a Clock.

Sir,

My behaviour towards you this morning was somewhat strange; but I shall tell you the cause of it, if you meet me at Ten this night in our Garden; the Back-door shall be open.

Yours *Lucinda*.

90 Oh heavens! certainly it can't be! *L, U, C, I, N, D, A*; that spells Woman. 'Twas never written so plain before. *Roebuck*,

thou'rt as true an Oracle, as she's a false one. Oh thou damn'd
Sybil! I have courted thee these three years, and cou'd never
obtain above a Kiss of the hand, and this fellow in an hour or
two has obtain'd *the back door open*. Mr. *Roebuck*, since I have
discover'd some of your Secrets, I'll make bold to open some
more of 'em.—But how shall I shake him off?—Oh, I have it;
I'll seek him instantly.

Exit.

Enter Roebuck *meeting the* Porter.

Roebuck. Here, you Sir, have you a Note for one *Roebuck?*

Porter. I had, Sir, but I gave it to him just now.   100

Roebuck. You lie, Sirrah, I am the Man.

Porter. I an't positive I gave it to the right person; but I'm
very sure I did; for he answer'd the Description the Page gave
to a T, Sir.

Roebuck. 'Twas well I met that Page, Dog, or now shou'd I
cut thy Throat, Rascal.

Porter. Bless your Worship, Noble Sir.

Exit.

Roebuck. At Ten, in the Garden! the back-door open!—Oh
the delicious place and hour! soft panting breasts! trembling
Joynts! melting Sighs! and eager Embraces!—Oh Extasie!—   110
But how to shake off *Lovewell?*—This is his nicely Vertuous!
Ha, ha, ha.—This is his innate Principle of Vertue? Ha, ha,
ha.

Enter Lovewell.

Lovewell. How now why so merry?

Roebuck. Merry! why, 'twou'd make a Dog split, Man; Ha,
ha, ha.—The Watch Sir, the Watch; Ha, ha, ha.

Lovewell. What of the Watch? you laugh by the hour; you'll
be run down by and by sure.

Roebuck. Ay, but I shall be wound up again. This Watch I
had for a Fee, Lawyer.—Shou'd I ever be try'd before this   120
Judge, how I shou'd laugh, to see how gravely his Goose-Caps
sits upon a pair of Horns. Ha, ha, ha.

Lovewell. Thou'rt Horn-mad. Prithee leave impertinence. I
receiv'd a Note just now.

Roebuck. A Note! 'Sdeath, what Note! what d'ye mean? who
brought it?

Lovewell. A Gentleman; 'tis a Challenge.

IV. iii. 121 Goose-Cap] O1; Goose-Caps

Roebuck. Oh, thanks to the Stars; I'm glad on't. (*Aside.*)

Lovewell. And you may be signally serviceable to me in this
130 affair. I can give you no greater testimony of my Affection,
than by making so free with you.

Roebuck. What needs all this formality? I'll be thy second,
without all this impertinence.

Lovewell. There's more than that, Friend.—In the first
place, I don't understand a Sword; and again, I'm to be call'd
to the Bar this Term, and such a business might prejudice me
extreamly. So, Sir, you must meet and fight for me.

Roebuck. Faith, *Lovewell*, I shan't stick to cut a Throat for
my Friend at any time, so I may do it fairly, or so.—The hour
140 and place?

Lovewell. This very Evening, in *Moorfields.*

Roebuck. Umph! How will you employ your self the while?

Lovewell. I'll follow you at a distance, lest you have any foul
play.

Roebuck. Which if you do.—No, faith *Ned*, since I'm to
answer an appointment for you, you must make good an
assignation for me. I'm to meet one of your Ladies at the
Fountain in the *Temple* to night. You may be called to the Bar
there, if you will. This Watch will tell you the hour, and shall
150 be your Pass-port. Let me have yours.—(*Changes Watches.*)

Lovewell. Oh, was that the Jest? Ha, ha, ha.—Well, I will
answer an Assignation for you sure enough. Ha, ha, ha.—How
readily does the Fool run to have his Throat cut? (*Aside.*)

Roebuck. How eagerly now does my moral Friend run to the
Devil, having hopes of Profit in the Wind! I have shabb'd him
off purely. [*Aside.*]—But prithee, *Ned*, where had you this fine
Jewel? (*Viewing one tied to the Watch.*)

Lovewell. Pshaw! a Trifle, a Trifle; from a Mistress.—Take
care on't tho. But hark ye, *George*; don't push too home; have a
160 care of whipping through the Guts.

Roebuck. Gad I'm afraid one or both of us may fall. But d'ye
hear, *Ned*, remember you sent me on this Errant, and are
therefore answerable for all mischief; if I do whip my
Adversary through the Lungs, or so remember you set me
upon't.

164 you] Q2; your

Lovewell. Well, honest *George*, you won't believe how much you oblige me in this Courtesie.

Roebuck. You know always I oblige my self by serving a Friend.—I never thought this Spark was a Coward before. (*Aside.*)

Lovewell. I never imagin'd this Fellow was so easie before.— 170 (*Aside.*) Well, good success to us both; and when we meet, we'll relate all Transactions that pass.

Roebuck. That you're a Fool. [*Aside.*]

Lovewell. That you're an Ass. [*Aside.*]

Exeunt severally, laughing.
Re-Enter Lovewell *crossing the Stage hastily*,
Mockmode *and* Lyrick *following him.*

Lyrick. Mr. *Lovewell*, a word w'ye.

Lovewell. Let it be short, pray Sir, for my bus'ness is urgent, and 'tis almost dark.

Lyrick. I'm reconcil'd to the 'Squire, and want only the Presentment of a Copy of Verses, to ingratiate my self wholly throughly. Let me have that piece I lent just now.   180

Lovewell. Ay, ay, with all my heart.—Here.—Farewell. (*Pulls the Poem hastily, and justles out a Letter with it, which* Mockmode *takes up.*)

[*Exit.*]

Lyrick. Now, Sir, here's a Poem, (which according to the way of us Poets) I say was written at fifteen; but between you and I it was made at five and twenty.

Mockmode. Five and twenty!—When is a Poet at Age, pray Sir?

Lyrick. At the third night of his first Play; for he's never a Man till then.

Mockmode. But when at years of discretion?

Lyrick. When they leave Writing, and that's seldom or 190 never.

Mockmode. But who are your Guardians?

Lyrick. The Criticks, who with their good will, wou'd never let us come to Age. But what have you got there?

Mockmode. By the Universe, I don't know; 'tis a Woman's hand; some *Billet-deux*, I suppose; it justl'd out of *Lovewell's* Pocket. We'll to the next Light, and read it.

Exeunt.

[ACT IV. Scene iv.]

SCENE *a dark Arbor in* Lucinda*'s Garden*

Enter Roebuck Solus.

Roebuck. Oh how I reverence a back-dore half open, half shut! 'Tis the narrow Gate to the Lovers Paradice; *Cupid* stood Centry at the entrance; *Love* was the Word, and he let me pass—Now is my friend pleading for Life; he has a puzzling Case to manage Ten to one he's Nonsuted; I have gull'd him fairly.

Enter Lovewell.

Lovewell. I've got in, thanks to my Stars, or rather the Clouds, whose influence is my best Friend at present. Now is *Roebuck* gazing, or rather groping about for a Fellow with a
10 long sword; and I know his fighting humour will be as mad to be baulk'd by an Enemy, as by a Mistress.

Roebuck. Hark, hark! I hear a Voice; it must be she.—*Lucinda!*

Lovewell. True to the touch, I find. Is it you, my Dear?

Roebuck. Yes, my Dear.

Lovewell. Let me embrace thee, my heart.

Roebuck. Come to my Arms.—(*Run into each others Arms. Finding the mistake, start back.*)

Lovewell. 'Slife! a Man!

Roebuck. 'Sdeath! a Devil!—And wert thou a Legion, here's a Wand shou'd conjure thee down—(*Draws.*)
20 *Lovewell.* We should find whose Charms is strongest. (*Draws.*)

> *They push by one another;* Roebuck *passes out at the* opposite door: *and as* Lovewell *is passing out on the other side of the Stage.*

Enter Leanthe.

Leanthe. Mr. *Roebuck?* Sir? Mr. *Roebuck?* (*With a Night-Gown over his Cloaths.*)

Lovewell. That's a Woman's Voice, I'll swear.—Madam?—

Leanthe. Sir.

Lovewell. Come, my dear *Lucinda;* I've staid a little too long; but making an Apology now were only lengthening the offence. Let's into the Arbor, and make up for the moments mispent.

Leanthe. Hold, Sir. Do you love this *Lucinda* you're so fond of hauling into the Arbor?

Lovewell. Yes, by all that's powerful.　　　　30

Leanthe. False, false *Roebuck!*—(*Aside.*)—I am lost.

Lovewell. Madam, do you love this *Roebuck*, that you open'd the Garden door to so late?

Leanthe. I'm afraid I do too well.

Lovewell. And did you never own an affection to another?

Leanthe. No, witness all those Powers you just now mention'd.

Lovewell. Revenge your selves, ye Heavens. Behold in me your Accuser and your Judge. Behold *Lovewell*, injur'd *Lovewell.*—This darkness, which opportunely hides your blushes, makes your shame more Monstrous.　　　　40

Leanthe. Ha! *Lovewell!* I'm vex'd 'tis he, but glad to be mistaken.—Now Female Policy assist me. [*Aside.*]

Lovewell. Yes, Madam, your silence proclaims you Guilty—Farewell Woman.

Leanthe. Ha, ha, ha.

Lovewell. What am I made your scorn?

Leanthe. Ha, ha, ha.—This happens better than I expected. —Ha, ha, ha.—Mr. *Lovewell!*

Lovewell. No Counter-plotting, Madam; the Mine's sprung already and all your deceit discovered.　　　　50

Leanthe. Indeed you're a fine fellow at discovering deceits, I must confess, that cou'd not find whether I was a Man or a Woman all this time.

Lovewell. What, the Page!

Leanthe. No Counter-plotting, good Sir, the Mine's sprung already.—Ah, Sir, I fancy Mr. *Roebuck* is better at discovering a Man from a Woman in the dark, than you.

Lovewell. This discovery is the greatest Riddle!—Prithee, Child, what makes thee disguis'd? But above all, what meant that Letter to *Roebuck*?　　　　60

Leanthe. Then I find you intercepted it.—Why, Sir, my Lady had a mind to put a trick upon the impudent Fellow, made him an Assignation, and sent me in her stead, to banter him, But when I tell her how you fell into the snare, and how jealous you were.—Ha, ha, ha.

Lovewell. Oh my little dear Rogue! was that the matter?—(*Hugs her.*) O' my Conscience thou'rt so soft, I believe thou art a Woman still.—But who was that Man I encountred just now?

70   *Leanthe.* A Man! 'Twas certainly *Roebuck.*—(*Aside.*) Some of the Footmen, I suppose.—Come, Sir, I must Conduct you out immediately, lest some more of 'em meet you.

                                  Conducts him to the door, and returns.

He certainly was here, and I have miss'd him.
Fortune delights with Innocence to play,
And loves to hoodwink those already blind.
Wary deceit can many by-ways tread,
To shun the blocks in Vertues open Road,
Whilst heedless Innocence still falls on Ruin
Yet, whilst by Love inspir'd, I will pursue;
80 What Men by Courage, we by Love can do.
Not even his falshood shall my Claim remove; ⎫
From mutual Fires none can true passion prove; ⎬
For like to like, is Gratitude, not Love. ⎭

The End of the Fourth Act.

ACT V. [Scene i.]

SCENE, *An Antichamber in* Lucinda's *house; The Flat Scene half open, discovers a Bed-Chamber;* Lucinda *in her Night-Gown, and reading by a Table.*

Enter Roebuck *groping his way.*

Roebuck. On what new happy Climate am I thrown? This house is Loves Labyrinth; I have stumbled into it by chance.—Ha! an Illusion! Let me look again.—Eyes, if you play me false, (*Looking about.*) I'll pluck ye out.—'Tis she; 'tis *Lucinda!* alone, undress'd, in a Bed-Chamber, between Eleven and Twelve a Clock.—A blessed opportunity!—Now if her innate Principle of Vertue defend her, then is my innate Principle of Manhood not worth Two-pence.—Hold, she comes forward.—

                Lucinda *approaches, reading.*

10   *Lucinda.* Unjust Prerogative of faithless Man,

Abusing Pow'r which partial Heaven has granted!
In former Ages, Love and Honour stood
As Props and Beauties to the Female Cause;
But now lie prostitute to scorn and sport.
Man, made our Monarch, is a Tyrant grown,
And Woman-kind must bear a second Fall.
   Roebuck. (*Aside.*) Ay, and a third, too, or I'm mistaken.—I
must divert this plaguy Romantick humour.
   Lucinda. While Vertue guided Peace, and Honour War,
Their Fruits and Spoils were off'rings made to Love.   20
   Roebuck. And 'tis so still; for (*Raising his Voice.*)
Beau with earliest Cherries Miss does grace,
And Soldier offers spoils of *Flanders* Lace.
   Lucinda. Ha!—Protect me Heav'ns! what art thou?
   Roebuck. A Man, Madam.
   Lucinda. What accursed Spirit has driven you hither?
   Roebuck. The Spirit of Flesh and Blood, Madam.
   Lucinda. Sir, what Encouragement have you ever received
to prompt you to this Impudence?
   Roebuck. Umph! I must not own the reception of a Note 30
from her.(*Aside.*) Faith, Madam, I know not whether to
attribute it to Chance, Fortune, my good Stars, my Fate, or
my Destiny: But here I am, Madam, and here I will be.
(*Taking her by the hand.*)
   Lucinda. (*Pulling her hand away.*) If a Gentleman, my
Commands may cause you to withdraw; If a Ruffian, my
Footmen shall dispose of you.
   Roebuck. Madam, I'm a Gentleman; I know how to oblige a
Lady, and how to save her Reputation. My Love and Honour
go link'd together; they are my Principles: and if you'll be my
Second, we'll engage immediately.   40
   Lucinda. Stand off, Sir; the name of Love and Honour are
burlesqu'd by thy Professing 'em. Thy Love is Impudence,
and thy Honour a Cheat. Thy Mien and Habit shew thee a
Gentleman? but thy behaviour is Brutal. Thou art a *Centaur*;
only one part Man, and the other Beast.
   Roebuck. Philosophy in Peticoats! No wonder Women wear
the Breeches; (*Aside.*) and, Madam, you are a Demi-Goddess;

V. i 26 hither] Q2; hitherto   35 to] Q2; [om.]

only one part Woman, t'other Angel; and thus divided, claim my Love and Adoration.

50   *Lucinda.* Honourable Love is the Parent of mankind; but thine is the Corruptor and Debaser of it.—The Passion of you Libertines is like your Drunkeness; heat of Lust, as t'other is of Wine, and off with the next Sleep.

Roebuck. No, Madam; an Hair of the same—is my Receipt —Come, come, Madam, all things are laid to rest that will disturb our Pleasure, whole Nature favours us; the kind indulgent Stars that directed me hither, wink at what we are about. 'Twere Jilting of Fortune to be now idle, and she, like a true Woman, once baulk'd, never affords a second oppor-
60 tunity.—I'll put out the Candle, the Torch of Love shall light us to Bed.

Lucinda. To Bed, Sir!—Thou hast Impudence enough to draw thy Rationality in Question. Whence proceeds it? From a vain thought of thy own Graces, or an opinion of my Vertue?—If from the latter, know that I am a Woman, whose modesty dare not doubt my Vertue; yet have so much Pride to support it, that the dying Groans of thy whole Sex at my feet shou'd not extort an immodest thought from me.

Roebuck. Your thoughts may be as modest as you please,
70 Madam.—You shall be as Vertuous to morrow morning as e're a Nun in *Europe*, the opinion of the World shall proclaim you such, and that's the surest Charter the most rigid Vertue in *England* is held by. The Night has no Eyes to see, nor have I a Tongue to tell: One kiss shall seal up my Lips for ever.

Lucinda. That uncharitable Censure of Women, argues the meaness of thy Conversation.

Roebuck. Her superior Vertue awes me into coldness. [*Aside.*]—'Slife! it can't be Twelve sure.—Night's a Lyar. (*Draws out his Watch.*)

Lucinda. Sir, if you won't be gone, I must fetch those shall
80 Conduct you hence.—! my Eyes are dazled sure, (*Passing by him towards the door, she perceives the Jewel ty'd to the Watch.*) Pray, Sir let me see that Jewel.

Roebuck. By Heavens she has a mind to't!—Oh, 'tis at your service with all my Soul.

Lucinda. Wrong not my Vertue by so poor a thought.—But answer directly, as you are a Gentleman, to what I now shall ask: whence had you that Jewel?

Roebuck. I exchanged Watches with a Gentleman, and had this Jewel into the bargain. He valu'd it not, 'twas a Trifle from a Mistress.   90

Lucinda. A Trifle said he?—Oh Indignation! slighted thus! —I'll put a Jewel out of his power, that he would pawn his Soul to retrieve.—If you be a Gentleman, Sir, whom Gratitude can work up to Love, or a Vertuous Wife reclaim, I'll make you a large return for that Trifle.

Roebuck. Hey-day! a Wife said she!

Lucinda. What's your Name, Sir? and of what Country?

Roebuck. My Name's *Roebuck*, Madam.

Lucinda. Roebuck.

Roebuck. 'Sdeath! I forgot my Instructions. [*Aside.*]—*Mock-* 100 *mode*, Madam.—*Roebuck Mockmode*, my Name, and Sir-name.

Lucinda. Mockmode my 'Squire! it can't be! But if it shou'd, I've made the better Exchange.—Of what Family are you, Sir?

Roebuck. Of *Mockmode*-Hall in *Shropshire*, Madam. My Father's lately dead; I came lately from the University; I have fifteen hundred Acers of as good fighting Ground as any in *England.*—'Twas lucky I met that Blockhead to day. (*Aside.*)

Lucinda. The very same.—And had you any directions to court a Lady in *London.*   110

Roebuck. Umph!—How shou'd I have found the way hither else, Madam. What the Devil will this come to? (*Aside.*)

Lucinda. My Fool that I dreamt of, I find a pretty Gentleman.—Dreams go by contraries.—Well, Sir, I am the Lady; and if your Designs are Honourable, I'm yours, take a turn in the Garden, till I send for my Chaplain, you must take me immediately, for if I cool, I'm lost for ever.

Exit.

Roebuck. I think I am become a very sober *Shropshire* Gentleman in good earnest; I don't start at the name of a Parson.—Oh Fortune! Fortune! what art thou doing? If thou 120 and my Friend will throw me into the arms of a fine Lady, and great Fortune, how the Devil can I help it! Oh but, Zoons, there's Marriage! Ay, but there's Money.—Oh but there are

Children; sqawling Children. Ay but then there are *Rickets*
and *Small-Pox*, which perhaps may carry them all away.—Oh
but there's Horns! Horns! Ay, but then I shall go to Heaven,
for 'tis but reasonable, since all Marriages are made in
Heaven, that all Cuckolds should go thither.—But then
there's *Leanthe*! That sticks. I love her, witness, Heaven, I love
130 her to that degree.—Pshaw, I shall whine presently. I love her
as well as any Woman; and what can she expect more? I can't
drag a Lover's Chain a hundred Miles by Land and a
hundred Leagues by Water.—Fortune has decreed it otherwise.—So lead on, blind Guide, I follow thee; and when the
blind lead the blind, no wonder they both fall into—Matrimony. (*Going out, meets* Leanthe.) Oh my dear auspicious little
Mercury! let me kiss thee.—Go tell thy Charming Mistress I
obey her Commands.

                                                      Exit.
                    Enter Leanthe.
    Leanthe. Her Commands! Oh Heavens! I must follow him.
(*Going.*)
140   *Lucinda.* Page, Page.
    Leanthe. Oh my curs'd Fortune! baulk'd again!—Madam.
    Lucinda. Call my Chaplain; I'm to be married presently.
    Leanthe. Married so suddenly! To whom, pray Madam?
    Lucinda. To the Gentleman you met going hence just now.
    Leanthe. Oh Heavens! your Ladiship is not in earnest,
Madam?
    Lucinda. What, is Matrimony to be made a Jest of? don't be
impertinent, Boy; call him instantly.
    Leanthe. What shall I do?—Oh, Madam, suspend it till the
150 morning, for Heaven's sake. Mr. *Lovewell* is in the House; I
met him not half an hour ago; and he will certainly kill the
Gentleman, and perhaps harm your Ladyship.
    Lucinda. *Lovewell* in my house! How came he hither?
    Leanthe. I know not, Madam. I saw him and talk'd to him;
he had his Sword drawn, and he threatned every body. Pray
delay it to night, Madam.
    Lucinda. No, I'm resolv'd; and I'll prevent his discovering
us; I'll put on a suit of your Cloaths, and order *Pindress* to
carry her Night-Gown to the Gentleman in the Garden, and

bid him meet me in the lower Arbor, in the West Corner, and 160
send the Chaplain thither instantly.

Exit.

Leanthe. Hold, Fortune, hold; thou hast entirely won;
For I am lost. Thus long I have been rack'd
On thy tormenting Wheel, and now my Heart-strings break.
Discovering who I am, exposes me to shame.
Then what on Earth can help me?

Enter Pindress.

Pindress. Oh Lord, Page, what's the matter? Here's old
doings, or rather new doings. Prithee let you and I throw in
our Two-pence a piece into this Marriage-Lottery.

Leanthe. You'll draw nothing but Blanks, I'll assure you, 170
from me.—But stay, let me consider o'th' bus'ness.

Pindress. No consideration; the bus'ness must be done hand
over head.

Leanthe. Well, I have one Card to play still; and with you,
Pindress. (*Takes her hand.*)

Pindress. You expect tho' that I shou'd turn up Trumps?

Leanthe. No, not if I shuffle right. (*Aside.*)—Well, *Pindress*,
'tis a Match. Be gone to the lower Arbor at the West Corner of
the Garden, and I'll come to thee immediately with the
Chaplain. You must not whisper, for we must pass upon the 180
Chaplain for my Lady and the Gentleman.—Haste.

Pindress. Shan't I put on my New Gown first?

Leanthe. No, no; you shall have a Green Gown for your
Wedding in the Arbor.

Pindress. A Green Gown?—Well, all Flesh is Grass.

Leanthe. Make haste, my spouse, fly.

Pindress. And will you come? will you be sure to come?—O
my little Green Gooseberry, my Teeth waters at ye.—

Exit.

Leanthe. Now Chance.—No, thou'rt blind.
Then Love, be thou my Guide, and set me right; 190
Tho' blind, like Chance, you have best Eyes by Night.

Exit.

[ACT V. Scene ii.]

SCENE Bullfinch's *House.*

Enter Lovewell, Brush, *and* Servant.

Lovewell. Mr. *Lyrick* abroad, saist thou? and *Mockmode* with him?

Servant. All abroad, my Mistress and all.

Lovewell. I don't understand this.—*Brush,* run to *Lucinda*'s Lodgings, and observe what's a doing there: I spy'd some hasty Lights glancing thro' the Rooms; I'll follow you presently.—

Exit Brush.

Can't you inform me which way they went.

Servant. Perhaps Mr. *Mockmode*'s man can inform ye.

10   *Lovewell.* Pray call him.

Servant. Mr. *Club,* Mr. *Club.*

Lovewell. What is the fellow deaf?

Servant. No, Sir; but he's asleep, and in bed.—Mr. *Club,* Mr. *Club.*

Club. Augh—(*Yawning.*) I'm asleep, I'm asleep; don't wake me.—Augh.

Servant. Here's a Gentleman wants ye.

Enter Club, *with his Coat unbutten'd, his Garter's unti'd, scratching and yawning, as newly waken'd from Bed.*

Club. Pox o' your *London*-breeding; what makes you waken a Man out of his sleep that way.

20   *Lovewell.* Where's your Master, pray Sir?

Club. Augh.—'Tis a sad thing to be broken of ones rest this way.

Lovewell. Can you inform me where your Master's gone?

Club. My Master?—Augh—(*Stretching and yawning.*)

Lovewell. Yes, Sir, your Master.

Club. My Master?—Augh—What a Clock is it, Sir? I believe 'tis past Midnight, for I have gotten my first sleep—Augh.—

Lovewell. Thou'rt asleep still, Blockhead. Answer me, or—

30   where's your Master?

Club. Augh—I had the pleasantest Dream when you call'd me—Augh—I thought my Master's great black Stone-horse, had broke loose among the Mares—Augh—and so, Sir, you call'd me—Augh—and so I waken'd.

Lovewell. Sirrah, (*Strikes him.*)—Now your dream's out, I hope.

Club. Zauns, Sir! what d'ye mean, Sir? My Master's as good a Man as you, Sir; Dem me, Sir?

Lovewell. Tell me presently, where your Master is, Sirrah, or I'll dust the secret out of your Jacket.   40

Club. Oh, Sir, your Name's *Lovewell*, Sir!

Lovewell. What then, Sir?

Club. Why then my Master is—where you are not, Sir.—My Master's in a fine Ladies Arms, and you are—here, I take it. (*Shrugging.*)

Lovewell. Has he got a Whore a Bed with him?

Club. He may be Father to the Son of a Whore by this time, if your Mistress *Lucinda* be one, Mr. *Lyrick* did his bus'ness, and my Master will do her bus'ness I warrant him, if o'th' right *Shropshire* breed which I'm sure he is, for my Mother nurs'd him on my Milk.   50

Lovewell. Two Calves suckl'd on the same Cow—Ha, ha, ha. Gramercy Poet; has he brought the Play to a Catastrophe so soon? A rare Executioner, to clap him in the Female Pillory already! Ha, ha, ha.

Club. Ay, Sir; and Pillory that you wou'd give your Ears for, I warrant you think my Master's over head and ears in the *Irish* Quagmire you wou'd have drown'd him in. But, Sir, we have found the bottom on't.

Lovewell. He may pass over the Quagmire, Sirrah; for there were Stepping-stones laid in his way.   60

Club. He has got over dry-shod, I'll assure you.—Pray, Sir, did not you receive a Note from *Lucinda*, the true *Lucinda*, to meet her at Ten in her Garden to Night.—Why don't you laugh now? Ha, ha, ha.

Lovewell. 'Sdeath, Rascal, What Intelligence cou'd you have of that?

Club. Hold, Sir, I have more Intelligence. You threw Mr. *Lyrick* his Poem in a hurrey in the Park, and justled that sweet Letter out of your Pocket, Sir. This Letter fell into my

70 Master's hands, Sir, and discovered your Sham, Sir, your
Trick, Sir. Now Sir, I think you're as deep in the Mud as he is
in the Mire.

Lovewell. Curs'd misfortune!—And where are they gone,
Sir? Quickly, the Truth, the whole Truth, Dog, or I'll spit you
like a Sparrow.

Club. I design to tell you, Sir. Mr. *Lyrick*, Sir, being my
Master's intimate Friend, or so, upon a Bribe of a hundred
Pounds, or so, has sided with him, taken him to *Lucinda's*
Garden in your stead, and there's a Parson, and all, and so
80 forth.—Now, Sir, I hope the Poet has brought the Play to a
very good Cata—Cata—what d'ye call him, Sir?

Lovewell. 'Twas he I incounter'd in the Garden.—'Sdeath!
Trick'd by the Poet! I'll cut off one of his Limbs, I'll make a
Synelepha of him; I'll—

Club. He, he, he!—Two Calves suck'd on the same Cow!—
He, he!—

Lovewell. Nay then I begin with you. (*Drubs him.*)

Club. Zauns! Murder! Dem me! Zauns! Murder! Zauns!

Runs off, and Lovewell *after him.*

[ACT V. Scene iii.]

SCENE *changes to the Anti-Chamber in* Lucinda's
house; a Hat, and Sword on the Table.

Enter Brush.

Brush. I have been peeping and crouching about like a Cat
a Mousing. Ha! I smell a Rat—A Sword and Hat!—There are
certainly a pair of Breeches appertaining to these, and may be
lap'd up in my Ladies Lavender, who knows!— (*Listens.*)

Enter Lovewell *in a hurry.*

Lovewell. What, Sir? What are you doing? I'm ruin'd,
trick'd.—

Brush. I believe so too, Sir.—See here.—(*Shews the Hat and
Sword.*)

Lovewell. By all my hopes, *Roebuck's* Hat and Sword. This is
mischief upon mischief. Run you to the Garden, Sirrah; and if

you find any body, secure 'em; I'll search the House.—I'm   10
ruin'd!—Fly.—*Roebuck?*—what hoa?—*Roebuck?*—hoa?
Enter Roebuck *unbutton'd; runs to* Lovewell, *and embraces him.*
Roebuck. Dear, dear *Lovewell*, wish me Joy, wish me Joy, my
Friend.
Lovewell. Of what, Sir?
Roebuck. Of the dearest, tenderest, whitest, softest Bride,
that ever blest Man's Arms. I'm all Air, all a *Cupid*, all Wings,
and must fly again to her embraces. Detain me not, my
Friend.
Lovewell. Hold, Sir; I hope you mock me; tho' that it self's
unkind.   20
Roebuck. Mock you!—By Heav'ns no; she's more than sense
can bear, or Tongue express.—Oh *Lucinda*! shou'd Heaven—
Lovewell. Hold, Sir; no more.
Roebuck. I'm on the Rack of Pleasure, and must confess all.
When her soft, melting white, and yielding Waste,
Within my pressing Arms was folded fast,
Our lips were melted down by heat of Love,
And lay incorporate in liquid kisses,
Whilst in soft broken, sighs, we catch'd each other's Souls.
Lovewell. Come, come, *Roebuck*, no more of this Extravagance. 30
—By Heav'n I swear you shan't marry her.
Roebuck. By Heaven I swear so too, for I'm married already.
Lovewell. Then thou'rt a Villain.
Roebuck. A Villain, Man!—Pshaw! that's Nonsense. A poor
fellow can no sooner get married, than you imagine he may be
call'd a Villain presently.—You may call me a Fool, a
Blockhead, or an Ass, by the Authority of Custom: But why a
Villain, for God's sake?
Lovewell. Did not you engage to meet and fight a Gentleman
for me in *Moorfields*?   40
Roebuck. Did not you promise to engage a Lady for me at
the Fountain, Sir?
Lovewell. This *Lucinda* is my Mistress, Sir.
Roebuck. This *Lucinda*, Sir; is my Wife.
Lovewell. Then this decides the matter.—Draw. (*Throws*
Roebuck *his Sword, and draws his own.*)
Roebuck. Prithee be quiet, Man, I've other bus'ness to mind
on my Wedding-night. I must in to my Bride. (*Going.*)

Lovewell. Hold, Sir; move a step, and by Heavens I'll stab thee.

50 *Roebuck.* Put up, put up; Pshaw, I an't prepar'd to dye; I an't, Devil take me.

Lovewell. Do you dally with me, Sir?

Roebuck. Why you won't be so unconscionable as to kill a Man so suddenly; I han't made my Will yet. Perhaps I may leave you a Legacy.

Lovewell. Pardon me Heaven's, if press'd by stinging taunts, my Passion urge my Arm to act what's foul. (*Offers to push at him.*)

Roebuck. Hold. (*Taking up his Sword.*) 'Tis safest making Peace, they say, with Sword in hand.—I'll tell thee what, *Ned*;
60 I wou'd not lose this Night's Pleasure for the honour of fighting and vanquishing the Seven Champions of *Christendom.* Permit me then but this Night to return to the Arms of my dear Bride, and faith and troth I'll take a fair Thrust with you to morrow morning.

Lovewell. What, beg a poor Reprieve for Life!—Then thou'rt a Coward.

Roebuck. You imagin'd the contrary, when you employ'd me to fight for ye in *Moorfields.*

Lovewell. Will nothing move thy Gall?—Thou'rt base,
70 ungrateful.

Roebuck. Ungrateful! I love thee, *Ned*; by Heavens, my Friend, I love thee: therefore name not that word again, for such a repetition wou'd over-pay all thy favours.

Lovewell. A cheap, a very cheap way of making acknowledgment, and therefore thou hast catch'd, which makes thee more ungrateful.

Roebuck. My Friendship even yet does balance Passion; but throw in the least grain more of an affront, and by heaven you turn the Scale.

80 *Lovewell.* (*Pausing.*) No, I've thought better; my Reason clears: She is not worth my Sword; a Bully only shou'd draw in her defence, for she's false, a Prostitute. (*Puts up his Sword.*)

Roebuck. A Prostitute! By Heaven thou ly'st. (*Draws.*)— Thou hast blasphem'd. Her Vertue answers the uncorrupted state of Woman; so much above Immodesty, that it mocks Temptation. She has convinc'd me of the bright Honour of her

Sex, and I stand Champion now for the fair Female Cause.

Lovewell. Then I have lost what naught on Earth can pay. Curse on all doubts, all Jealousies, that destroy our present happiness, by mistrusting the future. Thus mis-believers 90 making their Heaven uncertain, find a certain Hell.—And is she Vertuous?—sound the bold charge aloud, which does proclaim me Guilty.

Roebuck. By Heavens as Vertuous as thy Sister.

Lovewell. My Sister;—Ha!—I fear, Sir, your Marriage with *Lucinda* has wrong'd my Sister; for her you courted, and I heard she lov'd you.

Roebuck. I courted her, 'tis true, and lov'd her also; nay, my Love to her, rivall'd my Friendship tow'rds—; and had my Fate allow'd me time for thought, her dear remembrance 100 might have stopt the Marriage. But since 'tis past, I must own to you, to her, and all the World, that I cast off all former Passion, and shall henceforth confine my Love to the dear Circle of her Charming Arms from which I just now parted.

Enter Leanthe *in Woman's loose Apparel.*

Leanthe. I take you at your word. These are the Arms that held you.

Roebuck. Oh Gods and Happiness! *Leanthe!*

Lovewell. My Sister! Heavens! it cannot be.

Roebuck. By Heavens it can, it shall, it must be so—For none on Earth could give such Joys but she—Who wou'd have 110 thought my Joys cou'd bear increase? *Lovewell*, my Friend! this is thy Sister! 'tis *Leanthe*! my Mistress, my Bride, my Wife.

Leanthe. I am your Sister, Sir, as such I beg you to pardon the effects of violent passion, which has driven me into some imprudent Actions; But none such as may blot the honour of my Vertue, or Family. To hold you no longer in suspence, 'twas I brought the Letter from *Leanthe*; 'twas I manag'd the Intrigue with *Lucinda*; I sent the Note to Mr. *Roebuck* this afternoon; and I—

Roebuck. That was the Bride of happy me.   120

Lovewell. Thou art my Sister, and my Guardian-Angel; for thou hast bless'd thy self, and bless'd thy Brother. *Lucinda* still is safe, and may be mine.

Roebuck. May!—She shall be thine, my Friend.

Lovewell. Where is *Lucinda*?

Enter Mockmode.

Mockmode. Not far off; tho' far enough from you, by the
Universe.

Leanthe. You must give me leave not to believe you, Sir.

Mockmode. Oh Madam, I crave you ten thousand pardons
130 by the Universe, Madam.—Zauns, Madam, Dem me,
Madam. (*Offers to salute her awkwardly.*)

Lovewell. By your leave, Sir—(*Thrusts him back.*)

Roebuck. Ah, Cousin *Mockmode!*—How do all our Friends in
Shropshire?—

Mockmode. Now, Gentlemen, I thank you all for your Trick,
your Sham. You imagine I have got your Whore, Cousin, your
Crack. But Gentlemen, by the assistance of a Poet, your *Sheely*
is Metamorphos'd into the real *Lucinda*; which your Eyes shall
testifie. Bring in the Jury there.—Guilty or not Guilty?

Enter Lyrick *and* Trudge.

140 *Trudge.* Oh my dear *Roebuck!* (Trudge *seeing* Roebuck, *throws
off her Masque, flies to him, takes him about the Neck and kisses him.*)
And Faith is it you, dear Joy? and where have you been these
seven long years?

Mockmode. Zauns!—

Roebuck. Hold off, stale Iniquity.—Madam, you'll pardon
this?— (*To* Leanthe.)

Trudge. Indeed I won't live with that stranger. You
promised to marry me, so you did.—Ah Sir, *Neddy*'s a brave
Boy, God bless him; he's a whole arm full; Lord knows I had a
heavy load of him.

150 *Lovewell.* Guilty, or Not Guilty, Mr. *Mockmode?*

Mockmode. 'Tis past that; I am condemn'd, I'm hang'd in
the Marriage Noose.—Hark ye, Madam, was this the Doctor
that let you blood under the Tongue for the Quinsey.

Trudge. Yes, that it was, Sir.

Mockmode. Then he may do so again; for the Devil take me if
ever I breath a Vein for ye.—Mr. *Lyrick*, is this your Poetical
Friendship?

Lyrick. I had only a mind to convince you of your
'Squireship.

160 *Lovewell.* Now, Sister, my fears are over.—But where's
Lucinda? how is she dispos'd of?

V. iii 140 Roebuck] 1728; Lovewell

Leanthe. The fear she lay under of being discover'd by you, gave me an opportunity of imposing *Pindress* upon her instead of this Gentleman, whom she expected to wear one of *Pindress*'s Night-Gowns as a Disguise. To make the Cheat more current, she disguis'd her self in my Cloaths, which has made her pass on her Maid for me; and I by that opportunity putting on a Suit of hers, past upon this Gentleman for *Lucinda*, my next business is to find her out, and beg her pardon, eneavour her reconcilement to you, which the 170 discovery of the mistakes between both will easily effect.

Exit.

Roebuck. Well, Sir, (*To* Lyrick.) how was your Plot carried on?

Lyrick. Why this 'Squire (will you give me leave to call you so now?) this 'Squire had a mind to personate *Lovewell*, to catch *Lucinda.*—So I made *Trudge* to personate *Lucinda*, and snap him in this very Garden.—Now Sir, you'll give me leave to write your *Epithalamium.*

Mockmode. My *Epithalamium*! my *Epitaph*, Screech-Owl, for I'm Buried alive. But I hope you'll return my hundred pound 180 I gave you for marrying me.

Lyrick. No, But for Five hundred more I'll unmarry you. These are hard times, and men of industry must make Money.

Mockmode. Here's the Money, by the Universe, Sir; a Bill of Five hundred pound Sterling upon Mr. *Ditto* the Mercer in *Cheapside.* Bring me a Reprieve, and 'tis yours.

Lyrick. Lay it in that Gentleman's hands. (*Gives* Roebuck *the Bill.*) The Executioner shall cut the Rope. (*Goes to the door, and brings in* Bullfinch *dress'd like a Parson.*) Here's Revelation for you!—(*Pulls open the Gown.*)   190

Mockmode. Oh thou damn'd Whore of *Babylon*!

Lovewell. What, Pope *Joan* the second! were you the Priest?

Bullfinch. Of the Poet's Ordination.

Lyrick. Ay, ay, before the time of Christianity the Poets were Priests.

Mockmode. No wonder then that all the World were Heathens.

Lyrick. How d'ye like the Plot? wou'd it not do well for a

Play?—My Money, Sir.—(*To* Roebuck.)

200　*Roebuck.* No, Sir, it belongs to this Gentlewoman.—(*Gives it to* Trudge.) you have divorc'd her, and must give her seperate maintenance.—There's another turn of Plot you were not aware of, Mr. *Lyrick.*

Enter Lucinda, Leanthe, *and* Pindress.

Lucinda. You have told me Wonders.

Leanthe. Here are these can testifie the truth. This Gentleman is the real Mr. *Mockmode*, and much such another person as your dream represented.

Roebuck. I hope, Madam, you'll pardon my dissembling, since only the hopes of so great a purchase cou'd cause it.

210　*Lucinda.* Let my wishing you much Joy and Happiness in your Bride testifie my reconciliation; And at the request of your Sister, Mr. *Lovewell*, I pardon your past Jealousies. You threatned me, Mr. *Lovewell*, with an *Irish* Entertainment at my Wedding. I wish it present now, to assist at your Sisters Nuptials.

Leanthe. At my last going hence, I sent for 'em, and they're ready.

Lovewell. Call 'em in then.

An Irish *Entertainment of three Men and three
Women, dress'd after the* Fingallion *fashion.*

Lucinda. I must reward your Sister, Mr. *Lovewell*, for the
220　many Services done me as my Page. I therefore settle my Fortune and my self on you, on this Condition, That you make over your Estate in *Ireland* to your Sister, and that Gentleman.

Lovewell. 'Tis done; only with this Proviso, Brother, That you forsake your Extravagancies.

Roebuck. Brother, you know I always slighted Gold;
But most when offer'd as a sordid Bribe.
I scorn to be brib'd even to Vertue;
But for bright Vertues sake, I here embrace it. (*Embracing* Leanthe.)
I have espous'd all Goodness with *Leanthe*,
230　And am divorc'd from all my former Follies.

*Woman's our Fate. Wild and Unlawful Flames
Debauch us first, and softer Love reclaims.*

200 *Roebuck.*] Q2; *Lyr.*

Thus Paradice was lost by Woman's Fall;
But Vertuous Woman thus restores it all.

Exeunt omnes.

FINIS.

EPILOGUE:

Written and Spoke by *Jo. Haynes* in Mourning.

I Come not here, our Poets Fate to see,
He and his Play may both be damn'd for me.
No; Royal Theatre, I come to Mourn *for thee.*
And must these Structures then untimely fall
Whilst the other House stands and gets the Devil and all?
Must still kind Fortune through all Weathers steer 'em?
And Beauties bloom there spight of Edax, Rerum.
Vivitur Ingenio, *that damn'd Motto there* [Looking up at it.
Seduc'd me first to be a Wicked Player.
10   *Hard Times indeed, Oh* Tempora*! Oh* Mores*!*
I knew that Stage must down where not one whore is.
    But can you have the hearts tho'?—(pray now speak)
After all our Services to let us break,
You cannot do't unless the Devil's in ye,
What Arts, what Merit ha'n't we us'd to win ye?
First to divert ye with some new French *strowlers;*
We brought ye Bona Sere's, Barba Colar's. [Mocking the late
    singers.
   When their Male Throats no longer drew your Money,
We got ye an Eunuch's Pipe, Seignior Rampony.
20   *That Beardless Songster we cou'd ne're make much on;*
The Females found a damn'd Blot in his Scutcheon.
An Italian *now we've got of mighty Fame,*
Don Segismondo Fideli.—*There's Musick in his Name,*
His voice is like the Musick of the Spheres
It shou'd be Heavenly for the Price it bears. [20 *l.* a time.
He's a handsome fellow too, looks brisk and trim.
If he don't take ye, Then the Devil take him.
Besides least our white faces always mayn't delight ye;
We've Pickt up Gypsies now to please or fright ye.
30   *Lastly to make our House more Courtlier shine;*
As Travel does the Men of Mode refine,
So our Stage Hero's *did their* Tour *design.*
To mend their Manners *and course* English *Feeding;*

They went to Ireland *to improve their* Breeding:
Yet for all this, we still are at a loss,
Oh Collier! Collier! *Thou'st frighted away Miss* C—s
She to return our Foreigner's Complizance
At Cupid's *call, has made a* Trip *to* France.
Love's Fire Arm's *here are since not worth a sous,*
We've lost the only Touch-hole *of our* House.   ·40
    Losing that Jewel gave us a Fatal blow:
Well, if thin Audience must Jo. Haynes *undo,*
Well, if 'tis decreed, Nor can thy Fate, *O Stage*
Resist the Vows of this obdurate Age,
    I'll then grow wiser, leave off Playing the Fool,
And Hire this Play-House for a Boarding-School.
D'ye think the Maids *won't be in a sweet Condition*
When they are Under Jo. Haynes's *Grave Tuition*
They'll have no occasion then I'm sure to Play
They'll have such Comings *in another way.*   50

THE CONSTANT COUPLE

INTRODUCTION

SOURCES AND COMPOSITION

APPROXIMATELY a year after *Love and a Bottle* opened and the novella *The Adventures of Covent Garden* was published, Farquhar's second play, *The Constant Couple; or a Trip to the Jubilee* had its *première* at Drury Lane, probably in November 1699. Although scholars have speculated for almost three hundred years on whether *Love and a Bottle* with its wild Irish hero was written before Farquhar left Ireland, *The Constant Couple* is so entirely urbanized as to leave no doubt that he wrote it after he arrived in London.

Farquhar began work no earlier than spring or summer 1699, judging from internal evidence. The two public events central to the action of the play, that is, the statute disbanding the army and the Roman Jubilee, became important topics that spring. The Act of Parliament to disband the army had resounding social and economic effects. Except for a force in Ireland, all but 7,000 men were disbanded on 26 March 1699, the rest on or before 1 May.[1] Military men suddenly found themselves unemployed and impoverished. Interest in the Jubilee, a matter of far less consequence to Englishmen, erupted in England during the same spring. According to Richard Morton and William M. Peterson, news of the papal celebration had spread widely before the first official announcement in the *London Gazette* on 5–8 June 1699.[2] The Jubilee actually began on Christmas Eve 1699, only a month after the play opened.

As early as the *Biographia Dramatica*, *The Adventures of Covent Garden* was recognized as a source for *The Constant Couple*; Isaac Reed perceived the debt and noted it in his own copy of the *Adventures*, then expanded his published commentary, moralistically noting the lack of scruples on the part of early writers who borrowed from 'a piece without the slightest degree of merit', written by some 'contemptible' writer.[3] Leigh Hunt suspected Farquhar's authorship of the *Adventures* and recognized that Farquhar merely reused his own materials.[4] Subsequent scholars have acknowledged that Farquhar reused (or borrowed) the material in the *Adventures* in which the Captain changes clothes with the Porter for the scene in which Beau Clincher changes clothes with Tom Errand. Some have also seen the *novella* as a source for Lurewell, and fewer have included Standard.[5] The *Adventures* also provided two lines of poetry in III. i, with the single revision of the word 'most' to 'base'. Lines from the same poem had appeared in *Love and a Bottle*. Throughout his career Farquhar proved singularly thrifty with his poetry, reusing lines.

Critics have cited numerous other sources for the play, most of which have vague general similarities in stock characterizations or plot devices but not specific provable debts. Many critics have followed Genest in attributing the character of Lurewell and occasionally 'the outline of the two Clinchers' to D'Urfey's *Madame Fickle*. The older play had been on the stage since 1676. Archer believes Genest is probably right; Stonehill sees 'a decided resemblance' between the two jilts and believes the two Clinchers resemble Zekiel and Toby; James concurs; John Harrington Smith believes Farquhar took the theme from D'Urfey's comedy, and Bernbaum says Farquhar borrowed from *Madam Fickle* 'much of the play' including Lurewell, who weeps for her lost lover but spends her time spitefully entrapping and plaguing all the suitors she can attract.[6] James believes Farquhar may also have borrowed directly from William Rawley's *A Match at Midnight* (1633), a source for *Madame Fickle*.[7] Connely believes Angelica was 'only slightly suggested' by Furetière's Angelica,[8] and Allardyce Nicoll says that part of the play is derived from *Le Roman bourgeois* by Scarron (actually Furetière's *Le Roman bourgeois*, translated in 1671 as Scarron's *City Romance, Made English*, the acknowledged source of *The Adventures of Covent Garden*.[9]

Archer and Stonehill speculated whether Lurewell was modelled on Mary de la Riviere Manley, whose marriage was irregular at best. Although two of her plays had opened in 1696, there is no evidence that Farquhar knew her or indeed there is no evidence that Farquhar knew her or indeed portrayed his friends in his plays. Standard, however, asks Lurewell in the denouement, 'is not your real Name *Manly*?',

and she proves to be the daughter of Sir Oliver Manly.
However, as Stonehill points out, the name is a common one
in comedy, occurring not only in Wycherley's *Plain Dealer*, but
also in *Madame Fickle*.[10]

Critics have been sharply divided on the question of
Wildair. As early as 1700 a critic was complaining that
Wildair was borrowed from Etherege's Dorimant in *The Man
of Mode*;[11] Connely focused on another of Etherege's creations,
Sir Frederick Frollick of *The Comical Revenge*.[12] But most
observers have considered Wildair original, and many have
spoken of the character as a second self-portrait, as Giles
Jacob said, 'the Character of the Author in his politest
capacity',[13] in contrast with the untamed Irishman of *Love and
a Bottle*.

The 1733 *Memoirs of Wilks* says that Farquhar created the
part especially for his actor-friend.[14] Although Wildair
descended from extravagant rakes of the Restoration, characters
that both Farquhar and Wilks knew through their theatrical
experience, he was also distinctly original. Audiences perceived
the uniqueness, and applauded so enthusiastically that critics
immediately and continuously attacked the character as
derivative.[15] In fact, the play owed less to other works, the
author's own novella excluded, than most plays written during
the period. In a theatrical era noted for its translations,
adaptations, and borrowings, Farquhar wrote with unusual
originality.

Within two months, perhaps within a much shorter span,
Farquhar revised his comedy.[16] The confrontation between
Wildair and Angelica in Act V, Scene i, was drastically
altered, probably to preserve consistency in Sir Harry's
character as Robert Wilks interpreted him. In the first
version, Wildair, upon learning that Angelica is not a
prostitute, worships before the shrine of her chastity and talks
about 'Beauty without Art!' and 'Vertue without Pride!' in a
sentimental, highly emotional scene. The revision allows Sir
Harry to retain his crisp characterization; he 'Looks foolish
and hums a Song' when he discovers his mistake and chooses
marriage over a duel as 'the most daring Action of the two'
instead of marrying, as in the first version, so that 'chastest,
purest Passion with a large and fair Estate, can make

amends'. He no longer exults that 'The Day breaks glorious to my o'erclouded Thought, and darts its smiling Beams into my Soul'. The second version, far less sentimental than the first, avoids a highly emotional conversion and thereby retains consistency in the characterization of Sir Harry.

The revision occurred early during the first run or possibly during rehearsals, and was published in the second edition, which followed the first by less than two months. Although one would expect revisions made during rehearsal to find their way to the printer, there is considerable evidence that such was not always the case.[17] The remarkable theatrical popularity of the play on stage was responsible for the revised edition.

Farquhar must have spent considerable time around Drury Lane in the 1699–1700 season. He wrote an epilogue for Wilks on the occasion of his first theatrical appearance on his return to England. He revised the comedy within the next couple of months, and he wrote at least three other prologues and epilogues for performances during the same season.[18] The fact that he had written the epilogue for John Oldmixon's opera *The Grove*, which opened in January or February, could not prevent disaster at the box office; Oldmixon perhaps linked his failure to the overwhelming success of *The Constant Couple* a few months before. At any rate, he savagely attacked the successful comedy and its author in a prologue for Charles Gildon's alteration of *Measure for Measure*, which opened at Lincoln's Inn Fields probably in March. Farquhar smarted; he had been 'scurrilously . . . abus'd'[19] by Oldmixon, and he chose to vindicate his honour with the same weapon, in this case a prologue to *The Constant Couple* 'In Answer to my very Good Friend, Mr. *Oldmixon*; who, having Two PLAYS Damn'd at the Old House, had a mind to Curry-Favour, to have a Third Damn'd at the New'. The verbal volley was fired at a performance on 13 July and was subsequently published in the third edition on 20 August. Farquhar's tinkering with the play, in the revision and the new prologue, was unusual for him and for playwrights of his time; it is understandable in the light of the play's unprecedented success.

STAGE HISTORY

By autumn 1699, the theatrical warfare between Christopher Rich's company at Drury Lane and the renegade players who broke from the United Company in 1695 to perform at Lincoln's Inn Fields had cost both houses heavily. The best actors had deserted Drury Lane because of Rich's mismanagement; they were replaced by inexperienced youngsters. Betterton, Bracegirdle, and Barry were never surpassed in tragedy, but gradually the neophytes began to make a name for themselves in comedy. Drury Lane needed top actors to compete for audiences. Jane Rogers, who played Angelica in *The Constant Couple*, George Powell (Standard), William Pinkethman (Clincher Senior), and other cast members had never defected; William Bullock (Clincher Junior), John Mills (Vizard), and Benjamin Johnson (Smuggler) had all joined the company in its first season; Joe Haines (Tom Errand) had come in 1696–7. To their number Henry Norris (Dicky) and Robert Wilks were added, probably in the fall of 1699.[20] Wilks had played in London in 1693–4, then returned to the Smock Alley company for a highly successful career; there he came to know Farquhar, who tried acting between the end of his college career in 1696 and his departure for London in 1698. The Drury Lane company attempted to capitalize on Wilks's return; in Farquhar's epilogue celebrating Wilks's first performance after returning to London, the actor spoke openly of leaving behind his Dublin successes for the blandishments of London. By the time *The Constant Couple* opened, the Drury Lane company, with outstanding comedians such as Norris, Pinkethman, Haines, and Bullock and actors such as Wilks, was well prepared to challenge the established actors at Lincoln's Inn Fields.

The two houses waged the battle for audiences by mounting extravagant performances: they imported disastrously expensive musical artists and booked novelty acts; they spent heavily on scenery and machinery; and they staged elaborate operas. They also needed successful *premières*; in the three seasons from 1695 to 1698, the two houses launched a total of sixty-four new plays, ten of which can be termed successes.[21] Only ten *premières* occurred in 1698–9, and although *Love and a*

Bottle at least saw a third night, Motteux's adaptation of
Fletcher's operatic *The Island Princess* was the only new play
accounted a financial success. The theatrical difficulties were
intensified by the reformers who were by that season
increasingly nipping at the heels of the actors. It was not
surprising, then, that Drury Lane turned again to Farquhar,
who had achieved a moderate success the season before, for a
new vehicle for its comedians.

There is no evidence that the play was recognized as
remarkable before the opening. There was no unusual fanfare,
no puffing, no creation of new and impressive sets. But once
again musical ornamentation was an important item of
concern. New act tunes were commissioned, including a
rondeau, an air, a bourrée, a jig, and a slow air, and
presumably others no longer extant.[22] A country dance,
perhaps performed during the singing and dancing in v. iii,
was also created for the *Jubilee*. According to the published
text, Wilks sang '*Thus* Damon *knock'd at* Celia*'s Door*' in IV. ii
and '*Behold the Goldfinches*' in v. i, as well as an unspecified tune
in I. i and one designated as '*Let her wander*' in II. iii. However,
the publication of the music casts doubt on Wilks as
performer: *Mercurius Musicus* (1699) prints the song as 'A New
Song in the *Constant Couple*, or *a Trip to the Jubilee* Sett by
Mr. D. Purcell, and Sung by Mr. *Pate*'.[23] Cross published the
song as '*The Serenading Song in the CONSTANT COUPLE; or a
Trip to the Jubilee, written by Mr* George Farquhar, *Set by
Mr.* Daniel Purcel, *Sung by* Mr Freeman, *and exactly engrav'd by*
Tho. Cross'. Another edition, perhaps by Walsh, also claimed
Freeman was the singer. The settings by Purcell all begin
'Poor Damon'; a second setting, by Richard Leveridge, begins
'Thus Damon', the wording in the published text. One
engraving of Leveridge's setting says it was sung at the theatre
in Dublin. The unusual circumstance of two musical settings
within the first year is not readily explicable. Nor can the
singer be easily identified. Both Freeman and Pate performed
at Drury Lane in 1699–1700, and Wilks might also have sung
it, although the contemporary publication of the music
strongly suggests that a professional singer performed.

Another song, 'Come bring us Wine in Plenty', was
published at approximately the same time as the other music,

under the title '*A SONG to a Tune call'd a Trip to the* Jubilee'; the tune was set by Richard Lowe. The published play provides no clues as to whether the drinking song was included in the first run, was given to Wildair or someone else within the scenes of the play, or was sung *entr'acte*. But since Henry Playford advertised the song in the *Post Boy* as early as 30 March–2 April 1700, it was undoubtedly performed during the first season. The musical ornamentation for the play, including an additional song that is not part of the published text, suggests the same kind of commercial impulses that had shaped the production of *Love and a Bottle* the previous year.

The first known performance was staged 28 November 1699. The *première* was probably two or three weeks before that date, judging from the fact that the play was published early in December. It must have instantaneously struck success, for reputedly it played a phenomenal fifty-three nights in London and twenty-three in Dublin before the end of the season.[24] Farquhar himself, in the preface to *The Inconstant*, remarked that the *Trip* 'brought the Playhouse some fifty Audiences in five months'. Three to six nights was considered a success; nine nights was outstanding—and rare. If the statistics are accurate, *The Constant Couple* broke all performance records in its first season and held the record until *The Beggar's Opera* played sixty-two nights in 1728–9.

The reasons for the unprecedented success are difficult to pinpoint. Although Farquhar created a plot that was original, its component parts were familiar on stage—the kind of disguise, trickery, mistaken identities, and creaky solutions that shaped most comedies of the period. But *The Constant Couple* was clearly an actor's vehicle, designed to capitalize on the talents of Robert Wilks and other company members. Wilks had played many rakish roles before Sir Harry, including Palamede in Dryden's *Marriage à la Mode* in London[25] and Sir Frederick Frollick in Etherege's *The Comical Revenge*, Courtal in *She Would If She Could*, and Dorimant in *The Man of Mode* at Smock Alley.[26] He must have played numerous other sparks before 1699 because his subsequent roles include a great many from earlier plays, for example Wilmore in Behn's *The Rover*, Belmour in Congreve's *The Old Bachelour*, and Lorenzo in Dryden's *The Spanish Fryar*. However, his portrayal of Sir Harry was generally perceived as so delightful, so innovative, and so enjoyable that many people felt he rather than Farquhar was responsible for the incredible run. Critics consistently claimed his portrayal carried the play. Curll's *Life of Wilks*, for example, suggests that:

> Farquhar, by Writing gain'd Himself a Name
> And by *Wilks*, *Farquhar*, gain'd immortal Fame.[27]

Steele, in *Tatler*, no. 19, even more specifically attributed the success of the character to Wilks rather than Farquhar:

> This performance is the greatest instance that we can have of the irresistible force of proper action. The dialogue in itself has something too low to bear a criticism upon it; but Mr. Wilks enters into the part with so much skill, that the gallantry, the youth, the gaiety of a young man of a plentiful fortune, are looked upon with as much indulgence on the stage, as in real life, without any of those intermixtures of wit and humour, which usually prepossess us in favour of such characters in other plays.

But no one was more willing to attribute the success of the play to Wilks than Farquhar himself, who wrote in his Preface to the Reader of the published text:

> Mr. *Wilks*'s performance has set him so far above competition in the part of *Wildair*, that none can pretend to envy the Praise due to his Merit. That he made the Part, will appear from hence, that whenever the Stage has the misfortune to lose him, Sir *Harry Wildair* may go to the Jubilee.

So strongly was Wilks identified with Sir Harry in 1699 and for the next thirty years, that he was called Sir Harry Wildair in the theatrical pamphlets and poems of his time.[28]

But he was not the only actor permanently marked by success in *The Constant Couple*. The role of Dicky, Clincher Junior's witty little servant, who can 'powder a Wig, and pick up a Whore' as well as make telling comments against the upper class, earned Henry Norris the permanent nickname 'Jubilee Dicky'[29] and sped his career on its way. Playbills advertised him as Jubilee Dicky; for example, the *Daily Courant* bill for *Oroonoko* at Drury Lane, published on 19 June 1703, announced that the role of Daniel would be performed 'by Mr. Norris, commonly call'd *Jubilee Dicky*', and an advertisement on 26 October 1703 for *The Constant Couple* said it would be acted for the benefit of Mr Bullock and Jubilee Dicky. The dimunitive actor, with his 'comic, squeaking Voice',[30] popularized a minor role so successfully that both his own career and later stage productions showed the effect of his acting. Although strong arguments can be made against those critics who claim Wilks alone, not Farquhar, made Wildair a success, few would argue that Norris had not made the very most of a role that is far from remarkable on the page but apparently irresistible on stage. John Corye complained in the preface to *A Cure for Jealousie* that his play failed while 'we find an Audience crowding to a JUBILEE-FARCE, and Sweating to see DICKY play his Tricks'.

If the run actually extended to fifty-three performances during the first season, people must have returned to the theatre frequently. Lady Morley attended at least twice, on 13 February and 15 June.[31] The Duchess of Marlborough apparently commanded a performance; Abel Boyer's *Achilles; or Iphigenia in Aulis*, which opened shortly after *The Constant Couple*, failed, according to the advertisement for the second edition (1714), because 'the Dutchess of Marlborough, who at that Time bore an irresistable Sway, bespoke the Comedy then in Vogue, during the Run of *Iphigenia in Aulis*'.

One suspects the same fashionable auditors continued to return to the theatre in subsequent years, after the immediate vogue was past. *The London Stage*, which records only four performances in 1699–1700 of the acknowledged fifty-three and which remains sketchy until 1703, lists a total of 365 performances in the eighteenth century, the last on 29 May 1795. In the first decade for which we have reliable records, that is, 1703–13, the number of performances per season ranged from one to five, with two performances occurring in five of those ten seasons. However, the play ran twenty times in the 1729–30 season, and in the 1730s and 1740s it reached a total of 170 performances.

A tally by decade after the first season indicates steadily increasing, then rapidly decreasing, popularity, with a surge of interest in the 1780s. The rises and falls were, of course, precipitated by fashionable new productions built in large part around the actors who successfully played Sir Harry:

Decade	Performance count
1700–10	22 performances[32]
1710–20	35 performances
1720–30	51 performances[33]
1730–40	84 performances
1740–50	86 performances[34]
1750–60	30 performances
1760–70	10 performances
1770–80	6 performances
1780–90	33 performances
1790–1800	6 performances

If there is any truth to the estimate of more than fifty performances in 1699–1700, *The Constant Couple* ran more than 400 times in London during its first century.

Although no one can deny that Wilks and Norris, as well as their colleagues Pinkethman, Bullock, and others, enhanced the first production, the play was not merely an actors' vehicle, despite the asperity of the critics, for its popularity long outlived any of the actors that opened in it.

When Susannah Verbruggen, the original Lady Lurewell, died in childbirth, Anne Oldfield inherited the role. Curll tells the story, perhaps apocryphal considering its source, that Oldfield and Jane Rogers fought over the part and Wilks solved the problem by suggesting a competition in the role.[35] The Winston manuscript elaborates on the incident:

Wilks gave Mrs R parts to Mrs Oldfield upon her success which incenced her so much she left the Theatre & applied to Rich was engaged by him but the Town thinking Mrs R injured received Mrs O in her parts with catcalls & every mark of disapprobation for three months—it was at last agreed that each should choose a part the most approved and the audience should decide who was the best. the Nobility & Gentry agreed to this—Mrs Oldfᵈ choose Lady Loverule [i.e. Lurewell] Trip to Jubilee & play'd it and playd it with the greatest applause the next night Mrs R was to have her trial but she declined it & Mrs O playd the part. thus it ended.[36]

By whatever means Oldfield acquired the role, she continued to play it throughout her career, her final performance occurring in 1730; after her death, Christiana Horton, who had substituted for her on 15 October 1720, took on Lurewell.

Wilks reigned as Sir Harry for thirty years, owning the part to the extent that no one else dared attempt it, despite the popularity of the play. However, when Thomas Odell opened his theatre in Goodman's Fields in 1729, intent on wooing audiences from the established houses, competition began. The theatre opened on 27 October with a performance of *The Recruiting Officer*; by 20 December *The Constant Couple* was scheduled, with Henry Giffard as Sir Harry and his wife as Lurewell. An account in the *Daily Journal* of 22 December describes the audience's attitude:

... the Curiosity of the better Sort was a good deal raised, to see how it would fare in the Hands of a new Company, and were as agreeably surprized to see it play'd to a fine Audience, with universal Applause; and particularly the Parts of Wildair and Lurewell.

Goodman's Fields ran the play eighteen times that season and seven the next. Wilks, who was by 1729 about sixty-four years old, and who had played the role almost 150 times in London and at least eighteen in Dublin, did not wage any battle to keep the role. He had proclaimed that his performance of Sir Harry on 18 April 1723 would be his last, and he had kept his resolve the following season. But before Giffard's challenge, he had played the role twenty additional times. He assumed the role only once in 1729–30, and on 14 November 1730 he announced that he was performing it for the last time 'unless commanded'. The command came on 1 May 1731, from 'His Royal Highness, the Duke', and again on 8 December 1731 from the Prince of Wales. Wilks acted Sir Harry on 20 November 'At the particular Desire of several Ladies of Quality'. His final performance occurred on 20 March 1732, only six months before his death. By 1731 Lacy Ryan at Lincoln's Inn Fields was also performing Sir Harry. On 1 July 1731 Thomas Chapman tried the role at Richmond, and Theophilus Cibber first played it on 29 November. But while others attempted it, Giffard and Ryan played it regularly.

On 21 November 1740 a new era opened for the forty-year-old comedy. Peg Woffington took the role of Sir Harry. She had first tried the role in Dublin in April 1740, 'and charmed the town to an uncommon degree'.[37] John Rich invited her to Covent Garden the following season, where her debut in the role of Sir Harry caused a stir. Novelty obviously precipitated interest. Breeches roles for women were common, and Woffington herself excelled in them. But as Sir Harry, she was not acting the role of a woman in disguise; she was portraying a man. Apparently she played the role straight, and the audience was enchanted not by a travesty but by a genuinely fine performance of a male role. Hitchcock said she exhibited an 'elegant portrait of the Young Man of Fashion in a stile perhaps beyond the author's warmest ideas'.[38] By tradition 'the Ease, Manner of Address, Vivacity, and Figure of a young Man of Fashion was never more happily exhibited'.[39] Thomas Davies agreed that her 'ease, elegance, and propriety of deportment' as a dissipated, good-humoured rake won her reputation.[40] But James Boaden disagreed, claiming the travesty of the woman in a man's role gave the performance its innocent charm.[41] So completely did she captivate audiences that she played the role for ten consecutive nights, then performed it another five times during the season and regularly thereafter. Despite the fact that she advertised her last appearance in the role in March 1746, Woffington continued by popular demand for almost two decades, until January 1757, during her final season on stage. Other Wildairs tried the role during her nearly twenty years in the role—Giffard and Ryan, as well as Garrick, Foote, Cibber, 'a Gentleman from Ireland', Cushing, and Woodward. But none compared with her popularity.

After Woffington's triumph, several other women assumed the role of Wildair. Dorothy Jordan emulated Woffington's vogue of 1740 by playing the role twelve times in 1788–9. At least one observer attributed Mrs Jordan's success to her physical attributes, well displayed in the role:

. . . Mrs. Jordan sports now in Sir Harry one of the best legs in the kingdom. Sir Joshua Reynolds is a judge of legs, and has, like Paris with his apple, given his decree on that said leg.[42]

The critic of the *Morning Post* found her pleasant but 'by no means critically just', lacking the necessary 'graceful freedom of deportment', but the *European Magazine* took a harder view, finding her performance satisfactory but the tradition of females taking the role an offensive an disgusting deviation from propriety.[43] Such a strong sense of decorum must have been shared by many others, but it did not slow the parade of hopeful actresses attempting Farquhar's airy young gentleman. Despite the assault on the role by a total of seventeen actors and nine actresses during the century, only two, Wilks and Woffington, have been memorialized by theatre historians. A tally of all eighteenth-century Wildairs and their number of performances in London shows that many other actors, including Garrick and Cibber, each of whom once acted the role with Woffington as Lurewell, failed to make it their own. In some *London Stage* entries no cast-list exists. In the statistics below I have attributed performances, particularly to Giffard during his tenure, despite the lack of a cast-list. Performances for which there is no strong probability that a certain actor performed Sir Harry have not been included:

Actor	Span of performances	Performance count
Robert Wilks	1699–1732	Approximately 150[++]
Henry Giffard	1729–43	68
Lacy Ryan	1731–41	32
Thomas Chapman	1731	1 (Richmond)
Theophilus Cibber	1733–47	7
Peg Woffington	1740–57	73
David Garrick	1743	3
A Gentleman	1743	1
Mary Daniel	1745	2
Samuel Foote	1745–6	5
Ward (first name unknown)	1746	1
A Gentleman from Ireland	1747	1
Mrs John Cushing	1747	3
Mrs Phillips	1748	1 (Southwark)
Henry Woodward	1749–63	9
William Smith	1759	2
William O'Brien	1762–4	7
Thomas King	1763	1
James William Dodd	1766–92	7
Ann Barry	1771–2	4
Susan Greville	1776–82	2
Charlotte Walpole	1779	1
William Thomas Lewis	1785–6	5
Dorothy Jordan	1788–95	16

Actor	Span of performances	Performance count
Charlotte Goodall	1789–94	8
Catherine Ann Achmet	1789	3

The tally suggests the stage history of the play: its perennially comfortable niche in the repertory during Wilks's tenure, the successful attempts of Giffard and Ryan to bring it into public domain in Wilks's old age, the sudden vogue and long dominance of Woffington, all four actors contributing to the strong popularity in the second quarter of the century; then the struggle for a new Sir Harry, a role which never yielded to such fine actors as Garrick or Foote;[45] the exertion for novelty which brought to the stage an unknown Irishman and nine willing actresses; finally, the success of Dorothy Jordan, who temporarily breathed life once again into a play that had held the boards almost a century. One can add footnotes: command performances, benefits, a new prologue in 1731 on the anniversary of the Coronation, an epilogue by Joe Haines spoken in 1752 by Edward Shuter astride an ass, Woffington switching from Wildair to Lurewell on a couple of occasions, Woffington adding a minuet, O'Brien playing the role in 1763 to what Hopkins described as 'The worst House I ever saw', and Jordan regularly bringing in receipts around £200 in 1788–9. The immediate success that had drawn the barrage of criticism from contemporaries, particularly those at the rival house, was prelude to a long and solid, occasionally eruptive, success throughout the century.

The success in London was emulated on stages across the British Isles. Most particularly Dublin's Smock Alley theatre kept it among the repertory pieces for many years. Supposedly it played twenty-three times in Dublin during the first London season. Although its run cannot be traced with the clarity of the London performances, Smock Alley continued to host the play throughout the years, and brought to its audiences some remarkable Wildairs. Perhaps the most remarkable of all was George Farquhar, who returned to the theatre of his acting career for a benefit some time after 20 October 1704, when his regiment began arriving in Ireland, and certainly by 23 March 1705. Robert John Jordan estimates that the benefit performance occurred between 15 November and 25 March, the only time in 1704 in which the benefit could have been attended by the Duke of Ormonde, as Farquhar's biographer reports.[46] The impecunious Farquhar, failing to raise a subscription for his works as he had hoped, got permission from his Lord Lieutenant, Ormonde, to perform in a benefit. He was well paid for his efforts, raising £100 in a theatre in which £50 was considered good. However, his theatrical reputation was ill served; Chetwood and Wilkes report that 'his friends blushed to see him act it'.[47]

When Robert Wilks returned to Smock Alley in the summer of 1711, he played Sir Harry eighteen times in succession, excluding Sundays.[48] Woffington, who had first played the role at Smock Alley before coming to London, returned for the season of 1751–2, at a stipend of £400. Reportedly she played in four old plays, including *The Constant Couple*, playing each for about ten nights, and the theatre profited by more than £4,000, receiving an unprecedented £100 and more each night.[49] Thomas Sheridan, actor-manager of Smock Alley, apparently fared no better than Farquhar, or for that matter Garrick, when he tried the role on 21 November 1745 by command of the Earl of Chesterfield, then Lord Lieutenant; Garrick, who arrived in Dublin a few days later, wrote to Somerset Draper that Sheridan had 'hurt himself as an actor among his friends' by the performance,[50] which had drawn 'a most numerous and polite Audience', according to the *Dublin Journal*, despite the advanced prices.

The play was often acted during Sheridan's tenure at Smock Alley; Sheldon cites twenty-two performances in 1745–53; Wildair was played once by Garrick, twice by Bardin, three times by Woodward, once by Mrs Bland, and thirteen times by Woffington.[51]

The provincial towns were also exposed to *The Constant Couple* with some frequency. Sybil Rosenfeld lists fifteen performances in Norwich in 1710–58; Charles Macklin played Wildair in the summer of 1747. Performances are also recorded at York, Bath (eight nights between 1748 and 1756), Rochester, Canterbury (including a benefit for Macklin as Wildair and his wife as Lurewell in the 1736 season), Bristol (the Jacob's Well Theatre cleared a mere £4. 17s. 6d. on one performance),[52] and Leeds, where Mrs Jordan shocked the local ladies at her benefit in the summer of 1789.[53] The Irish towns also saw the old favourite; by mid century and thereafter performances are recorded at Belfast, Tralee, Kilkenny, Newry, Cork, Londonderry, Waterford, and Limerick; Thomas Sheridan played Sir Harry for his benefit in Cork in 1733, and Catherine Ann Achmet used the role for hers in Belfast in 1786.

The play, of course, did not die after the turn of the century, although its heyday was past. Other famous actors, including Robert William Elliston, attempted Sir Harry. But it was by then a museum piece, sometimes still featuring a woman as the male lead, sometimes a man. The play's astonishing longevity disproved Farquhar's prediction, in the preface of the first edition, that when the stage lost Wilks, Sir Harry would 'go to the Jubilee'; with youthful vitality Sir Harry stayed in London, with visits to the provinces, for more than a century.

REPUTATION AND INFLUENCE

The immediate critical reaction to *The Constant Couple* was contempt exacerbated by envy. Farquhar had felt the sting of early criticism by the time he wrote the preface to the printed edition, for he spoke in the final paragraph of two complaints against the play, that the sub-title *A Trip to the Jubilee* was a misnomer and that he had not adhered to the Rules, particularly classical ideals of decorum. However, he was more than ready to acknowledge 'the Beauties of this Play, especially those of the third Night'—financial success buoyed him. It was in fact the astounding commercial triumph of the play that set the critical hounds after him, failed playwrights and struggling actors of Lincoln's Inn Fields leading the way. His critics were relentlessly vociferous, condemning the play as farce and deploring its irregularities. His defenders cheerfully accepted the fact that the play was an actors' vehicle and argued one incontrovertible asset: audiences flocked to it. Susanna Centlivre, for example, allegedly Farquhar's mistress as well as theatrical colleague, conceded that the play had irregularities but concluded that box-office success was more desirable: '. . . I believe Mr. *Rich* will own, he got more by the *Trip to the Jubilee*, with all its Irregularities, than by the most uniform Piece the Stage cou'd boast of e'er since.' As long as audiences prefer wit and humour to regularities, 'why shou'd a Man torture, and wrack his Brain for what will be no Advantage to him?'[54] Abel Boyer called the *Trip to the Jubilee* 'a very taking, undigested medly of *Comedy* and *Farce*', but he added that Farquhar should not ridicule Aristotle and Horace since he owed his success to their rules, that is, to strict imitation of unchanging nature. Because Wildair, Angelica, Standard, and Smuggler are natural and well pursued, they 'justly met *with Applause*', but Lurewell and Clincher Senior have justly been condemned by good judges because they are unnatural.[55]

Albeit the mixed compliment was at best grudging, it was far more generous than most of Farquhar's competitors could manage. The prologues and epilogues to plays performed at Lincoln's Inn Fields not only that season but for several years, as well as prefaces written for publication, excoriated Farquhar and his foolish farce.[56] The attack that seems to have wounded Farquhar the most was John Oldmixon's prologue to Charles Gildon's adaptation of *Measure for Measure*. Farquhar had written the epilogue to Oldmixon's opera *The Grove* in January or February, a fact that did not deter Oldmixon from a savage attack in March. He condemned the audience for the taste that allowed success to Farquhar's play while art was praised but not attended at Lincoln's Inn Fields:

> In vain you Prais'd our Action, and our Wit;
> The best Applause is in a Crowded Pit.
> In vain you said, you did their *Farce* despise;
> Wit won the *Bays*, but *Farce* the Golden Prize.

Having admonished future bards to ignore Thought, Sense, and Plot in favour of Dance, Musick, and Scenes, Oldmixon specifically lampooned Farquhar by echoing *MacFlecknoe*:

> Good Sense was well receiv'd from *Honest Ben*;
> While none wou'd suffer *Flecknoes* Irish *Pen*.
> Yet, in his *Son*, Sleeping Monarch Reigns,
> And dreadful War, with Wit and Sense, Maintains.
> Study the *Smithfield-Bards* and him, with care;
> Like those Write non-sense, and, like these, you'll fare.

Farquhar was stung. He wrote to Susanna Carroll, later Mrs
Centlivre, 'You have heard, I suppose, Madam, how scurrilously I have been abus'd by Mr. — I am now busie about the
vindication of my Honour, and endeavouring to answer him
in his own Kind.'[57] He vindicated his honour through his
'New Prologue', first performed on 13 July 1700 and
published on 20 August in the third edition of the play.[58] But
Oldmixon was echoed for several years by other waspish
critics affiliated with Lincoln's Inn Fields. In the prologue to
George Granville's adaptation of *The Jew of Venice*, Dryden
complains about the low taste of audiences:

> Their sickly Judgments, what is just, refuse,
> And French Grimace, Buffoons, and Mimicks choose;
> Our Scenes desert, some wretched Farce to see;
> They know not Nature for they tast not Thee. [i.e. Shakespeare.]

The prologue to Gildon's *Love's Victim* again deplores Farquhar's
success:

> The forward pushing Spark in Plenty lives,
> By Farce he fattens, and by Nonsense Thrives
> While those whom Faction, nor Cabal support
> May starve by Sense, and thank their judgment for't.

As late as 1703 Charles Boyle, Earl of Orrery, was still
complaining about Farquhar's popularity, in the prologue to
As You Find It at Lincoln's Inn Fields:

> When to our Neighbours Joy th' exactest Play
> Must to a long and well writ Bill give Way.
> Or to th' Immortal *Trip* must yield the Day.

Mary Pix echoed his distaste the same year in the prologue to
Different Widows:

> Come, prithee let's be gon to *Drury-Lane*
> Thither in Crouds ye flock'd to see, Sir *Harry*, ⎫
> Or any Fop dress'd *All-A-Mode de Paris*;   ⎬
> So 'twas but *Droll*, it never could Miscarry.   ⎭

Nor did his enemies limit themselves to theatrical attacks;
satiric poetry also found a ready target in the popular appeal
of Farquhar. Daniel Kenrick, in his anonymously published
satire, *A New Session of the Poets*, typified Farquhar's tormentors;

he attacked him for vanity, for plagiarizing from Etherege, and for the sin of being born in Ireland:

> Flush'd with Success *Faqu—r* appear'd, and thought
> *Apollo* would, what all the Town, applaud.
> Then gave the Gaudy God that *Jubilee*,
> Which only in the Title Page we see.
> *Apollo* told him with a bended Brow,
> He'd borrow'd, from his Saint, Sir *George*, his Beau; }
> That *Dorimant* was Wildair long ago.
> That it would much disgrace the Throne of Wit,
> If on't an Irish Deputy should sit;
> And wonder'd why he'd longer here remain,
> Who in his Native Boggs might justly reign.

Four years later the author of *The Tryal of Skill: or, A New Session of the Poets* blasted Farquhar again for the same flaws and encouraged him to cling to his military employment and forget writing:

> Is it so then? said *Farquhar*, My Matters are safe,
>   By St. *Patrick* my Business is done,
> For it's known I have made Pit and Gallery laugh
>   Without any ones help but my own.
>
> My Jubilee *Dicky*, and Airy Sir *Harry*,
>   Will Vindicate what I have said,
> And none but myself has a Title to carry
>   The Laurels away on my Head.
>
> By your leave, Brother *Teague*, reply'd *Mac Fleckno*'s Ghost,
>   Our Country Men are better known,
> The Beauties are borrow'd of which you thus boast,
>   But the Faults, I dare swear, are your own.
>
> Tho' the Town allows, what you wou'd have 'em all take
>   For granted, with no one you joyn,
> Since none but a Man of your Judgment could make
>   Such Language to such a Design.
>
> And I can't but applaud the Resolve you have ta'en,
>   In the present employ which you chuse,
> For it's nobler in Red to make a Campaign,
>   Than to Butcher an innocent Muse.

The pervasiveness of barbed comments and vicious attacks on Farquhar and the longevity of the animosity towards him can be explained only in terms of the overwhelming theatrical success of his play. Of all the crimes of which he was accused—vanity, plagiarism and/or lack of creativity, Irish birth, and others—the unforgivable crime was success. If indeed the play was a negligible farce, why did so many commentators lambaste it for four or more years? The answer is, of course, that they did so because they were financially damaged by the success of Farquhar's play and the boost it gave the struggling company of neophytes at Drury Lane. *Love and a Bottle* was a far weaker play, but it received no animosity whatsoever because it was not catastrophically successful.

The tenor of the early, envious remarks, however, became the traditional critical stance in regard to the play. Farquhar's disregard for the Rules became an increasingly important theme. The play itself was treated at best as an attractive actors' vehicle, at worst as 'the lucky Result of an immature Undertaking'.[59]

Many references in periodical literature and miscellanies indicate that the play was so familiar that it could be alluded to with no explanation. Steele refers to Wilks's 'winning Emptiness of a young Man of Good-nature and Wealth' in the part of Sir Harry, and Addison, in a satirical Bill of Mortality, includes Dick Tastewell, 'slain by a Blush from the Queen's Box in the Third Act of the *Trip to the Jubilee*'.[60] Giles Jacob sees the play in terms of Wilks too, concluding that Wildair 'is the Character of the Author in his politest Capacity; but at best, it must be allow'd, that in the Representation, Mr. *Wilks*, by his sprightly Behaviour, vastly excells the Original'.[61] And Cibber says that judging merit by full houses, one would 'be reduc'd to allow, that the *Beggars Opera* was the best-written Play, and Sir *Harry Wildair* (as *Wilks* play'd it) was the best acted Part, that ever our *English* Theatre had to boast of. That Critick indeed, must be rigid, to a Folly, that would deny either of them, their due Praise, when they severally drew such Numbers after them; all their Hearers could not be mistaken. . . .'[62] Cibber's reluctant praise comes from a man who can appreciate the 'Beauties . . . of the third Night' and who, after all, managed the Drury Lane company and profited by the *Trip*. But neither he nor anyone else was willing to concede that the play had merit as a literary work, a fact that even Farquhar seems not to have realized. It was a successful piece of stagecraft, nothing more. The fact that it remained a successful piece of stagecraft for a century never changed that general evaluation of it. The one aspect that received critical attention was the character of Sir Harry, often compared to Dorimant, usually satirically but sometimes, for example by Thomas Davies, deemed on a par with his distinguished elder for gaiety and spirit.[63]

If fellow playwrights and critics would not praise Sir Harry, they were quick to imitate him. Wildair obviously owed a lot to his forebears, those 'extravagant rakes' that preceded him on the Restoration stage.[64] But Sir Harry was an original character, created from old materials but shaped by a new social and theatrical situation. 'An airy Gentleman, affecting humourous Gaiety and Freedom in his Behaviour', as he is described in the Dramatis Personae, he is also a war hero, a foppish follower of fashion, a skirt-chaser, and a good-humoured man of common sense and a slightly iconoclastic wit. The laughter is often at his expense, and yet he seems to savour every experience.[65] Wilks took the role and illuminated it with 'the irresistible force of proper action', thus assuring instant popularity for the play. Together the two friends created an inevitably influential stage character, for if Sir Harry appealed to audiences, he would be reborn many times. Farquhar himself wrote a sequel, *Sir Harry Wildair*, to exploit the popularity of the character. Not surprisingly, other playwrights courted fame by creating similar characters that would be ideal for Wilks to play. The strong influence of Wildair–Wilks on other comic heroes becomes obvious if one reads the plays of the early eighteenth century, the bad with the good. Short of that comprehensive undertaking, a few examples of conspicuous echoes will at least illustrate the effects; playwrights did not borrow lines, but they borrowed Wildair's characteristics, his ambience, even syllables of his name.

As Restoration rakes and the ladies they pursued, both 'extravagant' and 'judicious', were often called 'mad' or 'wild', the new heroes of the eighteenth century were sometimes labelled 'airy', meaning sprightly, vivacious, and buoyant. The term is not frequently used in the late seventeenth century,[66] but Wildair is described as 'airy' in the Dramatis Personae, and he earned that adjective from critics.[67] Centlivre must have been struck by the characteristic of airiness: Wilks played Sir James Courtly, 'an airy Gentleman given to Gaming' in *The Basset-Table* (1705); he would undoubtedly have played Belair, 'an Airy Spark', had *Love at a Venture* (1706) run in London instead of Bath; and he took the role of Sir George Airy in *The Busy Body* (1709).

References to sprightliness, briskness, good nature, and vivacity, all attributed to Sir Harry by fellow characters and Wilks by contemporary critics, accompany those to the airiness of new comic heroes. Thomas Baker's Bloom in the suppressed play, *An Act of Oxford* (1704), is, like Wildair, a gentleman-commoner of a good estate who is greeted by Captain Smart as 'My brisk young Commoner'. His self-mockery is reminiscent of Wildair: 'my Head's full o'Wind, Plays, Equipage, and fine Cloths'.[68] Mills rather than Wilks played Sir Harry Sprightly in Baker's *The Fine Lady's Airs* (1708) a few years later, but the two Sir Harrys certainly seem closely related when Sprightly says, 'The Ladies call me Mad Sir Harry, a Careless, Affable, Obliging Fellow'.[69] Wilks played Frederick, 'a young Gentleman, a great Lover of Court Modes, and the new Method of living, somewhat extravagant, but witty, good natur'd, and a Man of Honour'—the description fits Sir Harry perfectly—in Thomas D'Urfey's *The Old Mode and the New* (1703), and he acted Wilding, 'a brisk gay Gentleman of the Town', in Richard Wilkinson's *Vice Reclaim'd* (1703). The list could be continued at length; the point is that characters with new traits, characteristic of Wildair, described in terms associated with him, rapidly became standard comic heroes. And they differ from extravagant rakes as Harry does—through Farquhar's creation and Wilk's interpretation of him.

The new fine gentlemen also tend to be either noble officers back from the wars (doubtless an influence of contemporary events, not just of Sir Harry) or young men home from their travels. For example, Wilks played Freeman, 'a Noble Captain just back from Flanders' in William Burnaby's *The Reform'd Wife* (1700) and two of Steele's officers, Lieutenant Campley in *The Funeral* (1701) and Captain Clerimont in *The Tender Husband* (1705). Centlivre's Belair in *Love at a Venture* is 'a Gentleman just come from Travel'. The list of returnees from the wars or travels is extensive. Some earlier extravagant rakes were returning heroes; now their numbers multiply—Sir Harry may well have been their recruiting officer.

The characters do not merely imitate, they evolve from Sir Harry—rakishness is increasingly diminished to talk; one gets a stronger sense of appetite than experience. The love of French fashions that borders on foppery disappears as the fashions change. Like Sir Harry, the characters tend frequently to be interested in devout virgins rather than spirited adventuresses who happen to be chaste; even the 'gay couples' become considerably less witty—action tends to supplant dialogue as evidence of their *esprit*. Increasingly, they seem, like Wildair, to be decent at the core, but the decency does not become oppressive as it does with exemplary characters like Steele's Bevil Junior in *The Conscious Lovers*. They have fun; they like women; they are fallible; they get in scrapes. Sir Harry's eccentricities are toned down, but his youthful *joie de vivre* remains strong.

The plays mentioned will perhaps indicate the pervasiveness of Sir Harry's influence. The flops and failures of the early eighteenth century are full of Wildairs unfamiliar to any but the most fanatical readers of eighteenth-century plays. Even Farquhar's own heroes apart from Roebuck owe something to Sir Harry, and all were played by Wilks with the exception of Basil in his one afterpiece, *The Stage-Coach*. In the long run, the effect on characters in the period's most popular plays had a more lasting impact on English theatre through successive generations of playwrights who reached back into their own theatrical experiences when creating characters. Sir Harry's energy, his airiness, myopic intelligence, *joie de vivre*, good sense, good nature, and good humour, through his theatrical omnipresence and in ways that cannot be measured, filtered not only into the Plumes and Archers, Wildings and Airys, but, after decades of refinements and natural evolution through intervening characterizations, into the Charles Surfaces and Captains Absolute of later eighteenth-century drama.

Specific debts to *The Constant Couple* are incapable of proof because the play was not directly imitated; rather, it infiltrated the sensibilities of writers in the later eighteenth century. Familiarity with the play, however, is obvious. Sheridan, for example, was familiar with specific performances, as he demonstrates in *The Critic* when Puff explains the 'puff direct'; his commentary on the new play by 'Mr. Smatter, or Mr. Dapper—or any particular friend of mine' addresses the performance: 'Mr. Dodd was astonishingly great in the character of Sir Harry! That universal and judicious actor Mr. Palmer, perhaps never appeared to more advantage than in the Colonel. . . .'[70] If Sheridan admits to no borrowing himself, he is certainly aware that his contemporaries dipped frequently into Farquhar's plays.

But if the play influenced English authors as part of the collective theatrical experience, it affected German authors specifically through imitation. Critics generally assume that it was a source for Lessing's *Minna von Barnhelm*.[71] The general similarity between Colonel Standard and Telheim has often been noted, but J. G. Robertson believed the influence of Farquhar on the play, while undeniable, has been overestimated.[72] Like Standard, Telheim is an honourable and generous disbanded officer, who refuses to take advantage of his beloved after losing his commission. A ring is once again the instrument of revelation, but Robertson believes that *The Merchant of Venice* may well have influenced the plotting.

Stonehill sees influence on many German plays, not only *Minna von Barnhelm*, but also Gottlieb Stephanie's *Abgedankte Offiziere* and *Die Werber* (in which he also detects borrowings from *The Recruiting Officer*), Brandes's *Graf von Olsbach*, Moller's *Graf Waltron*, 'and a whole school of German Drama'.[73] The transmutation of Farquhar's characters and plot had come full circle when, on 24 July 1786, *The Disbanded*

Officer, James Johnstone's adaptation of *Minna von Barnhelm*, opened a successful run at the Haymarket.

The Constant Couple has never received serious critical attention. Early critics considered it an insult to dramatic art; later critics glanced at it before more seriously addressing *The Recruiting Officer* or *The Beaux Stratagem*; theatre historians remember it as a vehicle for Woffington and Jordan. Yet the pervasiveness of this play in the theatre created subtle subsurface influences on playwrights, actors, and managers who chose to obey the 'laws' prescribed by the taste of drama patrons.

THE TEXT

Three quarto editions were published during the first season. The first was published on 11 December 1699,[74] bearing the imprint of Ralph Smith and Bennet Banbury. The text is unusually clean for a first edition of the period, showing few of the obvious signs of a rushed printing job. Conceivably the immediate success and steady run delayed publication for a short period, allowing more time for printing than was usual for plays; conceivably the accuracy of the printer alone accounts for the cleanness of the first text.

The second edition, bearing the same imprint, appeared three weeks later, on 1 February 1700.[75] The title-page states that the printing was the second edition 'with a New Scene added to the part of *Wildair*'. Aside from the addition of the scene and the deletion of the original passage, Farquhar made no corrections. Obvious errors, even those a compositor might be expected to emend, are not corrected. Only the most obvious mistakes, the misspelling 'gaz'd' for 'graz'd', for example, are corrected by the compositor, and new mistakes are introduced, as in 'I sent his Letter backs by you' instead of 'Letters back'.

'The *Third Edition*; With a New *SCENE* | Added to the PART of *Wildair*; and a | New *PROLOGUE*' spoken in answer to Oldmixon's at Lincoln's Inn Fields on 13 July, was published 20 August 1700.[76] Two variant imprints were published, one reading 'Printed for *Ralph Smith* at the Bible under the *Piazza* of the *Royal | Exchange* in *Cornhill*, and Sold by *Bennet Banbury* at the *Blue Anchor |* in the *New Exchange* in the *Strand.* 1701.' (copy in the British Library) and the other reading 'Printed for *Ralph Smith* at the *Bible* under the *Piazza* of the | *Royal Exchange* in *Cornhill.* 1701.' and followed by advertisements for *Geography Rectify'd* and *An Abridgment of Sir Walter Raleigh's History of the World* (copies in the Bodleian, Folger, and Clark Libraries). The date 1701 on both title-pages is inexplicable since the publication clearly occurred in the summer of 1700. Although editions issued late in a year were often postdated to the next year, August is uncommonly early for such postdating. Aside from writing the new prologue, Farquhar had no hand in revising the third edition. At the time of its publication, he was in the Netherlands, for one of the letters in *Love and Business*, dated 10 August 1700, states that he landed at the Brill on that day (see vol. ii, p. 316), and other letters from the same voyage were sent in October. Perhaps he was paid for the new prologue; at any rate, he would have wanted it published. But like most authors of his period, he had no interest, financial or literary, in the later editions of his works.

The first quarto was published in eight gatherings, A–H⁴. The second was slightly reduced to the collational formula A–G⁴H². The third edition crowded type in order to print the new prologue within the bounds of the same number of leaves. The prologue was added in the prelims on A4, the epilogue moved to the end. The text was set from the second edition, which it follows page by page to p. 18, and then the conservation of space begins.

The fourth edition, misspelt 'Foutrh' on the title-page, published with Smith's imprint and the date 1704, was a hasty, careless reprint of the third. Many errors in spelling and omissions of words indicate the carelessness of the page-by-page reprint (exceptions of a word or syllable in pagination occur on pp. 17–18 and pp. 41–2). I have found no specific advertisements for the edition, although the playbills in the *Daily Courant* for 12 October and 29 December 1704 mention that the play is sold by Richard Wellington, a formulaic statement appearing regularly in the advertisements for performances at the time.

The fifth edition, not labelled as such, appeared in the *Comedies* issued by Lintott in 1708. The text includes the new scene but omits the new prologue; the second edition served as copy-text. The second and third octavo editions of the *Comedies* in 1711 and 1714 were also printed for Lintott.

Other editions followed frequently, a small octavo by Thomas Johnson in 1710, collected in *A Collection of the Best English Plays*; an incorrectly designated 'Fourth Edition' printed for Ralph Smith in 1716, another edition for Smith in 1721, an edition printed for John Clark in 1728, the 'Fifth Edition' in 1732, a 'Sixth' in 1735, and a 'Seventh' in 1738, all printed for Clarke and sold by William Feales, according to the imprint. A Dublin edition appeared in 1725, printed by S. Powell and George Risk, and an edition 'Printed for the Booksellers, in Town and Country' appeared in London in 1739. The work thereafter was regularly printed, of course, in editions of Farquhar's plays or works, as well as in separate editions, sometimes 'Marked with the Variations of the Manager's Book'.

The first edition serves as copy-text for the present edition. Into it I have introduced the revised scene from the second edition and the new prologue from the third. Other emendations from later editions have been based purely on the appropriateness of the wording, for Farquhar clearly had no hand in revising beyond the two editions. Because the first edition was unusually free of errors, very few emendations were necessary.

I have collated the following copies of *The Constant Couple*: first edition, Bodleian (two copies), Folger, Huntington, British Library; second edition, Folger, Huntington, University of Pennsylvania; third edition, Bodleian, Folger, British Library, Clark; fourth edition, Bodleian, Folger; *Comedies*, first edition, Clark; second edition, Library of Congress; third edition, Folger.

NOTES

1. *Statutes of the Realm*, vii. 522–4.
2. Richard Morton and William M. Petersen, 'The Jubilee of 1700 and Farquhar's "The Constant Couple" ', *N&Q*, 200 (1955), 521–5.

3. *Biographia Dramatica*, ii. 123–4.
4. Hunt, pp. lxiv–lxv.
5. Archer, p. 87 n. 1; Stonehill, i. 79; Kavanagh, p. 209; Rothstein, p. 18; James, pp. 102–5.
6. Genest, ii. 165; Archer, p. 32; Stonehill, i. 79; Kavanagh, p. 208; Smith, *Gay Couple*, p. 183; James, pp. 105–9; Ernest Bernbaum, *The Drama of Sensibility* (Boston, 1915; rept. 1958), p. 85 n. 3.
7. James, pp. 109–11.
8. Connely, p. 93.
9. Allardyce Nicoll, *A History of English Drama, 1660–1800* (Cambridge, 1952–9), vol. i, 1660–1700, p. 177.
10. Archer, p. 32; Stonehill, i, p. xx. There is some indication that Farquhar and Manley may have been acquaintances, at least later. Adario in the *New Atlantis*, who is misused by a lady through the promise of a military commission, may be a veiled reference to Farquhar. See Jordan, p. 252.
11. [Daniel Kenrick], *A New Session of the Poets, Occasion'd by the Death of Mr. Dryden* (London, 1700).
12. Connely, pp. 92–3.
13. [Giles Jacob], *The Poetical Register* (London, 1719), p. 98.
14. [Edmund Curll], *Memoirs of Wilks*, p. 24.
15. *A New Session of the Poets*, p. 5. The sentiment is echoed in *The Tryal of Skill: or A New Session of the Poets* (London, 1704), reprinted in *Poems on Affairs of State*, ed. Frank H. Ellis, p. 691:

> The Beauties are borrow'd of which you thus boast,
> But the Faults, I dare swear, are your own.

16. The revision was published in the second edition two or three months after the *première*. See G. W. Whiting, 'The Date of the Second Edition of *The Constant Couple*', *Modern Language Notes*, 49 (1932), 147–8.
17. For evidence, see Shirley Strum Kenny, 'The Publication of Plays', in Robert D. Hume (ed.), *The London Theatre World, 1600–1800* (Carbondale, Ill., 1980), pp. 315–20.
18. Shirley Strum Kenny, 'George Farquhar and "The Bus'ness of a Prologue"', *Theatre Survey*, 19 (1978), 152–3.
19. *Letters of Wit, Politicks, and Morality*, comp. Abel Boyer (London, 1701), p. 367, Letter XLII, 'Damon to Astrea', in 'Original Letters of Love and Gallantry'. Oldmixon's name was omitted when the letter was published.
20. No performances by Wilks are listed in *The London Stage* during the 1698–9 season, although the scantiness of evidence for those years allows strong possibilities for omissions. However, had he been in the company, it seems likely that he would have performed in *Love and a Bottle*. The *Biographical Dictionary* dates his arrival as 1699. I am indebted to Edward A. Langhans for pre-publication access to the Wilks biography.
21. Kenny, 'Theatrical Warfare, 1695–1710', pp. 130–6.
22. Price, pp. 156–7.
23. Cyrus Lawrence Day and Eleanore Boswell Murrie, *English Song-Books in 1651–1702 A Bibliography With a First-Line Index Of Songs* (Oxford, 1940), p. 354, no. 3351.
24. Wilkes, I. vi; *Biographia Dramatica*, i. 227.
25. Colley Cibber, *An Apology for the Life of Colley Cibber*, ed. B. R. S. Fone (Ann Arbor, Mich., 1968), pp. 131–2. Scholars disagree on whether Wilks actually returned to London during the season of 1698–9 or 1699–1700. The *London Stage* lists Wilks in the Drury Lane company in 1698–9 (i. 501).

26. Clark, pp. 113–14.
27. [Curll], p. 20.
28. See, for example, *The Female Tatler*, no. 41, 7–10 October 1709; 'Verses on Mrs. Oldfield's Death, Mr. Booth's Sickness; and the Declension of the Stage' in William Egerton, *Faithful Memoirs of . . . Mrs. Anne Oldfield* (London, 1731), Appendix V, p. 16; *To Diabebouloumenon* [sic]: *or, the Proceedings at the Theatre-Royal in Drury Lane* (London, 1723), *passim*.
29. *Life of Wilks*, p. 24; Benjamin Victor, *The History of the Theatres of London and Dublin, From the Year 1730 to the Present Time* (2 vols., London, 1761), ii. 65.
30. Victor, ii. 65–6.
31. Leslie Hotson, *Commonwealth and Restoration Drama* (Cambridge, Mass., 1928), p. 379.
32. Records for 1700–3 are far from complete.
33. Twenty performances occurred in 1729–30.
34. One more performance may have occurred on 26 Apr. 1749; the evidence is unclear.
35. [Curll], pp. 27–8.
36. Folger MSS Y. D. 23 (170?)
37. Hitchcock, i. 108.
38. Hitchcock, i. 108.
39. Victor, *History of the Theatres*, iii. 3.
40. Thomas Davies, *Memoirs of the Life of David Garrick, Esq.* (London, 1780), p. 306.
41. James Boaden, *The Life of Mrs. Jordan* (2 vols., London, 1831), i. 127.
42. Tate Wilkinson, *Memoirs of His Own Life* (4 vols., York, 1790), iv. 33.
43. *European Magazine*, May 1788, p. 372.
44. Ninety-nine performances are listed in the *London Stage*; Wilks acted the role at least fifty times that are not recorded.
45. For the failure of Garrick in the role, see Genest, iii. 36; Wilkinson, i. 112.
46. Jordan, p. 258.
47. Wilkes, I, pp. ix–x; Thomas Wilkes, *A General View of the Stage* (London and Dublin, 1759), p. 312; Chetwood, p. 154; Hitchcock, i. 32. The most accurate account is the Wilkes biography; Chetwood and Wilkes, *General View*, both incorrectly cite 1707 as the date.
48. *Biographical Dictionary*, forthcoming. Wilkes, *General View* says he played the role nineteen nights (p. 311).
49. Victor, *History of the Theatres*, i. 151; Hitchcock, i. 219–20; Esther K. Sheldon, *Thomas Sheridan of Smock-Alley* (Princeton, NJ, 1967),'p. 187.
50. Letter 40, dated 1 Dec. 1745, in *The Letters of David Garrick*, ed. David M. Little and George M. Kahrl (Cambridge, Mass., 1963), i. 69.
51. Sheldon, p. 409.
52. Sybil Rosenfeld, *Strolling Players and Drama in the Provinces, 1660–1765* (Cambridge, 1939), *passim*.
53. Philip W. Sergeant, *Mrs. Jordan: Child of Nature* (London, 1913), pp. 133–4.
54. Susanna Centlivre, Preface, *Love's Contrivance* (London, 1703).
55. [Abel Boyer], *The English Theophrastus: or, the Manners of the Age* (London, 1702), p. 13.
56. See, for example, the preface and epilogue to John Corye's *A Cure for Jealousie*, Dec. 1699; the prologue to Nicholas Rowe's *The Ambitious Stepmother*, Dec. 1700; the prologue to Boyle's *As You Find It*, 28 Apr. 1703; and the prologue to Mary Pix's *The Different Widows*, Nov. 1703.
57. *Letters of Wit, Politicks, and Morality*, vol. ii, p. 444.
58. For details, see Kenny, 'George Farquhar and the "Business of a Prologue" ', pp. 143–5.

59. William Burnaby, Letter 5 in *Letters of Wit, Politicks, and Morality*, published in *The Dramatic Works of William Burnaby*, ed. F. E. Budd (London, 1931), p. 456.
60. *Spectator*, no. 370, 5 May 1712; no. 377, 13 May 1712.
61. Jacob, p. 98.
62. Colley Cibber, *Apology*, p. 171.
63. Thomas Davies, *Dramatic Miscellanies* (London, 1784), p. 170.
64. See Robert John Jordan, 'The Extravagant Rake in Restoration Comedy', in Harold Love (ed.), *Restoration Literature: Critical Approaches* (London, 1972), pp. 69–90; Robert D. Hume, 'The Myth of the Rake in "Restoration" Comedy', *Studies in the Literary Imagination*, 10 (1977), 25–55.
65. Shirley Strum Kenny, 'Farquhar, Wilks, and Wildair; or, the "Metamorphosis of the Fine Gentleman" ', *Philological Quarterly*, 57 (1978), 46–65.
66. It occurs occasionally, for example, in James Carlile's *The Fortune Hunters* (London, 1689) and John Crowne's *The Country Wit* (London, 1675). For a discussion of adjectives, see Jordan, 'The Extravagant Rake', p. 75.
67. See, for example, the reference to 'Airy Sir Harry' in *The Tryal of Skill* in Ellis, p. 690.
68. Kenny, 'Farquhar, Wilks, and Wildair', p. 59.
69. Ibid.
70. *The Dramatic Works of Richard Brinsley Sheridan*, ed. Cecil Price (2 vols., Oxford, 1973), ii. 514–5. Palmer, in fact, played Colonel Standard only once, 3 May 1776.
71. See, for example, K. Elze, *Vermischte Blätter* (Köthen, 1865), pp. 93 ff.; E. Schmidt, *Lessing*, vol. i (Berlin, 1884), p. 481; P. Albrecht, *Lessings Plagiate* (6 vols., Hamburg, 1891–94), *passim*; D. Schmid, *George Farquhar* (Vienna, 1904), pp. 88 ff.
72. J. G. Robertson, 'Lessing and Farquhar,' *Modern Language Review*, 2 (1906–7), 57.
73. Stonehill, i. p. xix.
74. The *Post-Man* announced publication in the issue of 7–9 Dec. 1699 for Monday, i.e. 11 Dec. The advertisement was repeated 12–14 Dec. A scrap in James Winston's collection of miscellaneous theatrical papers c. 1660–1845 (Folger MSS Y.d. 23 [185] records in an eighteenth-century hand 'Mond. Dec. 11. 99 Farquhar's Constant Couple, publ. D.L.')
75. The *Post-Man*, 30 Jan.–1 Feb. 1700. See Whiting, pp. 147–8.
76. Advertisement in the *Post-Man*, 17–20 Aug. 1700, repeated 26–8 August.

Dodd del.   Geldar sculp.

Mrs. Barry as Sir Harry Wildair. Frontispiece, *The Constant Couple*, printed for Lowndes, Caslon, Nicoll, Bladon, and Corbett, 1777. Act II, Scene ii.

THE
CONSTANT COUPLE;
OR A
TRIP TO THE JUBILEE.
A
COMEDY

Sive favore tuli, sive hanc ego carmine famam
Jure tibi grates, candide lector, ago.
Ovid. *Tristia.* lib. 4 Eleg. 10

ABBREVIATIONS USED IN THE NOTES

Q1 First edition. London: Ralph Smith and Bennet Banbury, 1700.
Q2 Second edition. London: Ralph Smith and Bennet Banbury, 1700.
Q3 Third edition. London: Ralph Smith and Bennet Banbury, 1700.
Q4 Fourth edition. London: Ralph Smith, 1704.
O1 *Comedies*. First edition. London: Knapton, Smith, Strahan, and Lintott [1708].
1710 London: [T. Johnson], 1710.
1728 *Works*. Sixth edition. London: J. and J. Knapton, Lintott, Strahan, and Clark, 1728.

To the Honourable
Sir *ROGER MOSTYN* Baronet,
Of *Mostyn-Hall* in *Flintshire.*

SIR,

'Tis no small Reflection on Pieces of this nature, that Panegyrick is so much improv'd, and that Dedication is grown more an Art than Poetry; that Authors, to make their Patrons more than Men, make themselves less; and that Persons of Honour are forc'd to decline patronizing Wit, because their Modesty cannot bear the gross Strokes of Adulation.

But give me leave to say, Sir, that I am too young an Author to have learnt the Art of Flattery; and, I hope, the same Modesty which recommended this Play to the World, will also 10 reconcile my Addresses to You, of whom I can say nothing but what your Merits may warrant, and all that have the honour of your Acquaintance will be proud to vindicate.

The greatest Panegyrick upon you, Sir, is the unprejudiced and bare Truth of Your Character, the Fire of Youth, with the Sedateness of a Senatour, and the Modern Gaity of a fine *English* Gentleman, with the noble Solidity of the Antient *Britton.*

This is the Character, Sir, which all men, but your self, are proud to publish of You, and which more celebrated Pens 20 than mine should transmit to Posterity.

The Play has had some noble Appearances to honour its Representation; and to compleat the Success, I have presum'd to prefix so Noble a Name to usher it into the World. A stately Frontispiece is the Beauty of a Building. But here I must transverse *Ovid*:

> *Materia superabit Opus.*

I am,
Honourable Sir,
  Your most Devoted, and   30
     Humble Servant,
         Geo. Farquhar.

PREFACE to the READER.

An affected Modesty is very often the greatest Vanity, and Authors are sometimes prouder of their Blushes than of the Praises that occasion'd them. I shan't therefore, like a foolish Virgin, fly to be pursued, and deny what I chiefly wish for. I am very willing to acknowledg the Beauties of this Play, especially those of the third Night, which not to be proud of, were the heighth of Impudence: Who is asham'd to value himself upon such Favours, undervalues those who confer'd them.

As I freely submit to the Criticisms of the Judicious, so I
10 cannot call this an ill Play, since the Town has allow'd it such Success. When they have pardon'd my faults, 'twere very ill manners to condemn their Indulgence. Some may think (my Acquaintance in Town being too slender to make a Party for the Play) that the Success must be deriv'd from the pure Merits of the Cause. I am of another opinion: I have not been long enough in Town to raise Enemies against me; and the *English* are still kind to Strangers. I am below the Envy of great Wits, and above the Malice of little ones. I have not displeas'd the Ladies, nor offended the Clergy; both which are
20 now pleas'd to say, that a Comedy may be diverting without Smut and Profaneness.

Next to these Advantages, the Beauties of Action gave the greatest life to the Play, of which the Town is so sensible, that all will join with me in commendation of the Actors, and allow (without detracting from the merit of others) that the *Theatre Royal* affords an excellent and compleat set of Comedians. Mr. *Wilks*'s performance has set him so far above competition in the part of *Wildair*, that none can pretend to envy the Praise due to his Merit. That he made the Part, will appear from
30 hence, that whenever the Stage has the misfortune to lose him, Sir *Harry Wildair* may go to the Jubilee.

A great many quarrel at *the Trip to the Jubilee* for a *Misnomer*: I must tell them that perhaps there are greater Trips in the Play; and when I find that more exact Plays have had better success, I'll talk with the Criticks about *Decorums*, Ec. However, if I ever commit another fault of this nature, I'll endeavour to make it more excusable.

PROLOGUE, by a Friend.

Poets will think nothing so checks their Fury,
As Wits, Cits, Beaux, and Women for their Jury.
Our Spark's half dead to think what Medly's come,
With blended Judgments to pronounce his Doom.
'Tis all false Fear; for in a mingled Pit,
Why, what your grave Don thinks but dully writ,
His Neighbour i'th' great Wig may take for Wit.
Some Authors court the Few, the Wise, if any;
Our Youth's content, if he can reach the Many,
Who go with much like Ends to Church, and Play,   10
Not to observe what Priests or Poets say,
No! no! your Thoughts, like theirs, lie quite another way.
The Ladies safe may smile: for here's no Slander,
No Smut, no lewd-tongu'd Beau, no double Entendre.
'Tis true he has a Spark just come from France,
But then so far from Beau—why he talks Sense!
Like Coin oft carry'd out, but—seldom brought from thence.
There's yet a Gang to whom our Spark submits,
Your Elbow-shaking Fool, that lives by's Wits,
That's only witty tho, just as he lives by fits.
Who Lion-like through Bayliffs scours away,   20
Hunts in the Face a Dinner all the Day,
At Night with empty Bowels grumbles o're the Play.
And now the modish Prentice he implores,
Who with his Master's Cash stol'n out of Doors,
Imploys it on a Brace of—Honourable Whores;
While their good bulky Mother pleas'd sits by,
Bawd Regent of the Bubble Gallery.
Next to our mounted Friends we humbly move,
Who all your Side-box Tricks are much above,   30
And never fail to pay us—with your Love.
Ah Friends! Poor Dorset *Garden-house is gone,*
Our merry Meetings there are all undone:
Quite lost to us, sure for some strange Misdeeds
That strong Dog Sampson's *pull'd it o're our Heads,*

Snaps Rope like Thread; but when his Fortune's told him,
He'll hear perhaps of Rope will one day hold him:
At least I hope that our good-natur'd Town
Will find a way to pull his Prizes down.
40   *Well, that's all! Now Gentlemen for the Play,*
On second Thoughts I've but two words to say;
Such as it is for your Delight design'd,
Hear it, read, try, judg, and speak as you find.

Dramatis Personæ.

[MEN]

Sir Harry Wildair.	An airy Gentleman affecting humourous Gaity and Freedom in his Behaviour.	Mr. *Wilks.*
Standard.	A disbanded Colonel, brave and generous.	Mr. *Powel.*
Vizard.	Outwardly pious, otherwise a great Debauchee, and villanous.	Mr. *Mills.*
Smuggler.	An old Merchant.	Mr. *Johnson.*
Clincher Senior.	A pert *London* Prentice turn'd Beau, and affecting Travel.	Mr. *Pinkethman.*
Clincher Junior.	His Brother, educated in the Country.	Mr. *Bullock.*
Dicky.	His Man.	Mr. *Norris.*
Tom Errand.	A Porter.	Mr. *Haines.*

WOMEN.

Lurewell.	A Lady of a jilting Temper proceeding from a resentment of her Wrongs from Men.	Mrs. *Verbruggen.*
Lady Darling.	An old Lady, Mother to *Angelica.*	Mrs. *Powel.*
Angelica.	A Woman of Honour.	Mrs. *Rogers.*
Parly.	Maid to *Lurewell.*	Mrs. *Moor.*

Constable, Mob, Porter's Wife, Servants, [*Footmen, Butler,*] &c.

SCENE, *London.*

THE
CONSTANT COUPLE

ACT I. [Scene i.]

SCENE, *The Park.*

Enter Vizard *with a Letter,* Servant *following.*

Vizard. *Angelica* send it back unopen'd! say you?

Servant. As you see, Sir.

Vizard. The Pride of these vertuous Women is more insufferable, than the immodesty of Prostitutes—After all my Incouragement to slight me thus!

Servant. She said, Sir, that imagining your Morals sincere, she gave you access to her Conversation; but that your late Behaviour in her Company has convinc'd her, that your Love and Religion are both Hypocrisy, and that she believes your
10 Letter like your self, fair on the outside, foul within; so sent it back unopen'd.

Vizard. May Obstinacy guard her Beauty till Wrinkles bury it, then may Desire prevail to make her curse that untimely Pride her disappointed Age repents—I'll be reveng'd the very first opportunity—Saw you the old Lady *Darling*, her mother?

Servant. Yes, Sir, and she was pleas'd to say much in your Commendation.

Vizard. That's my Cue—An Esteem grafted in old Age is hardly Rooted out, Years stiffen their Opinions with their
20 Bodies, And old Zeal is only to be cozen'd by young Hypocrisy—Run to the Lady *Lurewell*s, and know of her Maid, Whether her Ladyship will be at home this Evening, Her Beauty is sufficient Cure for *Angelica*'s Scorn.

Exit Servant.
Vizard *pulls out a Book, reads, and walks about.*
Enter Smuggler.

Smuggler. Ay, there's a Pattern for the young Men o'th' times, at his Meditation so early, some Book of pious

Ejaculations, I'm sure.

Vizard. This *Hobbs* is an excellent Fellow! (*Aside.*) O Uncle *Smuggler!* to find you in this end o'th' Town is a Miracle.

Smuggler. I have seen a Miracle this Morning indeed, Cousin *Vizard.*   30

Vizard. What was it, pray Sir?

Smuggler. A Man at his Devotion so near the Court—I'm very glad Boy, that you keep your Sanctity untainted in this infectious place; the very Air of this Park is heathenish, and every Man's Breath I meet scents of Atheism.

Vizard. Surely Sir, some great Concern must bring you to this unsanctified end of the Town.

Smuggler. A very unsanctify'd Concern, truly Cousin.

Vizard. What is't?

Smuggler. A Law-Suit, Boy—Shall I tell you?—My Ship the 40 *Swan* is newly arriv'd from St. *Sebastians*, laden with *Portugal* Wines: Now the impudent Rogue of a Tide-waiter has the face to affirm, 'tis *French* Wines in *Spanish* Casks, and has indicted me upon the Statute—O Conscience, Conscience! These Tide waiters and Surveyors plague us more with their *French* Wines, than the War did with *French Privateers*—Ay, there's another Plague of the Nation—.

Enter Colonel Standard.

A red Coat and Feather.

Vizard. Colonel *Standard*, I'm your humble Servant.

Standard. May be not, Sir.   50

Vizard. Why so?

Standard. Because—I'm disbanded.

Vizard. How? broke!

Standard. This very morning, in *Hide Park*, my brave Regiment, a thousand Men that look'd like Lions yesterday, were scatter'd, and look'd as poor and simple as the Herd of Deer that graz'd beside 'em.

Smuggler. Tal, al, deral (*Singing.*) I'll have a Bonfire this night as high as the Monument.

Standard. A Bonfire! thou dry, wither'd, ill nature; had not 60 these brave Fellows Swords defended you, your House had been a Bonfire e're this about your Ears—Did not we venture our Lives, Sir?

I.i. 57 graz'd] Q2; gaz'd

Smuggler. And did not we pay you for your Lives, Sir?—
Venture your Lives! I'm sure we ventur'd our Money,
and that's Life and Soul to me—Sir, we'll maintain you no
longer.

Standard. Then your Wives shall, old *Acteon*: There are five
and thirty strapping Officers gone this Morning to live upon
70 free Quarter in the City.

Smuggler. O Lord! O Lord! I shall have a Son within these
nine Months born with a Leading staff in his hand—Sir, you
are—

Standard. What Sir?

Smuggler. Sir, I say that you are—

Standard. What Sir?

Smuggler. Disbanded Sir, that's all—I see my Lawyer
yonder.

Exit.

Vizard. Sir, I'm very sorry for your Misfortune.

80 *Standard.* Why so? I don't come to borrow Mony of you; if
you're my Friend, meet me this Evening at the *Rummer*, I'll
pay my Way, drink a Health to my King, Prosperity to my
Country; and away for *Hungary* to morrow Morning.

Vizard. What! you won't leave us?

Standard. What! a Souldier stay here! to look like an old pair
of Colours in *Westminster-Hall*, ragged and rusty! No, no—I
met yesterday a broken Lieutenant, he was asham'd to own
that he wanted a Dinner, but beg'd eighteen pence of me to
buy a new sheath for his Sword.

90 *Vizard.* O, but you have good Friends, Colonel!

Standard. O very good Friends! my Father's a Lord, and my
elder Brother a Beau.

Vizard. But your Country may perhaps want your Sword
agen.

Standard. Nay for that matter, let but a single Drum beat up
for Volunteers between *Ludgate* and *Charing-Cross*, and I shall
undoubtedly hear it at the Walls of *Buda*.

Vizard. Come, come, Colonel, there are ways of making
your Fortune at home—Make your Addresses to the Fair,
100 you're a Man of Honour and Courage.

Standard. Ay, my Courage is like to do me wondrous Service
with the Fair: This pretty cross Cut over my Eye will attract a
Dutchess—I warrant 'twill be a mighty Grace to my

Ogling—Had I us'd the Stratagem of a certain Brother
Colonel of mine, I might succeed.

Vizard. What was it, pray?

Standard. Why to save his pretty face for the Women, he
always turn'd his back upon the Enemy—He was a Man of
Honour for the Ladies.

Vizard. Come, come, the Loves of *Mars* and *Venus* will never 110
fail, you must get a Mistriss.

Standard. Prithee, no more on't—You have awakn'd a
thought, from which and the Kingdom I wou'd have stoln
away at once—To be plain, I have a Mistriss.

Vizard. And She's cruel?

Standard. No.

Vizard. Her Parents prevent your Happiness.

Standard. Nor that.

Vizard. Then she has no Fortune.

Standard. A large one, Beauty to tempt all Mankind, and 120
Virtue to beat off their Assaults. O *Vizard*! such a Creature!—
Hey Day! Who the Devil have we here!

Vizard. The Joy of the Play-house, and Life of the Park,

> *Enter Sir* Harry Wildair, *crosses the Stage singing,*
> *with Footmen after him.*

Sir *Harry Wildair* newly come from *Paris*.

Standard. Sir *Harry Wildair*! Did not he make a Campain in
Flanders some three or four years go?

Vizard. The same.

Standard. Why, he behav'd himself very bravely.

Vizard. Why not? Do'st think Bravery and Gaiety are
inconsistent? He's a Gentleman of most happy Circumstances, 130
born to a plentiful Estate, has had a genteel and easy
Education, free from the rigidness of Teachers, and Pedantry
of Schools. His florid Constitution being never ruffled by
misfortune, nor stinted in its Pleasures, has render'd him
entertaining to others, and easy to himself—Turning all
Passion into Gaiety of Humour, by which he chuses rather
to rejoice his Friends, than be hated by any; as you shall
see.

> *Enter* Wildair.

Wildair. Ha *Vizard*!

Vizard. Sir *Harry*! 140

Wildair. Who thought to find you out of the *Rubrick* so long;

I thought the Hypocrisy had been wedded to a Pulpit Cushion long ago—Sir, if I mistake not your Face, your Name is *Standard*.

Standard. Sir *Harry*, I'm your Humble Servant.

Wildair. Come, Gentlemen, the News, the News o'th Town; For I'm just arriv'd.

Vizard. Why, in the City end o'th Town we're playing the Knave to get Estates.

150 *Standard.* And in the Court end playing the Fool in spending 'em.

Wildair. Just so in *Paris*; I'm glad we're grown so modish.

Vizard. We are all so reform'd, that Gallantry is taken for Vice.

Standard. And Hypocrisy for Religion.

Wildair. Alamode de Paris. Agen.

Vizard. Not one Whore between *Ludgate* and *Aldgate*.

Standard. But ten times more Cuckolds than ever.

Vizard. Nothing like an Oath in the City.

160 *Standard.* That's a mistake; for my Major swore a hundred and fifty last night to a Merchant's Wife in her Bedchamber.

Wildair. P'shaw, this is trifling, tell me News, Gentlemen. What Lord has lately broke his Fortune at the Groomporters? or his Heart at *New-Market*, for the loss of a Race? What Wife has been lately suing in *Doctors-Commons* for Alimony? or what Daughter run away with her Fathers *Valet*? What Beau gave the noblest Ball at the *Bath*, or had the finest Coach in the *Ring*? I want News, Gentlemen.

Standard. Faith, Sir, these are no News at all.

170 *Vizard.* But pray, Sir *Harry*, tell us some News of your Travels.

Wildair. With all my heart—You must know then, I went over to *Amsterdam* in a *Dutch* Ship; I there had a *Dutch* Whore for five Stivers; I went from thence to *Landen*, where I was heartily drub'd in the Battle with the but-end of a *Swiss* Musket. I thence went to *Paris*, where I had half a dozen Intreagues, bought half a dozen new Suits, fought a couple of Duels, and here I am agen in *statu quo*.

Vizard. But we heard that you design'd to make the Tour of 180 *Italy*; what brought you back so soon?

Wildair. That which brought you into the World, and may

perhaps carry you out of it; a Woman.

Standard. What! Quit the Pleasures of Travel for a Woman!—

Wildair. Ay, Colonel, for such a Woman! I had rather see her *Ruell* than the Palace of *Lewis le Grand*: There's more Glory in her Smile, than in the *Jubilee at Rome*; and I would rather kiss her Hand than the *Pope's Toe*.

Vizard. You, Colonel, have been very lavish in the Beauty and Virtue of your Mistriss; and Sir *Harry* here has been no less eloquent in the Praise of his. Now will I lay you both ten 190 Guineas a piece, that neither of them is so pretty so witty, or so virtuous as mine.

Standard. 'Tis done.

Wildair. I'll double the Stakes—But, Gentlemen, now I think on't, how shall we be resolv'd? for I know not where my Mistriss may be found; she left *Paris* about a month before me, and I had an account—

Standard. How, Sir! left *Paris* about a month before you!

Wildair. Yes, Sir, and I had an account that she lodg'd somewhere in St. *James*'s.   200

Vizard. How is that, Sir? Somewhere in St. *James*'s, say you?

Wildair. Ay, but I know not where, and perhaps mayn't find her this fortnight.

Standard. Her Name, pray, Sir *Harry*.

Vizard. Ay, ay, her Name, perhaps we know her.

Wildair. Her Name! Ay—She has the softest, whitest Hand that ever was made of Flesh and Blood, her Lips so balmy sweet.

Standard. But her Name, Sir.

Wildair. Then her Neck and Breast;—her Breast so do 210 heave, so heave. (*Singing.*)

Vizard. But her Name, Sir, her Quality?

Wildair. Then her Shape, Colonel.

Standard. But her Name I want, Sir.

Wildair. Then her Eyes, *Vizard!*

Standard. P'shaw, Sir *Harry*, her Name, or nothing.

Wildair. Then if you must have it, she's call'd the Lady— But then her Foot, Gentlemen, she dances to a miracle. *Vizard,* you have certainly lost your Wager.

Vizard. Why you have lost your Senses; we shall never 220 discover the Picture unless you subscribe the Name.

Wildair. Then her Name is *Lurewell.*

Standard. S'Death, My Mistriss. (*Aside.*)

Vizard. My Mistriss by *Jupiter.* (*Aside.*)

Wildair. Do you know her, Gentlemen?

Standard. I have seen her, Sir.

Wildair. Can'st tell where she lodges? Tell me, dear
Colonel.

Standard. Your humble Servant, Sir.

                                          Exit Standard.

230   *Wildair.* Nay, hold Colonel, I'll follow you, and will know.

                                          Runs out.

Vizard. The Lady *Lurewell* his Mistriss! He loves her. But
she loves me—but he's a Baronet, and I plain *Vizard*; he has
Coach and six, and I walk a foot; I was bred in *London*, and he
in *Paris*—That very Circumstance has murder'd me—Then
some Stratagem must be laid to divert his Pretensions.

                                   Re-enter Wildair.

Wildair. Prithee, *Dick*, what makes the Colonel so out of
humour?

Vizard. Because he's out of Pay, I suppose.

Wildair. S'life that's true, I was beginning to mistrust some
240 Rivalship in the Case.

Vizard. And suppose there were, you know the Colonel can
fight, Sir *Harry.*

Wildair. Fight! Pshaw! but he can't dance, ha! We contend
for a Woman, *Vizard*! S'life man, if Ladies were to be gain'd by
Sword and Pistol only, what the Devil should all the Beaux
do?

Vizard. I'll try him farther (*Aside.*) But wou'd not you, Sir
Harry, fight for this Woman you so admire?

Wildair. Fight! Let me consider. I love her, that's true—but
250 then I love honest Sir *Harry Wildair* better. The Lady *Lurewell*
is divinely charming—right—but then a Thrust ith' Guts, or a
Middlesex Jury, is as ugly as the Devil.

Vizard. Ay, Sir *Harry*, 'twere a dangerous Cast for a Beau
Baronet to be tried by a parcel of greasy, grumbling, bartering
Boobies, who wou'd hang you purely because you're a
Gentleman.

Wildair. Ay, but on t'other hand, I have Mony enough to
bribe the Rogues with: So upon mature deliberation, I wou'd

fight for her—but no more of her. Prithee, *Vizard*, can't you
recommend a Friend to a pretty Mistriss by the by, till I can   260
find my own? you have store I'm sure; you cunning poaching
Dogs make surer game than we that hunt open and fair.
Prithee now, good *Vizard*.

Vizard. Let me consider a little—Now Love and Revenge
inspire my Politicks. (*Aside.*)

> *Pauses, whilst Sir* Harry *walks singing.*

Wildair. P'shaw! thou'rt as long studying for a new Mistriss,
as a Drawer is piercing a new Pipe.

Vizard. I design a new Pipe for you and wholesom Wine,
you'll therefore bear a little expectation.

Wildair. Ha! Say'st thou, dear *Vizard*.   270

Vizard. A Girl of sixteen, Sir *Harry*.

Wildair. Now sixteen thousand Blessings light on thee.

Vizard. Pretty and Witty.

Wildair. Ay, ay, but her Name, *Vizard*.

Vizard. Her Name! yes—she has the softest whitest Hand
that ever was made of Flesh and Blood, her Lips so balmy
sweet.

Wildair. Well, well, but where shall I find her, Man?

Vizard. Find her—but then her Foot, Sir *Harry*; she dances
to a Miracle.   280

Wildair. Prithee don't distract me.

Vizard. Well then, you must know, that this Lady is the
Curiosity and Ambition of the Town; her Name's *Angelica*. She
that passes for her Mother is a private Bawd, and call'd the
Lady *Darling*, she goes for a *Baronets* Lady (no disparagement
to your Honour, Sir *Harry*) I assure you.

Wildair. Pshaw, hang my Honour; but what Street, what
House?

Vizard. Not so fast, Sir *Harry*, you must have my Pasport for
your Admittance, and you'l find my Recommendation in a   290
Line or two will procure you very civil entertainment; I
suppose 20 or 30 pieces handsomly plac'd will gain the Point;
I'll ensure her sound.

Wildair. Thou dearest Friend to a man in necessity—Here
Sirrah, order my Coach about to St. *James*'s, I'll walk across
the Park. (*To his Servant.*)

> *Enter* Clincher Senior.

Clincher Senior. Here Sirrah, order my Coach about to St.
James's, I'll walk across the Park too—Mr. *Vizard*, your most
Devoted—Sir, (*To Wildair*.) I admire the mode of your
300 Shoulder-knot, methinks it hangs very emphatically, and
Carries an air of Travel in it; your Sword-knot too is most
Ornamentally modish, and bears a foreign Mein. Gentlemen,
My Brother is just arriv'd in Town, so that being upon the
Wing to kiss his Hands, I hope you'll pardon this abrupt
Departure of, Gentlemen, your most Devoted, and most
Faithful humble Servant.

Wildair. Prethee, dost know him?

Vizard. Know him! why 'tis *Clincher* who was Apprentice To
my Uncle *Smuggler*, the Merchant in the City.

310 *Wildair.* What makes him so Gay?

Vizard. Why, he's in mourning for his Father, the kind old
man In *Hertfordshire* 'tother day broke his Neck a Foxhunting;
the Son upon the news has broke his Indentures, Whip'd from
behind the Counter into the side Box, Forswears Merchandise,
where he must live by Cheating, And usurps Gentility, where
he may die by Raking. He keeps his Coach, and Liveries, *brace
of Geldings, Leash of Mistresses*, talks of nothing but Wines,
Intreagues, Plays, Fashions, and *going to the Jubilee*.

Wildair. Ha, ha, ha, how many pound of Pulvil must the
320 fellow Use in sweetning himself from the smell of Hops And
Tobacco, faugh—I'my Conscience methought, Like *Olivia*'s
Lover, he stunk of *Thames-street*. But now for *Angelica*, That's
her name? we'll to the *Princesse*'s Chocolate House, where you
shall write my Pasport, Aloons.

Exeunt.

[ACT I. Scene ii.]

SCENE, *Lady* Lurewell*'s Lodgings.*

Lurewell, *and her Maid* Parly.

Lurewell. Parly, my pocket Book—let me see—*Madrid,
Venice, Paris, London*—ay, *London*! they may talk What they will
of the hot Countries, but I find Love Most fruitful under this

Climate—In a Months space Have I gain'd—let me see, *Imprimis*, Colonel *Standard*.

Parly. And how will your Ladyship manage him?

Lurewell. As all Souldiers shou'd be manag'd, he shall serve me Till I gain my ends, then I disband him.

Parly. But he loves you, Madam.

Lurewell. Therefore I scorn him, I hate all that don't love 10 me, And slight all that do: would his whole deluding Sex Admir'd me, thus wou'd I slight them all; my Virgin and Unwary Innocence was wrong'd by faithless Man, But now glance Eyes, plot Brain, dissemble Face, Lye Tongue, and be a second *Eve* to tempt, seduce, and Damn the treacherous kind—Let me survey my Captives—The *Colonel* leads the Van, next Mr. *Vizard*, he courts me Out of the *Practice of Piety*, therefore is a Hypocrite: Then *Clincher* he adores me with Orangery, and is Consequently a Fool; then my old Merchant, Alderman *Smuggler*, he's a Compound of both—out of which 20 Medley of Lovers, if I don't make good Diversion—What d'ye think *Parly*?

Parly. I think, Madam, I'm like to be very virtuous in your Service, If you teach me all those Tricks that you use to your Lovers.

Lurewell. You're a Fool, Child; observe this, that tho a Woman swear, forswear, lie, dissemble, backbite, be proud, vain, malitious, any thing, if she secures the main Chance, she's still virtuous, That's a Maxim.

Parly. I can't be persuaded tho, Madam, but that you really 30 lov'd Sir *Harry Wildair* in *Paris*.

Lurewell. Of all the Lovers I ever had, he was my greatest Plague, for I cou'd never make him uneasy; I left him involv'd in a Duel upon my Account, I long to know whether the Fop be kill'd or not.

Enter Standard.

O Lord, no sooner talk of killing, but the Souldier is conjur'd up; you're upon hard Duty Colonel, to serve your King, your Country, and a Mistriss too.

Standard. The latter, I must confess, is the hardest; for in War, Madam, we can be relieved in our Duty; but in Love 40 who wou'd take our Post, is our Enemy; Emulation in Glory is transporting, but Rivals here intolerable.

Lurewell. Those that bear away the Prize in the Field, should boast the same success in the Bed-chamber; and I think, considering the weakness of our Sex, we should make those our Companions who can be our Champions.

Standard. I once, Madam, hop'd the Honour of defending you from all Injuries thro a Title to your lovely Person, but now my Love must attend my Fortune. This Commission, 50 Madam, was my Pasport to the Fair; adding a nobleness to my Passion, it stampt a value on my Love; 'twas once the life of Honour, but now its Hearse, and with it must my Love be buried.

Parly. What! Disbanded, Colonel?

Standard. Yes, Mrs. *Parly*.

Parly. Faugh, the nauseous Fellow, he stinks of Poverty already. (*Aside*.)

Lurewell. His misfortune troubles me, 'cause it may prevent my designs. (*Aside*.)

60 *Standard*. I'll chuse, Madam, rather to destroy my Passion by absence abroad, then have it starv'd at home.

Lurewell. I'm sorry, Sir, you have so mean an Opinion of my Affection, as to imagine it founded upon your Fortune.

And to convince you of your mistake, here I vow by all that's Sacred, I own the same Affection now as before. Let it suffice, my Fortune is considerable.

Standard. No, Madam, no, I'll never be a charge to her I love: The man that sells himself for Gold is the worst of Prostitutes.

70 *Lurewell*. Now were he any other Creature but a man, I cou'd love him. (*Aside*.)

Standard. This only last request I make, that no Title recommend a Fool, Office introduce a Knave, nor a Coat a Coward to my place in your Affections; so farewel my Country, and adieu my Love.

Exit.

Lurewell. Now the Devil take thee for being so honourable; Here *Parly*, call him back, I shall lose half my Diversion Else; now for a trial of Skill.

Re-enter Standard.

Sir, I hope you'll pardon my Curiosity, When do you take 80 your Journey?

Standard. To morrow Morning early, Madam.

Lurewell. So suddenly! which way are you design'd to travel?

Standard. That I can't yet resolve on.

Lurewell. Pray, Sir, tell me, pray Sir, I entreat you, why are you so obstinate?

Standard. Why are you so curious, Madam?

Lurewell. Because—

Standard. What?

Lurewell. Because, I, I,—   90

Standard. Because! what, Madam?—pray tell me.

Lurewell. Because I design—to follow you. (*Crying.*)

Standard. Follow me! by all that's great! I ne're was proud Before, but Love from such a Creature might Swell the vanity of the proudest Prince; follow me! By Heavens thou shalt not. What! expose thee to the Hazards of a Camp!—Rather I'll stay, and here bear The Contempt of Fools, and worst of Fortune.

Lurewell. You need not, shall not, my Estate for both is sufficient.   100

Standard. Thy Estate! no, I'll turn a Knave and purchase one my self; I'll cringe to that proud Man I undermine, and fawn on him that I wou'd bite to death; I'll tip my Tongue with Flattery, and smooth my Face with Smiles; I'll turn Pimp, Informer, Office-broker, nay Coward, to be great; and sacrifice it all to thee, my generous Fair.

Lurewell. And I'll dissemble, lye, swear, jilt, any thing but I'd reward thy Love, and recompence thy noble Passion.

Standard. Sir *Harry*, ha! ha! ha, poor Sir *Harry*, ha, ha, ha. Rather kiss her Hand than the *Pope*'s Toe, ha, ha, ha.   110

Lurewell. What Sir *Harry*? Colonel, What Sir *Harry*!

Standard. Sir *Harry Wildair*, Madam—

Lurewell. What! is he come over?

Standard. Ay, and he told me—but I don't believe a Syllable on't.

Lurewell. What did he tell you?

Standard. Only call'd you his Mistriss, and pretending to be extravagant in your Commendation, would vainly insinuate the praise of his own Judgment and good Fortune in a Choice—   120

Lurewell. How easily is the vanity of Fops tickled by our Sex!

Standard. Why, your Sex is the vanity of Fops.

Lurewell. O' my Conscience I believe so; this Gentleman, because he danc'd well, I pitch'd on for a Partner at a Ball in *Paris*, and ever since he has so persecuted me with Letters, Songs, Dances, Serenading, Flattery, Foppery, and Noise, that I was forc'd to fly the Kingdom—And I warrant he made you jealous.

130 *Standard.* Faith, Madam, I was a little uneasy.

Lurewell. You shall have a plentiful Revenge, I'll send him back all his foolish Letters, Songs and Verses, and you your self shall carry 'em, 'twill afford you opportunity of triumphing, and free me from his farther impertinence; for of all Men he's my Aversion. I'll run and fetch them instantly.

[*Exit.*]

Standard. Dear Madam, a rare Project, how I shall bait him like *Acteon*, with his own Dogs—Well, Mrs. *Parly*, 'tis order'd by *Act of Parliament*, that you receive no more pieces, Mrs. *Parly*—

140 *Parly.* 'Tis provided by the same Act, that you send no more Messages by me good Colonel; you must not pretend to send any more Letters, unless you can pay the Postage.

Standard. Come come! don't be Mercenary, take example by your Lady, be Honourable.

Parly. A lack a day, Sir, it shows as ridiculous and haughty for us to imitate our Betters in their Honour, as in their finery; leave Honour to Nobility that can support it: we poor Folks, Colonel, have no pretence to't; and truly, I think, Sir, that your Honour shou'd be cashier'd with your Leading-staff.

150 *Standard.* 'Tis one of the greatest curses of Poverty, to be the Jest of Chamber-maids!

Enter Lurewell.

Lurewell. Here's the Packet Colonel, the whole magazine of Love's Artillery. (*Gives him the Packet.*)

Standard. Which since I have gain'd, I will turn upon the Enemy; Madam, I'll bring you the News of my Victory this Evening. Poor Sir *Harry*! ha, ha, ha.

Exit.

Lurewell. To the right about as you were, march Colonel:

ha, ha, ha.
> *Vain Man, who boasts of study'd Parts and Wiles;* ⎫
> *Nature in us your deepest Art beguiles,*   ⎬   160
> *Stamping deep Cunning in our Frowns and Smiles.* ⎭
> *You toil for Art, your Intellects you trace;*
> *Woman without a Thought, bears Policy in her Face.*

[*The End of the First Act.*]

ACT II. [Scene i.]

SCENE, Clincher Junior's *Lodgings.*

Enter Clincher Junior *opening a Letter, Servant*
[Dicky] *following.*
Clincher Junior.—(*Reads.*)

Dear Brother;
> *I will see you presently, I have sent this Lad to wait on you, he can instruct you in the Fashions of the Town; I am your affectionate Brother,*
>
> Clincher.

Very well, and what's your Name, Sir?
Dicky. My Name is *Dicky*, Sir.
Clincher Junior. Dicky!
Dicky. Ay, *Dicky*, Sir.
Clincher Junior. Very well, a pretty Name! and what can you 10 do Mr. *Dicky?*
Dicky. Why Sir I can powder a Wig, and pick up a Whore.
Clincher Junior. O Lord! O Lord! a Whore! Why are there many Whores in this town?
Dicky. Ha, ha, ha, many Whores! there's a Question indeed; why Sir, there are above five hundred Surgeons in Town—Harkee Sir, do you see that Woman there in the Velvet Scarf, and red Knots?
Clincher Junior. Ay Sir, What then?
Dicky. Why she shall be at your Service in three minutes, 20 As I'm a Pimp.

Clincher Junior. O *Jupiter Ammon!* why she's a Gentlewoman.
Dicky. A Gentlewoman! Why so are all the Whores in Town, Sir.

Enter Clincher Senior.

Clincher Senior. Brother, you'r welcome to *London!*
Clincher Junior. I thought, Brother, you ow'd so much to the Memory of my Father, as to wear Mourning for his Death.
Clincher Senior. Why so I do Fool, I wear this because I have the Estate, And you wear that, because you have not the
30 Estate. You have cause to mourn indeed, Brother. Well Brother, I'm glad to see you, fare you well. (*Going.*)
Clincher Junior. Stay, stay Brother, where are you going?
Clincher Senior. How natural 'tis for a Country Booby to ask impertinent Questions. Harkee Sir, is not my Father dead?
Clincher Junior. Ay, ay, to my sorrow.
Clincher Senior. No matter for that, he is dead, and am not I a young powder'd extravagant English Heir?
Clincher Junior. Very right Sir.
Clincher Senior. Why then Sir, you may be sure that I am
40 going to the *Jubilee,* Sir.
Clincher Junior. Jubilee! what's that?
Clincher Senior. Jubilee! why the *Jubilee* is—faith I don't know what it is.
Dicky. Why the *Jubilee* is the same thing with our *Lord-Mayors* Day in the City; there will be *Pageants,* and *Squibs,* and *Rary Shows,* and all that Sir.
Clincher Junior. And must you go so soon Brother?
Clincher Senior. Yes, Sir, for I must stay a Month in *Amsterdam,* to study Poetry.
50 *Clincher Junior.* Then I suppose Brother, you travel through *Muscovy* to learn Fashions, Don't you, Brother?
Clincher Senior. Brother! Prithee *Robin* don't call me Brother; Sir will do every jot as well.
Clincher Junior. O *Jupiter Ammon!* why so?
Clincher Senior. Because People will imagin that you have a spight at me—But have you seen your Cousin *Angelica* yet, and her Mother the Lady *Darling?*
Clincher Junior. No, my Dancing Master has not been with me yet: How shall I salute them, Brother?
60 *Clincher Senior.* Pshaw, that's easy, 'tis only two Scrapes, a

Kiss, and your humble Servant: I'll tell you more when I
come from the *Jubilee*. Come along.

Exeunt.

[ACT II. Scene ii.]

SCENE, Lady Darling's *House.*

Enter Wildair *with a Letter.*

Wildair.   *Like Light and Heat incorporate we lay,*
　　　　We blest the Night, and curst the coming Day.
Well, if this Paper-kite flies sure, I'm secure of my Game—
Humph! the prettiest *Bordel* I have seen, a very stately genteel
one.

Footmen cross the Stage.

Hey day! Equipage too! Now for a Bawd by the Courtesy, and
a Whore with a *Coat of Arms*—s'Death, I'm afraid I've
mistaken the House.

Enter Lady Darling.

No, this must be the Bawd by her Bulk.
　Lady Darling. Your Business, pray Sir?　　　　　　　10
　Wildair. Pleasure, Madam.
　Lady Darling. Then, Sir, you have no business here.
　Wildair. This Letter, Madam, will inform you further; Mr.
Vizard sent it, with his humble Service to your Ladyship.
　Lady Darling. How does my Cousin, Sir?
　Wildair. Ay, her Cousin too, that's right Procuress agen.
[*Aside.*]
　Lady Darling. (*Reads.*) Madam—
　　　　　　Earnest Inclination to serve—Sir Harry—
　　　　　　Madam—Court my Cousin—Gentleman—
　　　　　　Fortune—. Your Ladyship's most humble　　20
　　　　　　Servant,
　　　　　　　　　　　　　　　　　Vizard.
　Sir, your Fortune and Quality are sufficient to recommend
you any where; but what goes farther with me, is the
recommendation of so sober and pious a young Gentleman as
Cousin *Vizard*.
　Wildair. A right sanctified Bawd o' my word. [*Aside.*]
　Lady Darling. Sir *Harry*, your Conversation with Mr. *Vizard*

argues you a Gentleman, free from the loose and vicious
30 Carriage of the Town; I'll therefore call my Daughter.

> *Exit.*

Wildair. Now go thy way for an illustrious Bawd of
Babylon—She dresses up a Sin so religiously, that the Devil
wou'd hardly know it of his making.

> *Re-enter* Lady Darling *with* Angelica.

Lady Darling. Pray Daughter use him civilly, such Matches
won't offer every Day.

> *Exit.*

Wildair. O all ye Powers of Love! an Angel! S'Death, what
Mony have I got in my Pocket, I can't offer her less than
twenty Guineas—and by *Jupiter* she's worth a hundred.

Angelica. 'Tis he! the very same! and his Person as agreeable
40 as his Character of good Humour—Pray Heav'n his Silence
proceed from respect.

Wildair. How innocent she looks! how wou'd that Modesty
adorn Virtue, when it makes even Vice look so charming!—By
Heav'n there is such a commanding Innocence in her looks,
That I dare not ask the Question. [*Aside.*]

Angelica. Now all the Charms of real Love and feign'd
Indifference assist me to engage his Heart, for mine is lost
already. [*Aside.*]

Wildair. Madam—I, I—Zoons, I cannot speak to her—But
50 she's a Whore, and I will [*Aside.*]—Madam in short,I, I—O
Hypocrisy! Hypocrisy! What a charming Sin art thou? [*Aside.*]

Angelica. He is caught, now to secure my Conquest [*Aside.*]
—I thought Sir, you had business to impart.

Wildair. Business to impart! how nicely she words it!
[*Aside.*] Yes Madam, Don't you, don't you love singing Birds,
Madam?

Angelica. That's an odd Question for a Lover [*Aside.*]—Yes,
Sir.

Wildair. Why then Madam, here is a Nest of the prettiest
60 Goldfinches that ever chirpt in a Cage; twenty young ones, I
assure you Madam.

Angelica. Twenty young ones! What then, Sir?

Wildair. Why then Madam, there are twenty young ones—
S'Life I think twenty is pretty fair.

Angelica. He's mad sure [*Aside.*]—Sir *Harry*, when you have

learn'd more Wit and Manners, you shall be welcome here
agen.

[Exit.]

Wildair. Wit and Manners!—I Gad now I conceive there is
a great deal of Wit and Manners in twenty Guineas—I'm sure
'tis all the Wit and Manners I have about me at present. What 70
shall I do?

Enter Clincher Junior, and Dicky.

What the Devil's here? another Cousin I warrant ye!
Harkee Sir, can you lend me ten or a dozen Guineas instantly?
I'll pay you fifteen for them in three hours upon my Honour.

Clincher Junior. These *London* Sparks are plaguy impudent!
this Fellow by his Wig and Assurance can be no less than a
Courtier.

Dicky. He's rather a Courtier by his borrowing.

Clincher Junior. Faith Sir, I han't above five Guineas about
me.   80

Wildair. What business have you here then Sir, for to my
knowledg twenty won't be sufficient.

Clincher Junior. Sufficient! for what Sir?

Wildair. What Sir? Why, for that Sir, what the Devil should
it be, Sir; I know your business notwithstanding all your
Gravity, Sir.

Clincher Junior. My Business! why my Cousin lives here.

Wildair. I know your Cousin does live there, and *Vizard's*
Cousin, and my Cousin, and every Bodies' Cousin—Harkee
Sir, I shall return immediately, and if you offer to touch her 90
till I come back, I shall cut your Throat, Rascal.

Exit.

Clincher Junior. Why the Man's mad sure.

Dicky. Mad, Sir, ay, why he's a Beau.

Clincher Junior. A Beau! what's that! are all Madmen
Beaux?

Dicky. No Sir, but most Beaux are Madmen. But now for
your Cousin; remember your three Scrapes, a Kiss, and your
humble Servant.

Exeunt, as into the House.

[ACT II. Scene iii.]

SCENE, *the Street.*

Enter Wildair, *Colonel* [Standard] *following.*

Standard. Sir *Harry*, Sir *Harry*.

Wildair. I'm in haste, Colonel; besides, if you're in no better humour than when I parted with you in the Park this morning, your Company won't be very agreeable.

Standard. You're a happy man, Sir *Harry*, who are never out of humour: Can nothing move your Gall, Sir *Harry*?

Wildair. Nothing but Impossibilities, which are the same as nothing.

Standard. What Impossibilities?

10   *Wildair.* The Resurrection of my Father to disinherit me, or an Act of Parliament against Wenching. A man of eight thousand Pound *per Annum* to be vext! No, no, Anger and Spleen are Companions for younger Brothers.

Standard. Suppose one call'd you Son of a Whore behind your back.

Wildair. Why then wou'd I call him Rascal behind his back, and so we're even.

Standard. But suppose you had lost a Mistriss.

Wildair. Why then I wou'd get another.

20   *Standard.* But suppose you were discarded by the Woman you love, that wou'd surely trouble you.

Wildair. You're mistaken, Colonel, my Love is neither romantically honourable, nor meanly mercenary, 'tis only a pitch of Gratitude; while she loves me, I love her; when she desists, the Obligation's void.

Standard. But to be mistaken in your Opinion, Sir, if the Lady *Lurewell* (only suppose it) had discarded you—I say only suppose it—and had sent your Discharge by me.

Wildair. P'shaw! that's another Impossibility.

30   *Standard.* Are you sure of that?

Wildair. Why 'twere a Solœcism in Nature, we're Finger and Thumb, Sir. She dances with me, sings with me, plays with me, swears with me, lies with me.

Standard. How Sir?

Wildair. I mean in an honourable way, that is, she lies for
me. In short, we are as like one another as a couple of
Guineas.

Standard. Now that I have rais'd you to the highest Pinnacle
of Vanity, will I give you so mortifying a Fall, as shall dash
your hopes to pieces [*Aside.*]—I pray your Honour to peruse 40
these Papers. (*Gives him the Packet.*)

Wildair. What is't, the Muster Roll of your Regiment,
Colonel?

Standard. No, no, 'tis a List of your Forces in your last Love
Campaign; and for your comfort all disbanded.

Wildair. Prithee, good Metaphorical Colonel, what d'ye
mean?

Standard. Read, Sir, read, these are the *Sybils* Leaves that
will unfold your Destiny.

Wildair. So it be not a false Deed to cheat me of my Estate, 50
what care I—(*Opening the Pacquet.*) Humph! my Hand! to the
Lady *Lurewell*—to the Lady *Lurewell*,—to the Lady *Lurewell*—
What Devil hast thou been tampering with to conjure up these
Spirits?

Standard. A certain Familiar of your Acquaintance Sir.

Wildair. (*Reading.*)—Madam, *my Passion—so natural—your
Beauty contending—Force of Charms—Mankind—Eternal Admirer
Wildair!—*I never was asham'd of my Name before.

Standard. What, Sir *Harry Wildair* out of humour, ha, ha, ha,
poor Sir *Harry*; more Glory in her Smile than in the *Jubilee* at 60
Rome, ha, ha, ha; but then her Foot, Sir *Harry*, she dances to a
miracle! ha, ha, ha! Fy, Sir *Harry*, a Man of your Parts write
Letters not worth a keeping! What say'st thou, my dear
Knight Errant? ha, ha, ha; you may go seek Adventures now
indeed.

Wildair. (*Sings.*)—Let her wander, &c.

Standard. You are jilted to some tune, Sir, blown up with
false Musick, that's all.

Wildair. Now why should I be angry that a Woman is a
Woman? since Inconstancy and Falshood are grounded in 70
their Natures, how can they help it?

Standard. Then they must be grounded in your Nature; for
you and she are Finger and Thumb, Sir.

Wildair. Here's a Copy of Verses too, I must turn Poet in

the Devil's name—Stay—S'death, what's here? This is her
Hand—Oh the charming Characters! My dear Wildair.
(*Reading.*) That's I—*this huff bluff Colonel*—that's he—*is the
rarest Fool in Nature*—the Devil he is! *and as such have I us'd him*—
with all my heart faith—*I had no better way of letting you know that
80 I lodg in* Pall Mall *near the* Holy Lamb—. [*Aside.*] Colonel, I'm
your most humble Servant.

Standard. Hold, Sir, you shan't go yet, I han't delivered half
my Message.

Wildair. Upon my faith but you have, Colonel.

Standard. Well, well, own your Spleen, out with it, I know
you're like to burst.

Wildair. I am so, by Gad, ha, ha, ha.

　　　Laugh, and point at one another.

Standard. Ay, with all my heart, ha, ha. Well, well, that's all
forc'd, Sir *Harry.*

90 *Wildair.* I was never better pleas'd in all my Life, by *Jupiter.*

Standard. Well, Sir *Harry*, 'tis prudence to hide your
Concern, when there's no help for't—: but to be serious now,
the Lady has sent you back all your Papers there—I was so
just as not to look upon 'em.

Wildair. I'm glad on't, Sir; for there were some things that I
would not have you see.

Standard. All this she has done for my sake, and I desire you
would decline any farther Pretensions for your own sake. So
honest, good natur'd Sir *Harry*, I'm your humble Servant.

　　　　　　　　　　　　　　　　　　　　Exit.

100 *Wildair.* Ha, ha, ha, poor Colonel!—O the delight of an
ingenious Mistriss! what a life and briskness it adds to an
Amour, like the Loves of mighty *Jove*, still sueing in different
shapes. A *Legerdemain Mistriss*, who, *presto, pass*, and she's
vanish'd, then *Hey*, in an instant in your Arms agen. (*Going.*)

　　　　　　　　　　Enter Vizard.

Vizard. Well met, Sir *Harry*, what news from the Island of
Love?

Wildair. Faith we made but a broken Voyage by your Card;
but now I am bound for another Port: I told you the Colonel
was my Rival.

110 *Vizard.* The Colonel! curs'd Misfortune! another! (*Aside.*)

Wildair. But the civilest in the world, he brought me word where my Mistriss lodges; the Story's too long to tell you now, for I must fly.

Vizard. What! have you given over all thoughts of *Angelica?*

Wildair. No, no, I'll think of her some other time, But now for the Lady *Lurewell*; Wit and Beauty calls.

That Mistriss ne're can pall her Lover's Joys,
Whose Wit can whet, when e're her Beauty cloys.
Her little amorous Frauds all Truths excel;
And make us happy, being deceiv'd so well.   120

Exit.

Vizard. (*Solus.*)—The Colonel my Rival too! how shall I manage? There is but one way—him and the Knight will I set a tilting, where one cuts t'others Throat, and the Survivor's hang'd: So there will be two Rivals pretty decently dispos'd of. Since Honour may oblige them to play the Fool, why should not Necessity engage me to play the Knave?

Exit.

[ACT II. Scene iv.]

SCENE, Lurewell*'s Lodgings.*

Lurewell *and* Parly.

Lurewell. Has my Servant brought me the Money from my Merchant?

Parly. No, Madam, he met Alderman *Smuggler* at *Charing-Cross*, who has promis'd to wait on you himself immediatly.

Lurewell. 'Tis odd, that this old Rogue shou'd pretend to love me, and at the same time cheat me of my Money.

Parly. 'Tis well, Madam, if he don't cheat you of your Estate; for you say the Writings are in his hands.

Lurewell. But what satisfaction can I get of him?

Enter Smuggler.

Mr. Alderman, your Servant, have you brought me any   10 Money, Sir?

Smuggler. Faith, Madam, trading is very dead; what with paying the Taxes, raising the Customs, Losses at Sea abroad, and maintaining our Wives at home, the Bank is reduc'd very low.

Lurewell. Come, come, Sir, these Evasions won't serve your turn, I must have Money, Sir,—I hope you don't design to cheat me.

Smuggler. Cheat you, Madam! have a care what you say:
20 I'm an Alderman, Madam; cheat you, Madam! I have been an honest Citizen these five and thirty years!

Lurewell. An honest Citizen! bear witness, *Parly*! I shall trap him in more Lies presently—. Come, Sir, tho I'm a Woman, I can take a course.

Smuggler. What Course, Madam? You'l go to Law, will ye? I can maintain a Suit of Law, be it right or wrong, these forty years, I'm sure of that, thanks to the honest Practice of the Courts.

Lurewell. Sir, I'll blast your Reputation, and so ruin your
30 Credit.

Smuggler. Blast my Reputation! he, he, he: why I'm a Religious Man, Madam, I have been very instrumental in the Reformation of Manners; ruin my Credit! ah, poor Woman: There is but one way, Madam,—you have a sweet leering Eye.

Lurewell. You instrumental in the Reformation! how?

Smuggler. *I whipt all the Whores Cut and Long-Tail, out of the Parish*—: Ah! that leering Eye! *Then I voted for pulling down the Play-house*—: Ah that Ogle, that Ogle!—*Then my own pious*
40 *Example*—Ah that Lip, that Lip.

Lurewell. Here's a Religious Rogue for you now!—as I hope to be sav'd I have a good mind to beat the old Monster. [*Aside.*]

Smuggler. Madam, I have brought you about a hundred and fifty Guineas (a great deal of Mony as times go) and—

Lurewell. Come, give it me.

Smuggler. Ah that hand, that hand, that pretty soft, white—I have brought it you see, but the condition of the Obligation is such, that whereas that leering Eye, that pouting Lip, that pretty soft Hand, that—you understand me, you
50 understand I'm sure you do, you little Rogue—

Lurewell. Here's a Villain now, so covetous that he won't wench upon his own Cost, but would bribe me with my own Mony. I will be reveng'd. [*Aside.*]—Upon my word Mr. Alderman you make me blush, what d'ye mean, pray?

Smuggler. See here, Madam (*Puts a piece of Mony in his*

Mouth.) *Buss and Guinea, buss and Guinea, buss and Guinea.*
Lurewell. Well, Mr. Alderman, you have such pretty yellow
Teeth, and green Gums, that I will, ha, ha, ha, ha.
Smuggler. Will you indeed, he, he, he, my little Cocket; and
when, and where, and how?   60
Lurewell. 'Twill be a difficult point, Sir, to secure both our
Honours, you must therefore be disguis'd, Mr. Alderman.
Smuggler. P'shaw! no matter, I am an old Fornicator, I'm
not half so Religious as I seem to be. You little Rogue, why
I'm disguis'd as I am, our Sanctity is all outside, all
Hypocrisy.
Lurewell. No man is seen to come into this House after
Night fall; you must therefore sneak in, when 'tis dark, in
Woman's Cloaths.
Smuggler. I gad so, cod so—I have a Suit a purpose, my   70
little Cocket, I love to be disguis'd, I cod I make a very
handsom Woman, I cod I do.
        Enter Servant, *whispers* Lurewell.
Lurewell. Oh! Mr. Alderman, shall I beg you to walk into
next Rome, here are some Strangers coming up.
Smuggler. Buss and Guinea first, ah my little Cocket.
                                                          Exit.
            Enter Wildair.
Wildair. My Life, my Soul, my all that Heaven can give.
Lurewell. Death's Life with thee, without thee Death to live.
Welcome, my dear Sir *Harry*, I see you got my Directions.
Wildair. Directions! in the most charming manner, thou
dear *Matchiavel* of Intreague.   80
Lurewell. Still brisk and airy I find, Sir *Harry.*
Wildair. The sight of you, Madam, exalts my Air, and makes
Joy lighten in my Face.
Lurewell. I have a thousand Questions to ask you, Sir *Harry*;
How d'ye like *France*?
Wildair. Ah! est le plus beau pais du monde.
Lurewell. Then what made you leave it so soon?
Wildair. Madam, Vous Voyez que je vous suy partout.
Lurewell. O Monsieur, je vouz suis fort obligee—But where's the
Court now?   90
Wildair. At *Marli*, Madam.
Lurewell. And where my Count *Le Valier*?

Wildair. His Body's in the Church of *Nostre Dame*, I don't know where his Soul is.

Lurewell. What Disease did he dye of?

Wildair. A *Duel*, Madam, I was his *Doctor*.

Lurewell. How d'ye mean?

Wildair. As most Doctors do, I kill'd him.

Lurewell. *En Cavalier*, my dear Knight Errant, well and how;
100 And how, what Intreagues, what Gallantries are carrying on in the *Beau Monde*?

Wildair. I should ask you that question, Madam, since your Ladyship makes the *Beau Monde* whereever you come.

Lurewell. Ah! Sir *Harry*, I've been almost ruin'd, pester'd to death here by the incessant Attacks of a mighty Colonel, he has besieg'd me as close as our Army did *Namur*.

Wildair. I hope your Ladyship did not surrender tho.

Lurewell. No, no, but was forc'd to capitulate; but since you are come to raise the Seige, we'll dance, and sing, and laugh.

110 *Wildair.* And love and kiss—*Montrez moy votre Chambre*.

Lurewell. *Attande, Attande, en peu*—I remember, Sir *Harry*, you promis'd me in *Paris* never to ask that impertinent Question agen.

Wildair. P'shaw, Madam, that was above two months ago; besides, Madam, Treaties made in *France* are never kept.

Lurewell. Wou'd you marry me, Sir *Harry*?

Wildiar. Oh! *Le marriage est une grand male*—but I will marry you.

Lurewell. Your Word, Sir, is not to be rely'd on: if a
120 Gentleman will forfeit his Honour in Dealings of Business, we may reasonably suspect his Fidelity in an Amour.

Wildair. My Honour in Dealings of Business! why, Madam, I never had any business in all my life.

Lurewell. Yes, Sir *Harry*, I have heard a very odd Story, and am sorry that a Gentleman of your Figure should undergo the Scandal.

Wildair. Out with it, Madam.

Lurewell. Why the Merchant, Sir, that transmitted your Bills of Exchange to you in *France*, complains of some indirect
130 and dishonourable Dealings.

Wildair. Who? old *Smuggler*!

Lurewell. Ay, ay, you know him I find.

Wildair. I have no less than reason, I think; why the Rogue has cheated me of above five hundred pound within these three years.

Lurewell. 'Tis your business then to acquit your self publickly, for he spreads the Scandal every where.

Wildair. Acquit my self publickly!—Here Sirrah, my Coach, I'll drive instantly into the City, and cane the old Villain round the *Royal Exchange*; he shall run the Gauntlet thro a 140 thousand brusht Beavers and formal Cravats.

Lurewell. Why he's in the House now, Sir.

Wildair. What, in this House?

Lurewell. Ay, in the next Room.

Wildair. Then, Sirrah, lend me your Cudgel.

Lurewell. Sir *Harry*, you won't raise a Disturbance in my House?

Wildair. Disturbance, Madam, No, no, I'll beat him with the Temper of a Philosopher; here, Mrs. *Parly*, shew me the Gentleman.   150

                                        Exit with Parly.

Lurewell. Now shall I get the old Monster well beaten, and Sir *Harry* pester'd next Term with Bloodsheds, Batteries, Costs and Damages, Sollicitors and Attornies; and if they don't teize him out of his good humour, I'll never plot agen.

                                                        Exit.

[ACT II. Scene v.]

SCENE, *Changes to another Room in the same House.*

Enter Smuggler.

Smuggler. O This damn'd Tide-waiter! A Ship and Cargo worth five thousand pound! why 'tis richly worth five hundred Perjuries.

                            Enter Wildair.

Wildair. Dear Mr. Alderman, I'm your most devoted and humble Servant.

Smuggler. My best Friend Sir *Harry*, you're welcome to *England*.

Wildair. I'll assure you Sir, there's not a Man in the King's Dominions I'm gladder to meet.

10 *Smuggler.* O Lord, Sir, you Travellers have the most obliging ways with you.

Wildair. There is a Business Mr. Alderman fall'n out, which you may oblige me infinitely by—I am very sorry that I'm forc'd to be troublesome; but necessity, Mr. Alderman.

Smuggler. Ay, Sir, as you say necessity—But upon my word, Sir, I am very short of Mony at present, but—

Wildair. That's not the matter, Sir, I'm above an Obligation that way, but the Business is, I am reduc'd to an indispensible necessity of being oblig'd to you for a Beating—Here take this

20 Cudgel.

Smuggler. A Beating Sir *Harry*! ha, ha, ha, I beat a Knight Baronet! an Alderman turn Cudgel-Player, ha, ha, ha.

Wildair. Upon my word, Sir, you must beat me, or I cudgel you, take your choice.

Smuggler. P'shaw, p'shaw, you jest.

Wildair. Nay, 'tis as sure as fate; so Alderman I hope you'll pardon my Curiosity.

Smuggler. Curiosity! Duce take your Curiosity, Sir, what d'ye mean.

30 *Wildair.* Nothing at all, I'm but in jest, Sir.

Smuggler. O, I can take any thing in jest, but a Man might imagine by the smartness of the Stroak, that you were in down right earnest.

Wildair. Not in the least, Sir, (*Strikes him.*) not in the least indeed Sir.

Smuggler. Pray good Sir, no more of your Jests, for they are the bluntest Jests that I ever knew.

Wildair. (*Strikes.*) I heartily beg your Pardon with all my Heart, Sir.

40 *Smuggler.* Pardon Sir, well Sir, that is satisfaction enough from a Gentleman; but seriously now if you pass any more of your Jests upon me, I shall grow angry.

Wildair. I humbly beg your permission to break one or two more. (*Striking him.*)

Smuggler. O Lord, Sir, you'll break my Bones: are you mad Sir; Murder, Felony, Manslaughter. (Wildair *knocks him down.*)

Wildair. Sir, I beg you ten thousand Pardons; but I am

absolutely compell'd to't upon my Honour, Sir; nothing can
be more averse to my Inclinations, than to jest with my
honest, dear, loving, obliging Friend, the Alderman.   50
     Striking him all this while, Smuggler *tumbles over and*
          over, and shakes out his Pocket-book on the Floor;
                    Lurewell *enters, takes it up.*
Lurewell. The old Rogue's Pocket-book, this may be of use.
(*Aside.*) O Lord, Sir *Harry*'s murdering the poor old Man—
Smuggler. O dear Madam, I was beaten in jest, 'till I am
murder'd in good earnest.
Lurewell. Well, well, I'll bring you off *Senior—Frapez, Frapez.*
Smuggler. O for Charity's sake, Madam, rescue a poor
Citizen.
Lurewell. O you barbarous Man, hold, hold, *Frapez, plus*
rudement, Frapez, I wonder you are not asham'd, (*Holding*
Wildair.) A poor reverend honest Elder—(*Helps* Smuggler *up.*) 60
It makes me weep to see him in this Condition, poor Man!
Now the Devil take you Sir *Harry*—For not beating Him
harder: Well, my Dear, you shall come at Night, and I'll make
you amends. (*Here Sir* Harry *takes Snush.*)
Smuggler. Madam, I will have amends before I leave the
Place, Sir; How durst you use me thus?
Wildair. Sir?
Smuggler. Sir, I say that I will have satisfaction.
Wildair. With all my Heart. (*Throws Snush into his Eyes.*)
Smuggler. O, Murder, Blindness, Fire; O Madam, Madam, 70
get me some Water, Water, Fire, Fire, Water.
                                        Exit with Lurewell.
Wildair. How pleasant is resenting an Injury without
Passion: 'Tis the Beauty of Revenge.
     Let Statesmen plot, and under Business groan,
     And settling publick Quiet lose their own;
     Let Soldiers drudg and fight for Pay or Fame,
     For when they're shot, I think 'tis much the same.
     Let Scholars vex their Brains with Mood and Tense,
     And mad with strength of Reason, Fools Commence.
     Losing their Wits in searching after Sense;   80
     Their Summum Bonum *they must toil to gain,*
     And seeking Pleasure, spend their Life in Pain.
                    62 For] Q2; Fear

I make the most of Life, no hour mispend,
Pleasure's the Means, and Pleasure is my End.
No Spleen, no Trouble shall my time destroy.
Life's but a Span; I'll every Inch enjoy.

Exit.

[*The End of the Second Act.*]

ACT III. [Scene i.]

SCENE, *The Street.*

Enter Standard *and* Vizard.

Standard. I bring him word where she lodg'd! I the Civilist Rival in the World! 'tis impossible.

Vizard. I shall urge it no further, Sir; I only thought Sir, That my Character in the World might add Authority To my Words without so many Repetitions.

Standard. Pardon me, Dear *Vizard*—Our Belief struggles hard, Before it can be brought to yield to the Disadvantage Of what we love; 'tis so great an Abuse to our Judgment, That it makes the Faults of our Choice our own failing. But what said
10 Sir *Harry*?

Vizard. He pitied the poor credulous Colonel, laugh'd heartily, Flew away with all the Raptures of a Bridegroom, repeating these Lines.

A Mistriss ne're can pall her Lover's Joys,
Whose Wit can whet when e're her Beauty cloys.

Standard. A *Mistriss ne're can pall!* By all my Wrongs he whores her! and I'm made their Property, Vengeance! *Vizard*, you must carry a Note from me to Sir *Harry*.

Vizard. What! a Challenge! I hope you don't design to fight?
20 *Standard.* What! wear the Livery of my King and Pocket an Affront! 'twere an abuse to his Sacred Majesty, a Souldier's Sword, *Vizard*, should start of it self to Redress its Master's Wrong.

Vizard. However, Sir, I think it not proper for me to carry any such Message between Friends.

Standard. I have ne're a Servant here, what shall I do?

Vizard. There's *Tom Errand*, the Porter, that plys at the *Blew Posts*, And who knows Sir *Harry* and his Haunts very well, You may send a Note by him.

Standard. Here, you, Friend.   30

Vizard. I have now some Business, and must take my Leave, I wou'd advise you nevertheless against this Affair.

Standard. No whispering now, nor telling of Friends to prevent us. He that disappoints a Man of an honourable Revenge, may love him foolishly like a Wife, but never value him as a Friend.

Vizard. Nay the Devil take him that parts you, say I.

Exit.

Enter Porter [Tom Errand] *running.*

Tom Errand. Did your Honour call a Porter?

Standard. Is your Name *Tom Errand?*

Tom Errand. People call me so, an't like your Worship—   40

Standard. D'ye know Sir *Harry Wildair?*

Tom Errand. Ay, very well Sir, he's one of my Masters; many a round half Crown have I had of his Worship, he's newly come home from *France*, Sir.

Standard. Go to the next Coffee-house, and wait for me. O Woman, Woman, how blest is Man, when favour'd by your Smiles, and how accurst when all those Smiles are found But wanton baits to sooth us to Destruction.

Thus our chief Joys with base Allays are curst,
And our best things, when once corrupted, worst.

Exit.   50

Enter Wildair *and* Clincher Senior *following.*

Clincher Senior. Sir, Sir, Sir, having some Business of Importance to communicate to you, I would beg your Attention to a trifling Affair that I wou'd impart to you.

Wildair. What is your trifling business of Importance pray sweet Sir?

Clincher Senior. Pray Sir, are the Roads deep between this and *Paris?*

Wildair. Why that Question, Sir?

Clincher Senior. Because I design to go to the *Jubilee*, Sir; I understand that you are a Traveller, Sir; there is an Air of 60 Travel in the Tie of your Cravat, Sir, there is indeed, Sir—I suppose, Sir, you bought this Lace in *Flanders.*

61 your] Q2; you

Wildair. No, Sir, this Lace was made in *Norway*.

Clincher Senior. Norway, Sir!

Wildair. Yes Sir, of the shavings of deal Boards.

Clincher Senior. That's very strange now, Faith—Lace made of the shavings of deal Boards; I Gad Sir, you Travellers see very strange things abroad, very incredible things abroad, indeed. Well, I'll have a Cravat of that very same Lace before
70 I come home.

Wildair. But Sir? what Preparations have you made for your Journey?

Clincher Senior. A Case of Pocket-pistols for the Bravo's—and a swimming Girdle.

Wildair. Why these, Sir.

Clincher Senior. O Lord, Sir, I'll tell you—suppose us in *Rome* now; away goes I to some Ball—for I'll be a mighty Beau. Then as I said, I go to some Ball, or some Bear-baiting, 'tis all one you know—then comes a fine *Italian Bona Roba*, and
80 plucks me by the Sleeve, *Siegniour Angle, Siegniour Angle,*—she's a very fine Lady, observe that—*Seigniour Angle,* says she,— *Siegniora,* says I, and trips after her to the corner of a Street, suppose it *Russel*-Street here, or any other Street; then you know I must invite her to the Tavern, I can do no less.—There up comes her Bravo, the *Italian* grows sawcy, and I give him an *English* douse of the Face. I can Box, Sir, Box tightly, I was a Prentice, Sir,—but then, Sir, he whips out his *Stilletto,* and I whips out my *Bull-Dog*—slaps him through, trips down Stairs, turns the corner of *Russel*-Street again, and
90 whips me into the Ambassador's Train, and there I'm safe as a Beau behind the Scenes.

Wildair. Was your Pistol charg'd, Sir?

Clincher Senior. Only a brace of Bullets, that's all, Sir, I design to shoot seven *Italians* a Week, Sir.

Wildair. Sir, you won't have Provocation.

Clincher Senior. Provocation, Sir! Zauns, Sir, I'll kill any Man for treading upon my Corn, and there will be a devilish Throng of People there; they say that all the Princes in *Italy* will be there.

100   *Wildair.* And all the Fops and Fidlers in *Europe*—but the use of your swimming Girdle, pray, Sir?

Clincher Senior. O Lord, Sir, that's easie. Suppose the Ship cast away; now, whilst other foolish People are busie at their Prayers, I whip on my swimming Girdle, claps a Months Provision into my Pockets, and sails me away like an Egg in a Duck's Belly.—And heark'ee, Sir, I have a new Project in my Head. Where d'ye think my swimming Girdle shall carry me upon this Occasion: 'Tis a new Project?

Wildair. Where, Sir?

Clincher Senior. To *Civita Vecchia*, Faith and Troth, and so save the Charges of my Passage! Well, Sir, you must Pardon me now, I'm going to see my Mistress.

Exit.

Wildair. This Fellow's an accomplish'd Ass before he goes abroad. Well! this *Angelica* has got into my Heart, and I can't get her out of my Head. I must pay her t'other Visit.

Exit.

[ACT III. Scene ii.]

SCENE, Lady Darling *'s House.*

Angelica sola.

Angelica. Unhappy State of Woman! whose chief Virtue is but Ceremony, and our much boasted Modesty but a slavish Restraint. The strict confinement on our Words makes our Thoughts ramble more; and what preserves our outward Fame, destroys our inward Quiet.—'Tis hard that Love shou'd be deny'd the privilege of Hatred; that Scandal and Detraction shou'd be so much indulg'd, yet sacred Love and Truth debarr'd our Conversation.

Enter Lady Darling, Clincher Junior, *and* Dicky.

Lady Darling. This is my Daughter, Cousin.

Dicky. Now, Sir, remember your three scrapes.

Clincher Junior. (*Saluting* Angelica.) One two, three, (*Kisses her.*) your humble Servant. Was not that right, *Dicky.*

Dicky. Ay faith, Sir, but why don't you speak to her.

Clincher Junior. I beg your pardon, *Dicky.* I know my distance, wou'd you have me speak to a Lady at the first sight?

Dicky. Ay, Sir, by all means, the first Aim is the surest.

Clincher Junior. Now for a good Jest, to make her laugh heartily—By *Jupiter Ammon* I'll go give her a Kiss. (*Goes towards her.*)

Enter Wildair, *Interposing.*

Wildair. 'Tis all to no purpose, I told you so before, your
20 pitiful Five Guinea's will never do—you may march, Sir, for as far as Five Hundred Pounds will go, I'll out-bid you.

Clincher Junior. What the Devil! the Mad-man's here again.

Lady Darling. Bless me, Cousin! what d'ye mean? Affront a Gentlemen of his Quality in my House.

Clincher Junior. Quality! why, Madam, I don't know what you mean by your Madmen, and your Beaux, and your Quality.—They're all alike I believe.

Lady Darling. Pray, Sir, walk with me into the next Room.

Exit Lady Darling *leading* Clincher Junior, Dicky *follows.*

Angelica. Sir, if your Conversation be no more agreeable
30 than 'twas the last time, I wou'd advise you to make it as short as you can.

Wildair. The Offences of my last Visit, Madam, bore their Punishment in the Commission; and have made me as uneasie 'till I receive Pardon, as your Ladyship can be 'till I sue for it.

Angelica. Sir *Harry* I did not well understand the Offence, and must therefore proportion it to the greatness of your Apology; if you wou'd therefore have me think it light, take no great Pains in an Excuse.

Wildair. How sweet must be the Lips that guard that
40 Tongue! [*Aside.*] Then, Madam, no more of past Offences, let us prepare for Joys to come; let this seal my Pardon. (*Kisses her Hand.*) And this (*Again.*) initiate me to farther Happiness.

Angelica. Hold, Sir,—one Question, Sir *Harry*, and pray answer plainly, d'ye love me?

Wildair. Love you! Does Fire ascend? Do Hypocrites Dissemble? Usurers love Gold, or Great Men Flattery? Doubt these, then question that I Love.

Angelica. This shows your Gallantry, Sir, but not your Love.

50 *Wildair.* View your own Charms, Madam, then judge my Passion; your Beauty ravishes my Eye, your Voice my Ear, and your Touch has thrill'd my melting Soul.

Angelica. If your Words be real, 'tis in your Power to raise an equal Flame in me.

Wildair. Nay then—I seize—

Angelica. Hold, Sir, 'tis also possible to make me detest and scorn you worse than the most profligate of your deceiving Sex.

Wildair. Ha! A very odd turn this. I hope, Madam, you only affect Anger, because you know your Frowns are Becoming. 60

Angelica. Sir *Harry*, you being the best Judge of your own Designs, can best understand whether my Anger shou'd be real or dissembled, think what strict Modesty shou'd bear, then judge of my Resentments.

Wildair. Strict Modesty shou'd bear! Why faith Madam, I believe the strictest Modesty may bear Fifty Guinea's, and I don't believe 'twill bear one Farthing more.

Angelica. What d'mean? Sir.

Wildair. Nay, Madam, what do you mean? If you go to that, I think now Fifty Guinea's is a very fine offer for your strict 70 Modesty, as you call it.

Angelica. 'Tis more Charitable, Sir *Harry*, to charge the Impertinence of a Man of your Figure, on his defect in Understanding, than on his want of Manners—I'm afraid you're Mad, Sir.

Wildair. Why, Madam, you're enough to make any Man mad. S'death, are not you a—

Angelica. What, Sir?

Wildair. Why, a Lady of—strict Modesty, if you will have it so. 80

Angelica. I shall never hereafter trust common Report, which represented you, Sir, a Man of Honour, Wit, and Breeding; for I find you very deficient in them all.

Exit.

Wildair. (*Solus.*) Now I find that the strict Pretences which the Ladies of Pleasure make to strict Modesty, is the reason why those of Quality are asham'd to wear it.

Enter Vizard.

Vizard. Ay, Sir *Harry*, have I caught you? well, and what Success.

Wildair. Success! 'tis a shame for you young Fellows in Town here, to let the Wenches grow so sawcy: I offer'd her 90

Fifty Guinea's, and she was in her Airs presently. I cou'd have had two Countesses in *Paris* for half the Money, and *Je vous remercie* in to the Bargain.

Vizard. Gone in her Airs say you? And did not you follow her?

Wildair. Whither shou'd I follow her?

Vizard. Into her Bed-Chamber, Man. She went on purpose; you a Man of Gallantry, and not understand that a Lady's best pleas'd when she puts on her Airs, as you call it.

100 *Wildair.* She talk'd to me of strict Modesty, and stuff.

Vizard. Certainly most Women magnify their Modesty, for the same reason that Cowards boast their Courage, because they have least on't. Come, come, Sir *Harry*, when you make your next Assault, incourage your Spirits with brisk *Burgundy*, if you succeed, 'tis well; if not, you have a fair excuse for your Rudeness. I'll go in, and make your Peace for what's past. Oh! I had almost forgot—Colonel *Standard* wants to speak with you about some Business.

Wildair. I'll wait upon him presently, d'ye know where he 110 may be found.

Vizard. In the *Piazza* of *Covent-Garden*, about an Hour hence, I promised to see him, and there you may meet him; to have your Throat cut. (*Aside.*) I'll go in and intercede for you.

Wildair. But no foul play with the Lady, *Vizard.*

Vizard. No fair play I can assure you.

Exit.

[ACT III. Scene iii.]

SCENE, *The Street before* Lurewell's Lodgings;
Clincher Senior *and* Lurewell *Coqueting in
the Balcony.*

Enter Standard.

Standard. How weak is Reason in disputes of Love? that daring Reason which so oft pretends to question Works of high Omnipotence, yet poorly truckles to our weakest Passions, and yields implicite Faith to foolish Love, paying

blind Zeal to faithless Womans Eyes. I've heard her Falshood
with such pressing Proofs, that I no longer shou'd distrust it.
Yet still my Love wou'd baffle Demonstration, and make
Impossibilities seem probable. (*Looks up.*) Ha! that Fool too!
what! stoop so low as that Animal.—'Tis true, Women once
fall'n, like Cowards in despair, will stick at nothing, there's no   10
Medium in their Actions. They must be bright as Angels, or
black as Fiends. But now for my Revenge, I'll kick her Cully
before her Face, call her a Whore, curse the whole Sex, and so
leave her.

Goes in.

Lurewell *comes down with* Clincher Senior.
The Scene changes to a Dining-Room.

Lurewell. O Lord, Sir, 'tis my Husband: What will become
of you?

Clincher Senior. Eh! Your Husband! Oh, I shall be murder'd:
What shall I do? Where shall I run? I'll creep into an Oven;
I'll climb up the Chimney; I'll fly; I'll swim;—I wish to the
Lord I were at the *Jubilee* now.—   20

Lurewell. Can't you think of any thing, Sir?

Enter Tom Errand.

What do you want, Sir?

Tom Errand. Madam, I am looking for Sir *Harry Wildair*; I
saw him come in here this Morning; and did imagine he might
be here still.

Lurewell. A lucky Hitt! [*Aside.*] Here Friend, change Clothes
with this Gentleman quickly: Strip.

Clincher Senior. Ay, ay, quickly strip: I'll give you Half a
Crown. Come here: So.

They change Clothes.

Lurewell. Now slip you, (*To* Clincher Senior.) down stairs,   30
and wait at the Door till my Husband be gone; And get you in
there (*To* Tom Errand.) till I call you.

Puts Tom Errand *into the next Room.*
Enter Standard.

Oh, Sir! Are you come? I wonder Sir, how you have the
Confidence to approach me after so base a Trick.

Standard. O Madam, all your Artifices won't prevail.

Lurewell. Nay Sir, Your Artifices won't avail. I thought, Sir,
that I gave you Caution enough against troubling me with Sir

Harry Wildair's Company when I sent his Letters back by you:
Yet you forsooth must tell him where I lodg'd, and expose me
40 again to his impertinent Courtship.

Standard. I expose you to his Courtship!

Lurewell. I'll lay my Life you'll deny it now: Come, come,
Sir, a pitiful Lye is as scandalous to a Red Coat as an Oath to
a Black. Did not Sir *Harry* himself tell me, that he found out by
you where I lodg'd?

Standard. You're all Lyes: First your Heart is false, your
Eyes are double; one Look belyes another: And then your
Tongue does contradict them all.—Madam, I see a little Devil
just now hammering out a Lye in your Pericranium.

50 *Lurewell.* As I hope for Mercy he's in the right on't. (*Aside.*)
Hold, Sir, You have got the Play-house Cant upon your
Tongue; and think that Wit may privilege your Railing: But I
must tell you, Sir, that what is Satyr upon the Stage, is ill
Manners here.

Standard. What is feign'd upon the Stage, is here in Reality.
Real Falshood. Yes, yes, Madam,—I expos'd you to the
Courtship of your Fool *Clincher* too? I hope your Female Wiles
will impose that upon me—also—

Lurewell. Clincher! Nay, now, you're stark mad. I know no
60 such Person.

Standard. O Woman in Perfection! not know him! 'Slife,
Madam, Can my Eyes, my piercing jealous Eyes be so
deluded? Nay, Madam, my Nose could not mistake him; for I
smelt the Fop by his Pulvilio from the Balcony down to the
Street.

Lurewell. The Balcony! Ha, ha, ha, the Balcony! I'll be
hang'd but he has mistaken Sir *Harry Wildair*'s Footman with
a new *French* Livery, for a Beau.

Standard. S'Death Madam, what is there in me that looks
70 like a Cully? Did I not see him?

Lurewell. No, no, you cou'd not see him; You're dreaming,
Colonel: Will you believe your Eyes, now, that I have rubb'd
them open?—Here, you Friend.

        Enter Tom Errand *in* Clincher Senior*'s Cloaths.*

Standard. This is Illusion all; My Eyes conspire against
themselves. 'Tis Legerdemain.

Lurewell. Legerdemain! Is that all your Acknowledgment

for your rude Behaviour?—Oh, what a Curse it is to love as I
do!—But don't presume too far, Sir, on my Affection: For such
ungenerous Usage will soon return my tir'd Heart.—Be gone
Sir (*To* Tom Errand.) to your impertinent Master, and tell 80
him I shall never be at leisure to receive any of his
troublesome Visits:—send to me to know when I shou'd be at
home!—Be gone Sir:—I am sure he has made me an
unfortunate Woman. (*Weeps.*)
    Standard. Nay, then there is no Certainty in Nature; and
Truth is only Falshood well disguis'd.
    Lurewell. Sir, had not I own'd my fond foolish Passion, I
shou'd not have been subject to such unjust Suspicions; But
'tis an ungrateful Return. (*Weeping.*)
    Standard. Now where are all my firm Resolves? I will believe 90
her just. My Passion rais'd my Jealousie; then why mayn't
Love be blind in finding faults as in excusing them?
[*Aside.*]—I hope, Madam, you'll pardon me, since Jealousie
that magnify'd my Suspicion is as much the Effect of Love as
my Easiness in being satisfy'd.
    Lurewell. Easiness in being satisfy'd! You Men have got an
insolent way of extorting Pardon, by persisting in your Faults.
No, no, Sir, cherish your Suspicions, and feed upon your
Jealousie: 'Tis fit Meat for your squeamish Stomach.
       With me all Women shou'd this Rule pursue: 100
       Who thinks us false, shou'd never find us true.
                                            Exit in a Rage.
    Enter Clincher Senior *in the Porter's* [Tom Errand'*s*] *Cloaths.*
    Clincher Senior. Well, Intriguing is the prettiest pleasantest
thing for a Man of my Parts:—How shall we laugh at the
Husband when he is gone?—How sillily he looks! He's in
labour of Horns already,—to make a Colonel a Cuckold!
'Twill be rare News for the Alderman. (*Aside.*)
    Standard. All this Sir *Harry* has occasion'd; but he's brave,
and will afford me just Revenge:—O! this is the Porter I sent
the Challenge by:—Well Sir, have you found him?
    Clincher Senior. What the Devil does he mean now?   110
    Standard. Have you given Sir *Harry* the Note, Fellow?
    Clincher Senior. The Note! What Note?

Standard. The Letter, Blockhead, which I sent by you to Sir
Harry Wildair, have you seen him?
Clincher Senior. O Lord, what shall I say now? [*Aside.*] Seen
him! Yes Sir.—No Sir.—I have Sir.—I have not Sir.
Standard. The Fellow's mad. Answer me directly Sirrah, or
I'll break your Head.
Clincher Senior. I know Sir *Harry* very well, Sir; but as to the
120 Note Sir, I can't remember a Word on't: Truth is, I have a
very bad Memory,
Standard. O Sir, I'll quicken your Memory. (*Strikes him.*)
Clincher Senior. Zauns, Sir, hold,—I did give him the Note.
Standard. And what Answer?
Clincher Senior. I mean Sir, I did not give him the Note.
Standard. What, d'ye banter, Rascal? (*Strikes him again.*)
Clincher Senior. Hold Sir, hold, He did send an Answer.
Standard. What was't Villain?
Clincher Senior. Why truly Sir, I have forgot it: I told you
130 that I had a very treacherous Memory.
Standard. I'll engage you shall remember me this Month,
Rascal.

　　　　　　　　　　　　　　　Beats him off, and Exit.
　　　　　　　Enter Lurewell *and* Parly.
Lurewell. Forthoon, forthoon, forthoon, This is better than I
expected; but Fortune still helps the Industrious.
　　　　　　　　Enter Clincher Senior.
Clincher Senior. Ah! The Devil take all Intriguing, say I, and
him who first invented Canes:—That curs'd Colonel has got
such a Knack of beating his Men, that he has left the Mark of
a Collar of Bandileers about my Shoulders.
Lurewell. O my poor Gentleman! And was it beaten?
140　*Clincher Senior.* Yes, I have been beaten: But where's my
Cloathes, my Cloaths?
Lurewell. What, you won't leave me so soon, my Dear, will
ye?
Clincher Senior. Will ye? If ever I peep into a Colonel's Tent
agen, may I be forc'd to run the Gauntlet:—But my Cloaths,
Madam.
Lurewell. I sent the Porter down stairs with them: Did not
you meet him?

---

133 *Forthoon, forthoon, forthoon*] Q4; *Fortboon, fortboon, fortboon*

Clincher Senior. Meet him! No, not I.

Parly. No? He went out of the Back-door, and is run clear 150
away I'm afraid.

Clincher Senior. Gone, say you? And with my Cloaths? my
fine *Jubilee* Cloaths?—O, the Rogue, the Thief!—I'll have
him hang'd for Murder:—But how shall I get home in this
Pickle?

Parly. I'm afraid, Sir, the Colonel will be back presently; for
he dines at home.

Clincher Senior. Oh, then I must sneak off! Was ever Man so
manag'd! to have his Coat well thrash'd, and lose his Coat
too?   160

Exit.

Lurewell. Thus the Noble Poet spoke Truth.
  Nothing sutes worse with Vice than want of Sense:
  Fools are still wicked at their own Expence.

Parly. Methinks Madam, the Injuries you have suffer'd by
Men must be very great, to raise such heavy Resentments
against the whole Sex.

Lurewell. The greatest Injury that Woman cou'd sustain;
They robb'd me of that Jewel, which preserv'd, exalts our Sex
almost to Angels: But, destroy'd, debases us below the worst
of Brutes, Mankind.   170

Parly. But I think, Madam, your Anger shou'd be only
confin'd to the Author of your Wrongs.

Lurewell. The Author! Alas, I know him not, which makes
my Wrongs the greater.

Parly. Not know him! 'Tis odd Madam, that a Man shou'd
rob you of that same Jewel you mention'd, and you not know
him.

Lurewell. Leave Trifling;—'tis a Subject that always sowres
my Temper; but since by thy faithful Service I have some
Reason to confide in your Secresie, hear the strange Relation: 180
—Some twelve, twelve Years ago I liv'd at my Father's House
in *Oxfordshire*, blest with Innocence, the ornamental, but weak
Guard of blooming Beauty: I was then just Fifteen, an Age oft
fatal to the Female Sex; Our Youth is tempting, our
Innocence credulous, Romances moving, Love powerful, and
Men are—Villains. Then it hapned that three young Gentlemen from the University coming into the Country, and being
benighted, and Strangers, call'd at my Father's: He was very

glad of their Company, and offer'd them the Entertainment of
190 his House.
  Parly. Which they accepted, no Doubt: Oh! these strouling
Collegians are never abroad, but upon some Mischief.
  Lurewell. They had some private Frolick or Design in their
Heads, as appear'd by their not naming one another, which
my Father perceiving, out of Civility, made no enquiry into
their Affairs, two of them had a heavy, pedantick, University
Air, a sort of disagreeable scholastick Boorishness in their
Behaviour, but the third!
  Parly. Ay! the third, Madam,—the third of all things, they
200 say, is very Critical.
  Lurewell. He was—but in short, Nature cut him out for my
undoing;—he seem'd to be about Eighteen.
  Parly. A fit Match for your Fifteen as cou'd be.
  Lurewell. He had a genteel Sweetness in his Face, a graceful
Comeliness in his Person, and his Tongue was fit to sooth soft
Innocence to ruine: His very Looks were Witty, and his
expressive Eyes spoke softer prettier things than Words cou'd
frame.
  Parly. There will be Mischief by and by; I never heard a
210 Woman talk so much of Eyes, but there were Tears presently
after.
  Lurewell. His Discourse was directed to my Father, but his
Looks to me. After Supper I went to my Chamber, and read
Cassandra, then went to Bed, and dreamt of him all Night, rose
in the Morning, and made Verses; so fell desperately in
Love—my Father was so pleas'd with his Conversation, that
he beg'd their Company next Day; they consented, and next
Night, *Parly*—
  Parly. Ay, next night,Madam,—next Night (I'm afraid)
220 was a Night indeed.
  Lurewell. He brib'd my Maid with his Gold out of her
Honesty, and me with his Rhetorick out of my Honour—she
admitted him to my Chamber, and there he vow'd, and swore,
and wep't, and sigh'd—and conquer'd. (*Weeps.*)
  Parly. Alack a day, poor Fifteen! (*Weeps.*)
  Lurewell. He swore that he wou'd come down from *Oxford* in
a Fortnight, and marry me.
  Parly. The old bait! the old bait—I was cheated just so my

self (*Aside.*) but had not you the Wit to know his Name all this
while?   230

Lurewell. Alas! what Wit had Innocence like mine? he told
me that he was under an Obligation to his Companions of
concealing himself then, but that he wou'd write to me in two
Days, and let me know his Name and Quality. After all the
binding Oaths of Constancy, joyning Hands, exchanging
Hearts, I gave him a Ring with this Motto, *Love and Honour*,
then we parted; but I never saw the dear Deceiver more.

Parly. No, nor never will, I warrant you.

Lurewell. I need not tell my Griefs, which my Father's
Death made a fair Pretence for; he left me sole Heiress and   240
Executrix to Three Thousand Pounds a Year; at last my Love
for this single Dissembler, turn'd to a hatred of the whole Sex,
and resolving to divert my Melancholy, and make my large
Fortune subservient to my Pleasure and Revenge, I went to
Travel, where in most Courts of *Europe* I have done some
Execution: Here I will play my last Scene; then retire to my
Country-house, live solitary, and die a Penitent.

Parly. But don't you still love this dear Dissembler?

Lurewell. Most certainly: 'Tis Love of him that keeps my
Anger warm, representing the Baseness of Mankind full in   250
View; and makes my Resentments work.—We shall have that
old impotent Lecher *Smuggler* here to Night: I have a Plot to
swinge him and his precise Nephew *Vizard*.

Parly. I think, Madam, you manage every body that comes
in your way.

Lurewell. No, *Parly*, those Men, whose Pretensions I found
just and honourable, I fairly dismist by letting them know my
firm Resolutions never to marry. But those Villains that
wou'd attempt my Honour, I've seldom fail'd to manage.

Parly. What d'ye think of the Colonel, Madam? I suppose   260
his Designs are honourable.

Lurewell. That Man's a Riddle; There's something of
Honour in his Temper that pleases: I'm sure he loves me too,
because he's soon jealous, and soon satisfied: But he's a Man
still.—When I once try'd his Pulse about Marriage, his Blood
ran as low as a Coward's: He swore indeed that he lov'd me,
but cou'd not marry me forsooth, because he was engag'd
elsewhere. So poor a Pretence made me disdain his Passion,

which otherwise might have been uneasie to me.—But, hang
270 him, I have teiz'd him enough:—Besides, *Parly*, I begin to be
tir'd of my Revenge;—but this Buss and Guinea I must maul
once more: I'll hansel his Woman's Cloaths for him. Go, get
me Pen and Ink; I must write to *Vizard* too.
    Fortune this once assist me as before.
    Two such Machines can never work in vain,
    As thy propitious Wheel, and my projecting Brain.

The End of the Third Act.

ACT IV. [Scene i.]

SCENE, *Covent-Garden.*

Wildair *and* Standard *meeting.*

Standard. I thought, Sir *Harry*, to have met you 'ere this in a
more convenient Place; but since my Wrongs were without
Ceremony, my Revenge shall be so too. Draw, Sir.
    Wildair. Draw, Sir! What shall I draw?
    Standard. Come, come, Sir, I like your facetious Humour
well enough: It shows Courage and Unconcern: I know you
brave; and therefore use you thus. Draw your Sword.
    Wildair. Nay, to oblige you I will draw: But the Devil take
me if I fight—Perhaps, Colonel, this is the prettiest Blade you
10 have seen.
    Standard. I doubt not but the Arm is good; and therefore
think both worth my Resentment. Come, Sir.
    Wildair. But, prithee Colonel, dost think that I am such a
Mad-man as to send my Soul to the Devil, and my Body to the
Worms upon every Fool's Errand?
    Standard. I hope you're no Coward, Sir.
    Wildair. Coward, Sir! I have eight thousand Pounds a year,
Sir.
    Standard. You fought in *Flanders* to my Knowledge.
20 *Wildair.* Ay, for the same Reason that I wore a Red Coat:
Because 'twas fashionable.
    Standard. Sir, you fought a *French Count* in *Paris.*

Wildair. True, Sir; he was a Beau, like my self: Now you're a Soldier, Colonel, and Fighting's your Trade; And I think it down-right Madness to contend with any Man in his Profession.

Standard. Come, Sir, no more Dallying: I shall take very unseemly Methods if you don't show your self a Gentleman.

Wildair. A Gentleman! Why there agen now. A Gentleman! I tell you once more, Colonel, that I am a Baronet, and have 30 eight thousand Pounds a Year. I can dance, sing, ride, fence, understand the Languages. Now, I can't conceive how running you through the Body shou'd contribute one Jot more to my Gentility. But, pray Colonel, I had forgot to ask you: What's the Quarrel?

Standard. A Woman, Sir.

Wildair. Then I put up my Sword. Take her.

Standard. Sir, my Honour's concern'd.

Wildair. Nay, if your Honour be concern'd with a Woman, get it out of her Hands as soon as you can. An honourable 40 Lover is the greatest Slave in Nature; some will say, the greatest Fool. Come, come, Colonel, this is something about the Lady *Lurewell*, I warrant; I can give you satisfaction in that Affair.

Standard. Do so then immediately.

Wildair. Put up your Sword first: You know I dare fight: But I had much rather make you a Friend than an Enemy. I can assure you this Lady will prove too hard for one of your Temper. You have too much Honour, too much in Conscience, to be a Favourite with the Ladies.   50

Standard. I am assur'd, Sir, she never gave you any Encouragement.—

Wildair. A Man can never hear Reason with a Sword in his Hand. Sheath your Weapon; and then if I don't satisfie you, sheath it in my Body.

Standard. Give me but Demonstration of her granting you any Favour, and 'tis enough.

Wildair. Will you take my Word?

Standard. Pardon me, Sir, I cannot.

Wildair. Will you believe your own Eyes?   60

Standard. 'Tis ten to one whether I shall or no: They have deceiv'd me already.

Wildair. That's hard.—But some means I shall devise for your Satisfaction.—We must fly this Place; else that Cluster of Mobb will overwhelm us.

Exeunt.

Enter Mobb, Tom Errand*'s* Wife *hurrying in*
Clincher Senior *in* Errand*'s Cloaths.*

Wife. O, the Villain, the Rogue, he has murder'd my Husband: Ah, my poor *Timothy*! (*Crying.*)

Clincher Senior. Dem your *Timothy*;—Your Husband has murder'd me, Woman: For he has carry'd away my fine *Jubilee*
70 Cloaths.

Wife. Ah, you Cut-Throat, have you not got his Cloaths upon your Back there?—Neighbours, don't you know poor *Timothy*'s Coat and Apron?

Mobb. Ay, ay, 'tis the same.

First Mobb. What shall we do with him, Neighbours?

Second Mobb. We'll pull him in pieces.

First Mobb. No, no; then we may be hang'd for Murder; but we'll drown him.

Clincher Senior. Ah, good People, pray don't drown me; for I
80 never learnt to swim in all my Life. Ah, this plaguy Intriguing!

Mobb. Away with him, away with him to the *Thames.*

Clincher Senior. Oh, if I had but my *Swimming Girdle* now.

Enter Constable.

Constable. Hold, Neighbours, I command the Peace.

Wife. O, Mr. *Constable*, here's a Rogue that has murder'd my Husband, and robb'd him of his Cloaths.

Constable. Murder and Robbery! then he must be a Gentleman. Hands off there, he must not be abus'd.—Give an Account of your self: Are you a Gentleman?

Clincher Senior. No, Sir, I am a Beau.

90 *Constable.* Then you have kill'd no body, I'm perswaded. How came you by these Cloaths, Sir?

IV.i. 67 *Timothy*] Mrs Errand's use of the name 'Timothy' for her husband, known as 'Tom Errand' elsewhere in the play, suggests an inconsistency, perhaps due to authorial carelessness. The fact that the name was not corrected in the editions revised according to theatrical changes suggests either further carelessness or perhaps an intentional use of the nickname 'Tom' for 'Timothy'. The original 'Timothy' stands in this edition, as it did in all early editions, although emendation to 'Thomas' would seem appropriate on grounds of consistency rather than bibliographical evidence.

Clincher Senior. You must know, Sir, that walking along, Sir, I don't know how, Sir; I can't tell where, Sir; and—so the Porter and I chang'd Cloaths, Sir.

Constable. Very well, the Man speaks Reason, and like a Gentleman.

Wife. But pray Mr. *Constable*, ask him how he chang'd Cloaths with him.

Constable. Silence, Woman, and don't disturb the Court.— Well, Sir, how did you change Cloaths?   100

Clincher Senior. Why, Sir, he pull'd off my Coat, and I drew off his: so I put on his Coat, and he puts on mine.

Constable. Why Neighbours, I don't find that he's guilty: Search him; and if he carries no Arms about him, we'll let him go.

> *They search his Pockets, and pull out his Pistols.*

Clincher Senior. O *Gemini*! my *Jubilee* Pistols.

Constable. What, a Case of Pistols! Then the Case is plain. Speak, what are you, Sir? whence come you, and whither go you?

Clincher Senior. Sir, I came from *Russel-street*, and am going 110 to the *Jubilee*.

Wife. You shall go to the Gallows, you Rogue.

Constable. Away with him, away with him to *Newgate* straight.

Clincher Senior. I shall go the *Jubilee* now indeed.

> *Exeunt.*

> *Re-enter* Wildair *and* Standard.

Wildair. In short, Colonel, 'tis all Nonsense: Fight for a Woman! Hard by is the Lady's House; if you please, we'll wait on her together: You shall draw your Sword, I'll draw my Snush-Box: You shall produce your Wounds receiv'd in War; I'll relate mine by *Cupid*'s Dart:—You shall look big; I'll 120 ogle:—You shall swear; I'll sigh:—You shall *sa, sa*, and I'll *coupee*; And if she flies not to my Arms, like a Hawk to its Pearch, my Dancing Master deserves to be damn'd.

Standard. With the generality of Women, I grant you, these Arts may prevail.

Wildair. Generality of Women! Why there agen you're out. They're all alike, Sir: I never heard of any one that was particular, but one.

Standard. Who was she, pray?

130   *Wildair.*   *Penelope*, I think she's call'd; and that's a Poetical Story too. When will you find a Poet in our Age make a Woman so chaste?

Standard. Well, Sir *Harry*, your facetious Humour can disguise Falshood, and make Calumny pass for Satyr: But you have promis'd me ocular Demonstration that she favours you: make that good, and I shall then maintain Faith and Female to be as inconsistent as Truth and Falshood.

Wildair. Nay, by what you have told me, I am satisfied that she imposes on us all; and *Vizard* too seems what I still

140 suspected him: but his Honesty once mistrusted, spoils his Knavery:—But will you be convinc'd if our Plot succeeds?

Standard. I rely on your Word and Honour, Sir *Harry*; which, if I doubted, my Distrust wou'd cancel the Obligation of their Security.

Wildair. Then meet me half an hour hence at the *Rummer*: You must oblige me by taking a hearty Glass with me toward the fitting me out for a certain Project which this Night I undertake.

Standard. I guess by the Preparation, that Woman's the

150 Design.

Wildair. Yes, faith,—I am taken dangerously ill with two foolish Maladies, Modesty and Love; the first I'll cure with *Burgundy*, and my Love by a Night's Lodging with the Damsel. A sure Remedy. *Probatum est.*

Standard. I'll certainly meet you, Sir.

Exeunt severally.

Enter Clincher Junior *and* Dicky.

Clincher Junior. Ah! *Dicky*, this *London* is a sad Place, a sad vicious Place: I wish that I were in the Country agen: And this Brother of mine! I'm sorry he's so great a Rake: I had rather see him dead than see him thus.

160   *Dicky.* Ay, Sir, He'll spend his whole Estate at this same *Jubilee*. Who, d'ye think lives at this same *Jubilee*?

Clincher Junior. Who pray?

Dicky. The *Pope*.

Clincher Junior. The Devil he does! my Brother go to the Place where the *Pope* dwells! he's bewitch'd sure.

Enter Tom Errand *in* Clincher Senior*'s Cloaths.*

Dicky. Indeed I believe he is, for he's strangely alter'd.

Clincher Junior. Alter'd! why he looks like a *Jesuit* already.

Tom Errand. This Lace will sell. What a Blockhead was the Fellow to trust me with his Coat! If I can get cross the Garden, down to the Water-side, I'm pretty secure. (*Aside.*)   170

Clincher Junior. Brother!—Alaw! O *Gemini*? are you my Brother?

Dicky. I seize you in the King's Name, Sir.

Tom Errand. O Lord, shou'd this prove some Parliament Man now!

Clincher Junior. Speak you Rogue, what are you.

Tom Errand. A poor Porter, Sir, and going of an Errand.

Dicky. What Errand? speak you Rogue.

Tom Errand. A Fools Errand, I'm afraid.

Clincher Junior. Who sent you?   180

Tom Errand. A Beau, Sir.

Dicky. No, no, the Rogue has murder'd your Brother, and stript him of his Cloaths.

Clincher Junior. Murther'd my Brother! O *Crimini*! O my poor *Jubilee* Brother!—stay, by *Jupiter Ammon*, I'm Heir: Tho' speak Sirrah, Have you kill'd him? Confess that you have kill'd him, and I'll give you Half a Crown.

Tom Errand. Who I, Sir? alack-a-day, Sir, I never kill'd any Man, but a Carrier's Horse once.

Clincher Junior. Then you shall certainly be Hang'd, but 190 confess that you kill'd him, and we'll let you go.

Tom Errand. Telling the Truth hangs a Man, but confessing a Lye can do no harm, besides, if the worst comes to the worst, I can but deny it agen—Well, Sir, since I must tell you, I did kill him.

Clincher Junior. Here's your Money, Sir,—but are you sure you kill'd him dead.

Tom Errand. Sir, I'll swear it before any Judge in *England*.

Dicky. But are you sure that he'd *Dead in Law*.

Tom Errand. Dead in Law! I can't tell whether he be *Dead in* 200 *Law*. But he's as dead as a Door Nail; for I gave him seven knocks on the Head with a Hammer.

Dicky. Then you have the Estate by the Statute. Any Man that's knock'd o'th' Head is *Dead in Law*.

Clincher Junior. But are you sure he was *Compos Mentis* when he was kill'd?

Tom Errand. I suppose he was, Sir, for he told me nothing to the contrary afterwards.

Clincher Junior. Hey!—then I go to the *Jubilee*—Strip, Sir,
210 strip. By *Jupiter Ammon* strip.

Dicky,. Ah! don't swear, Sir.

Clincher Junior. (*Puts on his Brother's Cloaths.*) Swear, Sir, *Zoons*, han't I got the Estate, Sir? Come, Sir, now I'm in Mourning for my Brother.

Tom Errand. I hope you'll let me go now, Sir.—

Clincher Junior. Yes, yes, Sir, but you must first do me the Favour, to swear positively before a Magistrate, that you kill'd him dead, that I may enter upon the Estate without any Trouble. By *Jupiter Ammon* all my Religion's gone, since I put
220 on these fine Cloaths—Hey, call me a Coach somebody.

Tom Errand. Ay, Master let me go, and I'll call one immediately.

Clincher Junior. No, no, *Dicky*, carry this Spark before a Justice,and when he has made Oath, you may discharge him. And I'll go see *Angelica*.

Exeunt Dicky *and* Tom Errand.

Now that I'm an Elder Brother, I'll Court, and Swear, and Rant, and Rake, and go to the *Jubilee* with the best of them.

Exit.

[ACT IV. Scene ii.]

SCENE, Lurewell's *House.*

Enter Lurewell *and* Parly.

Lurewell. Are you sure that *Vizard* had my Letter.

Parly. Yes, yes, Madam, one of your Ladyships Footmen gave it to him in the Park, and he told the Bearer, with all transports of Joy, that he wou'd be punctual to a Minute.

Lurewell. Thus most Villains, some time or other, are punctual to their Ruine; and Hypocrisie, by imposing on the

World, at last deceives it self. Are all things prepar'd for his
Reception.

Parly. Exactly to your Ladyships Order, the Alderman too
is just come, dress'd and cook'd up for Iniquity.   10

Lurewell. Then he has got Woman's Cloaths on.

Parly. Yes, Madam, and has pass'd upon the Family for
your Nurse.

Lurewell. Convey him into that Closet, and put out the
Candles, and tell him, I'll wait on him presently.

As *Parly goes to put out the Candle, somebody Knocks.*

Lurewell. This must be some Clown without Manners, or a
Gentleman above Ceremony. Who's there?

Wildair. (*Sings.*)

> Thus Damon *knock'd at* Celia*'s Door,*
> *He sigh'd, and beg'd, and wept, and swore.*
> > *The Sign was so,*   20
> > > (*Knocks.*)
> > *She answer'd, No,*
> > > (*Knocks thrice.*)
> > *No, no, no.*
> *Again he sigh'd, again he pray'd,*
> *No,* Damon, *no, I am afraid,*
> *Consider,* Damon, *I'm a Maid,*
> > *Consider,*
> > > *No,*
> > *I'm a Maid.*
> > *No,* &c.
> *At last his Sighs and Tears made way,*   30
> *She rose, and softly turn'd the Key,*
> *Come in, said she, but do not stay.*
> > *I may conclude*
> > *You will be rude,*
> > *But if you are, you may.*

[Wildair] *Enters.*

Exit Parly.

Lurewell. 'Tis too early for Serenading, Sir *Harry.*

Wildair. Wheresoever Love is, there Musick is proper,
there's an harmonious consent in their Natures, and when
rightly joyn'd, they make up the Chorus of Earthly Happiness.

40 *Lurewell.* But, Sir *Harry*, what Tempest drives you here at this Hour.

Wildair. No Tempest, Madam, but as fair Weather as ever entic'd a Citizens Wife to Cuckold her Husband in fresh Air. Love, Madam. (Wildair *taking her by the Hand.*)

Lurewell. As pure and white as Angels soft desires, is't not so?

Wildair. Fierce, as when ripe consenting Beauty Fires.

Lurewell. O Villain! what Privilege has Man to our Destruction, that thus they hunt our Ruine? (*Aside.*)

> *Wildair drops a Ring, she takes it up.*

(*Aside.*) If this be a Love Token, your Mistresses Favours hang
50 very loose about you, Sir.

Wildair. I can't justly, Madam, pay your Trouble of taking it up by any thing, but desiring you to wear it.

Lurewell. You Gentlemen have the cunningest ways of playing the Fool, and are so industrious in your Profuseness. Speak seriously, am I beholding to Chance or Design for this Ring?

Wildair. To design upon my Honour, and I hope my Design will succeed. (*Aside.*)

Lurewell. And what shall I give you for such a
    fine thing. ⎫
                     ⎬ (*Both sing.*)
Wildair. You'll give me another, you'll give me ⎭
60   *another fine thing.*

Lurewell. Shall I be free with you, Sir *Harry*.

Wildair. With all my Heart, Madam, so I may be free with you.

Lurewell. Then plainly, Sir, I shall beg the favour to see you some other time, for at this very Minute I have two Lovers in the House.

Wildair. Then to be as plain, I must be gone this Minute, for I must see another Mistress within these two Hours.

Lurewell. Frank and free.

70 *Wildair.* As you with me—Madam, your most humble Servant.

                                                       Exit.

Lurewell. Nothing can disturb his Humour. Now for my Merchant and *Vizard*.

                             Exit, and takes the Candles with her.
Enter Parly, *leading in* Smuggler, *dress'd in Woman's Cloaths.*

Parly. This way, Mr. Alderman.

Smuggler. Well, Mrs. *Parly*,—I'm oblig'd to you for this Trouble, here are a couple of Shillings for you. Times are hard, very hard indeed, but next time I'll steal a pair of silk Stockings from my Wife, and bring them to you—What are you fumbling about my Pockets for—?

Parly. Only settling the Pleats of your Gown, here, Sir; get 80 into this Closet, and my Lady will wait on you presently.

Puts him into the Closet, runs out, and returns with Vizard.

Vizard. Where wou'd'st thou lead me, my dear auspicious little Pilot?

Parly. You're almost in Port, Sir, my Lady's in the Closet, and will come out to you immediately.

Vizard. Let me thank thee as I ought. (*Kisses her.*)

Parly. Pshaw! who has hir'd me best? a couple of Shillings, and a couple of Kisses.

Exit.

Vizard. Propitious Darkness guides the Lovers Steps, and Night that shadows outward Sense, lights up our inward Joy. 90 Night! the great awful Ruler of Mankind, which, like the *Persian* Monarch hides its Royalty to raise the Veneration of the World. Under thy easie Reign Dissemblers may speak Truth; all slavish Forms and Ceremonies laid aside, and generous Villainy may act without Constraint.

Smuggler. (*Peeping out of the Closet.*) Bless me! what Voice is this?

Vizard. Our hungry Appetites, like the wild Beasts of Prey, now scour abroad, to gorge their craving Maws, the pleasure of Hypocrisie, like a chain'd Lyon, once broke loose, wildly 100 indulges its new Freedom, ranging through all unbounded Joys.

Smuggler. My Nephew's Voice! and certainly possess'd with an Evil Spirit, he talks as prophanely, as an Actor possess'd with a Poet.

Vizard. Ha! I hear a Voice, Madam,—my Life, my Happiness, where are you, Madam?

Smuggler. Madam! he takes me for a Woman too, I'll try him. [*Aside.*] where have you left your Sanctity, Mr. *Vizard*?

110   *Vizard.* Talk no more of that ungrateful Subject—I left it where it has only business with Day-light, 'tis needless to wear a Mask in the Dark.

   Smuggler. O the Rogue, the Rogue! [*Aside.*]—The World takes you for a very sober virtuous Gentleman.

   Vizard. Ay, Madam, that adds Security to all my Pleasures —with me a Cully-Squire may squander his Estate, and ne'er be thought a Spend-thrift—With me a Holy Elder may zealously be drunk, and toast his tuneful Nose in Sack, to make it hold forth clearer—But what is most my Praise, the 120 formal Rigid she that rails at Vice and Men, with me secures her loosest Pleasures, and her strictest Honour—she who with scornful Mien, and virtuous Pride, disdains the Name of Whore, with me can Wanton, and laugh at the deluded World.

   Smuggler. How have I been deceiv'd! then you are very great among the Ladies.

   Vizard. Yes, Madam, they know that like a Mole in the Earth, I dig deep but invisible, not like those fluttering noisie Sinners, whose Pleasure is the proclamation of their Faults, 130 those empty Flashes who no sooner kindle, but they must blaze to alarm the World. But come, Madam, you delay our Pleasures.

   Smuggler. He surely takes me for the Lady *Lurewell*—she has made him an Appointment too—but I'll be reveng'd of both [*Aside.*]—Well, Sir, what are these you are so intimate with.

   Vizard. Come, come, Madam, you know very well—those who stand so high, that the vulgar envy even their Crimes, whose Figure adds privilege to their Sin, and makes it pass unquestion'd; fair, high, pamper'd Females, whose speaking 140 Eyes, and piercing Voice, wou'd warm the Statue of a *Stoick*, and animate his cold Marble with the Soul of an *Epicure*, all ravishing, lovely, soft, and kind, like you.

   Smuggler. I am very lovely and soft indeed, you shall find me much harder than you imagine, Friend—Well, Sir, but I suppose your Dissimulation has some other Motive besides Pleasure.

   Vizard. Yes, Madam, the honestest Motive in the World, Interest—you must know, Madam, that I have an old Uncle, Alderman *Smuggler*, you have seen him, I suppose.

Smuggler. Yes, yes, I have some small Acquaintance with 150
him.

Vizard. 'Tis the most knavish, precise, covetous old Rogue,
that ever died of a Gout.

Smuggler. Ah! the young Son of a Whore. [*Aside.*] Well, Sir,
and what of him?

Vizard. Hell hungers not more for wretched Souls, than he
for ill-got Pelf—and yet (what's wonderful) he that wou'd
stick at no profitable Villainy himself, loves Holiness in
another—he prays all *Sunday* for the Sins of the Week past—he
spends all Dinner-time in too tedious Graces, and what he 160
designs a Blessing to the Meat, proves a Curse to his
Family—he's the most—

Smuggler. Well, well, Sir, I know him very well.

Vizard. Then, Madam, he has a swinging Estate, which I
design to Purchase as a Saint, and spend like a Gentleman. He
got it by Cheating, and shou'd lose it by Deceit. By the
pretence of my Zeal and Sobriety, I'll cozen the old Miser one
of these Days out of a Settlement, and Deed of Conveyance—

Smuggler. It shall be a Deed to convey you to the Gallows
then, you young Dog. (*Aside.*)   170

Vizard. And no sooner he's Dead, but I'll rattle over his
Grave with a Coach and Six, to inform his covetous Ghost
how genteelly I spend his Money.

Smuggler. I'll prevent you, Boy, for I'll have my Money
bury'd with me. (*Aside.*)

Vizard. Bless me, Madam, here's a Light coming this way, I
must fly immediately, when shall I see you, Madam.

Smuggler. Sooner than you expect, my Dear.

Vizard. Pardon me, dear Madam, I wou'd not be seen for
the World. I wou'd sooner forfeit my Life, nay, my Pleasure, 180
than my Reputation.

                                                            Exit.

Smuggler. Reputation! Reputation! that poor Word suffers a
great deal—Well! thou art the most accomplish'd Hypocrite
that ever made a grave plodding Face over a Dish of Coffee,
and a Pipe of Tobacco; he owes me for seven Years
maintenance, and shall pay me by seven Years Imprisonment;
and when I die, I'll leave him the Fee-Simple of a Rope and a
Shilling—who are these? I begin to be afraid of some

Mischief—I wish that I were safe within the City Liberties—
190 I'll hide my self. (*Stands close.*)

    Enter Butler, *with other* Servants *and Lights*.

Butler. I say there are Two Spoons wanting, and I'll search
the whole House—Two Spoons will be no small gap in my
Quarter's Wages—

Servant. When did you miss them, *James*?

Butler. Miss them. Why, I miss them now; in short they
must be among you, and if you don't return them, I'll go to
the Cunning-Man to Morrow-Morning; my Spoons I want,
and my Spoons I will have.

Servant. Come, come, search about. (*Search and discover*
200 Smuggler.) Ah! who's this?

Butler. Hark'ee, good Woman, what makes you hide your
self? What are you asham'd of.

Smuggler. Asham'd of! O Lord, Sir, I'm an honest Old
Woman that never was asham'd of any thing.

Butler. What are you, a Midwife then? Speak, did not you
see a couple of stray Spoons in your Travels?

Smuggler. Stray Spoons!

Butler. Ay, ay, stray Spoons; in short you stole them, and
I'll shake your old Limbs to pieces, if you don't deliver them
210 presently.

Smuggler. Bless me! a Reverend Elder of Seventy Years old
accus'd for *Petty-Larceny*! [*Aside.*]—why, search me, good
People, search me, and if you find any Spoons about me, you
shall burn me for a Witch.

Butler. Ay, ay, we will search you Mistress. (*They search and
pull the Spoons out of his Pockets.*)

Smuggler. Oh! the Devil, the Devil!

Butler. Where, where is he? Lord bless us, she is a Witch in
good earnest, may be.

Smuggler. O, it was some Devil, some *Covent-Garden*, or St.
220 *James*'s Devil, that put them in my Pocket.

Butler. Ay, ay, you shall be hang'd for a Thief, burnt for a
Witch, and then carted for a Bawd. Speak, what are you?

    Enter Lurewell.

Smuggler. I'm the Lady *Lurewell*'s Nurse.

Lurewell. What Noise is this?

Butler. Here is an old *Succubus*, Madam, that has stole two silver Spoons, and says, she's your Nurse.

Lurewell. My Nurse! O the Impudent old Jade, I never saw
the wither'd Creature before.

Smuggler. Then I'm finely caught. O Madam! Madam don't
you know me? Don't you remember Buss and Guinea?   230

Lurewell. Was ever such Impudence? I know thee! why
thou'rt as Brazen as a Bawd in the Side-Box—Take her before
a Justice, and then to *Newgate*, away.

Smuggler. O! consider, Madam, that I'm an Alderman.

Lurewell. Consider, Sir, that you're a Compound of Covetousness, Hypocrisy, and Knavery; and must be punish'd
accordingly—You must be in Petticoats, Gouty Monster,
must ye! You must Bufs and Guinea too, you must tempt a
Ladies Honour, old Satyr, away with him.

Hurry him off.

Still May our Sex thus Frauds of Men oppose,   240
Still may our Arts delude thee tempting Foes.
May Honour Rule, and never fall betray'd,
But Vice be caught in Nets for Virtue laid.

The End of the Fourth Act.

ACT V. [Scene i.]

SCENE, Lady Darling's *House.*

Lady Darling *and* Angelica.

Lady Darling. Daughter, since you have to deal with a Man
of so peculiar a Temper, you must not think the general Arts
of Love can secure him; you may therefore allow such a
Courtier some Incouragement extraordinary, without reproach
to your Modesty.

Angelica. I am sensible, Madam, that a formal Nicety
makes our Modesty sit awkard, and appears rather a Chain to
Enslave, than Bracelet to Adorn us—it shou'd show, when
unmolested, easie and innocent as a Dove, but strong and
vigorous as a Faulcon, when assaulted.   10

Lady Darling. I'm afraid, Daughter, you mistake Sir *Harry*'s Gaiety for Dishonour.

Angelica. Tho' Modesty, Madam, may Wink, it must not Sleep, when powerful Enemies are abroad—I must confess, that of all Mens, I wou'd not see Sir *Harry Wildair*'s Faults; nay, I cou'd wrest most suspicious Words a thousand ways, to make them look like Honour—but, Madam, in spight of Love I must hate him, and curse those Practices which taint our Nobility, and rob all virtuous Women of the bravest Men—

20 *Lady Darling.* You must certainly be mistaken, *Angelica*, for I'm satisfy'd Sir *Harry*'s designs are only to court, and marry you.

Angelica. His pretence, perhaps, was such, but Women now, like Enemies, are attack'd; whether by Treachery, or fairly Conquer'd, the Glory of Triumph is the same—pray, Madam, by what means were you made acquainted with his Designs?

Lady Darling. Means, Child! why my Cousin *Vizard*, who, I'm sure is your sincere Friend, sent him. He brought me this

30 Letter from my Cousin—

Gives her the Letter, which she opens.

Angelica. Ha! *Vizard*! then I'm abus'd in earnest—wou'd Sir *Harry*, by his Instigation, fix a base Affront upon me? no, I can't suspect him of so ungenteel a Crime—this Letter shall trace the Truth—(*Aside.*) my Suspicions, Madam, are much clear'd, and I hope to satisfy your Ladyship in my Management, when next I see Sir *Harry*.

Enter Servant.

Servant. Madam, here's a Gentleman below calls himself *Wildair*.

Lady Darling. Conduct him up. Daughter, I wont doubt

40 your Discretion.

Exit Lady Darling.

Enter Wildair.

Wildair. O, the Delights of Love and *Burgundy*—! Madam, I have toasted your Ladyship fifteen Bumpers successively, and swallow'd *Cupids* like Loches, to every Glass.

Angelica. And what then, Sir?

Wildair. Why then, Madam, the Wine has got into my Head; and the *Cupids* into my Heart: and unless by quenching quick my Flame, you kindly ease the Smart, I'm a lost Man, Madam.

Angelica. Drunkenness, Sir *Harry*, is the worst Pretence a Gentleman can make for Rudeness: For the Excuse is as 50 scandalous as the Fault:—Therefore pray consider who you are so free with, Sir; a Woman of Condition, that can call half a dozen Footmen upon Occasion.

Wildair. Nay, Madam, if you have a mind to toss me in a Blanket, half a dozen Chamber-maids would do better Service.—Come, come, Madam, tho' the Wine makes me lisp, yet has it taught me to speak plainer. By all the Dust of my ancient Progenitors I must this Night quarter my Coat of Arms with yours.

Angelica. Nay, then who waits there?   60

Enter Footmen.

Take hold of that mad Man, and bind him.

Wildair. Nay, then *Burgundy*'s the Word, and Slaughter will ensue. Hold,—do you know, Scoundrils, that I have been drinking victorious *Burgundy*? (*Draws.*)

Footmen. We know you're drunk, Sir.

Wildair. Then how have you the Impudence, Rascals, to assault a Gentleman with a couple of Flasks of Courage in his Head?

Footmen. Sir, we must do as our young Mistriss commands us.   70

Wildair. Nay, then, have among ye, Dogs.

Throws Money among them: They scramble and take it up:
He pelting them out, shuts the Door, and returns.

Rascals, Poultrons,—I have charm'd the Dragon, and now the Fruit's my own.

Angelica. O, the mercenary Wretches! This was a Plot to betray me.

Wildair. I have put the whole Army to flight: And, now take the General Prisoner. (*Laying hold on her.*)

Angelica. I conjure you, Sir, by the sacred Name of Honour, by your dead Father's Name, and the fair Reputation of your Mother's Chastity, that you offer not the least Offence.—Al- 80 ready you have wrong'd me past Redress.

Wildair. Thou art the most unaccountable Creature.

Angelica. What Madness, Sir *Harry*, what wild Dream of

loose Desire cou'd prompt you to attempt this Baseness? View
me well.—The Brightness of my Mind, methinks, shou'd
lighten outwards, and let you see your Mistake in my
Behaviour. I think it shines with so much Innocence in my
Face, that it shou'd dazzle all your vicious Thoughts: Think
not I am defenceless 'cause alone. Your very self is Guard
90 against your self: I'm sure there's somthing generous in your
Soul; My Words shall search it out, and Eyes shall fire it for
my own Defence.

Wildair. (*Mimicking.*) Tall ti dum, ti dum, tall ti didi,
didum. A Million to one now, but this Girl is just come flush
from reading the *Rival Queens*—I gad, I'll at her in her own
cant—

O my Statyra, O my Angry Dear, turn thy Eyes on me, behold thy
Beau in Buskins.

Angelica. Behold me, Sir, View me with a sober thought,
100 free from those fumes of Wine that throw a mist before your
Sight, and you shall find that every glance from my reproaching Eyes is arm'd with sharp Resentment, and with a vertuous
Pride that looks dishonour dead.

Wildair. This is the first Whore in *Heroicks* that I have met
with, (*Aside.*) look ye Madam, as to that slender particular of
your Vertue, we shan't quarrel about it, you may be as
Vertuous as any Woman in *England* if you please; you may say
your Pray'rs all the time—but pray Madam be pleas'd to
consider what is this same Vertue that you make such a
110 mighty Noise about—can your Vertue bespeak you a front
Row in the Boxes, No, for the Players can't live upon Vertue.
Can your Vertue keep you a Coach and Six, no, no, your
Vertuous Women walk a foot—can your Vertue hire you a
Pue in a Church? Why the very Sexton will tell you, no. Can
your Vertue stake for you at Picquet, no. Then what business
has a Woman with Vertue—Come, come, Madam, I offer'd
you fifty Guinea's,—there's a hundred—the Devil! Vertuous
still! Why 'tis a hundred, five score, a hundred Guinea's.

Angelica. O Indignation! Were I a Man you durst not use
120 me thus; but the Mean, poor Abuse you throw on me, reflects
upon your self, our Sex still strikes an awe upon the Brave,
and only Cowards dare affront a Woman.

Wildair. Affront! S'death Madam, a hundred Guinea's will set you up at Basset, a hundred Guinea's will furnish out your Lodgings with China; a hundred Guinea's will give you an Air of Quality; a hundred Guinea's will buy you a rich *Escritore* for your *Billet deux*, or a fine Common-Prayer-Book for your Vertue. A hundred Guinea's will buy a hundred fine things, and fine things are for fine Ladies; and fine Ladies are for fine Gentlemen; and fine Gentlemen are—I Gad this Burgundy 130 makes a Man speak like an Angel—Come, come, Madam, take it, and put it to what use you please.

Angelica. I'll use it, as I wou'd the base unworthy Giver, thus. (*Throws down the Purse, and stamps upon it.*)

Wildair. I have no mind to meddle in State Affairs; but these Women will make me a Parliament Man, spight of my Teeth, on purpose to bring in a Bill against their Extortion. She tramples under Foot, that Deity which all the World adores.—O the blooming pride of beautiful Eighteen! Pshaw, I'll talk to her no longer, I'll make my Markets with the Old 140 Gentlewoman, she knows Business better,—(*Goes to the Door.*) here you friend, pray desire the Old Lady to walk in.—Hearkee, by Gad, Madam, I'll tell your Mother.

Enter Lady Darling.

Lady Darling. Well, Sir *Harry*, and how d'ye like my Daughter, pray.

Wildair. Like her Madam!—hearkee will you take it? Why faith Madam!—take the Money, I say, or I gad, all's out.

Angelica. All shall out; Sir, you're a Scandal to the Name of Gentleman.

Wildair. With all my Heart, Madam—in short, Madam, 150 your Daughter has us'd me somewhat too familiarly, tho' I have treated her like a Woman of Quality.

Lady Darling. How Sir?

Wildair. Why, Madam, I have offer'd her a hundred Guineas.

Lady Darling. A hundred Guinea's! upon what Score?

Wildair. Upon what Score! Lord, Lord, how these Old Women love to hear Bawdy! Why faith Madam, I have ne're double Entandie ready at present, but I'll sing you a Song.

> *Behold the Goldfinches, tall al de rall,*   160
> *And a Man of my Inches, tall al de rall,*

You shall take um believe me, tall al de rall,
If you will give me, your tall al de rall.
A Modish Minuet Madam, that's all.

Lady Darling. Sir, I don't understand you.

Wildair. Ay, she will have it in plain Terms; then Madam, in downright *English*, I offer'd your Daughter a hundred Guinea's, to—

Angelica. Hold Sir, stop your abusive Tongue, too loose for
170 Modest Ears to bear.—Madam, I did before suspect that his Designs were base, now they're too plain; this Knight, this Mighty Man of Wit and Humours, is made a Tool to a Knave; *Vizard* has sent him of a Bully's Errand, to affront a Woman; but I scorn the Abuse, and him that offer'd it.

Lady Darling. How Sir, come to Affront us! d'ye know who we are, Sir.

Wildair. Know who ye are? Why, your Daughter there is Mr. *Vizard*'s Cousin, I suppose;—and for you Madam—now to call her Procuress Alamode *France.* (*Aside.*) *J'estime botre*
180 *Occupation.*—

Lady Darling. Pray Sir, speak *English.*

Wildair. Then to define her Office, Alamode *Londres*! (*Aside.*) I suppose your Ladiship to be one of those Civil, Obliging, Discreet, Old Gentlewomen, who keep their Visiting days for the Entertainment of their presenting Friends, whom they treat with Imperial Tea, a private Room, and a pack of Cards. Now I suppose you do understand me.

Lady Darling. This is beyond Sufferance; but say, thou abusive Man, what injury have you e're receiv'd from me or
190 mine, thus to engage you in this scandalous Aspersion.

Angelica. Yes Sir, what cause, what Motives could induce you thus to debase your self below your Rank.

Wildair. Hey day! Now Dear *Roxana*, and you my fair *Statyra*, be not so very Heroick in your Styles, *Vizard*'s Letter may resolve you, and answer all the impertinent Questions you have made me.

Both Women. We appeal to that.

Wildair. And I'll stand to't, he read it to me, and the Contents were pretty plain I thought.

200 *Angelica.* Here Sir, peruse it, and see how much we are injur'd, and you deceiv'd.

Wildair. (*Opening the Letter.*) But hold Madam (*To* Lady Darling.) before I read, I'll make some Condition—Mr. *Vizard* says here, that I wont scruple 30 or 40 pieces; Now Madam, if you have clapt in another Cypher to the account, and made it 3 or 4 Hundred, by Gad, I will not stand to't.

Angelica. Now can't I tell whether Disdain or Anger be the most just Resentment for this Injury.

Lady Darling. The Letter, Sir, shall answer you.

Wildair. Well then! (*Reads.*)   210

> *Out of my Earnest Inclination to serve your Ladyship*, and my Cousin Angelica,—Ay, ay the very Words, I can say it by heart—*I have sent Sir* Harry Wildair—*to court my Cousin.*— What the Devil's this? *Sent Sir* Harry Wildair *to court my Cousin*—he read to me a quite different thing—*He's a Gentleman of great Parts and Fortune.*—He's a Son of a Whore and a Rascal,—*and wou'd make your Daughter very Happy*, (*Whistles.*) *in a Husband.* (*Looks foolish, and hums a Song.*)

Oh poor Sir *Harry*, what have thy angry Stars design'd?

Angelica. Now Sir, I hope you need no Instigation to   220 Redress our Wrongs, since even the Injury points the way.

Lady Darling. Think Sir, that our Blood for many Generations, has run in the purest Channel of unsully'd Honour.

Wildair. Ay, Madam. (*Bows to her.*)

Angelica. Consider, what a tender Blossom is Female Reputation, which the least Air of foul Detraction blasts.

Wildair. Yes, Madam. (*Bows to t'other.*)

Lady Darling. Call then to mind your rude and scandalous Behaviour.

Wildair. Right, Madam. (*Bows again.*)   230

Angelica. Remember the base price you offer'd me.

                                                    Exit.

Wildair. Very true, Madam, was ever Man so Catechis'd.

Lady Darling. Then think that, *Vizard*, Villain *Vizard* caus'd all this, yet lives, that's all, farewell. (*Going.*)

Wildair. Stay Madam, (*To* Lady Darling.) one Word, is there no other way to redress your Wrongs, but by Fighting.

Lady Darling. Only one Sir, which if you can think of, you may do; you know the business I entertain'd you for.

219 thy] Q3; they   228 *Lady Darling*] Q3 [*Darl.*]; *Ear.*

Wildair. I understand you Madam.

Exit Lady Darling.

240 Here am I brought to a very pretty Dilemma; I must commit
Murder, or commit Matrimony, which is best now? A license
from *Doctors Commons*, or a Sentence from the *Old Baily*; If I kill
my Man, the Law hangs me; if I marry my Woman, I shall
hang my self;—but, Dam it,—Cowards dare fight, I'll marry,
that's the most daring Action of the two, so my dear Cousin
Angelica, have at you.

[*Exit.*]

[ACT V. Scene ii.]

SCENE *Newgate*, Clincher Senior solus.

Clincher Senior. How severe and melancholy are *Newgate*
Reflections? Last Week my Father died: Yesterday I turn'd
Beau: To day I am laid by the heels, and to morrow shall be
hung by the Neck.—I was agreeing with a Bookseller about
Printing an Account of my Journey through *France* to *Italy*; But
now, the History of my Travels thro' *Holborn* to *Tyburn*,—*The
last and dying Speech of Beau* Clincher, *that was going to the*
Jubilee.—*Come, a Half-peny a-piece.* A sad Sound, a sad Sound,
faith. 'Tis one Way to have a Man's Death make a great Noise
10 in the World.

Enter Smuggler *and* Gaoler.

Smuggler. Well, Friend, I have told you who I am: so send
these Letters into *Thames-street*, as directed; they are to
Gentlemen that will bail me.

Exit Gaoler.

Eh!—this *Newgate* is a very populous Place: Here's Robbery
and Repentance in every Corner.—Well, Friend, what are
you, a Cut-throat or a Bum-Bayliff?

Clincher Senior. What are you, Mistriss, a Bawd or a Witch?
Hearkee, if you are a Witch, d'ye see, I'll give you a hundred
Pounds to mount me on a Broom-staff, and whip me away to
20 the *Jubilee*.

Smuggler. The *Jubilee*! O, you young Rake-hell, what brought
you here?

Clincher Senior. Ah, you old Rogue, what brought you here, if you go to that?

Smuggler. I knew, Sir, what your Powdering, your Prinking, your Dancing and your Frisking wou'd come to.

Clincher Senior. And I knew what your Cozening, your Extortion, and your Smugling wou'd come to.

Smuggler. Ay, Sir, you must break your Indentures, and run to the Devil in a full Bottom Wig, must you?   30

Clincher Senior. Ay Sir, and you must put off your Gravity, and run to the Devil in Petticoats:—You design to swing in Masquerade, Master, d'ye?

Smuggler. Ay, you must go to Plays too, Sirrah: Lord, Lord, What Business has a Prentice at a Play-house, unless it be to hear his Master made a Cuckold, and his Mistriss a Whore? 'Tis ten to one now, but some malicious Poet has my Character upon the Stage within this Month: 'Tis a hard matter now, that an honest sober Man can't sin in private for this plaguy Stage. I gave an honest Gentleman five Guineas   40 my self towards writing a Book against it: And it has done no good, we see.

Clincher Senior. Well, well, Master, take Courage; our Comfort is, we have liv'd together, and shall die together, only with this difference, that I have liv'd like a Fool, and shall die like a Knave; and you have liv'd like a Knave, and shall die like a Fool.

Smuggler. No, Sirrah! I have sent a Messenger for my Cloaths, and shall get out immediately, and shall be upon your Jury by and by.—Go to prayers, you Rogue, go to   50 Prayers.

                                             Exit Smuggler.

Clincher Senior. Prayers! 'Tis a hard taking, when a Man must, say Grace to the Gallows.—Ah, this cursed Intriguing! Had I swung handsomely in a silken Garter now, I had died in my Duty; but to hang in Hemp, like the Vulgar, 'tis very ungenteel.

                         Enter Tom Errand.

A Reprieve, a Reprieve, thou dear, dear—damn'd Rogue, where have you been? Thou art the most welcome—Son of a Whore, where's my Cloaths?

Tom Errand. Sir, I see where mine are: Come, Sir, strip, Sir,   60 strip.

Clincher Senior. What, Sir, will you abuse a Gentleman?

Tom Errand., A Gentleman! ha, ha, ha, d'ye know where you are, Sir? Were all Gentlemen here,—I stand up for Liberty and Property.—*Newgate*'s a Common-wealth. No Courtier has Business among us; Come, Sir.

Clincher Senior. Well, but stay, stay till I send for my own Cloaths: I shall get out presently.

Tom Errand. No, no, Sir, I'll ha you into the Dungeon, and
70 uncase you.

Clincher Senior. Sir, you can't master me; for I'm twenty thousand strong.

Exeunt struggling.

[ACT V. Scene iii.]

The SCENE *changes to* Lady Darling*'s House.*

Enter Wildair *with Letters*, Servants *following.*

Wildair. Here, fly all around, and bear these as directed; you to *Westminster*,—you to St. *James*'s,—and you into the City.—Tell all my Friends a Bridegroom's Joy invites their Presence: Look all of ye like Bridegrooms also: All appear with hospitable Looks, and bear a Welcome in your Faces.—Tell 'em I'm married. If any ask to whom, make no Reply; but tell 'em that I'm married, that Joy shall crown the Day, and Love the Night. Be gone, fly.

Enter Standard.

A thousand Welcomes, Friend: my Pleasure's now compleat,
10 since I can share it with my Friend: Brisk Joy shall bound from me to you: Then back agen; and, like the Sun, grow warmer by Reflexion.

Standard. You're always pleasant, Sir *Harry*; but this transcends your self; whence proceeds it?

Wildair. Canst thou not guess? my Friend—whence flows all Earthly Joy? What is the Life of Man, and Soul of Pleasure?—*Woman*:—What fires the Heart with Transport, and the Soul with Raptures? *Lovely Woman.*—What is the Master Stroak and Smile of the Creation, but *Charming*
20 *Vertuous Woman?*—When Nature in the general Composition

first brought Woman forth, like a flush'd Poet, ravish'd with his Fancy, with Extasie: The blest, the fair Production.—Methinks, my Friend, you relish not my Joy. What is the Cause?

Standard. Canst thou not guess?—What is the Bane of Man, and Scourge of Life, but *Woman?*—What is the Heathenish Idol Man sets up, and is damn'd for worshipping? *Treacherous Woman:*—What are those whose Eyes, like Basilisks, shine beautiful for sure Destruction, whose Smiles are dangerous as the Grin of Fiends? But *false deluding Woman.*—Woman, whose Composition inverts Humanity; their Body's Heavenly, but their Souls are Clay.

Wildair. Come, come, Colonel, this is too much: I know your Wrongs receiv'd from *Lurewell*, may excuse your Resentments against her: But 'tis unpardonable to charge the Failings of a single Woman upon the whole Sex.—I have found one, whose Vertues—

Standard. So have I, Sir *Harry*; I have found one whose Pride's above yielding to a Prince: And if Lying, Dissembling, Perjury and Falshood be no Breaches in Woman's Honour, she's as innocent as Infancy.

Wildair. Well, Colonel, I find your Opinion grows stronger by Opposition, I shall now therefore wave the Argument, and only beg you for this Day to make a Show of Complaisance at least.—Here comes my Charming Bride.—

　　　　Enter Lady Darling *and* Angelica.

Standard. (*Saluting* Angelica.) I wish you, Madam, all the Joys of Love and Fortune.

　　　　Enter Clincher Junior.

Clincher Junior. Gentlemen and Ladies, I'm just upon the Spur, and have only a Minute to take my Leave.

Wildair. Whither are you bound, Sir?

Clincher Junior. Bound, Sir! I'm going to the *Jubilee*, Sir.

Lady Darling. Bless me, Cousin! how came you by these Cloaths?

Clincher Junior. Cloaths! Ha, ha, ha, the rarest Jest! Ha, ha, ha, I shall burst, by *Jupiter Ammon*, I shall burst.

Lady Darling. What's the Matter, Cousin?

Clincher Junior. The matter! Ha, ha, ha: why an honest Porter, ha, ha, ha, has knock'd out my Brother's Brains, ha, ha, ha.

Wildair. A very good Jest, i'faith, ha, ha, ha.

60 *Clincher Junior.* Ay Sir, but the best Jest of all is, he knock'd out his Brains with a Hammer, and so he is as dead as a Door-nail, ha, ha, ha.

Lady Darling. And do you laugh, Wretch?

Clincher Junior. Laugh! ha, ha, ha, Let me see e'er a younger Brother in *England* that won't laugh at such a Jest.

Angelica. You appear'd a very sober pious Gentleman some Hours ago.

Clincher Junior. Pshaw, I was a Fool then: but now, Madam, I'm a Wit: I can rake now.—As for your part, Madam, you
70 might have had me once:—But now, Madam, if you shou'd chance fall to eating Chalk, or gnawing the Sheets, 'tis none of my Fault—Now, Madam,—I have got an Estate, and I must go to the *Jubilee.*

Enter Clincher Senior *in a Blanket.*

Clincher Senior. Must you so, Rogue, must ye?—you will go to the *Jubilee*, will you?

Clincher Junior. A Ghost, a Ghost!—Send for the Dean and Chapter presently.

Clincher Senior. A Ghost! no, no, Sirrah, I'm an Elder Brother; Rogue.

80 *Clincher Junior.* I don't care a Farthing for that; I'm sure you're Dead in Law.

Clincher Senior. Why so, Sirrah, why so?

Clincher Junior. Because, Sir, I can get a Fellow to swear he knock'd out your Brains.

Wildair. An odd way of swearing a Man out of his Life.

Clincher Junior. Smell him, Gentlemen, he has a deadly Scent about him—

Clincher Senior. Truly the apprehensions of Death may have made me savour a little—O Lord—the Colonel! the apprehen-
90 sion of him may make me savour worse, I'm afraid.

Clincher Junior. In short, Sir, were you Ghost, or Brother, or Devil, I will go to the *Jubilee*, by *Jupiter Ammon.*

Standard. Go to the *Jubilee*! go to the *Bear-Garden*—the Travel of such Fools as you, doubly injures our Country, you expose our Native Follies, which ridicules us among Strangers, and return fraught only with their Vices, which you vend here

for fashionable Gallantry; a Travelling Fool is as dangerous as
a Home-bred Villain—Get ye to your Native Plough and
Cart, converse with Animals, like your selves, Sheep and
Oxen, Men are Creatures you don't understand. 100

Wildair. Let 'em alone, Colonel, their Folly will be now
diverting. Come, Gentlemen, we'll dispute this Point some
other time, I hear some Fiddles tuning; let's hear how they
can entertain us: Be pleas'd to sit.

Here Singing and Dancing. After which a Servant whispers Wildair.

Wildair. Madam, shall I beg you to entertain the Company
in the next Room for a Moment. (*To* Lady Darling.)

Lady Darling. With all my Heart—Come, Gentlemen.

Exeunt Omnes *but* Wildair.

Wildair. A Lady to enquire for me! Who can this be?

Enter Lurewell.

O, Madam, this Favour is beyond my Expectation, to come
uninvited to dance at my Wedding—What d'ye gaze at, 110
Madam?

Lurewell. A Monster—if thou art marry'd, thou'rt the most
perjur'd Wretch that e'er avouch'd Deceit.

Wildair. Hey day! why, Madam, I'm sure I never swore to
marry you, I made indeed a slight Promise, upon condition of
your granting me a small Favour, but you would not consent,
you know.

Lurewell. How he upbraids me with my Shame [*Aside.*]—
can you deny your binding Vows when this appears a Witness
'gainst your Falshood (*Shews a Ring.*) Methinks the Motto of 120
this sacred Pledge shou'd flash Confusion in your guilty
Face—read, read here the binding Words of Love and
Honour, Words not unknown to your perfidious Eyes.—tho'
utter Strangers to your treacherous Heart.

Wildair. The Woman's stark staring Mad, that's certain.
[*Aside.*]

Lurewell. Was it maliciously design'd to let me find my
Misery when past redress; to let me know you, only to know
you false—had not curs'd Chance show'd me the surprizing
Motto, I had been happy—The first Knowledge I had of you
was fatal to me, and this second worse. 130

Wildair. What the Devil's all this!—Madam, I'm not at

leisure for Rallery at present, I have weighty Affairs upon my
hands; the business of Pleasure, Madam, any other time—
(*Going.*)

Lurewell. Stay, I conjure you stay.

Wildair. Faith I can't, my Bride expects me; but hark'ee,
when the Honey-Moon is over, about a Month or two hence, I
may do you a small Favour.

Exit.

Lurewell. Grant me some wild Expressions, Heav'ns, or I
shall burst—Woman's Weakness, Man's Falshood, my own
140 Shame, and Love's Disdain, at once swell up my Breast—
Words, Words, or I shall burst. (*Going.*)

Enter Standard.

Standard. Stay, Madam, you need not shun my sight; for if
you are perfect Woman, you have Confidence to out-face a
Crime, and bear the Charge of Guilt without a Blush.

Lurewell. The charge of Guilt! what? making a Fool of you?
I've don't, and glory in the Act, the height of Female Justice
were to make you all hang or drown, dissembling to the
prejudice of Men is Virtue; and every Look, or Sigh, or Smile,
or Tear that can deceive is Meritorious.

150 *Standard.* Very pretty Principles truly—if there be Truth in
Woman, 'tis now in thee—Come, Madam, you know that
you're discover'd, and being sensible, you can't escape, you
wou'd now turn to Bay. That Ring, Madam, proclaims you
Guilty.

Lurewell. O Monster, Villain, perfidious Villain! has he told
you?

Standard. I'll tell it you, and loudly too.

Lurewell. O name it not—yes, speak it out, 'tis so just
Punishment for putting Faith in Man, that I will bear it all;
160 and let credulous Maids that trust their Honour to the
Tongues of Men, thus hear their Shame proclaim'd—Speak
now, what his busie Scandal, and your improving Malice both
dare utter.

Standard. Your Falshood can't be reach'd by Malice, nor by
Satyr; your Actions are the justest Libel on your Fame—your
Words, your Looks, your Tears, I did believe in spight of
common Fame. Nay, 'gainst my own Eyes, I still maintain'd
your Truth. I imagin'd *Wildair*'s boasting of your Favours to

be the pure result of his own Vanity, at last he urg'd your
taking Presents of him, as a convincing Proof of which you 170
Yesterday from him receiv'd that Ring—which Ring, that I
might be sure he gave it, I lent him for that purpose.

Lurewell. Ha! you lent him for that purpose!

Standard. Yes, yes, Madam, I lent him for that purpose—no
denying it—I know it well, for I have worn it long, and desire
you now, Madam, to restore it to the just Owner.

Lurewell. The just Owner, think Sir, think but of what
importance 'tis to own it, if you have Love and Honour in
your Soul. 'Tis then most justly yours, if not, you are a
Robber, and have stoln it basely.   180

Standard. Ha—your Words, like meeting Flints, have struck
a Light to show me something strange—but tell me instantly,
is not your real Name *Manly?*

Lurewell. Answer me first, did not you receive this Ring
about Twelve Years ago?

Standard. I did.

Lurewell. And were not you about that time entertain'd two
Nights at the House of Sir *Oliver Manly* in *Oxfordshire.*

Standard. I was, I was, (*Runs to her, and embraces her.*) the blest
remembrance fires my Soul with transport—I know the 190
rest—you are the charming She, and I the happy Man.

Lurewell. How has blind Fortune stumbled on the right!—
But where have you wander'd since, 'twas cruel to forsake me.

Standard. The particulars of my Fortune were too tedious
now; but to discharge my self from the stain of Dishonour, I
must tell you, that immediately upon my return to the
University, my Elder Brother and I quarrel'd; my Father, to
prevent farther Mischief, posts me away to Travel: I writ to
you from *London,* but fear the Letter came not to your Hands.

Lurewell. I never had the least account of you, by Letter or 200
otherwise.

Standard. Three Years I liv'd abroad, and at my Return,
found you were gone out of the Kingdom, tho' none cou'd tell
me whither; missing you thus, I went to *Flanders,* serv'd my
King 'till the Peace commenc'd; then fortunately going on
Board at *Amsterdam,* one Ship transported us both to *England.*
At the first sight I lov'd, tho' ignorant of the hidden
Cause—You may remember, Madam, that talking once of

Marriage, I told you I was engag'd; to your dear self I meant.

210 *Lurewell*. Then Men are still most Generous and Brave—and to reward your Truth, an Estate of Three Thousand Pounds a Year waits your acceptance; and if I can satisfie you in my past Conduct, and the reasons that engag'd me to deceive all Men, I shall expect the honourable performance of your Promise, and that you wou'd stay with me in *England*.

Standard. Stay, not Fame, nor Glory, e're shall part us more. My Honour can be no where more concern'd than here.

Enter Wildair, Angelica, *both* Clinchers.

Oh, Sir *Harry*, Fortune has acted Miracles, the Story's strange and tedious, but all amounts to this. That Woman's Mind is

220 charming as her Person, and I am made a Convert too to Beauty.

Wildair. I wanted only this to make my Pleasure perfect.

Enter Smuggler.

Smuggler. So, Gentlemen and Ladies, is my Gracious Nephew *Vizard* among ye?

Wildair. Sir, he dares not show his Face among such Honourable Company, for your Gracious Nephew is a—

Smuggler. What, Sir? Have a care what you say.

Wildair. A Villain, Sir.

Smuggler. With all my Heart—I'll pardon you the beating

230 me for that very Word. And pray, Sir *Harry*, when you see him next, tell him this News from me, that I have Disinherited him, that I will leave him as poor as a disbanded Quarter-Master. And this is the positive and stiff Resolution of Threescore and Ten, an Age that sticks as obstinately to its Purpose, as to the old Fashion of its Cloak.

Wildair. You see, Madam, (*To* Angelica.) how industriously Fortune has punish'd his Offence to you.

Angelica. I can scarcely, Sir, reckon it an Offence, considering the happy Consequences of it.

240 *Smuggler*. O, Sir *Harry*, he's as Hypocritical—

Lurewell. As your self, Mr. Alderman, how fares my good old Nurse, pray, Sir?

Smuggler. O Madam, I shall be even with you before I part with your Writings and Money, that I have in my Hands.

Standard. A word with you, Mr. Alderman, do you know this Pocket-Book?

Smuggler. O Lord, it contains an Account of all my secret Practices in Trading (*Aside.*) how came you by it, Sir.

Standard. Sir *Harry* here dusted it out of your Pocket, at this Lady's House, yesterday: It contains an Account of some secret Practices in your Merchandizing; among the rest, the Counterpart of an Agreement with a Correspondent at *Bourdeaux*, about transporting *French* Wine in *Spanish* Casks— First return this Lady all her Writings, then I shall consider, whether I shall lay your Proceedings before the Parliament or not, whose Justice will never suffer your Smuggling to go unpunish'd.

Smuggler. O my poor Ship and Cargo.

Clincher Senior. Hark'ee, Master, you had as good come along with me to the *Jubilee*, now.

Angelica. Come, Mr. Alderman, for once let a Woman advise; Wou'd you be thought an Honest Man, banish Covetousness, that worst Gout of Age; Avarice is a poor pilfering quality of the Soul, and will as certainly Cheat, as a Thief wou'd Steal—Wou'd you be thought a Reformer of the Times, be less severe in your Censures, less rigid in your Precepts, and more strict in your Example.

Wildair. Right, Madam, Vertue flows freer from Imitation, than Compulsion, of which, Colonel, your Conversion and Mine are just Examples.

> *In vain are musty Morals taught in Schools,*
> *By rigid Teachers, and as rigid Rules,*
> *Where Virtue with a frowning Aspect stands,*
> *And frights the Pupil from its rough Commands.*
> *But Woman—*
> *Charming Woman can true Converts make,*
> *We Love the Precepts for the Teachers sake.*
> *Virtue in them appears so bright, so gay,*
> *We hear with Transport, and with Pride obey.*

FINIS.

EPILOGUE, spoken by Mr. *Wilks*.

Now all depart, each his respective way,
To spend an Evening's Chatt upon the Play;
Some to Hippolito's, *one homeward goes,*
And one with loving she retires to th' Rose.
The amorous Pair in all things frank and free,
Perhaps may save the Play, in number three.
The tearing Spark, if Phillis *ought gainsays,*
Breaks th' Drawer's Head, kicks her, and murders Bays.
To Coffee *some retreat to save their Pockets,*
Others more generous damn the Play at Lockets.
But there, I hope, the Author's Fears are vain,
Malice ne're spoke in generous Champain.
That Poet merits an ignoble Death,
Who fears to fall over a brave Monteth.
The Privilege of Wine we only ask,
You'll taste again, before you damn the Flask.
Our Author fears not you; but those he may
Who in cold Blood, murder a Man in Tea.
Those Men of Spleen, who fond the World should know it,
Sit down, and for their two pence *damn a Poet.*
Their Criticism's good, that we can say fort't,
They understand a Play—too well to pay for't.
From Box to Stage, from Stage to Box they run,
First steal the Play, then damn it when they've done.
But now to know what Fate may us betide,
Among our Friends in Cornhil *and* Cheapside:
But those I think have but one Rule for Plays;
They'l say they'r good, if so the World says.
If it should please them, and their Spouses know it,
They straight enquire what kind of Man's the Poet.
But from Side-box we dread a fearful Doom,
All the good-natur'd Beaux are gone to Rome.
The Ladies Censure I'd almost forgot,
Then for a Line or two t'engage their Vote:
But that way's old, below our Author's Aim,
No less than his whole Play is Complement to them.

10
20
30

For their sakes then the Play can't miss succeeding,
Tho Criticks may want Wit, they have good Breeding.
They won't, I'm sure, forfeit the Ladies Graces,
By shewing their ill-nature to their Faces. 40
Our Business with good Manners may be done,
Flatter us here, and damn us when you're gone.

APPENDIX A

The scene between Angelica and Wildair, V. i. 93–246, was significantly revised in Q2 to reflect changes made either in rehearsal or very early in the first run. A few lines, including some in Vizard's letter, were retained. The original passage in Q1 is printed below.

Wildair. Ha! Her Voice bears a commanding Accent! Every Syllable is pointed.—By Heavens I love her:—I feel her piercing Words turn the wild Current of my Blood; and thrill through all my Veins.

Angelica. View me well: consider me with a sober Thought, free from those Fumes of Wine that cast a Mist before your Sight; and you shall find that every Glance from my reproaching Eye is arm'd with sharp Resentment, and with repelling Rays that look Dishonour dead.

10 *Wildair.* I cannot view you, Madam: For when you speak, all the Faculties of my charm'd Soul crowd to my attentive Ears; desert my Eyes, which gaze insensibly.—Whatever Charm inspires your Looks, whether of Innocence or Vice, 'tis lovely, past Expression.

Angelica. If my Beauty has power to raise a Flame, be sure it is a vertuous one: if otherwise, 'tis owing to the Foulness of your own Thought, which throwing this mean Affront upon my Honour, has alarm'd my Soul, and fires it with a brave Disdain.

20 *Wildair.* Where can the Difference lie 'twixt such Hypocrisie and Truth. Madam, whate'er my unruly Passion did at first suggest; I now must own you've turn'd my Love to Veneration, and my unmannerly Demands to a most humble Prayer.— Your surprizing Conduct has quench'd the gross material Flame; but rais'd a subtil piercing Fire, which flies like lambent Lightning, through my Blood, disdaining common Fuel, preys upon the nobler Part, my Soul.

Angelica. Grant, Heav'ns, his Words be true! (*Aside.*) Then, as you hope that Passion shou'd be happy, tell me without 30 Reserve, what Motives have engag'd you thus to affront my Virtue?

Wildair. Affront her Vertue! Ah, something I fear.—Your

Question, Madam is a Riddle, and cannot be resolv'd; but the
most proper Answer the old Gentlewoman can make, who
passes for your Mother.

Angelica. Passes for my Mother! O Indignation! Were I a
Man, you durst not use me thus:—But the mean poor Abuse
you cast on me, reflects upon your self: Our Sex still strikes an
Awe upon the Brave, and only Cowards dare affront a
Woman.   40

Wildair. Then, Madam, I have a fair Claim to Courage; for,
by all Hopes of Happiness, I ne'er was aw'd so much, nor ever
felt the Power of Fear before:—But since I can't dissolve this
Knot,—I'll cut it at a Stroak.

Vizard (who, I fear is a Villain) told me you were a
Prostitute; that he had known you, and sent a Letter,
intimating, my Designs to the old Gentlewoman, who, I
suppos'd had licens'd my proceedings by leaving us so oft in
private.

Angelica. That *Vizard* is a Villain, damn'd beyond the   50
Curses of an injur'd Woman, is most true; But, that his Letter
signified any dishonourable Proceedings, is as false.

Wildair. I appeal to that for Pardon or Condemnation: He
read it to me; and the Contents were as I have declar'd, only
with this Addition; That I wou'd scruple no price for the
Enjoyment of my Pleasure.

Angelica. No price! What have I suffer'd? to be made a
Prostitute for Sale!—'Tis an unequall'd Curse upon our Sex,
That Woman's Vertue shou'd so much depend on lying Fame,
and scandalous Tongues of Men.—Read that: Then judge   60
how far I'm injur'd, and you deceiv'd.

Wildair. (Reads.)

> *Out of my earnest Inclination to serve your Ladiship, and my*
> *Cousin* Angelica, *I have sent* Sir Harry Wildair *to court my*
> *Cousin.*—[The Villain read to me a clear different thing.]
> *He's a Gentleman of great Parts and Fortune:*—[Damn his
> Compliment.] *and wou'd make your Daughter very happy in a*
> *Husband.*—[O Lord, O Lord, what have I been doing!—]
> *I hope your Ladyship will entertain him as becomes his Birth and*
> *Fortune, and the Friend of, Madam,*

Your Ladyship's most Devoted   70
and Humble Servant,
V<small>IZARD</small>.

Angelica. Now, Sir,—I hope you need no Instigation to redress my Wrongs, since Honour points the Way.

Wildair. Redress your Wrongs! Instruct me, Madam: for all your Injuries ten-fold recoil'd on me. I have abus'd Innocence, murder'd Honour, stabb'd it in the nicest part: A fair Lady's Fame.—Instruct me, Madam: For my Reason's fled, and hides its guilty Face, as conscious of its Master's Shame.

80 *Angelica.* Think, Sir, that my Blood, for many Generations, has run in the purest Channel of unsully'd Honour.

Consider what a tender Flower is Woman's Reputation, which, the least Air of foul Detraction blasts.—Call then to mind your rude and scandalous Behaviour:—Remember the base Price you offer'd:—then think that *Vizard*, Villain *Vizard*, caus'd all this, yet lives. That's all.—Farewel.

(*Going.*)

Wildair. Stay, Madam; he's too base an Offering for such Purity: But Justice has inspir'd me with a nobler Thought.—I throw a purer Victim at your Feet, my honourable Love and
90 Fortune: If chastest, purest Passion, with a large and fair Estate, can make amends, they're yours this Moment.—The matrimonial Tye shall bind us Friends this Hour.—Nay, Madam, no Reply, unless you smile.—Let but a pleasing Look fore-run my Sentence: then raise me up to Joy.

Angelica. Rise, Sir, (*Smiling.*) I'm pleas'd to find my Sentiments of you, which were always *Generous*, so generously answer'd: And since I have met a Man above the common Level of your Sex, I think my self disengag'd from the Formality of mine, and shall therefore venture to inform you,
100 that with Joy I receive your honourable Love.

Wildair. Beauty without Art! Vertue without Pride! and Love without Ceremony! The Day breaks glorious to my o'erclouded Thought, and darts its smiling Beams into my Soul. My Love is heighten'd by a glad Devotion; and Vertue rarifies the Bliss to feast the purer Mind.

Angelica. You must promise me, Sir *Harry*, to have a care of *Burgundy* henceforth.

Wildair. Fear not, sweet Innocence; Your Presence, like a Guardian Angel shall fright away all Vice.

110   *In your sweet Eyes and Words there is a Charm*
        To settle Madness, or a Fiend disarm

Of all his Spite, his Torments and his Cares:
And make him change his Curses into Pray'rs.

Exeunt.

APPENDIX B

A New PROLOGUE,

In *Answer* to my very Good Friend, Mr. *Oldmixon*; who, having Two *PLAYS* Damn'd at the Old House, had a Mind to Curry-Favour, to have a Third Damn'd at the New.

> 'Tis hard, the Author of this PLAY in View,
> Shou'd be Condemn'd, purely for pleasing you:
> Charg'd with a Crime, which you, his Judges, own
> Was only this, that he has Pleas'd the Town.
> He touch'd no POET's Verse, nor DOCTOR's Bills;
> No foe to B----re, yet a Friend to Wills.
> No Reputation Stab'd, by Sow'r Debate;
> Nor had a Hand in Bankrupt Brisco's Fate:
> And, as an Ease to's Tender Conscience, Vows,
> He's none of those that Broke the t'other House:
> In Perfect Pity to their Wretched Cheer,
> Because his PLAY was Bad—he brought it here.
> The Dreadful Sin of Murder Cries Aloud; ⎫
> And sure these Poets ne'r can hope for Good, ⎬
> Who dipt their Barbarous Pens in that poor Houses Blood. ⎭
> 'Twas Malice all: No Malice like to Theirs,
> To Write Good PLAYS, purpose to Starve the Players.
> To Starve by's Wit, is still the Poet's due; ⎫
> But, here are Men, whose Wit, is Match'd by few; ⎬
> Their Wit both Starves Themselves, and others too. ⎭
> Our PLAYS are Farce, because our House is Cram'd;
> Their PLAYS all Good: For What?—because they'r Damn'd.
> Because we Pleasure you, you call us Tools;
> And 'cause you please your selves, they call you Fools.
> By their Good Nature, they are Wits, True Blew;
> And, Men of Breeding, by their Respects to you.
> To Engage the Fair, all other Means being lost,
> They Fright the Boxes, with Old Shakespear's GHOST:
> The Ladies, of such Spectres, should take heed;
> For, 'twas the DEVIL did Raise that Ghost indeed.

Their Case is hard, that such Despair can show; ⎫
They've Disoblig'd all Powers Above, they know; ⎬
And now must have Recourse to Powers below. ⎭
Let Shakespear *then lye still,* Ghosts *do no good:*
The Fair *are Better Pleas'd with Flesh and Blood:*
What is't to them, to mind the Antient's *Taste?*
But, the Poor Folks are Mad, and I'm in haste.

Runs off.

A SONG to a Tune Called a Trip to the Jubillee

Come bring us Wine in plenty,
  We've mony enough to Spend,
I hate to see y⁰ Pots empty,
  A Man cannot drink tos Friend.
Then Draw'r bring up more Wine,
  And merrily let it pass,
Weel drink till our faces doe Shine
  He that wont may look like an Ass
And we'el tell him so to his face,
  If he offers to baulk his glass,
For we defy all such dull Society.

Tis drinking makes us merry,
  And Mirth diverts all care;
A Song of high down derry,
  Is better then heavy air;
Make ready quickly my Boys,
  And fill up your glasses higher,
For we'el present with Huzas,
  And merrily all give Fire,
Since Drinkings our desire,
  And Friendship we admire,
For here we'el Stay, ne'er call Drawer whats to pay.

SIR HARRY WILDAIR

INTRODUCTION

SOURCES AND COMPOSITION

On 10 August 1700 NS Farquhar arrived in the Netherlands. After an illness which he described in correspondence as 'a very tedious Fit of Sickness, which had almost sent your Friend a longer Journey than he was willing to undertake at present', he remained there at least until 23 October, when he wrote to one of his female friends from the Hague.[1] His return to England cannot be precisely dated, and similarly nothing is known about when and where he wrote *Sir Harry Wildair*.[2]

The season of 1699–1700 had reflected in small ways the glory of being a successful playwright. He had written at least two additional prologues and two epilogues for Drury Lane. He had contributed letters to a collection published that spring. He had indulged in several amours, publicizing some of them in published letters. With *The Constant Couple* smashing performance records, one might well expect that he had worked on a sequel as well, and considering his working habits, he might well have finished it. In only one known instance, *The Stage-Coach*, did Farquhar struggle to write;[3] ordinarily, as he said, 'I can by Three Hours Study live One and Twenty with Satisfaction my self, and contribute to the Maintainance of more Families than some who have Thousands a Year.'[4] *The Beaux Stratagem*, for example, was supposedly created in a mere six weeks, as he lay on his death bed.

However, had the Drury Lane company had access to the play, probably the *première* would have been scheduled earlier than April. Centlivre's *Perjured Husband* had opened in October, and Trotter's *Love at a Loss* in November; in December Cibber's *Love Makes a Man* met with considerable success. Two more *premières*, Trotter's *The Unhappy Penitent* and Baker's *The Humours of the Age*, were staged in February and March. Given the dazzling success of *The Constant Couple* and the momentum it had provided Drury Lane in the drive for audiences, one would have expected the sequel to be rushed on stage, with the highest expectations, as early in the next season as possible.

Internal evidence also suggests a later date of composition if one assumes that references to contemporary events were drafted in the original rather than incorporated later. The play opens with an irreverent account of the 'News from the *Baltick*', a reference to the struggles between Charles XII of Sweden and Frederick of Denmark, in which an Anglo-Dutch squadron under Admiral Rooke participated effectively; from August to October 1700 this foreign news dominated foreign affairs accounts in London newspapers. Clincher in III. i reports the death of the Pope, which had occurred on 27 September. Wildair announces the death of the King of Spain in II. ii; Carlos died on 1 November. Standard speaks in III. i of the 'new Revolution in *Europe*', which ensued when Louis XIV proclaimed Philip V King of Spain on 24 November.

Farquhar's correspondence gives no clue to the date of composition. The weight of evidence, however, points to the probability that the play was not completed until Farquhar returned from his voyage, probably in late autumn or winter of 1700–1.

His object, first and foremost, was to recapture the success of the *Trip to the Jubilee*, a goal that dictated the title, *Sir Harry Wildair: Being the Sequel of the Trip to the Jubilee*. His only provable source was his own earlier play, from which he borrowed the audience's favourite characters, Sir Harry, Jubilee Dicky, Standard, Lurewell, Angelica, Parly, and Clincher, metamorphosed from Jubilee Beau to Politician. As James points out, the plot development also parallels the *Trip*, centring once again on the reformation of Lurewell's embittered coquetry and Wildair's airy rakishness.[5] But the reformations now must take place in the context of marriages, and the flawed behaviour exhibited by Lurewell and Wildair assumes more serious overtones because they are married.

The treatment of married couples, usually a necessity in the sequel to a comedy of Farquhar's era since comedies tended to end in multiple marriages, invites comparisons with other 'marriage comedies' of the period.[6] The 1690s witnessed the beginning of a change in the way at least some playwrights dealt with the institution of marriage, a change precipitated

by growing public interest in ecclesiastical separation and
parliamentary divorce.[7] Leading playwrights in the theatres,
notably Southerne, Cibber, Vanbrugh, and Farquhar, turned
to marriage rather than courtship as a focus in some of their
comedies, writing some 'problem plays', dealing with the hard
social realities of marriage and ending with resolutions such as
separation, and some 'solution plays', serious romantic works
ending happily in reconciliation.[8] *Sir Harry Wildair* fits the
latter category, as do the marriage plays of Cibber and Steele.

In a period replete with plays translated from or based on
Latin, French, and Spanish models, the marriage plays are
the original works of their authors or the original portions
thrust into adaptations. Vanbrugh, Cibber, and Steele, for
example, usually modelled their plays on English or foreign
antecedents, except in the marriage plays.[9] Broad similarities
exist between the marriage plays of 1690–1720, but specific
borrowings are not traceable; the genre itself created expectations that operate in these plays; at the same time, far more
originality existed in them than in any other category of
English-speaking drama of the era.

James compares *Sir Harry Wildair* to Vanbrugh's *The Relapse*
(1696) as well as Behn's *The Rover Part II* (1681) both sequels
that deal with a former rake returned to his rakish ways, both
sequels doubtless motivated by the popularity of the original
comedies.[10] The theme of the relapse of the rake or coquette of
the earlier play allows the audience to enjoy once again the
character traits that pleased the first time. But the characteristics are now embodied in a spouse rather than a lover, a fact
which engenders a new set of dramatic problems.

Sir Harry Wildair shares with other marriage plays a number
of general traits: the relapse of the hero or heroine (*The
Relapse*), the supposed death of one of the partners (*Love's Last
Shift*), the boredom of husbands married to chaste, beautiful
wives (*The Provok'd Wife, The Relapse, The Wives Excuse*), and
trickery and deception used to shock an erring mate back to
matrimonial bliss (*The Wives Excuse, Love's Last Shift, The
Provok'd Wife*). But these characteristics are shared generally,
not only in earlier plays but in those that followed *Sir Harry
Wildair*, such as Cibber's *The Careless Husband*, Steele's *The
Tender Husband*, and Vanbrugh and Cibber's *The Provok'd*

Husband. They must be considered contemporary influences at best, not sources.

Scholars have shown great indifference about source-hunting for *Sir Harry Wildair*. Stonehill, however, did say Lady Lurewell 'may be a reminiscence of Lady Lovemore in Thomas Jevon's *The Devil of a Wife*' (1686).[11] In fact *Sir Harry Wildair*, like most of Farquhar's plays, owed far less to foreign or English antecedents than is usual in the period. As in other works, Farquhar did not hesitate to reuse his own materials, in this case the characters developed in *The Constant Couple*. He knew contemporary theatre, and the marriage comedies provided the context in which he wrote his sequel. But he was not a borrower.

STAGE HISTORY

The play probably opened in April since publication was listed in the Easter Term Catalogue, in May 1701. Gottfried Finger was commissioned to compose a set of act tunes. He had contributed theatrical music for several years in London; during the 1700–1 season he had written music for three earlier performances at Drury Lane, Trotter's *Love at a Loss* in November, Cibber's *Love Makes a Man* in December, and Baker's *Humours of the Age* in March. For Farquhar's play he wrote a set of eight act tunes, an overture, two rondeaux, a jig, slow air, courante, gavotte, and hornpipe. The only music indicated in the printed text was a dance in v. vi to begin the 'new wedding'.

The players who had achieved such popularity in *The Constant Couple* continued in their original characters—Wilks as Sir Harry, Norris as Dicky, Pinkethman as Clincher, Mrs Verbruggen as Lurewell, and Mrs Rogers as Angelica. Mills, who had originally played Vizard, took over the role of Standard, created by Powell; Johnson moved from playing Smuggler to Fireball. Bullock, the original Clincher Junior was removed from the cast, and Cibber as the Marquis was added; the role of Parly (spelled Parley in the printed text of the second play), created by Mrs Moore, passed to Mrs Lucas.

The prologue was clearly written by Farquhar, who

reiterated the critical ideas earlier stated in *The Adventures of Covent Garden* and developed more fully in *A Discourse upon Comedy*. The epilogue 'By a Friend' was probably spoken by Cibber as the Marquis, the only character for whom the French accent would be appropriate.

Preparations, then, were considerably scaled down from those given his earlier plays. In particular, apart from the act tunes, no attention was given to music; no songs occur within the acts. Nor is there any reason to believe that sets and costumes received any unusual attention. The company relied on *The Constant Couple* to provide their audience for the sequel.

The play is unusually short; in printed form it stretches to a mere forty-eight pages, as opposed to fifty-six in *The Constant Couple* or sixty-four in *Love and a Bottle*. The brevity of the text caused W. J. Lawrence to speculate that *The Stage-Coach* originally ran as its afterpiece.[12] Lawrence pointed out that in the Stonehill text *Sir Harry Wildair* runs fourteen pages shorter than *The Constant Couple*, and *The Stage-Coach* runs fourteen pages. However, theatrical evidence clearly shows that the farce opened at Lincoln's Inn Fields, not at Drury Lane.[13]

One concludes that any decision on whether the play succeeded or not depends on which of a number of unreliable sources one chooses to follow, for of all seasons in the eighteenth century, 1700–1 is the one about which scholars know least. The *Daily Courant* did not regularly publish advertisements yet, and the records are too scanty for accurate assessments of runs. Abel Boyer, in a contemporary account, spoke of the '*Explosion*', that is, disappointing failure, of the sequel, in contrast with the great success of the *Trip*, which, he says, ought to have cured Farquhar of trumping up a new set of dramatic principles in opposition to those of Aristotle and Horace.[14] The author of *A New Miscellany of Original Poems, on Several Occasions*, published in London in 1701, perhaps refers to Farquhar's two plays of Sir Harry when he says:

Yet 'tis this false applause [of patrons] that has for a time Supported some wretched Authors in the World, has Crouded the Pit at their Plays, and engag'd an Audience as often as they desir'd it; . . . They wou'd not believe 'twas popular Cabal, which got their Farces Credit enough with the Fair and the Great, to keep 'em up for a Winter, Tho' they have afterwards shamefully Experienc'd, that 'tis not the Power of the Great nor the fair to maintain an ill Play, or an ill Poem a Long while against the opinion of the best Judges: they have seen the same Changeable Fortune, that lifted 'em up unexpectedly from the Lowest rank of Writers to compare with the Highest for Success, has sunk 'em again as fast into the Level which Nature design'd 'em for.

The resentment is echoed in the prologue to Charles Gildon's *Love's Victim*, which opened at Lincoln's Inn Fields at the same time as *Sir Harry Wildair* and was published a week later than Farquhar's play. However, there is no indication that the run was not successful.

Theatre historians have credited the play with a successful first run although, like all other plays of the period, it certainly could not compare with *The Constant Couple*. Giles Jacob claims that it was 'acted with great Applause'.[15] Theophilus Cibber gives the impression of success while reporting that Oldfield 'received as much reputation, and was as greatly admired in her part, as Wilks was in his';[16] Mrs Verbruggen, however, actually played the role, and Oldfield succeeded to the part of Lurewell only in *The Constant Couple*, not *Sir Harry Wildair*, which was never staged in the period between Verbruggen's death and Oldfield's. Archer says it ran nine nights to good houses; Stonehill cites a run of nine nights.[17]

The *London Stage* dates the opening at Drury Lane in April and lists performances on 2, 3, and 28 May 1701. Although one can only speculate on the length of the run, Farquhar clearly benefited from at least one third night and perhaps more. The lack of a preface in the printed edition leaves no indication from Farquhar himself concerning the relative success of the play, and he never mentioned it in other published works.

Following its first season, the play disappeared from the London stage for thirty-six years. In early 1737 it ran five times at Lincoln's Inn Fields, on 1–4 February and 15 March. Although *The Constant Couple* ran five times that season, there was no effort to run the two in sequence; *The Constant Couple* played on 5 January and 25 March, but not during the run of the sequel. Giffard and his wife played Sir Harry and Lurewell, and Pinkethman and Norris continued as Clincher

Senior and Dicky, while the roles of Standard, Angelica, and Parly varied in the two plays.

Some effort attended the revival. New costumes were advertised, and the main piece was followed by *Hymen's Triumph*, a new dramatic pantomime 'With New Cloaths, Scenes, Machines, and other Decorations' as well as 'Entire New Musick, composed by Mr. Jones'. The *Daily Advertiser* reported that one of the scene changes in the afterpiece miscarried on opening night, was immediately tried again, and executed so successfully that 'a general Clap continued for more than the Space of a Minute'. One way or another, interest in the bill was generated, but there is little indication that *Sir Harry Wildair* could have carried a five-night run alone. Nor was Giffard or anyone else tempted to try the old play again. It never reappeared on the eighteenth-century London stage, although Clark records a performance in Belfast in 1753.[18]

REPUTATION AND INFLUENCE

Sir Harry Wildair has been summarily dismissed by most critics as a sequel 'like most second parts very inferiour to the first',[19] 'a distinctly inferior play to its predecessor',[20] 'flat' and 'decidedly weak',[21] boring,[22] lacking in merit, lifeless in characterization, and poor in construction.[23] A few exceptions exist. Malcolm Elwin deemed the play flawed by the intrusion of Angelica as a ghost but 'of better calibre' than the original play.[24] James, while not ranking the sequel higher than the first play, believes it is wittier, the satire is more effective, and the play is more serious. He concludes that the play 'is too important a play to be passed off as just a poor sequel.'[25] Hazlitt finds the scene in which Lurewell tries to convince Sir Harry that Angelica has been unfaithful 'is not surpassed in modern comedy'.[26]

Nor have critics considered the play influential, although some credit has been given for its effect on later comedies in the marriage group. For example, John Harrington Smith claims Steele took from the play the general model for reclaiming a self-willed wife by a determined husband in *The*

Tender Husband.[27] One could mention other similarities: the husband Sir George Truman returning to his wife as a ghost in Addison's *The Drummer* (1716), the tender trap sprung by a loving husband (not only *The Tender Husband* and *The Provok'd Husband* but plays as late as George Colman's *The Jealous Wife*), tearful discoveries and reformations (most of these plays). But Farquhar cannot be proved a source for any of these devices any more than the earlier marriage plays can be shown to have affected him directly. Marriage plays were increasingly popular in the London theatre, and Farquhar, along with Southerne, Cibber, Vanbrugh, Steele, and others influenced the trends; but none of these writers can be proved directly responsible for setting them.

Farquhar's influence on Lessing and the German writers is well known, however, and Robertson points to the Marquis as 'an obvious model' for Riccaut de la Marlinière in Lessing's *Minna von Barnhelm*.[28]

THE TEXT

Sir Harry Wildair was listed in the Easter Term Catalogue in May 1701 as a quarto printed for J. Knapton at the Crown in St. Paul's Churchyard. The earliest extant newspaper advertisement, however, appeared on 30 September 1703, when Knapton advertised it with other plays. Nevertheless, we may conclude that it first appeared in or near May 1701.

Two impressions of at least some and possibly all formes of the first edition exist. The radical shifts in the same type that are visible in various copies indicate that the type was removed from the press, tied and stored, then reimpressed. In particular, evidence of tying and storing exists in inner and outer A, outer B, inner C, inner and outer D, inner and outer F, and inner G, with less clear indications of shifting type in inner B, outer C, inner and outer E, and outer G.

Corrections were made in three formes, outer A, outer B, and inner D. The stop-press correction of *tht* to *the* occurred on the running-title of D2^r, p. 19; the same incorrect spelling had occurred throughout the run on C2^r, p. 11, impressed earlier. The corrections in outer B were of a more serious nature, but still confined to titles easily noted and corrected: on B1^r the title was changed from 'THE | SECOND PART | OF THE | Constant Couple: | Or, A' to 'Sir Harry Wildair | Being the Sequel of the'. On B2ᵛ (p. 4) and B4ᵛ (p. 8) the running-title was corrected from '*The* Constant Couple: *Or*,' to '*Sir* Harry Wildair, *being*', and on B3 (p. 5) the running-title '*A Trip to the* Jubilee.' to '*the Sequel of the Trip to the* Jubilee.' (The error itself shows how closely the play was tied in people's minds to the earlier comedy.) Type shifts occur on these pages, suggesting that the corrections may have been made between impressions. Finally, a list of 'Plays Printed for and sold by *James Knapton*, at the *Crown* in St. *Paul's Churchyard*' contains significant revisions in some copies. In the Bodleian copy, 'viz.' follows '*bound or single*,'. Shadwell's plays are numbered 1 through 12, a blank line occurs after '12 Volunteers', and *Bellamira* and '*Dryden*'s Plays, in 4 Vol. 4°.' are listed. In other copies (Folger, University of Texas [two copies], University of Pennsylvania, British Library, Harvard, for example) Shadwell's plays are not numbered, 'Lost Lover' follows 'Volunteers', '*Anthony* and *Cleopatra*' replaces '*Bellamira*', '*Dryden*'s Plays' are advertised, and 'Fortune Hunters' is added to the end of the list. Neither performance nor publication history provides clues to which of the two lists came first; the plays are all old ones, and the decisions were made according to which ones were in stock, not according to which were newly performed or published.

At any rate, the two impressions followed each other rapidly, for copies of the uncorrected state of outer B (copies in the Folger, and Harvard, for example) are bound with the corrected state of inner D. Since a substantial number of extant copies have the incorrect version of outer B, one may conjecture that the corrections in running-titles occurred between impressions. The same running-titles were used in both impressions, another indication of the rapidity of reimpression.

Two presses were used in the first impression; a clear-cut distinction can be made between sheets B–D, which used the running-titles '*Sir* Harry Wildair, *being*' and '*the Sequel of the Trip to the* Jubilee.' and sheets E–G, which used '*Sir* Harry Wildair: *Or*,' and '*A Sequel to the Trip to the* Jubilee.'

The division of labour between two compositors matches

the two presses. The compositor who set B–D used the abbreviation *Fire.* for Fireball, *Mons.* for Monsieur Marquis, and *Stand.* for Standard; he also enclosed stage directions in square brackets when they were set flush right. The compositor who set E–G used *Fir., Marq.,* and in one scene *Lo.* (for Lord), and both *Stan.* and *Stand.*; he preceded but did not follow flush-right stage directions with a square bracket. No evidence exists for which of the two compositors set A.

An oddity occurs in the binding of the Harvard copy; sheet A was incorrectly folded first along its long rather than short axis; the result is a confusion of pages in the prelims (the title-page followed by the Epilogue in the A2 position, then the Dramatis Personae in the A2^v position, etc.) The misfolding may have occurred some time after original publication; it is not the kind of error one expects from a printing house.

The printing of the first edition was, then, routine. The text was not altered; the reimpression of some, perhaps all, formes was quickly undertaken, probably as a result of re-estimation of sales. Knapton's title list was updated, but the text itself received not so much as a glance. Knapton's stock must have lasted several years, for he continued to advertise the play, in the back of *The Inconstant* in 1702, for example, and in six advertisements for *Sir Giddy Whim* in the *Daily Courant* running from 25 September to 11 October 1703.

No other editions were published during Farquhar's lifetime. After his death new editions appeared regularly in editions of his dramatic works, but raised little other interest, even in 1737 when the play was revived. Editions appeared in the *Comedies* and *Works* sometimes solely with the Lintott imprint on the general title-page for the set, but the individual play carried the Knapton imprint on the title-page until 1760, after which Crowder, Lowndes, Caslon, and others bought into the ownership. Bell and Cawthorn published editions late in the century. A Dublin edition was printed by Powell for Risk and Smith in 1727 and again for Risk in 1743. But in Dublin as well as in London Farquhar's authorship rather than the intrinsic interest of the play accounts for publication after the initial season.

'Mr. Fingers Ayres in the Comedye of Sr. Hary Wild Hair'

were published as instrumental music, probably soon after the play opened.[29]

For the present edition, I have collated copies of the first edition in the Bodleian, British Library, Folger, University of Texas (two copies), University of Pennsylvania, and Harvard. I have also collated the first and second editions of the *Comedies*.

NOTES

1. *Love and Business*, vol. ii, pp. 360–1.
2. Stonehill claims Farquhar returned from the Netherlands with a draft of the sequel (i, p. xxiii), but he offers no proof.
3. Shirley Strum Kenny, 'The Mystery of Farquhar's *Stage-Coach* Reconsidered', *Studies in Bibliography*, 32 (1979), 224–5.
4. *Love and Business*, vol. ii, p. 352.
5. James, pp. 133–4.
6. See Robert L. Root Jr., *The Problematics of Marriage: English Comedy, 1688–1710*, Ph.D. dissertation, University of Iowa, 1975; Robert D. Hume, 'Marital Discord in English Comedy from Dryden to Fielding', *Modern Philology*, 74 (1977), 248–72; Shirley Strum Kenny, ' "Elopements, Divorce, and the Devil Knows What": Love and Marriage in English Comedy, 1690–1720', *South Atlantic Quarterly*, 78 (1979), 84–106.
7. Root, *passim*; Gellert Spencer Alleman, *Matrimonial Law and the Materials of Restoration Comedy* (Wallingford, Pa., 1942).
8. Hume, 'Marital Discord', p. 3.
9. Kenny, 'Elopements', p. 3.
10. James, p. 134.
11. Stonehill, i. 157.
12. W. J. Lawrence, 'The Mystery of "The Stage Coach" ', *Modern Language Review*, 27 (1932), 397.
13. Kenny, 'Mystery', pp. 221–6.
14. *The English Theophrastus*, p. 12.
15. Jacob, p. 99.
16. Theophilus Cibber, iii. 130.
17. Archer, p. 9; Stonehill, i. 159.
18. William Smith Clark, *The Irish Stage in the County Towns 1720 to 1800* (Oxford, 1965), p. 308.
19. Genest, ii. 234.
20. Archer, p. 9.
21. Hume, p. 446.
22. Rothstein, p. 49.
23. Stonehill, i, p. xxiii.
24. Elwin, pp. 188–9.
25. James, pp. 149–59.
26. Hazlitt, p. 86.
27. Smith, p. 202.
28. Robertson, p. 58.
29. See Price, p. 224.

G. Vand" Gucht Inv k Scul.

Wildair meets the Marquis in the fields. Frontispiece, *Sir Harry Wildair*, printed for the Knaptons and sold by Feales, 1735. Act V, Scene v.

SIR HARRY WILDAIR:

Being the Sequel of the Trip to the JUBILEE.

A
COMEDY.

ABBREVIATIONS USED IN THE NOTES

Q1   First edition. London: Knapton, 1701.

O1   *Comedies*. First edition. London: Knapton, Smith, Strahan, and Lintott [1708].

O2   *Comedies*. Second edition. London: Knapton, Smith, Strahan, and Lintott [1711].

To the Right Honourable the
Earl of *Albemarle*, &c.
Knight of the most Noble Order of the Garter.

My Lord,

My Pen is both a Novice in Poetry, and a Stranger at Court, and can no more raise it self to the Stile of *Panegyrick*, than it can stoop to the *Art of Flattery*; but if in the plain and simple Habit of Truth it may presume to mix with that Crowd of Followers that daily attend upon your Lordship's Favour, please to behold a Stranger, with this difference, that he pays more Homage to your Worth, than Adoration to your Greatness.

This distinction, my Lord, will appear too nice, and [10] *Metaphysical* to the World, who know your Lordship's Merit and Place to be so inseparable, that they can only differ as the Cause from the Effect; and this, my Lord, is as much beyond dispute, as that your Royal Master, who has made the noble Choice, is the most wise, and most discerning Prince in the Universe.

To present the World with a lively Draught of your Lordship's Perfections, I should ennumerate the Judgment, Conduct, Piety and Courage of our great and gracious King, who can only place his Favours on those shining Qualifications [20] for which his Majesty is so eminently remarkable himself; but this, my Lord, will prove the business of voluminous *History*, and your Lordship's Character must attend the Fame of your great Master in the *Memoires* of Futurity, as your faithful Service has hitherto accompanied the noble Actions of his Life.

The greatest Princes in all Ages have had their Friends and Favourites, with them to communicate and debate their Thoughts, so to exercise and ripen their Judgments; or sometimes to ease their Cares by imparting them. The great [30] *Augustus*, we read, in his project of settling the unweildy *Roman* Conquests on a fix'd Basis of Government, had the design laid, not in his Counsel, but his Closet; there we find him with

his two Friends *Mecænas* and *Agrippa*, his Favourite Friends,
Persons of sound Judgment and unquestionable Fidelity;
there the great Question is freely and reasonably debated,
without the noise of Faction, and constraint of Formality, and
there was laid that prodigious Scheme of Government that
soon recovered their bleeding Country, heal'd the Wounds of
40 the Civil War, blest the Empire with a lasting Peace, and stil'd
its Monarch, *Pater Patriæ*.

The Parallel, my Lord, is easily made; we have our *Cæsar*
too, no less renowned than the formention'd *Augustus*; he first
asserted our Liberties at home against Popery and Thraldom,
headed our Armies abroad with bravery and success, gave
Peace to *Europe*, and security to our Religion. And you, my
Lord, are his *Mecænas*, the private Councellour to those great
Transactions which have made *England* so formidable to its
Enemies, that (which I blush to own) it is grown jealous of its
50 Friends.

But here, my Lord, appears the particular Wisdom and
Circumspection of your Lordship's Conduct, that you so
firmly retain the favour of your Master without the envy of the
Subject; your Moderation and even Deportment between both
has secur'd to your Lordship the Ear of the King, and the
Heart of the People, the Nation has voted you their *Good Angel*
in all Suits and Petitions to their Prince, and their success fills
the three Kingdoms with daily Praises of your Lordship's
Goodness, and his Majesty's Grace and Clemency.

60 And now, my Lord, give me leave humbly to beg that
among all the good Actions of your Lordship's high and
happy Station, the encouragement of Arts and Literature may
not be solely excluded from the influence of your Favour. The
Polite *Mecænas*, whom I presum'd to make a Parallel to your
Lordship in the Favour of his Prince, had his *Virgil*, and his
Horace, and his time was mostly divided between the Emperor
and the Poet; he so manag'd his stake of Royal Favour, that as
Augustus made him Great, so the Muses fix'd him Immortal;
and *Maro*'s Excellency, my Lord, will appear the less wonder,
70 when we consider that his Pen was so cherish'd with Bounty,
and inspir'd by Gratitude.

But I can lay no claim to the Merits of so great a Person for
my access to your Lordship, I have only this to recommend

me without Art, void of Rhetorick, that I am a true lover of my
King, and pay an unfeign'd Veneration to all those who are
his trusty Servants and faithful Ministers; which infers that I
am, my Lord, with all submission,

Your Lordship's most devoted,
and most obedient humble Servant,

George Farquhar. 80

PROLOGUE.

Our Authors, have in most their late Essays,
Prologu'd their own, by damning other Plays;
Made great Harrangues to teach you what was fit
To pass for Humour, and go down for Wit.
Athenian *Rules must form an* English *Piece,*
And Drury-Lane *comply with ancient* Greece.
Exactness *only, such as* Terence *writ,*
Must please our masqu'd Lucretias *in the Pit.*
Our youthful Author swears he cares not a-Pin
For Vossius, Scaliger, Hedelin, *or* Rapin:
He leaves to learned Pens such labour'd Lays,
You are the Rules by which he writes his Plays.
From musty Books let others take their View,
He hates dull reading, but he studies You.
First, from you Beaux, his Lesson is Formality,
And in your Footmen there,—most nice Morality;
To pleasure them his Pegasus *must fly,*
Because they judge, and lodge, three Stories high.
From the Front-Boxes he has pick'd his Stile,
And learns, without a blush, to make 'em smile;
A Lesson only taught us by the Fair,
A waggish Action—but a modest Air.
Among his Friends here in the Pit, he reads
Some Rules that every modish Writer needs.
He learns from every Covent-Garden *Critick's Face,*
The modern Forms, of Action, Time, *and* Place.
The Action he's asham'd to name—d'ye see,
The Time, *is seven, the* Place, *is* Number Three.
The Masques *he only reads by* passant *Looks,*
He dares not venture far into their Books.
Thus then the Pit *and* Boxes *are his* Schools,
Your Air, your Humour, his Dramatick Rules.
Let Criticks censure then, and hiss like Snakes, ⎫
He gains his Ends, if his light Fancy takes ⎬
St. James's *Beaux, and* Covent-Garden *Rakes.* ⎭

Dramatis Personæ.

[MEN.]

Sir *Harry Wildair*,	Mr. *Wilks.*
Col. *Standard*,	Mr. *Mills.*
Fireball, a Sea-Captain,	Mr. *Johnson.*
Mons. Marquis, a sharping Refugee,	Mr. *Cibber.*
Beau-Banter,	Mrs. *Rogers.*
Clincher, the *Jubilee*-Beau turn'd Politician,	Mr. *Pinkethman.*
Dicky, Servant to *Wildair*,	Mr. *Norris.*
Shark, Servant to *Fireball*,	Mr. *Fairbank.*
[*Remnant*, a Taylor,]	
Ghost,	Mrs. *Rogers.*
Lord *Bellamy*,	Mr. *Simpson.*

WOMEN.

Lady *Lurewell*,	Mrs. *Verbruggen.*
Angelica,	Mrs. *Rogers.*
Parley,	Mrs. *Lucas.*

[Ladies,] Servants and Attendants.

SCENE *St. James*'s.

10

---

11 Lord *Bellamy*] This character, who appears in V. iv, is identified merely as *Lord* in speech prefixes. The text gives no indication of the name Bellamy.

SIR HARRY WILDAIR,
Being the Sequel of the
Trip to the JUBILEE.

ACT I.

SCENE *The Park.*

Enter Standard *and* Fireball *meeting.*

Standard. Hah, Brother *Fireball*! Welcome ashore. What! Heart whole? Limbs firm, and Frigat safe?

Fireball. All, all, as my Fortune and Friends cou'd wish.

Standard. And what News from the *Baltick*?

Fireball. Why, yonder are three or four young Boys i'th North, that have got Globes and Scepters to play with: They fell to Loggerheads about their Play-things; the *English* came in like *Robin Goodfellow*, cry'd *Boh*, and made'em be quiet.

Standard. In the next place then, you're to congratulate my
10 Success: You have heard, I suppose, that I've Marry'd a fine Lady with a great Fortune.

Fireball. Ay, ay; 'twas my first News upon my Landing, That Colonel *Standard* had marry'd the fine Lady *Lurewell*—A fine Lady indeed! A very fine Lady!—But Faith, Brother, I had rather turn Skipper to an *Indian Canoo*, than manage the Vessel you're Master of.

Standard. Why so, Sir?

Fireball. Because she'll run adrift with every Wind that blows: She's all Sail, and no Ballast—Shall I tell you, the
20 Character I have heard of a fine Lady? A fine Lady can laugh at the Death of her Husband, and cry for the loss of a Lap Dog. A fine Lady is angry without a Cause, and pleas'd without a Reason. A fine Lady has the Vapours all the

---

I. o.1–3 Sir . . . JUBILEE.] Q1 [cor.]; THE | SECOND PART | OF THE |
Constant Couple: | Or, A Q1 [uncor.]   4 *Standard.*] O1 [*Stand.*]; *Hand.*

Morning, and the Chollick all the Afternoon. The Pride of a
fine Lady is above the merit of an understanding Head; yet
her Vanity will stoop to the Adoration of a Peruke. And in
fine, A fine Lady goes to Church for fashion's sake, and to the
Basset-Table with Devotion; and her passion for Gaming
exceeds her vanity of being thought Vertuous, or the desire of
acting the contrary.—We Seamen speak plain, Brother.   30

Standard. You Seamen are like your Element, always
Tempestuous, too ruffling to handle a fine Lady.

Fireball. Say you so? Why then, give me thy Hand, honest
Frank; and let the World talk on, and be Damn'd.

Standard. The World talk, say you? What does the World
talk?

Fireball. Nothing, nothing at all—They only say what's
usual upon such Occasions: That your Wife's the greatest
Coquet about the Court, and your Worship the greatest
Cuckold about the City: That's all.   40

Standard. How, how, Sir!

Fireball. That she's a Coquet, and you a Cuckold.

Standard. She's an Angel in her self, and a Paradise to me.

Fireball. She's an *Eve* in her self, and a Devil to you.

Standard. She's all Truth, and the World a Liar.

Fireball. Why then, I'gad, Brother it shall be so, I'll back
again to *White*'s, and whoever dares mutter scandal of my
Brother and Sister, I'll dash his Ratefia in's Face, and call him
a Lyar. (*Going.*)

Standard. Hold, hold, Sir. The World is too strong for us. 50
Were Scandal and Detraction to be thorowly reveng'd, we
must murder all the Beaux, and poyson half the Ladies: Those
that have nothing else to say, must tell Stories; Fools over
Burgundy, and Ladies over *Tea*, must have something that's
sharp to relish their Liquor; Malice is the piquant Sauce of
such Conversation; and without it, their Entertainment wou'd
prove mighty insipid.—Now, Brother, why shou'd we pretend
to quarrel with all Mankind?

Fireball. Because that all Mankind quarrel with us.

Standard. The worst Reason in the World.—Wou'd you 60
pretend to devour a Lyon, because a Lyon wou'd devour you?

Fireball. Yes, if I cou'd.

Standard. Ay, that's right; If you cou'd! But since you have neither Teeth nor Paws for such an Encounter, lie quietly down, and perhaps the furious Beast may run over you.

Fireball. 'Sdeath, Sir! But I say, that whoever abuses my Brother's Wife, tho' at the back of the King's Chair, he's a Villain.

Standard. No, no, Brother; that's a contradiction: There's no 70 such thing as Villany at Court. Indeed if the practice of Courts were found in a single Person, he might be stil'd Villain with a vengeance; but Number and Power authorizes every thing, and turns the Villain upon their Accusers. In short, Sir, every Man's Morals, like his Religion now-adays, pleads liberty of Conscience; every Man's Conscience is his convenience, and we know no Convenience but Preferment.— As for instance, Who would be so complaisant as to thank an Officer for his Courage, when that's the Condition of his Pay? And who can be so ill-natur'd as to blame a Courtier for 80 espousing that which is the very tenure of his Livelyhood?

Fireball. A very good Argument in a very damnable Cause!—But, Sir, my bus'ness is not with the Court, but with You; I desire you, Sir, to open your Eyes, at least, be pleas'd to lend an Ear to what I heard just now at the *Chocolate-House.*

Standard. Brother.

Fireball. Well, Sir?

Standard. Did the Scandal please you when you heard it?

Fireball. No.

Standard. Then why shou'd you think it shou'd please me? 90 Be not more uncharitable to your Friends than to your Self, sweet Sir: If it made you uneasy, there's no question but it will torment me, who am so much nearer concern'd.

Fireball. But wou'd you not be glad to know your Enemies?

Standard. Pshaw! If they abus'd me, they're my Friends, my intimate Friends, my Table-Company, and Pot-Companions.

Fireball. Why then, Brother, the Devil take all your Acquaintance. You were so railly'd, so torn! there were a Hundred Ranks of sneering white Teeth drawn upon your Misfortunes at once; which so mangl'd your Wife's Reputation, 100 that she can never patch up her Honour while she lives.

Standard. And their Teeth were very white, you say?

Fireball. Very white! Blood, Sir, I say, they mangl'd your Wife's Reputation.

Standard. And I say, That if they touch my Wife's Reputation with nothing but their Teeth, her Honour will be safe enough.

Fireball. Then you wont hear it?

Standard. Not a Syllable. Listning after Slander, is laying Nets for Serpents, which when you have caught, will sting you to Death: Let 'em spit their Venom among themselves, and it hurts no body.   110

Fireball. Lord! Lord! How Cuckoldom and Contentment go together!—Fye, fye, Sir! consider you have been a Soldier, dignify'd by a Noble Post; distinguish'd by brave Actions, an Honour to your Nation, and a Terror to your Enemies.—Hell! That a Man who has storm'd *Namur*, shou'd become the Jest of a Coffee-Table!—The whole House was clearly taken up with the two important Questions, Whether the Colonel was a Cuckold; or *Kid* a Pyrate?

Standard. This I cannot bear. (*Aside.*)

Fireball. Ay, (says a sneering Coxcomb) the Colonel has 120 made his Fortune with a witness; he has secur'd himself a good Estate in this Life, and a Reversion in the World to come. Then (replies another) I presume he's oblig'd to your Lordship's Bounty for the latter part of the Settlement. There are others (says a third) that have play'd with my Lady *Lurewell* at Picket, besides my Lord; I have Capotted her my self two or three times in an Evening.

Standard. O Matrimonial Patience assist me!

Fireball. Matrimonial Patience! Matrimonial Pestilence.— Shake off these drowzy Chains that fetter your Resentments. 130 If your Wife has wrong'd ye, pack her off, and let her Person be as publick as her Character: If she be honest, revenge her Quarrel.—I can stay no longer: This is my Hour of Attendance at the *Navy-Office*; I'll come and Dine with you; in the mean time, Revenge; think on't.

Exit Fireball.

Standard. (*Solus.*) How easy is it to give Advice, and how difficult to observe it! *If your Wife has wrong'd ye, pack her off.* Ay, but how? The Gospel drives the Matrimonial Nail, and the Law clinches it so very hard, that to draw it again wou'd tear the Work to pieces.—That her Intentions have wrong'd me, 140 here's a young Bawd can witness.

Enter Parley, *running cross the Stage.*

Here, here, Mrs. *Parley*, Whither so fast?

Parley. Oh Lord! my Master!—Sir, I was running to Madamoiselle *Furbelo*, the *French* Milliner, for a new *Burgundy* for my Lady's Head.

Standard. No, Child, you're employ'd about an old fashion'd Garniture for your Master's Head, if I mistake not your Errand.

Parley. Oh, Sir! there's the prettiest fashion lately come
150 over! so airy, so *French*, and all that!—The Pinners are double ruffled with twelve pleats of a side, and open all from the Face; the Hair is frizl'd all up round the head, and stands as stiff as a bodkin. Then the Favourites hang loose upon the temples, with a languishing lock in the middle. Then the Caul is extremely wide, and over all is a Cor'net rais'd very high, and all the Lappets behind.—I must fetch it presently.

Standard. Hold a little, Child, I must talk with you.

Parley. Another time, Sir, my Lady stays for it.

Standard. One Question first—What Wages does my Wife
160 give you?

Parley. Ten Pound a Year, Sir; which Gad knows is little enough, considering how I slave from place to place upon her occasions. But then, Sir, my Perquisites are considerable; I make above two Hundred Pound a Year of her Old Cloaths.

Standard. Two Hundred Pound a Year by her Old Cloaths! What then must her New ones cost?—But what do you get by Visiting Gallants and Picket?

Parley. About a Hundred Pound more.

Standard. A Hundred Pound more! Now who can expect to
170 find a Lady's Woman honest, when she gets so much by being a Jade?—What Religion are you of, Mrs. *Parley*?

Parley. I can't tell.

Standard. What was your Father?

Parley. A Mountebank.

Standard. Where were you born?

Parley. In *Holland*.

Standard. Were you ever Christen'd?

Parley. No.

Standard. How came that?

180   *Parley.* My Parents were *Anabaptists*: they dy'd before I was Dip't; I then forsook their Religion, and ha' got ne'er a new

one since.

Standard. I'm very sorry, Madam, that I had not the Honour to know the worth of your Extraction sooner, that I might have pay'd you the Respect due to your Quality.

Parley. Sir, your humble Servant.

Standard. Have you any Principles?

Parley. Five Hundred.

Standard. Have you lost your Maidenhead?—(*She puts on her Masque and nods.*) Do you love Money?   190

Parley. Yaw, Mijn Heer.

Standard. Well, Mrs. *Parley*, now you have been so free with me, I tell you what you must trust to in return: Never to come near my House again. Be gone, Monster, fly—Hell and Furies! never Christen'd! her Father a Mountebank!

Parley. Lord, Sir, you need not be so furious. Never Christen'd! What then? I may be a very good Christian for all that, I suppose.—Turn me off! Sir, you sha'n't. Meddle with your Fellows; 'tis my Lady's business to order her Women.

Standard. Here's a young Whore for ye now! A sweet 200 Companion for my Wife! Where there's such a Hellish Confident, there must be damnable Secrets.—Be gone, I say.—My Wife shall turn you away.

Parley. Sir, she won't turn me away, she shan't turn me away, nor she can't turn me away. Sir, I say, she dare not turn me away.

Standard. Why, you Jade? Why?

Parley. Because I'm the Mistriss, not She.

Standard. You the Mistriss!

Parley. Yes, I know all her Secrets; and let her offer to turn 210 me off if she dares.

Standard. What Secrets do you know?

Parley. Humph! Tell a Wife's Secrets to her Husband!— Very pretty Faith!—Sure, Sir, you don't think me such a *Jew*; Tho' I was never Christen'd, I have more Religion than that comes to.

Standard. Are you faithful to your Lady for Affection or Interest?

Parley. Shall I tell you a Christian Lye, or a Pagan Truth?

Standard. Come, Truth for once. 220

Parley. Why then Interest, Interest. I have a great Soul,

which nothing can gain but a great Bribe.

Standard. Well, tho' thou art a Devil, thou art a very honest one.—Give me thy Hand, Wench. Should not Interest make you faithful to me as much as to others?

Parley. Honest to you! Marry for what? You gave me indeed two pityful pieces the Day you were marry'd, but not a Stiver since. One Gallant gives me Ten Guineas, another a Watch, another a pair of Pendants, a fourth a Diamond Ring; and my
230 Noble Master gives me—his Linnen to mend.—Faugh!—I'll tell you a Secret, Sir: Stinginess to Servants makes more Cuckolds, than ill nature to Wives.

Standard. And am I a Cuckold, *Parley?*

Parley. No, Faith, not yet; tho' in a very fair way of having the Dignity conferr'd upon you very suddenly.

Standard. Come, Girl, you shall be my Pensioner; you shall have a glorious Revenue; for every Guinea that you get for keeping of a Secret, I'll give you two for revealing it: You shall find a Husband once in your Life outdo all your Gallants in
240 Generosity. Take their Money, Child, take all their Bribes; give 'em hopes, make 'em Assignations; serve your Lady faithfully, but tell all to me. By which means she will be kept Chaste; you will grow Rich, and I shall preserve my Honour.

Parley. But what security shall I have for performance of Articles?

Standard. Ready payment, Child.

Parley. Then give me earnest.

Standard. Five Guineas. (*Giving her Money.*)

Parley. Are they right? No *Grays-Inn* pieces amongst 'em?—
250 All right as my Leg.—Now, Sir, I'll give you an earnest of my Service. Who d'ye think is come to Town?

Standard. Who?

Parley. Your old Friend, Sir *Harry Wildair.*

Standard. Impossible!

Parley. Yes, Faith, and as gay as ever.

Standard. And has he forgot his Wife so soon?

Parley. Why, she has been dead now above a Year.—He appear'd in the *Ring* last Night with such Splendor and Equipage that he Eclips'd the Beaux, dazl'd the Ladies, and
260 made your Wife dream all Night of Six *Flanders* Mares, Seven *French* Liveries, a Wig like a Cloak, and a Hat like a

Shittle-cock.

Standard. What are a Woman's Promises and Oaths?

Parley. Wind, Wind, Sir.

Standard. When I marry'd her, how heartily did she condemn her light preceding Conduct, and for the future vow'd her self a perfect Pattern of Conjugal Fidelity!

Parley. She might as safely Swear, Sir, That this Day se'night at four a Clock the Wind will blow fair for *Flanders.* 'Tis presuming for any of us all to promise for our Inclinations 270 a whole Week. Besides, Sir, my Lady has got the knack of Coquetting it; and once a Woman has got that in her Head, she will have a touch on't every where else.

Standard. An Oracle, Child. But now I must make the best of a bad Bargain; and since I have got you on my side, I have some hopes, that by constant disappointment and crosses in her Designs I may at last tire her into good Behaviour.

Parley. Well, Sir, the Condition of the Articles being duly perform'd, I stand to the Obligation; and will tell you farther, That by and by Sir *Harry Wildair* is to come to our House to 280 Cards, and that there is a Design laid to cheat him of his Money.

Standard. What Company will there be besides?

Parley. Why, the old Set at the Basset-Table; my Lady *Lovecards,* and the usual Company: They have made up a Bank of Fifteen Hundred *Louis-d'Ors* among 'em; the whole design lies upon Sir *Harry*'s Purse, and the *French* Marquis, you know, constantly *Taillés.*

Standard. Ay, the *French* Marquis; that's one of your Benefactors, *Parley*—the Persecution of Basset in *Paris* furnish'd 290 us with that Refugee, but the character of such a Fellow ought not to reflect on those who have been real sufferers for their Religion.—But take no notice. Be sure only to inform me of all that passes.—There's more Earnest for you; Be Rich and Faithful.

Exit Standard.

Parley. (*Solus.*) I am now not only Woman to the Lady *Lurewell,* but Steward to her Husband, in my double Capacity of knowing her Secrets, and commanding his Purse. A very pretty Office in a Family! *For every Guinea that I get for keeping a Secret, he'll give me two for revealing it.*—My comings-in at this 300

rate will be worth a Master in *Chancery*'s place, and many a
poor *Templar* will be glad to marry me with half my Fortune.
(*Going*.)

Enter Dicky, *meeting her*.

Dicky. Here's a Man much fitter for your purposes.

Parley. Bless me! Mr. *Dicky*!

Dicky. The very same in Longitude and Latitude; not a bit
diminish'd, nor a Hair's breadth increas'd.—Dear Mrs.
Parley, give me a Buss, for I'm almost starv'd.

Parley. Why so hungry, Mr. *Dicky*?

Dicky. Why, I han't tasted a bit this Year and half, Woman;
310 I have been wandring about over all the World, following my
Master, and come home to dear *London* but two Days ago.
Now the Devil take me if I had not rather kiss an *English* pair
of Pattins, than the finest Lady in *France*.

Parley. Then you're overjoy'd to see *London* again?

Dicky. Oh! I was just dead of a Consumption, till the sweet
smoke of *Cheapside*, and the dear perfume of *Fleet-Ditch*, made
me a Man again.

Parley. But how came you to live with Sir *Harry Wildair*?

Dicky. Why, seeing me a handsome personable Fellow, and
320 well qualify'd for a Livery, he took a fancy to my Figure, that
was all.

Parley. And what's become of your old Master?

Dicky. Oh! hang him, he was a Blockhead, and I turn'd him
off, I turn'd *Him* away.

Parley. And were not you very sorry for the loss of your
Mistriss, Sir *Harry*'s Lady? They say, she was a very good
Woman.

Dicky. Oh! the sweetest Woman that ever the Sun shin'd
upon. I cou'd almost weep when I think of her. (*Wiping his
Eyes*.)

330 *Parley*. How did she die, pray? I cou'd never hear how
'twas.

Dicky. Give me a Buss then, and I'll tell ye.

Parley. You shall have your Wages when your Work's done.

Dicky. Well then—Courage!—Now for a doleful Tale.—You
know that my Master took a freak to go see that foolish *Jubilee*
that made such a noise among us here; and no sooner said
than done; away he went; he took his fine *French* Servants to

wait on him, and left me, the poor *English* Puppy, to wait upon his Lady at home here.—Well; so far, so good—But scarce was my Master's back turn'd, when my Lady fell to sighing, 340 and pouting, and whining, and crying; and in short, fell sick upon't.

Parley. Well, well; I know all this already; and that she pluck'd up her Spirits at last, and went to follow him.

Dicky. Very well. Follow him we did, far, and far, and farther than I can tell, till we came to a place call'd *Montpellier*, in *France*; a goodly place truly.—But, Sir *Harry* was gone to *Rome*; there was our labour lost.—But, to be short, my poor Lady, with the tiresomness of Travelling, fell sick—and dy'd. (*Crying*.)

Parley. Poor Woman! 350

Dicky. Ay, but that was not all. Here comes the worst of the Story.—Those cursed barbarous Devils, the *French*, wou'd not let us bury her.

Parley. Not bury her!

Dicky. No, She was a Heretick Woman, and they wou'd not let her Corps be put in their holy Ground.—Oh! Damn their holy Ground for me.

Parley. Now had not I better be an honest Pagan as I am, then such a Christian as one of these?—But how did you dispose the Body? 360

Dicky. Why there was one Charitable Gentlewoman that us'd to visit my Lady in her sickness: She contriv'd the matter so, that she had her bury'd in her own private Chappel. This Lady and my self carry'd her out upon our own Shoulders through a back-door at the hour of Midnight, and laid her in a Grave that I dug for her with my own Hands; and if we had been catch'd by the Priests, we had gone to the Gallows without the benefit of Clergy.

Parley. Oh! the Devil take'em.—But what did they mean by a Heretick Woman? 370

Dicky. I don't know; some sort of a *Cannibal*, I believe. I know there are some *Cannibal* Women here in *England*, that come to the Playhouses in Masques; but let them have a care how they go to *France*. (For they are all Hereticks, I believe) But I'm sure my good Lady was none of these.

Parley. But how did Sir *Harry* bear the News?

Dicky. Why, you must know, that my Lady after she was bury'd sent me—

Parley. How! after she was bury'd!

380　*Dicky.* Pshaw! Why Lord, Mistriss, you know what I mean: I went to Sir *Harry* all the way to *Rome*; and where d'ye think I found him?

Parley. Where?

Dicky. Why, in the middle of a Monastery amongst a Hundred and fifty Nuns, playing at Hot-cockles. He was surpriz'd to see honest *Dicky*, you may be sure. But when I told him the sad Story, he roar'd out a whole Volley of *English* Oaths upon the spot, and swore that he would set fire on the Pope's Palace for the injury done to his Wife. He then flew 390　away to his Chamber, lock'd himself up for three Days; we thought to have found him dead; but instead of that, he call'd for his best Linnen, fine Wig, gilt Coach; and laughing very heartily swore again he wou'd be reveng'd, and bid them drive to the Nunnery; and he was reveng'd to some purpose.

Parley. How, how, dear Mr. *Dicky*?

Dicky. Why, in the matter of five Days he got six Nuns with Child, and left 'em to provide for their Heretick Bastards.— Ah plague on'em, they hate a dead Heretick, but they love a piping hot warm Heretick with all their Hearts.—So away we 400　came; and thus did he jog on, revenging himself at this rate through all the *Catholick* Countries that we pass'd, till we came home; and now, Mrs. *Parley*, I fancy he has some designs of Revenge too upon your Lady.

Parley. Who cou'd have thought that a Man of his light airy Temper wou'd have been so revengeful?

Dicky. Why, Faith, I'm a little malicious too: Where's the Buss you promis'd me, you Jade?

Parley. Follow me you Rogue.

Runs off.

Dicky. Allons.

Follows.

The End of the First Act.

ACT II. [Scene i.]

SCENE *A Lady's Apartment.*

Enter two Chambermaids.

First Chambermaid. Are all things set in order? The Toilet fix'd, the Bottles and Combs put in form, and the Chocolate ready?

Second Chambermaid. 'Tis no great matter whether they be right or not; for right or wrong we shall be sure of our Lecture; I wish, for my part, that my time were out.

First Chambermaid. Nay, 'tis a Hundred to One but we may run away before our time be half expir'd; and she's worse this Morning than ever.—Here she comes.

Enter Lurewell.

Lurewell. Ay, there's a couple of you indeed! But how, how 10 in the name of Negligence cou'd you two contrive to make a Bed as mine was last night? A wrinkle on one side, and a rumple on t'other; the Pillows awry, and the Quilt askew.—I did nothing but tumble about, and fence with the sheets all night long.—Oh!—my bones ake this morning as if I had lain all night on a pair of *Dutch* Stairs.—Go bring Chocolate.—And, d'ye hear? Be sure to stay an Hour or two at least.—Well! these *English* Animals are so unpolish'd! I wish the Persecution wou'd rage a little harder, that we might have more of these *French Refugees* among us. These Wenches are gone to *Smyrna* 20 for this *Chocolate.*

Enter the Maids with Chocolate.

And what made you stay so long?

Chambermaid. I thought we did not stay at all, Madam.

Lurewell. Only an hour and a half by the slowest Clock in *Christendom.*—And such Salvers and Dishes too! The Lard be merciful to me; what have I committed, to be plagu'd with such Animals?—Where are my new *Japan* Salvers?—Broke, o' my Conscience! all to pieces, I'll lay my life on't.

Chambermaid. No, indeed, Madam, but your Husband—

Lurewell. How! Husband, Impudence! I'll teach you 30 Manners. (*Gives her a box on the Ear.*) Husband! Is that your *Welsh* breeding? Han't the Colonel a name of his own?

Chambermaid. Well then, the Colonel. He us'd 'em this morning, and we han't got'em since.

Lurewell. How! the Colonel use my Things! How dare the Colonel use any thing of mine?—But his Campaign Education must be pardon'd.—And I warrant they were fisted about among his dirty Levee of Disbanded Officers?—Faugh! the very thoughts of them Fellows with their eager Looks, Iron
40 Swords, ty'd up Wigs, and tuck'd in Crevats makes me sick as Death.—Come, let me see.—(*Goes to take the Chocolate, and starts back.*) Heav'ns protect me from such a sight! Lord Girl! when did you wash your Hands last? And have you been pawing me all this Morning with them dirty Fists of yours? (*Runs to the Glass.*)—I must dress all over again.—Go, take it away, I shall swoon else.—Here, Mrs. Monster, call up my Tailer; and, d'ye hear? you Mrs. Hobbyhorse, see if the Company be come to Cards yet.

Enter the Tayler [Remnant].

Oh Mr. *Remnant!* I don't know what ails these Stays you
50 have made me; but something is the matter, I don't like'em.

Remnant. I'm very sorry for that, Madam. But what fault does your Ladiship find?

Lurewell. I don't know where the fault lies; but in short, I don't like'em; I can't tell how; the things are well enough made, but I don't like'm.

Remnant. Are they too wide, Madam?

Lurewell. No.

Remnant. Too straight, perhaps.

Lurewell. Not at all; they fit me very well; but—Lard bless
60 me! can't you tell where the fault lies?

Remnant. Why truly Madam, I can't tell;—But your Ladiship, I think, is a little too slender for the fashion.

Lurewell. How! too slender for the Fashion, say you?

Remnant. Yes, Madam; there's no such thing as a good shape worn among the Quality: Your fine Wastes are clear out, clear out, Madam.

Lurewell. And why did you not plump up my Stays to the fashionable size?

Remnant. I made'em to fit you, Madam.

70 *Lurewell.* Fit me! fit my Monkey.—What, d'ye think I wear Cloaths to please my self? Fit me! Fit the Fashion, pray; no

matter for me—I thought something was the matter, I wanted
of Quality-Air.—Pray, Mr. *Remnant*, let me have a bulk of
Quality, a spreading Contour. I do remember now, the Ladies
in the Appartments, the Birth-night were most of 'em two
Yards about.—Indeed, Sir, if you contrive my Things any
more with your scanty Chambermaids Air, you shall work no
more for me.

Remnant. I shall take care to please your Ladiship for the
future.   80

Exit.

Enter a Servant.

Servant. Madam, my Master desires—

Lurewell. Hold, hold, Fellow; for Gad's sake hold; If thou
touch my Cloaths with that Tobacco breath of thine, I shall
poyson the whole Drawing-Room. Stand at the Door pray,
and speak. (Servant *goes to the door and speaks.*)

Servant. My Master, Madam, desires—

Lurewell. Oh hideous! Now the Rascal bellows so loud, that
he tears my Head to pieces.—Here, Awkwardness, go take the
Booby's Message, and bring it to me. (Chambermaid *goes to
the Door, whispers and returns.*)

Chambermaid. My Master desires to know how your Ladyship 90
rested last Night, and if you are pleas'd to admit of a Visit this
Morning?

Lurewell. Ay.—Why this is civil.—'Tis an insupportable toil
tho' for Women of Quality to model their Husbands to good
Breeding.

Enter Standard.

Standard. Good morrow my dearest Angel. How have you
rested last night?

Lurewell. Lard, Lard, Colonel! What a Room have you
made me here with your dirty Feet! Bless me, Sir! will you
never be reclaim'd from your slovenly Campaign-Airs? 'Tis 100
the most unmannerly thing in nature to make a sliding Bow in
a Lady's Chamber with dirty Shoes; it writes Rudeness upon
the Boards.

Standard. A very odd kind of Reception this, truly!—I'm
very sorry, Madam, that the offences of my Feet should create
an aversion to my Company: But for the future I shall honour
your Ladyship's Appartment as the Sepulcher at *Jerusalem*,

and always come in barefoot.

Lurewell. Sepulcher at *Jerusalem*! Your Complement, Sir, is
110 very far fetch'd: But your Feet indeed have a very Travelling-
Air.

Standard. Come, come, my Dear, no serious disputes upon
Trifles, since you know, I never contend with you in matters of
Consequence. You are still Mistriss of your Fortune, and
Marriage has only made you more absolute in your Pleasure,
by adding one faithful Servant to your Desires.—Come, clear
your brow of that uneasy Chagrine, and let that pleasing Air
take place that first ensnar'd my Heart. I have invited some
Gentlemen to Dinner, whose Friendships deserve a welcome
120 look. Let their Entertainment shew how bless'd you have
made me by a plentiful Fortune, and the Love of so agreeable
a Creature.

Lurewell. Your Friends, I suppose, are all Men of Quality?

Standard. Madam, they are Officers, and Men of Honour.

Lurewell. Officers, and Men of Honour! That is, they will
daub the Stairs with their Feet, stain all the Rooms with their
Wine, talk Bawdy to my Woman, rail at the Parliament, then
at one another, fall to cutting of Throats, and break all my
China.

130 *Standard.* Admitting that I kept such Company, 'tis unkind
in you, Madam, to talk so severely of my Friends.—But my
Brother, my Dear, is just come from his Voyage, and will be
here to pay his Respects to you.

Lurewell. Sir, I shall not be at leisure to entertain a Person
of his *Wapping* Education, I can assure you.—

Enter Parley, *and whispers her.*

Sir, I have some business with my Woman; You may
entertain your Sea-monster by your self; you may command a
Dish of Pork and Pease, with a bowl of Punch, I suppose; and
so, Sir, much good may do you.—Come *Parley.*

Exeunt Lurewell *and* Parley.

140 *Standard.* Hell and Furies!

Enter Fireball.

Fireball. With all my Heart.—Where's your Wife, Brother?
—Ho'now Man What's the matter?—Is Dinner ready?

Standard. No.—I don't know.—Hang it; I'm sorry that I invited you:—For you must know that my Wife is very much out of order; taken dangerously ill of a sudden—so that—

Fireball. Pshaw! Nothing, nothing but a Marriage-qualm; breeding Children, or breeding Mischief? Where is she, Man? Prithee let me see her; I long to see this fine Lady you have got.

Standard. Upon my word she's very ill, and can't see any body.

Fireball. So ill that she can't see any body! What, she's not in labour sure! I tell you, I will see her.—Where is she? (*Looking about.*)

Standard. No, no Brother; she's gone abroad to take the Air.

Fireball. What the Devil! Dangerous sick, and gone out! So sick, that she'll see no body within, yet gone abroad to see all the World!—Ay, you have made your Fortunes with a Vengeance!—Then, Brother, you shall Dine with me at *Locket*'s; I hate these Family-Dinners, where a Man's oblig'd to, O Lard, Madam! No Apology, dear Sir.—'Tis very good indeed, Madam.—For your self, dear Madam.—Where between the rub'd Floor under foot, the China in one Corner, and the Glasses in another, a Man can't take two strides without hazard of his Life. Commend me to a Boy and a Bell; Coming, coming, Sir. Much noise, no Attendance, and a dirty Room, where I may eat like a Horse, drink like a Fish, and swear like a Devil. Hang your Family-Dinners; Come along with me.

> As they are going out, Enter Banter, *who seeing*
> *them, seems to retire.*

Standard. Who's that? Come in, Sir. Your business, pray Sir?

Banter. Perhaps, Sir, it may not be so proper to inform you; for you appear to be as great a Stranger here as my self.

Fireball. Come, come away, Brother; he has some bus'ness with your Wife.

Banter. His Wife! Gadso! a pretty fellow, a very pretty Fellow, a likely Fellow, and a handsome Fellow; I find nothing like a Monster about him; I wou'd fain see his Forehead tho'.—Sir your humble Servant.

Standard. Yours, Sir.—But why d'ye stare so in my Face?

180 *Banter.* I was told, Sir, That the Lady *Lurewell*'s Husband
had something very remarkable over his Eyes, by which he
might be known.

Fireball. Mark that, Brother. (*In his ear.*)

Standard. Your Information, Sir, was right: I have a cross
Cut over my left Eye that's very remarkable.—But pray, Sir,
by what marks are you to be known?

Banter. Sir, I am dignify'd and distinguish'd by the Name
and Title of *Beau Banter*; I'm younger Brother to Sir *Harry
Wildair*; and I hope to Inherit his Estate with his Humour; for
190 his Wife, I'm told, is dead, and has left no Child.

Standard. Oh, Sir! I'm your very humble Servant; you're not
unlike your Brother in the Face; but methinks, Sir, you don't
become his Humour altogether so well; for what's Nature in
Him looks like Affectation in you.

Banter. Oh Lard Sir! 'tis rather Nature in Me what is
acquir'd by Him; He's beholding to his Education for his Air:
Now where d'ye think my Humour was establish'd?

Standard. Where?

Banter. At *Oxford*.

200 *Standard.*}
Fireball. } At *Oxford*!

Banter. Ay; There have I been sucking my dear *Alma Mater*
these seven Years: Yet, in defiance to Legs of Mutton, small
Beer, crabbed Books, and four-fac'd Doctors, I can dance a
Minuet, court a Mistriss, play at Picket, or make a Paroli,
with any *Wildair* in *Christendome*. In short, Sir, in spight of the
University, I'm a pretty Gentleman.—Colonel Where's your
Wife?

Fireball. (*Mimicking him.*) *In spight of the University I'm a pretty
Gentleman.*—Then, *Colonel Where's your Wife?*—Hark ye, young
210 *Plato*, Whether wou'd you have, your Nose slit, or your Ears
cut?

Banter. First tell me, Sir, Which will you chuse, to be run
through the Body, or shot through the Head?

Fireball. Follow me, and I'll tell ye.

Banter. Sir, my Servants shall attend ye, if you have no
Equipage of your own.

Fireball. Blood, Sir!

Standard. Hold, Brother, hold; he's a Boy.

Banter. Look ye, Sir, I keep half a dozen Footmen that have no bus'ness upon Earth but to answer impertinent Questions: 220 Now, Sir, if your fighting Stomach can digest these six brawny Fellows for a Breakfast, their Master, perhaps, may do you the favour to run you through the Body for a Dinner.

Fireball. Sirrah, will you fight me? I received just now six Months Pay, and by this Light I'll give you the half on't for one fair blow at your Scull.

Banter. Down with your Money, Sir.

Standard. No, no, Brother; If you are so free of your Pay, get into the next Room; there you'll find some Company at Cards, I suppose; you may find opportunity for your Revenge, my 230 House protects him now.

Fireball. Well, Sir, the time will come.

                                       Exit.

Banter. Well said, Brazen-head.

Standard. I hope, Sir, you'll excuse the freedom of this Gentleman; his Education has been among the boisterous Elements, the Windd and Waves.

Banter. Sir, I value neither Him, nor his Wind and Waves neither; I'm priviledg'd to be very impertinent, being an *Oxonian*, and oblig'd to fight no Man being a *Beau*.

Standard. Sir, I admire the fredom of your Condition.—But 240 pray, Sir, have you seen your Brother since he came last over?

Banter. I han't seen my Brother these seven Years, and scarcely heard from him but by report of others. About a Month ago he was pleas'd to honour me with a Letter from *Paris*, importing his Design of being in *London* very soon, with a desire of meeting me here. Upon this I chang'd my Cap and Gown for a long Wig and Sword, and came up to *London* to attend him, went to his House, but that was all in Sables for the death of his Wife; there I was told, that he design'd to change his Habitation, because he wou'd avoid all remem- 250 brances that might disturb his quiet. You are the first Person that has told me of his Arrival, and I expect that you may likewise inform me where to wait on him.

Standard. And I suppose, Sir, this was the bus'ness that occasion'd me the Honour of this Visit.

Banter. Partly this, and partly an Affair of greater con-

222 Fellows] O1; Fellow

sequence. You must know, Sir, that tho' I have read Ten
thousand Lies in the University, yet I have learn'd to speak
the truth my self; and to deal plainly with you, the Honour of
260 this Visit, as you were pleas'd to term it, was design'd to the
Lady *Lurewell*.

Standard. My Wife, Sir?

Banter. My Lady *Lurewell*, I say, Sir.

Standard. But I say my Wife, Sir.—What!

Banter. Why, look ye, Sir; You may have the Honour of
being call'd the Lady *Lurewell*'s Husband; but you will never
find in any Author, either Ancient or Modern, that She's
call'd Mr. *Standard*'s Wife. 'Tis true you're a handsome young
Fellow, she lik'd you; she marry'd you; and tho' the Priest
270 made you both one Flesh, yet there's no small distinction in
your Blood. You are still a disbanded Colonel, and she is still
a Woman of Quality, I take it.

Standard. And you are the most impudent young Fellow I
ever met with in all my Life, I take it.

Banter. Sir, I'm a Master of Arts, and I plead the privilege
of my standing.

Enter a Servant, *and whispers* Banter.

Servant. Sir, the Gentleman in the Coach below says he'll be
gone unless you come presently.

Banter. I had forgot.—Colonel your humble Servant.

Exit.

280   *Standard.* Sir, you must excuse me for not waiting on you
down stairs.—An impudent young Dog.

Exit another way.

[ACT II. Scene ii.]

SCENE, *changes to another Appartment in the same House.*

Enter Lurewell, Ladies, Monsieur Marquis, *and*
Fireball, *as losing Gamesters, one after another, tearing
their Cards, and flinging 'em about the Room.*

Lurewell. Ruin'd! Undone! Destroy'd!

First Lady. Oh Fortune! Fortune! Fortune!

Second Lady. What will my Husband say?

Monsieur Marquis. Oh *malheur! malheur! malheur!*

Fireball. Blood and Fire, I have lost six Months Pay.

Monsieur Marquis. A Hundred and ten Pistols, sink me.

Fireball. Sink you! sink me, that have lost two Hundred and ten Pistols.—Sink you indeed!

Lurewell. But why wou'd you hazard the Bank upon one Card?   10

Monsieur Marquis. Because me had lose by de Card tree times before.—Look dere Madam, de very next Card had been our. Oh *Morbleu! qui sa?*

Lurewell. I rely'd altogether on your setting the Cards; you us'd to *Tailée* with success.

Monsieur Marquis. *Morbleu*, Madam, me nevre lose before: But dat *Monsieur* Sir *Arry*, dat *Chevalier Wildair* is de Devil.—Where is de *Chevalier?*

Lurewell. Counting our Money within younder.—Go, go, be gone; and bethink your self of some Revenge.—Here he   20 comes.

                    [*Exit* Monsieur Marquis.]
                 Enter Wildair.

Wildair. Fifteen hundred and seventy *Louis d'Ors.*—Tall dal de rall (*Sings.*) Look ye, Gentlemen, any body may dance to this Tune,—Tall dall de ral. I dance to the Tune of Fifteen hundred Pound, the most elevated piece of Musick that ever I heard in my Life; they are the prettiest Castagnets in the World. (*Chinks the Money.*) Here, Waiters, there's Cards and Candles for you; (*Gives the Servants Money.*) Mrs. *Parley*—here's Hoods and Scarfs for you; (*Gives her Money.*) And here's fine Coaches, splendid Equipage, lovely Women, and victorious   30 Burgundy for me.—Oh ye charming Angels! the Losers sorrow, and the Gainers joy; Get ye into my Pocket.—Now, Gentlemen and Ladies, I am your humble Servant.—You'll excuse me, I hope, the small Devotion here that I pay to my good Fortune.—Ho'now! Mute!—Why, Ladies, I know that Losers have leave to speak; but I don't find that they're privileg'd to be dumb.—*Monsieur!* Ladies! Captain! (*Claps the Captain* [Fireball] *on the shoulder.*)

Fireball. Death and Hell! Why d'ye strike me, Sir? (*Drawing.*)

Wildair. To comfort you, Sir.—You'r Ear, Captain.—The

40 King of *Spain* is dead.

Fireball. The King of *Spain* dead!

Wildair. Dead as *Julius Cæsar*; I had a Letter on't just now.

Fireball. Tall dall derall (*Sings.*) Look ye, Sir, pray strike me again if you please.—See here, Sir, you have left me but one solitary Guinea in the World. (*Puts it in his Mouth.*) Down it goes i'faith.—*Allons* for the *Thatch'd House* and the *Mediterranean.* —Tall dall derall.

Exit.

Wildair. Ha, ha, ha.—Bravely resolv'd, Captain.

Lurewell. Bless me, Sir *Harry*! I was afraid of a Quarrel. I'm 50 so much concern'd!—

Wildair. At the loss of your Money, Madam. But why, why should the Fair be afflicted? Your Eyes, your Eyes, Ladies, much brighter than the Sun, have equal Power with him, and can transform to Gold whate're they please. The Lawyer's Tongue, the Soldier's Sword, the Courtier's Flattery, and the Merchant's Trade, the Slaves that dig the Golden Mines for You. Your Eyes unty the Miser's knotted Purse. Melt into Coin the Magistrate's massy Chain. (*To one Lady.*)—Youth mints for you hereditary Lands (*To another.*)—And Gamesters 60 only win when they can lose to you. (*To Lurewell.*)—This Luck is the most Rhetorical thing in Nature.

Lurewell. I have a great mind to forswear Cards as long as I live.

First Lady. And I.

Exit.

Second Lady. And I.

Crying and Exit.

Wildair. What, forswear Cards! Why, Madam, you'll ruin our Trade.—I'll maintain, that the Money at Court circulates more by the Basset-Bank, than the Wealth of Merchants by the Bank of the City. Cards! the great Ministers of Fortune's 70 Power; that blindly shuffle out her thoughtless Favours, and make a Knave more pow'rful than a King.—What Adoration do these Pow'rs receive (*Lifting up a Card.*) from the bright Hands and Fingers of the Fair, always lift up to pay Devotion here! And then the pleasing Fears, the anxious Hopes and dubious Joy that entertain our Mind! The Capot at Picket, the Paroli at Basset;—And then Ombre! Who can resist the charms of Mattadors?

Lurewell. Ay, Sir *Harry*; and then the *Sept le Va, Quinze le Va,
& Trante le Va!*

Wildair. Right, right, Madam.   80

Lurewell. Then the Nine of Diamonds at Comet, three Fives
at Cribbidge, and Pam in Lanteraloo, Sir *Harry!*

Wildair. Ay, Madam, these are Charms indeed—Then the
pleasure of picking your Husbands Pocket over Night to play
at Basset next Day! Then the advantage a fine Gentleman
may make of a Lady's necessity, by gaining a Favour for fifty
Pistols, which a Hundred Years Courtship cou'd never have
produc'd.

Lurewell. Nay, nay, Sir *Harry*, that's foul play.

Wildair. Nay, nay, Madam, 'tis nothing but the Game; and   90
I have play'd it so in *France* a Hundred times.

Lurewell. Come, come, Sir, no more on't. I'll tell you in
three words, That rather forego my Cards, I'll forswear my
Visits, Fashions, my Monkey, Friends, and Relations.

Wildair. There spoke the spirit of True born *English* Quality,
with a true *French* Education.

Lurewell. Look ye, Sir *Harry*, I am well born, and I was well
bred; I brought my Husband a large Fortune; he shall
Mortgage, or I will Elope.

Wildair. No, no, Madam; there's no occasion for that. See   100
here, Madam!

Lurewell. What, the Singing Birds, Sir *Harry?* Let me see.

Wildair. Pugh, Madam, these are but a few.—But I cou'd
wish, *de tout mon ceur, for quelque Commoditie*, where I might be
handsomely plunder'd of 'em.

Lurewell. Ah! *Chevallier! tous jour obligeant Engageant & tout
sa.*—

Wildair. Allons, Allons, Madam, tout à votre service. (Pulls her.)

Lurewell. No, no, Sir *Harry*, not at this time o'day; you shall
hear from me in the Evening.   110

Wildair. Then, Madam, I'll leave you something to entertain
you the while. 'Tis a *French*-Pocket-book, with some Remarks
of my own upon the new way of making Love. Please to peruse
it, and give me your Opinion in the Evening.

Exit.

Lurewell. (*Opening the Book.*) A *French*-Pocket-book, with

Remarks upon the new way of making Love! Then Sir *Harry* is
turning Author, I find.—What's here?—Hi, hi, hi. A Bank
Bill for a Hundred Pound.—The new way of making
Love!—*Pardie cêt fort Gallant.*—One of the prettiest Remarks
120 that ever I saw in all my Life! Well now, that *Wildair*'s a
charming Fellow,—Hi, hi, hi.—He has such an Air, and such
a Turn in what he does! I warrant now there's a Hundred
home-bred Blockheads wou'd come,—Madam, I'll give you a
Hundred Guinea's if you'll let me.—Faugh! hang their
nauseous immodest Proceedings.—Here's a Hundred pound
now, and he never names the thing; I love an impudent Action
with an Air of modesty with all my heart.

Exit.

The End of the Second Act.

ACT III. [Scene i.]

SCENE *continues.*

Lurewell *and* Monsieur Marquis.

Lurewell. Well, *Monsieur*, and have you thought how to
retaliate your ill Fortune?

Monsieur Marquis. Madam, I have tought dat Fortune be
one blind Bich. Why shou'd Fortune be kinder to de *Anglis
Chevalier* dan to de *France Marquis*? Ave I not de *bon Grace*? ave I
not de *Personage*? ave I not de understanding? Can de *Anglis
Chevalier* dance bettre dan I? can de *Anglis Chevalier* fence
bettre dan I? can de *Anglis Chevalier* play Basset bettre dan I?
Den why shou'd Fortune be kinder to de *Anglis Chevalier* dan
10 de *France Marquis*?

Lurewell. Why? Because Fortune is blind.

Monsieur Marquis. Blind! Yes begar, and dumb, and deaf
too.—Vell den. Fortune give de *Anglis* man de Riches, but
Nature give de *France*-man de *Politique* to correct de unequal
Distribution.

Lurewell. But how can you correct it *Monsieur*?

Monsieur Marquis. *Ecoute*, Madam. Sir *Arry Wildair* his Vife is
dead.

Lurewell. And what advantage can you make of that?

Monsieur Marquis. Begar, Madam.—Hi, hi, hi.—De *Anglis*- 20
man's dead Vife sall Cuckol her Usband.

Lurewell. How, how, Sir! A dead Woman Cuckold her
Husband!

Monsieur Marquis. Mark! Madam. We *France*-men make a
de distinction between de design and de term of de Treaty.—
She canno touch his Head, but she can Cuckol his Pocket of
Ten tousan *Livres.*

Lurewell. Pray explain your self, Sir.

Monsieur Marquis. I have Sir *Arry Wildair* his Vife in my
Pocket.   30

Lurewell. How! Sir *Harry*'s Wife in your Pocket!

Monsieur Marquis. Hold, Madam; dere is an *autre* distinction
between de Design and de Term of de Treaty.

Lurewell. Pray, Sir, no more of your Distinctions, but speak
plain.

Monsieur Marquis. Wen de *France*-man's *Politique* is in his
Head, dere is noting but distinction upon his Tongue.—See
here, Madam! I ave de Picture of Sir *Arry* Vife in my Pocket.

Lurewell. Is't possible?

Monsieur Marquis. Voyez.   40

Lurewell. The very same, and finely drawn. Pray, *Monsieur,*
how did you purchase it?

Monsieur Marquis. As me did purchase de Picture, so me did
gain de Substance, de dear, dear Substance; by de *bon mien,*de
France Air, *Chantant, charmant, de Politique à la Tate,* and *Dançant
à la Pie.*

Lurewell. Lard bless me! How cunningly some Women can
play the Rogue! Ah! have I found it out! Now as I hope for
mercy I am glad on't. I hate to have any Woman more
Vertuous than my self.—Here was such a work with my Lady 50
Wildair's Piety! my Lady *Wildair*'s Conduct! and my Lady
Wildair's Fidelity forsooth!—Now dear *Monsieur*, you have
infallibly told me the best News that I ever heard in my Life.
Well, and she was but one of us? heh?

Monsieur Marquis. Oh, Madam! me no tell Tale, me no
scandalize de dead; de Picture be dumb, de Picture say
noting.

Lurewell. Come, come, Sir, no more distinctions; I'm sure it

was so. I wou'd have given the World for such a story of her
60 while she was living. She was Charitable forsooth! and she
was Devout forsooth! and every body was twitted i'th' Teeth
with my Lady *Wildair*'s Reputation; And why don't you mark
her Behaviour, and *her* Discretion? She goes to Church twice a
day,—Ah! I hate these Congregation-women. There's such a
fuss and such a clutter about their Devotion, that it makes
more noise than all the Bells in the Parish.—Well, but what
advantage can you make now of the Picture?

Monsieur Marquis. De advantage of ten tousan *Livres, pardie.*
—*Attendez vous,*Madam. Dis Lady she die at *Montpelier* in
70 *France*; I ave de Broder in dat City dat write me one Account
dat she dye in dat City, and dat she send me dis Picture as a
Legacy, wid a tousan *Base mains* to de dear *Marquis*, de
charmant Marquis, mon ceur le Marquis.

Lurewell. Ay, here was Devotion! here was Discretion! here
was Fidelity! *Mon ceur le Marquis!* Ha, ha, hi.—Well, but how
will this procure the Money?

Monsieur Marquis. Now, Madam, for de *France Politique.*

Lurewell. Ay, what is the *French* Politick.

Monsieur Marquis. Never to tell a Secret to a Voman.—
80 Madam, *je sui vôtre serviteur.*

Runs off.

Lurewell. Hold, hold, Sir; we shan't part so; I will have it.

Follows.

Enter Standard *and* Fireball.

Fireball. Hah! Look! look! Look ye there, Brother! See how
they Cocquet it! Oh! There's a Look! there's a Simper! there's
a Squeeze for you! Ay, now the *Marqui's* at it. *Mon ceur, ma foy,
pardie, allons.* Don't you see how the *French* Rogue has the
Head, and the Feet, and the Hands and the Tongue, all going
together?

Standard. (*Walking in disorder.*) Where's my Reason? Where's
my Philosophy? Where's my Religion now?
90 *Fireball.* I'll tell you where they are; in your Forehead,
Sir.—Blood! I say, Revenge.

Standard. But how, dear Brother?

Fireball. Why, stab him, stab him now.—*Italian, Spaniard*, I
say.

Standard. Stab him! Why, Cuckoldom's a *Hydra* that bears a

thousand Heads; and tho' I shou'd cut this one off, the
Monster still wou'd sprout. Must I murder all the Fops in the
Nation? and to save my Head from Horns, expose my Neck to
the Halter?

Fireball. 'Sdeath, Sir, can't you kick and cuff?—Kick one.   100

Standard. Cane another.

Fireball. Cut off the Ears of a third.

Standard. Slit the Nose of a fourth.

Fireball. Tear Crevats.

Standard. Burn Perukes.

Fireball. Shoot their Coach-horses.

Standard. A noble Plot.—But now it's laid, how shall we put
it in execution? for not one of these Fellows stirs about without
his *Guard-du-Corps*. Then they're stout as Heroes; for I can
assure you that a Beau with six Footmen shall fight you any   110
Gentleman in *Christendom*.

Enter Servant.

Servant. Sir, here's Mr. *Clincher* below, who begs the Honour
to kiss your Hand.

Standard. Ay, Why here's another Beau.

Fireball. Let him come, let him come; I'll shew you how to
manage a Beau presently.

Standard. Hold, hold, Sir; this is a simple inoffensive Fellow,
that will rather make us Diversion.

Fireball. Diversion! Ay. Why, I'll knock him down for
Diversion.   120

Standard. No, no; prithee be quiet; I gave *him* a surfeit of
Intriguing some Months ago before I was marry'd.—Here,
bid him come up. He's worth your Acquaintance, Brother.

Fireball. My Acquaintance! What is he?

Standard. A Fellow of a strange Wethercock-head, very
hard, but as light as the Wind; constantly full of the Times,
and never fails to pick up some humour or other out of the
publick Revolutions, that proves diverting enough. Some time
ago he had got the Travelling Maggot in his Head, and was
going to the *Jubilee* upon all occasions; but lately, since the   130
new Revolution in *Europe*, another spirit has possess'd him,
and he runs stark mad after News and Politicks.

Enter Clincher.

Clincher. News, news, Colonel! great—Eh! what's this

Fellow? methinks he has a kind of suspicious Air.—Your Ear,
Colonel—The Pope's dead.
   Standard. Where did you hear it?
   Clincher. I read it in the publick News. (*Whispering.*)
   Standard. Ha, ha, ha.—And why d'ye whisper it for a
Secret?
140 *Clincher.* Odso! Faith that's true.—But that Fellow there;
what is he?
   Standard. My Brother *Fireball*, just come home from the
Baltick.
   Clincher. Odso! Noble Captain, I'm your most humble and
obedient Servant, from the Poop to the Forecastle.—Nay, a
kiss o' 'tother side pray.—Now, dear Captain, tell us the
News.—Odso! I'm so pleas'd I have met you! Well, the News,
dear Captain.—You sail'd a brave Squadron of Men of War
to the *Baltick*.—Well, and what then? eh?
150 *Fireball.* Why then—we came back again.
   Clincher. Did you faith?—Foolish! foolish! very foolish! a
right Sea-Captain.—But what did you do? how did you Fight?
What Storms did you meet? and what Whales did you see?
   Fireball. We had a violent Storm off the Coast of *Jutland*.
   Clincher. Jutland! Ay, that's part of *Portugal*.—Well, and
so—you enter'd the *Sound*—and you maul'd *Copenhagen* 'faith.
—And then that pretty, dear, sweet, pretty King of *Sweden*!
What sort of Man is he, pray?
   Fireball. Why, tall and slender.
160 *Clincher.* Tall and Slender! much about my pitch? heh?
   Fireball. Not so gross, nor altogether so low.
   Clincher. No! I'm sorry for't; very sorry indeed.
        Here Parley *enters, and stands at the door;* Clincher
        beckens her with his Hands behind going backwards,
        and speaking to her and the Gentlemen by turns.
Well, and what more? and so you Bombarded *Copenhagen*.—
(Mrs. *Parley*)—Whiz, slap went the Bombs. (Mrs. *Parley*)—And
so—Well, not altogether so gross, you say.—(Here is a Letter
you Jade)—Very tall, you say? Is the King very tall?—(Here's
a Guinea you Jade.)—(*She takes the Letter, and* Standard *observes
him.*) Hem! hem! Colonel I'm mightily troubl'd with the
Ptysick of late.—Hem! hem! a strange stoppage of my breast
170 here. Hem! But now it is off again.—Well, but Captain, you

tell us no News at all.

Fireball. I tell you one piece that all the World knows, and still you are a stranger to it.

Clincher. Bless me! what can this be!

Fireball. That you are a Fool.

Clincher. Eh! witty, witty Sea-Captain. Odso! And I wonder, Captain, that your understanding did not split your Ship to pieces.

Fireball. Why so, Sir?

Clincher. Because, Sir, it is so very shallow, very *shallow.* 180 There's Wit for you Sir.—

Enter Parley, *who gives* Standard *a Letter.*

Odso! a Letter! then there's News.—What, is it the Foreign Post? What News, dear Colonel what News? Hark ye Mrs. *Parley* (*He talks with* Parley *while* Standard *reads the Letter.*)

Standard. The Son of a Whore! Is it he? (*Looks at* Clincher.)

(*Reads.*) Dear Madam,

> *I Was afraid to break open the Seal of your Letter, lest I shou'd violate the work of your fair Hands.*—(Oh! fulsome Fop.) *I therefore with the warmth of my Kisses thaw'd it asunder.* (Ay, here's such a turn of Style, as takes a fine Lady!) *I have no* 190 *News, but that the Pope's dead, and I have some Pacquets upon that Affair to send to my Correspondent in* Wales; *but I shall wave all bus'ness, and hasten to wait on you at the hour appointed, with the wings of a Flying-post.*
>
> *Yours,*
> Toby Clincher.

Very well, Mr. *Toby.*—Hark ye, Brother, this Fellow's a Rogue.

Fireball. A Damn'd Rogue.

Standard. See here! a Letter to my Wife! 200

Fireball. 'Sdeath! let me tear him to pieces.

Standard. No, no; We'll manage him to more advantage. Take him with you to *Locket*'s, and invent some way or other to fuddle him.—Here, Mr. *Clincher*, I have prevail'd on my Brother here to give you a very particular Account of the whole Voyage to the *Sound* by his own Journal, if you please to honour him with your Company at *Locket*'s.

Clincher. His own Journal! Odso, let me see it.

Standard. Shew it him.

210 *Fireball.* Here, Sir.

Clincher. Now for News—(*Reads.*) *Thursday, August* the 7th, from the 6th Noon to this Day Noon Winds variable, Courses *per* Traverse, true Course protracted, with all Impediments allow'd, is North 45 Degrees, West 60 Miles, difference of Latitude 42 Miles, departure West 40 Miles, Latitude *per* Judgment 54 Degrees 13 Minutes Meridian distance current from the bearing of the Land, and the Latitude is 88 Miles.—Odso! great News faith.—Let me see.—At Noon broke our Main-top-Sail-yard, being rotten in the Slings; two

220 Whales Southward.—Odso! a Whale! great News faith.— Come, come along, Captain.—But, d'ye hear? With this Proviso, Gentlemen, That I won't drink; for hark ye, Captain, between you and I, there's a fine Lady in the Wind, and I shall have the Longitude and Latitude of a fine Lady, and the—

Fireball. A fine Lady!—Ah the Rogue! (*Aside.*)

Clincher. Yes, a fine Lady, Colonel, a very fine Lady.— Come, no Ceremony, good Captain.

         Exeunt Fireball *and* Clincher.

Standard. Well, Mrs. *Parley*, how go the rest of our Affairs?

230 *Parley.* Why, worse and worse, Sir; here's more Mischief still, more Branches a sprouting.

Standard. Of whose planting, pray?

Parley. Why, that impudent young Rogue, Sir *Harry Wildair*'s Brother has commenc'd his Suit, and fee'd Counsel already.— Look here, Sir, two Pieces, for which, by Article, I am to receive Four.

Standard. 'Tis a hard Case now, that a Man must give four Guinea's for the good News of his Dishonour. Some Men throw away their Mony in Debauching other Mens Wives,

240 and I lay out mine to keep my own honest: But this is making a Man's Fortune!—Well, Child, there's your Pay; and I expect, when I come back, a true Account of how the Business goes on.

Parley. But suppose the Bus'ness be done before you come back?

Standard. No, no; she ha'n't seen him yet; and her Pride will preserve her against the first Assaults. Besides, I sha'n't stay.

         Exit Standard *and* Parley.

[ACT III. Scene ii.]

SCENE *changes to another Room in the same House.*

Enter Wildair *and* Lurewell.

Lurewell. Well now, Sir *Harry*, this Book you gave me! As I hope to breathe I think 'tis the best penn'd Piece I have seen a great while. I don't know any of our Authors have writ in so florid and genteel a Style.

Wildair. Upon the Subject, Madam, I dare affirm there is nothing extant more moving.—Look ye, Madam, I am an Author rich in Expressions; the needy Poets of the Age may fill their Works with Rhapsodies of Flames and Darts, their barren Sighs and Tears, their speaking Looks and amorous Vows, that might in *Chaucer*'s time, perhaps, have pass'd for 10 Love; but now 'tis only such as I can touch that noble Passion, and by the true, persuasive Eloquence, turn'd in the moving Stile of *Louis-d'Ors*, can raise the ravish'd Female to a Rapture.—In short, Madam, I'll match *Cowley* in softness, o'er-top *Milton* in sublime, banter *Cicero* in Eloquence, and Dr. *Swan* in Quibbling, by the help of that most ingenious Society, call'd the Bank of *England*.

Lurewell. Ay, Sir *Harry*, I begin to hate that old Thing call'd Love; they say 'tis clear out in *France*.

Wildair. Clear out, clear out, no Body wears it: And here 20 too, Honesty went out with the slash'd Doublets, and Love with the close-body'd Gowns. Love! 'tis so obsolete, so mean, and out of fashion, that I can compare it to nothing but the miserable Picture of *Patient Grizell* at the Head of an old Ballad—Faugh!

Lurewell. Ha, ha, hi.—The best Emblem in the World.— Come, Sir *Harry*, faith we'll run it down.—Love!—Ay, methinks I see the mournful *Melpomene* with her Handkerchief at her Eye, her Heart full of Fire, her Eyes full of Water, her Head full of Madness, and her Mouth full of Nonsense—Oh! 30 hang it.

Wildair. Ay, Madam. Then the doleful Ditties, piteous Plaints, the Daggers, the Poysons!—

Lurewell. Oh the Vapours!

Wildair. Then a Man must kneel, and a Man must

swear.—There is a Repose, I see, in the next Room. (*Aside.*)

Lurwell. Unnatural Stuff!

Wildair. Oh, Madam, the most unnatural thing in the
World; as fulsome as a Sack-Posset, (*Pulling her towards the*
40 *Door.*) ungenteel as a Wedding-Ring, and as impudent as the
naked Statue was in the Park. (*Pulls her again.*)

Lurwell. Ay, Sir *Harry*; I hate Love that's impudent. These
Poets dress it up so in their Tragedies, that no modest Woman
can bear it. Your way is much the more tolerable, I must
confess.

Wildair. Ay, ay, Madam; I hate your rude Whining and
Sighing; it puts a Lady out of countenance. (*Pulling her.*)

Lurewell. Truly so it does.—Hang their Impudence.—But
where are we going?

50 *Wildair.* Only to rail at Love, Madam.

Pulls her in.

Enter Banter.
Lurewell *comes back.*

Banter. Hey! who's here?

Lurewell. Pshaw! prevented! by a Stranger too! Had it been
my Husband now.—Pshaw! [*Aside.*]—Very familiar, Sir.

Banter. Madam, you have dropt your Hat. (Banter *takes up*
Wildair*'s Hat, that was dropt in the Room.*)

Lurewell. Discover'd too by a Stranger!—What shall I do?
[*Aside.*]

Wildair. (*From within.*)—Madam, you have got the most
confounded Pens here! Can't you get the Colonel to write the
Superscriptions of your Letters for you?

Lurewell. Bless me, Sir *Harry*! don't you know that the
60 Colonel can't write *French*? Your time is so precious!

Wildair. Shall I direct by way of *Roan* or *Paris*?

Lurewell. Which you will.

Banter. Madam, I very much applaud your choice of a
Secretary; he understands the Intrigues of most Courts in
Europe they say.

Enter Wildair *with a Letter.*

Wildair. Here, Madam, I presume 'tis right.—This Gentleman a Relation of yours, Madam?—Dem him. (*Aside.*)

Banter. Brother, your humble Servant.

Wildair. Brother; By what Relation, Sir?

70 *Banter.* Begotten by the same Father, born of the same

Mother, Brother Kindred, and Brother Beau.

Wildair. Hey-day! how the fellow strings his Genealogy!—
Look ye, Sir, you may be Brother to *Tom Thumb* for ought I
know; but if you are my Brother, I cou'd have wish'd you in
your Mother's Womb for an hour or two longer.

Banter. Sir, I receiv'd your Letter at *Oxford*, with your
Commands to meet you in *London*; and if you can remember
your own hand, there 'tis. (*Gives a Letter.*)

Wildair,. (*Looking over the Letter.*) Oh! pray, Sir, let me
consider you a little.—By *Jupiter* a pretty Boy, a very pretty 80
Boy; a handsome Face, good Shape, (*Walks about and views
him.*) well dress'd.—The Rogue has a good Leg too!—Come
kiss me, Child.—Ay, he kisses like one of the Family, the right
Velvet Lip.—Can'st thou Dance, Child?

Banter. Ouy, Monsieur.

Lurewell. Hey-day! *French* too! Why sure, Sir, you cou'd
never be bred at *Oxford*!

Banter. No, Madam, my Cloaths were made in *London*.—
Brother, I have some Affairs of Consequence to communicate,
which require a little privacy.   90

Lurewell. Oh, Sir! I beg your pardon, I'le leave you.—Sir
Harry, you'll stay Supper?

Wildair. Assurement Madam.

Banter. Yes, Madam, we'll both stay.

                                        Exit [Lurewell.]

Wildair. Both!—Sir, I'le send you back to your Mutton-
Commons again. How now?

Banter. No, no; I shall find better Mutton-Commons by
messing with You, Brother.—Come, Sir *Harry*: If you stay, I
stay; If you go, *allons.*

Wildair. Why, the Devil's in this young fellow.—Why 100
Sirrah, hast thou any thoughts of being my Heir? Why, you
Dog, you ought to Pimp for me; you shou'd keep a Pack of
Wenches o' purpose to hunt down Matrimony. Don't you
know, Sir, that lawful Wedlock in Me is certain Poverty to
You? Look ye, *Sirrah*, come along; and for my disappointment
just now, if you don't get me a new Mistress to night, I'le
marry to morrow, and won't leave you a Groat.—Go, Pimp,
like a dutiful Brother.

                            Pushes him out, and Exit.
               [*The End of the Third Act.*]

ACT IV. [Scene i.]

SCENE *a Tavern.*

Enter Fireball *hauling in* Clincher.

Fireball. Come, Sir; not drink the King's Health!

Clincher. Pray now, good Captain, excuse me. Look here, Sir; the (*Pulling out his Watch.*) critical Minute, the critical Minute, faith!

Fireball. What d'ye mean, Sir?

Clincher. The Lady's critical Minute, Sir—Sir, your humble Servant. (*Going.*)

Fireball. Well! the Death of this *Spanish* King will—

Clincher. (*Returning.*) Eh! What's that of the *Spanish* King?
10 Tell me, dear Captain, tell me.

Fireball. Sir, if you please to sit down, I'll tell you that old Don *Carlos* is Dead.

Clincher. Dead!—Nay, then—(*Sits down.*)—Here, Pen and Ink, Boy; Pen and Ink presently; I must write to my Correspondent in *Wales* strait.—Dead! (*Rises, and walks about in Disorder.*)

Fireball. What's the matter, Sir?

Clincher. Politicks, Politicks, stark mad with Politicks.

Fireball. 'Sdeath, Sir, what have such Fools as you to do with Politicks?
20 *Clincher.* What, Sir? The Succession!—Not mind the Succession.

Fireball. Nay, that's minded already; 'tis settl'd upon a Prince of *France.*

Clincher. What, settl'd already!—The best News that ever came into *England*—Come, Captain, faith and troth Captain, here's a Health to the Succession.

Fireball. Burn the Succession, Sir. I won't drink it—What! Drink Confusion to our Trade, Religion and Liberties!

Clincher. Ay, by all means.—As for Trade, d'ye see? I'm a
30 Gentleman, and hate it mortally. These Tradesmen are the most impudent Fellows we have, and spoil all our good Manners. What have we to do with Trade?

Fireball. A trim Politician truly!—And what do you think of our Religion, Pray?

Clincher. Hi, hi, hi—Religion!—And what has a Gentleman
to do with Religion pray?—And to hear a Sea-Captain talk of
Religion! That's Pleasant, Faith.

Fireball. And have you no regard to our Liberties, Sir?

Clincher. Pshaw! Liberties! That's a Jest. We Beaux shall
have liberty to Whore and Drink in any Government, and 40
that's all we care for.—

Enter Standard.

Dear Collonel, the rarest News!

Standard. Damn your News, Sir; why are not you Drunk by
this?

Clincher. A very civil Question truly!

Standard. Here, Boy, bring in the Brandy—Fill.

[*Boy brings bottle and fills glass for* Clincher.]

Clincher. This is a Piece of Politicks that I don't so well
comprehend.

Standard. Here, Sir; now drink it off, or (*Draws.*) expect your
Throat cut.   50

Clincher. Ay, ay; this comes o'the Succession; Fire and
Sword already.

Standard. Come, Sir, off with it.

Clincher. Pray, Colonel, what have I done to be burnt alive?

Standard. Drink, Sir, I say—Brother, manage him, I must
be gone.

Aside to Fireball, *and Exit.*

Fireball. Ay, Drink, Sir.

Clincher. Eh! What the Devil; attack'd both by Sea and
Land!—Look ye, Gentlemen, if I must be Poyson'd, pray let
me chuse my own Dose—Were I a Lord now, I shou'd have 60
the Privilege of the Block, and as I'm a Gentleman, pray stifle
me with Claret at least; don't let me die like a Bawd, with
Brandy.

Fireball. Brandy! You Dog, abuse Brandy! Flat Treason
against the Navy-Royal.—Sirrah, I'll teach you to abuse the
Fleet.—Here, *Shark.*

Enter Shark.

Get Three or Four of the Ships Crew, and Press this Fellow
aboard the *Belzebub.*

Shark. Ay, Master.   *Exit.*

70 *Clincher.* What, aboard the *Belzebub*!—Nay, nay, dear
Captain, I'll chuse to go to the Devil this way—Here, Sir,
your good Health;—and my own Confusion, I'm afraid.
(*Drinks it off.*) Oh! Fire! Fire! Flames! Brimstone and
Tobacco! (*Beats his Stomach.*)

Fireball. Here, quench it, quench it then. [*Refills the glass.*]—
Take the Glass, Sir.

Clincher. What, another Broadside! Nay, then I'm sunk
downright.—Dear Captain, give me Quarter; consider the
present juncture of Affairs; you'll spoil my Head, ruin my
80 Politicks; faith you will.

Fireball. Here, *Shark.*

Clincher. Well, well, I will drink.—The Devil take *Shark* for
me. (*Drinks.*) Whiz, Buz. Don't you hear it? Put your Ear to
my Breast, and hear how it whizzes like a hot Iron.—Eh! Bless
me, how the Ship rouls!—I can't stand upon my Legs,
faith.—Dear Captain, give me a Kiss—Ay, burn the Succession.
—Look ye, Captain, I shall be Sea-Sick presently. (*Falls into*
Fireball's *Arms.*)

        Enter Shark *and another with a Chair.*

Fireball. Here, in with him.

Shark. Ay, ay, Sir.—Avast, avast.—Here, Boy.—No *Nants*
90 left.— (*Topes the Glass.*)

Fireball. Bring him along.

Clincher. Politicks, Politicks, Brandy Politicks.

                                [*Exeunt.*]

[ACT IV. Scene ii.]

SCENE *changes to* Lurewell's *Appartment.*

Enter Lurewell *and* Parley.

Lurewell. Did you ever see such an impudent young Rogue
as that *Banter*? He follow'd his Brother up and down from
Place to Place so very close, that we cou'd not so much as
whisper.

Parley. I reckon, Sir *Harry* will dispose of him now, Madam,
where he may be secur'd.—But I wonder, Madam, why

Clincher comes not, according to his Letter! 'tis near the Hour.

Lurewell. I wish, *Parley*, that no harm may befal me to Day; for I had a most frightful Dream last Night; I dreamt of a Mouse.   10

Parley. 'Tis strange, Madam, you shou'd be so much afraid of that little Creature that can do you no harm!

Lurewell. Look ye, Girl, we Women of Quality have each of us some darling Fright.—I now hate a Mouse; my Lady *Lovecards* abhors a Cat; Mrs. *Fiddlefan* can't bear a Squirrel; the Countess of *Picquet* abominates a Frog; and my Lady *Swimair* hates a Man.

Enter Monsieur Marquis *running.*

Monsieur Marquis. Madam! Madam! Madam! *Pardie voyez.* —*L'Argent! L'Argent!* (*Shews a Bag of Mony.*)

Lurewell. As I hope to breathe he has got it.—Well, but   20 how? How, dear *Monsieur?*

Monsieur Marquis. Ah, Madam! Begar *Monsieur* Sir *Arry* be one *Pigeaneau.*—*Voyez*, Madam; me did tell him dat my Broder in *Montpelier* did furnise his Lady wid ten tousan *Livres* for de expence of her *Travaille*; and dat she not being able to write wen she was dying, did give him de Picture for de Certificate and de Credential to receive de Mony from her Husband. Mark ye?

Lurewell. The best Plot in the World.—You told him, that your Brother lent her the Mony in *France*, when her Bills, I   30 suppose, were delay'd.—You put in that, I presume?

Monsieur Marquis. Ouy, ouy, Madam.

Lurewell. And that upon her Death-Bed she gave your Brother the Picture, as a Certificate to Sir *Harry* that she had receiv'd the Mony, which Picture your Brother sent over to you, with Commission to receive the Debt?

Monsieur Marquis. Assurement.—Dere was de *Politique*, de *France Politique!*—See, Madam, wat he can do, de *France Marquis!* He did make de *Anglise* Lady Cuckle her Husband wen she was living, and sheat him when she was dead, Begar: 40 Ha, ha, ha.—Oh! *Pardie, cette bon.*

Lurewell. Ay.—But what did Sir *Harry* say?

Monsieur Marquis. Oh! begar *Monsieur Chevalier* he love his Vife; he say, dat if she take up a hundre tousan *Livres*, he

33 your] O1; our

wou'd repay it; he knew de Picture, he say, and order me de
Money from his Stewar.—Oh *notre Dame! Monsieur* Sir *Arry* be
one Dupe.

Lurewell. Well but, *Monsieur*, I long to know one thing. Was
the Conquest you made of his Lady so easy? What Assaults
50 did you make? And what Resistance did she shew?

Monsieur Marquis. Resistance against de *France Marquis!*
Voyez, Madam; dere was tree *deux-yeux*, one Serenade, an 'two
Capre; dat was all, begar.

Lurewell. Chatillionte! There's nothing in nature so sweet to a
longing Woman, as a malicious Story.—Well, *Monsieur!* 'tis
about a thousand Pounds; we go Snacks.

Monsieur Marquis. Snacke! *Pardie*, for what? why Snacke,
Madam? Me will give you de Present of fifty *Louis-d'Ors*; dat is
ver' good Snacke for you.

60 *Lurewell.* And you'll give me no more?—Very well!

Monsieur Marquis. Ver' well! Yes, begar, 'tis ver' well.—
Considre, Madam, me be de poor *Refugé*, me'ave noting but
de religious *Charite* and de *France Politique*, de fruit of my own
Address, dat is all.

Lurewell. Ay, an Object of Charity with a thousand Pound
in his Fist! Emh! (*Knocking below.*) Oh *Monsieur!* that's my
Husband, I know his knock. He must not see you. Get into the
Closet till by and by;

Hurries him in.

and if I don't be reveng'd upon your *France Politique*, then have
70 I no *English Politique.*—Hang the Money; I wou'd not for twice
a thousand Pouind forbear abusing this Virtuous Woman to
her Husband.

Enter Parley.

Parley. 'Tis Sir *Harry*, Madam.

Lurewell. As I cou'd wish. Chairs.

Enter Wildair.

Wildair. Here, Mrs. *Parley*, in the first place I sacrifice a
Louis-d'Or to thee for good luck.

Parley. A Guinea, Sir, will do as well.

Wildair. No, no, Child; *French* Money is always most
successful in Bribes, and very much in fashion, Child.

Enter Dicky, *and runs to Sir* Harry.

80 *Dicky.* Sir, will you please to have your own Night-Caps?

Wildair. Sirrah!

Dicky. Sir, Sir! shall I order your Chair to the back-door by Five a Clock in the Morning!

Wildair. The Devil's in the Fellow. Get you gone.

Dicky runs out.

Now, dear Madam, I have secur'd my Brother, you have dispos'd the Colonel, and we may rail at Love till we han't a Word more to say.

Lurewell. Ay, Sir *Harry.*—Please to sit a little, Sir.—You must know I'm in a strange Humour of asking you some Questions.—How do you like your Lady, pray Sir? 90

Wildair. Like her!—Ha, ha, ha.—So very well faith, that for her very sake I'm in love with every Woman I meet.

Lurewell. And did Matrimony please you extremely?

Wildair. So very much, that if Polygamy were allow'd, I wou'd have a new Wife every Day.

Lurewell. Oh, Sir *Harry*! This is Raillery. But your serious Thoughts upon the Matter pray.

Wildair. Why then, Madam, to give you my true Sentiments of Wedlock: I had a Lady that I marry'd by chance, she was Vertuous by chance, and I lov'd her by great chance. Nature 100 gave her Beauty, Education an Air, and Fortune threw a young Fellow of Five and Twenty in her Lap.—I courted her all Day, lov'd her all Night; she was my Mistress one Day, my Wife another: I found in One the variety of a Thousand, and the very confinement of Marriage gave me the Pleasure of Change.

Lurewell. And she was very Vertuous?

Wildair. Look ye, Madam, you know she was Beautiful. She had good Nature about her Mouth, the Smile of Beauty in her Cheeks, sparkling Wit in her Forehead, and sprightly Love in 110 her Eyes.

Lurewell. Pshaw! I knew her very well; the Woman was well enough. But you don't answer my Question, Sir.

Wildair. So Madam, as I told you before, she was Young and Beautiful, I was Rich and Vigorous; my Estate gave a Lustre to my Love, and a Swing to our Enjoyment; round, like the Ring that made us one, our golden Pleasures circl'd without end.

Lurewell. Golden Pleasures! Golden Fiddlesticks.—What

120 d'ye tell me of your canting Stuff? Was she Vertuous, I say?

Wildair. Ready to burst with Envy; but I will torment thee a little. (*Aside.*) So, Madam, I powder'd to please her, she dress'd to engage me; we toy'd away the Morning in amorous Nonsense, loll'd away the Evening in the Park or the Play-house, and all the Night—Hem!—

Lurewell. Look ye, Sir, answer my Question, or I shall take it ill.

Wildair. Then, Madam, there was never such a Pattern of Unity.—Her Wants were still prevented by my Supplies; my
130 own Heart whisper'd me her Desires, 'cause she her self was there; no Contention ever rose, but the dear Strife of who shou'd most oblige; no Noise about Authority; for neither wou'd stoop to Command, 'cause both thought it Glory to Obey.

Lurewell. Stuff! stuff! stuff!—I won't believe a Word on't.

Wildair. Ha, ha, ha. Then, Madam, we never felt the Yoak of Matrimony, because our Inclinations made us One; a Power superiour to the Forms of Wedlock. The Marriage-Torch had lost its weaker Light in the bright Flame of mutual
140 Love that join'd our Hearts before; Then—

Lurewell. Hold, hold, Sir; I cannot bear it; Sir *Harry*, I'm afronted.

Wildair. Ha, ha, ha. Afronted!

Lurewell. Yes, Sir; 'tis an afront to any Woman to hear another commended; and I will resent it.—In short, Sir *Harry*, your Wife was a—

Wildair. Buz, Madam.—No Detraction.—I'll tell you what she was.—So much an Angel in her Conduct, that tho' I saw another in her Arms, I shou'd have thought the Devil had
150 rais'd the Phantom, and my more conscious Reason had given my Eyes the Lye.

Lurewell. Very well! Then I an't to be believ'd, it seems.—But, d'ye hear, Sir?

Wildair. Nay, Madam, do you hear? I tell you 'tis not in the power of Malice to cast a blot upon her Fame; and tho' the Vanity of our Sex and the Envy of yours conspir'd both against her Honour, I wou'd not hear a Syllable. (*Stopping his Ears.*)

Lurewell. Why then, as I hope to breathe, you shall hear

it.—The Picture! the Picture! the Picture! (*Bawling aloud.*)

Wildair. Ran, tan, tan. A Pistol-bullet from Ear to Ear.   160

Lurewell. That Picture which you had just now from the *French Marquis*, for a thousand Pound; that very Picture did your very Vertuous Wife send to the *Marquis* as a Pledge of her very vertuous and dying Affection. So that you are both robb'd of your Honour, and cheated of your Money. (*Aloud.*)

Wildair. Louder, louder, Madam.

Lurewell. I tell you, Sir, your Wife was a Jilt; I know it, I'll Swear it.—She Vertuous! She was a Devil.

Wildair. (*Sings.*) Fal, al, deral.

Lurewell. Was ever the like seen! He won't here me.—I   170 burst with Malice, and now he won't mind me! [*Aside.*]—Won't you hear me yet?

Wildair. No, no, Madam.

Lurewell. Nay, then I can't bear it. (*Burst out a Crying.*)—Sir, I must say that you're an unworthy Person, to use a Woman of Quality at this rate, when she has her Heart full of Malice; I don't know but it may make me Miscarry. Sir, I say again and again, that she was no better than one of us, and I know it; I have seen it with my Eyes, so I have.

Wildair. Good Heav'ns deliver me, I beseech thee. How   180 shall I 'scape!

Lurewell. Will you hear me yet? Dear Sir *Harry*, do but hear me; I'm longing to speak.

Wildair. Oh! I have it.—Hush, hush, hush.

Lurewell. Eh! What's the matter?

Wildair. A Mouse! a Mouse! a Mouse!

Lurewell. Where? Where? Where?

Wildair. Your Pettycoats, your Pettycoats, Madam.

                    Lurewell *shrieks, and runs off.*

Wildair. Oh my Head! I was never worsted by a Woman before.—But I have heard so much as to know the *Marquis* to   190 be a Villain. (*Knocking.*) Nay then, I must run for't. (*Runs out and returns.*)—The Entry is stopt by a Chair coming in, and something there is in that Chair that I will discover, if I can find a place to hide my self. (*Goes to the Closet-door.*) Fast! I have Keys about me for most Locks about St. *James*'s.—Let me see.—(*Tries one Key.*)—No, no; this opens my Lady

IV. ii. 189 Woman] O1; Women

Planthorn's Back-door.—(*Tries another.*)—Nor this; this is the
Key to my Lady *Stakeall*'s Garden. (*Tries a Third.*) Ay, ay, this
does it Faith.

> *Goes into the Closet, and peeps out.*

Enter Shark *and another with* Clincher *in a Chair;* Parley.

200　*Parley.* Hold, hold, Friend; who gave you Orders to lug in
your dirty Chair into the House?

Shark. My Master, Sweetheart.

Parley. Who is your Master, Impudence?

Shark. Every Body, Sawce-Box.—And for the present here's
my Master; and if you have any thing to say to him, there he is
for ye. (*Lugs* Clincher *out of the Chair, and throws him upon the
Floor.*) Steer away, *Tom.*

> *Exeunt.*

Wildair. What the Devil, Mr. *Jubilé*, is it you?

Parley. Bless me! the Gentleman dead! Murder! Murder!

> *Enter* Lurewell.

210　*Lurewell.* Protect me! What's the matter, *Clincher*?

Parley. Mr. *Clincher*, are you dead, Sir?

Clincher. Yes.

Lurewell. Oh! then 'tis well enough.—Are you drunk, Sir?

Clincher. No.

Lurewell. Well! certainly I'm the most unfortunate Woman
living: All my Affairs, all my Designs, all my Intrigues,
miscarry.—Faugh! the Beast! But, Sir, what's the matter with
you?

Clincher. Politicks.

220　*Parley.* Where have you been, Sir?

Clincher. Shark?

Lurewell. What shall we do with him, *Parley*? If the Colonel
shou'd come home now, we were ruin'd.

> *Enter* Standard.

Oh inevitable Destruction!

Wildair. Ay, ay; unless I relieve her now, all the World can't
save her.

Standard. Bless me! what's here? Who are you, Sir?

Clincher. Brandy.

Standard. See there, Madam!—Behold the Man that you
230 prefer to me! And such as He are all those Top-Gallants that
daily haunt my House, ruin your Honour, and disturb my

Quiet.—I urge not the Sacred Bond of Marriage; I'll wave your earnest Vows of Truth to me, and only lay the Case in equal Ballance; and see whose Merit bears the greater weight, his or mine?

Wildair. Well argu'd, Colonel.

Standard. Suppose your self freely disingag'd, unmarry'd, and to make a choice of him you thought most worthy of your Love; wou'd you prefer a Brute? a Monkey? one destin'd only for the Sport of Man?—Yes; take him to your Bed; there let 240 the Beast disgorge his fulsom Load in your fair lovely Bosom, snore out his Passion in your soft Embrace, and with the Vapours of his sick Debauch perfume your sweet Appartment.

Lurewell. Ah nauseous! nauseous! Poyson!

Standard. I ne're was taught to set a value on my self: But when compar'd to him, there Modesty must stoop, and Indignation give my words a loose, to tell you, Madam, that I am a Man unblemish'd in my Honour, have nobly serv'd my King and Country; and for a Lady's Service, I think that Nature has not been defective.   250

Wildair. Egad I shou'd think so too; the Fellow's well made.

Standard. I'm young as He, my Person too as fair to outward view; and for my Mind, I thought I cou'd distinguish right, and therefore made a choice of you.—Your Sex have bless'd our Isle with Beauty, by distant Nations priz'd; and cou'd they place their Loves aright, their Lovers might acquire the Envy of Mankind, as well as They the Wonder of the World.

Wildair. Ay, now he coaxes.—He will conquer unless I relieve her in time; She begins to melt already.

Standard. Add to all this, I love you next to Heav'n; and by 260 that Heav'n I swear, the constant study of my Days and Nights have been to please my dearest Wife. Your Pleasure never met controul from me, nor your Desires a frown.—I never mention'd my distrust before, nor will I now wrong your discretion so as e're to think you made him an appointment.

Lurewell. Generous, generous Man! (*Weeps.*)

Wildair. Nay, then 'tis time for me; I will relieve her.—(*He steals out of the Closet, and coming behind* Standard, *claps him on the Shoulder.*) Colonel your humble Servant.—

Standard. Sir *Harry*? How came you hither?

Wildair. Ah poor Fellow! Thou hast got thy Load with a 270 Witness; but the Wine was humming strong; I have got a touch on't my self. (*Reels a little.*)

Standard. Wine, Sir *Harry*! What Wine?

Wildair. Why, 'twas new *Burgundy*, heady Stuff: But the Dog was soon gone, knock'd under presently.

Standard. What, then Mr. *Clincher* was with you it seems? Eh?

Wildair. Yes faith, we have been together all this Afternoon; 'Tis a pleasant foolish Fellow. He wou'd needs give me a
280 Welcome to Town, on pretence of hearing all the News from the *Jubilee*. The Humour was new to me; so to't we went.—But 'tis a weak-headed Coxcomb; two or three Bumpers did his Business.—Ah Madam! What do I deserve for this? (*Aside to* Lurewell.)

Lurewell. Look ye there, Sir; you see how Sir *Harry* has clear'd my Innocence.—I'm oblig'd t'ye, Sir; but I must leave you to make it out.

To Wildair *and Exit.*

Standard. Yes, yes; he has clear'd you wonderfully.—But pray, Sir.—I suppose you can inform me how Mr. *Clincher* came into my House? Eh?
290 *Wildair.* Ay. Why, you must know that the Fool got presently as drunk as a Drum: so I had him tumbl'd into a Chair, and order'd the Fellows to carry him Home. Now you must know he lodges but three Doors off; but the Boobies it seems mistook the Door, and brought him in here, like a Brace of Loggerheads.

Standard. Oh, yes! Sad Loggerheads, to mistake a Door in *James*'s for a House in *Covent-Garden*. Here.

Enter Servants.

Take away that Brute.—

Servants *carry off* Clincher.

And you say 'twas new Burgundy, Sir *Harry*, very strong?
300 *Wildair.* Egad there is some trick in this matter, and I shall be discover'd. (*Aside.*) Ay, Colonel; but I must be gone, I'm engaged to meet.—Colonel, I'm your humble Servant. (*Going.*)

Standard. But, Sir *Harry*, where's your Hat? Sir?

Wildair. Oh *Morbleu*! These Hats, Gloves, Canes, and Swords, are the ruin of all our designs. (*Aside.*)

Standard. But where's your Hat, Sir *Harry*?

Wildair. I'll never Intrigue again with any thing about me

but what is just bound to my Body. How shall I come
off?—Hark ye, Colonel in your Ear; I wou'd not have your
Lady hear it.—You must know, just as I came into the Room 310
here, what shou'd I spy but a great Mouse running a-cross
that Closet-door. I took no notice, for fear your Lady should
be frighted, but with all my force (d'ye see?) I flung my Hat at
it, and so threw it into the Closet, and there it lies.

Standard. And so, thinking to kill the Mouse, you flung your
Hat into that Closet?

Wildair. Ay, ay; that was all. I'll go fetch it.

Standard. No, Sir *Harry*, I'll bring it out.

Goes into the Closet.

Wildair. Now have I told a matter of twenty Lyes in a
Breath. [*Aside.*]   320

Standard. Sir *Harry*, is this the Mouse that you threw your
Hat at?

Standard *comes in with the Hat in one Hand, and*
hawling in the Monsieur Marquis *with the other.*

Wildair. I'm amaz'd!

Monsieur Marquis. *Pardie*, I'm amaze too.

Standard. Look ye, *Monsieur Marquis*, as for your part, I shall
cut your Throat, Sir.

Wildair. Give me leave, I must cut his Throat first.

Monsieur Marquis. Wat! Bote cut my Troat! Begar, *Messiers*,
I have but one Troat.

Enter Parley, *and runs to* Standard.

Parley. Sir the *Monsieur* is Innocent; he came upon another 330
design. My Lady begins to be penitent, and if you make any
noise, 'twill spoil all.

Standard. Look ye, Gentlemen, I have too great a confidence
in the Vertue of my Wife, to think it in the power of you, or
you, Sir, to wrong my Honour: But I am bound to guard her
Reputation so that no attempts be made that may provoke a
Scandal; Therefore, Gentlemen, let me tell you 'tis time to
desist.

Exit.

Wildair. Ay, ay; so 'tis faith.—Come *Monsieur*, I must talk
with you, Sir.   340

Exeunt.

[*The End of the Fourth Act.*]

ACT V. [Scene i.]

SCENE Standard*'s House.*

Enter Standard *and* Fireball.

Standard. In short, Brother, a Man may talk till Dooms-day
of Sin, Hell, and Damnation; but your Rhetorick will ne're
convince a Lady that there's any thing of the Devil in a
handsome Fellow with a fine Coat. You must shew the
Cloven-Foot, expose the Brute, as I have done; and tho' her
Vertue sleeps, her Pride will surely take th' Alarm.

Fireball. Ay, but if you had let me cut off one of the Rogue's
Ears before you sent him away.—

Standard. No, no; the Foot has serv'd my turn, without the
10 Scandal of a publick Resentment; and the effect has shewn
that my Design was right; I've touch'd her very heart, and she
relents apace.

Enter Lurewell *running.*

Lurewell. Oh! my Dear, save me! I'm frighted out of my
Life.

Fireball. Blood and Fire! Madam, who dare touch you?
(*Draws his Sword and stands before her.*)

Lurewell. Oh, Sir! A Ghost! a Ghost! I have seen it twice.

Fireball. Nay then, we Soldiers have nothing to do with
Ghosts; send for the Parson. (*Sheaths his Sword.*)

Standard. 'Tis fancy, my Dear, nothing but fancy.

20 *Lurewell.* Oh dear Colonel! I'll never lie alone again; I'm
frighted to death; I saw it twice; twice it stalk'd by my
Chamber-door, and with a hollow Voice utter'd a piteous
Groan.

Standard. This is strange! Ghosts by day-light!—Come, my
Dear, along with me; don't shrink; we'll see to find this Ghost.

Exeunt.

[ACT V. Scene ii.]

SCENE *changes to the Street.*

Enter Wildair, Monsieur Marquis, *and* Dicky.

Wildair. Dicky.

Dicky. Sir.

Wildair. Do you remember any thing of a thousand Pounds lent to my Wife in *Montepelier* by a *French* Gentleman?

Monsieur Marquis. Ouy, *Monsieur Dicky*, you remembre de Gentilman, he was one *Marquis.*

Dicky. Marqui, Sir! I think for my part that all the Men in *France* are *Marqui's*. We met above a thousand *Marqui's*, but the Devil a one of 'em cou'd lend a thousand Pence, much less a thousand Pound.   10

Monsieur Marquis. Morbleu, que dit vous, Bougre le Chien?

Wildair. Hold, Sir, pray answer me one Question. What made you fly your Country?

Monsieur Marquis. My Religion, *Monsieur.*

Wildair. So you fled for your Religion out of *France*, and are a downright Atheist in *England?* A very tender Conscience truly!

Monsieur Marquis. Begar, *Monsieur*, my Conscience be ver' tendre; he no suffre not his Mastre to starve, *pardie.*

Wildair. Come, Sir, no Ceremony; refund.   20

Monsieur Marquis. Refunde! Vat is dat refunde? *Parle François, Monsieur?*

Wildair. No, Sir; I tell you in plain *English*, return my Mony, or I'll lay you by the Heels.

Monsieur Marquis. Oh! begar dere is de *Anglis*-man now. Dere is de Law for me. De Law! *Ecoute, Monsieur* Sir *Arry.—Voyez sa.—*De *France* Marquis scorn de Law. My Broder lend your Vife de Mony, and here is my Witness. (*Draws.*)

Wildair. Your Evidence, Sir, is very positive, and shall be examin'd: But this is no place to try the Cause; we'll cross the   30 Park into the Fields; you shall throw down the Mony between us, and the best Title, upon a fair hearing, shall take it up.—*Allons!*

Exit.

Monsieur Marquis. O! *de tout mon cœur.—Allons! Fient à la tate,* begar.

Exit.

[ACT V. Scene iii.]

SCENE Lurewell's *Apartment.*

Enter Lurewell *and* Parley.

Lurewell. Pshaw! I'm such a frightful Fool! 'Twas nothing but a Fancy.—Come, *Parley*, get me Pen and Ink, I'll divert it. Sir *Harry* shall know what a Wife he had, I'm resolv'd. Tho' he wou'd not hear me speak, he'll read my Letter sure. (*Sits down to write.*)

Ghost. (*From within.*)—Hold.

Lurewell. Protect me!—*Parley*, don't leave me.—But I won't mind it.

Ghost. Hold.

Lurewell. Defend me! don't you hear a Voice?

10   *Parley.* I thought so, Madam.

Lurewell. It call'd to hold. I will venture once more. (*Sits down to write.*)

Ghost. Disturb no more the quiet of the Dead.

Lurewell. Now 'tis plain. I heard the Words.

Parley. Deliver us, Madam, and forgive us our Sins! what is it?

Ghost *enters,* Lurewell *and* Parley *shriek, and run to
a corner of the Stage.*

Ghost. Behold the airy Form of wrong'd *Angelica*,
Forc'd from the Shades below to vindicate her Fame.
Forbear, malicious Woman, thus to load
With scandalous Reproach the Grave of Innocence.
20   Repent, vain Woman!
Thy Matrimonial Vow is register'd above,
And all the Breaches of that solemn Faith
Are register'd below. I'm sent to warn thee to repent.
Forbear to wrong thy injur'd Husband's Bed,
Disturb no more the quiet of the Dead.

Stalks off.

Lurewell *swoons, and* Parley *supports her.*
Parley. Help! help! help!

Enter Standard *and* Fireball.

Standard. Bless us! What, Fainting! What's the matter!
Fireball. Breeding, Breeding, Sir.
Parley. Oh, Sir! We're frighted to Death; here has been the
Ghost again.   30
Standard. Ghost! Why you're mad sure! What Ghost!
Parley. The Ghost of *Angelica*, Sir *Harry Wildair*'s Wife.
Standard. *Angelica!*
Parley. Yes, Sir; and here it preach'd to us the Lord knows
what, and murder'd my Mistress with meer Morals.
Fireball. A good hearing, Sir; 'twill do her good.
Standard. Take her in, *Parley.*

Parley *leads out* Lurewell.

What can this mean, Brother?
Fireball. The meaning's plain. There's a design of Communication between your Wife and Sir *Harry*, so his Wife is 40
come to forbid the Banns; that's all.
Standard. No, no, Brother. If I may be induc'd to believe the
walking of Ghosts, I rather fancy that the rattle-headed
Fellow her Husband has broke the poor Lady's Heart; which,
together with the Indignity of her Burial, has made her uneasy
in her Grave.—But whatever be the cause, it's fit we
immediately find out Sir *Harry*, and inform him.

Exeunt.

[ACT V. Scene iv.]

SCENE *the Park.*

Company Walking; Wildair and Monsieur Marquis
passing hastily over the Stage, one calls.

Lord. Sir Harry.
Wildair. My Lord?—*Monsieur* I'll follow you, Sir.

Exit Monsieur Marquis.

Lord. I must talk with you, Sir.

Wildair. Pray, my Lord, let it be very short; for I was never in more haste in my Life.

Lord. May I presume, Sir, to enquire the cause that detain'd you so late last Night at my House?

Wildair. More mischief again!—Perhaps, my Lord, I may not presume to inform you.

10 *Lord.* Then perhaps, Sir, I may presume to extort it from you.

Wildair. Look ye, my Lord, don't frown; it spoils your Face.—But, if you must know, your Lady owes me Two hundred Guinea's, and that Sum I will presume to extort from your Lordship.

Lord. Two hundred Guinea's! Have you any thing to shew for it?

Wildair. Ha, ha, ha. Shew for it, my Lord! I shew'd Quint and Quatorz for it; and to a Man of Honour that's as firm as a 20 Bond and Judgment.

Lord. Come, Sir, this won't pass upon me; I'm a Man of Honour.

Wildair. Honour! Ha, ha, ha.—'Tis very strange! that some Men, tho' their Education be never so Gallant, will ne'er learn Breeding!—Look ye, my Lord, when you and I were under the Tuition of our Governors, and convers'd only with old *Cicero*, *Livy, Virgil, Plutarch,* and the like; why then such a Man was a Villain, and such a one was a Man of Honour: But now, that I have known the Court, a little of what they call the *Beau-monde*, 30 and the *Belle-esprit,* I find that Honour looks as ridiculous as *Roman* Buskins upon your Lordship, or my full Peruke upon *Scipio Africanus.*

Lord. Why shou'd you think so, Sir?

Wildair. Because the World's improv'd, my Lord, and we find that this Honour is a very troublesom and impertinent Thing.—Can't we live together like good Neighbours and *Christians,* as they do in *France*? I lend you my Coach, I borrow yours; you Dine with me, I Sup with you; I lie with your Wife, and you lie with mine.—Honour! That's such an Impertinence! 40 —Pray, my Lord, hear me. What does your Honour think of murdering your Friend's Reputation? making a Jest of his Misfortunes? cheating him at Cards, debauching his Bed, or the like?

Lord. Why, rank Villany.

Wildair. Pish! pish! Nothing but good Manners, excess of good Manners. Why, you han't been at Court lately. There 'tis the only practise to shew our Wit and Breeding.—As for Instance; your Friend reflects upon you when absent, because 'tis good Manners; raillies you when present, because 'tis witty; cheats you at Picquet, to shew he has been in *France*; and 50 lies with your Wife, to shew he's a Man of Quality.

Lord. Very well, Sir.

Wildair. In short, my Lord, you have a wrong Notion of Things. Shou'd a Man with a handsom Wife revenge all Affronts done to his Honour, poor *White*, *Chaves*, *Morris*, *Locket*, *Pawlet*, and *Pontack*, were utterly ruin'd.

Lord. How so, Sir?

Wildair. Because, my Lord, you must run all their Customers quite through the Body. Were it not for abusing your Men of Honour, Taverns, and Chocolate-houses cou'd not subsist; 60 and were there but a round Tax laid upon Scandal and false Politicks, we Men of Figure wou'd find it much heavier than Four Shillings in the Pound.—Come, come, my Lord; no more on't, for Shame; your Honour is safe enough; for I have the Key of its back Door in my Pocket.

                                                    Runs off.

Lord. Sir, I shall meet you another time.

                                                    Exit.

[ACT V. Scene v.]

SCENE *the Fields.*

Enter Monsieur Marquis *with a Servant carrying his fighting Equipage, Pumps, Cap, &c. He dresses himself accordingly, and flourishes about the Stage.*

Monsieur Marquis. Sa, sa, sa; *fient a la Tate. Sa; Embaracade; Quart sur redouble.* Hey!
                    Enter Wildair.
Wildair. Ha, ha, ha; The Devil! Must I fight with a

Tumbler? These *French* are as great Fops in their Quarrels, as
in their Amours.

Monsieur Marquis. Allons! allons! Stripe, Stripe.

Wildair. No, no, Sir; I never strip to engage a Man; I Fight
as I Dance.—Come, Sir, down with the Money.

Monsieur Marquis. Dere it is, *pardie. (Lays down the Bag between*
10 *'em.)—Allons!*—

> *Enter* Dicky, *and gives* Wildair *a Gun.*

Morbleu! que sa?

Wildair. Now, *Monsieur*, if you offer to stir, I'll shoot you
through the Head.—*Dicky*, take up the Money, and carry it
home.

Dicky. Here it is faith. And if my Master be kill'd, the
Money's my own.

Monsieur Marquis. Oh *Morbleu*! de *Anglis*-man be one Coward.

Wildair. Ha, ha, ha. Where is your *France Politique* now?
Come, *Monsieur*; you must know I scorn to fight any Man for my
20 own; but now we're upon the level; and since you have been at
the trouble of putting on your Habiliments, I must requite your
pains. So come on, Sir. (*Lays down the Gun, and uses his Sword.*)

Monsieur Marquis. Come on! For wat? Wen de Money is
gone! De *France*-man fight where dere is no profit! *Pardonnez
moy, pardie. (Sits down to pull off his Pumps.)*

Wildair. Hold, hold, Sir; you must Fight. Tell me how you
came by this Picture?

Monsieur Marquis. (Starting up.) Wy den, begar, *Monsieur
Chevalier*, since de Money be gone, me will speak de
30 *verite*;—*Pardie, Monsieur*, me did make de Cuckle of you, and
your Vife send me de Picture for my pain.

Wildair. Look ye Sir, if I thought you had Merit enough to
gain a Lady's Heart from me, I wou'd shake hands
immediately, and be Friends: But as I believe you to be a vain
scandalous Lyar, I'll cut your Throat.

> *They Fight.*
> *Enter* Standard *and* Fireball, *who part 'em.*

Standard. Hold, hold, Gentlemen.—Brother, secure the
Marquis.—Come, Sir *Harry*, put up; I have something to say to
you very serious.

Wildair. Say it quickly then; for I am a little out of humour,
40 and want something to make me laugh.

As they talk, Monsieur Marquis *dresses, and* Fireball
helps him.

Standard. Will what's very serious make you laugh?

Wildair. Most of all.

Standard. Pshaw! Pray, Sir *Harry*, tell me, What made you
leave your Wife?

Wildair. Ha, ha, ha. I knew it.—Pray, Colonel, What makes
you stay with your Wife?

Standard. Nay, but pray answer me directly; I beg it as a
favour.

Wildair. Why then, Colonel, you must know we were a pair
of the most happy, toying, foolish people in the World, till she 50
got, I don't know how, a Crotchet of Jealousy in her Head.
This made her frumpish; but we had ne're an angry word: She
only fell a crying over Night, and I went for *Italy* next
Morning.—But pray no more on't.—Are you hurt, *Monsieur*?

Standard. But, Sir *Harry*, you'll be serious when I tell you
that her Ghost appears.

Wildair. Her Ghost! Ha, ha, ha. That's pleasant faith.

Standard. As sure as Fate, it walks in my House.

Wildair. In your House. Come along, Colonel. By the Lard
I'll kiss it. 60

Exeunt Wildair *and* Standard.

Monsieur Marquis. Monsieur le Capitain, Adieu.

Fireball. Adieu! No, Sir, you shall follow Sir *Harry*.

Monsieur Marquis. For wat?

Fireball. For what? Why, d'ye think I'm such a Rogue as to
part a Couple of Gentlemen when they're fighting, and not see
'em make an end on't; I think it a less Sin to part Man and
Wife.—Come along, Sir.

Exit pulling Monsieur Marquis.

[ACT V. Scene vi.]

SCENE Standard*'s House.*

Enter Wildair *and* Standard.

Wildair. Well then! This, it seems, is the inchanted Chamber.

The Ghost has pitch'd upon a handsome Appartment however.—Well, Colonel, When do you intend to begin?

Standard. What, Sir?

Wildair. To laugh at me; I know you design it.

Standard. Ha! By all that's powerful there it is.

Ghost *walks cross the Stage.*

Wildair. The Devil it is!—Emh! Blood, I'll speak to't.—*Vous, Mademoiselle Ghost, parle vous François?*—No! Hark ye, Mrs. *Ghost,* Will your Ladyship be pleas'd to inform us who you
10 are, that we may pay you the Respect due to your Quality?

Ghost *returns.*

Ghost. I am the Spirit of thy departed Wife.

Wildair. Are you faith? Why then here's the Body of thy living Husband, and stand me if you dare. (*Runs to her and Embraces her.*)—Ha! 'tis Substance I'm sure.—But hold, Lady *Ghost,* stand off a little, and tell me in good earnest now, Whether you are alive or dead?

Angelica. (*Throwing off her Shroud.*)—Alive! alive! (*Runs and throws her Arms about his Neck.*) and never liv'd so much as in this moment.

20 *Wildair.* What d'ye think of the Ghost now, Colonel? (*She hangs upon him.*) Is it not a very loving Ghost?

Standard. Amazement!

Wildair. Ay, 'tis amazement truly—Look, ye, Madam; I hate to converse so familiarly with Spirits: Pray keep your distance.

Angelica. I am alive; indeed I am.

Wildair. I don't believe a word on't. (*Moving away.*)

Standard. Sir *Harry,* you're more afraid now than before.

Wildair. Ay, most Men are more afraid of a living Wife than
30 a dead one.

Standard. 'Tis good manners to leave you together however.

Exit.

Angelica. 'Tis unkind, my Dear, after so long and tedious an absence, to act the Stranger so. I now shall dye in earnest, and must for ever vanish from your sight. (*Weeping and going.*)

Wildair. Hold, hold, Madam. Don't be angry, my Dear; you took me unprovided; Had you but sent me Word of your coming, I had got three or four Speeches out of *Oroonoko* and the *Mourning Bride* upon this occasion, that wou'd have

charm'd your very Heart. But we'll do as well as we can; I'll
have the Musick from both Houses; *Pawlet* and *Locket* shall 40
contrive for our Taste; we'll charm our Ears with *Abell*'s
Voice; feast our Eyes with one another; and thus, with all our
Senses tun'd to Love, we'll hurl off our Cloaths, leap into Bed,
and there—Look ye, Madam, if I don't welcome you home
with Raptures more natural and more moving than all the
Plays in *Christendom*—I'll say no more.

Angelica. As mad as ever.

Wildair. But ease my Wonder first, and let me know the
Riddle of your Death.

Angelica. Your unkind Departure hence, and your avoiding 50
me abroad, made me resolve, since I cou'd not live with You,
to die to all the World besides; I fancy'd, that tho' it exceeded
the force of Love, yet the Power of Grief perhaps might change
your Humour, and therefore had it given out that I dy'd in
France; my Sickness at *Montpelier*, which indeed was next to
Death, and the Affront offer'd to the Body of our Ambassador's
Chaplain at *Paris*, conduc'd to have my Burial private. This
deceiv'd my Retinue; and by the Assistance of my Woman,
and your faithful Servant, I got into Man's Cloaths, came
home into *England*, and sent him to observe your Motions 60
abroad, with Orders not to undeceive you till your return.—
Here I met you in the Quality of Beau *Banter*, your busie
Brother, under which Disguise I have disappointed your
Design upon my Lady *Lurewell*; and in the Form of a Ghost
have reveng'd the Scandal she this Day threw upon me, and
have frighted her sufficiently from lying alone. I did resolve to
have frighted you likewise, but you were too hard for me.

Wildair. How weak, how squeamish, and how fearful are
Women .when they want to be humour'd! and how Extravagant, how daring, and how provoking, when they get the 70
impertinent Maggot in their Head!—But by what means, my
Dear, cou'd you purchase this double Disguise? how came you
by my Letter to my Brother?

Angelica. By intercepting your Letters all since I came
home. But for my Ghostly Contrivance, good Mrs. *Parley*
(mov'd by the Justness of my Cause, and a Bribe) was my
chief Engineer.

Enter Fireball *and* Monsieur Marquis.

Fireball. Sir *Harry*, if you have a mind to fight it out, there's your Man; If not, I have discharg'd my Trust.

80 *Wildair.* Oh, *Monsieur*! Won't you salute your Mistress, Sir?

Monsieur Marquis. Oh, *Morbleu*! Begar me must run to some oder Countrey now for my Religion.

Angelica. Oh! what the *French Marquis*! I know him.

Wildair. Ay, ay, my Dear, you do know him; and I can't be angry, because 'tis the Fashion for Ladies to know every Body: But methinks, Madam, that Picture now! Hang it, considering 'twas my Gift, you might have kept it.—But no matter; my Neighbors shall pay for't.

Angelica. Picture, my Dear! Cou'd you think I e'er wou'd
90 part with that? No; of all my Jewels this alone I kept, 'cause 'twas given by you. (*Shews the Picture.*)

Wildair. Eh! wonderful! —and what's this? (*Pulling out t'other Picture.*)

Angelica. They're very much alike.

Wildair. So like that one might fairly pass for t'other.—*Monsieur Marquis, ecouté.*—You did lie wid my Vife, and she did give you de Picture for your Pain? Eh? Come, Sir, add to your *France Politique* a little of your Native Impudence, and tell us plainly how you came by't.

Monsieur Marquis. Begar, *Monsieur Chevalier*, wen de *France*-
100 man can tell no more Lie, den vill he tell Trute.—I was acquaint wid de Paintre dat draw your Lady's Picture, an' I give him ten Pistole for de Copy.—An so me have de Picture of all de Beauty in *London*; and by dis *Politique* me have de Reputation to lie wid dem all.—

Wildair. When perhaps your Pleasure never reach'd above a Pit-Masque in your Life.

Monsieur Marquis. An' begar, for dat matre, de natre of Women, a Pit-Masque is as good as de best. De Pleasure is noting, de Glory is all, *Alamode de France*.

             Struts out.

110 *Wildair.* Go thy ways for a true Pattern of the Vanity, Impertinence, Subtlety, and Ostentation of thy Country.— Look ye, Captain, give me thy hand; once I was a Friend to *France*; but henceforth I promise to sacrifice my Fashions, Coaches, Wigs, and Vanity, to Horses, Arms, and Equipage, and serve my King in *propria persona*, to promote a vigorous

War, if there be occasion.

Fireball. Bravely said, Sir *Harry*: And if all the Beaux in the Side-boxes were of your mind, we wou'd send 'em back their *L'Abbe*, and *Balon*, and shew 'em a new Dance to the Tune of *Harry the Fifth*.   120

Enter Standard, Lurewell, Dicky, *and* Parley.

Wildair. Oh Colonel! Such Discoveries!

Standard. Sir, I have heard all from your Servant; honest *Dicky* has told me the whole Story.

Wildair. Why then let *Dicky* run for the Fiddles immediately.

Dicky. Oh, Sir! I knew what it would come to; they're here already, Sir.

Wildair. Then, Colonel, we'll have a new Wedding, and begin it with a Dance.—Strike up.

A Dance here.

Standard. Now, Sir, *Harry*, we have retriev'd our Wives; Yours from Death, and mine from the Devil; and they are at   130 present very honest. But how shall we keep 'em so?

Angelica. By being good Husbands, Sir; and the great Secret for keeping Matters right in Wedlock, is never to quarrel with your Wives for Trifles; for we are but Babies at best, and must have our Play-things, our Longings, our Vapours, our Frights, our Monkeys, our China, our Fashions, our Washes, our Patches, our Waters, our Tattle, and Impertinence; therefore I say 'tis better to let a Woman play the Fool, than provoke her to play the Devil.

Lurewell. And another Rule, Gentlemen, let me advise you   140 to observe, Never to be Jealous; or if you shou'd, be sure never to let your Wife think you suspect her; for we are more restrain'd by the Scandal of the Lewdness, than by the Wickedness of the Fact; and once a Woman has born the Shame of a Whore, she'll dispatch you the sin in a moment.

Wildair. We're oblig'd to you, Ladies, for your Advice; and, in return, give me leave to give you the definition of a good Wife, in the Character of my own.

The Wit of her Conversation never outstrips the Conduct of her Behaviour: She's affable to all Men, free with no Man, and   150 only kind to me: Often chearful, sometimes gay, and always pleas'd, but when I am angry; then sorry, not sullen: The Park, Play-house, and Cards, she frequents in compliance with Custom; but her Diversions of Inclination are at home: She's more cautious of a remarkable Woman, than of a noted Wit, well knowing that the Infection of her own Sex is more catching than the Temptation of ours: To all this, she is beautiful to a Wonder, scorns all Devices that engage a Gallant, and uses all Arts to please her Husband.

160
  So, spite of Satyr 'gainst a marry'd Life,
   A Man is truly blest with such a Wife.

FINIS.

EPILOGUE,

By a Friend.

Ventre bleu! *vere is dis dam Poet? vere?*
Garzoon! me vil cut off all his two Ear:
Je suis *Enrage—now he is not here.*
He has affront de French! Le Villaine bête.
De French! your best Friend!—you suffre dat?
Parbleu! Messieurs a serait fort *Ingrate!*
Vat have you English, *dat you can call your own?*
Vat have you of grand Plaisire *in dis Towne,*
Vidout it come from France, *dat will go down?*
Picquet, Basset; *your Wine, your Dress, your Dance;*   10
'Tis all you see, tout Alamode de France.
De Beau dere buy a hondre knick, knack;
He carry out Wit, but seldome bring it back:
But den he bring a Snuff-Box Hinge, so small
De Joynt, you can no see de Vark at all,
Cost him five Pistole, dat is sheap enough,
In tree year it sal save, alf an ounce of Snoffe.
De Coquet she ave her Ratafia dere,
Her Gown, her Complexion, Deux yeux, *her Lovere;*
As for de Cuckold—dat indeed you can make here.   20
De French *it is dat teach the Lady wear*
De short Muff, wit her vite Elbow bare;
*De Beau de large Muff, with his sleeve down dere.** ⎫   *Pointing to
                                                              his Fingers.*
We teach your Vife, to ope dere Husbands Purses,
To put de Furbalo round dere Coach, and dere Horses.
Garzoon! vee teach you every ting de Varle:
For vy den your damn Poet dare to snarle?
Begar, me vil be revenge upon his Play,
Tre tousand Refugee (Parbleu ce'st vray)
Sal all come here, and dam him upon his tird day.   30

THE STAGE-COACH

INTRODUCTION

SOURCES AND COMPOSITION

FACTS about the composition of *The Stage-Coach* are exceedingly scarce. The Dublin quarto, dated 1704, named Farquhar as author on the title-page. The first London edition was published anonymously on 3 or 4 May 1705.[1] Two more anonymous London editions were published in 1709. No London edition of Farquhar's *Comedies* or *Works* included the farce until 1736 when it was printed in the seventh edition of the *Dramatick Works*; it did not reappear in a London edition of the *Works* until 1772. All later single editions of the farce, both in Dublin and London, however, identified Farquhar as the author. *A Compleat Catalogue Of All the Plays That Were Ever Yet Printed in the English Language* (London: W. Mears, 1719), listed the farce along with Farquhar's other seven plays under his name.

Scholars have traditionally attributed *The Stage-Coach* to a collaboration between Farquhar and Peter Anthony Motteux, a transplanted Frenchman who wrote for the English stage. The tradition that Motteux collaborated on the farce originated in print in a memoir published in the sixth edition of Farquhar's *Works* in London in 1728, more than a quarter of a century after the *première*, twenty-one years after Farquhar died, and ten years after Motteux was murdered. The joint attribution has persisted; questions have not concerned whether Motteux was involved but rather what the relationship of the two authors was. The 1728 Memoirs, reprinted in the next three editions of the *Works* (1736, 1742, 1760) and the sixth Dublin edition of the *Poems, Letters, and Essays* (1728), claimed Farquhar 'assisted Mr. *Motteux*' in the composition. Thomas Whincop said Farquhar wrote 'a great Part' of it, Motteux the rest,[2] and the *Biographia Dramatica* said Farquhar was assisted by Motteux.[3] Twentieth-century critics have consistently accepted the authenticity of Motteux's particiɔation. But no one has satisfactorily answered the question of what Motteux contributed.

Lacking concrete contemporary evidence of collaboration, one must look toward internal evidence and bibliographical clues. In fact, such evidence does suggest that Motteux had a hand. Most notably, the 'Stage-Coach Song' set by John Eccles, was probably contributed by Motteux: the song's short lines, jingling rhythms, and feminine rhymes are entirely consistent with his style in other songs, for example, the 'Mountebank Song' in *Farewel Folly*:

> *Here are People and Sports,*
> *Of all Sizes and Sorts,*
> *Coach'd Damsel with Squire,*
> *And Mob in the Mire;*
> *Tarpawlions,*
> *Trugmullions,*
> *Lords, Ladies, Sows, Babies,*
> *And Loobies in Scores;* . . . .

Farquhar's songs, on the other hand, were quite different in structure and tone. He wrote witty satire, love songs, and a few humorous lyrics such as drinking songs, but never with the short lines, jogging tunes, and frequent feminine rhymes that became a trademark for Motteux.

Other details characteristic of Motteux also suggest his participation. For example, at the bottom of the page of Dramatis Personae in both quartos a note says 'the time of action is the same as that of representation'. Notations of the duration of a play's action occur in none of Farquhar's other plays, and they are not customary in the period. However, they occur in the same location in five of Motteux's plays and operas.[4]

Moreover, Motteux wrote the prologue printed with *The Inconstant*, and in it he made a specific if oblique reference to *The Stage-Coach*. He compared the theatrical bill to a bill of fare, a common metaphor in the period:

> Like hungry Guests a sitting Audience looks:
> Plays are like Suppers: Poets are the Cooks. . . .
> Each Act, a Course; Each Scene, a different Dish. . . .
> Your surly Scenes, where Rant and Bloodshed joyn,
> Are Butcher's Meat, a Battel's a Sirloyn.

Your Scenes of Love, so flowing, soft, and chaste,
Are Water-gruel, without Salt or Taste.
Baudy's fat Ven'son, which, tho stale, can please: . . .
Your Rarity for the fair Guests to gape on
Is your nice *Squeaker*, or *Italian* Capon; . . .
An Op'ra, like an Olio, nicks the Age;
Farce is the Hasty-Pudding of the Stage.
For when you're treated with indifferent Cheer,
Ye can dispense with slender Stage-Coach Fare. . . .
But Comedy, That, That's the darling Cheer.
This Night we hope you'll an Inconstant bear:
Wild Fowl is lik'd in Playhouse all the year. . . .

In the context of the prologue, 'Stage-Coach Fare' refers to performances of the farce, one of many specific references to contemporary events in the theatre. Motteux's jesting reference suggests an 'inside joke' between the two authors, who had not publicly been identified as the creators of the farce.

Circumstances of the publication of the London quarto also suggest Motteux's influence (see The Text below), as does the fact that the farce opened at Lincoln's Inn Fields, since Motteux but not Farquhar contributed other plays to Betterton's company.

Whether Farquhar had a collaborator or not, he seems to have suffered the agonies of authorship more with *The Stage-Coach* than with his more ambitious efforts. In a letter published in *Love and Business* he lamented the pangs of authorship in a punning, metaphorical bit of verse:

But now Madam, hear my misfortune

> *The Angry Fates and dire Stage-Coach*
> *Upon my Liberty incroach,*
> *To bear me hence with many a Jog*
> *From thee my charming dear* Incog.
> *Unhappy Wretch! at once who feels*
> *O'returns of Hack, and Fortune's Wheels.*

This is my Epitaph, Madam, for now I'm a dead Man, and the Stage-Coach may most properly be call'd my Herse, bearing the Corps only of deceas'd *F—r*; for his Soul is left with you, whom he loves above all Womankind; . . .

The *Stage-Coach* which encroached upon his liberty was, of course, the farce he struggled to adapt. The jolting and jogging of the stagecoach is cursed in the farce and celebrated in Motteux's comical song, which is full of 'Jogging' and 'Jolting', tumbling and jumbling, until 'up Tails all'. The 'Hack', a pun on the coach for hire, also refers of course to hireling writers, like Motteux, like Jean de la Chapelle, and perhaps like Farquhar as he seemed to himself in his labours to anglicize the farce. The effort of the adaptation was 'killing' him, *The Stage-Coach* would finish him, hence would serve as his hearse: with puns of this witty, jocular sort, Farquhar filled the correspondence.

Perhaps composition proved so agonizing to him because he was attempting something he had never tried before, conceivably at the encouragement of Motteux, an old hand at Anglicizing French plays. The source was Jean de la Chapelle's farce *Les Carrosses d'Orléans*, which had opened in Paris in 1681, when Motteux was an eighteen-year-old resident of Rouen. It had recently been published in La Chapelle's *Œuvres* (1700). Farquhar's first three plays had been remarkably original compositions for the turn of the eighteenth century; never before had he tried his hand at translation, an art that kept many of his fellow playwrights profitably occupied. Yet this minor farce, adapted from the French, is the only one of his plays about which complaints of writer's woes survive.

Perhaps the constraints imposed on his imagination by the limitations of translation proved irksome, for after the first scene he wandered increasingly from the mother text. The first scene is a loose translation, with lines, often *double entendres*, added. The passengers are Anglicized from the original provincial girl, the woman who must frequently halt the coach to relieve herself, the Dutchman (adapted to Macahone), and other type characters. The romantic triangle endures, but the plot itself significantly changes. The dialogue, quite spare in La Chapelle, is expanded and enriched with specifically British coloration. The tentativeness in the translated dialogue of the first scene matures to a recognition that the farce must be Anglicized to succeed on stage. But Farquhar obviously did not find translation or adaptation compatible with his creative instincts; after *The Inconstant*, his modernization of Fletcher's *The Wild Goose Chase*, he returned to original plots.

No prologue, epilogue, or dedication appear in Q1, published in Dublin, but all three appear in Q2, the first London edition. The prologue borrows in part from Farquhar's epilogue to John Oldmixon's *The Grove* (1700), a plagiarism in keeping with Farquhar's tendency to husband his rhymed lines, but one of which Motteux also would have been capable. The epilogue, however, is borrowed, almost verbatim, from the prologue to Thomas Goffe's *The Careless Shepherdess*, published in 1656. Accidentals of the epilogue mirror the 1656 edition of Goffe's play so closely that it is evident someone carefully copied the earlier text when the material was 'stolen bodily', as Lawrence says.[5]

The unsigned dedication seem uncharacteristic of either man. Robert Newton Cunningham finds it lacks 'the extravagant flattery' characteristic of Motteux.[6] Lawrence points out that Farquhar signed his dedications and suggests it might be a publisher's dedication,[7] but publishers did not write dedications in quarto plays at the time. Motteux, in fact, also signed his dedications, but no one signed this one. Samuel Bagshaw remains a mystery; one Samuel Bagshaw, Esq. was named Sheriff for Derby in 1701. Another Samuel Bagshaw of Ford Hall, Derbyshire, perhaps the son of the Revd William Bagshawe (d. 1702), left a will dated 7 September 1706. Another Samuel Bagshawe of Ford died in 1712.[8] Moreover, the text of the dedication makes no sense in the context of Farquhar's life: the author complains of being, like Ben Jonson, 'assaulted with the Ignorance of partial and prejudicial Readers; as has sufficiently appeared by a piece I lately Publish't, which . . . is hated for speaking Truth'; no such criticism of Farquhar for a satirical publication would have existed, for he had published no signed satire. He was not ordinarily one to complain of attacks anyway. Nor can the dedication be assigned with any assurance to Motteux; it remains inexplicable.

Farquhar probably wrote *The Stage-Coach* in 1700 or 1701. *Love and Business*, in which the 'dire Stage-Coach' letter appeared, was published by Bernard Lintott on 28 February

1702, but in Lintott's memorandum book of 'Copies when purchased', he entered a payment of £3 4s. 6d. for Farquhar's 'Letters and Poems', i.e. *Love and Business*, on 3 July 1701.[9] The only fully dated letters in the collection came from Holland in August and October 1700. The only dated love-letter, one which appears later in the collection than the reference to *The Stage-Coach*, is dated simply 'Hague, October the 23d. New Stile', that is, 23 October 1700, when he was in Holland. The sequence of love-letters was probably written over a period of time in 1700. He requested the return of the correspondence because he had 'promis'd to equip a Friend with a few Letters to help out a Collection for the Press', a reference either to the agreement with Lintott or to one of the collections to which he earlier contributed. Since the letter was probably written in 1700 or perhaps 1701, the farce which encroached on his liberty must have dated from the same period.

If in fact Farquhar's love-letter and presumably his writer's agonies originated from Holland, any sort of full collaboration with Motteux seems unlikely. One suspects, particularly in the light of publication evidence described below and in awareness of the frequency with which other persons wrote songs for Farquhar's plays, that Motteux's part was minimal, decorative (although perhaps he originally recommended the project), and late, after the worst of the task had been painfully accomplished. Farquhar's authorial complaints, the decreasing reliance on La Chapelle's original, the Anglicization of the characters, particularly Macahone, and Farquhar's byline on the Dublin first quarto suggest that Farquhar was primarily responsible for the adaptation; the prologue which borrowed from another of his prologues could be attributed to either writer; the epilogue, 'Stage-Coach Song', and time designation on the cast-list page all point to Motteux; the dedication cannot be attributed convincingly to either.

STAGE HISTORY

The precise date of the first London performance cannot be ascertained. No advertisement of the *première* exists, and the farce was not published in London until 1705, several years after the play was first mounted. Evidence indicates that the opening occurred some time between autumn 1700 and February 1702. The reference in the printed prologue to *The Inconstant*, published 11 March 1702, proves that the farce had played by the end of February. An enigmatic reference in the preface to *The Inconstant* to the 'civility' of the Lincoln's Inn Fields company on the author's sixth night also suggests a prior performance.[10] The text of the play offers a final clue to dating. The Dublin quarto contains the line 'Come out here, I Charge you in the Kings Name?', a reference to King William, who died 8 March 1702; the London quarto substitutes 'Come out here. I charge you to come out, I am an Officer, What—won't you come out, in the Queens name. . . .' The Dublin quarto, printed from Farquhar's manuscript (see The Text below), again suggests that the play first ran before early March 1702, and it could not have run until after Farquhar's return from Holland, that is, no earlier than November 1700.

The farce opened at Lincoln's Inn Fields, although Farquhar never previously or subsequently mounted a play with Betterton's company. Not only his plays but all his known prologues and epilogues for other writers' plays were performed by the Drury Lane company or the group of actors that left Drury Lane for the Queen's Theatre in the Haymarket in 1706. His loyalty to a single troupe of actors was rare; most playwrights other than those who also were actors or managers willingly wrote for either house or both. Motteux, unlike Farquhar, sold six of his theatrical pieces to Lincoln's Inn Fields, five to Drury Lane, and one to the Queen's Theatre.

No original cast list exists in the Dublin quarto, which derived from Farquhar himself. The cast list in the London quarto, which probably derived from Motteux (see The Text below), records the cast in the 1703–4 season, the only season in which all the listed actors performed at Lincoln's Inn Fields:[11] Freeman played Micher, Booth Basil, Doggett Somebody, Tattnel Macahone, Pack Fetch, Trout Tom Jolt, Leigh the Constable, Mrs Prince Isabella, and Mrs Hunt Dolly. However, theatrical practice suggests that most of the actors would have continued in their roles, and so the printed cast would give some notion of the original run.

Whether the play opened in the winter or spring of 1701 or in the 1701–2 season, Booth probably played Captain Basil, Freeman his uncle Micher, Pack his servant Basil, and Mrs Prince Isabella. Tattnel, who played Macahone, and Mrs Hunt, who played Dolly in the 1703–4 production recorded in the London quarto, were not in the company in either 1700–1 or 1701–2, so unquestionably other actors first created those roles. Conceivably if the play opened in 1700–1, Bowen could have played Macahone, for he was in the company that season, and he definitely played the role in the Drury Lane production of 17 May 1709 and later performances. Although he chose not to perform for 'some months' during 1700 because of disputes with the other sharers at Lincoln's Inn Fields,[12] on 6 March 1701 he gave a highly praised performance in the comparable role of Teague in *The Committee*. However, by the following season he had moved to Drury Lane. Facts about the casts of later performances provide no indication of who played Isabella, however.

If the play opened in 1701–2, the roles of Nicodemus Somebody, Tom Jolt, and the Constable were played by actors other than Doggett, Trout, and Leigh, who were not in the company that season. Doggett and Pack regularly played the role of Nicodemus in later years at the two houses; both appeared in the performance recorded in the London quarto, but Pack played Fetch to Doggett's Somebody. The *London Stage* lists Pack at Lincoln's Inn Fields in 1701–2, but no actual performances are recorded for him, and the *Biographical Dictionary* gives no indication that he performed there during the season. Nor would one expect him to be demoted from the larger part to the smaller in subsequent performances. Evidence suggests, then, that Pack was not the original Somebody.

In fact, casting evidence leads one to suspect that the play may well have opened after November in the 1700–1 season rather than the subsequent year. Actors in the repertory companies tended to play the same roles year after year. Five changes in the cast of a nine-character farce would be unusual. Moreover, the four half-sheet broadside engravings of the 'Stage-Coach Song' are all titled 'Mr Doggets Comical Song in the Farce call'd the Stage Coach', another reason to believe that Doggett was the original Nicodemus Somebody and that, hence, the first performances occurred in the 1700–1 season.

Despite the insoluble questions concerning the original cast, the printed texts provide unusually full indications of the properties that were used, including a cloak-bag, pistols, a bottle of brandy, a bandbox, other luggage, a mask, a fan, a bill, lights, a small trunk, and a constable's staff. Nightcaps and nightgowns are indicated as costuming for the late-night scenes.

The only known music from the original play is the comical stagecoach song. Most likely written by Motteux, it was set by John Eccles and sung by Doggett in the role of Nicodemus Somebody, according to the separately published half-sheet broadside engravings of the song (no date).

Although little else is known about the first run, theatrical historians have consistently agreed that the farce was well received. Wilkes claims it ran ten nights,[13] and later scholars have reiterated his statement. Early records of the afterpiece are non-existent, however. The first performance recorded in the *London Stage* is 2 February 1704, when the farce served as afterpiece to *The Country Wit* at Lincoln's Inn Fields. In the past, this performance has been accepted traditionally by scholars as a night during the first run; the advertisement for it referred to *The Stage-Coach* as 'the last new Farce', suggesting it was relatively new. But since Lincoln's Inn Fields was still advertising irregularly in 1704, one suspects that many early performances have not been recorded. The next recorded performance occurred on 29 April, and others followed on 16 October 1704, 16 November 1705, and two in the spring of 1707. Contemporary commentary, however, suggests far greater popularity than the listings in the *London Stage* attest. The prologue to *The Different Widows* (1703), for example, complains of the vitiated taste of audiences and the need to substitute '*Irish Farce*' for tragedies:

> *Finding your Palates so much out of tast,*
> *We fairly ventur'd for a lucky Cast;*
> *And* Wit *being grown by Prohibition scarce,*
> *Regal'd you here too with an* Irish Farce.
> *Twas* Farce, *and therefore pleas'd You; for a while,*
> *Our* Teague, *and* Nicodemus *made you smile:*[14]

Even the Prologue to *The Inconstant* suggests unrestrained popularity.

The Philips prologue and epilogue (see Appendix B) were most likely first performed during the 1704–5 season, perhaps at the recorded performance on 16 October 1704 at Lincoln's Inn Fields. A reference in the prologue to the importation of foreign entertainers suggest that the performance occurred before 9 April 1705 when the Lincoln's Inn Fields company moved to the Queen's Theatre and the sentiments expressed became obsolete. Stonehill discovered the two poems in the Dublin edition of 1775 and called their existence a 'mystery'. Lawrence later concluded that they had adorned the ballad opera and benefitted the author of the adaptation, 'John Chetwood' or more probably William Rufus Chetwood, the Drury Lane prompter, in 1730 at Drury Lane.[15] But in fact Samuel Philips, a few years Farquhar's junior, probably wrote the pieces for a benefit for Farquhar or perhaps even Motteux during the 1704–5 season. Philips or Phillips, having matriculated at St John's College, Oxford, on 30 June 1703 and been sent down within the year, came to London soon thereafter. He seems to have turned actor in the summer of 1704 and regular contributor to the *Diverting Post* by January 1705.[16] Contemporary references in Philips's prologue and epilogue corroborate the dating.

The Drury Lane company undertook a new production of the farce on 17 May 1709. The performances evoked sufficient interest to warrant not one but two distinct editions, both seemingly pirated and both listing the Drury Lane cast: Norris playing Micher, Booth as Basil, Pack as Somebody, Bowen as Macahone, Carnaby as Fetch, Bullock as Tom Jolt, Leigh as the Constable, Mrs Bradshaw as Isabella, and Mrs Baker as Dolly. During the next two seasons both Drury Lane and the Queen's Theatre mounted productions, with Pack playing Nicodemus for the Drury Lane company and Doggett continuing in the role at the Queen's Theatre. Advertisements ordinarily neglected to list other players, for the competition clearly focused on a popularity contest between the country squires. The *London Stage* lists five performances in the spring of 1709, all at Drury Lane, eleven in 1709–10, including eight at the Queen's, two at Drury

Lane, and one at Greenwich with Nicodemus played by 'a Gentleman for his Diversion'; and four in 1710–11, one at the Queen's and three at Drury Lane.

Again it is possible that all performances were not advertised and that consequently the *London Stage* does not record the full number. Charles Johnson commented disparagingly on the popularity of *The Stage-Coach* in the preface to *The Force of Friendship*, which opened 20 April 1710 and was probably published in May. His ire suggests the farce maintained the kind of grating popularity thar irked the prologist of *The Different Widows* in 1703. Johnson condemned the age for lacking a taste for tragedy and preferring 'Whipt Cream' to intellectual nourishment:[17]

. . . no Audience now can bear the Fatigue of two Hours good Sense tho' *Shakespear* or *Otway* endeavour to keep 'em awake, without the promis'd Relief of the *Stage-Coach*, or some such solid Afterlude, a few Lines indeed are now and then forced down their Throats by the Help of this Gewgaw, 'tis tack'd to the Tragedy or rather the Tragedy to that, for 'tis the *Money Bill*; the Actors may design it as a Desert, but they generally find the Palates of their Guests so vitiated that they make a Meal of Whipt Cream, and neglect the more substantial Food which was design'd for their Nourishment. . . .

Johnson's remarks suggest that perhaps the *London Stage* falls short of a full listing of performances of the farce. He speaks, for example, of its supporting tragedy and mentions its playing with Otway and Shakespeare although perhaps that reference should not be taken literally. The performances listed in the *London Stage* primarily served as afterpieces to comedies, with only three performances on programmes with tragedies, two with *The Unhappy Favourite* and one with *The Fatal Marriage*. Moreover, the number of listings would not really warrant the animosity Johnson displays. One can only suspect that the *London Stage*, particularly in the early years, lacks sufficient evidence to provide an accurate picture of the intense popularity of the little afterpiece.

During the next decade, however, in the seasons from 1711 to 1721, the farce justified Johnson's earlier remarks, for it ran fifty times, thirty-six of the performances at Drury Lane. On 19 May 1719 it ran at both Drury Lane and Lincoln's

Inn Fields. Although little evidence of casting is extant,
Pack apparently continued playing Nicodemus. At least by
23 October 1716 Joseph Miller tried the role, and he played
the squire on numerous later occasions. Increasingly the farce
followed tragedies, including *Cato*, *The Fair Penitent*, *The Duke
of Guise*, *The Distrest Mother*, *The Orphan*, *Titus Andronicus* (seven
times), *The Fatal Marriage*, and *Timon of Athens*.

The next nine seasons, down to spring 1730, witnessed
twenty-four more known performances of *The Stage-Coach*,
nineteen of them at Drury Lane. Miller continued in the role
of Nicodemus, and at least once and probably more frequently
Hallam played Macahone. The farce ordinarily followed
comedies, but it also shared the bill with *Venice Preserv'd*, *The
Fatal Marriage*, *The Unhappy Favourite*, *Virtue Betrayed*, and *The
Mourning Bride*.

The Stage-Coach entered a new phase of its theatrical history
in spring 1730 when the farce was moulded into a ballad
opera. The season had been one of intense competition due in
part to the opening of a fourth major house, the theatre in
Goodman's Fields. Lincoln's Inn Fields was still profiting
from the unprecedented popularity of *The Beggar's Opera*,
which opened on 29 January 1728 and which spawned
imitations for years. The 1729–30 season pitted old favourite
comedies such as Farquhar's full-length plays, which ran a
total of fifty-seven times,[18] against musical fluff such as *Bayes's
Opera*, *The Lover's Opera*, and *The Beggar's Wedding*. A number of
afterpieces were laced with songs to modernize and enliven
them. Then on 30 April 1730 the Haymarket scored a
lucrative triumph by mounting Fielding's double bill of *The
Author's Farce* and *Tom Thumb*; by the end of the season, *Tom
Thumb* had played forty-one times. Nothing could seem more
logical, given the commercial successes of the past few years,
than to rig the perennially popular afterpiece *The Stage-Coach*
with some ballad tunes, newly set with lyrics that strove to be
merry, devil-may-care, satirical, sometimes witty, and often
suggestive, as imitative as possible of the formula created by
The Beggar's Opera. So closely did the adapter cling to *The
Beggar's Opera* in fitting new lyrics to the sixteen old familiar
tunes that he chose some of the tunes used by Gay, 'An old
Woman Cloathed in Gray' and 'O ponder well'. He inserted

the same kinds of lyrics: flirtatious bouts of sexual innuendo (Airs I and II), comic songs sung in character (Airs IV, XIV, and XVI), satirical commentary on society (Airs V, XI, XII, and XIII), and love songs (Airs VI and XVII, which is sung in recitativo).[19] The operatic version was, then, a coldly calculated and altogether normal response to the financial triumphs of *The Beggar's Opera*, *Tom Thumb*, and contemporary imitations.

The retooled afterpiece opened on 13 May 1730 at Drury Lane, where the old version had played as recently as 8 January.[20] The singer and actor James Excell made his 'first appearance on any stage' as Jolt the coachman, whose part had been fitted out with three airs, doubtless to capitalize on Excell's talents.[21] Miller continued to play Nicodemus, Roberts took the role of Basil, Williams played Macahone, Norris Micher, Oates Fetch, Harper the Landlord, the young Kitty Clive (still Miss Raftor) Isabella, and Mrs Heron Dolly. Lest the frequently performed *Timoleon* and the new 'opera' lacked sufficient drawing power, the programme was embellished with a new prologue addressed to the Freemasons, a new epilogue spoken by a five-year-old girl, three dances, and Handel's *Water Music* with a preamble on the kettle drums by Benjamin Baker.

No incontrovertible proof exists for the authorship of the adaptation, but the evidence points strongly to the prompter William Rufus Chetwood.[22] Chetwood had created *The Lover's Opera*, an original one-act afterpiece adorned with forty airs 'made to Old Ballad Tunes and Country Dances'. The afterpiece had opened at Drury Lane on 14 May 1729 with a cast that included four of the players in the operatic *Stage-Coach*, Miller, Oates, Harper, and Clive. The opening performance was designated as a benefit for Chetwood. *The Lover's Opera* proved highly successful, judging from the number of performances. It had been performed thirteen times in the 1729–30 season before the opening of *The Stage-Coach Opera*. The *première* of the adaptation contained 'new Songs to old Ballad Tunes and Country Dances' also, and it too was designated a benefit for Chetwood. For a *première* to benefit the prompter would be extremely unlikely unless in fact he was the creator or adapter of the new piece. Chetwood was, of course, eager to increase the profits of his benefit night through the addition of music, dancing, and the novel epilogue.

On 17 July 1730 the opera was performed at Goodman's Fields, with Excell still singing the role of Jolt. The Drury Lane season had ended on 21 May, and a number of afterpieces had been picked up by Goodman's Fields, including *Flora* and *Phebe* (*The Beggar's Wedding*), not to mention the performance there of *The Beggar's Opera*. Still, it was unusual to use a play during its first year of performance; obviously the troupe at Goodman's Fields considered *The Stage-Coach* as a play of some decades. The following season Goodman's Fields mounted the afterpiece twelve times from 22 February to 28 April; during the 1731–2 season, the company gave three more performances. The cast advertised for 27 April 1732 included Miller as Somebody, Excell as Jolt, Collett as Micher, Jenkins as Basil, Rosco as Fetch, Morgan as Macahone, Mrs Roberts as Isabella, and Mrs Palmer as Dolly. In 1732–3, Covent Garden produced the operatic version, attributed the farce to Farquhar, and cast the piece entirely anew.

After that the farce was often performed at Goodman's Fields and Covent Garden (with performances at Richmond and Lincoln's Inn Fields) until 1745–6, when Drury Lane again ran its old standby. Statistics by five-year periods show four performances during 1733–8, eight in 1738–43 (all at Covent Garden), thirty in 1743–8, and six more by 18 February 1751. On 24 January 1746 the farce ran at two houses, both Drury Lane and Goodman's Fields. A performance at Drury Lane occurred on 11 May 1764, and a final one was given at Covent Garden on 16 April 1787, advertised as *The Stage-Coach; or, Inn in an Uproar*, altered from Farquhar. Three women appear in the cast list, indicating that the play may well have been newly revised for this performance, since only two appear in Farquhar's original. The farce continued to share bills primarily with comedies, often dating from Farquhar's own period, and sometimes it ran with his full-length works. But on occasion it also shared an evening with *Tamerlane*, *The Fair Penitent*, or even *Comus*. The hardiness of the farce as an afterpiece for fifty years is remarkable, considering the slightness of the original over which Farquhar suffered. Its stage history suggests, as so many facts of theatrical history do, that as heartily as Farquhar displeased the critics, he understood the paying customers, even those that came to the theatre two generations after he had died.

REPUTATION AND INFLUENCE

One can imagine that the thought of a twentieth-century scholar seriously discussing the reputation of *The Stage-Coach* might well send its author into paroxysms of laughter; indeed, even a twentieth-century scholar cannot but smile. Only now have scholars undertaken serious and often humourless research on the 'popular culture' of times past.

To talk about the 'reputation' of the farce is to discuss something that did not, in fact, exist, for *The Stage-Coach* was beneath reputation based on critical grounds. It was a bagatelle, never to be confused with a work of art. It was 'Whipt Cream', a 'Gewgaw', not only farce but *'Irish Farce'*. But it was also, as Charles Johnson noted, a *'Money Bill'*, produced in London on 182 known occasions and probably many more that have not been recorded. If it was negligible drama, it was also profitable theatre.

Not until the twentieth century did scholars begin looking into the complex theatrical and publication history of the little farce. Lawrence then claimed that the ultimate vogue for it 'brought about the firm establishment of the principle of the afterpiece early in the eighteenth century',[23] a view which Leo Hughes denies.[24] But most scholars who have discussed the farce have mulled the questions of composition without critical comment.

Certainly the success of *The Stage-Coach* as a short farcical afterpiece encouraged imitation. It originated at a time when afterpieces were still rare: Avery records that of 225 programmes in 1704–5, only ten were double bills.[25] It continued to prosper in changing times, adapting itself to contemporary modes through revision and adaptation. Afterpieces indeed became commonplace, but to claim that *The Stage-Coach* directly caused or contributed to that trend can only be speculation, for contemporary writers and critics did not even think to discuss it. Moreover, specific incontrovertible borrowings by later writers do not exist. As a gauge of the tenor of the times, *The Stage-Coach* is extremely useful, but one can scarcely prove it a significant shaping influence.

THE TEXT

The unusual publishing history of *The Stage-Coach* defies all the common expectations for eighteenth-century play publishing. Ordinarily plays were published within a few weeks or months of the first production. They were republished either when revivals renewed interest or when the collected works of the author were published and republished. Ordinarily republished texts derived from the first or later editions, with revisions occurring when the author submitted rewritten passages or additions or requested omissions; sometimes, for example in the 1730s and again late in the century, texts were supposedly corrected according to the prompt-book; in most cases the marking of deletions with inverted commas was the major distinction between these and earlier editions. Finally, first editions were regularly London editions; Dublin editions tend to be cheap imitations. *The Stage-Coach* follows none of these 'rules'.

The most surprising single fact about the publication is that three distinct manuscripts underlay the printed editions, one used for the first Dublin edition, one for the first London edition, and one for a London edition of 1735,which had been preceded by several intervening editions. A second strange fact is that the play was only once published with the *Works* of Farquhar, in the *Works* of 1736, although the memoirs published in some of the other editions identified him as author. Third, startling interrelationships between some Dublin and London editions and performances were inexplicable. Moreover, no logical relationships exist between dates of performance and dates of publication for the farce.

The first quarto (Q1) was published in Dublin in 1704 with the imprint 'Printed, and are to be Sold by the Booksellers', an imprint often used for unauthorized editions. The second quarto (Q2) was published in London by Benjamin Bragg on 3 or 4 May 1705. Both state that the play was first acted at

Lincoln's Inn Fields. The third text that derived from a manuscript was published for W. Feales in 1735, and copies were included in the *Dramatick Works* of 1736. Each of these three texts has its own unique authority.[26] All other editions of intervening and later times were derived from these three texts. Except for the lyrics of the 1730 operatic version published in 1761, none of the other texts can be considered textually significant. The relationship of the three underlying manuscripts to each other and to the authors can be determined through a combination of bibliographical and biographical evidence.[27]

The title-page of Q1 reads: THE | Stage-Coach. | A | FARCE. | As it was ACTED at the | Theatre in *Lincolns-Inn-Fields.* | By Her MAJESTIES Servants. || *Written by Mr.* George Farquhar. || *DUBLIN*: | Printed, and are to be Sold by the Book-| sellers, 1704, Price 4 *d.* The entire quarto consists of two four-leaf gatherings, A–B⁴. The dramatis personae on A1ᵛ lists the characters' names but not the actors. The one-act text begins on A2 and concludes on B4ᵛ.

The title-page of Q2 reads: THE | STAGE-COACH | A | COMEDY: | As it was | Acted at the New Theatre | IN | LINCOLNS-INN-FIELDS. | BY | Her Majesties Servants. || *LONDON*: | Printed, and are to be Sold by *Benjamin Bragg*, at the | *Blew-Ball* in *Ave-Mary-Lane.* 1705. There are six quarto gatherings, A–F⁴, without running-titles. Several oddities should be noted: first, Farquhar's name does not appear on the title-page although it would certainly have attracted buyers. Second, the farce has metamorphosed into a 'Comedy'. The peculiarities continue within the text. The one-act farce of sixteen pages has swollen to a three-act 'comedy' of thirty-nine pages, and the fourpence price has likewise swollen to a shilling.[28] A five-page dedication to Samuel Bagshaw is printed on A2ʳ–A4ʳ, and a prologue and epilogue appear on F2ᵛ–F4ʳ. The dramatis personae lists a cast that could only have appeared during the performances in 1703–4, that is, the previous season, because the actors were not all in the company in 1704–5 or indeed in any other season.

To stretch the short piece to a three-act comedy, the printer used large type and huge margins. The length of pages varies strikingly, a result, no doubt of the effort to extend the length of the printed piece. The first page of Act I has only nine lines, and some pages of uninterrupted text have seventeen or eighteen lines, while others bear a more normal thirty-two or thirty-three. Notably, nineteen of the twenty-five entrances begin a new page. This unusual practice, reminiscent of the French division of plays into scenes according to entrances, contributes significantly to the widely varying page-lengths and the lack of continuity in format. For example, p. 10, the beginning of Act II, contains a total of eleven lines; the next page, which opens with Isabella's entrance, contains twenty-five lines. Similarly, p. 14 contains thirty-three lines of text, but p. 15 contains only sixteen; the entrance of Micher is carried over to begin p. 16, despite the fact that p. 15 is only half as long as the facing p. 14.

Biographical evidence places Farquhar in Dublin on military duty when Q1 appeared there as well as when Q2 was issued in London. Robert John Jordan has shown that Farquhar arrived in Dublin some time after 20 October 1704 and was still there at least as late as 27 July 1705.[29] Farquhar's brother was a bookseller in Dublin, a fact that argues against the usual scepticism toward Dublin editions, particularly those issued 'by the Booksellers' rather than under a specific imprint. Farquhar's established presence in Dublin, his brother's business, and the fact that he was not named as author in the London edition render strikingly credible the possibility that he may have been the source for the Dublin edition but not the London one. Moreover, Farquhar was by this time consistently publishing with Lintott, one of the biggest drama-text enterpreneurs of his day in London. *Love and Business* (28 February 1702), *The Inconstant* (Knapton, Strahan, and Lintott, 12 March 1702), *The Twin Rivals* (29 December 1702), *The Recruiting Officer* (25 April 1706), and *The Beaux Stratagem* (27 March 1707) were all issued under Lintott's imprint; Farquhar contracted with no other London bookseller to publish plays during these years.[30] Again, biography suggests scepticism about any connection between Farquhar and Q2.

Biographical and textual evidence points instead toward that 'thrifty Cit' Motteux as Bragg's source for the manuscript copy-text for the London edition, although the possibility of an unknown purveyor cannot be rejected out of hand. First of all, Motteux seems not only to have been in London but to have had frequent contact with Bragg during the period Farquhar was in Dublin, for Bragg had published one of his plays anonymously as well as one of his songs. In the *Diverting Post* for 20–7 January 1705, he printed the 'Mountebank Song', and on 6 February he published anonymously *The Amorous Miser: or, the Younger the Wiser* which is either an early draft or a piracy of Motteux's *Farewel Folly*, performed at Drury Lane on 18 January 1705 but not published under that title until 1707.

Another reason to suspect the Frenchman is that although the two editions vary in ways that preclude any form of derivation from the same manuscript, some of the variants are either foolish compositorial misreadings of the manuscript or bad stabs at English colloquialisms. Some Q2 expressions have a foreign flavour. For example, the phrase 'Club this Matter' in Q1, meaning divide the bill of expenses, becomes 'Curry this Club' in Q2, a reading that makes no sense. 'But this is a rare time to quit Scores with him', that is, get even with him, in Q1 becomes in Q2 'but this is a rare time to kill Horses with him', an inexplicable line in the context. Some of the errors could derive from a misreading of a messy manuscript—'quit Scores' might well look like 'kill Horses' in some hands. But they could not derive from a printed version.

The dedication and plagiarized epilogue further argue against Farquhar's hand in Q2, but they argue neither for nor against Motteux as Bragg's source (see Sources and Composition above). Still the relationship of Motteux and Bragg, the curious foreign flavour of some mistaken phrases, Motteux's role in authorship, and the strong possibility that the Frenchman could have supplied the prologue, epilogue, and dedication give credence to the possibility that Motteux provided Bragg the manuscripts for both *The Stage-Coach* and *The Amorous Miser*. At any rate, by fair means or foul, Bragg acquired a manuscript, probably one that was difficult to read, as printer's copy, but he did not get it from Farquhar.

Two octavo editions were published in 1709. The first, 1709a, occurs in two states. A reprint of Q2, the edition bears a revised cast list to match the playbill for 17 May 1709, the first recorded performance at Drury Lane, and the title-page reads, 'As it was Acted at the Theatre-Royal in Drury-Lane'. One state (copy in the Bodleian, shelf-marked Vet. A4 e. 1108) has the collational formula A–D⁴. The dedication to Bagshaw appears on A2ʳ–A3ᵛ, the prologue on A4ʳ, the dramatis personae on A4ᵛ. The other state (copy in the Folger, shelfmarked PR 2823 1710b Sh. Col.) has the collational formula A²B–D⁴ and differs only in the omission of the dedication. B1 is paginated as 9, as in the Bodleian copy. Two settings of sheet B exist. The Folger copy is full of errors through B, but sheet C shows considerably more compositorial skill. Edition 1709b, is a reprint of 1709a. The title-page carries the same information, with the addition of the price (3*d.*); the cast list is identical. The collational formula for 1709b (copy at the Houghton Library, Harvard, shelf-marked EC75.Sh668.750eb) is A–C⁴. A2ʳ contains the prologue, A2ᵛ the Dramatis Personae, and A3ʳ begins the text. The epilogue appears on C4ʳ⁻ᵛ. The composition is far neater and more intelligent than in 1709a. No evidence to identify the printer exists, but Henry Hills was in his heyday as pirate in 1709 and might be considered a suspect.

Curll published an edition in 1718, which listed the same cast and theatre, but which was, perhaps surprisingly, a reprint of Q1. Two new Dublin editions appeared in 1719 and 1728, also reprints of Q1; the first bore the imprint 'Printed for George Risk at the Corner of Castle-Lane in Dames-Street, near the Horse-Guard, 1719' and the second 'Printed by S. Powell for George Risk, at Shakespear's-head, the Corner of Castle-lane in Dame's-street, M DCC XXVIII'. All three editions include 'The Life and Character of Mr. *George Farquhar*', which begins 'Mr. *George Farquhar* was a Gentleman by Birth . . .' , and all three contain the Philips prologue and epilogue as well as the 'Song of a Trifle' from *The Beaux Stratagem*. The prologue and epilogue add yet another bizarre element to the unusual publication history of *The Stage-Coach*. They probably predated Q2 but were not included. Having predated 1709a and 1709b by several years, they were not included in those editions which presumably attempt to reflect the Drury Lane production of 1709. How, then, did the prologue and epilogue survive to appear in Curll's edition of

1718 and the Dublin edition of 1719, and how did they become available for printing at that time? Although the temptations to speculation are almost irresistible, no proof exists for their provenance. The thirteen verses of 'The Trifle', published in these editions but not included in Farquhar's *Works* or *Comedies* add yet one more inexplicable note to the publishing history. Did Curll find these papers through the theatre? Did they somehow derive from Farquhar's original papers when the play was first published in Dublin? What was the connection between Curll's edition and those in Dublin? Mysteries persist.

But a more remarkable surprise lay ahead in the two duodecimo editions of 1735, labelled as farce rather than comedy and bearing the imprint 'London: Printed for W. Feales, at Rowe's-Head, over-against St. Clement's Church in the Strand. M.DCC.XXXV'. The first of these, 1735a (two copies in the Bodleian, three in the Folger, and one in the British Library, shelf-marked 11771.b.15.), is, in fact, a third distinct text, the copy for which was not Q1, Q2, or any text derived from either of them; the second, 1735b (copy in the British Library, shelf-marked 1507/424), derived from 1735a. They both contain 'Some Memoirs of Mr. *George Farquhar*', as published in the sixth edition of the *Works*, which begin in this edition, 'It is observ'd, that the World . . .' . The title-page names Farquhar as author, calls the play a farce instead of a comedy, and cites Drury Lane as the theatre. The collational formula for 1735a is 12°: A^{12}B^8. The Memoirs appear on A3^r–A6^r, the Dramatis Personae on A6^v. The text begins on A7^r and concludes on B5^v; the following pages contain a catalogue of plays published by Tonson and Feales. A frontispiece by van der Gucht faces the title-page. The collational formula for 1735b is 12°: A^6 B^6. The memoirs appear on A2^r–3^v, the dramatis personae on the lower half of A3^v, the text on A4^r–B6^r. No prologue or epilogue appears in either edition. One would expect in 1735a a reprint of an earlier edition of the farce, but such is not the case; 1735a agrees with Q1 in some readings, Q2 in others, but in still other variants it agrees with neither. For instance, a stage direction in Q1 reads '*Peeps in the Empty Purse and throws it down*'. Q2 substitutes '*the Pot*' for '*the Empty Purse and*'; 1735a reads '*the empty Pot, and*'. Again, Q1 reads 'see what your Uncle will say to you'; Q2 'odd you'll make a rare Wife, if you'; and 1735a 'See what your Uncle will say to you! You'll make a rare Wife, faith, if you . . .'. Q1 reads 'Whimbled', Q2 'dwindled', 1735a 'whindled'. Q1 reads 'I Charge you in the Kings Name?', Q2 'I charge you to come out, I am an Officer, What—won't you come out, in the Queens name,'; and 1735a 'I charge ye come out: I'm an Officer won't you come out in the King's Name?' The list could be extended at great length.

The notion of authorial or editorial revisions so long after Farquhar and Motteux died lacks credibility. Another manuscript was printer's copy. The most logical explanation is a playhouse copy, that of Drury Lane. The farce had played there fifty-three times by 1735, and it had first played there with some of the original cast. Between 1704 and 1735 it played only eight times at Lincoln's Inn Fields, according to available records, and the last of those performances was in 1720.

But perhaps strangest of all is the fact that the published version was not the operatic version, which had opened at Drury Lane in 1730 and was the version performed during the 1730s. The 'opera' had, in fact, been performed only once at Drury Lane before moving on to Goodman's Fields and Covent Garden; the most recent performance had been at Richmond on 2 September 1734. Nevertheless, the publication of a new edition, taken not from a prior edition but rather from a playhouse copy, would lead one to expect a contemporary prompt copy as copy-text. Instead, the 1735 editions probably actually reflect the earliest performances at Drury Lane, in the spring of 1709. Although Farquhar had died in 1707, his relationship with Drury Lane and particularly Robert Wilks was so close that the manuscript may have had some claim to original authority.

There is, of course, no absolute proof that the playhouse copy was the source for 1735a, but no other explanation is convincing. Furthermore, editions of other plays in the early 1730s published under Feale's imprint seem to have had a close relationship to the Drury Lane theatre. Other Farquhar plays published between 1728 and 1735 were revised, seemingly according to the prompt-book. The best example, perhaps, is the exclusion of a scene in *The Beaux Stratagem* cut during or immediately after its first season. In some instances Feales's editions seem to anticipate Bell's later editions. That 1735a represented the version that ran at Drury Lane from 1709 on, then, seems extremely likely.

The Stage-Coach never appeared in the *Comedies* or *Works* until the seventh edition of the *Dramatick Works* in 1736. Probably the farce did not appear in the earlier editions for the simple reason that neither Lintott nor his associates in the collected editions owned the copyright. The first edition of the *Comedies* appeared 27 March 1708,[31] after Farquhar's death. Lintott made appropriate arrangements for all seven full-length comedies (he owned the rights to four of them). Whether it was possible to buy rights to *The Stage-Coach* or whether Lintott even knew it was part of the canon we cannot know. Its copyright, however, expired 10 April 1731 according to the Copyright Act of 1710. When the next edition of the *Dramatick Works* appeared in 1736, *The Stage-Coach* was included for the first time. Later London editions of the *Works* continued to ignore *The Stage-Coach*.

In 1761 a Dublin edition of *The Stage-Coach Opera* appeared. The title-page cited Drury Lane, claimed the piece was 'Written Originally by Mr. George Farquhar', and bore the imprint of Peter Wilson, John Exshaw, and Hulton Bradley. The duodecimo has the collational formula A–B⁶C⁴. A1ᵛ contains the dramatis personae, the text runs from A2ʳ to C1ʳ, followed by the Philips epilogue and prologue and 'The Trifle'. Within the text are embedded seventeen songs, the 'Stage-Coach Song' plus sixteen new airs with lyrics written to old familiar tunes (see Appendix C). The Dublin edition of 1728 served as copy-text for this edition. Once again the discrepancy between the time of first performance, in this case 1730, and the time of publication is astonishing. Moreover, the operatic version was never published in London where it was so frequently performed. The only other edition of it appeared in the Dublin edition of the *Works* in 1775, published by Thomas Ewing.

Four more London editions appeared, two published by T. Lowndes in 1766, and 1772, one by W. Oxlade in 1775, and another by Wenman in 1778. None bear any textual significance.

A family tree showing all the textual deviations of *The Stage-Coach* is complex and multi-branched:

MS A (Farquhar)   MS B (Motteux?)   MS C (Drury Lane 1709?)

Q1	Q2	1735a
1718	1709a	1735b
Du 1719	1709b	1766
Du 1728		1772
Du 1761		1775
Du 1775		1778

At least four half-sheet broadside engravings of the 'Stage-Coach Song, were published: (1) 'Mᴿ Dogget's *Comicall* Song *in the* Farce *calld the* Stage Coach', copy in the British Library; (2) 'Mᴿ Doggets *Comicall* SONG *in the Farce call'd the | Stage* Coach Sett by Mᴿ John Eccles', copies in the British Library, Folger; (3) 'Mᴿ Doggets *Comicall* SONG *in the Farce call'd the* Stage | Coach Set by Mᴿ John Eccles *and exactly engrav'd by* D. Wright', copies in the Bodleian, British Library; and (4) '*Mᴿ Doggets Comicall SONG in the Farce call'd the Stage-Coach, Set by Mᴿ* John Eccles *and exactly engrav'd by* T. Cross', copy in the Rowe Music Library, King's College, Cambridge. The engravings print the fourth verse of the play texts as the third verse and the third as fourth. All include a flute line. No indication of dating exists on any of the broadsides. Daniel Wright the elder began musical publishing *c.*1709, according to Charles Humphries and William C. Smith, whereas Thomas Cross published *c.*1683–1733.[32] The broadsides, however, were probably actually published in the period before the 1709 performances at Drury Lane, and perhaps as early as 1700–1, for clearly Doggett, not Pack, was the unchallenged possessor of the role of Nicodemus and the song that enhanced that role.

The first Dublin edition serves as copy-text for the present edition because it derived directly from Farquhar. The dedication, prologue, and epilogue of Q2 appear in Appendix

A, the Philips prologue and epilogue in Appendix B, and the songs in the operatic version in Appendix C. I have collated the following copies: Q1 Harvard, University of Texas; Q2 Bodleian, Harvard, Folger, Texas (two copies) Huntington; 1709a Bodleian, Folger; 1709b Harvard; 1718 (microcard, *Three Centuries of British Drama*); Dublin 1719 Chicago; Dublin 1728 Bodleian, Princeton; 1735a Bodleian (two copies), Folger (three copies), British Library; 1735b British Library; Dublin 1761 Bodleian; 1766 British Library; 1775, Folger; Dublin 1775 Princeton; and 1778 British Library.

NOTES

1. The *Daily Courant* for 4 May 1705 advertised the play as published 'This day'; the *Post-Man* for 3–5 May 1705 advertised it as published 'on Thursday last', i.e. 3 May.
2. *A Compleat List of All the English Dramatic Poets*, appended to Thomas Whincop's *Scanderbeg: Or, Love and Liberty* (London, 1747), p. 231.
3. *Biographia Dramatica*, iii, 298. The author felt, however, that the farce 'is nothing more than a plagiarism' from *Les Carrosses d'Orléans*.
4. 'Time of Action from Noon till Night', *Love's a Jest* (1696); 'The Time of Action from 5 to 8 in the Evening', *Beauty in Distress* (1698); 'The Time of Action, the same with that of the Representation', *The Temple of Love* (1706); 'The Time of Action about Three Days', *Thomyris* (1707); 'The Time of Action three Hours', *Love's Triumph* (1708).
5. Lawrence, p. 392.
6. Robert Newton Cunningham, *Peter Anthony Motteux, 1663–1718*, (Oxford, 1933), p. 143.
7. Lawrence pp. 394–5.
8. *Calendar of State Papers Domestic*, Anne 1 (1702–3), p. 522. I am indebted to Linda Merians for information on this Bagshawe. *Hand-List of the Bagshawe Muniments Deposited in the John Rylands Library* (Manchester, 1955).
9. Nichols, viii, 296.
10. For a full discussion, see Kenny, 'Mystery', pp. 219–36.
11. Tattnel and Mrs Hunt were not in the company in 1700–1; Doggett, Leigh, Tattnel, Trout, and Mrs Hunt were not in 1701–2; Trout, Tattnel, and Mrs Hunt were not in 1702–3; and Doggett, Tattnel, and Mrs Prince were not in 1704–5.
12. *London Stage*, Part 2, i. 8.
13. Wilkes, i, p. ix.
14. Prologue, Mary Pix, *The Different Widows* (London, 1703). The prologue was reprinted in *The Works of Rochester and Roscommon* (London, 1703) as 'Prologue to Different Widows, supposedly by Capt. B—n'.
15. Stonehill, ii. 5; Lawrence, p. 397.
16. For details of his curious career, see Kenny, 'Mystery', pp. 234–5.
17. Motteux used the same metaphor in the prologue to *The Inconstant*.
18. *The Constant Couple* played twenty times, twice at Drury Lane and eighteen times at Goodman's Fields, where Giffard was the first actor ever to challenge Wilks for

the role of Sir Harry. *The Beaux Stratagem* played nineteen times, three times at Drury Lane, five at Lincoln's Inn Fields, six at Goodman's Fields, four at the Haymarket, and once at the Front Long Room. *The Recruiting Officer* ran fifteen times, once at Drury Lane, five times at Lincoln's Inn Fields, eight times at Goodman's Fields, and once at Southwark. Drury Lane ran *The Inconstant* three times.

19. No contemporary editions of the new version were published. I have assumed that the Dublin edition of 1761, the first published operatic version, reflects the performance. Nothing in the stage history suggests another revision of the old farce. Moreover, the close imitation and the distribution of the songs to actors suggest that this was the version of 1730.

20. Stonehill claims (ii. 5) that the ballad opera 'probably originated' in an Irish version and cites a production 'with new songs, and greatly enlarged' at Smock Alley on 2 Apr. 1730 for the benefit of the Widow Eastham and the box-keeper Le Roux, repeated ('never performed but once') on 13 May 1731 for Thomas Griffith's benefit. Lawrence (p. 395) repeats the information and surmises that the opera was first produced in Dublin, the work of an Irish author. He mentions that the performance on 2 Apr. 1730 was performed under the old title.

21. For a discussion of James Excell, see the *Biographical Dictionary*, v. 130–1.

22. The *Biographical Dictionary* attributes *The Stage Coach Opera* as presented at Goodman's Fields on 17 July 1730 to Chetwood, but offers no explanation of the attribution. The entry says that the work was not printed (iii. 192). Wilkes falsely reports that a few years after Farquhar died, the play was revived 'with several additional songs, wrote by the late John Chetwood, and was performed 18 nights, with applause' (i. p. ix). Stonehill claims the operatic version was performed at Smock Alley on 2 Apr. 1730 and that the lyrics were possibly written by Thomas Griffith (ii. 5).

23. Lawrence, p. 392.

24. Leo Hughes, *A Century of English Farce* (Princeton, NJ, 1956), p. 245.

25. *London Stage*, Part 2, i, p. cxvii. It seems likely that records for some performances of afterpieces no longer exist, however.

26. Stonehill, the only twentieth-century editor who has reprinted the farce, collated only Q1 and Q2. He chose Q2 as copy-text but did not discuss his choice.

27. For a full discussion of the facts, see Kenny, 'Mystery', pp. 219–36.

28. Advertisements, *Daily Courant*, 4 and 7 May 1705.

29. Jordan, pp. 253–60.

30. The half-sheet broadside of Farquhar's 'Prologue Spoken by Mr. Wilks, At the Opening of the Theatre in the Hay-Market, October the 15th, 1706' was printed by Bragg in 1706. See Shirley Strum Kenny, 'A Broadside Prologue by Farquhar', *Studies in Bibliography*, 25 (1972), 179.

31. Advertisement, *Daily Courant*, 27 Mar. 1708.

32. Charles Humphries and William C. Smith, *Music Publishing in the British Isles* (London, 1954), pp. 342, 122.

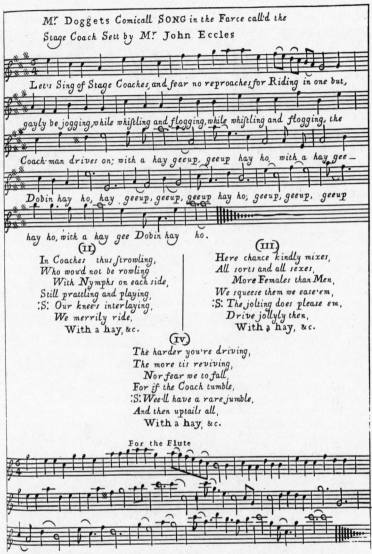

'Let's Sing of Stage Coaches', Mr. Dogget's Comical Song in the *Stage-Coach*. Set by John Eccles. By permission of the Folger Shakespeare Library.

THE
STAGE-COACH

A

FARCE.

As it was ACTED at the

Theatre in *Lincolns-Inn-Fields*.

By Her MAJESTIES Servants.

ABBREVIATIONS USED IN THE NOTES

Q1	First Dublin edition. Dublin: Booksellers, 1704.
Q2	First London edition. London: Bragg, 1705.
1709a	London: Booksellers, 1709.
1709b	London: Booksellers, 1709.
1718	London: Curll, 1718.
1735a	London: Feales, 1735.
1735b	London: Feales, 1735.
1761	*The Stage-Coach Opera*. Dublin: Wilson, Exshaw, Bradley, 1761.

Dramatis Personæ.

Micher. The Old Uncle.
Isabella. His Niece.
Squire Somebody.
Basil. A Captain, in Love with *Isabella*.
Fetch. His Man.
Tom Jolt. The Stage-Coach-man.
Dolly. The Maid.
Macahone. An Irish-man.
Landlord.
Servants.
Several Guests in the *Inn*.
Hostler.

The time of *Action*, the same with the time of *Representation*.

THE
Stage-Coach.

ACT I.

Scene an *Inn*.
Enter Fetch *with a Cloak-bag and Pistols.*

Fetch. Here! House! Where are you all!—Now we've Supp'd
I'll see if my Master's Bed be ready:—*Tom, John, Robin,* Where
a Plague are ye? All Deaf?—No Attendance in these Country-
Inns;—This is worse than the *Rose-Tavern* after Play, the *Sun-
Tavern* after Change, or the *Devil-Tavern* after Church.

Enter Dolly.

Dolly. D'ye call Sir?

Fetch. Call Sir? What a plague—Egad 'tis a pretty Girl—
Heark you Child, Do you serve Travellers upon the Road
here?

10   *Dolly.* Yes Sir.

Fetch. Kiss me then.

Dolly. That's the Chambermaid's Business; D'you want
any thing else?—I'm in haste:

Fetch. What Room does my Master lie in?

Dolly. The *Castle.*

Fetch. And what Room do I lie in?

Dolly. The *Garret.*

Fetch. Very well! And what Room do you lie in?

Dolly. Under ye.

20   *Fetch.* Say no more;—I'll but take a Dram to digest my
Supper;—Lay these things in my Master's Chamber, then I'll
talk with you in yours.

Dolly. Are your Pistols Charg'd? (*Takes the Things.*)

Fetch. Yes, yes, we always go Charg'd Child; A Brace of
Bullets I'll assure you.

Exit Dolly.

I. 4 after Play, the *Sun-Tavern*] Q2 [after Play; the Sun Tavern]; [om.]
21 Master's] Q2 [Masters]; Master

Enter Captain Basil.

Captain. What a tedious, tiresome, dull, jolting, Vehicle is a
Stage-Coach! We that are in it, are more Fatigu'd than the
Beasts that Draw it.—This unluky Hurt, *Fetch*, that I've got
lately, has hindr'd my Riding Post, and thrown me into this
confounded Company.—A Big-belly'd Farmers Daughter, an 30
Irish-Wit, a Canting *Quaker*, a City Whore, and a Country
Parson.

Fetch. And a Disbanded Captain, Sir, for want of a
Strowling Lawyer, or a Nurse and a Child, to make up a
clever Stage-Coach-Sett.

Captain. Aye, the Swell'd Country Puss plagu'd me with her
Screaming and Wry Faces, The profound *Teague* with his
Nonsense, The *Quaker* with the Spirit, The Whore with Flesh,
And the Fat Parson with both.

Fetch. Truly Sir, I pity'd you; for I don't think there was in 40
the whole Company a Man of Parts, but You and I.

Captain. But must I be Tormented Two Days more with
this Coach, before I get to *London*?

Fetch. Too true, Sir.

Captain. How can you tell?

Fetch. No body better Sir: My Father in *London* has an
Employment about the Coaches.

Captain. What's his Employment?

Fetch. Sir, He's a very worthy Citizen, that attends at
Blossoms-Inn, in Quality of a Ticket-Porter.   50

Captain. I must get to *London* sooner, or I ruin my
Affairs;—Let me talk with the Coach-man; if it be possible I'll
make him Stretch for me: Call him hither.

Exit Fetch.

Pshaw, here's that *Irish* Booby.

Enter Macahone, *Staring about him.*

Macahone. Be me Shoul, 'tis a braw House, sure the
Shentelman of the Tavern must be some Person of Quality,—
Oh! My dear Maishter Captain, I am your most loving and
mush honoured Friend.

Captain. Our Acquaintance, Sir, is a little too short for so
much Familiarity.   60

Macahone. Our Acquaintance too short Dear Joy, it ish
Threescore Miles long; And by Shaint *Patrick*, I would be very

Joiful for being your especial Friend, because I am afraid we shall never meet again.

Captain. May I crave your Name, Sir?

Macahone. My Name ish *Torlough Rauwer Macahone*, of the Parish of *Curough a Begely*, in the County of *Tiperary*, Eshquire; Where is my Mansion House, for me and my Predecessors after me.

70 *Captain.* Very well. And pray, Sir, what Affairs carry you to *London.*

Macahone. No Affairs my Dear Joy; For I have Transacted my Business in *London*, before I came there.

Captain. That's somewhat an odd way of doing Business.

Macahone. Be me Shoul Sir, it is the quickest way, tho' I was going to *London* to macke my Fortune.

Captain. How, Sir?

Macahone. Why by the Law, Friend, or Physick, or a Merchants Wife, or Back-Gammon, or any of these honourable 80 Professions; 'tis all the same to *Macahone*, Fait: But I have made my Fortune already, be me Goships Hand.

Captain. How, pray Sir?

Macahone. Because, my Dear Joy, you are my Intimate Friend, and a Stranger I will Communicate that Secret into your Stomack: The fine Lady in the Coach, Madam *Strowler*, is a Rich Merchants Wife in *Vinegar-Yard*, by *Drury-Lane* in *London*, and she is fallen in down-right Affections with me, and Treats me with mighty Civility, permitting me to Pay the Reckoning for her in every place.

90 *Captain.* Honest *Jenny* the Player has snapt this Booby, and e'en let her make a Hand of him. (*Aside.*) Are you sure she's Rich? (*To him.*)

Macahone. Be me Shoul, She shou'd me a Diamond as Big as a Potatoe; and I'faith it look'd almost as Clear as Glass; and she keeps her Flying Chariot too, she told me so her self: And be me Shoul I am so Cunning, that if anoder had told me so, I had not believ'd him.

Captain. Your'e plaguy Cunning indeed, Sir.

Macahone. O Ara Dear Joy, wee are all so; Upon me Shoul, 100 let an *Irish-man* alone for mauking his Fortune: He is as Cunning as no Man alive.—But me Dear Joy, I wish I was after going to Bed to digest my Supper;—Here are Two Beds

in your Chamber, and pray, my dear Friend, tell me, do you
intend to lie in 'em both?

Captain. 'Tis probable, Sir, I shall use but one.

Macahone. Then Sir, with your leave and permission, I shall
use the to'ther:—But pray let me not Incommode your
Person, if you intend to lie in both the Beds.

Captain. Not at all Sir,—Booby. (*Aside.*)

Macahone. Sir, I am your most obliging Servant.   110

Captain. Coxcomb. (*Aside.*)

Macahone. I render you many tanks.

Exit Macahone.

Enter Jolt *and* Fetch.

Captain. Honest Jolt, How is't? What shall I give thee to
Drink?

Jolt. Thank you Master. What you please; here's rare *Nants*
in the House. A Cogue or so, wou'd do no harm.

Captain. Here *Fetch*; bring us Half a Pint.

Exit Fetch.

Well *Jolt*, Canst do a Man a Kindness upon Occasion?

Jolt. A Kindness! Ay Master an that be all—We Coach-
men are all mighty Civil Fellows, you know.   120

Captain. Are your Horses good?

Jolt. Good special Cattle, Master: A *London* Doctor wou'd
have set up his Coach with them, if we had trusted to the fall
of the Leaf:—And but t'other Day here, One of your Stock-
Jobbers Hir'd 'em for an Election;—E' Cod they had almost
got him the place.

Enter Fetch *with Brandy.*

Captain. Here *Jolt*, pull it off. (*Gives* Jolt *the Brandy.*)

Jolt. Your Health Master. (*Drinks.*) Rare Stuff, after my
Twelve Eggs and Pound of Bacon.

Captain. Well *Jolt*, can I be at *London* by to Morrow Night? 130

Jolt. To Morrow Night,—Ay, Master, (*Drinks.*) If you can
Flye.

Captain. See here, *Jolt*. (*Pulls out a Purse.*)—My Business is
so pressing, a good share of this Purse is thine, if thou wilt
hasten our Journey.

Jolt. If that be all, (*Drinks all.*)—'Tis done.—We are to be

131 *Drinks*] Q2; *Shrinks*

in *London* the Day after to Morrow by Ten a Clock at
Night,—Now, Master, to oblige you, I'll be there by Nine.

Captain. Is the Fellow Mad?—I tell thee I must be there to
140 Morrow.

Jolt. Aye, so you may, if you can; 'Tis a long way,
Master,—The Roads are deep, and I wont spoil my Horses,
they're dearer to me, poor Beasts, than my Wife and Children.

Fetch. Silly Fool! Thou hast no more Sense than these
Horses! Why there's enough in that Purse to Bribe thy very
Master, the Duke of *Mantua*, and Two or Three *German*
Princes.

Jolt. Well, what there's in't, there's in't. (*Peeps in the Empty
Purse and throws it down.*) What do you Prate for; These Beau
150 Foot-Men Are as Cock a hoop of late, as if they had places at
Court.—I'm an honest Man;—Bribes won't pass i'the Country
now,—Besides I must not baulk my Stages.—The Inn-
keepers have Brib'd me already. (*Aside.*)

Exit Jolt.

Captain. Well, tho' it kills me, I must ride Post.

Fetch. But pray Sir, what makes you in so much haste?

Captain. Why this Letter from my Mistress. (*Reads.*)

> *You've heard, I've lost my dear Mother; My Uncle* (to whose
> Care I am left,) *not considering your Pretensions, is resolv'd to
> Marry me to another; But what's worse, the Old Gentleman has*
160 *got my Writings, and I must seem to comply with his desires: if
> you would prevent my being made a most Unfortunate Creature,
> flie to my Relief, my Dear* Basil, *with all the speed which your
> Love and my Distress require.*

ISABELLA

I'm afraid I shall come too late. Run to the Post-House, get us
Horses; and we'll mount this Moment.—But whom have we
here?

Fetch. Some of the Company that came in the *London* Coach;
that Supp'd on t'other side o'th House.

Enter Squire Somebody, *bringing a Band-box with
other Luggage, a Mask and a Fann.*

170 *Squire Somebody.* Come Mrs. *Isbel*, I've got your things. Bless

us, what a parcel of Luggage these Women carry about 'em; and the poor Lover here, must be subject to the Slavery of Band-boxes.—Mrs. *Isbel*, why don't you come away;—I'm as tir'd as a *Scotch* Peddlar under his Pack.

        Enter Isabella. *She Starts seeing the Captain.*

Isabella. Ha!

Squire Somebody. Ha! Whats the matter my dear Wife that is to be?

Isabella. I miss my Watch; I fear I've lost it in the Room where we Supp'd, pray go and see.

Squire Somebody. Aye by all means,—Here, look to your 180 things, there are Strangers about.

        Exit Squire Somebody, *having laid down the things.*

Captain. Ha! What do I see? Look, *Fetch*, Is not that *Isabella?*

Isabella. My Dear *Basil!* (*Meet and Embrace.*)

Captain. My *Isabella*, what Miracle has brought you hither?

Isabella. You receiv'd my Letter?

Captain. There it is; and it has brought me so far in my Journey to you.

Isabella. My Uncle, who knows you only by Name; dreading your return to *London*, has thought fit to hurry me down to the Country-house of that Block-head, that I sent just now on a 190 Fools Errand, under pretence of losing my Watch; My Uncle is at the Bar, Haggling with the Land-lady, and is to come up presently into the Room where we lie. Now if you can find a way to rescue me from the Old Knave and the Young Fool,—But here he comes,—He's the Son of Sir *Aminadab Somebody* in *Lancashire*.

        Enter Squire Somebody.

Squire Somebody. Gone, Gone, No Watch to be found; O Lord, Gentlewoman, See what your Uncle will say to you, lose your things so aforehand.—I won't lend you mine.

Isabella. You need not Sir,—For the Watch is found again, I 200 had only put it in the wrong Pocket.

Squire Somebody. And that's Thirty Pound in mine.(*Aside.*)

Captain. Sure I should know that Voice and Face too.—Sir, are not you Related to the Family of the *Somebodies?*

Squire Somebody. Yes, Sir: My Father is Sir *Aminadab*

Somebody, Baronet: And I am his Eldest Son by the First
Venter, *Nicodemus Somebody*, Esquire.

　　Captain. Sir, I am proud to embrace the Son of my old
Friend, Sir *Aminadab.*—Pray Sir, what Lady is that with you?
210　*Squire Somebody.* 'Tis only my Mistress, at your Service,—
We want but a Parson, A Wedding Dinner, A Pair of Clean
Sheets, and a Sack Posset, to send us the way of all Flesh.

　　Captain. Then Sir, upon your Account, I'll presume to pay
my Respects to the Lady. (*Salutes* Isabella.)

　　Squire Somebody. Sir, You're a very respectful Person;—Well,
how d'you like her? Won't she make a rare Tit, for Young
Somebody? She's a little in the Dumps at present, but we shall
Dump her out of that.

　　Captain. What, out of Humour, and so near her Marriage?
220　*Squire Somebody.* Aye, There was a certain Captain that
lov'd her, and she lov'd that certain Captain. Now I can't tell
how the Devil this Fellow had Wimbled himself into the
Mother's Favour, and had got her Consent. But as good luck
wou'd have it, the Old Woman was pleased to go, where all
Old Women shou'd go. And so Mr. *Micher* being a very honest
Man, and mighty fit for a Guardian, but having a deadly
Aversion to a Red-Coat;—Struck up a Bargin with the Father
for me, and we're going down to our House, to take Possession
of the Premises:—So this Scoundrel of an Officer is like to be
230　Disbanded; and she, forsooth, is vexed, because she can't
Serve under him.—Ha, ha, ha, (*Laughs.*) Poor Dog, he's Broke
of all sides.

　　Captain. Ha, ha, ha, Silly Fellow;—He'll Hang himself,
that's certain; What should Soldiers do else in time of Peace?

　　Squire Somebody. Aye, my dear Friend, I should be glad if
they were all Hang'd,—But for the sake of the *French*,—Perhaps
you may know the same Captain,—'Tis one *Basil*, a poor
Insignificant Ring-leader of Fifty Rogues. Ha, ha, ha.

　　Captain. Basil! I know him: Bloody Rogues he led indeed.
240　*Squire Somebody.* And he the saddest Rogue of 'em all! Ha,
ha, ha. (*Laughs.*)

---

211 but] Q2; put　　222 Wimbled] ed.; Whimbled 'Whimble' does not appear in
the *NED*. Figuratively 'wimble' means to insinuate oneself into. Q2 reads 'dwindled',
which clearly is incorrect. The 1735a text uses 'whindled', meaning whined or
whimpered, another very plausible reading.　　224 Woman] Q2: Women

Captain. Ha, ha, ha. (*Laughs.*)

Isabella. If you thought this Captain over-heard you, you durst not talk at that rate.

Squire Somebody. Durst not, say you? Odsookers, I fear neither Man, Woman, nor Child;—And I wou'd tell him so to his Face.—When my Friend stands by me here. (*Shaking the* Captain *by the Hand.*)

Captain. Softly, Madam. My Friend *Nicodemus Somebody*, is a Person whom you ought to regard;—In time you'll have no cause to complain.   250

Squire Somebody. Ah, dear Sir, You do me more Honour than I deserve. But don't you think now, that I am much more for her turn, than this same Raggamuffin?

Captain. There's no Comparison, Sir; and I think no body can tell better than I. So I can assure the Lady, this is like to be the last trouble you shall give her.

Squire Somebody. Well said faith. E'cod I've got a good Friend here, and did not think on't.

Isabella. Aye, But if *Basil* were here, he wou'd be too hard for you and your Friend both.   260

Captain. Why, What wou'd you do, if *Basil* were here?

Isabella. I wou'd run away with him to the next Parson, and leave *Nicodemus* here in the Lurch.

Squire Somebody. *Nicodemus* thanks you with all his Heart.— Did not I tell you now, how she was bewitch'd by this Captain? The Devil's in these Captains, I believe.—God, I've mind to be a Captain too.—Udsookers, now think on't, my dear Friend, I am Captain already of the Militia. (*And that's a kind of a Captain.*) And do you think that we that pay them, are not better than they?   270

Isabella. Well, But we cou'd do it, Sir, and you never the wiser; For while my Uncle and you were fast a Sleep, I cou'd steal out of my Chamber, fly into *Basil*'s Arms, and he shou'd have a Coach ready to hurry me to *London*, before you were awake the next Morning.

Squire Somebody. Udsookers, she's a cunning Jade, for all that. I shall have a rare Wife of her.

Captain. Well, well, Madam, I understand you; We shall take care of that Matter.

245 not] Q2; [om.]

280   *Squire Somebody.* Aye, aye, so we will; my dear Friend here, and I, shall watch your Waters;—I'll warrant you.—Oh! Here's Uncle *Micher.*

        Enter Micher, *with a Bill in his Hand.*

  Micher. Ha! The Cut-throat Dogs! Here's a Bill for you: That Fat Jade at the Bar will Score her self to the Devil before any Sollicitor, Taylor, Physick, or Tipple-Poysoner in *Europe.* (*Gives the Bill to the Squire.*)

  Squire Somebody. (*Reads.*) *For Bread and Beer* 8 s. 10d.—Here's as much bread and Drink as wou'd serve the *French* in *Spittle-Fields* for a Week.—*For a Calves Head and Bacon* 10 s. *For a Boild Pig and Colliflowers,*—That I bespoke. 9 s. *For a Red-Herring,*—

290 That was yours, Uncle,—1 s. *For a Bottle of Harts-horn,*—That was your Supper, Mistress,—7 d. Hey day! What's here;— *Mull'd-Sack, Dumplings, Cheese, Oranges, Toast and Butter, Fruit, Sallad, Wine, Cards, Brandy, Tarts and Tobacco. In all, Two Pound, Thirteen Shillings, and Three Pence, Three Farthings,—Besides Fire.* The De'el Fire the House.

  Micher. Well, How shall we Club this Matter? There's the Old Woman that has the Kings-Evil; And to'ther that stops the Coach every Minute, to go behind a Bush, they wont pay as much as we.

300   *Squire Somebody.* E'cod but they shall: And for you Mistress, you shall pay but a Crown, because you Eat nothing; And that you may not think your hardly dealt by, I'll Sing you the Song that makes it Stage-Coach-Law.

A SONG.

(I.)

    Let's Sing of Stage-Coaches,
    And fear no Reproaches,
      For Riding in one,
    But daily by Jogging,
:S: *While Whistling and Flogging,*
    While Whistling and Flogging,
310   *The Coachman drives on:*
      With a Hay Geeup, geeup hay ho,
      With a Hay gee Dobin, hay ho;

281 Waters] Q2; Water   298 Minute] Q2; Minuet

Hay, geeup, geeup geeup, hay ho,
Geeup, geeup, geeup, hay ho,
With a hay gee Dobin, *hay ho.*

(II.)

In Coaches thus Strowling,
Who wou'd not be rowling
   With Nimphs on each side,
Still prattling and playing,
:S: *Our Knees interlaying,*   320
We merrily ride.
   With a Hay, &c.

(III.)

Here Chance Kindly mixes,
All Sorts and all Sexes,
   More Females than Men,
We Squeeze them, we Ease them,
:S: *The Jolting does please them,*
Drive Jollily then.
   With a Hay, &c.

(IV.)

The harder you're Driving,   330
The more 'tis reviving;
   Nor fear we to fall,
For if the Coach Tumble
:S: *Wee'll have a rare Jumble,*
Wee'll have a rare Jumble,
   And then up Tails all.
With a Hay Geeup, geeup hay ho,
With a hay gee Dobin, hay ho,
Hay, geeup, geeup, geeup hay ho,
Geeup, geeup, geeup, hay ho,   340
   With a hay gee Dobin hay ho.

Micher. Well, Now let's go to Bed, that we may be the sooner out of this confounded Inn next Morning.

Squire Somebody. Well, My dear Friend, Sir, The best Friends must part, tho' it be Man and Wife:—But if you can

step home with me, 'tis but hard by, about Fourscore and Ten
Miles off, and stay there a Week, I'll make you so Drunk, you
shan't find the way back again in a Month.

    Captain. Sir, You must excuse me; I am otherwise engag'd.

350 *Squire Somebody.* Good Night, Sir.

Exit Squire Somebody.

    Isabella. Good Night, Sir.

Exit with Micher, who hands her off.

    Captain. Your Servant, Madam,—I hope you'll be in a
better Humour to Morrow.—Ha! *Fetch*, here's Fortune for
you.—Now my dear Lad run and at any Rate, get us some
Calash, Chariot, Coach, any thing to hurry us to *London*.—Flie!
—In the mean time, I'll run to my Chamber and get every
thing ready.

Exeunt severally.

Enter Jolt, the Coachman.

    Jolt. Hush! Mum's the word, there's a plaguy Candle
stands in my sight,—Out, Informer, I'll spoil your Peeping.

360 (*Puts it out.*)—The House is full, and Beds are scarce, therefore
I can't lie in my own. So good Wife at Home, by your leave!
We Travellers are forc'd sometimes to lie Two in a Bed;—'Tis
main dark: Rare Driving now in a deep Road and a rough
Way.—Odsnigs if *Dolly* now shou'd be Skittish, and won't let
me? I'll knock at her Chamber Door however; and if the Door
will open, Well said Door! I'll enter: And if *Dolly* will do like
the rest of her Crew, Well said *Dolly!*—Pox on't, here's a
Light, 'tis not yet right Catterwauling time:—So I'll sheer off
till anon.

Exit Jolt.

Enter Captain with his Things, and Fetch with a Candle.

370 *Captain.* Well, *Fetch?*

    Fetch. I've done your Business, Sir,—I've found in this very
Inn a Calash, with Four good Horses, that shou'd have gone
Empty to *London* to Morrow Morning. I've agreed with the
Coachman to go with you immediately:—He'll be ready at a
Whistle.

    Captain. That was lucky; And I've got my things here; they
shall lie till *Isabella* comes out:—I wish she were here.

360 (Puts it out.)] Q2 (puts it out); [om.]   368 off] 1718; of

Fetch. Sir! Sir! I think I here a Noise?

Captain. Put out the Candle then; And let us step into that Corner, for here we must wait for her. (Fetch *puts out the*   380 *Candle.*)

Re-enter Jolt.

Jolt. Now the Coast is clear,—I have had a strange hankering after this same *Doll* this great while, and for her sake I have set up here at the *Angel* now: If she won't be civil, d'you see, I'll carry my Guests to the *Saracen's-Head*, where I shall have the Hostler to take care of my Horses, and the Maid to take care of me.—Now for her Door.

Fetch. Ods my life, Sir, we've forgot one thing; the Gate is lock'd up by this time: How shall we get out?

Captain. What shall we do?

Jolt. Hush: I hear something:—Shou'd this be some Rogue   390 now creeping in to *Dolly!*—I'll put a Spoke in his Wheel. (*Aside.*)

Fetch. I've thought on't. The Maid's a good tractable Wench: She'll do what we'll have her.

Jolt. Will she, faith, ye Dog? Sirrah, I'll take care of that. (*Aside.*)

Fetch. I'll knock at her Door: for a piece of Money, I'll warrant you, she'll do the Job.

Jolt. Perhaps I may do your Job first, you catterwauling Son of a Whore. (*Aside.*)

Fetch. 'Tis well if I scape a good dab on the Nose here. (*Groping about.* Jolt *strikes him with the but end of his Whip.*) Confound that Post; 'tis deadly hard:—Her Door is on this   400 side, I'm sure. (Jolt *strikes him again.*) Ha! what's that?—another Post?—Ware Nose the third time.—Oh, sure here's the Door: I'll knock. (*Hits* Jolt *in the Teeth.*) *Dolly, Dolly!*—Plague on't, she's asleep.—Sure I'm right.—Where's the Key-hole?—Oh, I've found it. (*He puts his finger in* Jolt's *mouth, who bites it.*) Oh, the Devil, the Devil; help, help, Sir! I've got my Finger here in a Rat-trap.

Captain. Where art thou? (Jolt *lets hs fingers go, and lays 'em on with his Whip.*)

Jolt. Gee, gee, gee, ho, hay, gee, ho. (*As whipping his Horses.*)

Fetch. Murther, murther, help, help.   410

Captain. Hold, hold, you Dog, or I'll kill you. (*Draws.*)

Jolt. Gee, oh, gee, gee, hay gee hoh. (*Whips on.*)

Fetch. Murther, murther, help! the Devil lays me on.

Enter Hostler *with a Light.*

Hostler. What's the matter! what's the matter?

Jolt. Come on, gee, gee ho, my Hearts. (*Whips on.*)

Hostler. What a Deuce d'you mean, Master *Jolt?*

Jolt. What's the matter? what's all this bustle for? (*Yawning.*)

Hostler. What, are you drunk, or dreaming?

Jolt. What wou'd you have? where am I!—Oh, oh, is it you,
420 *Phil* the Hostler? Odsnigs, I thought I had been a Bed, I
dream'd that my Coach stuck in *Hockley the Hole*, and I was
licking my Horses till I made 'em smoak again. I beg your
pardon, Gentlemen, for taking you for my Beasts.

Enter Dolly.

Dolly. What's the matter here? Are not you asham'd to
disturb People at this time of Night?

Fetch. You're come in good time, Child, to save that Rogue
a beating; for now we've other business.—A word with you.
(*Takes her aside.*)

Captain. Get thee gone, Sirrah, or I'll cut your Ears off, you
Dog. (*To* Jolt.) And you here, with your light, go off, and leave
430 us to our business. (Jolt *retires to the Door.*)

Exit Hostler *with light.*

Jolt. Odzookers, now they're driving the Bargain. Icod I'll
over-turn the Coach to morrow in a Slough, to cool that Dog
of a Captain's Courage in a Puddle.

Exit Dolly.

Fetch. The Town's our own, Sir; I've given *Dolly* a Guinea,
she consents, and I've got the Key. (*Holds the Key in his hand.*)

Jolt. The Key! a plague on her Lock. Now has the Minx
granted at once what she has deny'd me this Twelvemonth;
but that Guinea is the Devil at a Keyhole: I warrant it would
open a thousand Spring Locks in *Covent-Garden.*—I'll watch,
440 and see what all this will come to. (*Aside.*)

Enter Isabella *with a small Trunk.*

Isabella. He shou'd be here.—*Captain.* (*In a low voice.*)

Captain. My Dear. (*In a low voice.*)

Jolt. My Dear! ah the damn'd Jade:—She's come out to
him now. (*Aside.*)

Enter Micher, *groping his way.*

Micher. Does she walk in her sleep? Where can she go at this time of Night?—I'll watch her. (*Aside.*)

Isabella. Captain! where are you? (*In a low voice.*)

Captain. Here, here.

Micher. Captain! Sure she can't have her Captain here. (*Aside.*)

Jolt. Odsnigs they're going to't; but I'll spoil their sport. 450 (*Aside.*) (*The* Captain *and* Isabella *meet.*)

Isabella. Come, I'm got out at last; and what's more, I've got the Writings. (Micher *meets* Jolt, *they lay hold on each other.*)

Micher. Ah, you young Baggage, have I caught you? Lights, lights here.

Isabella. Sir, I hear my Uncle's voice.—Let's lose no time.

Captain. Let's away, my Dear.—*Fetch*, take up the things.

Exeunt Captain *and* Isabella.

Fetch *taking up the things, drops the Key, and Exit.*

Micher. Lights here, lights.

Enter Hostler *with a Candle.*

Hostler. What's the matter here again?

Micher. Ha! what a Devil? who are you? (*Looks on* Jolt.)

Jolt. And who are you, an that be all?   460

Micher. Where's my Niece? Ah, you Pimp, you're in the Plot too. Where's that damn'd Rogue the *Captain*?

Jolt. Your Niece! The *Captain* has other work in hand: But this is a rare time to quit scores with him. (*Aside.*) (*To* Micher.) If you want the *Captain*, Sir, you'll find him in that Room with his Whore.

Micher. His Whore! the Dog make my Niece his Whore! Get a Constable,—help, a Constable.

Enter Squire Somebody *yawning.*

Squire Somebody. Here, what a Devil's the matter? Can't you let a body sleep among ye.   470

Micher. Ah, *Nicodemus*, we're all undone; the *Captain* here has got away your mistress into that Room,—and what they are doing Heaven knows.

Squire *goes to the door, and listens.*

Squire Somebody. Ha! I hear some noise; I hear some noise within: Why don't you break the Door, Uncle?

Micher. Why don't you?

Squire Somebody. She's your Niece.

Micher. She's your Wife, that's to be.

Squire Somebody. I can't tell that now.

480 *Micher.* A Constable, let's have a Constable. ⎫
Squire Somebody. A Constable, a Constable. ⎬ *Together.*

Jolt. I'll run and call up my Landlord; he's a Constable.

Exit Jolt.

> *Here one appears at the Window or Balcony; and*
> *after he has spoke another appears on the opposite*
> *side, in Night-Caps.*

In a Masculine Voice. What's the matter there? A Man may as well sleep in a Paper Mill, as in one of these confounded Inns.

Feminine Voice. What noise is that below? Are the People mad?

> *Here several People pop out at several Windows and*
> *Balconies, with Night-Caps, and cry all at once in*
> *different Keys.*

Omnes. Are ye all distracted here? Is the Devil in the People? What's the matter below? Why do you make such a 490 noise? Will no body tell us the meaning of this Uproar?

Squire Somebody. Nothing, nothing, Mistress; no harm, only a Gentleman who's making me a Cuckold before my time.

Enter Landlord *and* Jolt, *with a Leaver in his Hand,* Servants.

Landlord. Here, Where are these People?

Squire Somebody. Here, Sir; In that Room.

Landlord. Come out here, I Charge you in the Kings Name? Why then stay where you are, in the Devils Name.—Break open the Door. (Jolt *Breaks open the Door.*)

Landlord. Why don't you go in?

Jolt. Why don't you go in? You are an Officer.

500 *Landlord.* Then I Command you to go in before me.

Jolt. Let the *Squire* go in; 'Tis his Business.

Squire Somebody. Let my Uncle go in; 'Tis more his than mine.

Micher. Come, we'll all go in; tho' he be a Captain, he's but one.

They all step into the Room.

Enter Dolly at another Door.

Dolly. What can they be Searching for in my Chamber?

Re-enter Squire Somebody, Micher, &c.

Squire Somebody. The Devil a thing is there; but an Old Pair of Boddice, A Broken-back Chair, A Quire of Ballads, A Flock-Bed, And a Green Chamber-Pot.

Dolly. Why, Gentlemen, The People that you want are 510 gone: They took the Key from me, and went out.

Squire Somebody. Gone! O ye Skies. *Sic transit Gloria Mundi.*

Micher. Here, here, let's follow 'em.

Squire Somebody. Ay, ay, Horses, Coaches, Spurs, Whips, Spatterdashes, Gambadoes, Boots and Sashoons;—Away.

Landlord. (*Finds the Key.*) Hold, hold, Gentlemen; What's here? The Key of the Great Gate!—They must be in the House still, if the Maid did not let 'em out.

Dolly. Not I, upon my word, Sir.

Landlord. Then they must have dropt the Key; and are in 520 the House still.

Squire Somebody. Huzza! Have at 'em there; Swords, Halberts, Quarter-Staves, Muskets, Pikes, and Pocket-Pistols.

Micher. Find 'em out, find 'em out then.

                         Exeunt Landlord, Jolt, *and* Servants.
Why don't you go help 'em, Nephew?

Squire Somebody. Uncle, I stay to keep you Company.

                    Enter Captain, *in a Night-Gown.*

Captain. What's the meaning of all this Noise?

Squire Somebody. Ah! My dear Friend, stand by me now. (*Runs to the* Captain *and Embraces and Kisses him.*) Who shou'd be here, but that damn'd Rogue of a Captain that we talk'd of; 530 and has run away with my Mistress.

Captain. The Devil he did! And how will you use him when he's found?

Squire Somebody. Use him! I'll Pump him, I'll Souse him, Flea him, Carbonade him, and Eat him alive.

Captain. But hark you, Sir; Don't make such a Noise, you'll disturb my Wife.

Squire Somebody. What, Sir! Are you Married?

Captain Somebody. Married; and Bedded, since I saw you.

Squire Somebody. To whom?   540

            Enter Isabella *and all the rest, except* Macahone.

Captain. To this Lady, Sir.

                    530 of] Q2: off

Squire Somebody. Uncle.

Micher. Nephew.

Squire Somebody. Speak, you're the Older Man.

Micher. Married, it can't be! How cou'd you be Married so suddenly?

Captain. Very luckily, Sir; We intended, indeed, to have had it done more Decently: But my Blockhead dropt the Key, and being stopp'd that way, we saw a Light in the Ministers 550 Chamber, that travell'd with me;—we went up, found him Smoaking his Pipe; he first gave us his Blessing, and then lent us his Bed.

Squire Somebody. He was a very Civil Gentleman.

Micher. Sir this won't pass upon me. What Evidence have you for this?

Enter Macahone.

Macahone. Be me Shoul he needs no Evidence, for I am one: I was call'd to be a Witness: His Man did Waken me before I was a Sleep: And if you will believe no body, you may go up and ask the Minishter.

560 *Captain.* And in return, my Dear Country-man, I'll take care to do you Service in Relation to your pretended Merchants Wife.

Micher. Then since it is so, much good may't do you with your No-Fortune.—Her Mother did not leave her a Groat.

Squire Somebody. I am glad on't, with all my heart.

Isabella. Sir, it will appear otherwise by my Writings.

Micher. Writings! What Writings? I've no Writings of yours.

Captain. No more you have, Sir; for here they are. (*Shews them.*)

570 *Micher.* Confusion! Then I know what I have lost.

Squire Somebody. And so do I too: I've lost my Labour; I've lost my Friend, I've lost my Uncle; and I've lost my Wife.

> But since the Coach such Novelties has bred,
> The Squire *Unmarried,* and the Captain *Wed,*
> I'll be Reveng'd and go,—I'll go to Bed.

Exeunt Omnes.

FINIS.

APPENDIX A

Q2: TITLE-PAGE, DEDICATION, DRAMATIS PERSONAE, PROLOGUE,
AND EPILOGUE

THE

STAGE-COACH

A

COMEDY:

As it was

Acted at the New Theatre

IN

LINCOLNS-INN-FIELDS.

BY

Her Majesties Servants.

LONDON:
Printed, and are to be Sold by *Benjamin Bragg,* at the
Blew-Ball in *Ave-Mary-Lane.* 1705.

THE
Epistle Dedicatory
TO
Samuel Bagshaw, Esquire.

SIR,

When the Age declineth from her primitive Vertue, and the Silken Wits of the Time (as Learned *Johnson* calls 'em) disgracing Nature, and Harmonious Poesie, are transported with many illiterate and prodigious Births, it is not safe to appear without Protection. I have read that *Lucilius* (one, who in his time, had the repute of a Learned Person) was wont to say, that he would not have his Writings Read or Perus'd, either by Learned or Illiterate Readers; because the former
10 might have a more clear notion and conception of things than himself, the latter understood nothing. But I shall assume the Confidence to be of a different Opinion from him; and insert this Petition into my Letany, that I may meet with Learned and Judicious Readers. Ignorance being the only Enemy that I can fear; it being (as my Lord *Verulam* has well observ'd) infallibly true, that he that hath no Vertue himself, ever envieth Vertue in others; for Mens Minds will either feed upon their own Good, or upon others Evil, and who wanteth one will prey upon the other, at least, strive to come at even
20 Hand, by depressing it with black mouth'd Obloquy and Detraction. With these (as with evil Genius) the most Learned and Deserving Men have ever been haunted, and as dark Shadows do no less attend Beautiful than Deformed Bodies in brightest Sun-shine, so as well the best Men, as their best Actions, are still waited on by (those Brats of Ignorance or Malice) Detraction and Calumnies. For confirming the Truth of which, I shall need no farther to search the Rolls of Antiquity, than to look back upon those Times, in which *Johnson* (that Son of Wit) did by the clear and piercing Rays of
30 his Wit and Judgment, dissipate all mists of Ignorance, and reform the Errors of the Stage; and yet, though he shined so

bright in Wits Horizon, were there not wanting some barren
Clods of dull Earth, who being uncapable of receiving the least
Ray of Wit themselves from his quickening Influence, (as
Niobe preferr'd her own earthly Brood before *Apollo* and *Diana*,
the Cœlestial Twins of *Latona*) dar'd prefer the spurious issue
of their own Brain before this great *Apollo*, and endeavour'd to
Eclipse the Glory of his Heavenly Endowments, but with how
bad success they attempted it, his Incomparable Play (the
Poetaster) made in derision of them, sufficiently declares. And 40
although like a petty inconsiderable Star, I could not expect to
be taken notice of in the presence of that glorious Sun, nor
dare to entertain such high Conceptions of my self, as to hope
to be named with him; yet I'll take the Confidence to declare
to the World, that tho' my weak Abilities can hold no
proportion with those rich Gifts of Nature, of which he was
Master, yet I can Glory, I resemble him in this, that I am
assaulted with the Ignorance of partial and prejudicial
Readers; as has sufficiently appeared by a piece I lately
Publish't, which because it looked upon all with an Impartial 50
Eye, and (remote from servile Flattery) spared not nearest
Relations, taxing not their Persons but their Vices, is hated for
speaking Truth, but those gall'd Camels whom it toucht to the
quick, their Anger I as much scorn as pity. But (Worthy Sir) I
too much press upon the assurance of your Patience, by
dwelling so long upon a Subject which derogates from what is
Customary in Dedications, but since Dedicators of late, make
the praises they give their Patrons so extravagant, that they
become Abuses, I shall omit Writing what I think. Only this,
Works of this Nature have always assumed this priviledge, to 60
aspire the noblest for their Protectors, and (thank Heaven) in
all Ages there wants not a succession of some candid
Dispositions, who (in spight of Malice and Ignorance) dare
countenance Poetry, and the Professors. How such an
Excellent and Divine part of Humanity should fall under the
least Contempt, or arm the petulancy of Writers to declaim
against her, I know not, but I guess the Reason, that having
their Souls darkned, and rejoycing in their Errors, are
offended at the Lustre of those Arts that would enlighten
them: but the Fates have not so ill befriended our Studies, as 70
to expose them to Contempt, without the Protection of such

whose Ability of Judgment can both wipe off all Aspersions, and dignifie Desert. Amongst the worthy Patrons of Learning, that can best vindicate her Worth, you are not the least; and because Custom and Respect to Noble Friends, gives a priviledge to Dedicate our Endeavours where they may find Admittance, I have made bold to present this Piece to your noble Patronage.

(Sir,) You have the Fame for Piety and Love to your
80 Country, and have so equally ballanc'd your Actions in these distemper'd Times, that you have not only merited the Title *Apollo* gave to *Socrates*, but have drawn all Mens Eyes, Loves and Admiration upon you. Amongst the number of which your Honourers, I humbly tender this Offering; and though it is naked of Worth, yet the property of your Acceptance will be shelter sufficient to it, and him, who, next to your Pardon, shall endeavour to deserve the Title of,

S I R,

Your most Humble,
90   and Faithful Servant,
In all observance.

Dramatis Personæ

[MEN]

Micher, Uncle to the Squire.	Mr. *Freeman*.
Captain *Basil*, in Love with *Isabella*.	Mr. *Booth*.
Squire *Somebody*, a Clownish Country Gentleman, pretender to *Isabella*.	Mr. *Dogget*.
Macahone, an *Irishman*.	Mr. *Tattnal*.
Fetch, Servant to Captain *Basil*.	Mr. *Pack*.
Tom. Jolt, the Stage-Coach-Man.	Mr. *Trout*.
Constable.	Mr. *Lee*.

WOMEN.

Isabella, Niece to *Micher*, in Love with Captain *Basil*.	Mrs. *Prince*.
Dolly, Maid of the Inn.	Mrs. *Hunt*.

10

SCENE:

An Inn between *London* and *Chester*, The Time of Action the same with that of Representation.

PROLOGUE.

Poets in former Days, without Disputes,
Turn'd Men to Gods, transform'd the Gods to Brutes:
Our Poets change the Scene, but with this odds,
Make Men the Brutes; make nothing of the Gods.
'Tis but a Word with them, hey—presto——pass,
Jove's made a Bull, an Alderman as Ass.
Strange Wonders still have been perform'd this way,
As you have seen in many a careless Play.
The Beau, that's all the Morning charm'd, to view
In his dear Glass, his Wig, his Shape, his Shooe;
That courts his smiling form with easie Leer,
Pleased with his Likeness there,—he hates it here.
I've known a Lady rise, perhaps, at Six,
Slip on her Gown, and to her Toylet fix,
For some four Hours, nay five, to chuse her Airs,
But first she lays out half an Hour at Prayers.
With Paint, and Pins, and Wash, she makes a pother,
This Curls awry, and this, and that, and to'other.
And what's all this for?—faith 'tis past my reach!
Oh!——
She must be fine, to hear the Doctor preach.
A Lady, if undrest at Church, looks silly,
One cannot be devout in dishabilly.
This Lady shure must strangely love her Toylet,
And yet a Poet, at one dash shall spoil it.
In short, they can do any thing to please ye,
I've known an Audience meet here, gay and easie,
In Humour good, as ever here was seen,
And in an Hour, the House intire has been,
By charms of dullness, murder'd with the Spleen. $\Big\}$

EPILOGUE.

Praise a fair Day at Night, the Proverb says,
And 'tis the Evening that must Crown all Plays.
When first this Farce was acted, 'twas unknown
To th' Author, and before 'twas Feathered, flown;
He now consents, that you shou'd see't once more,
Cause it hath more faults, than it had before.
He knows there is a snarling Sect i'th'Town,
That do condemn all Wit, except their own;
Were this Farce ne're so good, it shou'd not take,
Nothing must pass that Gentlemen do make.   10
As in the Pit I sate, I heard one say,
There ne're was poorer Language in a Play
And told his Neighbour, that much he fear'd the vile
Composure wou'd go near to spoil his Stile:
Another Damn'd the Scene with full mouth'd Oaths,
Because it was not dress'd in better Cloaths;
And rather wish'd each Actor might be mute,
Then he should lose the sight of a fine Suit.
Oh Wit! and Judgment both! what they do raise
To Prejudice, is here the greatest praise.   20
Would it be proper, think you, for a Swain
To put on Buskins, and a lofty Strain?
Or should a home bred Maid such Phrases vent,
As at the Court, your Ladies Compliment?
Or Country Putt, he who did never know,
The Art of Dress, or Beau, Lord like to go
In Silks or Sattins? Or a serving Lass,
Wear by her side a Watch, or Looking-Glass?
Faith Gentlemen, such Solecisms as these,
Might have done well in the Antipodes;   30
It argues a strange Ignorance to call
Every thing foolish, that is Natural.
If only Monsters please you, you must go   ⎫
Not to the Stage, but to a Bartholomew Show,   ⎬
Where Elephant, Ox, Ass, and Rider grow.   ⎭
The Author aims not to shew Wit, but Art,

Nor did he strive to Pen the Speech, but Part.
He could have Writ high Lines, and this I know,
His pains were double to descend so low.
Good Voices fall and rise; and Virgil, *who*
Did Georgicks *make, did Write the* Æneids *too.*
The Picture of a Beggar, and a King,
Do equal praises to a Painter bring,
Meadows and Groves in Landskips please the Eye,
As much as Court, or City Bravery.
In short, be pleas'd or not, he begs no Fame.
He sought your Mirth, more than a Poets Name.

FINIS.

APPENDIX B

PROLOGUE

*Spoken upon the Revival of this Comedy, at the
Theatre in* Lincolns-Inn-Fields, *some Years
since, when acted for the Benefit of the*
AUTHOR.
Written by Mr. *Samuel Philips.*

Like some abandon'd Mistress of the Town,
By long Enjoyment stale and nauseous grown,
A thousand little cunning Tricks she trys,
T'appear more tempting in her Lover's Eyes;
Study's each Hour new Arts t' increase her Charms,
And draw him back to her once lovely Arms;
But all in vain, in vain the Nymph does labour,
And racks Invention to regain your Favour,
Nothing will do, since you're resolv'd to leave her.

This is our Case; what Projects han't we try'd,   10
In hopes you'd stick the closer to our Side?
Both Day and Night toil'd with incessant Pains,
T'increase your Pleasures, and augment our Gains:
Nay, when we found we'd nothing here wou'd do,
We ransack'd the whole Globe to find out new,
And all for such ungrateful Souls as you.
Do what we cou'd, you left us hear alone,
Our Fate and your Unkindness to bemoan.
The poor Monimia *you unpity'd, mourn'd,*
Her moving Sighs, alas! were all return'd,   20
By a more piercing, ecchoing, hollow Sound.

Yet after all th' Unkindness you have shown,
(Such easy Fools as we were never known)

8 *your*] ed.; *you*

We'd persevere again, renew our Toil,
Wou'd you but crown our Labours with a Smile;
And, as a Proof, we here this Night present you
With something New, *which will, we hope, content you:*
And if at last, this the stray'd Town reclaims,
We're fully satisfy'd for all our Pains;
Your once-lov'd Stage its drooping Head shall raise,
And from its Rival *boldly snatch the Bays.*
But yet, if after all you'll not relent, ⎫
But stedfastly are on our Ruin bent, ⎬
Don't with the Guilty slay the Innocent. ⎭
To Night, at least, let's your Compassion share, ⎫
And out of Charity be pleas'd to spare ⎬
The half-starv'd Poet, *tho' you damn the* Player. ⎭

30

EPILOGUE

Spoken by Captain Basil.
Written by Mr. Philips.

At length, Gallants, With whipping, and much flogging,
And Ribs most sorely bruis'd by Jolts and Jogging;
Safely am I arriv'd at th' Land of Matrimony,
(A Land, I'm told, that flows with Milk and Honey)
In which, accompany'd with my loving Wife,
I intend to travail out the small Remains of Life:
If I've mistook the Path, and gone amiss,
And 'stead of th' promis'd Land of Happiness,
Find it a barren, curss'd, uneven Soil,
O'er-run with Bryars, and not worth my Toil;   10
How shall I curse the Authors of my Sin,   ⎫
Who with fine gilded Words first drew me in,   ⎬
And noos'd the cred'lous Wretch fast in the Marrige Gin? ⎭
But all in vain, for there is no Relief
To heal my Sorrows, and correct my Grief;
No Pray'rs, no Tears can wash away my Crime,   ⎫
Nothing will do, unless aloft I climb,   ⎬
And fairly rouse my self a second Time: ⎭
Yet that, perhaps, may like the first, deceive;
Therefore let what will come, I'll e'en contented live.   20

    If my kind Spouse t' Incontinency is given,
That's not amiss, for Cuckolds go to Heaven:
Besides, of late, a Cuckold and a Rogue
Are the two only Men wh'are most in Vogue.
To Cuckoldom the Citizens lay claim,   ⎫
They, cunning Knaves, (submitting all to Gain)   ⎬
Know 'tis the chief Step to a golden Chain;   ⎭
And, I dare say, there's not one to be found,
But first wore Horns, and then the Scarlet Gown.
To Roguery the Courtiers most pretend,   30
Yet it finds neighb'ring Cit no backward Friend;

That, like the other, to Preferment leads,
Then sure he cannot fail that both Paths treads.
The latter—
As being an Officer, *I understand,*
Knows how to Cheat, as well as to Command:
Yet I don't doubt but that my Spouse is kind,
And then too soon I shall the former find.

APPENDIX C

AIR I. *Every Man take a Glass in his* Hand.
[following l. 25 of text]

Fetch. Every Man that would stand on his Guard,
    Should be loaded with Bullets a Brace,
    Cock and prime, and be always prepar'd
    For a sudden Rencounter, or Chace:
If a stout Son of *Mars* should his Faulchion wield;
Or an *Amazon* bold should display her Shield,
      Let him bravely defy,
      And with Courage let fly,
And no doubt but he wins the Field.

AIR II. *On Enfield* Common. [following Air I.]

Dolly. Oh, have a Care, Sir,
      A Virgin spare, Sir,
    And lay your thundring Engine softly down,
      Your bold attacking,
      Will send you packing,
    And Conquest will procure but small Renown;
      Yet if a Maiden,
      With Troubles laden,
    Shou'd face the Danger your stout Heart wou'd yield,
      Sir,
      Your Heat and Fire,
      Wou'd soon expire,
    You'd hardly stand the Charge—but quit the Field,
      Sir.

AIR III. Muirland Willy. [following l. 53]

    How tedious do the Moments pass
      In Expectation of our Joy;
    But hasty Time oft shakes his Glass,
      If Pleasure we employ.

10

Too rigid Fate, you deal us Bliss
   Swift as rapid Torrents flow,
But Care and Anguish you dismiss,
   Like Snails, by creeping slow.

AIR IV. *Dame of* Honour. [following l. 120]

There's ne'er a Coachman drives a Coach,
   But what's an honest Fellow;
At your least Beck, we soon approach,
   Or when your Servants bellow.
     We use our Fare
     With tender Care,
Go fast, or slow, to ease you:
     If Maids are kind,
     We know your Mind,
10   And softly drive to please you.

AIR V. *Tho' Claret be a* Blessing. [following l. 126]

You'll find in ev'ry Nation
By shining Gold's Persuasion;
   A Fool is fit
   (With Wealth) to sit,
Far higher than his Station:
   Be ne'er so dull,
   If Purse is full,
Votes will come whene'er they call:
   Tho' the Fools
10   Are but Tools
For the Wise to work withal.

AIR VI. *Tell me, tell me, dearest Creature.*
   [following 'Fools,—' l. 196]

Isabella.   If we lose the fair Occasion,
     I no more shall bless thy Sight;
Basil.   Love avert the dire Vexation,
     And secure my Soul's Delight:
Isabella.   Vain is idle Invocation,
     While our Foes their Strength unite;

Basil.   But we'll mock their Combination,
             Flying thro' the Shades of Night.

AIR VII. *From the* Italian. [following l. 247]

      Think not to affright
      A Man of my Might,
         By threatning Wounds and Scars,
      I'll swell and look bluff,
      Vapour and huff
         Spite of your Bully of *Mars*.
Isabella. Remember the Jest
      Befel the bold Beast,
         Array'd in the Lion's Skin,
      When Spite of Harangues   10
      Bruises and Bangs
      Shew'd the dull Coward within.

AIR VIII. *Last Part of the Dutch* Skipper.
[following l. 275]

      When a Lady is fir'd by a Hero brave,
         With Invention quick
         She will frame a Trick,
      To cheat a dull Fool, and a sordid Knave,
         And fly to her Love's Defence.
      Secure in their Folly she boasts her Scheme,
      And sees them insult on the fancy'd Dream,
         'Till suffering quickens their Sense.

AIR IX. *O ponder well, Etc.* [following *Europe*, l. 285]

Micher. This Jade will score herself to Hell,
         If she such Bills does make.
Squire. Then get the Priest that Tale to tell,
         And she may warning take.

AIR X. [following l. 303]

      Let's sing of *Stage-Coaches*,
         And fear no Reproaches,

For riding in one;
But daily be jogging,
While whistling and flogging,
While whistling and flogging,
The Coachman drives on:
With a Hey, geeup, geeup, hey ho;
With a Hey gee *Dobbin*, hey ho;
Hey, geeup, geeup, geeup, hey ho,
Geeup, geeup, geeup, hey ho,
With a hey gee *Dobbin*, hey ho.

In Coaches thus strolling,
Who wou'd not be rolling,
   With Nymphs on each Side;
Still prattling and playing,
Our Knees interlaying,
We merrily ride:
   With a Hey, &c.

Here Chance kindly mixes,
All Sorts and all Sexes,
   More Females than Men;
We squeeze them, we ease them,
The Jolting does please them;
Drive jollily then:
   With a Hey, &c.

The harder you're driving,
The more 'tis reviving;
   Nor fear we to fall;
For if the Coach tumble,
We'll have a rare Jumble,
We'll have a rare Jumble,
And then up Tails all:
With a Hey, geeup, geeup, hey ho,
With a hey gee *Dobbin*, hey ho;
Hey, geeup, geeup, geeup, hey ho,
Geeup, geeup, geeup, hey ho,
With a hey gee *Dobbin*, hey ho.

AIR XI. *Daniel* Cooper. [following *Dolly!*—, l. 367]

> The Great may fancy as they will,
>   Only they have Pleasure,
> The poor Man he enjoys it still,
>   In a greater Measure:
> Labour fits us for Delight,
>   Hunger comes by Fasting.
> He ne'er eats with Appetite,
>   Whose Meal is everlasting.

AIR XII. *The Scotch* Tune. [following l. 433]

Dolly. Since Bribes are Fashions of each Day,
>   Why then shou'd I be out?
> Both High and Low the Game will play,
>   No Conscience makes a Doubt.
> Your Coin I'll take but as my Due,
>   'Tis Vales in such a Case,
> And all well know there's very few
>   But tack it to their Place.

AIR XIII. *There was three Lads in London* Town.
[following l. 492]

Macahone. In City, Town, and Country too,
>   A Cuckold is no wonder;
> 'Tis more than any one can do,
>   To keep a Woman under;
> Your Horns, dear Joy, will grace your Head,
>   And fit you for high Station;
> A Wife will save your Soul, when Dead,
>   And fait you're in de Fashion.

AIR XIV. *An old Woman cloathed in* Grey.
[following Name? l. 496]

> *Authority Hard-head* here calls
>   A Constable famous for Might,
> I silence all Squables and Brawls,
>   And snore in my Chair ev'ry Night;

And therefore strait open the Door,
    And let me your Crimes understand,
Or as I'm a Son of a Whore,
    I'll punish you all by this Hand.

AIR XV. *To* Chloe *the Kind and the* Easy.
[following l. 506]

How wretched were *Dolly's* Condition,
    If under the Bed
    Her Lover were hid,
Expecting the Hour of Fruition;
And panting with eager Haste,
    Instead of a whispering Voice,
Awak'd by a boist'rous Noise,
    His Heart wou'd so beat,
    It wou'd surely defeat
His hopes, tho' the Storms are past.

AIR XVI. *Under the Green Wood* Tree [following l. 559]

Macahone. He needs no Evidensh, dear Joy,
        For fait now I am one,
    I was awak'd by dat brave Boy, [*Pointing to* Fetch.
    'Fore I to Sleep was gone.
    I saw de Parson say de Grace,
    In Troth now this is true,
        De Meat was drest
        And of de best,
    And fait he did fall too.

AIR XVII. [following l. 569]

Captain. }	Thrice happy we by Love and *Hymen* joyn'd.
Isabella. }	
Captain.	Souls cementing,
Isabella.	Hearts contenting,
Both.	Free and yet confin'd.
Captain.	While you, my fairest,
Isabella.	You, my dearest,
Both.	Gently rule my Mind.

Captain.	No more my absent Fair,
	With jealous dread tormenting;
Isabella.	No more shall Rivals dare,
	My trembling Heart invest.
Captain.	Cares ever pleas'd and pleasing,
Isabella.	Joys evermore increasing,
Both.	Swell my tuneful Breast.
Captain.	With Raptures warming,
Isabella.	Charm'd and Charming,
Both.	Thou its only Guest.

10

THE INCONSTANT

INTRODUCTION

No details are known about the composition of *The Inconstant*. Farquhar had returned from Holland in the winter of 1700–1. *The Stage-Coach* probably opened during the winter or spring. On 24 July 1701 *Letters of Wit, Politicks and Morality*, to which Farquhar contributed correspondence, was published.[1] Farquhar was apparently very much involved in publishing correspondence, for on 3 July 1701 he contracted with Lintott to publish *Love and Business* and 'A Discourse upon Comedy In Fourteen Letters';[2] the miscellany appeared on 28 February 1702, only shortly after the *première* of *The Inconstant*. Perhaps these miscellanies kept him from theatrical endeavours; at any rate, there is no evidence that he wrote prologues between summer 1700 and autumn 1702 with the exception of 'A Prologue on the propos'd Union of the Two Houses', spoken probably in 1701 and then published in *Love and Business*.

Farquhar said in the Preface to *The Inconstant* that he had invested 'half a years pains' in the play. If the statement is true, he began work in or near August, a fact which might explain why there are no known minor works, even prologues or epilogues, for the autumn and winter of 1701–2.

Although little is known about the circumstances of composition, the primary source of the play is obvious. Farquhar claimed in the Preface that he 'took the hint from *Fletcher*'s *Wild Goose Chase*'. Adaptations like *The Inconstant* as well as translations like *The Stage-Coach* were more the rule than the exception at the turn of the eighteenth century. Translations of foreign works, modernizations of earlier English works, and the merging of borrowed plots and characterizations from several old plays in a new piece were standard procedures for playwrights, even the best. Perhaps the rapidity of such authorship helped meet the strong demand for plays in a time in which the companies waged intense competition. The reliance of Farquhar on earlier

models for *The Stage-Coach* and *The Inconstant*, then, is
surprising only in terms of his own unusual originality, not in
terms of the theatre of his time. Like his contemporaries,
Farquhar adapted with considerable freedom, Anglicizing
characterizations and liberally retooling the materials he
worked with. In both pieces, he diverged increasingly from the
original as the adaptation progressed.

In *The Inconstant*, Farquhar reduced Fletcher's cast of twelve
characters to eight by combining some characters and
omitting others. La Castre, in some respects joined with
Nantolet, became Old Mirabel; Mirabell, Young Mirabel; De
Gard Dugard; Pinac and Belleur together Duretete; Oriana
Oriana; Rosalura and Lillia-Bianca together Bisarre. Several
characters disappeared, and Petit and Lamorce were added,
with Petit taking on some of the functions of Lugier, the
footboy, and Lillia's servant. The dependence on Fletcher's
original contains nothing that is plagiarism 'in its coarser or
burglarious forms', as Arthur Colby Sprague expressed it.
Sprague contends that at the lowest estimate seven of
Farquhar's sixteen scenes are wholly original, and three or
four more might well be added to that category.[3] In fact,
Farquhar borrowed few lines, although he relied on Fletcher's
plot outline in the early acts. By the third act he had diverged
considerably, and Acts IV and V are almost entirely original.

Farquhar claims in the Preface to have taken Oriana's
rescue of Mirabel in Act V from 'an Adventure of *Chevalier de
Chastillon* in *Paris*' which was 'universally known'. Stonehill
identifies Alexis-Henri, Chevalier and afterwards Marquis de
Châtillon, who lived from 1650 to 1737. Scholars, however,
have romanticized the incident into an autobiographical
adventure. The *Biographia Dramatica* says the incident 'owes its
origin, it is said, to an affair of the like nature, in which the
author had himself some concern when on military duty
abroad' (ii. 322), a bit of creative biography that was copied in
Hazlitt's remarks in Samuel French's edition of the play, and
in William Winter's account.

In the Prologue Motteux reused the metaphor of the feast
frequently applied to theatrical fare, for example in the
Prologue to *Love Without Interest* (April 1699), the Epilogue to
Feign'd Friendship (probably May 1699), and the prologue to

Cibber's *Love Makes a Man* (9 January 1701). An excerpt from Cibber's prologue indicates how close the similarities were:

Since Plays are but a kind of Publick Feasts,
Where Tickets only make the welcome Guests;
Methinks, instead of Grace, we shou'd prepare
Your Tastes in Prologue, with our Bill of Fare.
When you foreknow each Course, tho' This may teize you,
'Tis five to One, but One o'th'Five may please you.

Farquhar's originality, however, could never be suppressed, not even when he set out deliberately to adapt an older work. Although he nowhere complains of authorial pains in creating *The Inconstant* as he did for *The Stage-Coach*, he chose in his final three plays to return to the originality in plots that had marked his first three.

STAGE HISTORY

The paucity of information about the season 1701–2 leaves the printed text as the primary authority on the first production. The quarto was advertised in the Term Catalogue in February 1702: 'In a few days will be published the last new Comedy, call'd *The Inconstant*. Acted at the Theatre Royal.' The act tunes were published by John Walsh on 5 March.[4] The quarto was published on 11 March.[5] Furthermore, when *Love and Business* was advertised in the *Post Man* of 26–8 February 1702, Farquhar was identified as the author of *The Inconstant*, a clear indication that the play had opened before then. Judging from the data Judith Milhous and Robert D. Hume have accrued, the average time between the *première* and publication of a play in the 1690s was approximately one month.[6] From all indications, then, *The Inconstant* must have opened in February, as the *London Stage* estimates. It came during a lean season: with six *premières*, in 1701–2, Drury Lane scored only with Steele's *Funeral*; Lincoln's Inn Fields produced no successful comedies although *Tamerlane*, which opened during the season, may have had a long run.

Some embellishments to *The Inconstant* were provided in the theatre. A song, 'Since *Celia* tis not in our Power', by an unidentified 'Mr. O—r' was set by Daniel Purcell to be performed by the singer Hughes. A second song, 'Prethee *Phillis*', described as 'The new Song' was given to professional singers in v. ii., but no music has been found. Purcell's act tunes included an overture, three airs, two minuets, a march, a hornpipe, and a gavotte.[7] A prologue different from the printed one was added, and Nicholas Rowe was engaged to write the epilogue.

Predictably Wilks played Young Mirabel, Jane Rogers Oriana, Norris the comic servant, and Mills Dugard. Pinkethman took Old Mirabel, and Bullock, rather surprisingly, played Duretete to Mrs Verbruggen's Bisarre. Mrs Kent rounded out the cast as Lamorce. The scenes were mostly common ones drawn out of stock—a tavern, a large parlour and other rooms, a street scene—but a monastery set and a scene in front of the theatre were also required.

According to the printed Preface, the *première* performance was first marred by shocking impromptu additions to the prologue by its performer and then disrupted by noisy expressions of contempt from some gentlemen in the pit. Nevertheless, the audience as a whole seem to have received the play favourably. Thomas Brown, in 'A Criticism On several Modern Plays, in a Letter to Mr. Dennis' claimed that the comedy expired after two or three nights,[8] but Farquhar in the Preface says the play ran six successive nights. Still he considered the run neither victory nor defeat; he complained that the audience preferred the charms of a 'French lady' and her company of dancers who achieved an apparently triumphant run that has not been recorded by theatrical historians.

The play might have proved hardier in its first season had not King William died on 8 March. The theatres had to close until after the coronation on 23 April. Farquhar indicated in the Preface his expectation that the run would continue when the theatres reopened; nothing in the sparse extant records indicates whether in fact his hopes for a longer run were realized.

The next recorded run of *The Inconstant*, in fact, did not occur until fourteen years later when Lincoln's Inn Fields revived the play for three nights in December. The receipts, which averaged about £22 an evening, did not encourage a flurry of performances. Another seven years lapsed before

Drury Lane ran the play for three nights with the original Mirabel father and son, Pinkethman and Wilks.

But by the third decade of the century, when theatrical competition had expanded, *The Inconstant*, which had been performed only a dozen known times in its first twenty-eight years, gained a comfortable niche in the repertory. The comedy ran every season from 1729 to 1737 and again was performed annually, usually several times, from 1751 to 1758. A tally of performances by decade shows the rises and falls of the play's frequency on stage:

1729–39	25 performances
1739–49	7 performances
1749–59	31 performances
1759–69	18 performances
1769–79	7 performances
1779–89	5 performances
1789–1800	26 performances

The statistics are unusual, for most of Farquhar's plays swelled in the number of performances in the decades at mid century and then declined. The vacillations were in part responses to the popularity of certain actors; for example, Young Mirabel was never played by Wilks after 1723 but became a standard role for later actors: Giffard played it twenty-six times, Palmer nineteen, Smith thirty-five, and Wroughten twenty-five, and it was attempted on one or two occasions by Roberts, 'a Gentleman of the Temple', Yarrow, Hallam, Dexter, Farren, Pope, and Talbot. The Duretete–Bisarre sub-plot grew very popular on stage. Duretete became a favourite role, performed originally by Bullock but later undertaken by Garrick among many others, and Kitty Clive and Frances Abington were among those who played Bisarre. Peg Woffington, noted for her breeches parts, became one of many Orianas.

The Inconstant remained in the repertory in London throughout the nineteenth century, its popularity apparently unaffected by what some critics deemed quaintness. The acting version of the text published by Oxberry in 1822 indicated fully not only stage directions and stage business but also costuming (Old Mirabel, for example, wore a puce-coloured spotted suit with embroidered loops; Bisarre, a spangled muslin dress, festooned up with roses).

Furthermore, the play travelled well to Dublin and other Irish towns, including Belfast, Kilkenny, Newry, Cork, Londonderry, and Ennis; the second half of the century saw frequent performances in Ireland.[9] It also crossed the ocean in fine fettle. It played at the theatre on Cruger's Wharf, New York, on 1 January 1759. Later a three-act version was devised and played at the John Street theatre in 1795. Other performances were given, including ones in 1829; in 1832 with Charles Kemble as Mirabel and Fanny Kemble as Bisarre; at Burton's theatre in 1857; and at the Arch Street Theatre in Philadelphia in 1858. Perhaps the most notable American productions were those by Augustin Daly in 1872 and again in 1889. The latter production, which played nightly with two matinees a week, was a great success. In it the monastery scene was removed; III. ii, the scene of Duretete's great anger was replaced, having been cut earlier; and the entire play was compressed into four acts. In America the play's sub-title became 'Wine Works Wonders'. Many English actors played roles in American productions, but according to William Winter the part of Mirabel 'is inseparably entwined' with the name of James E. Murdoch.[10]

The Inconstant developed remarkable durability; it was far more important in the repertory of the last decades of the century than in its earliest years, and it continued to flourish in the nineteenth century. It evolved with the times, and perhaps it mellowed, as with maturity it gained popularity. Had the King's death not darkened the theatre in the spring of 1702, perhaps the stage history of the play would have been different. But as events occurred, Farquhar never lived to know that *The Inconstant* would prove yet another perennial repertory piece.

REPUTATION AND INFLUENCE

The Inconstant had already been reviled in print by critics before opening night. The author of *A Comparison Between the Two Stages* was the first of many critics to complain both that

Farquhar borrowed from Fletcher and that he did not follow
Fletcher closely enough:

> . . . he vamps it up, and with some wretched Interpolations of his
> own, passes it for New, but I'll undertake to mark out his from
> *Fletcher*'s, as evidently as I can perceive the River *Dee* runs thro' the
> great Lake in *Wales*. . . . If *Fletcher* had not the misfortune to be in
> *English*, he had escap'd this Highway Man.[11]

Tom Brown repeated the complaints about the originality
that marked the adaptation:

> For the *Irish* so maul'd the *English Author*, that *Fletcher* and the *Wild-
> Goose Chace* cou'd not be seen through it.[12]

Moreover, early followers of Collier condemned the immorality of the piece. *A Representation of the Impiety and
Immorality of the English Stage* (London, 1704) condemns
'detestable lewd Expressions' in *The Inconstant* as well as other
plays, quoting some of them lest anyone overlook their
immorality.

The revival at Drury Lane in 1723 prompted a letter from
'Menander' in *Pasquin*, no. 75 (22 October 1723) in which he
criticized both the performance and the play, complimenting
Farquhar while attacking the play. Oddly enough, Menander
spoke of borrowing from the French, presumably of the
incident in Act V, but did not refer to Fletcher:

> The Author of that Play was not without a great deal of light
> Humour of his own, which he has drop'd in a good Measure in this,
> to borrow somewhat much worse from the *French*, in the Place of it;
> by which Means this happens to be the least entertaining of his
> Comedies.
> The Plot of the Play is indeed nothing at all.

With great irony Menander suggests that the play is both silly
and immoral:

> This, it seems, is *the way to win him*; that is, a Young Fellow may
> reasonably be allow'd to marry the Lady he is in love with, and
> contracted to, after she has very seasonably sav'd his Throat from
> being cut, especially if she brings him Ten Thousand Pounds in her
> Pocket.

The reputation of *The Inconstant* improved, however, with

passing time. Hazlitt considered it much superior to *The Recruiting Officer*.[13] Leigh Hunt, on the other hand, scorned the adaptation, calling it pleasant but far inferior to the Fletcher original:

> . . . compared with the 'Wild Goose Chace', it is not a whit livelier, nor indeed so lively, nor has it anything of the other's robust and masterly expression or imagination. It is, in truth, with the exception of the highly interesting adventure that is taken from a fact in the history of a French gentleman, neither more nor less than Fletcher's play with all the poetry taken out of it. . . .[14]

Winter considered the continuing popularity of *The Inconstant* proof of its superiority to Farquhar's other works with the possible exceptions of *The Recruiting Officer* and perhaps *The Beaux Stratagem*. However, he felt the piece needed cutting and alterations to be performed, for Farquhar 'did not scruple sometimes to write in a licentious vein and to use expressions which in these days would offend the audience'.[15]

Twentieth-century critics have by and large continued the discussion of the adaptation, some ranking Farquhar as clearly inferior to Fletcher, some preferring the tightening of structure in the adaptation, some finding it heavily sentimental, and at least one, James, finding it one of Farquhar's lightest comedies. They have not taken the play as seriously as did their nineteenth-century predecessors, and they have not, with the exception of James, critically analysed it. Instead, they have tended to discuss the scope and kind of adaptation before rushing on to discuss the later plays.

One could scarcely argue for early influence on other English dramatists, for the play was rarely in the public eye for almost three decades. The feast or bill of fare continued as a metaphor for the theatre, but since it predates *The Inconstant*, a specific debt is incapable of proof in such cases as William Walker's *Marry, or do Worse*, which opened on 1 November 1703. The possibility of specific imitation of Motteux's piece seems more likely in the prologue to Susanna Centlivre's *Love's Contrivance* (4 June 1703) because of her alliance with Farquhar, but the metaphor was such a commonplace that she would not really have needed to borrow it—it was in the public domain.

More importantly, the characterizations and plotting devices were fairly commonplace. Disguise and trickery; winsome,
woeful girls courageously tracking their chosen mates; lively,
witty couples in the sub-plots; heavy fathers and pert
servants—all were part of the common stock of comedy at the
turn of the century. Therefore, to claim specific borrowings
would be perilous if not foolhardy.

The German playwrights, however, borrowed frequently
from the English in the eighteenth century. Lessing's brother
Karl Lessing published *Der Wildfang*, a comedy apparently
adapted from *The Inconstant*.[16]

THE TEXT

Only one text appeared during Farquhar's lifetime, the quarto
of 1702. The play, advertised in the Term Catalogue of
February 1702, appeared on 11 March with the imprint of
James Knapton, George Strahan, and Bernard Lintott. The
advertised price was 1s. 6d.[17]

The *quarto* (Q) has the collational formula A^4 $a^2(-a^2)$ B–F^4
F^{*2} ($-F^{*2}$) G–H^4 K–M^4. In most copies the pagination is (10)
1–42 41–56 65 87–8 68–9 91–2 72–87 *88*. Pages 1–40 occupy
sheets B–F; F^*1^{r-v} are numbered 41–2; pages 41–56 occur in
sheets G and H (proper pagination ordinarily for these
gatherings, although rendered incorrect because of the addition
of F*); no I gathering exists. Outer K is numbered 65, 68, 69,
72, the proper sequence if an I gathering had occurred. Inner
K is misnumbered 87, 88, 91, and 92, but one Huntington
copy (shelfmarked 131321) has corrected numeration on inner
K of 66, 67, 70, 71. Sheets L–M are numbered 73–*88*. There
are no running-titles or press figures.

Compositorial duties were divided between at least three
compositors and probably three printing houses. Whether the
division of labour was purely the result of the co-operative
venture of the three booksellers who shared in the edition or
whether some urgency encouraged rapid setting of the text,
the job was done quickly, and none of the compositors seemed
to be aware of what was happening in the other parts of the
book. One compositor or one shop handled sheets B–F*, a
second composed G–H, and a third K–M; which of the three

printed the prelims cannot be determined. The copy was cast off so inaccurately that the first section required the addition of F*1 and the added prelims in a1, although the setting of other sheets, for example H, required a reduction in the number of lines on some pages so that the copy could be extended to fill out the sheet. In general there was little regularity in the length of pages in different parts of the book. The compositor of K–M clearly did not know that Oriana was a character when he began setting K1: he set the first words, 'Or: your' flush left as speech text although in fact '*Or.*' should have been indented as the heroine's speech prefix, followed by 'Your' as the first word of her speech. Obviously the compositor was newly facing the text, not having set earlier parts of the play.

The disjointed pagination also demonstrates the lack of co-ordination between compositors. The addition of F*, numbered 41–2, was not known by the compositor of G–H; indeed those portions were probably already set when the need for F* arose. The omission of sheet I, perhaps a result of bad casting-off, had not been expected when sheets K–M were assigned signatures and appropriate page numbers, causing the omission of page numbers 57–64, ordinarily found in I gatherings. But even division of the copy between shops cannot explain why inner K should be numbered 87, 88, 91, 92. In a regular quarto, p. 87 would fall on inner M (M4), p. 88 on outer M (M4^v), p. 91 on inner N (N2^r), and p. 92 on outer N (N2^v). In no case would the odd numbers 87 and 91 fall on versos, and the even numbers 88 and 92 fall on rectos. Even if such an obvious error were made by some unwitting apprentice, one would expect immediate correction. But most extant copies contain the strangely incorrect pagination.

The three compositors are identifiable through spelling and abbreviation practices. For example, two of the compositors consistently used the spelling 'Mirabel', but the compositor of K–M chose 'Mirable' four times and 'Mirabell' twice in stage directions although 'Mirabel' appears in the text of speeches. The compositor of B–F* used both *Or.* and *Ori.* as speech prefixes for Oriana and *Old M.*, *O. M.*, and *Old. Mir.* (once) for Old Mirabel, sometimes mixing forms on the same page; the compositor of G–H used *Or.* and *Old M.* consistently; the compositor of K–M, *Ori.* as well as *O. Mir.* and *O. M.* (once). Moreover, the compositor of K–M frequently began sentences with lower-case type, omitted end punctuation, mispunctuated series by omitting commas after the first term (for example, 'Vigour Youth, and Fortune'), and misplaced apostrophes ('hee'r' for 'here' or 'e'm' for 'em').

An oddity occurs in a two-leaf M gathering in one copy (Clark, shelf-marked PR1269 1693) in which only the pages of outer M appear: M1^r of the Clark copy contains the regular M1^r; M1^v contains M2^v (p. 84, the end of the play); M2^r is M3^r (p. 85, the song 'Since Cælia 'tis not in our power'); and M2^v contains the advertisement which appeared on M4^v (p. *88*) of most copies. The word 'Happiness' on p. 84, l. 20 reads 'Happiuess' in the Clark copy. Apparently, the outer forme of M in the Clark copy was backed by another copy of outer M, then cut into two half-sheets for binding.

Some copies (Huntington, Harvard, Clark) have a variant in the advertisement for Lintott on p. *88* (M4^v). After the advertisement for *Vindicius Liberius*, the words 'price 3 s.' are added, and an additional advertisement is inserted for '*Amintor*: Or a Defence of *Milton*'s life' by John Toland. Lintott, then, must have been responsible for sheets K–M since he added a book to his list during the printing of M, not an addition for which one could expect Knapton or Strahan to stop the press.

No such proof exists for assigning responsibility for B–F* and G–H. One does notice, however, that the first compositor set the first five sheets of text, finishing with the end of Act III, and the other two together set the other five sheets of text. Conceivably, although there is no proof, Knapton, who brought out *Sir Harry Wildair*, the most recently published Farquhar play, contracted for *The Inconstant*, then shared with Strahan and Lintott. If such were the case, one would expect that the first half of the text was Knapton's responsibility, Strahan handled G–H, and Lintott, of course, set K–M. Regardless of how the copy-text was divided, clearly communication between the three houses during the period of composition was not adequate.

One final oddity about Q is that several extant copies have a peculiar mark drawn by hand on the title-page. The mark is composed of two adjoining circles; the one on the left shaded in a distinctive way, the one on the right including emanating rays (copies at the British Library, Folger, University of Texas, Huntington). It seems likely that the mark was used to distinguish those copies printed for one of the three partners in the venture.

Q was the only edition published during Farquhar's lifetime. It has served as copy-text for this edition. The fourteen-year lapse before the play reappeared on stage left no incentive to publish it except in the collected editions of the *Comedies* and *Works*, in which it appeared consistently. None of these later editions, however, is textually significant. As interest in the stage-piece flourished, editions continued to be published in the late eighteenth and nineteenth centuries.

'A Song in ye Comedy call'd ye Inconstant or ye way to win him Sung by Mr. Hughes Sett by M^r. D. Purcell' was issued as a half-sheet broadside. The instrumental music by Daniel Purcell was published in four parts by John Walsh on 5 March[18] to be sold for 1*s*. 6*d*.

For the present edition, I have collated the following copies of Q: Bodleian, British Library, Folger, Harvard, Library of Congress, University of Texas (three copies), Clark (two copies), Huntington (two copies). I also collated at least one other copy of all editions through 1736.

NOTES

1. Advertisement, *Flying Post*, 22–4 July 1701.
2. Nichols, VIII, 293, 296.
3. Arthur Colby Sprague, *Beaumont and Fletcher on the Restoration Stage* (Cambridge, Mass., 1926), pp. 248–9.
4. Advertisement, *Post Boy*, 3–5 Mar. 1702: 'The Instrumental musick, in 4 parts, perform'd in the new Comedy, called, the Inconstant, or the Way to win him. Compos'd by Mr. D. Purcell, Price 1s. 6d.'
5. Advertisement, *English Post*, 9–11 Mar. 1702: 'This day is publish'd. . . .'
6. Judith Milhous and Robert D. Hume, 'Dating Play Premières from Publication Data, 1660–1700', *Harvard Library Bulletin*, 22 (1974), 397.
7. The music, in four parts, was printed by Walsh in *Harmonia Anglicana*, iii (London, 1702). (An imperfect copy may be found in the Royal College of Music. See Price, p. 181.)
8. *The Fourth Volume of the Works of Mr. Thomas Brown* (London, 1711), pp. 237–8.
9. See Stockwell, pp. 68–9; Esther K. Sheldon, *Thomas Sheridan of Smock-Alley* (Princeton, 1967), *passim*; Smith, *1720–1780*, *passim*.
10. William Winter, *Old Shrines and Ivy* (New York, 1892), pp. 258–60.
11. *A Comparison Between the Two Stages* (London, 1702), pp. 173–7.

12. Brown, p. 238.
13. Hazlitt, p. 89.
14. Hunt, p. lxxiii.
15. Winter, p. 255.
16. J. G. Robertson, 'Lessing and Farquhar', *Modern Language Review*, 2 (1906–7), 56–7.
17. Advertisement, *English Post*, 9–11 Mar. 1702.
18. Advertisement, *Post Boy*, 3–5 Mar. 1702.

'Since Celia 'tis not in our Power', from *The Inconstant*. Set by Daniel Purcell.

THE

INCONSTANT:

OR,

The way to win him.

A

COMEDY.

In nova fert Animus Mutatas dicere formas Corpora.

Ovid. *Metamorphoses.*

ABBREVIATIONS USED IN THE NOTES

Q First edition. London: Knapton, Strahan, and Lintott, 1702.

O1 *Comedies*. First edition. London: Knapton, Smith, Strahan, and Lintott [1708].

O2 *Comedies*. Second edition. London: Knapton, Smith, Strahan, and Lintott [1711].

O3 *Comedies*. Third edition. London: Knapton, Smith, Strahan, and Lintott [1714].

1718 *Works*. Fourth edition. London: Knapton, Smith, Strahan, and Lintott, 1718.

1728 *Works*. Sixth edition. J. and J. Knapton, Lintott, Strahan, and Clark, 1728.

1736 *Dramatick Works*. Seventh edition. London: Knapton, Strahan, Lintott, and Feales, 1736.

To
Richard Tighe, Esq.

SIR,

Dedications are the only Fashions in the World that are more dislik'd for being Universal; and the reason is, that they very seldom fit the persons they were made for; but I hope to avoid the common Obloquy in this address, by laying aside the Poet in every thing but the *Dramatick Decorum* of suiting my Character to the Person.

From the Part of *Mirabel* in this Play, and another Character in one of my former, people are willing to Compliment my performance in drawing a gay, splendid, 10 generous, easie, fine young Gentleman. My Genius, I must confess, has a bent to that kind of description; and my Veneration for you, Sir, may pass for unquestionable, since in all these happy Accomplishments, you come so near to my darling Character, abating his Inconstancy.

What an unspeakable Blessing is Youth and Fortune, when a happy Understanding comes in, to moderate the desires of the first, and to refine upon the advantages of the latter; when a Gentleman is Master of all Pleasures, but a Slave to none; who has Travell'd, not for the Curiosity of the Sight, but for 20 the Improvement of the Mind's Eye; and who returns full of every thing but himself—An Author might say a great deal more, but a Friend, Sir, nay, an Enemy must allow you this.

I shall here, Sir, meet with two obstacles, your Modesty and your Sense; the first as a *Censor* upon the Subject, the second as a Critick upon the Stile; but I am obstinate in my purpose, and will maintain what I say to the last drop of my Pen; which I may the more boldly undertake, having all the World on my side; nay, I have your very self against you, for by declining to hear your own Merit, your Friends are authoriz'd the more to 30 proclaim it.

Your Generosity and Easiness of Temper is not only obvious in your common affairs and Conversation, but more plainly evident in your darling Amusement, that opener and

dilater of the Mind, Musick;—from your affection for this
delightful study we may deduce the pleasing harmony that is
apparent in all your actions; and be assur'd, Sir, that a person
must be possess'd of a very Divine Soul, who is so much in
love with the entertainment of Angels.

40   From your Encouragement of Musick, if there be any
Poetry here, it has a claim, by the right of Kindred, to your
favour and affection. You were pleas'd to honour the
Representation of this Play with your appearance at several
times, which flatter'd my hopes that there might be something
in it which your good Nature might excuse. With the Honour
I here intend for my self, I likewise consult the Interest of my
Nation, by showing a person that is so much a Reputation and
Credit to my Country. Besides all this, I was willing to make a
handsome Compliment to the place of my Pupilage; by
50 informing the World that so fine a Gentleman had the seeds of
his Education in the same University, and at the same time
with,

    S I R,

                        Your most faithful and
                          most humble Servant,
                         George Farquhar.

PREFACE

To give you the History of this Play, wou'd but cause the Reader and the Writer a trouble to no purpose; I shall only say, that I took the hint from *Fletcher*'s *Wild Goose Chase*; and to those who say, that I have spoyl'd the Original, I wish no other injury, but that they wou'd say it again.

As to the success of it, I think 'tis but a kind of *Cremona* business, I have neither lost nor won, I pushed fairly, but the *French* were prepossess'd, and the charms of *Gallick* Heels, were too hard for an *English* Brain; but I am proud to own, that I have laid my Head at the Ladies Feet. The favour was 10 unavoidable, for we are a Nation so very fond of improving our Understanding, that the instruction of a Play does no good, when it comes in Competition with the Moral of Minuet. *Pliny* tells us in his *Natural History*, of Elephants that were taught to dance on the Ropes, if this could be made practicable now, what a number of *Subscriptions* might be had to bring the great *Mogul* out of *Fleetstreet*, and make him dance between the Acts.

I remember that about two years ago, I had a Gentleman from *France*, that brought the Playhouse some fifty Audiences 20 in five Months, then why shou'd I be surpriz'd to find a *French* Lady do as much: 'Tis the prettiest way in the World of despising the *French* King, to let him see that we can afford Money to bribe away his Dancers, when he poor Man has exhausted all his Stock, in buying off some pitiful Towns and Principalities; *cum multis alijs*: What can be a greater Compliment to our generous Nation, than to have the Lady upon her *retour* to *Paris*, boast of their splendid entertainment in *England*, of the complaisance, liberality and good nature of a People, that thronged her House so full, that she had not room to stick 30 a Pin; and left a poor Fellow that had the misfortune of being one of themselves, without one farthing, for half a years pains that he had taken for their entertainment.

There were some Gentlemen in the Pit the first night, that

12 instruction] 1728 (Instruction); instructions

took the hint from the Prologue to damn the Play; but they made such a noise in the execution, that the People took the outcry for a reprieve, so that the darling mischief was overlay'd by their over-fondness of the Changling; 'tis somewhat hard, that Gentlemen shou'd debase themselves
40 into a faction of a dozen to stab a single Person, who never had the resolution to face two men at a time, if he has had the misfortune of any misunderstanding with a particular Person, he has a particular Person to answer it; but these Sparks wou'd be remarkable in their resentment, and if any body falls under their displeasure, they scorn to call him to a particular account, but will very honourably burn his House, or pick his Pocket.

The *New House* has perfectly made me a Convert by their civility on my sixth night; for, to be Friends, and reveng'd at
50 the same time, I must give them a Play, that is—when I write another; for faction runs so high, that I cou'd wish the Senate wou'd suppress the Houses, or put in force the Act against bribing Elections, that House which has the most favours to bestow will certainly carry it, spight of all Poetical Justice that wou'd support t'other.

I have heard some People so extravagantly angry at this Play, that one wou'd think they had no reason to be displeased at all; whilst some (otherwise men of good sense) have commended it so much, that I was afraid they ridicul'd me; so
60 that between both, I am absolutely at a loss what to think on't, for tho the cause has come on six days successively, yet the tryal, I fancy is not determin'd. When our devotion to *Lent* and our Lady is over, the business will be brought on again, and then we shall have fair play for our Money.

There is a Gentleman of the first Understanding, and a very good Critick, who said of Mr *Wilks*, that in this part he out-acted himself, and all men that he ever saw. I wou'd not rob Mr *Wilks*, by a worse expression of mine, of a Compliment that he so much deserves.

70 I had almost forgot to tell you, that the turn of Plot in the last Act is an Adventure of *Chevalier de Chastillon* in *Paris*, and matter of fact, but the thing is so universally known, that I think this advice might have been spar'd, as well as all the rest of the Preface, for any good it will do either to me or the Play.

[PROLOGUE]

The Prologue that was spoke the first night receiv'd such additions from Mr— who spoke it, that they are best if bury'd and forgot. But the following Prologue is literally the same that was intended for the Play, and written by Mr *Motteux*.

Like hungry Guests a sitting Audience looks:
Plays are like Suppers: Poets are the Cooks.
The Founders you; The Table is this Place.
The Carvers, We; The Prologue is the Grace.
Each Act, a Course; Each Scene, a different Dish.
Tho we're in Lent, *I doubt you're still for Flesh.*
Satire's the Sauce, high-season'd, sharp, and rough:
Kind Masques and Beaux, I hope you're Pepper-proof.
Wit is the Wine; but 'tis so scarce the true,
Poets, like Vintners, balderdash and brew.   10
Your surly Scenes, where Rant and Bloodshed joyn,
Are Butcher's Meat, a Battel's a Sirloyn.
Your Scenes of Love, so flowing, soft, and chaste,
Are Water-gruel, without Salt or Taste.
Baudy's fat Ven'son, which, tho stale, can please:
Your Rakes love hogoes *like your damn'd* French Cheese.
Your Rarity for the fair Guests to gape on
Is your nice Squeaker, *or* Italian *Capon;*
Or your French *Virgin-Pullet, garnish'd round,*
And drest with Sauce of some—four hundred pound.   20
An Op'ra, like an Olio, nicks the Age;
Farce is the Hasty-Pudding of the Stage.
For when you're treated with indifferent Cheer,
Ye can dispense with slender Stage-Coach Fare.
A Pastoral's Whipt Cream; Stage-Whims, meer Trash;
And Tragicomedy, half Fish, half Flesh.
But Comedy, That, That's the darling Cheer. ⎫
This Night we hope you'll an Inconstant bear: ⎬
Wild Fowl is lik'd in Playhouse all the year. ⎭
 Yet since each Mind betrays a diff'rent Taste, ⎫   30
And ev'ry Dish scarce pleases ev'ry Guest, ⎬
If ought you relish, do not damn the rest. ⎭
This Favour crav'd, up let the Musick strike:
You're welcome all—Now fall to where you like.

Dramatis Personæ

[MEN]

Old Mirabel.	An aged old Gentleman of an odd compound, between the Peevishness incident to his years, and his Fatherly fondness towards his Son.	Mr. *Penkithman.*
Mirabel.	His Son.	Mr. *Wilks.*
Duretete.	An honest good natur'd Fellow, that thinks himself a greater Fool than he is.	Mr. *Bullock.*
10 *Dugard.*	Brother to *Oriana.*	Mr. *Mills.*
Petit.	Servant to *Dugard,* afterwards to his Sister.	Mr. *Norris.*

WOMEN.

Oriana.	A Lady contracted to *Mirabel* who wou'd bring him to Reason.	Mrs. *Rogers.*
Bisarre.	A whimsical Lady, friend to *Oriana,* admir'd by *Duretete.*	Mrs. *Verbruggen.*
Lamorce.	A Woman of Contrivance.	Mrs. *Kent.*

[*Maid, Fiddler, Singers, Page.*] 4 *Bravo's,* 2 *Gent.,* and 2 *Ladies.*
20   *Soldiers, Servants* and *Attendants.*

ACT I. [Scene i.]

SCENE *the Street.*

Enter Dugard, *and his man*, Petit, *in riding habits.*

Dugard. Sirrah, what's a Clock?

Petit. Turn'd of eleven, Sir.

Dugard. No more! we have rid a swinging pace, from *Nemours* since two this morning! *Petit*, run to *Rousseau*'s, and bespeak a Dinner at a *Lewis d'Or* a head, to be ready by one.

Petit. How many will there be of you, Sir?

Dugard. Let me see, *Mirabel* one, *Duretete* two, my self three—

Petit. And I four.

Dugard. How now Sir, at your old travelling familiarity! 10 when abroad, you had some freedom for want of better Company; but among my friends at *Paris* pray remember your distance—Be gone, Sir—

Exit Petit.

This fellow's Wit was necessary abroad, but he's too cunning for a Domestick; I must dispose of him some way else—who's here? old *Mirabel*, and my Sister! my dearest Sister!

Enter Old Mirabel *and* Oriana.

Oriana. My Brother! Welcome.

Dugard. Monsieur Mirabel! I'm heartily glad to see you.

Old Mirabel. Honest Mr *Dugard*, by the Blood of the *Mirabels* I'm your most humble Servant. 20

Dugard. Why, Sir, you cast your Skin sure, you're brisk and gay, lusty health about you, no sign of Age but your silver hairs.

Old Mirabel. Silver hairs! then they are Quicksilver hairs, Sir. Whilst I have Golden Pockets, let my Hairs be Silver an they will. Adsbud, Sir, I can dance, and sing, and drink, and—no, I can't wench. But Mr *Dugard*, no news of my Son *Bob* in all your Travels?

Dugard. Your Son's come home, Sir.

30   *Old Mirabel.* Come home! *Bob* come home! by the Blood of
the *Mirabels*, Mr *Dugard*, what say ye.

Oriana. Mr *Mirabel* return'd, Sir?

Dugard. He's certainly come, and you may see him within
this hour or two.

Old Mirabel. Swear it, Mr *Dugard*, presently swear it.

Dugard. Sir, he came to Town with me this morning, I left
him at the *Bagnieurs*, being a little disorder'd after riding, and
I shall see him again presently.

Old Mirabel. What! and he was asham'd to ask Blessing
40 with his Boots on. A nice dog! Well, and how fares the young
Rogue, he!

Dugard. A fine Gentleman, Sir. He'll be his own Messenger.

Old Mirabel. A fine Gentleman! But is the Rogue like me
still?

Dugard. Why yes Sir, he's very like his Mother, and as like
you as most modern Sons are to their Fathers.

Old Mirabel. Why, Sir, don't you think that I begat him?

Dugard. Why yes Sir; you marry'd his Mother, and he
inherits your Estate. He's very like you, upon my word.

50   *Oriana.* And pray, Brother, what's become of his honest
Companion, *Duretete*?

Dugard. Who? the Captain? The very same he went abroad;
he's the only *French* man I ever knew that cou'd not change.
Your Son, Mr *Mirabel*, is more oblig'd to Nature for that
fellow's composition than for his own; for he's more happy in
Duretete's Folly than his own Wit. In short, they are as
inseparable as Finger and Thumb, but the first instance in the
world, I believe, of opposition in Friendship.

Old Mirabel. Very well; will he be home to Dinner, think ye?

60   *Dugard.* Sir, he has order'd me to bespeak a Dinner for us at
Rousseau's at a *Lewidore* a head.

Old Mirabel. A *Lewidore* a head! Well said *Bob*; by the Blood
of the *Mirabels*, *Bob*'s improv'd. But Mr *Dugard*, was it so civil
of *Bob* to visit *Monsieur Rousseau* before his own Natural Father?
Eh! hearkee, *Oriana*, what think you now of a fellow that can
eat and drink ye a whole *Lewidore* at a sitting? he must be as
strong as *Hercules*; Life and Spirit in abundance. Before gad I
don't wonder at these men of Quality, that their own Wives
can't serve 'em. A *Lewidore* a head, 'tis enough to stock the

whole Nation with Bastards, 'tis faith. Mr *Dugard*, I leave you 70
with your Sister.

Exit.

Dugard. Well, Sister, I need not ask you how you do, your
looks resolve me; fair, tall, well shap'd; you're almost grown
out of my remembrance.

Oriana. Why truly Brother I look pretty well, thank Nature
and my Toylet; I have scap'd the Jaundice, Green Sickness,
and the Small Pox; I eat three meals a day, am very merry
when up, and sleep soundly when I'm down.

Dugard. But, Sister, you remember that upon my going
abroad you wou'd chuse this old Gentleman for your 80
Guardian; he's no more related to our Family than *Prester
John*, and I have no reason to think you mistrusted my
management of your Fortune, therefore pray be so kind as to
tell me without reservation the true cause of making such a
choice.

Oriana. Lookee Brother, you were going a rambling, and
'twas proper lest I shou'd go a rambling too, that some body
shou'd take care of me. Old *Monsieur Mirabel* is an honest
Gentleman, was our Father's Friend, and has a young Lady in
his House, whose company I like, and who has chosen him for 90
her Guardian as well as I.

Dugard. Who, *Madamoiselle Bisarre?*

Oriana. The same; we live merrily together without Scandal
or Reproach; we make much of the old Gentleman between
us, and he takes care of us; we eat what we like, go to Bed
when we please, rise when we will, all the week we dance and
sing, and upon *Sundays* go first to Church and then to the
Play—Now, Brother, besides these motives for chusing this
Gentleman for my Guardian, perhaps I had some private
reasons.   100

Dugard. Not so private as you imagine, Sister; your love to
young *Mirabel*; no secret, I can assure you, but so publick that
all your friends are asham'd on't.

Oriana. O' my word then my friends are very Bashful; tho
I'm afraid, Sir, that those people are not asham'd enough at
their own crimes, who have so many blushes to spare for the
faults of their Neighbours.

Dugard. Ay, but Sister, the people say—

Oriana. Pshaw, hang the people, they'll talk Treason, and
110 profane their Maker, must we therefore infer that our King is
a Tyrant, and Religion a Cheat. Lookee Brother, their Court
of Enquiry is a Tavern, and their Informer, Claret: They think
as they drink, and swallow Reputations like Loches, a Lady's
health goes briskly round with the Glass, but her Honour is
lost in the Toast.

Dugard. Ay, but Sister, there is still something—

Oriana. If there be something, Brother, 'tis none of the
people's something; Marriage is my thing, and I'll stick to't.

Dugard. Marriage! young *Mirabel* Marry! he'll build
120 Churches sooner; take heed, Sister, tho your Honour stood
proof to his home-bred assaults, you must keep a stricter
Guard for the future; he has now got the foreign Ayre and the
Italian Softness; his Wit's improv'd by Converse, his Behaviour
finish'd by Observation, and his Assurance confirm'd by
Success. Sister, I can assure you he has made his Conquests;
and 'tis a plague upon your Sex, to be the soonest deceiv'd by
those very men that you know have been false to others.

Oriana. Then why will you tell me of his Conquests; for I
must confess there is no title to a Womans favour so engaging
130 as the repute of a handsom dissimulation; there is something
of a pride to see a fellow lye at our feet, that has triumph'd
over so many; and then, I don't know, we fancy he must have
something extraordinary about him to please us, and that we
have something engaging about us to secure him, so we can't
be quiet; till we put our selves upon the lay of being both
disappointed.

Dugard. But then, Sister, he's as fickle—

Oriana. For Gads sake, Brother, tell me no more of his
faults, for if you do I shall run mad for him: Say no more, Sir,
140 let me but get him into the bands of Matrimony, I'll spoyl his
wandring, I warrant him. I'll do his business that way, never
fear.

Dugard. Well, Sister, I won't pretend to understand the
engagements between you and your Lover; I expect, when you
have need of my counsel or assistance, you will let me know
more of your affairs. *Mirabel* is a Gentleman, and as far as my
Honour and Interest can reach, you may command me to the
furtherance of your happiness; in the mean time, Sister, I have

a great mind to make you a present of another humble
Servant; a fellow I took up at *Lyons*, who has serv'd me 150
honestly ever since.

Oriana. Then why will you part with him?

Dugard. He has gain'd so insufferably on my good humour
that he's grown too familiar; but the Fellow's cunning, and
may be serviceable to you in your affair with *Mirabel*. Here he
comes.

Enter Petit.

Well Sir, have you been at *Rousseau*'s?

Petit. Yes Sir, and who shou'd I find there, but Mr *Mirabel*
and the Captain hatching as warmly over a Tub of Ice, as two
Hen-Pheasants over a brood—they wou'd let me bespeak 160
nothing, for they had din'd before I came.

Dugard. Come Sir, you shall serve my Sister, I shall still
continue kind to you, and if your Lady recommends your
diligence upon tryal, I'll use my interest to advance you, you
have sense enough to expect preferment—Here Sirrah, there's
ten Guineas for thee, get thyself a Drugget Sute and a Puff
Wig, and so—I dub thee Gentlemen Usher—Sister, I must go
put my self in repair, you may expect me in the evening—Wait
on your Lady home, *Petit*.

Exit.

Petit. A Chair, a Chair, a Chair.   170

Oriana. No, no, I'll walk home, 'tis but next door.

Exeunt.

[ACT I. Scene ii.]

SCENE *a Tavern, discovering Young* Mirabel *and*
Duretete *rising from Table.*

Mirabel. Welcome to *Paris* once more, my dear Captain, we
have eat heartily, drank roundly, paid plentifully, and let it go
for once; I lik'd every thing but our Women, they look'd so
lean and tawdry, poor Creatures! 'tis a sure sign the Army is
not paid—Give me the plump *Venetian*, brisk and sanguine,
that smiles upon me like the glowing Sun, and meets my lips
like sparkling Wine, her Person shining as the Glass, and
Spirit like the foaming Liquor.

Duretete. Ay, *Mirabel, Italy* I grant you; but for our Women
10 here in *France*, they are such thin brawn-faln Jades, a man
may as well make a Bed-fellow of a Cane-Chair.

Mirabel. France! a light unseason'd Country, nothing but
Feathers, Foppery and Fashions; we're fine indeed, so are our
Coach-Horses; Men say we're Courtiers, Men abuse us; that
we are wise and politick, *non credo Seigneur*: That our Women
have Wit, Parrots; meer Parrots, Assurance and a good
Memory sets them up—there's nothing on this side the *Alps*
worth my humble service t'ee—Ha *Roma la Santa, Italy* for my
Money; their Customs, Gardens, Buildings, Paintings, Musick,
20 Policies, Wine and Women! the Paradice of the World;—not
pester'd with a parcel of precise old gouty fellows, that would
debar their Children every pleasure that they themselves are
past the sense of; commend me to the *Italian* familiarity—Here,
Son, there's fifty Crowns, go pay your Whore her weeks
allowance.

Duretete. Ay, these are your Fathers for you, that understand
the necessities of young men; not like our musty Dads, who
because they cannot fish themselves, would muddy the Water,
and spoil the sport of them that can. But now you talk of the
30 plump, what d'e think of a *Dutch* woman?

Mirabel. A *Dutch* Woman, too compact, nay, every thing
among 'em is so; a *Dutch* Man is thick, a *Dutch* Woman is
squab, a *Dutch* Horse is round, a *Dutch* Dog is short, a *Dutch*
Ship is broad bottom'd; and, in short, one wou'd swear the
whole products of the Country were cast in the same Mold
with their Cheeses.

Duretete. Ay, but *Mirabel*, you have forgot the *English*
Ladies.

Mirabel. The Women of *England* were excellent, did they not
40 take such unsufferable pains to ruine what Nature has made
so incomparably well; they wou'd be delicate Creatures
indeed, cou'd they but throughly arrive at the *French* mein, or
entirely let it alone, for they only spoyl a very good air of their
own, by an awkard imitation of ours; their Parliaments and
our Taylors give Laws to their three Kingdoms. But come,
Duretete, let us mind the business in hand, Mistresses we must
have, and must take up with the Manufacture of the place,
and upon a competent diligence we shall find those in *Paris*

shall match the *Italians* from top to toe.

Duretete. Ay *Mirabel*, you will do well enough, but what will 50
become of your friend; you know I am so plauguey bashful, so
naturally an Ass upon these occasions, that—

Mirabel. Pshaw, you must be bolder, man; Travel three
years, and bring home such a Baby as Bashfulness! A great
lusty Fellow! and a Souldier! fye upon't.

Duretete. Lookee Sir, I can visit, and I can ogle a little—as
thus or thus now. Then I can kiss abundantly, and make a
shift to—but if they chance to give me a forbidding look; as
some Women you know have a Devilish cast with their
Eyes—or if they cry—what d'e mean? what d'e take me for? 60
fye Sir, remember who I am, Sir—a Person of Quality to be
us'd at this rate!—Igad I'm struck as flat as a Frying-pan.

Mirabel. Words o' course! never mind 'em, turn you about
upon your heel with a jaunty air, hum out the end of an old
Song, cut a cross caper, and at her again.

Duretete. (*Imitates him.*) No, hang it, 'twill never do—oons
what did my Father mean by sticking me up in an University,
or to think that I should gain any thing by my Head, in a
Nation whose genius lyes all in their Heels—Well, if ever I
come to have Children of my own, they shall have the 70
education of the Country, they shall learn to dance before they
can walk, and be taught to sing before they speak.

Mirabel. Come, come, throw off that Childish Humour, put
on assurance, there's no avoiding it; stand all hazards, thou'rt
a stout lusty Fellow, and hast a good Estate, look bluff, hector,
you have a good Side-box Face, a pretty impudent Face, so
that's pretty well—this Fellow went abroad like an Ox, and is
return'd like an Ass. (*Aside.*)

Duretete. Let me see now, how I look. (*Pulls out a Pocket
Glass, and looks on't.*) A Side-Box face, say you?—egad I don't 80
like it, *Mirabel*—fye, Sir, don't abuse your Friends, I cou'd not
wear such a face for the best Countess in Christendom.

Mirabel. Why can't you, Blockhead, as well as I?

Duretete. Why, thou hast impudence to set a good face upon
any thing, I wou'd change half my Gold for half thy Brass,
with all my Heart. Who comes here, odso, *Mirabel*, your
Father.

Enter Old Mirabel.

Old Mirabel. Where's *Bob*, dear *Bob*?

Mirabel. Your Blessing, Sir.

90   *Old Mirabel.* My Blessing! Dam'ye you young Rogue; why did not you come see your Father first, Sirrah? My dear Boy, I am heartily glad to see thee, my dear Child, faith—Captain *Duretete*, by the Blood of the *Mirabels* I'm yours, well my Lads, ye look bravely efaith—*Bob*, hast got any Money left?

Mirabel. Not a farthing, Sir.

Old Mirabel. Why, then I won't gi'thee a souse.

Mirabel. Sir, I did but jest, here's ten *Pistoles*.

Old Mirabel. Why, then here's ten more, I love to be Charitable to those that don't want it—well, and how d'ee like 100 *Italy*, my Boys?

Mirabel. O the Garden of the World, Sir, *Rome*, *Naples*, *Venice*, *Milan*, and a thousand others—all fine.

Old Mirabel. Ay, say you so? And they say, that *Chiari* is very fine too.

Duretete. Indifferent, Sir, very indifferent; a very scurvy Air, the most unwholsome to a *French* Constitution in the World.

Mirabel. Pshaw, nothing on't, these rascally Gazeteers have misinform'd you.

Old Mirabel. Misinform'd me! Oons, Sir, were not we 110 beaten there?

Mirabel. Beaten, Sir! the *French* beaten!

Old Mirabel. Why, how was it, pray, sweet Sir?

Mirabel. Sir, the Captain will tell you.

Duretete. No, Sir, your Son will tell you.

Mirabel. The Captain was in the action, Sir.

Duretete. Your Son saw more than I, Sir, for he was a looker on.

Old Mirabel. Confound ye both for a brace of Cowards; here are no *Germans* to overhear you, why don't ye tell me how it 120 was?

Mirabel. Why, then you must know, that we march'd up a body of the finest, bravest, well-drest Fellows in the Universe; our Commanders at the head of us, all Lace and Feather, like so many Beaux at a Ball,—I don't believe there was a man of 'em, but cou'd dance a *Charmer*, *Morblew*.

Old Mirabel. Dance! very well, pretty Fellows, faith!

Mirabel. We caper'd up to their very Trenches, and there

saw peeping over a parcel of Scare-crow, Olive colour'd, Gun-
powder Fellows, as ugly as the Devil.

Duretete. Igad, I shall never forget the looks of 'em, while I 130
have breath to fetch.

Mirabel. They were so civil indeed as to welcome us with
their Cannon; but for the rest, we found 'em such unmannerly
rude unsociable Dogs, that we grew tir'd of their Company,
and so we e'n danc'd back again.

Old Mirabel. And did ye all come back?

Mirabel. No, two or three thousand or us stay'd behind.

Old Mirabel. Why, *Bob,* why?

Mirabel. Pshaw—because they cou'd not come that night;
—but come Sir, we were talking of something else; pray how 140
does your lovely Charge, the fair *Oriana?*

Old Mirabel. Ripe, Sir, just ripe; you'll find it better
engaging with her than with the *Germans,* let me tell you—and
what wou'd you say, my young *Mars,* if I had a *Venus* for thee
too? Come *Bob,* your Apartment is ready, and pray let your
Friend be my Guest too, you shall command the House
between ye, and I'll be as merry as the best of you.

Mirabel. Bravely said, Father;
   Let Misers bend their Age with niggard Cares,
   And starve themselves to pamper hungry Heirs;   150
   Who, living, stint their Sons what Youth may crave,
   And make 'em Revel o're a Father's Grave.
   The Stock on which I grew, does still dispense
   Its Genial Sap into the blooming Branch;
   The Fruit, he knows, from his own Root is grown,
   And therefore sooths those Passions once his own.

[*The*] *End of the First Act.*

ACT II. [Scene i.]

SCENE Old Mirabel*'s House.*

Oriana *and* Bisarre.

Bisarre. And you love this young Rake, d'ee?

Oriana. Yes.

Bisarre. In spight of all his ill usage?

Oriana. I can't help it.

Bisarre. What's the matter w'ye?

Oriana. Pshaw.

Bisarre. Umh—before that any young, lying, swearing, flattering, Rakelly Fellow shou'd play such Tricks with me, I wou'd wear my Teeth to the stumps with Lime and
10 Chalk—O, the Devil take all your *Cassandra*'s and *Cleopatra*'s for me—Prithee mind your Ayres, Modes, and Fashions; your Stayes, Gowns and Fourbeleau's. Harkee, my Dear, have you got home your Fourbeleau'd Smocks yet?

Oriana. Prithee be quiet, *Bisarre*; you know I can be as mad as you, when this *Mirabel* is out of my head.

Bisarre. Pshaw, wou'd he were out, or in, or some way to make you easie—I warrant now, you'll play the Fool when he comes, and say you love him; eh!

Oriana. Most certainly; I can't dissemble, *Bisarre*—besides,
20 'tis past that, we're contracted.

Bisarre. Contracted! alack a day, poor thing. What, you have chang'd Rings, or broken an old *Broad-piece* between you! Hearkee, Child, han't you broke something else between ye?

Oriana. No, no, I can assure you.

Bisarre. Then what d'e whine for? Whilst I kept that in my power, I wou'd make a Fool of any Fellow in *France*. Well, I must confess, I do love a little Coquetting with all my heart; my business shou'd be to break Gold with my Lover one hour, and crack my Promise the next; he shou'd find me one day
30 with a Prayer-Book in my hand, and with a Play-Book another. He shou'd have my consent to buy the Wedding Ring, and the next moment wou'd I Laugh in his face.

Oriana. O, my Dear, were there no greater Tye upon my Heart, than there is upon my Conscience, I wou'd soon throw

the Contract out a doors; but the mischief on't is, I am so fond
of being ty'd, that I'm forc'd to be just, and the strength of my
Passion keeps down the Inclination of my Sex—But here's the
Old Gentleman.

[*Enter* Old Mirabel.]

Old Mirabel. Where's my Wenches? Where's my two little
Girls, eh! Have a care, look to your selves, faith, they're a 40
coming, the Travellers are a coming. Well! which of you two
will be my Daughter-in-Law now? *Bisarre, Bisarre*, what say
you, Mad-cap? *Mirabel* is a pure wild Fellow.

Bisarre. I like him the worse.

Old Mirabel. You lye, Honey, you like him the better,
indeed you do; what say you, my t'other little Filbert, he?

Oriana. I suppose the Gentleman will choose for himself,
Sir.

Old Mirabel. Why that's discreetly said, and so he shall.

Enter Mirabel *and* Duretete, *they salute the Ladies.*

Bob, hearkee, you shall marry one of the Girls, Sirrah. 50

Mirabel. Sir, I'll marry 'em both, if you please.

Bisarre. He'll find that one may serve his turn. (*Aside.*)

Old Mirabel. Both! Why, you young Dog, d'ee banter
me?—come Sir, take your choice—*Duretete*, you shall have
your choice too, but *Robin* shall choose first. Come Sir, begin.

Mirabel. Well, I an't the first Son that has made his
Father's Dwelling a Bawdy-house—let me see.

Old Mirabel. Well! which d'e like?

Mirabel. Both.

Old Mirabel. But which will you marry? 60

Mirabel. Neither.

Old Mirabel. Neither!—Don't make me angry now, *Bob*—
pray don't make me angry—Lookee Sirrah, if I don't dance at
your Wedding to morrow, I shall be very glad to cry at your
Grave.

Mirabel. That's a Bull, Father.

Old Mirabel. A Bull! Why how now, ungrateful Sir, did I
make thee a Man, that thou shou'dst make me a Beast?

Mirabel. Your pardon Sir, I only meant your expression.

Old Mirabel. Hearkee *Bob*, learn better Manners to your 70

II. i. 45 the] O1; he

Father before strangers: I won't be angry this time—but oons,
if ever you do't again, you Rascal; remember what I say.

Exit.

Mirabel. Pshaw, what does the old Fellow mean by mewing
me up here with a couple of green Girls. Come, *Duretete*, will
you go?

Oriana. I hope, Mr *Mirabel*, you han't forgot—

Mirabel. No, no, Madam, I han't forgot, I have brought you
a thousand little *Italian* Curiosities; I'll assure you, Madam, as
far as a hundred *Pistoles* wou'd reach, I han't forgot the least
80 Circumstance.

Oriana. Sir, you misunderstood me.

Mirabel. Odso, the Relicks, Madam, from *Rome*. I do
remember now you made a Vow of Chastity before my
departure; a Vow of Chastity, or something like it; was it not,
Madam?

Oriana. O Sir, I'm answer'd at present.

Exit.

Mirabel. She was coming full mouth upon me with her
Contract—wou'd I might dispatch the t'other.

Duretete. Mirabel—that Lady there, observe her, she's won-
90 drous pretty faith, and seems to have but few words; I like her
mainly; speak to her, man, prithee speak to her.

Mirabel. Madam, here's a Gentleman, who declares—

Duretete. Madam, don't believe him, I declare nothing—
What the Devil do you mean, man?

Mirabel. He says, Madam, that you are beautiful as an
Angel.

Duretete. He tells a damn'd lye, Madam; I say no such
thing; are you mad, *Mirabel*? Why, I shall drop down with
shame.

100 *Mirabel.* And so, Madam, not doubting but your Ladyship
may like him as well as he does you, I think it proper to leave
you together. (*Going,* Duretete *holds him.*)

Duretete. Hold, hold—why *Mirabel*, Friend, sure you won't
be so barbarous as to leave me alone. Prithee speak to her for
your self, as it were. Lord, Lord, that a *French*-man should
want impudence!

Mirabel. You look mighty Demure, Madam—She's deaf,

107 mighty] O1; ~

Captain.

Duretete. I had much rather have her dumb.

Mirabel. The Gravity of your Ayre, Madam, promises some 110
extraordinary fruits from your Study, which moves us with a
curiosity to enquire the Subject of your Ladyship's contem-
plation. Not a word?

Duretete. I hope in the Lord she's Speechless, if she be, she's
mine this moment—*Mirabel*, d'ee think a Womans silence can
be natural?

Bisarre. But the forms that Logicians introduce, and which
proceeds from simple ennumeration is dubitable, and proceeds
only upon admittance—

Mirabel. Hoyty toyty! what a plague have we here: *Plato* in 120
Petticoats!

Duretete. Ay, ay, let her go on, man, she talks in my own
Mother Tongue.

Bisarre. 'Tis expos'd to invalidity from a contradictory
instance, looks only upon common operations, and is infinite
in its termination.

Mirabel. Rare Pedantry.

Duretete. Axioms, axioms, self-evident principles.

Bisarre. Then the Idea's wherewith the mind is preoccupate
—O Gentlemen, I hope you'll pardon my Cogitation, I was 130
involv'd in a profound point of Philosophy; but I shall discuss
it somewhere else, being satisfy'd that the subject is not
agreeable to you Sparks, that profess the vanity of the times.

Exit.

Mirabel. Go thy way, Goodwife *Bias*: Do you hear, *Duretete*,
dost hear this starcht piece of austerity?

Duretete. She's mine, man; she's mine; my own Talent to a
T. I'll match her in Dialecticks faith. I was seven years at the
University, man; nurst up with *Barbara, Celarunt, Darii ferio,
Baralipton*. Did you never know, man, that 'twas Metaphysicks
made me an Ass? it was faith. Had she talk'd a word of 140
Singing, Dancing, Plays, Fashions, or the like, I had founder'd
in the first step; but as she is—*Mirabel*, wish me Joy.

Mirabel. You don't mean Marriage, I hope?

Duretete. No, no, I'm a man of more Honour.

Mirabel. Bravely resolv'd, Captain; now for thy Credit,
warm me this frozen Snow-ball, 'twill be a Conquest above

the *Alps*.

Duretete. But will you promise to be always near me?

Mirabel. Upon all occasions, never fear.

150   *Duretete.* Why then you shall see me in two moments make an Induction from my Love to her Hand, from her Hand to her Mouth, from her Mouth to her Heart, and so conclude in her Bed, *Categorimatice.*

Exit.

Mirabel. Now the Game begins, and my Fool is enter'd—but here comes one to spoyl my sport, now shall I be teiz'd to death with this old-fashion'd Contract. I shou'd love her too if I might do it my own way, but she'll do nothing without Witnesses forsooth: I wonder Women can be so immodest.

Enter Oriana.

Well, Madam, why d'ye follow me?

160   *Oriana.* Well Sir, why do you shun me?

Mirabel. 'Tis my humour, Madam, and I am naturally sway'd by inclination.

Oriana. Have you forgot our Contact, Sir?

Mirabel. All I remember of that Contract is, that it was made some three years ago, and that's enough in Conscience to forget the rest on't.

Oriana. 'Tis sufficient, Sir, to recollect the passing of it, for in that circumstance, I presume, lyes the force of the obligation.

170   *Mirabel.* Obligations, Madam, that are forc'd upon the Will are no tye upon the Conscience; I was Slave to my passion when I pass'd the Instrument, but the recovery of my freedom makes the Contract void.

Oriana. Sir, you can't make that a Compulsion which was your own choice; besides, Sir, a subjection to your own desires has not the vertue of a forcible constraint: And you will find, Sir, that to plead your passion for the killing of a man will hardly exempt you from the Justice of the punishment.

Mirabel. And so, Madam, you make the sin of Murder and
180 the Crime of a Contract the very same, because that Hanging and Matrimony are so much alike.

Oriana. Come, Mr *Mirabel*, these expressions I expected from the Raillery of your Humour, but I hope for very different sentiments from your Honour and Generosity.

Mirabel. Lookee Madam, as for my Generosity, 'tis at your service with all my heart: I'll keep you a Coach and six Horses if you please, only permit me to keep my Honour to my self; for I can assure you, Madam, that the thing call'd Honour is a Circumstance absolutely unnecessary in a natural Corres- pondence between Male and Female, and he's a Mad-man 190 that lays it out, considering its scarcity, upon any such trivial occasions. There's Honour requir'd of us by our Friends, and Honour due to our Enemies, and they return it to us again, but I never heard of a Man that left but an inch of his Honour in a Woman's keeping, that cou'd ever get the least account on't—Consider, Madam, you have no such thing among ye, and 'tis a main point of Policy to keep no Faith with Reprobates—thou art a pretty little Reprobate, and so get thee about thy business.

Oriana. Well Sir, even all this I will allow to the gayety of 200 your temper; your Travels have improv'd your talent of Talking, but they are not of force, I hope, to impair your Morals.

Mirabel. Morals! Why there 'tis again now—I tell thee, Child, there is not the least occasion for Morals in any business between you and I—don't you know that of all Commerce in the World there is no such Couzenage and Deceit as in the Traffick between Man and Woman; we study all our lives long how to put tricks upon one another—What is your business now from the time you throw away your 210 Artificial Babies, but how to get Natural ones with the most advantage?—No Fowler lays abroad more Nets for his Game, nor a Hunter for his Prey, than you do to catch poor innocent Men—Why do you sit three or four hours at your Toylet in a morning? only with a villanous design to make some poor Fellow a Fool before night. What are your languishing looks, your study'd airs and affectations, but so many baits and devices to delude Men out of their dear Liberty and Freedom—What d'ee sigh for, what d'ee weep for, what d'ee pray for? Why for a Husband: that is, you implore Providence 220 to assist you in the just and pious design of making the wisest of his Creatures a Fool, and the head of the Creation a Slave.

Oriana. Sir, I am proud of my power, and am resolv'd to use it.

Mirabel. Hold, hold, Madam, not so fast—as you have variety of Vanities to make Coxcombs of us; so we have Vows, Oaths, and Protestations of all sorts and sizes to make Fools of you. As you are very strange and whimsical Creatures, so we are allow'd as unaccountable ways of managing you. And this,
230 in short, my dear Creature, is our present condition, I have sworn and ly'd briskly to gain my ends of you; your Ladyship has patch'd and painted violently to gain your ends of me—but since we are both disappointed, let us make a Drawn Battel, and part clear of both sides.

Oriana. With all my heart, Sir; give me up my Contract, and I'll never see your face again.

Mirabel. Indeed I won't, Child:

Oriana. What Sir, neither do one nor t'other?

Mirabel. No, you shall dye a Maid, unless you please to be
240 otherwise upon my terms.

Oriana. What do you intend by this, Sir?

Mirabel. Why, to starve you into Complyance; lookee, you shall never marry any man; and you had as good let me do you a kindness as a stranger.

Oriana. Sir, you're a—

Mirabel. What am I, Mistress?

Oriana. A Villain, Sir.

Mirabel. I'm glad on't—I never knew an honest fellow in my life but was a Villain upon these occasions—han't you
250 drawn your self now into a very pretty dilemma? Ha, ha, ha; the poor Lady has made a Vow of Virginity, when she thought of making a Vow for the contrary. Was ever poor Woman so cheated into Chastity?

Oriana. Sir, my Fortune is equal to yours, my Friends as powerful, and both shall be put to the Test, to do me Justice.

Mirabel. What! you'll force me to marry you, will ye?

Oriana. Sir, the Law shall.

Mirabel. But the Law can't force me to do any thing else, can it?

260 *Oriana.* Pshaw, I despise thee,—Monster.

Mirabel. Kiss and be friends then—don't cry, Child, and you shall have your Sugar-plumb—Come, Madam, d'e think I cou'd be so unreasonable as to make ye fast all your life long;

263 as to] O1; to as

no, I did but jest, you shall have your liberty; here, take your Contract, and give me mine.

Oriana. No, I won't.

Mirabel. Eh! What, is the Girl a Fool?

Oriana. No Sir, you shall find me cunning enough to do my self Justice; and since I must not depend upon your Love, I'll be reveng'd, and force you to marry me out of Spight.   270

Mirabel. Then I'll beat thee out of spight; make a most confounded Husband.

Oriana. O Sir, I shall match ye: A good Husband makes a good Wife at any time.

Mirabel. I'll rattle down your China about your ears.

Oriana. And I'll rattle about the City to run you in debt for more.

Mirabel. Your face-mending Toylet shall fly out of the Window.

Oriana. And your face-mending Perriwig shall fly after it.   280

Mirabel. I'll tear the Fourbelow off your Cloaths, and when you swoon for vexation, you shan't have a penny to buy a Bottle of Harts-horn.

Oriana. And you, Sir, shall have Harts-horn in abundance.

Mirabel. I'll keep as many Mistresses as I have Coach-horses.

Oriana. And I'll keep as many Gallants as you have Grooms.

Mirabel. I'll lye with your Woman before your face.

Oriana. Have a care of your Valet behind your back.   290

Mirabel. But, sweet Madam, there is such a thing as a Divorce.

Oriana. But, sweet Sir, there is such a thing as Alimony, so Divorce on, and spare not.

                                                                Exit.

Mirabel. Ay, that Separate Maintenance is the Devil—there's their refuge—o' my Conscience one wou'd take Cuckoldom for a meritorious action, because the Women are so handsomely rewarded for't.

                                                                Exit.

[ACT II. Scene ii.]

SCENE *changes to a large Parlour in the same House.*

Enter Duretete *and* Petit.

Duretete. And she's mighty peevish, you say?

Petit. O Sir, she has a Tongue as long as my Leg, and talks so crabbedly, you wou'd think she always spoke *Welsh*.

Duretete. That's an odd language, methinks, for her Philosophy.

Petit. But sometimes she will sit you half a day without speaking a word, and talk Oracles all the while by the wrinkles of her Forehead, and the motions of her Eye-brows.

Duretete. Nay, I shall match her in Philosophical Ogles, faith; that's my Talent: I can talk best, you must know, when I say nothing.

Petit. But d'e ever laugh, Sir?

Duretete. Laugh! won't she endure laughing?

Petit. Why she's a Critick, Sir, she hates a Jest, for fear it shou'd please her; and nothing keeps her in humour but what gives her the Spleen. And then for Logick, and all that, you know—

Duretete. Ay, ay, I'm prepar'd, I have been practising hard words and no sense this hour to entertain her.

Petit. Then place your self behind this Screen, that you may have a view of her behaviour before you begin.

Duretete. I long to engage her, lest I shou'd forget my lesson.

Petit. Here she comes, Sir, I must fly.

Exit Petit *and* Duretete *stands peeping behind the Curtain.*
Enter Bisarre *and Maid.*

Bisarre. (*With a Book.*) Pshaw, hang Books, they sowre our Temper, spoil our Eyes, and ruin our Complexions. (*Throws away the Book.*)

Duretete. Eh! the Devil such a word there is in all *Aristotle*. [*Aside.*]

Bisarre. Come Wench, let's be free, call in the Fiddle, there's no body near us.

Enter Fiddler.

Duretete. Wou'd to the Lord there was not. [*Aside.*]

Bisarre. Here, Friend, a Minuet!—quicker time; ha—wou'd 30
we had a man or two.

Duretete. (*Stealing away.*) You shall have the Devil sooner,
my dear dancing Philosopher. [*Aside.*]

Bisarre. Uds my life—here's one. (*Runs to* Duretete *and hales
him back.*)

Duretete. Is all my learned preparation come to this?

Bisarre. Come Sir, don't be asham'd, that's my good
Boy—you're very welcome, we wanted such a one—Come,
strike up—I know you dance well, Sir, you're finely shap'd
for't—Come, come, Sir, quick, quick, you miss the time else.

Duretete. But, Madam, I come to talk with you.   40

Bisarre. Ay, ay, talk as you dance, talk as you dance, come.

Duretete. But we were talking of Dialecticks.

Bisarre. Hang Dialecticks—Mind the time—quicker Sirrah
(*To the* Fiddler.) Come—and how d'e find your self now, Sir?

Duretete. In a fine breathing sweat, Doctor.

Bisarre. All the better, Patient; all the better—Come Sir,
sing now, sing, I know you sing well; I see you have a singing
face; a heavy dull Sonato face. [*Aside.*]

Duretete. Who I sing?

Bisarre. O you're modest, Sir—but come, sit down, closer, 50
closer. Here, a Bottle of Wine—come Sir, fa, la, la, sing, Sir.

Duretete. But Madam, I came to talk with you.

Bisarre. O Sir, you shall drink first. Come, fill me a
bumper—here Sir, bless the King.

Duretete. Wou'd I were out of his Dominions—by this
Light, she'll make me drunk too. [*Aside.*]

Bisarre. O pardon me, Sir, you shall do me right, fill it
higher—now Sir, can you drink a health under your Leg?

Duretete. Rare Philosophy that, faith. [*Aside.*]

Bisare. Come, off with it, to the bottom—now how d'e like 60
me, Sir?

Duretete. O, mighty well, Sir.

Bisarre. You see how a Woman's fancy varies, sometimes
splenatick and heavy, then gay and frolicksome—and how d'e
like the humour?

Duretete. Good Madam let me sit down to answer you, for I
am heartily tir'd.

Bisarre. Fye upon't; a young man, and tir'd; up for shame,

and walk about, action becomes us—a little faster, Sir—what
70 d'e think now of my Lady *La Pale*, and Lady *Coquet* the Duke's
fair Daughter? ha! are they not brisk Lasses; then there is
black Mrs *Bellair*, and brown Mrs *Bellface*.

Duretete. They are all strangers to me, Madam.

Bisarre. But let me tell you Sir, that brown is not always
despicable—O Lard Sir, if young Mrs *Bagatell* had kept
herself single till this time o' day, what a Beauty there had
been; and then you know, the charming Mrs *Monkeylove*, the
fair Gem of *St. Germains*.

Duretete. Upon my Soul, I don't.

80 *Bisarre.* And then you must have heard of the *English* Beau
Spleenamore, how unlike a Gentleman—

Duretete. Hey—not a syllable on't, as I hope to be sav'd
Madam.

Bisarre. No! why then play me a Jigg, come Sir.

Duretete. By this Light, I cannot, faith, Madam, I have
sprain'd my Leg.

Bisarre. Then sit you down Sir, and now tell me what's your
business with me? What's your errand? quick, quick, dispatch
—odso, may be, you are some Gentleman's Servant, that have
90 brought me a Letter, or a Haunch of Venison.

Duretete. 'Sdeath, Madam, do I look like a Carrier?

Bisarre. O, cry you mercy Sir, I saw you just now, I mistook
you, upon my word; you are one of the Travelling Gentlemen
—and pray Sir, how do all our impudent friends in *Italy*?

Duretete. Madam, I came to wait on you with a more serious
intention than your entertainment has answer'd.

Bisarre. Sir, your intention of waiting on me was the
greatest affront imaginable, howe're your expressions may
turn it to a Complement: Your visit, Sir, was intended as a
100 Prologue to a very scurvy Play, of which Mr *Mirabel* and you
so handsomely laid the Plot—*Marry! no, no, I'm a man of more*
Honour. Where's your Honour, where's your Courage now?
Ads my life Sir, I have a great mind to kick you—go, go to your
fellow Rake now, rail at my Sex, and get drunk for vexation,
and write a Lampoon—but I must have you to know Sir, that
my Reputation is above the Scandal of a Libel, my Vertue is

II. ii. 84 *Bisarre.*] O1 (*Bis.*); *Bus.*

sufficiently approv'd to those whose opinion is my interest;
and for the rest let them talk what they will, for when I please
I'll be what I please, in spight of you and all mankind, and so
my dear *Man of Honour*, if you be tir'd, con over this lesson,   110
and sit there till I come to you.

Runs off.

Duretete. Tum ti dum. (*Sings.*) Ha, ha, ha, *ads my life, I have a
great mind to kick you*—oons and Confusion! (*Starts up.*) Was
ever man so abus'd—ay, *Mirabel* set me on.

Enter Petit.

Petit. Well Sir, how d'e find your self?

Duretete. You Son of a nine-ey'd Whore d'e come to abuse
me, I'll kick you with a vengeance, you Dog.

Petit *runs off, and* Duretete *after him.*

[*The End of the Second Act.*]

ACT III. [Scene i.]

SCENE *Continues.*

Old Mirabel *and the Young* [Mirabel].

Old Mirabel. Bob, come hither, *Bob.*

Mirabel. Your pleasure, Sir?

Old Mirabel. Are not you a great Rogue? Sirrah.

Mirabel. That's a little out of my Comprehension, Sir, for
I've heard say that I resemble my Father.

Old Mirabel. Your Father is your very humble Slave—I tell
thee what, Child, thou art a very pretty fellow, and I love thee
heartily; and a very great Villain, and I hate thee mortally.

Mirabel. Villain, Sir? then I must be a very impudent one,
for I can't recollect any passage of my life that I'm asham'd of.   10

Old Mirabel. Come hither, my dear Friend; do'st see this
Picture? (*Shews him a little Picture.*)

Mirabel. Oriana's? Pshaw!

Old Mirabel. What Sir, won't you look upon't?—*Bob*, dear
Bob, prithee come hither now—dost want any Money, Child?

Mirabel. No, Sir.

Old Mirabel. Why then here's some for thee; come here now—how canst thou be so hard-hearted, an unnatural, unmannerly Rascal (don't mistke me, Child, I an't angry) as
20 to abuse this tender, lovely, good-natur'd dear Rogue—Why, she sighs for thee, and crys for thee, pouts for thee, and snubs for thee, the poor little heart of it is like to burst—come, my dear Boy, be good-natur'd like your nown Father, be now—and then see here, read this—the Effigies of the lovely *Oriana*, with ten thousand pound to her Portion—ten thousand pound, you Dog; ten thousand pound, you Rogue; how dare you refuse a Lady with ten thousand pound, you impudent Rascal?

Mirabel. Will you hear me speak, Sir?
30 *Old Mirabel.* Hear you speak, Sir! if you had ten thousand Tongues, you cou'd not out-talk ten thousand pound, Sir.

Mirabel. Nay Sir, if you won't hear me, I'll be gone! Sir, I'll take Post for *Italy* this moment.

Old Mirabel. Ah! the Fellow knows I won't part with him. [*Aside.*] Well Sir, what have you to say?

Mirabel. The universal Reception, Sir, that Marriage has had in the World is enough to fix it for a publick good, and to draw every body into the Common Cause; but there are some Constitutions, like some Instruments, so peculiarly singular,
40 that they make tolerable Musick by themselves, but never do well in a Consort.

Old Mirabel. Why this is Reason, I must confess, but yet 'tis Nonsense too; for tho you shou'd reason like an Angel, if you argue your self out of a good Estate you talk like a Fool.

Mirabel. But Sir, if you bribe me into bondage with the Riches of *Cræsus*, you leave me but a Beggar for want of my Liberty.

Old Mirabel. Was ever such a perverse Fool heard? 'Sdeath Sir, why did I give you Education? was it to dispute me out of
50 my senses? Of what Colour now is the Head of this Cane? you'll say 'tis white, and ten to one make me believe it too—I thought that young fellows study'd to *get* Money.

Mirabel. No Sir, I have study'd to despise it; my Reading was not to make me rich, but happy, Sir.

Old Mirabel. There he has me agen now. [*Aside.*] But Sir, did not I marry to oblige you?

Mirabel. To oblige me, Sir, in what respect, pray?

Old Mirabel. Why to bring you into the World, Sir; wa'n't that an obligation?

Mirabel. And because I wou'd have it still an obligation, I 60 avoid Marriage.

Old Mirabel. How is that, Sir?

Mirabel. Because I wou'd not curse the hour I was born.

Old Mirabel. Lookee Friend, you may perswade me out of my designs, but I'll command you out of yours; and tho you may convince my Reason that you're in the right, yet there is an old attendant of sixty three, call'd positiveness, which you nor all the Wits in *Italy* shall ever be able to shake; so Sir, you're a Wit, and I'm a Father, you may talk, but I'll be obey'd.   70

Mirabel. This it is to have the Son a finer Gentleman than the Father, they first give us breeding that they don't understand, then they turn us out of doors 'cause we are wiser than themselves. But I'm a little afore-hand with the old Gentleman. [*Aside.*] Sir, you have been pleas'd to settle a thousand pound Sterling a year upon me, in return of which I have a very great honour for you and your Family, and shall take care that your only and beloved Son shall do nothing to make him hate his Father, or to hang himself. So, dear Sir, I'm your very humble Servant.   80

Runs off.

Old Mirabel. Here, Sirrah, Rogue, *Bob*, Villain.

Enter Dugard.

Dugard. Ay Sir, 'tis but what he deserves.

Old Mirabel. 'Tis false Sir, he don't deserve it; what have you to say against my Boy, Sir?

Dugard. I shall only repeat your own words.

Old Mirabel. What have you to do with my words? I have swallow'd my words already; I have eaten them up, and how can you come at 'em, Sir?

Dugard. Very easily, Sir; 'tis but mentioning your injur'd Ward, and you will thrown them up again immediately.   90

Old Mirabel. Sir, your Sister was a foolish young Flirt to trust any such young, deceitful, rakehelly Rogue like him.

Dugard. Cry you mercy, Old Gentleman, I thought we shou'd have the words again.

Old Mirabel. And what then! 'tis the way with young
Fellows to *slight* old Gentlemen's words, you never mind 'em
when you ought—I say that *Bob*'s an honest Fellow, and who
dares deny it?

Enter Bisarre.

Bisarre. That dare I, Sir—I say that your Son is a wild,
100 foppish, whimsical, impertinent Coxcomb, and were I abus'd
as this Gentleman's Sister, I wou'd make it an *Italian* Quarrel,
and poyson the whole Family.

Dugard. Come Sir, 'tis no time for trifling, my Sister is
abus'd, you are made sensible of the affront, and your Honour
is concern'd to see her redress'd.

Old Mirabel. Lookee, Mr *Dugard*, good words go farthest. I
will do your Sister Justice, but it must be after my own rate,
no body must abuse my Son but my self. For altho *Robin* be a
sad Dog, yet he's no body's Puppy but my own.

110 *Bisarre.* Ay, that's my sweet-natur'd, kind old Gentleman—
(*Wheadling him.*) We will be good then, if you'll joyn with us in
the plot.

Old Mirabel. Ah, you coxeing young Baggage, what plot can
you have to wheadle a fellow of sixty three?

Bisarre. A plot that sixty three is only good for, to bring
other people together, Sir; and you must act the *Spaniard*,
'cause your Son will least suspect you; and if he shou'd, your
authority protects you from a Quarrel, to which *Oriana* is
unwilling to expose her Brother.

120 *Old Mirabel.* And what part will you act in the business,
Madam?

Bisarre. My self, Sir; my Friend is grown a perfect Change-
ling; these foolish hearts of ours spoil our heads presently; the
Fellows no sooner turn Knaves but we turn Fools; but I am
still my self, and he may expect the most severe usage from
me, 'cause I neither love him nor hate him.

Exit.

Old Mirabel. Well said, Mrs Paradox; but Sir, who must
open the matter to him?

Dugard. *Petit*, Sir, who is our Engineer General. And here
130 he comes.

Enter Petit.

Petit. O Sir, more discoveries; are all friends, about us?

Dugard. Ay, ay, speak freely.

Petit. You must know Sir—ods my life I'm out of breath; you must know, Sir—you must know—

Old Mirabel. What the Devil must we know, Sir?

Petit. That I have (*Pants and blows.*) brib'd, Sir, brib'd—your Son's Secretary of State.

Old Mirabel. Secretary of State—who's that, for heaven's sake?

Petit. His *Valet-de-Chambre*, Sir; you must know, Sir, that the   140 intreague lay folded up with his Masters Cloaths, and when he went to dust the Embroider'd Suit, the secret flew out of the right Pocket of his Coat, in a whole swarm of your Crambo Songs, short-footed Odes, and long-legg'd Pindaricks.

Old Mirabel. Impossible!

Petit. Ah Sir, he has lov'd her all along; there was *Oriana* in every line, but he hates Marriage: Now Sir, this plot will stir up his Jealousie, and we shall know by the strength of that how to proceed farther. Come Sir, let's about it with speed.

> *'Tis expedition gives our King the sway;*   150
> *For expedition too the* French *give way;*
> *Swift to attack, or swift to run away.*

Exeunt.

[ACT III. Scene ii.]

Enter Mirabel *and* Bisarre, *passing carelessly by one another.*

Bisarre. I wonder, what she can see in this fellow to like him? (*Aside.*)

Mirabel. I wonder, what my Friend can see in this Girl to admire her? (*Aside.*)

Bisarre. A wild, foppish extravagant Rakehell. (*Aside.*)

Mirabel. A light whimsical impertinent Mad-cap. (*Aside.*)

Bisarre. Whom do you mean, Sir?

Mirabel. Whom do you mean, Madam?

Bisarre. A Fellow that has nothing left to re-establish him

III. ii. 1–6 The four lines are meant to be overheard. The stage direction '*Aside.*' has been retained to indicate that the speakers do not address one another.

10 for a humane Creature, but a prudent Resolution to hang
himself.

Mirabel. There is a way, Madam, to force me to that
Resolution.

Bisarre. I'll do't with all my heart.

Mirabel. Then you must marry me.

Bisarre. Lookee Sir, don't think your ill manners to me shall
excuse your ill usage of my Friend; nor by fixing a quarrel
here, to divert my zeal for the absent; for I'm resolv'd, nay, I
come prepar'd to make you a Panegyrick, that shall mortifie
20 your pride like any Modern Dedication.

Mirabel. And I, Madam, like a true Modern Patron, shall
hardly give you thanks for your trouble.

Bisarre. Come Sir, to let you see what little foundation you
have for your dear sufficiency, I'll take you to pieces.

Mirabel. And what piece will you chuse?

Bisarre. Your Heart, to be sure, 'cause I shou'd get
presently rid on't; your Courage I wou'd give to a Hector,
your Wit to a lewd Play-maker, your Honour to an Attorney,
your Body to the Physicians, and your Soul to their Master.

30 *Mirabel.* I had the oddest Dream last night of the Dutchess
of *Burgundy*, methought the Fourbelows of her Gown were
pinn'd up so high behind, that I cou'd not see her Head for
her Tail.

Bisarre. The Creature don't mind me! [*Aside.*] do you think,
Sir, that your humorous Impertinence can divert me? No Sir,
I'm above any pleasure that you can give, but that of seeing
you miserable. And mark me, Sir; my Friend, my injur'd
Friend shall yet be doubly happy, and you shall be a Husband
as much as the rites of Marriage, and the breach of 'em can
40 make you. (*Here* Mirabel *pulls out a* Virgil, *and reads to himself
while she speaks.*)

Mirabel. (*Reading.*) *At Regina dolos, quis fallere possit amantem.
Dissimulare etiam sperasti, perfide, tantum* (Very true.) *Posse nefas.*
By your favour, Friend *Virgil*, 'twas but a Rascally trick of
your Hero to forsake poor Pug so inhumanely.

Bisarre. I don't know what to say to him. [*Aside.*] The
Devil—what's *Virgil* to us, Sir?

22 your] O₁; you

Mirabel. Very much, Madam, the most apropo in the world—for, what shou'd I chop upon, but the very place where the perjur'd Rogue of a Lover and the forsaken Lady are batteling it tooth and nail. Come, Madam, spend your 50 Spirits no longer, we'll take an easier method: I'll be *Æneas* now, and you shall be *Dido*, and we'll rail by Book. Now for you, Madam *Dido*.

Nec te noster amor, nec te data dextera quondant
Nec Moritura tenet crudeli funere Dido—Ah poor *Dido*
(*Looking at her.*)

Bisarre. Rudeness, affronts, impatience! I cou'd almost start out even to Manhood, and want but a Weapon as long as his to fight him upon the spot. What shall I say? [*Aside.*]

Mirabel. Now she rants, *quæ quibus anteferam, jam jam nec Maxima Juno.* 60

Bisarre. A Man! No, the Womans Birth was spirited away.

Mirabel. Right, right, Madam, the very words.

Bisarre. And some pernicious Elf left in the Cradle with humane shape to palliate growing mischief. (*Both speak together, and raise their voices by degrees.*)

Mirabel. Perfide, sed duris genuit te Cautibus horrens
Caucasus, hircanæque admorunt Ubera Tigres.

Bisarre. Go Sir, fly to your midnight Revels—

Mirabel. Excellent
I sequere Italiam ventis, pete regna per undas
Spero equidem mediis, si quid pia numina possunt. (*Together* 70 *again.*)

Bisarre. Converse with Imps of Darkness of your make, your Nature starts at Justice, and shivers at the touch of Vertue. Now the Devil take his Impudence, he vexes me so, I don't know whether to cry or laugh at him.

Mirabel. Bravely perform'd, my Dear *Lybian*; I'll write the Tragedy of *Dido*, and you shall act the part; but you do nothing at all unless you fret your self into a fit; for here the poor Lady is stifled with Vapours, drops into the Arms of her Maids, and the cruel barbarous deceitful Wanderer is in the very next line call'd *Pious Æneas*—there's Authority for you. 80

Sorry indeed Æneas stood
To see her in a Pout;

74 or] O1; at

> But Jove *himself, who ne're thought good*
> *To stay a second bout,*
> *Commands him off, with all his crew,*
> *And leaves poor* Dy, *as I leave you.*

　　　　　　　　　　　　　　　　　　　　　　Runs off.

Bisarre. Go thy ways for a dear, mad, deceitful, agreeable
Fellow. O' my Conscience I must excuse *Oriana.*
　　That Lover soon his Angry Fair disarms,
90　　*Who slighting pleases, and whose Faults are Charms.*

　　　　　　　　　　　　　　　　　　　　　　　　[*Exit.*]

[ACT III. Scene iii.]

Enter Petit, *runs about to every door, and knocks.*

Petit. Mr *Mirabel*, Sir, where are you? no where to be
found?

　　　　　　　　　　Enter Mirabel.

Mirabel. What's the matter, *Petit.*

Petit. Most critically met—ah Sir, that one who has
follow'd the game so long, and brought the poor Hare just
under his paws, shou'd let a Mungril Cur chop in, and run
away with the Puss.

Mirabel. If your Worship can get out of your Allegories, be
pleas'd to tell me in three words what you mean.

10　*Petit.* Plain, plain, Sir. Your Mistress and mine is going to
be marry'd.

Mirabel. I believe you lye, Sir.

Petit. Your humble Servant, Sir. (*Going.*)

Mirabel. Come hither, *Petit.* Marry'd! say you?

Petit. No, Sir, 'tis no matter; I only thought to do you a
service, but I shall take care how I confer my favours for the
future.

Mirabel. Sir, I beg you ten thousand pardons. (*Bowing low.*)

Petit. 'Tis enough, Sir—I come to tell you, Sir, that *Oriana*
20　is this moment to be sacrific'd; marry'd past redemption.

Mirabel. I understand her, she'll take a Husband out of
spight to me, and then out of love to me she will make him a
Cuckold; 'tis ordinary with women to marry one person for

the sake of another, and to throw themselves into the arms of
one they hate, to secure their pleasure with the man they love.
But who is the happy man?

Petit. A Lord, Sir.

Mirabel. I'm her Ladyship's most humble Servant; a Train
and a Title, hey! room for my Lady's Coach, a front Row in
the Box for her Ladyship; Lights, Lights for her Honour—now 30
must I be a consant attender at my Lords Levee, to work my
way to my Lady's Couchee—a Countess, I presume, Sir—

Petit. A *Spanish* Count, Sir, that Mr *Dugard* knew abroad, is
come to *Paris*, saw your Mistress yesterday, marries her to
day, and whips her into *Spain* to morrow.

Mirabel. Ay, is it so, and must I follow my Cuckold over the
Pyrenees; had she marry'd within the precincts of a *Billet deux* I
wou'd be the man to lead her to Church; but as it happens, I'll
forbid the Bans. Where is this mighty Don?

Petit. Have a care, Sir, he's a rough cross-grain'd piece, 40
and there's no tampering with him; wou'd you apply to
Mr *Dugard*, or the Lady herself, something might be done, for
it is in despight to you, that the business is carry'd so hastily.
Odso, Sir, here he comes. I must be gone.

Exit.

[ACT III. Scene iv.]

Enter Old Mirabel *drest in a* Spanish *habit, leading* Oriana.

Oriana. Good my Lord, a nobler choice had better suited
your Lordships merit. My person, rank, and circumstance
expose me as the publick theme of Raillery, and subject me to
so injurious usage, my Lord, that I can lay no claim to any
part of your regard, except your pity.

Old Mirabel. Breathes he vital air, that dares presume
With rude behaviour to profane such excellence!
Show me the man—
And you shall see how sudden my Revenge
Shall fall upon the head of such presumption. 10
Is this thing one? (*Strutting up to* Mirabel.)

III. iii. 39 Bans] ed.; Banes

Mirabel. Sir?

Oriana. Good my Lord.

Old Mirabel. If he, or any he!

Oriana. Pray, my Lord, the Gentleman's a stranger.

Old Mirabel. O your pardon, Sir—but if you had—remember, Sir—the Lady now is mine, her injuries are mine therefore, Sir, you understand me—Come, Madam.

　　　　　　　　　　　　Leads Oriana *to the door, she goes off,*
　　　　　　　　Mirabel *runs to his Father, and pulls him by the Sleeve.*

Mirabel. Ecoute, Monsieur Le Count.

20　*Old Mirabel.* Your business, Sir?

Mirabel. Boh.

Old Mirabel. Boh! What Language is that, Sir?

Mirabel. *Spanish*, my Lord.

Old Mirabel. What d'e mean?

Mirabel. This, Sir. (*Trips up his heels.*)

Old Mirabel. A very concise Quarrel truly—I'll bully him [*Aside.*]—*Trinidado Seigniour*, give me fair play. (*Offering to rise.*)

Mirabel. By all means, Sir. (*Takes away his Sword.*) Now *Seigniour*, where's that bombast look, and fustian face your 30　Countship wore just now? (*Strikes him.*)

Old Mirabel. The Rogue Quarrels well, very well, my own Son right [*Aside.*]—but hold Sirrah, no more jesting, I'm your Father, Sir, your Father.

Mirabel. My Father! then by this light I cou'd find in my heart to pay thee. (*Aside.*) Is the Fellow mad? Why sure Sir, I han't frighted you out of your senses?

Old Mirabel. But you have, Sir.

Mirabel. Then I'll beat them into you again. (*Offers to strike him.*)

Old Mirabel. Why Rogue—*Bob*, dear *Bob*, don't you know 40　me, Child?

Mirabel. Ha, ha, ha, the Fellow's downright distracted, thou Miracle of Impudence, wou'dst thou make me believe that such a grave Gentleman as my Father wou'd go a Masquerading thus: That a person of threescore and three wou'd run about in a Fools Coat to disgrace himself and Family! Why you impudent Villain, do you think I will suffer such an affront to pass upon my honour'd Father, my worthy

Father, my dear Father? 'Sdeath Sir, mention my Father but
once again, and I'll send your soul to my Grandfather this
minute. (*Offering to stab him.*)   50

Old Mirabel. Well, well, I am not your Father.

Mirabel. Why then Sir, you are the sawcy hectoring
Spaniard, and I'll use you accordingly.

Old Mirabel. The Devil take the *Spaniards*, Sir; we have all
got nothing but blows since we began to take their part.

    Enter Dugard, Oriana, Maid, Petit. Dugard *runs to*
    Mirabel, *the rest to the old Gentleman.*

Dugard. Fye, fye, *Mirabel*, murder your Father!

Mirabel. My Father! What is the whole Family mad? Give
me way, Sir. I won't be held.

Old Mirabel. No! nor I neither, let me be gone, pray.
(*Offering to go.*)

Mirabel. My Father!   60

Old Mirabel. Ay, you Dog's face, I am your Father, for I
have bore as much for thee, as your Mother ever did.

Mirabel. O ho! then this was a trick it seems, a design, a
contrivance, a stratagem—oh! how my Bones ake!

Old Mirabel. Your Bones, Sirrah, why yours?

Mirabel. Why Sir, han't I been beating my own flesh and
blood all this while? O Madam, (*To* Oriana.) I wish your
Ladyship Joy of your new Dignity. Here was a Contrivance
indeed.

Petit. The Contrivance was well enough, Sir, for they   70
impos'd upon us all.

Mirabel. Well, my dear *Dulcinea*, did your *Don Quixote* battel
for you bravely? My Father will answer for the force of my
Love.

Oriana. Pray Sir, don't insult the misfortunes of your own
creating.

Dugard. My Prudence will be counted Cowardice if I stand
tamely now—(*Comes up between* Mirabel *and his Sister.*) Well,
Sir!

Mirabel. Well, Sir! do you take me for one of your Tenants, 80
Sir, that you put on your Landlord face at me?

Dugard. On what presumption, Sir, dare you assume thus?
(*Draws.*)

       III. iv. 63 was] O1; was was

Mirabel. What's that to you, Sir. (*Draws.*)

Petit. Help, help, the Lady faints. (Oriana *falls into her* Maids *arms.*)

Mirabel. Vapours, vapours, she'll come to herself; if it be an angry fit; a Dram of *Assa fœtida*—if Jealousie, Harts-horn in Water—if the Mother, burnt Feathers—if Grief, Ratafia—if it be strait Stayes, or Corns, there's nothing like a Dram of plain Brandy.

Exit.

90　*Oriana.* Hold off, give me air—O my Brother, wou'd you preserve my life, endanger not your own; wou'd you defend my Reputation, leave it to it self; 'tis a dear Vindication that's purchas'd by the Sword; for tho our Champion prove Victorious, yet our Honour is wounded.

Old Mirabel. Ay, and your Lover may be wounded, that's another thing. But I think you're pretty brisk again, my Child.

Oriana. Ay Sir, my indisposition was only pretence to divert the quarrel; the capricious taste of your Sex excuses this artifice in ours.

100　　　*For often, when our chief perfections fail,*
　　　　Our chief defects with foolish men prevail.

Exit.

Petit. Come, Mr *Dugard*, take Courage, there is a way still left to fetch him again.

Old Mirabel. Sir, I'll have no Plot that has any Relation to *Spain*.

Dugard. I scorn all Artifice whatsoever; my Sword shall do her Justice.

Petit. Pretty Justice truly! suppose you run him thro the Body; you run her thro the Heart at the same time.

110　*Old Mirabel.* And me thro the Head—rot your Sword, Sir, we'll have Plots; come, *Petit*, let's hear.

Petit. What if she pretended to go into a Nunnery, and so bring him about to declare himself.

Dugard. That, I must confess, has a face.

Old Mirabel. Face! a face like an Angel, Sir. Ads my life Sir, 'tis the most beautiful Plot in Christendom. We'll about it immediately.

Exeunt.

83 *Mirabel*] ed.; *Old Mirabel* [*O.M.*]

[ACT III. Scene v.]

SCENE *the Street*.

Duretete *and* Mirabel.

Duretete. (*In a passion*.) And tho I can't dance, nor sing, nor talk like you, yet I can fight, you know, Sir.

Mirabel. I know thou canst, man.

Duretete. 'Sdeath Sir, and I will: Let me see the proudest man alive make a Jest of me!

Mirabel. But I'll engage to make you amends.

Duretete. Danc'd to death! baited like a Bear; ridicul'd! threatn'd to be kick'd! Confusion. Sir, you set me on, and I will have satisfaction, all mankind will point at me.

Mirabel. I must give this Thunderbolt some passage, or 10 'twill break upon my own head (*Aside*.)—lookee *Duretete*, what do these Gentlemen laugh at?

Enter two Gentlemen.

Duretete. At me to be sure—Sir, what made you laugh at me?

First Gentleman. You're mistaken, Sir, if we were merry we had a private reason.

Second Gentleman. Sir, we don't know you.

Duretete. Sir, I'll make you know me; mark and observe me, I won't be nam'd, it shan't be mention'd, not even whisper'd in your Prayers at Church. 'Sdeath Sir, d'ye smile?   20

First Gentleman. Not I, upon my word.

Duretete. Why then look grave as an Owl in a Barn, or a Fryar with his crown a shaving.

Mirabel. Don't be Bully'd out of your humour, Gentlemen; the Fellow's mad, laugh at him, and I'll stand by you. (*Aside to the* Gentlemen.)

First Gentleman. Igad and so we will.

Both. Ha, ha, ha.

Duretete. Ha, ha, ha, very pretty. (*Draws*.) She threaten'd to kick me. Ay, then, you Dogs, I'll murther you.

Fights, and beats them off, Mirabel *runs over to his side*.

III. ii. 25 laugh] O1; laugh'd

30 *Mirabel.* Ha, ha, ha, bravely done, *Duretete*, there you had him, Noble Captain, hey, they run, they run, *Victoria*, *Victoria*—ha, ha, ha—how happy am I in an excellent Friend! tell me of your Virtuoso's and men of sense, a parcel of sowre-fac'd splenatick Rogues—a man of my thin Constitution shou'd never want a Fool in his company: I don't affect your fine things that improve the understanding, but hearty laughing to fatten my Carcass: And o' my Conscience, a man of sense is as melancholy without a Coxcomb, as a Lyon without his Jackall; he hunts for our diversion, starts game for 40 our Spleen, and perfectly feeds us with pleasure.

> *I hate the man who makes acquaintance nice,*
> *And still discreetly plagues me with advice;*
> *Who moves by Caution, and Mature delays,*
> *And must give Reasons for whate're he says.*
> *The man, indeed, whose converse is so full,*
> *Makes me attentive, but it makes me dull.*
> *Give me the Careless Rogue, who never thinks,*
> *That plays the fool as freely as he drinks.*
> *Not a Buffoon, who is Buffoon by trade,*
50 > *But one that Nature, not his Wants have made.*
> *Who still is merry, but does ne'r design it;*
> *And still is ridicul'd, but ne'r can find it.*
> *Who when he's most in earnest, is the best;*
> *And his most grave expression, is the Jest.*

Exeunt.

[*The*] *End of the Third Act.*

ACT IV. [Scene i.]

SCENE Old Mirabel's *House.*

Enter Old Mirabel *and* Dugard.

Dugard. The Lady Abbess is my Relation, and privy to the Plot: Your Son has been there, but had no admittance beyond the privilege of the Grate, and there my Sister refus'd to see

54.1 *Exeunt*] ed.; *Exit*

him. He went off more nettled at his repulse, than I thought
his gayety cou'd admit.

Old Mirabel. Ay, Ay, this Nunnery will bring him about, I
warrant ye.

Enter Duretete.

Duretete. Here, where are ye all?—O, Mr. *Mirabel*, you have
done fine things for your Posterity—And you, Mr. *Dugard*,
may come to answer this—I come to demand my Friend at 10
your Hands; restore him, Sir, or—(*To* Old Mirabel.)

Old Mirabel. Restore him! why d'ee think I have got him in
my Trunk, or my Pocket?

Duretete. Sir, he's Mad, and you're the cause on't.

Old Mirabel. That may be; for I was as mad as he when I
begat him.

Dugard. Mad, Sir; what de'e mean?

Duretete. What do you mean, Sir, by shutting up your Sister
yonder, to talk like a Parrot thro a Cage?—Or a Decoy-Duck,
to draw others into the Snare? Your Son, Sir, because she has 20
deserted him, he has forsaken the World; and, in three Words,
has—

Old Mirabel. Hang'd himself!

Duretete. The very same; turn'd Fryar.

Old Mirabel. You Lie, Sir, 'tis ten times worse. *Bob* turn'd
Fryar!—Why shou'd the Fellow shave his foolish Crown,
when the same Razor may cut his Throat?

Duretete. If you have any Command, or you any Interest
over him, lose not a minute! He has thrown himself into the
next Monastery, and has order'd me to pay off his Servants, 30
and discharge his Equipage.

Old Mirabel. Let me alone to Ferret him out; I'll Sacrifice
the Abbot, if he receives him; I'll try whether the Spiritual or
the Natural Father has the most right to the Child.—But, dear
Captain, what has he done with his Estate?

Duretete. Settled it upon the Church, Sir.

Old Mirabel. The Church! Nay then the Devil won't get him
out of their Clutches.—Ten Thousand *Livres* a Year upon the
Church! 'tis downright Sacrilege.—Come Gentlemen, all
hands to work; for half that Sum, one of these Monasteries 40
shall protect you, a Traitor Subject from the Law, a
Rebellious Wife from her Husband, and a Disobedient Son

from his own Father.

Exit.

Dugard. But will you persuade me, that he's gone to a Monastery!

Duretete. Is your Sister gone to the *Filles Repenties*? I tell you, Sir, she's not fit for the Society of Repenting Maids.

Dugard. Why so, Sir?

Duretete. Because she's neither one, nor t'other; she's too old 50 to be a Maid, and too young to Repent.

Exit, Dugard *after him.*

[ACT IV. Scene ii.]

SCENE *the inside of a Monastery.*

Oriana *in a Nun's habit*; Bisarre.

Oriana. I hope, *Bisarre*, there is no harm in Jesting with this Religious Habit?

Bisarre. To me, the greatest Jest in the Habit, is taking it in earnest: I don't understand this Imprisoning People with the Keys of *Paradise*, nor the merit of that Virtue which comes by constraint.—Besides, we may own to one another, that we are in the worst Company when among our selves; for our private Thoughts run us into those desires, which our Pride resists from the Attacks of the World; and, you may remember, the 10 first Woman then met the Devil, when she retired from her Man.

Oriana. But I'm reconcil'd methinks to the Mortification of a Nunnery; because I fansie the Habit becomes me.

Bisarre. A well-contriv'd Mortification, truly, that makes a Woman look ten times handsomer than she did before!—Ah, my Dear, were there any Religion in becoming Dress, our Sex's Devotion were rightly plac'd; for our Toylets wou'd do the Work of the Altar; we shou'd all be Canoniz'd.

Oriana. But don't you think there is a great deal of Merit, in 20 Dedicating a Beautiful Face and Person to the Service of Religion?

Bisarre. Not half so much, as devoting 'em to a pretty
Fellow: If our Femality had no business in this World, why
was it sent hither? Let us dedicate our beautiful Minds to the
Service of Heaven. And for our handsom Persons, they
become a Box at the Play, as well as a Pew in the Church.

Oriana. But the vicissitudes of Fortune, the inconstancy of
Man, with other disappointments of Life, require some Place
of Religion, for a refuge from their Persecution.

Bisarre. Ha, ha, ha, and do you think there is any Devotion 30
in a Fellow's going to Church, when he takes it only for a
Sanctuary? Don't you know, that Religion consists in a
Charity with all Mankind; and that you should never think of
being Friends with Heaven, till you have Quarrell'd with all
the World. Come, come, mind your Business, *Mirabel* loves
you, 'tis now plain, and hold him to't; give fresh Orders that
he shan't see you: We get more by hiding our Faces
sometimes, than by exposing them; a very Mask you see whets
Desire, but a pair of keen Eyes thro' an Iron Gate, fire double
upon 'em, with View and Disguise. But I must be gone upon 40
my Affairs, I have brought my Captain about again.

Oriana. But why will you trouble your self with that
Coxcomb?

Bisarre. Because he is a Coxcomb; had not I better have a
Lover like him, that I can make an Ass, than a Lover like
yours, to make a Fool of me. (*Knocking below.*) A Message from
Mirabel, I'll lay my Life. (*She runs to the Door.*) Come hither,
Run, thou Charming Nun, come hither?

Oriana. What's the News? (*Runs to her.*)

Bisarre. Don't you see who's below?   50

Oriana. I see no Body but a Fryar.

Bisarre. Ah! thou poor blind *Cupid*! O my Conscience these
Hearts of ours spoil our Heads instantly; the Fellows no
sooner turn Knaves, than we turn Fools. A Fryar! don't you
see a Villanous genteel Mien under that Cloak of Hypocrisie,
the loose careless Air of a tall Rakehelly Fellow?

Oriana. As I live *Mirabel* turn'd Fryar! I hope in Heav'n he's
not in earnest.

Bisarre. In earnest! ha, ha, ha, are you in earnest? Now's
your time; this disguise has he certainly taken for a Pasport, to 60
get in and try your Resolutions; stick to your Habit to be sure;

treat him with Disdain, rather than Anger; for Pride becomes
us more than Passion: Remember what I say, if you wou'd
yield to advantage, and hold out the Attack; to draw him on,
keep him off to be sure.

> *The cunning Gamesters never gain too fast,*
> *But lose at first, to win the more at last.*

Exit.

Oriana. His coming puts me into some Ambiguity, I don't
know how; I don't fear him, but I mistrust my self; wou'd he
70 were not come, yet I wou'd not have him gone neither; I'm
afraid to talk with him, but I love to see him tho'.

> *What a strange Power has this fantastick Fire,*
> *That makes us dread even what we most Desire!*
> *Enter* Mirabel *in Fryars Habit.*

Mirabel. Save you, Sister—Your Brother, young Lady,
having a regard to your Souls Health, has sent me to prepare
you for that sacred Habit by Confession.

Oriana. That's false, the Cloven Foot already. (*Aside.*) My
Brother's Care I own; and to you, sacred Sir, I confess, that
the great crying Sin which I have long indulg'd, and now
80 prepare to expiate, was Love. My morning Thoughts, my
evening Prayers, my daily Musings, nightly Cares, was Love!
My present Peace, my future Bliss; the Joys of Earth, and
hopes of Heaven, I all contemn'd for Love!

Mirabel. She's downright stark Mad in earnest; Death and
Confusion, I have lost her. (*Aside.*) You confess your fault,
Madam, in such moving Terms, that I could almost be in love
with the Sin.

Oriana. Take care Sir; Crimes, like Virtues, are their own
rewards; my chief Delight became my only Grief; he in whose
90 Breast I thought my Heart secure turn'd Robber, and
despoil'd the Treasure that he kept.

Mirabel. Perhaps that Treasure he esteems so much, that
like a Miser, tho' afraid to use it, he reserves it safe.

Oriana. No, holy Father; who can be Miser in another's
Wealth that's Prodigal of his own, his Heart was open, shar'd
to all he knew, and what, alas, must then become of Mine?
But the same Eyes that drew the Passion in, shall send it out
in Tears, to which now hear my Vow—

Mirabel. (*Discovering himself.*) No, my fair Angel, but let me

Repent; here on his Knees behold the Criminal, that vows 100
Repentance his. Ha! No concern upon her! [*Aside.*]

Oriana. This Turn is odd, and the time has been that such a
sudden Change wou'd have surpris'd me into some Confusion.

Mirabel. Restore that happy Time, for I am now return'd to
my self, I want but Pardon to deserve your Favour, and here
I'll fix till you Relent, and give it.

Oriana. Grovelling, sordid Man; why wou'd you Act a thing
to make you kneel, Monarch in Pleasure to be Slave to your
Faults? Are all the Conquests of your wandring Sway, your
Wit, your Humour, Fortune, all reduc'd to the base Cringing 110
of a bended Knee? Servil and Poor! I—*Love it.* (*Aside.*)

Mirabel. I come not here to justifie my Fault but my
Submission, for tho' there be a meaness in this humble
Posture, 'tis nobler still to bend when Justice calls, than to
resist Conviction.

Oriana. No more—thy oft repeated violated Words reproach
my weak Belief, 'tis the severest Calumny to hear thee speak;
that humble Posture which once cou'd raise, now mortifies my
Pride; How can'st thou hope for Pardon from one that you
Affront by asking it?   120

Mirabel. (*Rises.*) In my own Cause no more, but give me
leave to intercede for you against the hard Injunctions of that
Habit, which for my Fault you wear.

Oriana. Surprising Insolence! My greatest Foe pretends to
give me Counsel; but I am too warm upon so cool a Subject.
My Resolutions, Sir, are fix'd, but as our Hearts were united
with the Ceremony of our Eyes, so I shall spare some Tears to
the Separation, (*Weeps.*) That's all; farewel.

Mirabel. And must I lose her? No (*Runs, and Catches her.*)
Since all my Prayers are vain, I'll use the nobler Argument 130
of Man, and force you to the Justice you refuse; you're mine
by Pre-contract: And where's the Vow so sacred to disanul
another? I'll urge my Love, your Oath, and plead my Cause
'gainst all Monastick Shifts upon the Earth.

Oriana. Unhand me Ravisher! Would you profane these
holy Walls with Violence? Revenge for all my past Disgrace
now offers, thy Life should answer this, wou'd I provoke the
Law: Urge me no farther, but be gone.

Mirabel. Unexorable Woman, let me Kneel again. (*Kneels.*)

IV. ii 130 Woman] O1: Women

Enter Old Mirabel.

140   *Old Mirabel.* Where, where's this Counterfeit Nun?

Oriana. Madness, Confusion, I'm Ruin'd?

Mirabel. What do I hear, (*Puts on his Hood.*) What did you say Sir?

Old Mirabel. I say she's a Counterfeit, and you may be another for ought I know, Sir; I have lost my Child by these Tricks, Sir.

Mirabel. What Tricks Sir?

Old Mirabel. By a pretended Trick Sir? A Contrivance to bring my Son to Reason, and it has made him stark Mad; I
150 have lost him, and a thousand Pound a Year.

Mirabel. (*Discovering himself.*) My dear Father, I'm your most humble Servant.

Old Mirabel. My Dear Boy, (*Runs and kisses him.*) Welcome. *Ex Inferis* my Dear Boy, 'tis all a Trick, she's no more a Nun than I am.

Mirabel. No?

Old Mirabel. The Devil a bit.

Mirabel. Then kiss me again my Dear Dad, for the most happy News.—And now most venerable holy Sister. (*Kneels.*)
160   *Your Mercy and your Pardon I implore,*
         For the Offence of asking it before.
Lookee, my Dear Counterfeiting Nun, take my Advice, be a Nun in good earnest; Women make the best Nuns always when they can't do otherwise. Ah, my Dear Father, there is a Merit in your Sons behaviour that you little think; the free Deportment of such Fellows as I, makes more Ladies Religious, than all the Pulpits in *France*.

Oriana. O, Sir, how unhappily have you destroy'd what was so near Perfection; he is the Counterfeit, that has deciev'd you.
170   *Old Mirabel.* Ha! Lookee Sir, I recant, she is a Nun.

Mirabel. Sir, Your humble Servant, then I'm a Fryar this moment.

Old Mirabel. Was ever an Old Fool so Banter'd by a brace o' Young ones; hang you both, you're both Counterfeits, and my Plots spoil'd, that's all.

[*Exit.*]

Oriana. Shame, and Confusion, Love, Anger, and Disappointment, will work my Brain to Madness. (*Throws off her Habit.*)

                                                                    Exit.

Mirabel. Ay, Ay, thrown by the Rags, they have serv'd a turn for us both, and they shall e'en go off together. (*Takes off his Habit.*)

> *Thus the Sick Wretch, when tortur'd by his Pain,*   180
> *And finding all Essays for Life are Vain;*
> *When the Physician can no more design,*
> *Then call the t'other Doctor, the divine.*
> *What Vows to Heaven, wou'd Heaven restore his Health;*
> *Vows all to Heaven, his Thoughts, his Actions, Wealth;*
> *But if restor'd to Vigour as before*
> *His Health refuses what his Sickness swore.*
> *The Body is no sooner Rais'd, and Well,*
> *But the weak Soul relapses into Ill;*
> *To all its former swing of Life is led,*   190
> *And leaves its Vows and Promises in Bed.*

                    Exit, Throwing away the Habit.

[ACT IV. Scene iii.]

SCENE *changes to* Old Mirabel*'s House*;

Duretete *with a Letter.*

Duretete. (*Reads.*)
> *My Rudeness was only a Proof of your Humour, which I have found so agreeable; that I own my self Penitent, and willing to make any Reparation upon your first appearance to*
>   Bisarre.

Mirabel swears she Loves me, and this confirms it, then farewel Gallantry, and welcome Revenge; 'tis my turn now to be upon the Sublime, I'll take her off, I warrant her.
                    Enter Bisarre.
Well Mistress, do you love me?
Bisarre. I hope, Sir, you will pardon the Modesty of—
Duretete. Of what? Of a Dancing Devil?—Do you love me, I   10
say.

Bisarre. Perhaps I—

Duretete. What?

Bisarre. Perhaps I do not.

Duretete. Ha! Abus'd again! Death Woman, Ill—

Bisarre. Hold, hold, Sir, I do, I do!

Duretete. Confirm it then, by your Obedience stand there; and Ogle me now, as if your Heart, Blood, and Soul, were like to fly out at your Eyes—First, the direct surprise. (*She looks full* 20 *upon him.*) Right, next the *Deux yeux par oblique.* (*She gives him the side Glance.*) Right, now depart, and Languish. (*She turns from him, and looks over her Shoulder.*) Very well, now Sigh. (*She Sighs.*) Now drop your Fan a purpose. (*She drops her Fan.*) Now take it up again Come now, confess your Faults, are not you a Proud—say after me.

Bisarre. Proud.

Duretete. Impertinent.

Bisarre. Impertinent.

Duretete. Ridiculous.

30 *Bisarre.* Ridiculous.

Duretete. Flurt.

Bisarre. Puppy.

Duretete. Soons Woman, don't provoke me, we are alone, and you don't know but the Devil may tempt me to do you a Mischief, ask my Pardon immediately.

Bisarre. I do, Sir, I only mistook the word.

Duretete. Cry then, ha, you got e're a Hankerchief?

Bisarre. Yes, Sir.

Duretete. Cry then Hansomly, cry like a Queen in a Trajedy.

She pretending to Cry, burst out a Laughing, and
Enter two Ladies *Laughing.*

40 *Bisarre.* Ha, ha, ha.

Ladies both. Ha, ha, ha.

Duretete. Hell broke loose upon me, and all the Furies flutter'd about my Ears! Betray'd again!

Bisarre. That you are upon my word, my dear Captain, ha, ha, ha.

Duretete. The Lord deliver me.

First Lady. What! Is this the mighty Man with the Bull Face that comes to frighten Ladies? I long to see him Angry; come begin.

Duretete. Ah, Madam, I'm the best natur'd Fellow in the 50
World.

Second Lady. A Man! We're mistaken, a Man has Manners;
the aukard Creature is some Tinkers Trull in a Perriwig.

Bisarre. Come Ladies, let's examine him. (*They lay hold on
him.*)

Duretete. Examine! The Devil you will!

Bisarre. I'll lay my Life, some great Dayry Maid in Man's
Cloaths.

Duretete. They will do't—lookee, dear *Christian* Women,
pray hear me.

Bisarre. Will you ever attempt a Ladies Honour again? 60

Duretete. If you please to let me get away with my Honour,
I'd do any thing in the World.

Bisarre. Will you persuade your Friend to Marry mine?

Duretete. O yes, to be sure.

Bisarre. And will you, do the same by me.

Duretete. Burn me if I do, if the Coast be clear.

Runs out.

Bisarre. Ha, ha, ha, this Visit Ladies, was Critical for our
Diversion, we'll go make an end of our Tea.

Exeunt.

[ACT IV. Scene iv.]

Enter Mirabel *and* Old Mirabel.

Mirabel. Your Patience, Sir, I tell you I won't Marry, and
tho' you send all the Bishops in *France* to perswade me, I shall
never believe their Doctrine against their Practice.

Old Mirabel. But will you disobey your Father, Sir?

Mirabel. Wou'd my Father have his youthful Son lie lazing
here, bound to a Wife, chain'd like a Monkey to make sport to
a Woman, subject to her Whims, Humours, Longings,
Vapours, and Capriches, to have her one Day Pleas'd, to
Morrow Peevish, the next Day Mad, the fourth Rebellious;
and nothing but this succession of Impertinence for Ages 10

IV. iii. 52 *Second Lady*] ed. (2 *Lady* in O1); 2. *Ladies*
IV. iv. 1 *Mirabel.*] O2 (*Mir.*); [om.]

together. Be Merciful, Sir, to your own Flesh and Blood.

Old Mirabel. But, Sir, did not I bear all this, why should not you?

Mirabel. Then you think, that Marriage like Treason should attaint the whole Blood; pray consider, Sir, is it reasonable, because you throw your self down from one Story, that I must cast my self headlong from the Garret Window, you wou'd compel me to that state, which I have heard you curse your self, when my Mother and you have Battel'd it for a
20 whole Week together.

Old Mirabel. Never but once you Rogue, and that was when she long'd for six *Flanders* Mares; Ay, Sir, then she was breeding of you, which show'd what an expensive Dog I shou'd have of you.

Enter Petit.

Well *Petit*, how do's she now?

Petit. Mad, Sir, *con Pompos*—Ah Mr. *Mirabel*, you'll believe that I speak Truth, now, when I confess that I have told you hitherto nothing but Lies, our jesting is come to a sad earnest, she's downright distracted.

Enter Bisarre.

30   *Bisarre.* Where is this mighty Victor?—The great Exploit is done, go triumph in the Glory of your Conquest, inhumane barbarous Man! O, Sir, (*To the Old Gentleman.*) Your wretched Ward has found a tender Guardian of you, where her young Innocence expected protection, here has she found her Ruin.

Old Mirabel. Ay, The Fault is mine, for I believe that Rogue won't Marry, for fear of begetting such a disobedient Son as his Father did. I have done all I can, Madam, and now can do no more than run Mad for Company. (*Crys.*)

Enter Dugard *with his Sword drawn.*

Dugard. Away! Revenge, Revenge.

40   *Old Mirabel.* Patience, Patience, Sir. (Old Mirabel *holds him.*) *Bob*, draw. (*Aside.*)

Dugard. Patience! The Cowards virtue, and the brave Man's failing when thus provok'd—Villain.

Mirabel. Your Sisters Frenzy shall excuse your Madness;

---

38 *Crys*] All editions retain the stage direction. However, Old Mirabel is unlikely to weep, even if he threatens to run mad. Bisarre does not seem a weeper, but perhaps she is the one intended to cry.

and to shew my concern for what she suffers, I'll bear the
Villain from her Brother—Put up your Anger with your
Sword; I have a Heart like yours, that swells at an Affront
received, but melts at an Injury given; and if the lovely
Oriana's Grief be such a moving Scene, 'twill find a part within
this Breast perhaps, as tender as a Brothers.   50

Dugard. To prove that soft Compassion for her Grief,
endeavour to remove it.—There, there, behold an Object
that's Infective; I cannot view her but I am as mad as she,

Enter Oriana *mad, held by two Maids, who put her in a Chair.*

a Sister that my dying Parents left with their last Words and
Blessing to my Care. Sister, dearest Sister. (*Goes to her.*)

Old Mirabel. Ay, poor Child, poor Child, d'ye know me?

Oriana. You! you are *Amadis de Gaul*, Sir;—Oh! oh my
Heart! were you never in Love, fair Lady? And do you never
Dream of Flowers and Gardens?—I Dream of walking Fires,
and tall Gigantick Sighs. Take heed, it comes now—What's   60
that? Pray stand away: I have seen that Face sure—How light
my head is?

Mirabel. What piercing Charms has Beauty, ev'n in Madness; these suddain starts of undigested Words, shoot thro' my
Soul with more perswasive Force, than all the study'd Art of
labour'd Eloquence. [*Aside.*]—Come, Madam, try to repose a
little.

Oriana. I cannot; for I must be up to go to Church, and I
must Dress me, put on my new Gown, and be so fine, to meet
my Love. Hey, ho!—will not you tell me where my Heart lies   70
Bury'd?

Mirabel. My very Soul is touch'd [*Aside.*]—Your hand, my
Fair.

Oriana. How soft and gentle you feel?—I'll tell you your
Fortune, Friend.

Mirabel. How she stares upon me!

Oriana. You have a flattering Face; but 'tis a fine one—I
warrant you have five Hundred Mistresses—Ay, to be sure, a
Mistress for every Guinea in his Pocket—Will you pray for
me? I shall die to morrow—and will you Ring my Passing-   80
Bell?

Mirabel. O Woman, Woman, of Artifice created! whose Nature, even distracted, has a Cunning: In vain let Man his Sense, his Learning boast, when Womans Madness over-rules his Reason. Do you know me, injur'd Creature.

Oriana. No,—but you shall be my intimate Acquaintance in the Grave. (*Weeps.*)

Mirabel. Oh Tears, I must believe ye; sure there's a kind of Simpathy in Madness; for even I, obdurate as I am, do feel my
90 Soul so toss'd with Storms of Passion, that I could cry for help, as well as she—(*Wipes his Eyes.*)

Oriana. What! have you lost your Lover? No, you mock me, I'll go home and pray.

Mirabel. Stay, my fair Innocence, and hear me own my Love so loud, that I may call your Senses to their place, restore 'em to their charming happy Functions, and reinstate my self into your Favour.

Bisarre. Let her alone, Sir, 'tis all too late; she trembles, hold her, her Fits grow stronger by her talking; don't trouble
100 her, she don't know you, Sir.

Old Mirabel. Not know him! what then? she loves to see him for all that.

Enter Duretete.

Duretete. Where are you all? What the Devil! Melancholly, and I here; are ye sad, and such a ridiculous Subject, such a very good Jest among ye, as I am?

Mirabel. Away with this Impertinence; this is no place for Bagatel; I have murder'd my Honour, destroy'd a Lady, and my desire of reparation, is come at length too late: See there.

Duretete. What ails her?
110 *Mirabel.* Alas, she's Mad.

Duretete. Mad! dost wonder at that? By this Light, they're all so; they're cozening Mad, they're brawling Mad, they're proud Mad; I just now came from a whole World of Mad Women, that had almost—What is she Dead?

Mirabel. Dead! Heav'ns forbid.

Duretete. Heav'ns further it; for till they be cold as a Key, there's no trusting them; your'e never sure that a Woman's in earnest, till she be nail'd in her Coffin. Shall I talk to her? Are you mad, Mistress?
120 *Bisarre.* What's that to you, Sir?

Duretete. Oon's, Madam, are you there?

Runs off.

Mirabel. Away, thou wild Buffoon; how poor and mean this Humour now appears? His Follies and my own I here disclaim; this Ladies Frenzy has restor'd my Senses, and was she perfect now, as once she was, (before you all I speak it) she shou'd be mine; and as she is, my Tears and Prayers shall wed her.

Dugard. How happy had this Declaration been some hours ago?

Bisarre. Sir, she beckons to you, and waves us to go off; 130 come, come, let's leave 'em.

Exeunt Omnes, *but* Mirabel *and* Oriana.

Oriana. Oh, Sir!

Mirabel. Speak, my charming Angel, if your dear Senses have regain'd their order; speak, Fair, and bless me with the News.

Oriana. First let me bless the Cunning of my Sex, that happy counterfeited Frenzy that has restor'd to my poor labouring Breast, the dearest best-belov'd of Men.

Mirabel. Tune all ye Spheres, your Instruments of Joy, and carry round your spacious Orbs, the happy Sound of *Oriana's* 140 Health; her Soul whose Harmony was next to yours, is now in Tune again; the counterfeiting Fair has play'd the Fool.

> *She was so Mad to Counterfeit for me;* ⎫
> *I was so Mad to pawn my Liberty.*   ⎬
> *But now we both are well, and both are Free.* ⎭

Oriana. How, Sir? Free!

Mirabel. As Air, my Dear *Bedlamite*; what, Marry a Lunatick! Look, my Dear, you have counterfeited Madness so very well this bout, that you'l be apt to play the Fool all your Life-long—Here, Gentlemen.   150

Oriana. Monster! you won't disgrace me?

Mirabel. O my Faith, but I will; here, come in, Gentlemen —A Miracle, a Miracle, the Woman's dispossest, the Devil's vanisht.

Enter Old Mirabel *and* Dugard.

Old Mirabel. Bless us, was she Possest?

124–5 was she] O1; [om.] ~

Mirabel. With the worst of Demons, Sir, a Marriage Devil,
a horrid Devil. Mr. *Dugard*, don't be surpriz'd, I promis'd my
Endeavours to Cure your Sister. No Mad Doctor in *Christendom*
could have done it more effectually. Take her into your
160 Charge; and have a care she don't relapse; if she should
employ me again, for I am no more infallible than others of
the Faculty, I do cure sometimes.

Oriana. Your remedy most barbarous Man, will prove the
greatest poyson to my health, for tho' my former frenzy was
but Counterfeit, I now shall run into a real Madness.

　　　　　　　　　　　　　　　Exit, Old Mirabel *after*.

Dugard. This was a turn beyond my knowledge; I'm so
confus'd, I know not how to resent it.

　　　　　　　　　　　　　　　　　　　　　　Exit.

Mirabel. What a dangerous precipice have I scap'd? Was
not I just now upon the brink of Destruction?

　　　　　　　　　　　Enter Duretete.

170 O my Friend, let me run into thy Bosom; no Lark escap'd
from the devouring pounces of a Hawk, quakes with more
dismal apprehensions.

Duretete. The matter Man?

Mirabel. Marriage, Hanging, I was just at the Gallows foot,
the running Noose about my Neck, and the Cart wheeling
from me—Oh—I shan't be my self this Month again.

Duretete. Did not I tell you so? They are all alike, Saints or
Devils; their counterfeiting can't be reputed a Deceit, for 'tis
the Nature of the Sex, not their Contrivance.

180 *Mirabel.* Ay, ay: There's no living here with security; this
House is so full of Stratagem and Design, that I must abroad
again.

Duretete. With all my Heart, I'll bear thee Company, my
Lad, I'll meet you at the Play; and we'll set out for *Italy* to
morrow Morning.

Mirabel. A Match: I'll go pay my Complement of leave to
my Father presently.

Duretete. I'm afraid he'll stop you.

Mirabel. What, pretend a Command over me after his
190 Settlement of a Thousand Pound a Year upon me: No, no, he

has passed away his Authority with the Conveyance; the Will
of a living Father is chiefly obeyed for sake of the dying one.

> *What makes the World attend and crowd the Great?*
> *Hopes, Interest, and Dependance, make their State.*
> *Behold the Anti-chamber filled with Beaux,*
> *A Horse's Levee thronged with Courtly Crows.*
> *Tho' grumbling Subjects make the Crown their sport,*
> *Hopes of a Place, will bring the Sparks to Court.*
> *Dependance, even a Father's sway secures,*
> *For tho' the Son rebels, the Heir is yours.*   200

The End of the Fourth Act.

ACT V. [Scene i.]

SCENE *the Street before the Play-House.*

Mirabel *and* Duretete *as coming from the Play.*

Duretete. How dy'e like this Play?

Mirabel. I lik'd the Company; the Lady, the rich Beauty in
the front Box had my attention, these impudent Poets bring
the Ladies together to support them, and to kill every body
else,

> *For Deaths upon the Stage the Ladies cry,*
> *But ne're mind us that in the Audience die:*
> *The Poets Hero shou'd not move their pain,*
> *But they shou'd weep for those their eyes have slain.*

Duretete. Hoity, toity, Did *Phillis* inspire you with all this?   10

Mirabel. Ten times more, the Play-house is the Element of
Poetry, because the Region of Beauty, the Ladies, methinks
have a more inspiring triumphant Air in the Boxes than any
where else, they sit commanding on their Thrones with all
their Subject Slaves about them. Their best Cloaths, best
Looks, shining Jewels, sparkling Eyes, the Treasure of the
World in a Ring. Then there's such a hurry of Pleasure to
transport us, the Bustle, Noise, Gallantry, Equipage, Garters,
Feathers, Wigs, Bows, Smiles, Oggles, Love, Musick and
Applause. I cou'd wish that my whole Life long were the first   20
Night of a New Play.

Duretete. The Fellow has quite forgot this Journey, have you bespoke Post-Horses?

Mirabel. Grant me but three days, Dear Captain, one to discover the Lady, one to unfold my self, and one to make me happy; and then I'm yours to the World's End.

Duretete. Hast thou the Impudence to promise thy self a Lady of her Figure and Quality in so short a time.

Mirabel. Yes Sir—I have a confident Address, no disagree-
30 able Person, and Five hundred *Lewidors* in my Pocket.

Duretete. Five hundred *Lewidores*! You an't mad?

Mirabel. I tell you she's worth Five Thousand, one of her Black Brilliant Eyes is worth a Diamond as big as her head. I compar'd her Necklace with her looks, and the living Jewels out-sparkel'd the dead ones by a Million.

Duretete. But you have own'd to me, that abating *Oriana*'s pretentions to Marriage, you lov'd her passionately, then how can you wander at this rate?

Mirabel. I long'd for a Partridge t'other day off the King's
40 Plate, but d'e think because I cou'd not have it I must eat nothing.

Duretete. Prethee *Mirabel*, be quiet. You may remember what narrow scapes you have had abroad by following Strangers, you forget your leap out of the *Curtesan*'s Window at *Bollognia* to save your fine Ring there.

Mirabel. My Ring's a trifle, there's nothing we possess comparable to what we desire—be shy of a Lady barefac'd in the front Box with a Thousand Pound in Jewels about her Neck! for shame, no more.

Enter Oriana *in Boy's Cloaths with a Letter.*

50 *Oriana.* Your Name, *Mirabel* Sir?

Mirabel. Yes Sir.

Oriana. A letter from your Unkle in *Picardy.* (*Gives the Letter.*)

Mirabel. (*Reads.*) *The Bearer is the Son of a Protestant Gentleman,*
who flying for his Religion, left me the charge of this Youth [a
pretty Boy] *he's fond of some hansom Service that may afford*
him opportunity of Improvement, your Care of him will Oblige;
Yours.

Hast a mind to Travel Child?

Oriana. 'Tis my desire Sir, I shou'd be pleas'd to serve a
60 Traveller in any Capacity.

Mirabel. A hopeful Inclination; you shall along with me into *Italy*, as my Page.

Duretete. I don't think it safe; the Rogue's too hansome—(*Noise without.*) The Play's done, and some of the Ladies come this way.

Enter Lamorce *with her Train born up by a* Page.

Mirabel. Duretete, The very Dear, Identical She.

Duretete. And what then?

Mirabel. Why 'tis she.

Duretete. And what then Sir?

Mirabel. Then! why,—looke Sirrah the first piece of service 70 I put you upon is to follow that Lady's Coach, and bring me word where she lives. (*To* Oriana.)

Oriana. I don't know the Town Sir, and am afraid of loosing my self.

Mirabel. Pshaw!

Lamorce. Page, what's become of all my People?

Page. I can't tell Madam I can see no sign of your Ladyship's Coach.

Lamorce. That fellow is got into his old Pranks, and fall'n drunk somewhere, none of the Footmen there? 80

Page. Not one Madam.

Lamorce. These Servants are the plague of our lives, what shall I do?

Mirabel. By all my hopes Fortune Pimps for me; now *Duretete* for a piece of Gallantry.

Duretete. Why you won't sure?

Mirabel. Won't! Brute! Let not your Servants neglect, Madam, put your Ladyship to any inconvenience, for you can't be disappointed of an equipage whilst mine waits below and wou'd you honour the Master so far, he would be proud 90 to pay his attendance.

Duretete. Ay, to be sure. (*Aside.*)

Lamorce. Sir, I won't presume to be troublesom for my Habitation is a great way off.

Duretete. Very true Madam, and he's a little engaged, besides Madam a hackney-Coach will do as well Madam.

Mirabel. Rude beast be quiet. (*To* Duretete.) The farther

from home Madam, the more Occasion you have for
Guard—pray Madam—

100   *Lamorce.* Lard Sir—(*He seems to press, she to decline it in dumb
show.*)

    Duretete. Ah! the Devil's in his impudence, now he whedles,
she smiles, he flatters, she simpers, he swears, she believes,
he's a Rogue and she's a Wh—in a moment.

    Mirabel. Without there, my Coach; *Duretete*, wish me Joy.
(*Hands the Lady out.*)

    Duretete. With you a Surgeon! here you little *Picard*, go
follow your Master and he'll lead you—

    Oriana. Whether Sir?

    Duretete. To the Accademy Child, tis the fashion with Men
of Quality to teach their Pages their Exercises—go.

110   *Oriana.* Won't you go with him too Sir, that Woman may
do him some harm I don't like her!

    Duretete. Why how now, *Tages* do you start up to give laws
of a sudden; do you pretend to rise at Court and disaprove the
pleasures of your betters: Looke Sirrah, if ever you wou'd rise
by a great Man, be sure to be with him in his little Actions,
and as a step to your advancement follow your Master
immediately, and make it your hope that he go to a Baudy-
House.

    Oriana. Heavens forbid.

Exit.

120   *Duretete.* Now wou'd I sooner take a Cart in Company of
the Hangman, than a Coach with that Woman: What a
strange antipathy have I taken against these Creatures, a
Woman to me is aversion upon aversion, Cheese, a Cat, a
breast of Mutton, the squeeling of Children, the grinding of
Knives, and the snuff of a Candle.

Exit.

103 Rogue] O1; Rouge

[ACT V. Scene ii.]

SCENE *a handsom Apartment.*

Enter Mirabel *and* Lamorce.

Lamorce. To convince me Sir, that your service was somthing more than Good breeding, please to lay out an hour of your Company upon my desire, as you have already upon my necessity.

Mirabel. Your desire Madam, has only prevented my request, my hours! make 'um yours Madam, eleven, twelve, one, two, three, and all that belong to those happy Minutes.

Lamorce. But I must trouble you Sir to dismiss your retinue because an Equipage at my door at this time of night will not be consistent with my Reputation.   10

Mirabel. By all means Madam, all but one little Boy—here Page, order my Coach and Servants home, and do you stay; [*To* Oriana *offstage.*] 'tis a foolish Country Boy that knows nothing but Innocence.

Lamorce. Innocence Sir, I shou'd be sorry if you made any sinister Constructions of my freedom.

Mirabel. O Madam, I must not pretend to remark upon any bodies freedom, having so intirely forfeited my own.

Lamorce. Well Sir, 'twere convenient towards our easy Correspondence, that we enter'd into a free confidence of each   20
other by a mutual declaration of what we are, and what we think of one Another;—now Sir what are you?

Mirabel. In three words Madam—I am a Gentleman, I have five hundred pound in my pocket, and a clean shirt on.

Lamorce. And your Name is—

Mirabel. Mustapha—now Madam the Inventory of your Fortunes.

Lamorce. My Name is *Lamorce*; my Birth Noble; I was married young to a proud, rude, sullen, imperious fellow; the Husband spoyled the Gentleman; crying ruin'd my Face till at   30
last I took heart, leapt out of a window, got away to my Friends, sue'd my Tyrant, and recovered my Fortune—I lived

V. ii. 29 married] O1; mared

from fifteen to twenty to please a Husband, from twenty to
forty I'm resolved to please my self, and from thence upwards
I'll humour the World.

Mirabel. The Charming wild Notes of a Bird broke out of its
Cage!

Lamorce. I mark'd you at the Play, and something I saw of a
well-furnished careless agreeable Tour about you. Methought
40 your Eyes made their mannerly demands with such an Arch
Modesty, that I dont know how—but I'm elop'd, ha, ha, ha,
I'm Elop'd.

Mirabel. Ha, ha, ha, I rejoyce in your good fortune with all
my heart.

Lamorce. O now I think on't Mr. *Mustapha*, you have got the
finest Ring there, I cou'd scarcely believe it right, pray let me
see it.

Mirabel. Hum! yes Madam 'tis, 'tis right—but, but, but, it
was given me by my Mother, an Old Family Ring, Madam,
50 an Old-fashioned Family Ring.

Lamorce. Ay Sir—if you can entertain your self with a Song
for a moment I'll wait on you, come in there.

Enter Singers.

Call what you please Sir.

[*Exit.*]

Mirabel. The new Song—*Prethee* Phillis, &c.

SONG.

Certainly the Stars have been in a strange intreaguing
humour when I was born—Ay, this night shou'd I have had a
Bride in my Arms, and that I shou'd like well enough, but
what shou'd I have to morrow night? the same. And what next
night the same, and what next night the very same, Soop for
60 breakfast, Soop for dinner, Soop for supper, and Soop for
breakfast again—but here's variety.

> *I love the fair who freely gives her heart*
> *That's mine by tyes of Nature not of Art;*
> *Who boldly owns what e're her thoughts indite,*
> *And is too modest for Hypocrite.*

*Lamorce appears at the door, as he runs towards
her, four* Bravoes *step in before her. He starts back.*

She comes, she comes—Hum, hum—Bitch,—Murder'd, murder'd to be sure! The Cursed Strumpet! to make me send away
my Servants—no body near me! These Cut-throats make
always sure work. What shall I do? I have but one way.
[*Aside.*] Are these Gentlemen your Relations Madam?   70
     Lamorce. Yes Sir.
     Mirabel. Gentlemen, your most humble servant, Sir your
most faithful, yours Sir, with all my heart; your most
obedient—come Gentlemen. (*Salutes all round.*) Please to
sit—no ceremony, next the Lady pray Sir.
     Lamorce. Well Sir, and how do'e like (*They all sit.*) my friend?
     Mirabel. O Madam the most finish'd Gentlemen! I was
never more happy in good Company in my life, I suppose Sir,
you have traveld?
     First Bravo. Yes Sir.   80
     Mirabel. Which way? may I presume?
     First Bravo. In a Western Barge Sir.
     Mirabel. Ha, ha, ha, very pretty, facetious pretty Gentleman!
     Lamorce. Ha, ha, ha, Sir, you have got the prettiest Ring
upon your finger there—
     Mirabel. Ah Madam, 'tis at your service with all my heart.
(*Offering the ring.*)
     Lamorce. By no means Sir, a family Ring! (*Takes it.*)
     Mirabel. No matter Madam, Seven hundred pound, by this
Light. (*Aside.*)
     Second Bravo. Pray Sir, what's a Clock?   90
     Mirabel. Hum! Sir I forgot my Watch at home.
     Second Bravo. I thought, I saw the string of it just now.
     Mirabel. Ods my life Sir, I beg your pardon, here it is—but
it don't go. (*Puting it up.*)
     Lamorce. O dear Sir, and *English* Watch! *Tompions* I presume.
     Mirabel. Do'e like it Madam—no Ceremony—'tis at your
service with all my heart and soul—*Tompions*! hang ye. (*Aside.*)
     First Bravo. But Sir, above all things I admire the fashion
and make of your Sword hilt.
     Mirabel. I'm mighty glad you like it Sir.   100
     First Bravo. Will you part with it Sir?
     Mirabel. Sir I won't sell it.

First Bravo. Not sell it Sir.

Mirabel. No Gentlemen,—but I'll bestow it with all my heart. (*Offering it.*)

First Bravo. O Sir we shall rob you.

Mirabel. That you do I'll be sworn. (*Aside.*) I have another at home, pray Sir—Gentlemen you'r too modest, have I any thing else that you fancy—Sir, will you do me a favour (*To the* 110 First Bravo.) I am extreamly in love with that Wig which you wear, will you do me the favour to change with me.

First Bravo. Looke Sir, this is a family Wig, and I wou'd not part with it, but if you like it—

Mirabel. Sir your most humble servant. (*They change wigs.*)

First Bravo. Madam your most humble slave. (*Goes up fopishly to the Lady salutes her.*)

Second Bravo. The Fellows very liberal shall we murder him?

First Bravo. What! let him scape, to hang us all. And I to lose my Wig, no, no, I want but a hansom pretence to quarrel with him, for you know we must act like Gentlemen! here 120 some Wine—(*Wine here.*) Sir your good health. (*Pulls* Mirabel *by the Nose.*)

Mirabel. Oh Sir, your most humble servant, a pleasant frolick enough to drink a mans health and pull him by the Nose, ha, ha, ha, the pleasantest pretty humour'd Gentleman.

Lamorce. Help the Gentleman to a Glass. (Mirabel *drinks.*)

First Bravo. How do'e like the Wine Sir?

Mirabel. Very good o the Kind Sir, but I'll tell ye what I find, were all inclin'd to be frolicksome, and I gad for my own part I was never more disposed to be merry, let's make a night on't, ha!—this Wine is pretty! but I have such *Burgundy* at 130 home! looke Gentlemen, let me send for a dozen flaskes of my *Burgundy*, I defie *France* to Match it—'twill make us all life, all air, pray Gentlemen.

Second Bravo. Eh! shall us have his *Burgundy*?

Bravoes. Yes faith, we'll have all we can, heer, call up the Gentlemans Servant—What think you *Lamorce*?

Lamorce. Yes, yes,—your Servant is a foolish Country Boy Sir, he understands nothing but Innocence?

Mirabel. Ay, ay Madam—here Page,

Enter Oriana.

take this Key and go to my Butler, order him to send half a
dozen flasks of the red *Burgundy*, mark't a thousand, and be 140
sure you make hast, I long to entertain my Friends here, my
very good Friends.

Omnes. Ah dear Sir—

First Bravo. Here Child take a glass of Wine—your Master
and I have chang'd Wigs, Honey, in a frolick,—Where had
you this pretty Boy, honest *Mustapha.*

Oriana. Mustapha!

Mirabel. Out of *Picardy*—this is the first errand he has made
for me, and if he do's it right, I'll encourage him.

Oriana. The red *Burgundy* Sir!   150

Mirabel. The red, Markt a thousand, and be sure you make
hast.

Oriana. I shall Sir.

                                                      Exit.

First Bravo. Sir you were pleas'd to like my Wigg! have you
any fancy for my Coat—look'e Sir, it has serv'd a great many
honest Gentlemen very faithfully.

Mirabel. Not so faithfully, for I'm afraid it has got a scurvy
trick of leaving all its Masters in Necessity—the Insolence of
these Dogs is beyond their Cruelty. (*Aside.*)

Lamorce. You'r Melancholy Sir.   160

Mirabel. Only concern'd Madam, that I shou'd have no
Servant here but this little Boy—he'll make some confounded
blunder I'll lay my life on't, I wou'd not be disappointed of my
Wine for the Universe.

Lamorce. He'll do well enough Sir, but supper's ready, will
you please to eat a bit Sir?

Mirabel. O Madam, I never had a better stomach in my life.

Lamorce. Come then,—we have nothing but a plate of Soop.

Mirabel. Ah! the Marriage Soop I cou'd dispense with now.
(*Aside.*)

                                    Exit handing the Lady.

Second Bravo. That Wigg won't fall to your Share.   170

First Bravo. No, no, we'll settle that after Supper, in the
mean time the Gentleman shall wear it.

Second Bravo. Shall we dispatch him?

Third Bravo. To be sure, I think he knows me.

First Bravo. Ay, ay, Dead Men, tell no Tales, I wonder at
the Impudence of the *English* Rogues That will hazard the
meeting a Man at the Barr, that they have Encounter'd upon
the road, I han't the Confidence to Look a Man in the face
after I have done him an Injury, therefore we'll Murder him.

Exeunt.

[ACT V Scene iii.]

SCENE *Changes to* Old Mirabel'*s House.*

Enter Duretete.

Duretete. My Friend has forsaken me, I have abandon'd my
Mistress, my time lyes heavy on my hands, and my Money
burns in my Pocket—but now I think on't my *Mirmidons* are
upon duty to night, I'll fairly stroal down to the Guard, and
Nod away the night with my honest Lieutenant over a flask of
Wine a Rakehelly story, and a pipe of Tobacco. (*Going off*,
Bisarre *meets him.*)

Bisarre. Who comes there, stand.

Duretete. Hey day, now she's turnd Dragoon!

Bisarre. Look'e Sir, I'm told you intend to Travel again—I
10　design to wait on you as far as *Italy.*

Duretete. Then I'll Travel into *Wales.*

Bisarre. Wales! what Countrey's that?

Duretete. The Land of Mountains child, where you're never
out of the way, cause there's no such thing as a high road.

Bisarre. Rather always in a high road, 'cause you Travel all
upon Hills—but as it will, I'll Joy along with you.

Duretete. But we intend to sail to the *East-Indies.*

Bisarre. East or *West*, 'tis all one to me, I'm tight and light,
and the fitter for sailing.

20　*Duretete.* But suppose we take thro' *Germany*, and drink
hard.

Bisarre. Suppose I take thro' *Germany*, and drink harder
than you.

Duretete. Suppose I go to a Baudy-house.

V. iii. 12 *Bisarre*] O1 (*Bis.*); *Bur.*

Bisarre. Suppose I show you the way.

Duretete. 'Sdeath Woman, will you go to the Guard with me, and smoak a Pipe?

Bisarre. Alloons Don.

Duretete. The Devil's in the Woman,—suppose I hang my self.   30

Bisarre. There I'll leave you.

Duretete. And a happy riddance, the Gallows is wellcome.

Bisarre. Hold, hold Sir, (*Catches him by the arm going.*) one word before we part.

Duretete. Let me go Madam—or I shall think that you're a Man and perhaps may examine you.

Bisarre. Stir if you dare, I have still Spirits to attend me and can raise such a muster of Faries as shall punish you to death—come Sir, stand there now and Oggle me. (*He frowns upon her.*) Now a languishing sigh. (*He groans.*) Now run and   40
take up my Fan, faster. (*He runs and takes it up.*) Now play with it handsomely.

Duretete. Ay, ay. (*He tears it all in pieces.*)

Bisarre. Hold, hold, dear humorous, Coxcomb, Captain, spare my fan and I'll—why you rude inhumane Monster, don't you expect to pay for this.

Duretete. Yes Madam there's twelve pence, for that's the price on't.

Bisarre. Sir, it cost a Guiney.

Duretete. Well Madam you shall have the sticks again.   50
                              Throws them to her, and Exit.

Bisarre. Ha, ha, ha, rediculous below my concern. I must follow him however to know if he can give me any news of *Oriana.*

                                                              Exit.

[ACT V. Scene iv.]

SCENE *changes to* Lamorces *Lodgings.*

Enter Mirabel Solus.

Mirabel. Bloody Hellhounds I overheard you,—was not I two hours ago the happy, gay, rejoycing—*Mirabel*? how did I

plume my hopes in a fair coming prospect of a long scene of
years? life courted me with all the Charms of Vigour Youth,
and Fortune; And to be torn away from all my promised Joys,
is more than Death. The manner too, by Villains—O my
Oriana, this very moment might have Blest me in thy Arms,
and my poor Boy, the Innocent Boy!—Confusion!—But hush,
they come, I must dissemble. Still—no News of my Wine
10 Gentlemen?

Enter the Four Bravoes.

First Bravo. No Sir, I belive Your Country Booby has Lost
himself and we Can wait no Longer fort—true Sir, You'r a
pleasant Gentleman, but I suppose You undersand our
Business?

Mirabel. Sir I may go near to guess at your Employments,
You Sir, are a Lawyer. I presume, You a Physitian, You a
Scrivener, You a Stock Jobber—all Cutthroats IGad. (*Aside.*)

Fourth Bravo. Sir, I am a Broken Officer, I was Cashir'd at
the head of the Army for a Coward, So I took up the trade of
20 Murder to retrieve the Reputation of my Courage.

Third Bravo. I am a Souldier too, and wou'd serve my King,
but I don't like the quarrel, and I have more honour than to
fight in a bad Cause.

Second Bravo. I was bred a Gentleman, and have no Estate,
but I must have my Whore and my Bottle, thro' the prejudice
of Education.

First Bravo. I am a Ruffian, too by the prejudice of
Education, I was bred a Butcher. In short Sir, if your Wine
had come, we might have trifled a little longer—come Sir,
30 which Sword will you fall by, mine Sir—(*Draws.*)

Second Bravo. Or mine—(*Draws.*)

Third Bravo. Or mine—(*Draws.*)

Fourth Bravo. Or mine—(*Draws.*)

Mirabel. I Scorn to beg my Life, but to be Butcher'd thus!
[*Aside.*] (*Knocking.*) O, there's the Wine—this moment for my
Life or Death. [*Aside.*]

Enter Oriana.

Lost, for ever lost!—where's the Wine Child? (*Faintly.*)

Oriana. Coming up Sir. (*Stamps.*)

Enter Duretete *with his Sword drawn, and six of the*
Grand Musqueteers with their Peeces presented, the
Ruffians drop their Swords.

Oriana *goes off.*

Mirabel. The Wine, the Wine, the Wine. Youth, Pleasure,
Fortune, Days and Years are now my own again—Ah my dear 40
Friends, Did not I tell you this Wine wou'd make me
merry?—Dear Captain, these Gentlemen are the best Natur'd,
Facetious, Witty Creatures that ever you knew.

Enter Lamorce.

Lamorce. Is the Wine come Sir.

Mirabel. O yes Madam, the Wine is come—see there—
(*Pointing to the Souldiers.*) Your Ladyship has got a very fine
Ring upon your Finger.

Lamorce. Sir, 'Tis at your Service.

Mirabel. O ho, is it So? thou dear Seven Hundred Pound,
thou'rt wellcome home again with all my Heart—adsmylife 50
Madam, You have got the finest built Watch there, *Tompions* I
presume.

Lamorce. Sir you may wear it.

Mirabel. O Madam, by no means, 'tis too much—rob you of
all—(*Taking it from 'er.*) good dear Time, thou'rt a precious
thing. I'm glad I have retriev'd thee. (*Putting it up.*) What, my
Friends neglected all this while! Gentlemen You'll pardon my
Complaisance to the Lady—how now—is it so Civil to be out
of Humour at my Entertainment, and I so pleased with yours;
Captain you'r surpriz'd at all this! But we're in our frolicks 60
you must know—Some Wine here.

Enter Servant with Wine.

Come, Captain this worthy Gentleman's health. (*Tweaks the*
First Bravo *by the Nose, he roars.*) But now where—where's my
Dear Deliverer, my Boy, my Charming Boy?

First Bravo. I hope some of our Crew below stairs have
dispatch'd him.

Mirabel. Villain, what say'st thou? dispatch'd! I'll have ye
all tortur'd, rack'd, torn to pieces alive, if you have touch'd my
Boy—here, Page, Page, Page.

Runs out.

60 we're] O1; were

70   *Duretete.* Here Gentlemen, be sure you secure those fellows.

First Bravo. Yes Sir, we know you and your Guard will be very civil to us.

Duretete. Now for you Madam—he, he, he—I'm so pleas'd to think that I shall be reveng'd of one Woman before I dye—well Mistris Snap-dragon, which of these Honourable Gentlemen is so happy to call you Wife.

First Bravo. Sir, she shou'd have been mine to Night, cause *Sampre* here had her last night. Sir she's very true to us all four.

Duretete. Take 'em to Justice.

> *The Guards carry off the* Bravoes.

> *Enter* Old Mirabel, Dugard, Bisarre

80   *Old Mirabel.* *Robin, Robin,* where's *Bob*, where's my Boy?— what, is this the Lady? a pretty Whore faith!—hearkey Child, because my son was so civil as to oblige you with a Coach, I'll treat you with a Cart; indeed I will.

Dugard. Ay Madam—and you shall have a swinging Equipage; three or four thousand Footmen at your heels at least.

Duretete. No less becomes her quality.

Bisarre. Faugh! the monster.

Duretete. Monster, Ay, you'r all a little monstrous, let me
90 tell you.

> *Enter* Mirabel.

Old Mirabel. Ah my dear *Bob*, art thou safe Man?

Mirabel. No, no Sir, I'm ruin'd, the saver of my life is lost.

Old Mirabel. No, no, he came and brought us the news.

Mirabel. But where is he—

> *Enter* Oriana.

ha: (*Runs and embraces her.*) my dear preserver what shall I do to recompence your trust—Father, Friend, Gentlemen behold the Youth that has reliev'd me from the most ignominious death, from the scandalous poniards of these bloody Ruffians, where to have fall'n wou'd have defam'd my memory with vile
100 reproach—my life, estate, my all is due to such a favour— Command me Child, before ye all, before my late, so kind indulgent Stars I swear, to grant what'ere you ask.

Oriana. To the same Stars indulgent now to me, I will

appeal as to the Justice of my Claim, I shall demand but what
was mine before—the Just performance of your Contract to
Oriana. (*Discovering her self.*)

Omnes. Oriana.

Oriana. In this disguise I resolved to follow you abroad,
Counterfited that Letter that got me into your service, and so
by this strange turn of fate I became the Instrument of your 110
Preservation, few Common servants wou'd have had such
Cunning, My Love Inspired me with the meaning of your
Message, Cause my Concern for your safety made me suspect
Your Company.

Duretete. Mirabel You'r Caught.

Mirabel. Caught! I scorn the thought of Imposition, the
tricks and artful Cunning of the Sex I have despis'd, and
broke thro' all Contrivance. Caught! No, 'tis my Voluntary
Act, this was no Humane Stratagem, But by my providental
Stars designed to show the Dangers, wandring Youth Incurs 120
by the persuit of an unlawful Love, to plunge me headlong in
the snares of Vice, and then to free me by the hands of Virtue,
here on my knees I humbly beg my fair preservers pardon, my
thanks are needless, for my self I owe. And now for ever do
protest me yours.

Old Mirabel. Tall, all, di, dall (*Sings.*) kiss me Daughter—
No, you shall kiss me first (*To* Lamorce.) for you'r the cause
on't, well *Bisarre*, what say you to the Captain?

Bisarre. I like the Beast well enough, but I don't understand
his paces so well as to venture him in a strange Road.   130

Old Mirabel. But Marriage is so beaten a path that you
can't go wrong.

Bisarre. Ay, 'tis so beaten that the way is spoiled.

Duretete. There is but one thing shou'd make me thy
husband—I cou'd Marry thee to Day for the priviledge of
beating thee to Morrow.

Old Mirabel. Come come, you may agree for all this,
Mr. *Dugard*, are not you pleas'd with this?

Dugard. So pleas'd, that if I thought it might secure your
Sons affection to my sister; I wou'd double her fortune.   140

Mirabel. Fortune! has not she given me mine; my life,
estate, my all, and what is more her vertuous self—vertue in
this so advantagous light has her own sparkling Charms more

tempting far than glittering Gold or Glory. Behold the Foil (*Pointing to* Lamorce.) that sets this brightness off. (*To* Oriana.) Here view the pride (*To* Oriana.) and scandal of the Sex. (*To* Lamorce.) There (*To* Lamorce.) the false Meteor whose Deluding light leads Mankind to destruction here (*To* Oriana.) the bright shining Star that guides to a Security of
150 Happiness. A Garden and a single She (*To* Oriana.) was our first fathers bliss, the Tempter (*To* Lamorce.) and to wander was his Curse.

  What liberty can be so Tempting there (*To* Lamorce.)
  As a soft, vertuous, Amorous bondage here. (*To* Oriana.)

SONG.

By Mr. *O—r.*

Set by Mr. *Daniel Purcell.*

I.

Since, Cælia *'tis not in our power*
To tell how long our lives may last,
Begin to love this very hour
You've lost too much in what is past.

II.

For since the power we all obey
160 *Has in your breast my heart confind,*
Let me my body to it lay,
In vain you'd part what Nature Joynd.
       [FINIS.]

151 Tempter] O1; Temper

EPILOGUE.

Written by *Nicholas Rowe*, Esq;

AND

Spoken by Mr. *Wilks*.

From Fletcher*'s great Original to day*
We took the hint of this our Modern Play;
Our Author from his Lines has strove to Paint
A Witty, Wild, Inconstant, free Gallant
With a Gay Soul, with Sense, and Will to rove ⎫
With Language, and with Softness fram'd to move ⎬
With little Truth, but with a World of Love. ⎭
Such forms on Maids in Morning Slumbers wait, ⎫
When fancy first instructs their hearts to beat, ⎬
When first they wish, and Sigh for what they ⎭   10
   know not yet.
Frown not ye Fair to think your Lovers may
Reach your cold hearts by some unguarded way
Let Villeroy*'s misfortune make you wise*
There's danger still in Darkness and Surprize
Tho' from his Ramparts he defy'd the Foe
Prince Eugene *found an Aquaduct below.*
With easy freedom, and a gay Address,
A pressing Lover seldom wants Success:
Whilst the respectfull like the Greek *sits down,*   20
And wastes a ten years Seige before one Town.
For her own Sake let no forsaken Maid,
Our Wanderer for want of Love Upbraid.
Since 'tis a Secret, none shou'd er'e confess
That they have lost the happy Pow'r to please.
If you Suspect the Rogue inclin'd to break,
Break first, and swear You've turn'd him off a week;

Epilogue. 0.2 *Nicholas*] ed.; *Nathaniel*. Although all editions, including Stonehill, read
'Nathaniel', Nicholas Rowe, must have been the author. He was active in London
theatre at the time, *Tamerlane* having opened at Lincoln's Inn Fields, probably in
December 1701.

As Princes when they resty States-men doubt,
Before they can Surrender turn 'em out.
30 *What er'e you think grave Uses may be made,*
And much even for inconstancy be said.
Let the Good Man for Marriage rites design'd, ⎫
With Studious Care and Diligence of Mind, ⎬
Turn over every page of Woman kind. ⎭
Mark Every Sense, and how the reading Vary,
And when he knows the worst on't—Let him Marry.

A New PROLOGUE,

In Answer *to my very Good Friend, Mr.* Oldmixon; *who, having Two* PLAYS *Damn'd at the Old House, had a Mind to Curry-Favour, to have a Third Damn'd at the New.*

> *'Tis hard, the* Author *of this* PLAY *in View,*
> *Shou'd be Condemn'd, purely for pleasing you:*
> *Charg'd with a* Crime, *which you, his* Judges, *own*
> *Was only this, that he has Pleas'd the Town.*
> *He touch'd no* POET's *Verse, nor* DOCTOR's *Bills;*
> *No foe to B—re, yet a Friend to* Wills.
> *No* Reputation *Stab'd, by Sow'r Debate;*   10
> *Nor had a Hand in* Bankrupt Brisco's *Fate:*
> *And, as an Ease to's* Tender Conscience, *Vows,*
> *He's none of those that Broke the t'other House:*
> *In Perfect Pity to their Wretched Cheer,*
> *Because his* PLAY *was Bad—he brought it here.*
> *The Dreadful Sin of* Murder *Cries Aloud;*
> *And sure these* Poets *ne'r can hope for Good,*
> *Who dipt their Barbarous* Pens *in that poor Houses Blood.*
> *'Twas Malice all: No Malice like to Theirs,*
> *To Write Good* PLAYS, *purpose to Starve the* Players.   20
> *To Starve by's* Wit, *is still the* Poet's *due;*
> *But, here are Men, whose* Wit, *is Match'd by few;*
> *Their* Wit *both Starves Themselves, and others too.*
> *Our* PLAYS *are* Farce, *because our* House *is Cram'd;*
> *Their* PLAYS *all Good: For what?—because they'r Damn'd.*
> *Because we Pleasure you, you call us Tools;*
> *And 'cause you please your selves, they call you Fools.*
> *By their Good Nature, they are* Wits, *True Blew;*
> *And, Men of Breeding, by their Respects to you.*
> *To Engage the* Fair, *all other Means being lost,*   30
> *They Fright the* Boxes, *with Old* Shakespear's *GHOST:*
> *The* Ladies, *of such* Spectres, *should take heed;*
> *For, 'twas the* DEVIL *did Raise that* Ghost *indeed.*
> *Their Case is hard, that such Despair can show;*
> *They've Disoblig'd all Powers Above, they know;*

And now must have Recourse to Powers Below.
Let Shakespear *then lye still,* Ghosts *do no good;*
The Fair *are Better Pleas'd with Flesh and Blood:*
What is't to them, to mind the Antient*'s Taste?*
40 *But the Poor Folks are Mad, and I'm in haste.*

[*Runs off.*

THE TWIN-RIVALS

INTRODUCTION

ON 14 December 1702, less than a year after the *première* of *The Inconstant*, *The Twin-Rivals* appeared. Farquhar had provided the prologue for Francis Manning's *All for the Better*, which opened in late October or early November 1702, and the epilogue to Charles Gildon's *The Patriot*, which opened in late November or early December.

In *The Twin-Rivals*, Farquhar turned a direction he had not previously explored. The unexpected success of Richard Steele's *The Funeral*, which opened at Drury Lane in late November or early December 1701, only a couple of months before *The Inconstant*, may have influenced Farquhar's decision to create an entirely new kind of play. Steele had created a melodramatic main plot concerning the attempts of a villainess to gain the inheritance which rightly belongs to her stepson, as Young Wou'dbe attempts to take over his elder brother's inheritance; in both cases, the blocking character is a genuinely evil person and a serious threat to the hero. In both, the language reverberates with the pathos of the hero's situation. Lord Hardy laments:

Now indeed, I am Utterly Undone, but to expect an Evil softens the weight of it when it happens, and pain no more than pleasure is in reality so great as in expectation: But what will become of me? How shall I keep my Self ev'n above Worldly want?[1]

Elder Wou'dbe mourns in a similar key:

My Father dead! my Birth-right lost! How have my drowsie Stars slept o'er my Fortune? . . . but why should I repine? Let Man but view the Dangers he has past, and few will fear what Hazards are to come.

In both plays unprincipled lawyers intentionally manipulate wills to distort the intent of the deceased, thus providing an opportunity to satirize the legal profession. In both there are two couples in the love-plots, the 'disinherited' son and his seriously devoted young lady as well as his military companion and a slightly livelier match. An attempted rape in each play darkens the tone of the love plots; in each a woman (Lady Brumpton, Midnight) has planned the crime.

Although there are no specific echoes that prove Farquhar owed a debt to Steele, the two comedies are distinct enough from other comedies of the period to suggest at least that Farquhar was aware of the unusual qualities of Steele's play. Most of the 'sentimental' or 'soft' comedies of the turn of the century dwelled on domestic incompatibility. The melo-dramatic intensity created by actual or attempted crimes against people—stolen inheritances or attempted rapes—was exceedingly rare in 1702. If Farquhar did not borrow lines from Steele, he may well have been moved to the experimentation in *The Twin-Rivals* by the success of his contemporary.

Still, as Stonehill says, *The Twin-Rivals* is 'a play of great originality'.[2] One can find analogues in other plays, but no incontrovertible sources. Several critics, for example, have pointed to Teague in *The Committee* as a forerunner of Teague in *The Twin-Rivals*.[3] Stonehill also notes that bawd-midwives had appeared in the plays of Middleton, Dekker, and Brome, but he finds nothing approaching plagiarism in these 'slight similarities'.[4]

James links *The Twin-Rivals* to *Volpone*, noting the use of the name Wou'dbe, 'evidently taken over from Sir Politick Would-be', and the defences of poetry in the prefaces of the two plays. Both comedies, he says, explore sins of greed and lust: Young Wou'dbe, like Volpone, is driven by those dual motives. Midnight, like Mosca, while seemingly trying to fulfil the master's desires, is really a parasite manipulating the plot; in their machinations both act as bawds. Subtleman, like Voltore, is a dishonest lawyer. However, James admits that the specific influence of Volpone on *The Twin-Rivals* is somewhat difficult to trace; he does not specify whether the Jonson play was source or analogue but concludes that it 'helps us to understand the tone of *The Twin-Rivals* better'.[5]

If one looks toward Renaissance playwrights, however, Farquhar's familiarity with Shakespeare's plays, as repeatedly demonstrated in allusions and parodied lines, suggests that the twins from the comedies and the conniving hunchbacked

Gloucester of *Richard III*, have somehow been welded into the highly original character of Young Wou'dbe.[6] Although *The Comedy of Errors* and *Twelfth Night* were not in the repertory, Shakespeare's *Richard III* had been adapted by Colley Cibber for Drury Lane, and opened in late December 1699 or January 1700, about a month after the *première* of *The Constant Couple*. Cibber, who played Richard in the adaptation, was the original Young Wou'dbe as well.

Farquhar himself, in the preface, attributed to Mr Longueville the idea of the twins on which the plot was formed as well as some of the dialogue of Teague and Subtleman. The identity of Longueville has eluded scholars. Tom Brown claimed that 'the two Authors had great Contention for the Infamy of writing it: And the *Gallic*, and *Hibernian* Wits are grown irreconcileable Enemies about the Matter.'[7] Since Brown knew Farquhar at this period, one could assume that Longueville probably was a Frenchman. The *Biographia Britannica*, however, identifies him as an Irish fencing master who laboured on a comedy without success. Stonehill, following the *DNB*, identifies him as William Longueville (1639–1721), a lawyer from Buckinghamshire who lived in Covent Garden. A Peter Longueville was apparently the author of *The Hermit*, prose fiction first published in 1727. Henry V. Longueville was made a peer in 1700. Farquhar may refer to a Frenchman, however, when he speaks of 'Foreign Assistance', or he may merely mean outside help.

Farquhar also plants a tantalizing suggestion that Richmore was modelled on an individual. He mentions that 'Some People are apt to say' that the characterization points at a specific person although he himself sees 'nothing but what is very general in his Character, except his Marrying his own Mistress'. If Farquhar intended a direct satire, no one has identified the target.

Although one can perceive echoes from earlier works, *The Twin-Rivals* is, as Stonehill claims, highly original. The twin brothers, one good and one seemingly disfigured by his own evil, were certainly unique, albeit Farquhar attributes the idea to Longueville. The cunning bawd-midwife as a menacing counterpart to the bumbling young valet as manipulator of the action was a highly unusual and successful character. The tense plots of theft and rape, foreshadowed in *The Funeral*, were unusual comic fare. Having suffered cruel accusations of plagiarism from the early success of *The Constant Couple* through the run of *The Inconstant*, Farquhar experimented now with a radically new kind of comedy.

STAGE HISTORY

The Twin-Rivals met with resistance even before opening night. Farquhar reports in the preface that 'There was an *Odium* cast upon this Play before it appear'd, by some Persons who thought it their Interest to have it suppress'd.' Although Farquhar claims to have written the play in response to Collier's strictures, condemnations of immorality, centring perhaps on the creation of the bawd-midwife, were hurled at the play in rehearsal. Farquhar complains, with unusual bitterness, that English audiences 'take all Innovations for Grievances; and, let a Project be never so well laid for their Advantage, yet the Undertaker is very likely to suffer by't'.

The play was mounted without the kind of ornamentation accorded some of Farquhar's earlier works. Motteux, who had collaborated in *The Stage-Coach* and written the prologue for *The Inconstant*, contributed a prologue which exploits a martial metaphor to describe the siege the critics make on plays as well as the author's attempt to 'hold the fort' for three or, better yet, six days. The critical skirmishes which preceded the opening may well have precipitated the prologue although the embattled theatre of the period produced many prologues complaining of the critics' attacks. The epilogue, apparently written by Farquhar himself, referred to the prologue, an indication that it was written later. William Croft or Crofts, who had provided the overture and act tunes for *The Funeral*, was commissioned to provide act music, including an overture, allemande, trumpet air, two marches, hornpipe, air, Scotch air, and farewell.[8] No songs, however, were written for *The Twin-Rivals* although all Farquhar's previous plays except *Sir Harry Wildair* had included singing within the acts.[9] Nor were the sets and costumes extraordinary; all were probably drawn out of the common stock.

The cast drew upon actors completely familiar with

Farquhar's plays. Wilks, who had played all of Farquhar's heroes at Drury Lane since his triumph as Sir Harry Wildair, took the role of Elder Wou'dbe. Wilks traditionally played the airy, debonair, devil-may-care character, a type-casting that accounts for his playing Campley rather than the hero Lord Hardy in *The Funeral*. In *The Twin-Rivals*, however, he plays a far more serious-minded hero, who speaks portentous lines, such as 'No, perfidious Man; all Kindred and Relation I disown; the poor Attempts upon my Fortune I cou'd pardon, but thy base Designs upon my Love I never can forgive.' Jane Rogers played opposite him, as she had done numerous times before, including the role of Angelica in the two Sir Harry plays, Oriana in *The Inconstant* and Lady Harriot recently in *The Funeral*; she had also played Lucinda in *Love and a Bottle*. Teague was played by William Bowen, a master of the Irish comic roles, who may have played Macahone in the first London production of *The Stage-Coach*[10] as he did in later years and who played Teague in *The Committee* for his own benefit on 6 March 1701. Cibber took the role of Young Wou'dbe, Mills played Trueman, and Pinkethman portrayed Subtleman. The controversial role of Midnight was played by William Bullock, a comedian noted for his skirt roles, who had played Kate Matchlock in *The Funeral* as well as comic roles in Farquhar's plays, including Mockmode in *Love and a Bottle*, Clincher Junior in *The Constant Couple*, and Duretete in *The Inconstant*. Jane Rogers played Constance, and Mrs Hook took Aurelia. It is striking that Anne Oldfield, discovered by Farquhar according to theatrical tradition, played in none of his plays until *The Recruiting Officer*, although she would have been a likely choice for Aurelia, a role she played in the revival twenty-three years later.

The *première* on 14 December 1702 was disrupted when 'a Rencounter happen'd on the Stage of the Play-House in Drury-Lane, between Mr. Fielding and Mr. Goodyar, in which the former was Wounded', an incident followed the next night by a duel near the other theatre in which a man was killed.[11] Whether the duel affected attendance or not, the first run disappointed Farquhar. Although some early biographers termed the run a 'very good Success',[12] which ran thirteen nights according to Wilkes,[13] Farquhar commented on the thinness of the galleries. Advertisements in the *Daily Courant* were still fairly irregular at this point, and only one was inserted for the new play. The next Drury Lane advertisement ran eight days later; it is possible that *The Twin-Rivals* continued for three nights or even six, but no one, including its author, considered it a 'very good Success'.

The bitterness of Farquhar's preface to the printed play conveys his disappointment at the failure. Not since *The Constant Couple* had the bright young Irishman hit the taste of the audiences, if one excludes the negligible anonymous farce *The Stage-Coach*. Both *Sir Harry Wildair* and *The Inconstant* had received more condemnation than praise. Carped at repeatedly for plagiarism of one kind or another, Farquhar was attacked for immorality when he created what seemed a rigorously moral and sharply original piece, in which he attempted to counter 'The Success and Countenance that Debauchery has met with in Plays'. London audiences were not ready for Farquhar's comedy, which in many ways prefigured trends of the future: the use of villains discovered in the end and punished, virtuous maidens in danger of violently losing their chastity, serious heroes in tense difficulties, great dangers that evoke 'generous Pity of a painted Woe', before concluding with 'a Joy too exquisite for Laughter'.[14]

The play consequently disappeared from the London stage for fourteen years.[15] The first revival occurred at Lincoln's Inn Fields in 1716–17, with Elrington as Elder Wou'dbe, Bullock Jr. as Young Wou'dbe, and Mrs Rogers still playing Constance. From 1716 to 1779 *The Twin-Rivals* ran a total of 117 times.[16] In the years 1716–26 it ran twenty-eight times, concentrated into six seasons; the longest run occurred at Lincoln's Inn Fields in 1716–17 (eleven performances) and the second longest at Drury Lane in 1725–6 (seven performances). After December 1726 it was not performed in London again until summer of 1735, but after that it played every season for thirteen years for a total of fifty-five performances, including ten performances in 1735–6 and eight in 1738–9. During the next eleven seasons, 1748–59, the comedy ran at least once every season except 1755–6, for a total of twenty-five performances. A decade passed before the comedy reopened, to play four times in 1769–70 and two in

1770–1; it disappeared for eight seasons and then played three last times in 1778–80. The comedy was performed a total of twenty times at Lincoln's Inn Fields in the four seasons from 1716 to 1720; forty-one times at Drury Lane between 1725 and 1746, twice more in 1758, and once in 1771; six times at the Haymarket in 1735–7; once at James Street in 1742; five times at Covent Garden, starting in 1739.

When Lincoln's Inn Fields revived the old play in 1716, Husband and Mrs Rogers took their original roles as Richmore and Constance, and Bullock played the Alderman. But the prompt-book was a purchased copy of the printed play, and as a result the role of Midnight, played by Pack, was labelled 'Mandrake', as printed in the quarto, a name that continued to be used while the play ran at Lincoln's Inn Fields. But when Drury Lane reran the comedy in 1725, the company must have turned to the original prompt-book, for the character was called Mrs Midnight regularly at Drury Lane. The Haymarket picked up the same Midnight and even added a 'Midwife's Maid' played on 14 January 1736 by a Mrs Westley in her first stage appearance. The confusion caused by the variation in the name is perhaps best illustrated by the advertisements at Covent Garden, which first advertised 'Mrs Mandrake' on 12 April 1739 and then switched to 'Mother Midnight' on 5 May 1740. From then on the character was regularly called 'Midnight' on stage and in advertisements.

The role of Midnight-Mandrake was traditionally played by a man, first Bullock, then Pack, Harper, Topham, Stoppelaer, Turbett, and Paget until 1747. Eventually, however, some women tried it; Mrs Marshall at Drury Lane in 1739 was the first female Midnight, followed by Mrs Bridges, Mrs Copin, Miss Macklin, Mrs Bambridge, and Mrs Pitt. Teague was another very popular role, played by many comedians, including Bowen, Knapp, Miller, Jones, Oates, Macklin, Barrington (fresh from Smock Alley in Dublin), James, Yates, Lewis Hallam, Theophilus Cibber, Morris, Saunders (also from Smock Alley), Moody, and Egan. By 1752 Barrington had added to the role a song in character, and when the play returned to Drury Lane in 1771 Moody was given songs.

The Twin-Rivals also played at Smock Alley; Sheldon lists

thirteen performances in 1747–58.[17] Some of the same performers acted in both London and Dublin, for example, Barrington as Teague and Miss Copin as Midnight. Clark also records three performances in Belfast, one in Kilkenny, and two in Cork in 1753–81.[18] No one seemed to 'own' the roles of *The Twin-Rivals* as, for example, Wilks long owned Sir Harry; casting changes occurred frequently. Furthermore, adornments were constantly added, not only between the scenes but even within the scenes, with the introduction of new songs and new characters. It was a vehicle for introducing new actors, sometimes professional, occasionally amateur. It was frequently chosen for benefits, and five performances were given by royal command, in 1725, 1737, twice in 1739, and 1755. All in all, *The Twin-Rivals* was a dependable staple of eighteenth-century repertory theatre, retooled regularly for modernity and sparkle, but also comfortably well tried and reliable.

REPUTATION AND INFLUENCE

Perhaps lack of success brought Farquhar surcease from the steady barrage of condemnation by critics of *The Constant Couple*. Whatever the reason, *The Twin-Rivals* captured little attention from the prologuists and essayists who maligned Farquhar's earlier work. Later critics have been generally favourable, if not very interested. In general, the play has been praised for its regularity,[19] strength and liveliness,[20] artistry,[21] and originality.[22] Critics have wondered at its early lack of popularity; blame has been assigned to its morality and poetic justice. Farquhar did not, certainly, at least in his own day, enhance his reputation by his attempt to answer Collier's demands. He may even have earned, through his portrayal of the evil hunchback, Pope's ire, which led him to condemn the playwright's pert, low dialogue. In the twentieth century, however, the play has been addressed seriously by a few critics, including James and Rothstein.

Whether the play influenced later works is a matter of some complexity. Like *The Funeral*, *The Twin-Rivals* was an experiment in a new form for a new era, the seemly age of Queen Anne. These and many other comedies of the period turned to serious problems, in these two cases the lawful inheritance of an estate but in others marriage, filial obligations, and other forms of domestic responsibility. Farquhar, like Steele, experimented with deeply serious, probing examinations of the social mores of London before retreating to lighter approaches to the same subject-matter, Farquhar with *The Twin-Rivals* followed by *The Recruiting Officer*, Steele with *The Funeral* and *The Lying Lover* followed by *The Tender Husband*. Their work affected each other as well as other playwrights of the period.

As *The Funeral* may have suggested themes and treatments for *The Twin-Rivals*, so Farquhar's play seems to have foreshadowed *The Lying Lover*. Both authors spoke in the preface of writing a play to answer the accusations of Collier. Farquhar said he 'endeavour'd to show, that an *English* Comedy may Answer the strictness of Poetical Justice', and Steele said he 'thought therefore it would be an honest Ambition to attempt a Comedy, which might be no improper Entertainment in a Christian Commonwealth'. Farquhar said the most serious objection against his play 'is the Importance of the Subject, which necessarily leads into Sentiments too grave for Diversion, and supposes Vices too great for Comedy to Punish'; Steele said that the anguish and sorrow depicted 'are, perhaps, an Injury to the Rules of Comedy; but I am sure they are a Justice to those of Morality'. Both authors agree that these matters are appropriate to the theatre. If the characters are too low for the heroic, Farquhar explains, they must drop into comedy.

The Twin-Rivals and *The Lying Lover* include prison scenes, although with a significant difference: Elder Wou'dbe has been cheated out of his inheritance and thus goes to debtor's prison whereas Young Bookwit ends in jail after a riotous duel. (Goldsmith's Honeywood also goes to debtor's prison in *The Good-Natur'd Man* of 1768.) But the differences in structure, plot, themes, and characterizations are far more striking than the similarities.

Addison's *Cato* in 1713 echoes one scene in *The Twin-Rivals*: Juba observes unnoticed as Marcia with her friend Lucia mourns his supposed death just as Elder Wou'dbe watches Constance and Aurelia lament his own death. Both Juba and Elder Wou'dbe were rendered by Wilks, but Mrs Rogers had been replaced by Mrs Oldfield in Addison's tragedy. Constance wails, 'I am become so fond of Grief, that I would fly where I might enjoy it all, and have no Interruption in my darling Sorrow', and Marcia similarly laments, 'I will indulge my sorrows, and give way | To all the pangs and fury of despair.' The tender emotions aroused by the misplaced grief are heightened to admissions of love by the discovery that the mourned one lives.

The rape prevented in the nick of time is a motif not only foreshadowed in *The Funeral* but also increasingly used in comedies as the century progressed. The titillation of peril, in fact, focusing on duels and attempted rapes, provided the dramatic excitement in comedies that were no longer very funny. The development of melodramatic comedy did not immediately follow Farquhar's exposure of vice in *The Twin-Rivals*; yet there are chronological correlations to be made between the rising stage popularity of his play and the growing number of melodramatic comedies full of the threat of bodily harm.

THE TEXT

On 22 December 1702, eight days after the *première* performance, Lintott paid Farquhar £15 for publication rights.[23] On Tuesday, 29 December, *The Twin-Rivals* was published, at a price of 1*s*. 6*d*.[24] 'Mr Croft's Aires in the Comedy calld the twinn Rivalls', in four parts, had been published by John Walsh and John Hare for 1*s*. 6*d*. no more than three days after the opening, by 17 December.[25]

The quarto has the collational formula A^2 a^4 $B-I^4$ K^2. The running-title, recto and verso, is *The Twin-Rivals*. The composition and printing are ordinary. Two compositors worked on the text, one setting B–E, and a second F–K. The compositor of B–E used the spellings 'Clearaccount' and 'Wou'dbe' regularly; the compositor of F–K preferred 'Clear-Account' and 'Woudbee' The compositor of B–D usually set the scene description at the beginning of an act or scene on a line separate from the listing of characters on stage; the second compositor did not. The first usually began stage directions with capital letters; the second often used lower-case letters.

The second compositor reduced the type size in K to save pages, changing the number of lines per page from approximately 38 or 39 to 44 or 45. As a result the two-leaf A gathering could be imposed in the same forme. There is no clearcut compositorial evidence for the prelims; the spellings 'Wou'dbee' and 'Clear-Account' appear in the Dramatis Personae. The printing seems entirely ordinary; a few pieces of type were pulled from the forme during the course of printing, but that was not unusual.

The relative cleanness of the composition suggests a fairly clear copy-text. An abbreviation for 'Midnight' must have caused the consistent speech prefix 'Mandrake'. One peculiarity in composition is that III. ii. I leaves a blank rather than inserting a date in the heading of a letter: '*Monday the*   1702'. The manuscript must have omitted the date because the opening had not been scheduled.

Lintott was by this time advertising his dramatic texts rather intensively, both in the newspapers and in his own published works. The title-page of *The Twin-Rivals* bore advertisements for *Love and Business* at 2*s.* and *The Inconstant* at 1*s.* 6*d.* Lintott also advertised frequently in the *Daily Courant* and other newspapers, featuring *The Twin-Rivals* more than ten times in a month and about fifty by the end of 1704.

The present edition uses Q as copy-text but introduces significant substantive revisions in the 1728 edition although ignoring indifferent readings. Editions of the plays, particularly those issued by Lintott and Feales, in the period extending approximately from 1728 to 1736, seem to have been corrected according to the prompt-book at Drury Lane although they are not identified on the title-page as theatrical texts.[26] *The Beaux Stratagem* of 1728, for example, contains revisions marked with a note explaining that the changes were made on stage during the first run, a claim made plausible by the fact that the player whose part was removed had left the company at least by the next season. The 1735 version of *The Stage-Coach* was entirely different from earlier editions; it probably derived from Drury Lane, although the play had originally run at Lincoln's Inn Fields (see pp. 337–9 above). Similarly, revisions in the 1728 edition of *The Twin-Rivals* seem to have promptbook authority. Although the 1728 edition did not derive from a later edition than Q, the copy-text must have been marked with revisions from the playhouse. As a result, indifferent substantive readings, most likely attributable to compositors, whether those reflecting intermediate texts or those that accrued in 1728, have not been considered authoritative, but substantive readings that could only have been inserted into an edition used as copy-text have been incorporated into the present text.

The most notable revision is the use of 'Midnight' for 'Mandrake' throughout the play; a number of bits of evidence suggest that the character was called 'Midnight' on stage at Drury Lane even during the first run. For example, in a Folger copy of the first edition, shelf-marked Prompt T33, containing emendations in two eighteenth-century hands, 'Mandrake' is consistently emended to 'Midnight' except for one emendation to 'Mother' in Richmore's line, 'Dost thou know her, my dear, *Mandrake*?' (I. ii. 50). Although there is no possible way to ascertain whether the holograph is Farquhar's as the Folger cataloguer speculated, the contemporaneity of the hand suggests a close relationship to the original production.

Certainly 'Midnight' is a more appropriate name for the character than 'Mandrake'. The term 'mandrake' is used allusively, according to the *OED*, as a term of abuse, a narcotic, or a noisome growth; the examples tie the word to men. 'Mother-Midnight', however, according to contemporary cant dictionaries, meant a 'Midwife (often a Bawd)'.[27] The tag-name, then, is entirely appropriate to the character.

Following the 1728 London edition, authoritative texts of the *Works* read 'Midnight', and, as has been pointed out earlier, companies returned to the original character's name after Drury Lane revived the play in 1725. But critics and editors until now have used the wording of Q, that is, 'Mandrake', in discussing the play. Since the weight of evidence suggests that Q used 'Mandrake' in error, the character is consistently called 'Midnight' in this edition.

Another revision in 1728 adds credence to the idea that the text was corrected according to the original promptbook. In the blank in III. ii. 1 the date of '14*th of* December' was inserted after '*Monday the*' and before '1702'. That date had not only been a Monday but had been the opening night for

The Twin-Rivals. Although there is no reason to suspect anyone in 1728 would have been aware of either fact, the reproduction of the date in the promptbook would not be at all surprising. One other notable if less dramatic example of revisions in 1728 is the substitution of 'one for my Purpose' for 'my Countryman' in Subtleman's line, 'There's a Fellow that has Hunger and the Gallows pictur'd in his Face, and looks like my Countryman' (III. ii. 84–6).

I have incorporated revisions from an edition that appeared twenty-one years after Farquhar's death with all due trepidation. Yet the evidence for promptbook corrections dating to the original production is so strong that I have gone against all my instincts as a textual scholar to introduce revisions that make this text reflect the first staged production as opposed to the first printed version.

I have collated the following editions: Q, Bodleian, British Library, Folger (three copies), Library of Congress (compared with copies in the Huntington, Clark, and University of Texas collections); *Comedies* 1708, Clark; 1711, Library of Congress; 1714, Folger; 1718, Folger (two copies); 1721, Bodleian; 1728, Library of Congress; 1736, Folger, copy in my collection. I have also examined copies of all other editions including one with no date 'PRINTED FOR THE COMPANY', Bodleian; Dublin 1726, Folger; 1739, 'Printed for the Booksellers in Town and Country', British Library; and later editions.

NOTES

1. *The Funeral*, II. i. 1–4, in *The Plays of Richard Steele*, ed. Shirley Strum Kenny (Oxford, 1971), p. 38.
2. Stonehill, i. 281.
3. Stonehill, i. 281, calls him an 'embryo Teague'; Kavanagh, p. 211, says Farquhar 'may have got some hint from Howard'. James, pp. 200–1, says that Farquhar 'of course' borrowed Teague from *The Committee* but then shows how widely the characters differ.
4. Stonehill, i. 281.
5. James, pp. 94–8.
6. The possible relationship to Richard is mentioned by Rothstein, p. 63.
7. 'A Criticism On Several Modern Plays, in a Letter to Mr. Dennis', in Brown, iv. 237.
8. Price, pp. 228–9.
9. The poem of Elder Wou'dbe in prison, of IV. iii. 1–8, was printed in *Songs of the Dramatists*. However, no music has been found to suggest the lines were sung.
10. See p. 324 above.
11. *Daily Courant*, 17 Dec. 1702.

12. Jacobs, p. 99.

13. Wilkes, i, p. viii.

14. Epilogue, *The Lying Lover*, Preface to *The Conscious Lovers*, in Steele, pp. 189, 299.

15. It is notable that Steele's next play, *The Lying Lover*, a year later, which also claimed to answer Collier's complaints and also included a prison scene, disappeared until 1746 when it played four nights and expired for ever. See Steele, p. 105.

16. *London Stage, passim.*

17. Sheldon, pp. 470–1.

18. Clark, *1720–1800*, p. 308.

19. *Biographia Dramatica*, i. 232; Wilkes, p. 10.

20. Archer, p. 10.

21. Winter, Preface to Daly's edition of *The Inconstant*, 1889.

22. Hume, pp. 464–5; Kavanaugh, p. 218; Rothstein, p. 70. A contemporary critic, however, complained:

> His fame he built on mighty D'avenant's wit,
> And lately own'd a play, that he ne'er writ:

and a marginal note identifies *The Twin-Rivals* (*Religio Poetae: or A Satire on the Poets* [London, 1703]).

23. Nichols, viii. 296.

24. Advertisements promising publication appeared in the *Daily Courant* on 18 Dec. and 26 Dec., and on 29 Dec. the advertisement in the *Daily Courant* read 'This day is publish'd . . .', as did the one in the *Post Boy* for 29–31 Dec.

25. Advertisement, *Post Man*, 15–17 Dec. 1702.

26. See Shirley Strum Kenny, 'The Printing of Plays', pp. 326–7.

27. *A New Canting Dictionary* (London, 1725). A similar definition occurs in *A New Dictionary of the Terms Ancient and Modern of the Canting Crew* (London, 1690).

The rescue of Aurelia. Frontispiece, *The Twin-Rivals*, *The Comedies of George Farquhar*, printed for Lintott, [1711]. Act V, Scene iii.

THE
TWIN-RIVALS.
A
COMEDY.

Sic vos non vobis.

ABBREVIATIONS USED IN THE NOTES

Q1   First edition. London: Lintott, 1703.
O1   *Comedies*. First edition. London: Knapton, Smith, Strahan, and Lintott [1708].
O2   *Comedies*. Second edition. London: Knapton, Smith, Strahan, and Lintott [1711].
1728   London: Lintott, 1728. In *Works*, Sixth edition, London: J. and J. Knapton, Lintott, Strahan, and Clark, 1728.

THE
DEDICATION:
TO
HENRY BRET Esq;

 The Commons of *England* have a Right of Petitioning, and
since by your Place in the Senate you are oblig'd to Hear and
Redress the Subject, I presume upon the Priviledge of the
People, to give you the following Trouble.

 As Prologues introduce Plays on the Stage, so Dedications
usher them into the great Theatre of the World; and as we
choose some Stanch Actor to Address the *Audience*, so we pitch
upon some Gentleman of Undisputed Ingenuity to Recommend us to the *Reader*. Books, like Metals, require to be
Stampt with some valuable Effigies before they become 10
Popular and Current.

 To Escape the Cricks I resolv'd to take Sanctuary with
one of the best, One who differs from the Fraternity in this,
That his good Nature is ever Predominant; Can discover an
Author's smallest Fault, and Pardon the greatest.

 Your Generous Approbation, *Sir*, Has done this Play
Service, but has Injur'd the Author; For it has made him
insufferably Vain, and he thinks himself Authoriz'd to stand
up for the Merit of his Performance, when so great a Master of
Wit has Declar'd in its Favour. 20

 The Muses are the most Coquetish of their Sex, Fond of
being Admir'd, and always putting on their best Ayrs to the
finest Gentleman: But alas, *Sir*! Their Addresses are Stale, and
their fine Things but Repetition; for there is nothing new in
Wit, but what is found in your own Conversation.

 Cou'd I Write by the help of Study, as you Talk without it,
I wou'd venture to say something in the usual Strain of
Dedication; But as you have too much Wit to suffer it, and I

17 has] O1; nas

too little to undertake it, I hope the World will Excuse my
30 Deficiency, and you will Pardon the Presumption of,

S I R,

Your most Oblig'd,
and most humble Servant,
GEORGE FARQUHAR.

Decemb. 23.
1702.

THE
PREFACE.

The Success and Countenance that Debauchery has met
with in Plays, was the most Severe and Reasonable Charge
against their Authors in Mr. *Collier's short View*; and indeed
this Gentleman had done the *Drama* considerable Service, had
he Arraign'd the Stage only to Punish it's Misdemeanours,
and not to take away it's Life; but there is an Advantage to be
made sometimes of the Advice of an Enemy, and the only way
to disappoint his Designs, is to improve upon his invective,
and to make the Stage flourish by vertue of that Satyr, by
which he thought to suppress it.   10

I have therefore in this Piece, endeavour'd to show, that an
English Comedy may Answer the strictness of Poetical Justice,
but indeed, the greater share of the *English* Audience; I mean,
that Part which is no farther read than in Plays of their own
Language, have imbib'd other Principles, and stand up as
vigorously for the old Poetick Licence, as they do for the
Liberty of the Subject. They take all Innovations for
Grievances; and, let a Project be never so well laid for their
Advantage, yet the Undertaker is very likely to suffer by't. A
Play without a Beau, Cully, Cuckold, or Coquet, is as Poor an   20
Entertainment to some Pallats, as their *Sundays* Dinner wou'd
be without Beef and Pudding. And this I take to be one
Reason that the Galleries were so thin during the Run of this
Play. I thought indeed to have sooth'd the Splenetick Zeal of
the City, by making a Gentleman a Knave, and Punishing
their great Grievance—A *Whoremaster*; but a certain Virtuoso of
that Fraternity has told me since, that the Citizens were never
more disappointed in any Entertainment, for (said he)
however Pious we may appear to be at home, yet we never go
to that end of the Town, but with an intention to be Lewd.   30

There was an *Odium* cast upon this Play before it appear'd,
by some Persons who thought it their Interest to have it
suppress'd. The Ladies were frighted from seeing it by
formidable Stories of a Midwife, and were told no doubt, that

they must expect no less than a *Labour* upon the Stage; but I hope the examining into that Aspersion will be enough to wipe it off, since the Character of the Midwife is only so far Touch'd, as is necessary for carrying on the Plot, she being principally Decipher'd in her Procuring Capacity; and I dare
40 not affront the Ladies so far, as to imagine they cou'd be offended at the exposing of a Baud.

Some Criticks Complain, that the Design is defective for want of *Clelia*'s Appearance in the Scene; but I had rather they should find this Fault, than I forfeit my Regard to the Fair, by showing a Lady of Figure under a Misfortune; for which Reason I made her only Nominal, and chose to expose the Person that Injur'd her; and if the Ladies don't agree that I have done her Justice in the End, I'm very sorry for't.

Some People are apt to say, That the Character of *Richmore*
50 points at a particular Person; tho' I must confess, I see nothing but what is very general in his Character, except his Marrying his own Mistress; which, by the way, he never did, for he was no sooner off the Stage, but he chang'd his Mind, and the poor Lady is still in *Statu Quo*, but upon the whole Matter, 'tis Appliction only makes the Asse; And Characters in Plays, are like *Long-Lane* Cloaths, not hung out for the Use of any particular People, but to be bought by only those they happen to fit.

The most material Objection against this Play, is the
60 Importance of the Subject, which necessarily leads into Sentiments too grave for Diversion, and supposes Vices too great for Comedy to Punish. 'Tis said, I must own, that the business of Comedy is chiefly to Ridicule Folly; and that the Punishment of Vice falls rather into the Province of Tragedy; but if there be a middle sort of Wickedness, too high for the *Sock*, and too low for the *Buskin*, is there any Reason that it shou'd go unpunish'd? What are more Obnoxious to Humane Society, than the Villanies expos'd in this Play; the Frauds, Plots and Contrivances upon the Fortunes of Men,
70 and the Vertue of Women, but the Persons are too mean for the Heroick, Then what must be do with them? Why, They must of necessity drop into Comedy: For it is unreasonable to

57 those] O1; that

imagine that the Law-givers in Poetry wou'd tye themselves up from Executing that Justice which is the Foundation of their Constitution; or to say, That exposing Vice is the business of the *Drama*, and yet make Rules to screen it from Persecution.

Some have ask'd the Question, Why the Elder *Wou'd-be*, in the Fourth Act, should Counterfeit Madness in his Confinement, don't mistake, there was no such thing in his Head; and the Judicious cou'd easily perceive, that it was only a start of Humour put on to divert his Melancholy; and when Gayety is strain'd to cover Misfortune, it may very Naturally be overdone, and rise to a semblance of Madness, sufficient to impose on the Constable, and perhaps on some of the Audience; who taking every thing at sight, impute that as a Fault, which I am bold to stand up for, as one of the most Masterly stroaks of the whole Piece.

This I think sufficient to obviate what Objecteons I have heard made; but there was no great occasion for making this Defence, having had the Opinion of some of the greatest Persons in *England*, both for Quality and Parts, that the Play has Merit enough to hide more Faults than have been found; and I think their Approbation sufficient to excuse some Pride that may be incident to the Author upon this Performance.

I must own my self oblig'd to Mr. *Longueville* for some Lines in the part of *Teague*, and something of the Lawyer; but above all, for his hint of the Twins, upon which I form'd my Plot: But having paid him all due Satisfaction and Acknowledgment, I must do my self the Justice to believe, that few of our Modern Writers have been less beholden to Foreign Assistance in their Plays, than I have been in the following Scenes.

PROLOGUE.

By Mr. *Motteux.*

And Spoken by Mr. *Wilks.*

An Alarm Sounded.

With Drums and Trumpets in this Warring Age,
A Martial prologue shou'd Alarm the Stage.
New Plays—E're Acted; A full Audience near,
Seem Towns invested, when a Siege they fear.
Prologues are like a Forlorn-Hope sent out
Before the Play, to Skirmish, and to Scout:
Our Dreadful Foes the Criticks, when they spy
They Cock, they Charge, they Fire—Then back they fly.
The Siege is laid—There Gallant Chiefs abound,   ⎫
10 *Here—Foes Intrench'd, there—Glittering Troops around,*   ⎬
And the loud Batt'ries Roar—From yonder rising ground.   ⎭
In the First Act, brisk Sallies, *(miss or hit)*   ⎫
With Vollies of Small Shot, or Snip-Snap Wit   ⎬
Attack, and Gaul the Trenches of the Pit.   ⎭
The next—The Fire continues, but at length
Grows less, and slackens like a Bridegroom's strength.
The Third; Feints, Mines, and Countermines abound,   ⎫
Your Critick-Engineer's Safe under ground   ⎬
Blow up our Works, and all our Art Confound.   ⎭
20 *The Fourth—Brings on most Action, and 'tis sharp,*   ⎫
Fresh Foes crowd on, at your Remisness carp,   ⎬
And desp'rate, tho' unskill'd, insult our Counterscarp. ⎭
Then comes the last; the Gen'ral Storm is near,
The Poet-Governor now quakes for fear;
Runs wildly up and down, forgets to huff,
And wou'd give all h'as plunder'd—to get off.
*So—*Don *and* Monsieur—Bluff *before the Siege,*
Were quickly tam'd—At Venlo, *and at* Liege:
'Twas Viva Spagnia! Vive France! *Before*
30 *Now,* Quartier! Monsieur! Quartier! Ah! Senor!
But what your Resolution can withstand?

You Master all, and Awe the Sea and Land.
In War—Your Valour, makes the strong submit;
Your Judgment humbles all Attempts in Wit.
What Play, what Fort, what Beauty can endure
All fierce Assaults, and always be secure!
Then grant 'em gen'rous Terms who dare to write,
Since now—That seems as desp'rate as to fight:
If we must yield—Yet e're the day be fixt,
Let us hold out the Third—And, if we may, the Sixth.   40

Dramatis Personæ

MEN.

Elder Wou'dbe,	Mr. *Wilks.*
Young Wou'dbe,	Mr. *Cibber.*
Richmore,	Mr. *Husband.*
Trueman,	Mr. *Mills.*
Subtleman,	Mr. *Pinkethman.*
Balderdash,	
and	
Alderman,	Mr. *Johnson.*
Clearaccount, a *Steward,*	Mr. *Fairbank.*
10 *Fairbank,* a Goldsmith,	Mr. *Minns.*
Teague,	Mr. *Bowen.*

WOMEN.

Constance,	Mrs. *Rogers.*
Aurelia,	Mrs. *Hook.*
Midnight,	Mr. *Bullock.*
Steward's *Wife,*	Mrs. *Moor.*

Constable, Watch, [*Valet, Comick,*
Frisure, Mob, Servants] &c.

SCENE, *LONDON.*

14 *Midnight*] 1728; Mandrake. The character's name is changed throughout the play. See Introduction, p. 490 above.

ACT I. SCENE I.

Lodgings.

The Curtain drawn up, discovers Young Wou'dbe
a Dressing, and his Valet *Buckling his Shooes.*

Young Wou'dbe. Here is such a Plague every Morning with
Buckling Shooes, Gartering, Combing, and Powdering, Pshaw!
Cease thy Impertinence, I'll dress no more to day—Were I an
honest Brute, that rises from his Litter, shakes himself, and so
is Drest, I could bear it?
                    Enter Richmore.

Richmore. No further yet, *Wou'dbe*? 'tis almost One.

Young Wou'dbe. Then blame the Clockmakers, they made it
so; the Sun has neither Fore nor Afternoon—Prithee, What
have we to do with Time? Can't we let it alone as Nature
made it? Can't a Man Eat when he's Hungry, go to Bed when   10
he's Sleepy, Rise when he Wakes, Dress when he pleases,
without the Confinement of Hours to enslave him?

Richmore. Pardon me, Sir, I understand your Stoicism—You
have lost your Money last Night.

Young Wou'dbe. No, no, Fortune took care of me there—I
had none to lose.

Richmore. 'Tis that gives you the Spleen.

Young Wou'dbe. Yes, I have got the Spleen; and something
else.—Hearkee—(*Whispers.*)

Richmore. How!—   20

Young Wou'dbe. Positively. The Lady's kind Reception was
the most severe usage I ever met with—Shan't I break her
Windows—*Richmore*?

Richmore. A mighty Revenge truly: Let me tell you, Friend,
That breaking the Windows of such Houses, are no more than
Writing over a Vintner's Door, as they do in *Holland*—*Vin te
koop*—'Tis no more than a Bush to a Tavern, a Decoy to
Trade, and to draw in Customers; but upon the whole matter,
I think, a Gentleman shou'd put up an Affront got in such
little Company; for the Pleasure, the Pain, and the Resentment,   30
are all alike scandalous.

Young Wou'dbe. Have you forgot, *Richmore*, how I found you one Morning with the *Flying Post* in your hand, hunting for Physical Advertisements?

Richmore. That was in the days of *Dad*, my Friend, in the days of dirty Linnen, Pit-Masks, Hedge-Taverns, and Beef-Stakes; but now I fly at nobler Game; the Ring, the Court, *Pawlet*'s and the *Park*: I despise all Women that I apprehend any danger from, less than the having my Throat cut; and
40 shou'd scruple to Converse even with a Lady of Fortune, unless her Virtue were loud enough to give me Pride in exposing it.—Here's a Letter I received this Morning; you may read it. (*Gives a Letter.*)

Young Wou'dbe. (*Reads.*) *If there be Solemnity in protestation, Justice in Heaven, or Fidelity on Earth, I may still depend on the Faith of my* Richmore—*Tho' I may conceal my Love, I no longer can hide the Effects on't from the World—Be careful of my Honour, remember your Vows, and fly to the Relief of the Disconsolate,* CLELIA.

The Fair, the courted, blooming *Clelia*!
50 *Richmore.* The credulous, troublesome, foolish *Clelia*. Did you ever read such a fulsome Harangue—Lard Sir, I am near my time, and want your Assistance—Do's the silly Creature imagine that any Man wou'd come near her in those Circumstances, unless it were Doctor *Chamberlain*—You may keep the Letter.

Young Wou'dbe. But why wou'd you trust it with me? you know I can't keep a Secret that has any Scandal in't.

Richmore. For that reason I communicate: I know thou art a perfect *Gazette*, and will spread the News all over the Town:
60 For you must understand, that I am now Besieging another; and I would have the Fame of my Conquests upon the Wing, that the Town may Surrender the sooner.

Young Wou'dbe. But if the report of your Cruelty goes along with that of your Valour, you'll find no Garrison of any Strength will open their Gates to you.

Richmore. No, no, Women are Cowards, and Terrour prevails upon them more than Clemency: My best pretence to my success with the Fair, is my using 'um ill; 'Tis turning their own Guns upon 'um, and I have always found it the

most successful Battery to assail one Reputation by sacrificing 70
another.

Young Wou'dbe. I cou'd Love thee for thy Mischief, did I not
Envy thee for thy success in't.

Richmore. You never attempt a Woman of Figure.

Young Wou'dbe. How can I? This confounded Hump of mine
is such a Burthen at my Back, that it presses me down here in
the Dirt and Diseases of *Covent-Garden*, the low Suburbs of
Pleasure—Curst Fortune! I am a younger Brother, and yet
cruelly depriv'd of my Birth-right of a handsome Person;
seven thousand a year in a direct Line, wou'd have straitn'd 80
my Back to some purpose—But I look, in my present
Circumstances, like a Branch of another kind, grafted only
upon the Stock which makes me grow so Crooked.

Richmore. Come, come, 'tis no Misfortune, your Father is so
as well as you.

Young Wou'dbe. Then why shou'd not I be a Lord as well as
he? had I the same Title to the Deformity I cou'd bear it.

Richmore. But how do's my Lord bear the Absence of your
Twin-Brother?

Young Wou'dbe. My Twin-Brother! Ay, 'twas his crouding 90
me that spoil'd my Shape, and his coming half an Hour before
me that ruin'd my Fortune—My Father Expell'd me his
House some two years ago, because I would have persuaded
him that my Twin-Brother was a Bastard—He gave me my
Portion, which was about Fifteen Hundred Pound, and I have
spent Two Thousand of it already. As for my Brother, he
don't care a farthing for me.

Richmore. Why so, pray?

Young Wou'dbe. A very odd reason—Because I hate him.

Richmore. How should he know that? 100

Young Wou'dbe. Because he thinks it reasonable it shou'd be
so.

Richmore. But did your Actions ever express any Malice to
him?

Young Wou'dbe. Yes: I wou'd fain have kept him Company,
but being aware of my Kindness, he went·abroad: He has
Travel'd these Five years, and I am told, is a grave sober
Fellow, and in danger of Living a great while; All my hope is,
that when he gets into his Honour and Estate, the Nobility

110 will soon kill him by Drinking him up to his Dignity—But come, *Frank*, I have but two Eye-Sores in the World, a Brother before me, and a Hump behind me, and thou art still laying 'um in my way: Let us assume an Argument of less severity—Can'st thou lend me a Brace of Hundred Pounds?

Richmore. What wou'd you do with 'um?

Young Wou'dbe. Do with 'um!—There's a question indeed—Do you think I wou'd Eat 'um?

Richmore. Yes, o 'my Troth, wou'd you, and Drink 'um together—Lookee, Mr. *Wou'dbe*, Whilst you kept well with 120 your Father, I cou'd have ventur'd to have Lent you Five Guinea's—But as the case stands, I can assure you, I have lately paid off my Sister's Fortunes, and—

Young Wou'dbe. Sir, This put off looks like an Affront; and you know I don't use to take such things.

Richmore. Sir, Your Demand is rather an Affront, when you know I don't use to give such things.

Young Wou'dbe. Sir, I'll Pawn my Honour.

Richmore. That's Mortgag'd already for more than it is worth; You had better Pawn your Sword there, 'twill bring 130 you forty Shillings.

Young Wou'dbe. 'Sdeath, Sir—(*Takes his Sword off the Table.*)

Richmore. Hold, Mr. *Wou'dbe*,—Suppose I put an end to your Misfortunes all at once?

Young Wou'dbe. How, Sir?

Richmore. Why, go to a Magistrate, and Swear you wou'd have Robb'd me of Two Hundred Pounds—Lookee, Sir, You have been often told that your Extravagance wou'd some time or other be the Ruin of you; and it will go a great way in your Indictment, to have turn'd the Pad upon your Friend.

140 *Young Wou'dbe.* This usage is the heighth of Ingratitude from you, in whose Company I have spent my Fortune.

Richmore. I'm therefore a witness, that it was very ill Spent—Why wou'd you keep Company, be at equal Expences with me that have fifty times your Estate? What was Gallantry in me, was Prodigality in you; Mine was my Health, because I cou'd pay for't; your's a Disease, because you cou'd not.

Young Wou'dbe. And is this all I must expect from our Friendship?

I. i. 111 Eye-Sores] O1 (Eye-sores); Eye-Pores

Richmore. Friendship! Sir, There can be no such thing without an Equality.   150

Young Wou'dbe. That is, there can be so such thing when there is occasion for't.

Richmore. Right Sir,—Our Friendship was over a Bottle only, and whilst you can pay your Club of Friendship, I'm that way your humble Servant, but when once you come borrowing, I'm this way—your humble Servant.

Exit.

Young Wou'dbe. Rich, big, proud, arrogant Villain! I have been twice his Second, thrice Sick of the same Love, and thrice Cur'd by the same Physick, and now he drops me for a Trifle—That an honest Fellow in his Cups shou'd be such a   160 Rogue when he's Sober—The narrow hearted Rascal has been drinking Coffee this Morning. Well! thou dear Solitary Half-Crown, adieu—Here *Jack,*

Enter Servant.

Take this; Pay for a Bottle of Wine, and bid *Balderdash* bring it himself.

Exit Servant.

How melancholly are my poor Breeches, not one Chink!—Thou art a villanous Hand, for thou hast Pickt my Pocket—This Vintner now has all the Marks of an honest Fellow, a broad Face, a copious Look, a strutting Belly, and a jolly Mien. I have brought him above Three Pound a Night for   170 these two years successively—The Rogue has Money I'm sure, if he will but lend it.

Enter [Servant *and*] Balderdash *with a Bottle and Glass.*

Oh, Mr. *Balderdash,* good morrow.

Balderdash. Noble Mr. *Wou'dbe,* I'm your most humble Servant—I have brought you a Whetting-Glass, the best *Old Hock* in *Europe;* I know 'tis your drink in a Morning.

Young Wou'dbe. I'le Pledge you, Mr. *Balderdash.*

Balderdash. Your Health, Sir. (*Drinks.*)

Young Wou'dbe. Pray Mr. *Balderdash,* tell me one thing, but first sit down, Now tell me plainly what you think of me?   180

Balderdash. Think of you, Sir! I think that you are the honestest, noblest Gentleman, that ever drank a Glass of Wine; and the best Customer that ever came into my House.

Young Wou'dbe. And you really think as you speak.

Balderdash. May this Wine be my Poison, Sir, if I don't speak from the bottom of my Heart.

Young Wou'dbe. And how much Money do you think I have spent in your House?

Balderdash. Why truly, Sir, by a moderate Computation, I
190 do believe that I have handled of your Money, the best part of Five Hundred Pounds within these two years.

Young Wou'dbe. Very well! And do you think that you lie under any Obligation for the Trade I have promoted to your Advantage?

Balderdash. Yes, Sir; And if I can serve you in any respect, pray Command me to the utmost of my Ability.

Young Wou'dbe. Well! Thanks to my Stars, there is still some honesty in Wine. Mr. *Balderdash*, I embrace you and your kindness: I am at present a little low in Cash, and must beg
200 you to lend me a Hundred Pieces.

Balderdash. Why truly Mr. *Wou'dbe*, I was afraid it would come to this, I have had it in my Head several times to caution you upon your Expences, but you were so very genteel in my House, and your Liberality became you so very well, that I was unwilling to say any thing that might check your Disposition; but truly, Sir, I can forbear no longer to tell you, that you have been a little too Extravagant.

Young Wou'dbe. But since you reap'd the benefit of my Extravagance, you will I hope consider my Necessity.

210 *Balderdash.* Consider your Necessity! I do with all my Heart, and must tell you moreover, that I will be no longer Accessary to it: I desire you, Sir, to frequent my House no more.

Young Wou'dbe. How, Sir!

Balderdash. I say, Sir, that I have an Honour for my good Lord your Father, and will not suffer his Son to run into any Unconvenience; Sir, I shall order my Drawers not to serve you with a drop of Wine—Wou'd you have me Connive at a Gentleman's Destruction?

220 *Young Wou'dbe.* But methinks, Sir, that a Person of your nice Conscience should have caution'd me before.

Balderdash. Alas! Sir, it was none of my Business; Wou'd

you have me be sawcy to a Gentleman that was my best
Customer? Lackaday, Sir, Had you Money to hold it out still,
I had been hang'd rather than be rude to you—But truly, Sir,
When a Man is ruin'd, 'tis but the Duty of a *Christian* to tell
him of it.

Young Wou'dbe. Will you lend me the Money, Sir?

Balderdash. Will you pay me this Bill, Sir?

Young Wou'dbe. Lend me the Hundred Pound, and I will 230
pay the Bill—

Balderdash. Pay me the Bill, and I will not lend the Hundred
Pound, Sir,—But pray consider with your self, now Sir,
Wou'd not you think me an errant Coxcomb, to trust a Person
with Money that has always been so extravagant under my
Eye? Whose Profuseness I have seen, I have felt, I have
handled? Have not I known you, Sir, throw away Ten Pound
of a Night upon a Covey of Pit-Partridges, and a Setting Dog?
Sir, you have made my House an ill House; my very Chairs
will bear you no longer—In short, Sir, I desire you to frequent 240
the *Crown* no more, Sir.

Young Wou'dbe. Thou Sophisticated Tun of Iniquity; Have I
fatned your Carkass, and swell'd your Bags with my vital
Blood? Have I made you my Companion to be thus saucy to
me? But now I will keep you at your due distance. (*Kicks him.*)

Servant. Wellcome Sir!

Young Wou'dbe. Well said *Jack.* (*Kicks him again.*)

Servant. Very wellcome Sir! I hope we shall have your
Company another time. Welcome Sir.

He's kick'd off.

Young Wou'dbe. Pray wait on him down Stairs, and give him 250
a wellcome at the Door too.

Exit Servant.

This is the Punishment of Hell; The very Devil that tempted
me to the Sin, now upbraids me with the Crime—I have
villainously murder'd my Fortune; and now its Ghost, in the
lank shape of Poverty haunts me: Is there no Charm to
Conjure down the Fiend?

Re-enter Servant.

Servant. Oh Sir, Here's sad News.

Young Wou'dbe. Then keep it to thy self, I have enough of
that already.

260 *Servant.* Sir, you will hear it too soon.

Young Wou'dbe. What! Is *Broad* below?

Servant. No, no, Sir; better Twenty such as he were hang'd. Sir, your Father's Dead.

Young Wou'dbe. My Father;—Good night, my Lord; Has he left me any thing?

Servant. I heard nothing of that, Sir.

Young Wou'dbe. Then I believe you heard all there was of it; let me see—My Father dead! And my Elder Brother Abroad!—If Necessity be the Mother of Invention, she was 270 never more Pregnant than with me. (*Pawses.*) Here, Sirrah, run to Mrs. *Midnight*, and bid her come hither presently.

Exit Servant.

That Woman was my Mother's Midwife when I was Born, and has been my Bawd these Ten years. I have had her Endeavours to corrupt my Brother's Mistress; and now her Assistance will be necessary to Cheat him of his Estate; for she's famous for understanding the Right-side of a Woman, and the Wrong-side of the Law.

Exit.

[ACT I. Scene ii.]

SCENE *changes to* Midnight's *House*.

Midnight *and* Maid.

Midnight. Who is there?

Maid. Madam.

Midnight. Has any Message been left for me to day?

Maid. Yes, Madam: Here has been one from my Lady *Stillborn*, that desir'd you not to be out of the way, for she expected to cry out every Minute.

Midnight. How! Every Minute!—Let me see—(*Takes out her Pocket-Book.*) *Stillborn*—Ay—She reckons with her Husband from the first of *April*; and with Sir *James*, from the first of 10 *March*—Ay, She's always a Month before her Time. (*Knocking at the Door.*) Go see who's at the Door—

Maid. Yes, Madam.

Exit Maid.

Midnight. Well! Certainly there is not a Woman in the
World so willing to oblige Mankind as my self; and really I
have been so ever since the Age of Twelve, as I can
remember—I have Deliver'd as many Women of great Bellies,
and helped as many to 'um as any Person in *England*; But my
Watching and Cares have broken me quite, I am not the same
Woman I was forty years ago.

Enter Richmore.

Oh, Mr. *Richmore*! You're a sad Man, a barbarous Man, so   20
you are—What will become of poor *Clelia*, Mr. *Richmore*? The
poor Creature is so big with her Misfortunes, that they are not
to be born. (*Weeps.*)

Richmore. You, Mrs. *Midnight*, are the fittest Person in the
World to ease her of 'um.

Midnight. And won't you Marry her, Mr. *Richmore*.

Richmore. My Conscience won't allow it; for I have Sworn
since, to Marry another.

Midnight. And will you break your Vows to *Clelia*?

Richmore. Why not, when she has broke her's to me?   30

Midnight. How's that, Sir?

Richmore. Why; She Swore a Hundred times never to grant
me the Favour, and yet you know she broke her Word.

Midnight. But she lov'd Mr. *Richmore*, and that was the
Reason she forgot her Oath.

Richmore. And I love Mr. *Richmore*, and that is the reason I
forgot mine—Why shou'd she be Angry that I follow her own
Example, by doing the very same thing from the very same
Motive?

Midnight. Well, well! Take my Word, you'll never thrive—I   40
wonder how you can have the Face to come near me, that am
the Witness of your horrid Oaths and Imprecations! Are not
you afraid that the guilty Chamber above-stairs shou'd fall
down upon your Head?—Yes, yes, I was Accessary, I was so;
But if ever you involve my Honour in such a Villany the
second time—Ah, poor *Clelia*! I lov'd her as I did my own
Daughter—You seducing Man—(*Weeps.*)

Richmore. Hey, ho, My *Aurelia*!

Midnight. Hey, ho, she's very pretty.

Richmore. Dost thou know her, my dear, *Midnight*?   50

Midnight. Hey, ho, she's very pretty—Ah, you're a sad

Man—Poor *Clelia* was handsome, but indeed, Breeding, Pukeing, and Longing, has broken her much—'Tis a hard Case, Mr. *Richmore*, for a young Lady to see a Thousand Things, and long for a Thousand Things, and yet not dare to own that she Longs for One—She had like to have Miscarried t'other day for the Pith of a Loyn of Veal—Ah, you barbarous Man—

Richmore. But my *Aurelia*! Confirm me that you know her,
60 and I'll Adore thee.

Midnight. You would fling Five Hundred Guinea's at my Head, that you knew as much of her as I do: Why, Sir, I brought her into the World; I have had her sprawling in my Lap: Ah! She was as plump as a Puffin, Sir.

Richmore. I think she has no great Portion to value her self upon; her Reputation only will keep up the Market: We must first make that Cheap, by crying it down, and then she'll part with it at an easie Rate.

Midnight. But won't you provide for poor *Clelia*?

70 *Richmore.* Provide! Why han't I taught her a Trade? Let her Set up when she will, I'le engage her Customers enough, because I can answer for the Goodness of the Ware.

Midnight. Nay, But you ought to Set her up with Credit, and take a Shop; that is, Get her a Husband—Have you no pretty Gentleman your Relation now that wants a young virtuous Lady with a hansome Fortune? No young *Templer* that has Spent his Estate in the Study of the Law, and Starves by the Practice? No Spruce Officer that wants a handsome Wife to make Court for him among the Major-Generals? Have
80 you none of these, Sir?

Richmore. Pho, pho, Madam—You have tir'd me upon that subject. Do you think a Lady that gave me so much trouble before Possession shall ever give me any after it—No, no, Had she been more Obliging to me when I was in her Power, I shou'd be more Civil to her, now she's in mine: My Assiduity before-hand was an over-Price; had she made a Merit of the matter, she shou'd have yielded sooner.

Midnight. Nay, nay, Sir; Tho' you have no regard to her Honour, yet you shall protect mine: How d'ee think I have

secur'd my Reputation so long among the People of best 90
Figure, but by keeping all Mouths stopt? Sir, I'll have no
Clamours at me—Heavens help me, I have Clamours enough
at my Door early and late in my t'other Capacity: In short,
Sir, a Husband for *Clelia*; or I Banish you my presence for
ever.

Richmore. Thou art a necessary Devil, and I can't want thee.
(*Aside.*)

Midnight. Lookee, Sir; 'Tis your own Advantage; 'tis only
making over your Estate into the Hands of a Trustee; and tho'
you don't absolutely Command the Premises, yet you may
exact enough out of 'um for Necessaries, when you will.   100

Richmore. Patience a little, Madam—I have a young Nephew
that is Captain of Horse: He Mortgag'd the last Morsel of his
Estate to me, to make up his Equipage for the last Campagne.
Perhaps you know him; he's a brisk Fellow, much about
Court, Captain *Trueman*.

Midnight. *Trueman*! Adsmylife, he's one of my Babies—I can
tell you the very Minute he was Born—precisely at three a
Clock next St. *George*'s Day, *Trueman* will be Two and Twenty,
a Stripling, the prettiest, good natur'd Child, and your
Nephew! He must be the Man, and shall be the Man; I have a 110
kindness for him.

Richmore. But we must have a Care; the Fellow wants
neither Sense nor Courage.

Midnight. Phu, phu, Never fear her part, she shan't want
Instructions, and then for her Lying-in, a little abruptly, 'tis
my Business to reconcile Matters there, a Fright or a Fall
excuses that: Lard Sir, I do these things every day.

Richmore. 'Tis pitty then to put you out of your Road; and
Clelia shall have a Husband.

Midnight. Spoke like a Man of Honour—And now I'le serve 120
you again. This *Aurelia*, you say—

Richmore. O she distracts me! Her Beauty, Family, and
Virtue, make her a noble Pleasure.

Midnight. And you have a mind for that reason to get her a
Husband?

Richmore. Yes, faith: I have another young Relation at

93 my] O1; my my

Cambridge, he's just going into Orders; and I think such a fine
Woman, with Fifteen Hundred Pound, is a better Presentation
than any Living in my Gift; and why should he like the Cure
130 the worse that an Incumbent was there before?

Midnight. Thou art a pretty Fellow—At the same Moment
you wou'd perswade me that you love a Woman to Madness,
are you contriving how to part with her.

Richmore. If I lov'd her not to Madness, I shou'd not run
into these Contradictions—Here, my Dear Mother, *Aurelia*'s
the Word—(*Offering her Money.*)

Midnight. Pardon me, Sir; (*Refusing the Money.*) Did you ever
know me Mercenary—No, no, Sir; Virtue is its own Reward.

Richmore. Nay, But Madam, I owe you for the Teeth
140 Powder you sent me.

Midnight. O, that's another matter, Sir; (*Takes the Money.*) I
hope you lik't it, Sir?

Richmore. Extreamly Madam—but it was somewhat dear of
Twenty Guineas. (*Aside.*)

Enter Servant.

Servant. Madam, Here is Mr. *Wou'dbe*'s Footman below
with a Message from his Master.

Midnight. I come to him presently: Do you know that
Wou'dbe loves *Aurelia*'s Cousin and Companion, Mrs. *Constance*
with the great Fortune, and that I sollicite for him?

150 *Richmore.* Why, She's Engag'd to his Elder Brother: Besides,
Young Wou'dbe has no Money to prosecute an Affair of such
Consequence—You can have no hopes of Success there, I'm
sure.

Midnight. Truly, I have no great hopes; But an industrious
Body you know, wou'd do any thing rather than be Idle: The
Aunt is very near her Time, and I have Access to the Family
when I please.

Richmore. Now I think on't; Prithee get the Letter from
Wou'dbe that I gave him just now; It wou'd be proper to our
160 Designs upon *Trueman*, that it shou'd not be expos'd.

Midnight. And you show'd *Clelia*'s Letter to *Wou'dbe*?

Richmore. Yes.

Midnight. Eh, you barbarous Man—Who the Devil wou'd
oblige you—What pleasure can you take in exposing the poor
Creature? Dear little Child, 'tis pity; indeed it is.

Richmore. Madam, the Messenger waits below; so I'll take
my leave.

Exit.

Midnight. Ah, you're a sad Man.

Exit.

The End of the First Act.

ACT II. [Scene i.]

SCENE *the Park.*

Constance *and* Aurelia.

Aurelia. Prithee Cousin *Constance*, be chearful; Let the Dead
Lord sleep in Peace, and look up to the Living; Take Pen, Ink,
and Paper, and write immediately to your Lover, that he is
now a Baron of *England*, and that you long to be a Baroness.

Constance. Nay, *Aurelia*, there is some regard due to the
Memory of the Father, for the Respect I bear the Son; besides,
I don't know how, I cou'd wish my young Lord were at home
in this juncture: This Brother of his—Some Mischief will
happen—I had a very ugly Dream last Night—In short, I am
Eaten up with the Spleen, my Dear.   10

Aurelia. Come, come; walk about and divert it, the Air will
do you good; think of other People's Affairs a little—When did
you see *Clelia?*

Constance. I'm glad you mention'd her; Don't you observe
her Gayety to be much more forc'd than formerly, her
Humour don't sit so easily upon her.

Aurelia. No, nor her Stays neither, I can assure you.

Constance. Did you observe how she devour'd the Pome-
granates yesterday?

Aurelia. She talks of Visiting a Relation in *Leicestershire.*   20

Constance. She fainted away in the Country-Dance to'ther
Night.

Aurelia. Richmore shun'd her in the Walk last Week.

Constance. And his Footman laugh'd.

Aurelia. She takes *Laudanum* to make her Sleep a Nights.

Constance. Ah, poor Clelia! What will she do Cousin?

Aurelia. Do! Why nothing till the Nine Months be up.

Constance. That's cruel, *Aurelia*. How can you make merry with her Misfortunes? I am positive she was no easy
30 Conquest; some singular Villany has been practis'd upon her.

Aurelia. Yes, yes, the Fellow wou'd be practising upon me too, I thank him.

Constance. Have a care, Cousin, he has a promising Person.

Aurelia. Nay, for that matter, his promising Person may as soon be broke as his promising Vows: Nature indeed has made him a Gyant, and he Wars with Heaven like the Giants of old—

Constance. Then why will you admit his Visits?

Aurelia. I never did,—But all the Servants are more his
40 than our own: He has a Golden Key to every Door in the House; besides, he makes my Uncle believe that his Intentions are honourable; and indeed he has said nothing yet to disprove it—But Cousin, Do you see who comes yonder, sliding along the Mall?

Constance. Captain *Trueman*, I protest; The Campagne has improv'd him, he makes a very clean well furnish'd figure.

Aurelia. Youthful, easie, and good Natur'd, I cou'd wish he wou'd know us.

Constance. Are you sure he's well-bred?

50 *Aurelia.* I tell you he's good Natur'd, and I take good Manners to be nothing but a natural Desire to be easie and agreeable to whatever Conversation we fall into; and a Porter with this is Mannerly in his way; and a Duke without it, has but the Breeding of a Dancing-Master.

Constance. I like him for his Affection to my young Lord.

Aurelia. And I like him for his Affection to my young Person.

Constance. How, how, Cousin? You never told me that.

Aurelia. How shou'd I? He never told it me, but I have
60 discover'd it by a great many Signs and Tokens, that are better Security for his Heart than Ten Thousand Vows and Promises.

Constance. He's *Richmore*'s Nephew.

Aurelia. Ah! Wou'd he were his Heir too—He's a pretty Fellow—But then he's a Soldier, and must share his time with his Mistress, Honour, in *Flanders*—No, no, I'm resolv'd

against a Man 'that disappears all the Summer, like a
Woodcock.

        As these last words are spoken, Trueman *enters*
           behind them, as passing over the Stage.

Trueman. That's for me, whoever spoke it. (*The Ladies turn
about.*) Aurelia! (*Surpris'd.*)   70

Constance. What, Captain, You're afraid of every thing but
the Enemy.

Trueman. I have reason, Ladies, to be most Apprehensive
where there is most Danger: The Enemy is satisfied with a Leg
or an Arm, but here I'm in hazard of loosing my Heart.

Aurelia. None in the World, Sir, no Body here Designs to
Attack it.

Trueman. But suppose it be Assaulted, and taken already,
Madam.

Aurelia. Then we'll return it without Ransom.   80

Trueman. But suppose, Madam, the Prisoner choose to stay
where it is.

Aurelia. That were to turn Deserter, and you know Captain,
what such deserve—

Trueman. The Punishment it undergoes this moment—Shot
to Death—

Constance. Nay, then, 'tis time for me to put in—Pray, Sir,
Have you heard the News of my Lord *Wou'dbe*'s Death?

Trueman. People mind not the Death of others, Madam,
that are Expiring themselves. (*To* Constance.) Do you 90
consider Madam, the Penalty of Wounding a Man in the
Park? (*To* Aurelia.)

Aurelia. Hey day! Why Captain, d'ee intend to make a *Vigo*
Business of it, and break the Boom at once? Sir, if you only
Rally, pray let my Cousin have her share; or if you wou'd be
particular, pray be more Respectful, not so much upon the
Declaration, I beseech you, Sir.

Trueman. I have been, fair Creature, a perfect Coward in
my Passion; I have had hard Strugglings with my Fear before
I durst Engage, and now perhaps behave but too desperately. 100

Aurelia. Sir, I am very sorry you have said so much; for I
must punish you for't, tho' it be contrary to my Inclination—
Come, Cousin, Wil you walk?

Constance. Servant, Sir.   *Exeunt Ladies.*

Trueman. Charming Creature!—*I must punish you for't, tho' it be contrary to my Inclination*—Hope and Despair in a Breath. But I'll think the best.

Exit.

[ACT II. Scene ii.]

SCENE *Changes to* Young Wou'dbe's *Lodgings.*

Young Wou'dbe *and* Midnight *meeting.*

Young Wou'dbe. Thou Life and Soul of Secret Dealings, Wellcome.

Midnight. My Dear Child, Bless thee—Who wou'd have imagin'd that I brought this great Rogue into the World? He makes me an old Woman I protest—But adso, my Child, I forgot; I'm sorry for the loss of your Father, sorry at my Heart, poor Man. (*Weeps.*) Mr. *Wou'dbe*, Have you got a drop of Brandy in your Closet? I an't very well to day.

Young Wou'dbe. That you shan't want; But please to sit my
10 dear Mother—Here, *Jack*, the Brandy-Bottle—Now Madam —I have occasion to use you in Dressing up a handsom Cheat for me.

Midnight. I defie any Chamber-Maid in *England* to do it better—I have drest up a Hundred and Fifty Cheats in my time.

Enter Jack *with the Brandy Bottle.*

Here, Boy, this Glass is too big, carry it away, I'll take a Sup out of the Bottle.

Young Wou'dbe. Right Madam—And my Business being very urgent—In three Words, 'tis this—
20 *Midnight.* Hold Sir, till I take Advice of my Council. (*Drinks.*) There is nothing more comfortable to a poor Creature, and fitter to revive wasting Spirits, than a little Plain-Brandy: I an't for your Hot-Spirits, your *Rosa Solis*, your *Ratafia*'s, your Orange-Waters, and the like—A moderate Glass of cool *Nants* is the thing—

Young Wou'dbe. But to our Business, Madam—My Father is

II. ii. 16 Here] O1; Hete   25 the] O1; the the

dead, and I have a mind to Inherit his Estate.

Midnight. You put the Case very well.

Young Wou'dbe. One of two things I must chuse—Either to be a Lord or a Beggar. 30

Midnight. Be a Lord to chuse—Tho' I have known some that have chosen both.

Young Wou'dbe. I have a Brother that I love very well; but since one of us must want, I had rather he should Starve than I.

Midnight. Upon my Conscience, dear heart, you're in the right on't.

Young Wou'dbe. Now your Advice upon these Heads.

Midnight. They be Matters of weight, and I must consider, (*Drinks.*) Is there a Will in the Case? 40

Young Wou'dbe. There is; which excludes me from every Foot of the Estate.

Midnight. That's bad—Where's your Brother?

Young Wou'dbe. He's now in *Germany*, in his way to *England*, and is expected very soon.

Midnight. How soon?

Young Wou'dbe. In a Month or less.

Midnight. O ho! A Month is a great while; our Business must be done in an hour or two—We must—(*Drinks.*) Suppose your Brother to be Dead; nay, he shall be actually 50 Dead—and my Lord, my humble Service t'ee—

Young Wou'dbe. O Madam, I'm your Ladyship's most devoted—Make your Words good, and I'll—

Midnight. Say no more, Sir; You shall have it, you shall have it.

Young Wou'dbe. Ay, but how, Dear Mrs. *Midnight?*

Midnight. Mrs. *Midnight!* Is that all?—Why not Mother, Aunt, Grandmother: Sir, I have done more for you this Moment, than all the Relations you have in the World.

Young Wou'dbe. Let me hear it. 60

Midnight. By the strength of this potent Inspiration, I have made you a Peer of *England*, with Seven Thousand Pound a year—My Lord, I wish you Joy. (*Drinks.*)

Young Wou'dbe. The Woman's mad, I believe. [*Aside.*]

Midnight. Quick, quick, my Lord! Counterfeit a Letter presently from *Germany*, that your Brother is kill'd in a Duel; Let it be directed to your Father, and fall into the Hands of the Steward when you are by: What sort of Fellow is the Steward?

Young Wou'dbe. Why, A timerous half-honest Man, that a
70 little Perswasions will make a whole Knave: He wants Courage to be thoroughly Just, or entirely a Villain—but good Backing will make him either.

Midnight. And he shan't want that! I tell you the Letter must come into his hands when you are by; upon this you take imediate Possession, and so you have the best part of the Law of your side.

Young Wou'dbe. But suppose my Brother comes in the mean time?

Midnight. This must be done this very moment: Let him
80 come when you're in Possession, I'll warrant we'll find a way to keep him out.

Young Wou'dbe. But, how, my dear Contriver?

Midnight. By your Father's Will, Man, your Father's Will—That is, One that your Father might have made, and which we will make for him—I'll send you a Nephew of my own, a Lawyer, that shall do the Business; Go, get into Possession, Possession, I say; let us have but the Estate to back the Suit, and you'll find the Law too strong for Justice, I warrant you.

90 *Young Wou'dbe.* My Oracle! How shall we Revel in Delight when this great Prediction is accomplish'd—But one thing yet remains, My Brother's Mistress, the Charming *Constance*—Let her be mine—

Midnight. Pho, pho, She's yours a Course; she's Contracted to you; For she's engaged to Marry no Man but my Lord *Wou'dbe*'s Son and Heir; Now you being the Person, she's recoverable by Law.

Young Wou'dbe. Marry her! No, no, She's Contracted to him, 'twere Injustice to rob a Brother of his Wife, an easier favour
100 will satisfie me.

Midnight. Why, truly, as you say, that favour is so easie, that I wonder they make such a Bustle about it—But get you gone and mind your Affairs, I must about mine—Oh—I had forgot—Where's that foolish Letter you had this Morning from *Richmore?*

Young Wou'dbe. I have posted it up in the *Chocolate*-House.

Midnight. Yaw, (*Shrieks.*) I shall fall into Fits; hold me—

Young Wou'dbe. No, no, I did but Jest; Here it is—But be assur'd Madam, I wanted only time to have expos'd it.

Midnight. Ah! You barbarous Man, Why so? 110

Young Wou'dbe. Because, When Knaves of our Sex, and Fools of yours meet, they make the best Jest in the World.

Midnight. Sir; The World has a better share in the Jest when we are the Knaves and you the Fools—But lookee, Sir, If ever you open your Mouth about this Trick—I'll discover all your Tricks; therefore Silence and Safety on both sides.

Young Wou'dbe. Madam, You need not doubt my Silence at present; because my own Affairs will employ me sufficiently; so there's your Letter. (*Gives the Letter.*) And now to write my own. 120

Exit.

Midnight. Adieu, my Lord. Let me see: (*Opens the Letter and Reads.*) *If there be Solemnity in Protestations*—That's Foolish, very Foolish—Why shou'd she expect Solemnity in Protestations? um, um, um. *I may still depend on the Faith of my* Richmore—Ah, poor *Clelia!*—um, um, um. *I can no longer hide the Effects on't from the World*—The Effects on't! How Modestly is that Exprest? Well 'tis a pretty Letter, and I'll keep it.—

Puts the Letter in her Pocket, and Exit.

[ACT II. Scene iii.]

SCENE *Lord* Wou'dbe's *House.*

Enter Steward, *and his* Wife.

Wife. You are to blame, you are much to blame, Husband, in being so scrupulous.

Steward. 'Tis true: This foolish Conscience of mine has been the greatest Bar to my Fortune.

Wife. And will ever be so. Tell me but one that Thrives, and

111 our] O1; your   112 yours] O1; ours

I'll show you a hundred that Starve by it—Do you think 'tis
Fourscore Pound a year makes my Lord *Gowty*'s Steward's
Wife live at the rate of Four Hundred? Upon my word, my
Dear, I'm as good a Gentlewoman as she, and I expect to be
10 maintain'd accordingly: 'Tis Conscience I warrant, that Buys
her the Point-Heads, and Diamond Necklace?—Was it
Conscience that Bought her the fine House in *Jermain*-street?
Is it Conscience that enables the Steward to Buy when the
Lord is forced to Sell?

Steward. But what wou'd you have me do?

Wife. Do! Now's your time; That small Morsel of an Estate
your Lord bought lately, a thing not worth mentioning; take it
towards your Daughter *Molly*'s Portion—What's two Hundred a
year; 'twill never be mist.

20 *Steward.* 'Tis but a small matter, I must confess; and as a
Reward for my past faithful Service, I think it but reasonable I
shou'd Cheat a little now.

Wife. Reasonable! All the reason that can be, If the
ungrateful World won't reward an honest Man, Why let an
honest Man reward himself—There's Five Hundred Pound
you receiv'd but two days ago, lay them aside—You may
easily sink it in the Charge of the Funeral—Do my dear now,
Kiss me, and do it.

Steward. Well, You have such a Winning way with you!
30 But, my Dear, I'm so much afraid of my young Lord's coming
home; he's a cunning close Man they say, and will examine
my Accounts very narrowly.

Wife. Ay, my Dear, Wou'd you had the younger Brother to
deal with? you might manage him as you pleas'd—I see him
coming. Let us weep, let us weep. (*They pull out their
Hankerchiefs, and seem to mourn.*)

Enter Young Wou'dbe.

Steward. Ah, Sir; We have all lost a Father, a Friend, and a
Supporter.

Young Wou'dbe. Ay, Mr. *Steward*, We must submit to Fate, as
he has done. And it is no small addition to my Grief, honest
40 Mr. Clearaccount, that it is not in my Power to supply my
Father's place to you and yours—Your Sincerity and Justice
to the Dead, Merits the greatest regard from those that
Survive him—Had I but my Brother's Ability, or he my

Inclinations—I'll assure you Mrs. *Clearaccount* you shou'd not
have such cause to Mourn.

Wife. Ah, Good Noble, Sir!

Steward. Your Brother, Sir, I hear, is a very severe Man.

Young Wou'dbe. He is what the World calls a Prudent Man,
Mr. *Steward*: I have often heard him very severe upon Men of
your Business; and has declar'd, That for Form's sake indeed 50
he wou'd keep a Steward, but that he wou'd Inspect into all
his Accounts himself.

Wife. Ay, Mr. *Wou'dbe*, you have more Sense than to do
these things; You have more Honour than to trouble your
Head with your own Affairs—Wou'd to Heavens we were to
serve you.

Young Wou'dbe. Wou'd I cou'd serve you, Madam—Without
Injustice to my Brother.

Enter a Servant.

Servant. A Letter for my Lord *Wou'dbe.*

Steward. It comes too late, alas! for his perusal, let me see it. 60
(*Opens, and Reads.*)

Franckfort, Octob. 10. New Style.

Franckfort! Where's *Franckfort*, Sir?

Young Wou'dbe. In *Germany*: The Letter must be from my
Brother, I suppose he's a coming home.

Steward. 'Tis none of his Hand. Let me see. (*Reads.*)

> My Lord
> *I am troubled at this unhappy Occasion of sending to your*
> *Lordship; Your Brave Son, and my Dear Friend, was yesterday*
> *unfortunately kill'd in a Duel by a* German *Count*—

I shall love a *German* Count as long as I live [*Aside.*]—My 70
Lord, my Lord, now I may call you so, since your Elder
Brother's—Dead.

Young Wou'dbe and Wife. How?

Steward. Read there. (*Gives the Letter,* Young Wou'dbe *peruses*
it.)

Young Wou'dbe. Oh, my Fate! A Father and a Brother in one
day! Heavens! 'Tis too much—Where is the fatal Messenger?

Servant. A Gentleman, Sir; who said, he came Post on

purpose. He was afraid the Contents of the Letter wou'd
unqualifie my Lord for Company; so he would take another
80 time to wait on him.

Young Wou'dbe. Nay, then 'tis true; and there is Truth in
Dreams. Last Night I dreamt—

Wife. Nay, my Lord, I Dreamt too; I Dreamt I saw your
Brother Drest in a long Minister's Gown, (Lord bless us) with
a Book in his Hand walking before a Dead Body to the Grave.

Young Wou'dbe. Well, Mr. *Clearaccount*, get Mourning ready.

Steward. Will your Lordship have the old Coach cover'd, or
a new one made.

Young Wou'dbe. A new one—The old Coach with the Grey
90 Horses, I give to Mrs. *Clearaccount* here; 'tis not fit she shou'd
walk the Streets.

Wife. Heav'ns bless the *German* Count, I say [*Aside.*]—But
my Lord—

Young Wou'dbe. No reply, Madam, You shall have it—And
receive it but as the earnest of my Favours—Mr. *Clearaccount*, I
double your Salary, and all the Servants Wages, to moderate
their Grief for our great Losses—Pray, Sir, Take Order about
these Affairs.

Steward. I shall, my Lord.

Exeunt Steward *and* Wife.

100 *Young Wou'dbe.* So! I have got Possession of the Castle, and
if I had but a little Law to fortifie me now, I believe we might
hold it out a great while. Oh! Here comes my Attorney—Mr.
Subtleman, your Servant—

Enter Subtleman.

Subtleman. My Lord, I wish you Joy; my Aunt *Midnight* has
sent me to receive your Commands.

Young Wou'dbe. Has she told you any thing of the Affair?

Subtleman. Not a word, my Lord.

Young Wou'dbe. Why then—Come nearer—Can you make a
Man right Heir to an Estate during the Life of an Elder
110 Brother?

Subtleman. I thought you had been the Eldest.

Young Wou'dbe. That we are not yet Agreed upon; for you
must know, there is an impertinent Fellow that takes a fancy
to Dispute the Seniority with me—For, lookee, Sir, My
Mother has unluckily Sow'd discord in the Family by bringing

forth Twins; My Brother, 'tis true, was First-Born; but I believe from the bottom of my Heart, I was the First-Begotten.

Subtleman. I understand—You are come to an Estate and Dignity, that by Justice indeed is your own, but by Law it falls 120 to your Brother.

Young Wou'dbe. I had rather, Mr. *Subtleman*, it were his by Justice and mine by Law, for I wou'd have the strongest title, if possible.

Subtleman. I am very sorry there shou'd happen any Breach between Brethren—So I think it wou'd be but a *Christian* and Charitable Act to take away all farther Disputes, by making you true Heir to the Estate by the last Will of your Father, Lookee—I'll divide Stakes—You shall yield the Eldership and Honour to him, and he shall quit his Estate to you. 130

Young Wou'dbe. Why, as you say, I don't much care if I do grant him the Eldest, half an hour is but a trifle; But how shall we do about this Will? Who shall we get to prove it?

Subtleman. Never trouble your self for that, I expect a Cargoe of Witnesses and Usquebaugh by the first fair Wind.

Young Wou'dbe. But we can't stay for them, it must be done immediately.

Subtleman. Well, well; We'll find some Body I warrant you, to make Oath of his last Words.

Young Wou'dbe. That's impossible; For my Father died of an 140 Apoplexy, and did not Speak at all.

Subtleman. That's nothing, Sir: He's not the first Dead Man that I have made to Speak.

Young Wou'dbe. You're a great Master of Speech, I don't question, Sir, and I can assure you there will be Ten Guineas for every Word you Extort from him in my Favour.

Subtleman. O Sir; That's enough to make your Great Grandfather Speak.

Young Wou'dbe. Come then, I'll carry you to my Steward, He shall give you the Names of the Mannors, and the true 150 Titles and Denominations of the Estate, and then you shall go to work.

Exeunt.

[ACT II. Scene iv.]

SCENE *Changes to the Park.*

Richmore *and* Trueman *meeting.*

Richmore. O, brave Cuz! You're very happy with the fair, I find. Pray which of those two Ladies you encounter'd just now, has your Adoration?

Trueman. She that Commands by forbidding it: And since I had Courage to declare to her self, I dare now own it to the World; *Aurelia*, Sir, is my Angel.

Richmore. Ha! (*A long Pause.*) Sir, I find you're of every Body's Religion; but methinks you make a bold Flight at first; Do you think your Captain's pay will Stake against so high a
10 Gamester?

Trueman. What do you mean?

Richmore. Mean, Bless me, Sir, Mean—You're a Man of mighty Honour we all know—But I'll tell you a Secret—The thing is publick already.

Trueman. I shou'd be Proud that all Mankind were acquainted with it; I shou'd Despise the Passion that cou'd make me either asham'd or afraid to own it.

Richmore. Ha, ha, ha, Prithee Dear Captain, no more of these Rodomontado's; You may as soon put a Standing Army
20 upon us—I'll tell you another Secret—Five Hundred Pound is the least Peny.

Trueman. Nay, To my knowledge, she has Fifteen Hundred.

Richmore. Nay, To my knowledge, she took Five.

Trueman. Took Five! How? Where?

Richmore. In her Lap, in her Lap, Captain; Where shou'd it be.

Trueman. I'm amaz'd.

Richmore. So am I; That she cou'd be so unreasonable—Fifteen Hundred Pound! 'Sdeath! Had she that Price from you?
30 *Trueman.* 'Sdeath, I meant her Portion.

Richmore. Why, What have you to do with her Portion?

Trueman. I lov'd her up to Marriage, by this Light.

Richmore. Marriage! Ha, ha, ha, I love the Gipsey for her

Cunning—A Young, Easie, Amorous, Credulous Fellow of
two and twenty, was just the Game she wanted, I find she
presently singled you out from the Herd.

Trueman. You distract me.

Richmore. A Soldier too, that must follow the Wars abroad,
and leave her to Engagements at home.

Trueman. Death and Furies; I'll be reveng'd.   40

Richmore. Why? What can you do? You'll challenge her,
Will you?

Trueman. Her Reputation was spotless when I went over.

Richmore. So was the Reputation of Mareschal *Boufflers*; but
d'ee think, that while you were beating the *French* abroad, that
we were idle at home—No, no, we have had our Sieges, our
Capitulations, and Surrendries, and all that—We have cut
our selves out good Winter Quarters as well as you.

Trueman. And are you billetted there?

Richmore. Lookee *Trueman*; You ought to be very trusty to a   50
secret, that has sav'd you from Destruction—In plain terms, I
have buryed Five hundred Pounds in that little spot, and I
should think it very hard, if you took it over my Head.

Trueman. Not by a Lease for Life I can assure you, but I
shall—

Richmore. What! You han't Five hundred Pounds to give?
Lookee, since you can make no Sport, spoil none. In a year or
two, she dwindles to a perfect Basset-Bank, every body may
play at it that pleases, and then you may put in for a piece or
two.   60

Trueman. Dear Sir; I could worship you for this.

Richmore. Not for this, Nephew; for I did not intend it, but I
came to seek you upon another affair—Were not you at Court
last Night?

Trueman. I was.

Richmore. Did not you talk to *Clelia*, my Lady *Taper*'s Niece?

Trueman. A fine Woman.

Richmore. Well! I met her upon the Stairs, and handing her
to her Coach, she asked me, if you were not my Nephew, and
said two or three warm Things that persuade me she likes   70
you? Her Relations have Interest at Court, and she has
Money in her Pocket.

Trueman. But—This Devil *Aurelia* still sticks with me.

Richmore. What then? The way to Love in one Place with Success, is to Marry in another with Convenience. *Clelia* has Four Thousand Pound: This applied to your reigning Ambition, whether Love or Advancement, will go a great way: And for her Virtue and Conduct, be assur'd, that no Body can give a better account of it than my self.

80   *Trueman.* I am willing to believe from this late Accident, that you consult my Honour and Interest in what you propose, and therefore I am satisfied to be govern'd.

Richmore. I see the very Lady in the Walk—We'll about it.

Trueman. I wait on you.

                      Exeunt.

[ACT II. Scene v.]

SCENE *Changes to Lord* Wou'dbe's *House.*

Young Wou'dbe, Subtleman, *and* Steward.

Young Wou'dbe. Well, Mr. *Subtleman*, You are sure the Will is firm and good in Law?

Subtleman. I warrant you, my Lord: And for the last Words to prove it, here they are—Lookee Mr. *Clearaccount*—Yes— That is an Answer to the Question that was put to him, (you know) by those about him when he was a Dying—Yes, or no, he must have said; so we have chosen, Yes—*Yes, I have made my Will, as it may be found in the Custody of Mr.* Clearaccount *my Steward; and I desire it may stand as my last Will and Testament*—Did 10 you ever hear a Dying Man's Words more to the purpose? An Apoplexy! I tell you, my Lord had Intervals to the last.

Steward. Ay, But how shall these Words be prov'd?

Subtleman. My Lord shall speak 'um now.

Young Wou'dbe. Shall he faith?

Subtleman. Ay, now—If the Corps ben't Bury'd—Lookee, Sir; These Words must be put into his Mouth, and drawn out again before us all; and if they won't be his last Words then;—I'll be Perjur'd.

Young Wou'dbe. What! Violate the Dead! It must not be, Mr. 20 *Subtleman.*

Subtleman. With all my heart, Sir! But I think you had

better violate the Dead of a Tooth or so, than violate the Living of Seven Thousand Pound a Year.

Young Wou'dbe. But is there no other way?

Subtleman. No Sir: Why? D'ee think Mr. *Clearaccount* here will hazard Soul and Body to Swear they are his last Words, unless they be made his last Words: For my part, Sir; I'll Swear to nothing but what I see with my Eyes come out of a Man's Mouth.

Young Wou'dbe. But it looks so Unnatural.   30

Subtleman. What! To open a Man's Mouth, and put in a Bit of Paper—This is all.

Young Wou'dbe. But the Body is cold, and his Teeth can't be got asunder.

Subtleman. But what occasion has your Father for Teeth now? I tell you what—I knew a Gentleman, three Day's Buried, taken out of his Grave, and his Dead Hand set to his Last Will, (unless some Body made him sign another afterwards) and I know the Estate to be held by that Tenure to this day; and a firm Tenure it is; for a Dead Hand holds   40 fastest; and let me tell you, Dead Teeth will fasten as hard.

Young Wou'dbe. Well, well; Use your Pleasure, you understand the Law best.

                  Exit Subtleman *and* Steward.

Young Wou'dbe. What a mighty Confusion is brought into Families by sudden Deaths? Men should do well to settle their Affairs in time—Had my Father done this before he was taken Ill, what a trouble had he sav'd us? But he was taken suddenly, poor Man.

                  Re-enter Subtleman.

Subtleman. Your Father still bears you the old Grudge, I find; It was with much strugling he consented; I never knew a   50 Man so loth to Speak in my life.

Young Wou'dbe. He was always a Man of few Words.

Subtleman. Now I may safely bear Witness, my self; as the Scrivener there present—I love to do things with a clear Conscience. (*Subscribes.*)

Young Wou'dbe. But the Law requires three Witnesses.

Subtleman. O! I shall pick up a Couple more, that perhaps may take my Word for't—But is not Mr. *Clearaccount* in your Interest?

60   *Young Wou'dbe.* I hope so.

Subtleman. Then he shall be one; A Witness in the Family
goes a great way; besides these Foreign Evidences are risen
confoundedly since the Wars: I hope if mine escape the
Privateers, to make a Hundred Pound an ear of every Head of
'um—But the Steward is an honest Man, and shall save you
the Charges.

Exit.

Young Wou'dbe. (*Solus.*) The Pride of Birth, the Heats of
Appetite, and Fears of Want, are strong Temptations to
Injustice—But why Injustice?—The World has broke all
70 Civilities with me; and left me in the Eldest State of Nature,
Wild, where Force, or Cunning first created Right. I cannot
say I ever knew a Father;—'Tis true, I was Begotten in his
Life-time, but I was Posthumous Born, and Liv'd not till he
Died—My Hours indeed, I numbred, but ne'er enjoy'd 'em,
till this Moment—My Brother! What is Brother? We are all
so; and the first two were Enemies—He stands before me in
the Road of Life to Rob me of my Pleasures—My Senses,
form'd by Nature for Delight, are all alarm'd—My Sight, my
Hearing, Taste, and Touch, call loudly on me for their
80 Objects, and they shall be satisfy'd.

Exit.

The End of the Second Act.

ACT III. [Scene i.]

SCENE *A Levee.*

*Young Wou'dbe Dressing, and several Gentlemen whispering
him by turns.*

Young Wou'dbe. Surely the greatest Ornament of Quality is a
clean and a numerous Levee; Such a Croud of Attendance for
the cheap Reward of Words and Promises distinguishes the
Nobility from those that Pay Wages to their Servants.

A Gentleman Whispers.

Sir, I shall speak to the Commissioners, and use all my Interst
I can assure you, Sir.

Another Whispers.

Sir, I shall meet some of your Board this Evening; let me see you to morrow.

A Third Whispers.

Sir, I'll consider of it—That Fellow's Breath Stinks of Tobacco. (*Aside.*) O, Mr. *Comick*, your Servant.   10

Comick. My Lord, I wish you Joy; I have something to show your Lordship.

Young Wou'dbe. What is it, pray, Sir?

Comick. I have an Elegy upon the Dead Lord, and a Panegyrick upon the Living one—*In utrumque paratus*, my Lord.

Young Wou'dbe. Ha, ha, Very pritty Mr. *Comick*—But pray, Mr. *Comick*, Why don't you write Plays. It wou'd give one an opportunity of serving you.

Comick. My Lord, I have writ one.   20

Young Wou'dbe. Was it ever Acted?

Comick. No, my Lord, But it has been a Rehearsing these Three Years and a half.

Young Wou'dbe. A long time. There must be a great deal of Business in it surely.

Comick. No, my Lord, None at all—I have another Play just finish'd, but that I want a Plot for't.

Young Wou'dbe. A Plot! You shou'd read the *Italian*, and *Spanish* Plays, Mr. *Comick*—I like your Verses here mightily— Here, Mr. *Clearaccount*.   30

Comick. Now for Five Guineas at least. (*Aside.*)

Young Wou'dbe. Here, give Mr. *Comick*, give him—Give him the *Spanish* Play that lies in the Closet Window—*Captain*, Can I do you any Service?

Captain. Pray, my Lord, Use your Interest with the General for that vacant Commission: I hope, my Lord, the Blood I have already lost, may intitle me to spill the Remainder in my Countries Cause.

Young Wou'dbe. All the reason in the World—*Captain*, You may depend upon me for all the Service I can.   40

Gentleman. I hope your Lordship won't forget to Speak to the General about that vacant Commission, altho' I have never made a Campagne; yet my Lord, my Interest in the Country can raise me Men; which I think shou'd prefer me to

that Gentleman whose Bloody Disposition frightens the poor
People from Listing.

Young Wou'dbe. All the Reason in the World, Sir; You may
depend upon me for all the Service in my Power—*Captain*,
I'll do your Business for you—Sir, I'll speak to the General; I
50 shall see him at the House—(*To the Gentleman.*)

Enter a Citizen. [Alderman.]

Oh, Mr. *Alderman.*—Your servant—Gentlemen all, I beg your
Pardon.

Exeunt Levee.

Mr. *Alderman*, Have you any Service to Command me?

Alderman. Your Lordship's humble Servant—I have a
favour to beg. You must know, I have a Graceless Son, a
Fellow that Drinks and Swears Eternally, keeps a Whore in
every corner of the Town: In short, he's fit for no kind of thing
but a Soldier—I am so tir'd of him, that I intend to throw him
into the Army, let the Fellow be ruin'd, if he will.

60 *Young Wou'dbe.* I commend your Paternal Care, Sir—Can I
do you any Service in this Affair?

Alderman. Yes, my Lord: There is a vacant Company in
Colonel Whatdeecalum's Regiment, and if your Lordship
wou'd but Speak to the General.

Young Wou'dbe. Has your Son ever serv'd?

Alderman. Serv'd! Yes, my Lord; He's an Ensign in the
Train-Bands now.

Young Wou'dbe. Has he ever signaliz'ed his Courage?

Alderman. Often, often, my Lord; But one day particularly,
70 you must know, his Captain was so busie Shipping off a
Cargoe of Cheeses, that he left my Son to Command in his
Place—Wou'd you believe it my Lord? He charg'd up
Cheapside in the Front of the Buff-Coats with such Bravery and
Courage, that I could not forbear wishing in the Loyalty of my
Heart, for Ten Thousand such Officers upon the *Rhine*—Ah!
My Lord, We must employ such Fellows as him, or we shall
never humble the *French* King—Now, My Lord, If you cou'd
find a convenient time to hint these things to the General.

Young Wou'dbe. All the reason in the World, Mr. *Alderman*,
80 I'll do you all the Service I can.

III. i. 67 now] 1728; [om.]   70 off] O2; of

Alderman. You may tell him; He's a Man of Courage, fit for the Service; and then he loves Hardship—He Sleeps every other Night in the *Round-House.*

Young Wou'dbe. I'll do you all the Service I can.

Alderman. Then, My Lord, He Salutes with his Pike so very handsomly, it went to his Mistress's Heart, t'other day—Then he Beats a Drum like an Angel.

Young Wou'dbe. Sir, I'll do you all the Service I can—(*Not taking the least notice of the* Alderman *all this while, but Dressing himself in the Glass.*)

Alderman. But, My Lord, The hurry of your Lordship's Affairs may put my Business out of your Head; therefore, my Lord, I'll presume to leave you some *Memorandum.*

Young Wou'dbe. I'll do you all the Service I can. (*Not minding him.*)

Alderman. Pray my Lord, (*Pulling him by the Sleeve.*) Give me leave for a *Memorandum*; My Glove, I suppose will do: Here, My Lord, Pray remember me—

Lays his Glove upon the Table, and Exit.

Young Wou'dbe. I'll do you all the Service I can—What, Is he gone? 'Tis the most rude familiar Fellow—Faugh, What a greasie Gauntlet is here—(*A Purse drops out of the Glove.*) Oh! no, no, the Glove is a clean well made Glove, and the owner of it, the most respectful Person I have seen this Morning, he knows what distance (*Chinking the Purse.*) is due to a Man of Quality,—but what must I do for this? *Frisure* (*To his Valet.*) do you remember what the *Alderman* said to me!

Frisure. No my Lord, I thought your Lordship had.

Young Wou'dbe. This Blockhead thinks a Man of Quality can mind what People say,—when they do somthing, 'tis another Case; here, hall him back,

Exit Frisure.

he talk'd somthing of the General, and his Son, and Train-Bands, I know not what stuff.

Re-enter Alderman *and* Frisure.

Oh, Mr. *Alderman*, I have put your *Memorandum* in my Pocket

Alderman. Oh, my Lord, you do me too much Honour.

Young Wou'dbe. But Mr. *Alderman*, the business you were talking of; it shall be done, but if you gave a short Note of it to my Secretary, it would not be amiss—but Mr. *Alderman*, han't you the fellow to this Glove, it fits me mighty well (*Putting on the Glove.*) it looks so like a Challenge to give a Man an odd Glove—and I wou'd have nothing that looks like Enmity between you and I Mr. *Alderman.*

Alderman. Truly my Lord, I intended the other Glove for a
120 *Memorandum* to the Collonel, but since your Lordship has a mind to't—(*Gives* the Glove.)

Young Wou'dbe. Here *Frisure*, lead this Gentleman to my Secretary, and bid him take a Note of his Business.

Alderman. But, my Lord, *don't* do me all the Service you can now.

Young Wou'dbe. Well! I *won't* do you all the Service I can—
　　　　　　　　　　　　　　　　　　Exit Alderman.
these Citizens have a strange Capacity of Solliciting sometimes.
　　　　　　　　　　Enter Steward.

Steward. My Lord, here are your Taylor, your Vintner, your Bookseller, and half a Dozen more with their Bills at the Door,
130 and they desire their Money.

Young Wou'dbe. Tell 'em, Mr. *Clearaccount*, that when I was a Private Gentleman, I had nothing else to do but to run in Debt, and now that I have got into a higher Rank, I'm so very busy, I can't pay it—as for that Clamorous Rogue of a Taylor speak him fair, till he has made up my Liveries—then about a Year and a half hence, I shall be at leisure to put him off; for a Year and a half longer.

Steward. My Lord, there's a Gentleman below calls himself Mr. *Basset*, he says your Lordship owes him fifty Guinea's
140 that he won of you at Cards.

Young Wou'dbe. Look'ee Sir—the Gentleman's Money is a Debt of Honour, and must be paid immediately.

Steward. Your Father thought otherwise, my Lord, he always took care to have the poor Tradesmen satisfy'd, whose only subsistence lay in the Use of their Money, and was used to say, That nothing was honourable but what was honest.

Young Wou'dbe. My Father might say what he pleas'd, he was a Noble Man of very singular Humours—but in my Notion, there are not two things in Nature more different than
150 Honour and Honesty—now your Honesty is a little Mechan-

nick Quality, well enough among Citizens, People that do
nothing but Pittiful Mean Actions according to Law—but
your Honour fly's a much higher Pitch, and will do any thing
that's free and spontaeous, but scorns to Level it self to what is
only just.

Steward. But I think it a little hard to have these Poor
People starve for want of their Money, and yet pay this
sharping Rascal fifty Guinea's.

Young Wou'dbe. Sharping Rascal! What a Barbarism that is?
why he wears as good Wiggs, as fine Linnen, and keeps as   160
good Company as any at *White*'s; and between you and I Sir,
this sharping Rascal, as you are pleased to call him, shall
make more Interest among the Nobility with his Cards and
Counters, than a Soldier shall with his Sword and Pistol. Pray
let him have fifty Guineas immediately.

Exeunt.

[ACT III. Scene ii.]

SCENE, *The Street*;

Elder Wou'dbe *writing in a Pocket-Book, in a Riding Habit.*

Elder Wou'dbe. Monday the 14*th of* December, 1702. *I arrived
safe in* London, *and so concluding my Travels.—(Putting up his
Book.)*

 Now welcome Countrey, Father, Friends,
 My Brother too, (if Brothers can be Friends:)
 But above all, my charming Fair, my *Constance.*
 Thro' all the Mazes of my wandring Steps,
 Thro' all the various Climes that I have run;
 Her Love has been the Loadstone of my Course,
 Her Eyes the Stars that pointed me the Way.
 Had not her Charms my Heart intire possest,   10
 Who knows what *Circe*'s artful Voice and Look

161 you] 1728; Him   162 him] O1; nim

III. ii. 1 14*th of December.*] 1728; *om.* The date printed in 1728, a Monday, was the
date of the opening performance. Since this seems a remarkable coincidence, one
must conclude that the date, like 'Midnight', originated in the Drury Lane prompt-
copy. The copy-text for Q1 would not have been the promptbook.

Might have ensnar'd my travelling Youth,
And fixt me to Inchantment?
Enter Teague *with a Port-Mantel. He throws it
down and sits on it.*
Here comes my Fellow-Traveller. What makes you sit upon
the Port-Mantel, *Teague?* You'll rumple the things.

Teague. Be me Shoule, Maishter, I did carry the Port-
Mantel till it tir'd me; and now the Port-Mantel shall carry
me till I tire him.

Elder Wou'dbe. And how d'ye like *London,* *Teague,* after our
20 Travels?

Teague. Fet, dear Joy, 'tis the Bravest Plaase I have sheen in
my Peregrinations, exshepting my nown brave Shitty of
Carick-Vergus.—uf, uf, dere ish a very fragrant Shmell hereabouts.—Maishter, shall I run to that Paishtry-Cooks for shix
penyworths of boil'd Beef?

Elder Wou'dbe. Tho' this Fellow travell'd the World over he
would never lose his Brogue nor his Stomach. [*Aside.*]—Why,
you Cormorant, so hungry and so early!

Teague. Early! Deel tauke me, Maishter, 'tish a great deal
30 more than almost pasht twelve a-clock.

Elder Wou'dbe. Thou art never happy unless thy Guts be
stuft up to thy Eyes.

Teague. Oh Maishter, dere ish a dam way of distance, and
the deel a bit between.
Enter Young Wou'dbe *in a Chair, with four or
five Footmen before him, and passes over
the Stage.*
Elder Wou'dbe. Hey day—who comes here? with one, two,
three, four, five Footmen! Some young Fellow just tasting the
sweet Vanity of Fortune.—Run, *Teague,* inquire who that is.

Teague. Yes, Maishter, (*Runs to one of the Footmen.*) Sir, will
you give my humble Shervish to your Maishter, and tell him
40 to send me word fat Naam ish upon him.

Footman. You wou'd know fat Naam ish upon him?

Teague. Yesh, fet would I.

Footman. Why, what are you, Sir?

16–17 Port-Mantel] Farquhar used the northern dialect for 'portmanteau'; O2 and
all subsequent editions emended to 'Port-Manteau', a far more common usage. I have
retained the original spelling throughout.　　　30 pasht] 1728; [*om.*]

Teague. Be me Shoul I am a Shentleman bred and born, and dere ish my Maishter.

Footman. Then your Master would know it?

Teague. Arah, you Fool, ish it not the saam ting?

Footman. Then tell your Master 'tis the young Lord *Woud'be* just come to his Estate by the Death of his Father and elder Brother.   50

                                 Exit Footman.

Elder Wou'dbe. What do I hear?

Teague. You hear that you are dead, Maishter; fere vil you please to be buried?

Elder Wou'dbe. But art thou sure it was my Brother?

Teague. Be me Shoul it was him nown self; I know'd him fery well, after his Man told me.

Elder Wou'dbe. The Business requires that I be convinc'd with my own eyes; I'll follow him, and know the Bottom on't.—Stay here till I return.

Teague. Dear Maishter, have a care upon your shelf: now 60 they know you are dead, by my Shoul they may kill you.

Elder Wou'dbe. Don't fear; none of his Servants know me; and I'll take care to keep my Face from his sight. It concerns me to conceal my self, till I know the Engines of this Contrivance.—Be sure you stay till I come to you; and let no body know whom you belong to.

                                       Exit.

Teague. Oh, oh, hon, poor *Teague* is left all alone. (*Sits on the Port-Mantel.*)

             Enter Subtleman *and* Steward.

Subtleman. And you won't swear to the Will?

Steward. My Conscience tells me I dare not do't with Safety.

Subtleman. But if we make it lawful, what shou'd you fear? 70 We now think nothing against Conscience, till the Cause be thrown out of Court.

Steward. In you, Sir, 'tis no Sin; because 'tis the Principle of your Profession: but in me, Sir, 'tis downright Perjury indeed.—You can't want Witnesses enough, since Money won't be wanting—and you must lose no time; for I heard just now, that the true Lord *Wou'dbe* was seen in Town, or his Ghost.

Subtleman. It was his Ghost, to be sure; for a Nobleman

80 without an Estate, is but the Shadow of a Lord.—Well; take
no care: leave me to my self; I'm near the *Friars*, and ten to
one, shall pick up an Evidence.

Steward. Speed you well, Sir.

Exit.

Subtleman. There's a Fellow that has Hunger and the
Gallows pictur'd in his Face, and looks like one for my
Purpose.—How now, honest Friend, what have you got under
you there?

Teague. Noting, dear Joy.

Subtleman. Nothing? Is it not a Port-mantel?

90   *Teague.* That is noting to you.

Subtleman. The Fellow's a Wit.

Teague. Fel am I: my Granfader was an *Irish* Poet.—He did
write a great Book of Verses concerning the Vars between St.
Patrick and the Wolf-Dogs.

Subtleman. Then thou art poor, I'm afraid.

Teague. Be me Shoul, my sole Generation ish so.—I have
noting but thish poor Portmantel, and dat it shelf ish not my
own.

Subtleman. Why, who does it belong to?

100 *Teague.* To my Maishter, dear Joy.

Subtleman. Then you have a Master.

Teague. Fet have I, but he's dead.

Subtleman. Right!—And how do you intend to live.

Teague. By eating, dear Joy, fen I can get it, and by sleeping
fen I can get none.—tish the fashion of *Ireland*.

Subtleman. What was your Master's Name, pray?

Teague. I will tell a Lee now; but it shall be a true one.
[*Aside.*] *Macfadin*, dear Joy, was his Naam. He vent over with
King *Jamish* into *France*.—He was my Master once.—Dere ish
110 de true Lee; noo. (*Aside.*)

Subtleman. What Employment had he?

Teague. Je ne scay pas.

Subtleman. What! you can speak *French*?

Teague. Ouy Monsieur;—I did travel *France*, and *Spain*, and
Italy;—Dear Joy, I did kish the Pope's Toe, and dat will

85–6 one for my Purpose] 1728; my Countryman. The revision in 1728, an edition
with significant authority, makes sense. There is no reason to believe Subtleman is
Irish, the only reason he could have to speak of 'my Countryman'.

excuse me all the Sins of my Life; and fen I am dead, St. *Patrick* will excuse the rest.

Subtleman. A rare Fellow for my purpose. (*Aside.*) Thou look'st like an honest Fellow; and if you'll go with me to the next Tavern, I'll give thee a Dinner, and a Glass of Wine.   120

Teague. Be me Shoul, 'tis dat I wanted, dear Joy; come along, I will follow you.

Runs out before Subtleman *with the Portmantel on his Back. Exit*
Subtleman.

Enter Elder Wou'dbe.

Elder Wou'dbe. My Father dead! my Birth-right lost! How have my drowsie Stars slept o'er my Fortune? Ha! (*Looking about.*) my Servant gone! The simple, poor, ungrateful Wretch, has left me. — I took him up from Poverty and Want; and now he leaves me just as I found him.—My Cloaths and Money too!—but why should I repine? Let Man but view the Dangers he has past, and few will fear what Hazards are to come. That Providence that has secur'd my Life from   130 Robbers, Shipwreck, and from Sickness, is still the same; still kind whilst I am just.—My Death, I find, is firmly believ'd; but how it gain'd so universal Credit, I fain wou'd learn.—Who comes here?—honest Mr. *Fairbank*! my Father's Goldsmith, a Man of Substance and Integrity. The Alteration of five years Absence, with the Report of my Death, may shade me from his Knowledge, till I enquire some News.

Enter Fairbank.

Sir, your humble Servant.

Fairbank. Sir, I don't know you. (*Shunning him.*)

Elder Wou'dbe. I intend you no harm, Sir; but seeing you   140 come from my Lord *Woud'be*'s House, I would ask you a Question or two.—Pray what Distemper did my Lord die of?

Fairbank. I am told it was an Apoplexy.

Elder Wou'dbe. And pray Sir, what does the World say? Is his Death lamented?

Fairbank. Lamented! my Eyes that Question shou'd resolve; Friend,—Thou knew'st him not; else thy own Heart had answer'd thee.

Elder Wou'dbe. His Grief, methinks, chides my defect of filial Duty; [*Aside.*] but I hope, Sir, his Loss is partly recompens'd   150 in the Merits of his Successor.

Fairbank. It might have been; but his eldest Son, Heir to his Vertue and his Honour, was lately and unfortunately kill'd in *Germany*.

Elder Wou'dbe. How unfortunately, Sir?

Fairbank. Unfortunately for him and us.—I do remembar him.—He was the mildest, humblest, sweetest Youth.—

Elder Wou'dbe. Happy indeed, had been my part in Life, if I had left this Humane Stage, whilst this so spotless and so fair
160 Applause, had crown'd my going off. (*Aside.*) Well, Sir.

Fairbank. But those that saw him in his Travels, told such Wonders of his Improvement, that the Report recall'd his Father's Years; and with the Joy to hear his *Hermes* prais'd, he oft wou'd break the Chains of Gout and Age; and leaping up with strength of greenest Youth, cry, *My* Hermes *is my self: methinks I live my sprightly Days agen, and I am young in him.*

Elder Wou'dbe. Spite of all Modesty, a Man must own a Pleasure in the hearing of his Praise. (*Aside.*)

Fairbank. You're thoughtful, Sir:—Had you any Relation to
170 the Family we talk of?

Elder Wou'dbe. None, Sir, beyond my private Concern in the publick Loss.—But pray, Sir, what Character does the present Lord bear?

Fairbank. Your Pardon, Sir. As for the Dead, their Memories are left unguarded, and Tongues may touch them freely: but for the Living, they have provided for the Safety of their Names by a strong Inclosure of the Law. There is a thing call'd *Scandalum Magnatum*, Sir.

Elder Wou'dbe. I commend your Caution, Sir; but be assur'd
180 I intend not to entrap you.—I am a poor Gentleman; and having heard much of the Charity of the old Lord *Wou'dbe*,I had a mind to apply to his Son; and therefore enquir'd his Character.

Fairbank. Alas, Sir, things are chang'd: That House was once what Poverty might go a Pilgrimage to seek, and have its Pains rewarded.—The Noble Lord, the truly Noble Lord, held his Estate, his Honour, and his House, as if they were only lent upon the Interest of doing good to others. He kept a Porter, not to exclude, but serve the Poor. No Creditor was
190 seen to guard his going out, or watch his coming in: No craving Eyes, but Looks of smiling Gratitude.—But now, that

Family, which like a Garden fairly kept, invited every
Stranger to its Fruit and Shade, is now run o'er with
Weeds:—Nothing but Wine and Revelling within, a Crowd of
noisie Creditors without, a Train of Servants insolently
proud.—Wou'd you believe it, Sir, as I offer'd to go in just
now, the rude Porter push'd me back with his Staff.—I am at
this present (thanks to Providence and my Industry) worth
twenty thousand Pounds. I pay the fifth part of this to
maintain the Liberty of the Nation; and yet this Slave, the   200
impudent *Swiss* Slave, offer'd to strike me.

Elder Wou'dbe. 'Twas hard, Sir, very hard:—And if they
us'd a Man of your Substance so roughly, how will they
manage me, that am not worth a Groat?

Fairbank. I wou'd not willingly defraud your Hopes of what
may happen.—If you can drink and swear, perhaps—

Elder Wou'dbe. I shall not pay that price for his Lordship's
Bounty wou'd it extend to half he's worth.—Sir, I give you
thanks for your Caution, and shall steer another Course.

Fairbank. Sir, you look like an honest, modest Gentleman.   210
Come home with me; I am as able to give you a Dinner as my
Lord: and you shall be very welcome to eat at my Table every
Day, till you are better provided.

Elder Wou'dbe. Good Man (*Aside.*) Sir, I must beg you to
excuse me to day: but I shall find a time to accept of your
Favours, or at least to thank you for 'em.

Fairbank. Sir, you shall be very welcome when ever you
please.

Exit.

Elder Wou'dbe. Gramercy Citizen! Surely if Justice were an
Herald, she wou'd give this Tradesman a nobler Coat of Arms   220
than my Brother.—But I delay: I long to vindicate the
Honour of my Station, and to displace this bold Usurper:—But
one Concern, methinks is nearer still, my *Constance*! Shou'd she
upon the Rumour of my death, have fixt her Heart elsewhere,
—then I were dead indeed: But if she still proves true,—
Brother, sit fast.

> *I'll shake your Strength, all Obstacles remove,*
> *Sustain'd my Justice, and inspir'd by Love.*

Exit.

[ACT III. Scene iii.]

SCENE, *An Apartment.*

Constance, Aurelia.

Constance. For Heaven'sake, Cousin, cease your impertinent
Consolation: It but makes me angry, and raises two Passions
in me instead of one. You see I commit no Extravagance, my
Grief is silent enough: my Tears make no noise to disturb any
body. I desire no Companion in my Sorrows: leave me to my
self, and you comfort Me.—

Aurelia. But, Cousin, have you no regard to your Reputation?
this immoderate Concern for a young Fellow. What will the
World say? You lament him like a Husband.—

10   *Constance.* No; you mistake: I have no Rule nor Method for
my Grief; no Pomp of black and darkned Rooms; no formal
Month for Visits on my Bed. I am content with the slight
Mourning of a broken Heart; and all my Form is Tears.
(*Weeps.*)

Enter Midnight.

Midnight. Madam *Aurelia*, Madam, don't disturb her.—
Every thing must have its vent. 'Tis a hard case to be cross'd
in ones first Love: But you shou'd consider, Madam (*To*
Constance.) that we are all born to die, some young, some old.

Constance. Better we all dy'd young, than be plagued with
Age, as I am. I find other folks Years are as troublesome to us
20   as our own.

Midnight. You have reason, you have cause to mourn. He
was the handsomest Man, and the sweetest Babe, that I know;
tho' I must confess too, that *Ben* had much the finer
Complection when he was born: but then *Hermes*, O yes,
Hermes had the Shape that he had.—But of all the Infants that
I ever beheld with my Eyes, I think *Ben* had the finest Ear,
Wax-work, perfect Wax-work; and then he did so sputter at
the Breast.—His Nurse was a hale, well-complection'd
sprightly Jade as ever I saw; but her Milk was a little too stale;
30   tho' at the same time 'twas as blue and clear as a Cambrick.

Aurelia. Do you intend all this, Madam, for a Consolation to my Cousin?

Midnight. No, no, Madam, that's to come.—I tell you, fair Lady, you have only lost the Man; the Estate and Title are still your own; and this very moment I wou'd salute you Lady *Wou'dbe*, if you pleas'd.

Constance. Dear Madam, your Proposal is very tempting: let me but consider till to morrow, and I'll give you an Answer.

Midnight. I knew it, I knew it; I said when you were born you wou'd be a Lady; I knew it. To morrow you say. My Lord 40 shall know it immediately.

Exit.

Aurelia. What d'ye intend to do, Cousin?

Constance. To go into the Countrey this moment, to be free from the Impertinence of Condolence, the Persecution of that Monster of a Man, and that Devil of a Woman.—O *Aurelia*, I long to be alone. I am become so fond of Grief, that I would fly where I might enjoy it all, and have no Interruption in my darling Sorrow.

Enter Elder Wou'dbe *unperceiv'd.*

Elder Wou'dbe. In Tears! perhaps for me! I'll try—

(*Drops a Picture, and goes back to the Entrance,*
and listens.)

Aurelia. If there be ought in Grief delightful, don't grudge 50 me a share.

Constance. No, my dear *Aurelia*, I'll ingross it all. I lov'd him so, methinks I should be jealous if any mourned his death besides my self. What's here! (*Takes up the Picture.*) Ha! see Cousin—the very Face and Features of the Man! Sure some officious Angel has brought me this for a Companion in my Solitude.—Now I'm fitted out for Sorrow. With this I'll sigh, with this converse, gaze on his Image till I grow blind with weeping.

Aurelia. I'm amaz'd! how came it here?   60

Constance. Whether by Miracle or humane Chance, 'tis all alike; I have it here: Nor shall it ever separate from my Breast.—It is the only thing cou'd give me Joy; because it will increase my Grief.

Elder Wou'dbe. (*Entring.*) Most glorious Woman! Now I am fond of Life.

Aurelia. Ha! what's this? Your Business, pray Sir!

Elder Wou'dbe. With this Lady. (*Goes to* Constance, *takes her Hand and kneels.*) Here let me worship that Perfection, whose
70 Vertue might attract the listning Angels, and make 'em smile to see such Purity, so like themselves in humane shape.

Constance. Hermes?

Elder Wou'dbe. Your living *Hermes*, who shall dye yours too.

Constance. Now Passion, powerful Passion, would bear me like a Whirlwind to his Arms;—but my Sex has bounds. [*Aside.*]—'Tis wondrous, Sir.

Elder Wou'dbe. Most wondrous are the Works of Fate for Man, and most closely laid is the Serpentine Line that guides him into Happiness,—that hidden Power which did permit
80 those Arts to cheat me of my Birthright, had this Surprize of Happiness in store, well knowing that Grief is the best Preparative for joy.

Constance. I never found the true Sweets of Love, till this Romantick turn, dead and alive! my Stars are Poetical. For Heavens sake, Sir, unriddle your Fortune.

Elder Wou'dbe. That my dear Brother must do; for he made the *Enigma*.

Aurelia. Methinks I stand here like a Fool all this while: Wou'd I had some body or other to say a fine thing or two to
90 me.

Elder Wou'dbe. Madam, I beg ten thousand Pardons: I have my Excuse in my Hand.

Aurelia. My Lord, I wish you Joy.

Elder Wou'dbe. Pray Madam, don't trouble me with a Title till I am better equipt for it. My Peerage wou'd look a little shabby in these Robes.

Constance. You have a good Excuse, my Lord: you can wear better when you please.

Elder Wou'dbe. I have a better Excuse, Madam.—These are
100 the best I have.

Constance. How, my Lord?

Elder Wou'dbe. Very true, Madam; I am at present, I believe, the poorest Peer in *England.*—Hearkee, *Aurelia*, prithee lend me a Piece or two.

Aurelia. Ha, ha, ha; poor Peer indeed! he wants a Guinea.

Constance. I'm glad on't with all my Heart.

Elder Wou'dbe. Why so, Madam?

Constance. Because I can furnish you with five thousand.

Elder Wou'dbe. Generous Woman!

Enter Trueman.

Ha, my Friend too!   110

Trueman. I'm glad to find you here, my Lord: here's a current Report about Town that you were kill'd. I was afraid it might reach this Family; so I came to disprove the Story by your Letter to me by last Post.

Aurelia. I'm glad he's come; now it will be my turn, Cousin.

Trueman. Now, my Lord, I wish you Joy; and I expect the same from you.

Elder Wou'dbe. With all my heart; but upon what score?

Trueman. The old score, Marriage.

Elder Wou'dbe. To whom?   120

Trueman. To a neighbour-Lady here. (*Looking* at Aurelia.)

Aurelia. Impudence! (*Aside.*) The Lady mayn't be so near as you imagine, Sir.

Trueman. The Lady mayn't be so near as you imagine, Madam.

Aurelia. Don't mistake me, Sir: I did not care if the Lady were in *Mexico.*

Trueman. Nor I neither, Madam.

Aurelia. You're very short, Sir.

Trueman. The shortest Pleasures are the sweetest, you   130
know.

Aurelia. Sir, you appear very different to me, from what you were lately.

Trueman. Madam, you appear very indifferent to me, to what you were lately.

Aurelia. Strange! (*This while* Constance *and* Wou'dbe *entertain one another in dumb show.*)

Trueman. Miraculous!

Aurelia. I cou'd never have believ'd it.

Trueman. Nor I, as I hope to be sav'd.

Aurelia. Ill Manners!   140

III. iii. 134 indifferent] The word is revised to 'different' in 1728. However, the use of 'to what you were lately' in l. 116, as opposed to 'from what you were lately' in l. 115 casts doubt. The adjective 'indifferent' is also a more stinging attack on Aurelia.

Trueman. Worse.

Aurelia. How have I deserv'd it, Sir?

Trueman. How have I deserv'd it, Madam?

Aurelia. What?

Trueman. You.

Aurelia. Riddles!

Trueman. Women!—My Lord, you'll hear of me at *White's*. Farewel.

Runs off.

Elder Wou'dbe. What, *Trueman* gone!

150 *Aurelia.* Yes. (*Walks about in Disorder.*)

Constance. Bless me! what's the matter, Cousin?

Aurelia. Nothing.

Constance. Why are you uneasie?

Aurelia. Nothing.

Constance. What ails you then?

Aurelia. Nothing.—I don't love the Fellow,—yet to be affronted,—I can't bear it.

Bursts out a crying, and runs off.

Constance. Your Friend, my Lord, has affronted *Aurelia*.

Elder Wou'dbe. Impossible! His regard to me were sufficient
160 Security for his good behaviour here, tho' it were in his Nature to be rude elsewhere.—She has certainly us'd him ill.

Constance. Too well rather.

Elder Wou'dbe. Too well? have a care Madam;—that with some Men is the greatest provocation to a Slight.

Constance. Don't mistake, my Lord, her Usage never went further than mine to you; and I should take it very ill to be abus'd for it.

Elder Wou'dbe. I'll follow him, and know the cause of it.

Constance. No, my Lord, I'll follow her, and know it:
170 Besides, your own Affairs with your Brother require you at present.

Exeunt.

[*The End of the Third Act.*]

ACT IV. [Scene i.]

SCENE, *Lord* Wou'dbe's *House.*

Young Wou'dbe *and* Subtleman.

Young Wou'dbe. Return'd! Who saw him? who spoke with
him? he can't be return'd.

Subtleman. My Lord, he's below at the Gate parlying with
the Porter, who has private Orders from me to admit no body
till you send him word, that we may have the more time to
settle our Affairs.

Young Wou'dbe. 'Tis a hard case, Mr. *Subtleman*, that a Man
can't enjoy his Right without all this Trouble.

Subtleman. Ay, my Lord, you see the Benefit of Law now,
what an Advantage it is to the Publick for securing of 10
Property.—Had you not the Law o' your side, who knows
what Devices might be practis'd to defraud you of your
Right.—But I have secur'd all.—The Will is in true form; and
you have two Witnesses already to swear to the last words of
your Father.

Young Wou'dbe. Then you have got another?

Subtleman. Yes, yes, a right one,—and I shall pick up
another time enough before the Term,—and I have planted
three or four Constables in the next Room, to take care of your
Brother if he shou'd be boisterous.   20

Young Wou'dbe. Then you think we are secure.

Subtleman. Ay, ay; let him come now when he pleases.—I'll
go down and give orders for his Admittance.

Young Wou'dbe. Unkind Brother! to disturb me thus, just in
the swing and stretch of my full Fortune! Where is the Tye of
Blood and Nature, when Brothers will do this? Had he but
staid till *Constance* had been mine, his Presence or his Absence
had been then indifferent.

Enter Midnight.

Midnight. Well, my Lord, (*Pants as out of breath.*) you'll ne'er
be satisfied till you have broken my poor heart. I have had 30
such ado yonder about you with Madam *Constance.*—But she's
your own.

Young Wou'dbe. How! my own? Ah, my dear Helpmate, I'm afraid we are routed in that Quarter: my Brother's come home.

Midnight. Your Brother come home! then I'll go travel. (*Going.*)

Young Wou'dbe. Hold, hold, Madam, we are all secure; we have provided for his Reception; your Nephew *Subtleman* has stopt up all Passages to the Estate.

40 *Midnight.* Ay, *Subtleman* is a pritty, thriving, ingenious Boy. Little do you think who is the Father of him. I'll tell you; Mr. *Moabite* the rich *Jew* in *Lombard-street.*

Young Wou'dbe. Moabite the *Jew?*

Midnight. You shall hear, my Lord,—One Evening as I was very grave in my own House, reading the—*weekly Preparation* —ay, it was the *weekly Preparation,* I do remember particularly well.—What hears me I—but pat, pat, pat very softly at the Door. Come in, cries I, and presently enters Mr. *Moabite,* follow'd by a snug Chair, the Windows close drawn, and in it 50 a fine young Virgin just upon the point of being deliver'd.— We were all in a great hurly burly for a while, to be sure; but our Production was a fine Boy.—I had fifty Guineas for my Trouble; the Lady was wrapt up very warm, plac'd in her Chair, and re-conveigh'd to the Place she came from. Who she was, or what she was, I cou'd never learn, tho' my Maid said that the Chair went thro' the Park—but the Child was left with me—the Father wou'd have made a *Jew* on't presently, but I swore, if he committed such a Barbarity on the Infant, that I wou'd discover all—so I had him brought up a good 60 *Christian,* and bound Prentice to an Attorney.

Young Wou'dbe. Very well!

Midnight. Ah, my Lord, there's many a pretty Fellow in *London* that knows as little of their true Father and Mother as he does; I have had several such Jobbs in my time—there was one *Scotch* Nobleman that brought me four in half a year.

Young Wou'dbe. Four! and how were they all provided for?

Midnight. Very handsomly indeed; they were two Sons and two Daughters, the eldest Son rides in the first Troop of Guards, and the 'tother is a very pretty Fellow, and his 70 Father's *Valet de Chambre.*

Young Wou'dbe. And what is become of the Daughters, pray?

Midnight. Why one of 'em is a Manto maker, and the
Youngest has got into the Playhouse—Ay, ay, my Lord, let
Subtleman alone, I'll warrant, he'll manage your Brother,
adsmylife here's somebody coming, I would not be seen.

Young Wou'dbe. 'Tis my Brother, and he'll meet you upon
the Stairs, adso, get into this Closet till he be gone. (*Shuts her
into the Closet.*)
              Enter Elder Wou'dbe *and* Subtleman.
My Brother! dearest Brother, welcome! (*Runs and embraces
him.*)

Elder Wou'dbe. I can't dissemble, Sir, else I wou'd return
your false Embrace.   80

Young Wou'dbe. False Embrace! still suspicious of me! I
thought that five Years Absence might have cool'd the
unmanly Heats of our childish days—that I am overjoy'd at
your Return, let this testify, this Moment I resign all Right
and Title to your Honour, and salute you Lord.

Elder Wou'dbe. I want not your Permission to enjoy my
Right, here I am Lord and Master without your Resignation;
and the first Use I make of my Authority, is, to discard that
rude bull-fac'd Fellow at the Door; where is my Steward,
                    Enter Steward.
Mr. *Clearaccount*, let that pamper'd Sentinel below this Minute 90
be discharg'd—Brother, I wonder you cou'd feed such a
swarm of lazy idle Drones about you, and leave the poor
industrious Bees that fed you from their Hives, to starve for
want—*Steward*, look to't, if I have not Discharges for every
Farthing of my Father's Debts upon my Toylet to morrow
morning, you shall follow the Tipstaff I can assure you.

Young Wou'dbe. Hold, hold, my Lord, you usurp too large a
Power, methinks, o'er my Family.

Elder Wou'dbe. Your Family!

Young Wou'dbe. Yes, my Family, you have no Title to lord it 100
here—Mr. *Clearaccount*, you know your Master.

Elder Wou'dbe. How! a Combination against me!—Brother,
take heed how you deal with one that, cautious of your
Falshood, comes prepar'd to meet your Arts, and can retort
your Cunning to your Infamy: Your black unnatural Designs
against my Life before I went abroad, my Charity can pardon;
but my Prudence must remember to guard me from your

Malice for the future.

Young Wou'dbe. Our Father's weak and fond Surmise! which
110 he upon his Death-bed own'd; and to recompence me for that
injurious unnatural Suspicion, he left me sole Heir to his
Estate—Now, my Lord, my House and Servants are—at your
Service.

Elder Wou'dbe. Villany beyond Example! have I not Letters
from my Father, of scarce a Fortnight's Date, where he
repeats his Fears for my Return, least it should again expose
me to your Hatred.

Subtleman. Well, well, these are no Proofs, no Proofs, my
Lord; they won't pass in Court against positive Evidence—here
120 is your Father's Will, *signatum & sigillatum*, besides his last
Words to confirm it, to which I can take my positive Oath in
any Court of *Westminster*.

Elder Wou'dbe. What are you, Sir?

Subtleman. Of *Clifford*'s-Inn, my Lord, I belong to the Law.

Elder Wou'dbe. Thou art the Worm and Maggot of the Law,
bred in the bruis'd and rotten parts, and now art nourish'd on
the same Corruption that produc'd thee—the *English* Law as
planted first, was like the *English* Oak, shooting its spreading
Arms around to shelter all that dwelt beneath its shade—but
130 now whole Swarms of Caterpillars, like you, hang in such
Clusters upon every Branch, that the once thriving Tree now
sheds infectious Vermin on our Heads.

Young Wou'dbe. My Lord, I have some Company above, if
your Lordship will drink a Glass of Wine, we shall be proud of
the Honour, if not, I shall attend you at any Court of
Judicature whenever you please to summon me. (*Going.*)

Elder Wou'dbe. Hold sir,—perhaps my Father's dying
Weakness was impos'd on, and he has left him Heir; if so, his
Will shall freely be obey'd. (*Aside.*)—Brother, you say you
140 have a Will.

Subtleman. Here it is. (*Shewing a Parchment.*)

Elder Wou'dbe. Let me see it.

Subtleman. There's no President for that, my Lord.

Elder Wou'dbe. Upon my Honour I'll restore it.

Young Wou'dbe. Upon my Honour but you shan't—(*Takes it
from* Subtleman *and puts it in his Pocket.*)

Elder Wou'dbe. This over-caution, Brother, is suspicious.

Young Wou'dbe. Seven thousand Pound a Year is worth looking after.

Elder Wou'dbe. Therefore you can't take it ill that I am a little inquisitive about it—Have you Witnesses to prove my 150 Father's dying Words.

Young Wou'dbe. A Couple, in the House.

Elder Wou'dbe. Who are they?

Subtleman. Witnesses my Lord—'tis unwarrantable to enquire into the Merits of the Cause out of Court—my Client shall answer no more Questions.

Elder Wou'dbe. Perhaps, Sir, upon a satisfactory Account of his Title, I intend to leave your Client to the quiet Enjoyment of his Right, without troubling any Court with the Business; I therefore desire to know what kind of Persons are these 160 Witnesses.

Subtleman. Oho, he's a coming about (*Aside.*) I told your Lordship already, that I am one, another is in the House, one of my Lord's Footmen.

Elder Wou'dbe. Where is this Footman?

Young Wou'dbe. Forthcoming.

Elder Wou'dbe. Produce him.

Subtleman. That I shall presently—The day's our own, Sir, (*To* Young Wou'dbe.) but you shall engage first to ask him no cross Questions. 170

Exit Subtleman.

Elder Wou'dbe. I am not skill'd in such: But pray Brother, did my Father quite forget me, left me nothing.

Young Wou'dbe. Truly, my Lord, nothing—he spake but little, left no Legacies.

Elder Wou'dbe. 'Tis strange! he was extreamly just, and lov'd me too—but, perhaps—

Enter Subtleman *with* Teague.

Subtleman. My Lord, here's another Evidence.

Elder Wou'dbe. Teague!

Young Wou'dbe. My Brother's Servant! (*They all four stare upon one another.*)

Subtleman. His Servant! 180

Teague. Maishter! see here Maishter, I did get all dish (*Chinks Money.*) for being an Evidensh dear Joy, an be me shoule I will give the half of it to you, if you will give me your

Permission to maake swear against you.

Elder Wou'dbe. My Wonder is divided between the Villany of the Fact, and the Amazement of the Discovery. *Teague!* my very Servant! sure I dream.

Teague. Fet, dere is no dreaming in the cashe, I'm sure the Croon pieceish are awake, for I have been taaking with dem
190 dish half hour.

Young Wou'dbe. Ignorant, unlucky Man, thou hast ruin'd me; why had not I a sight of him before.

Subtleman. I thought the Fellow had been too ignorant to be a Knave.

Teague. Be me shoule, you lee, dear Joy—I can be a Knave as well as you, fen I think it conveniency.

Elder Wou'dbe. Now Brother! Speechless! Your Oracle too silenc'd! Is all your boasted Fortune sunk to the guilty blushing for a Crime? but I scorn to insult—let Disappoint-
200 ment be your Punishment: But for your Lawyer there—*Teague*, lay hold of him.

Subtleman. Let none dare to attach me without a legal Warrant.

Teague. Attach! no dear Joy, I cannot attach you—but I can catch you by the Troat, after the fashion of *Ireland.* (*Takes* Subtleman *by the Throat.*)

Subtleman. An Assault! An Assault!

Teague. No, no, tish nothing but choaking, nothing but choaking.

Elder Wou'dbe. Hold him fast *Teague*—Now Sir (*To* Young
210 Wou'dbe.) because I was your Brother you wou'd have betray'd me; and because I am your Brother, I forgive it,—dispose your self as you think fit,—I'll order Mr. *Clearaccount* to give you a thousand Pounds. Go take it, and pay me by your Absence.

Young Wou'dbe. I scorn your beggarly Benevolence: Had my Designs succeeded, I wou'd not have allow'd you the weight of a Wafer, and therefore will accept none.—As for that Lawyer, he deserves to be Pillory'd, not for his Cunning in deceiving you; but for his Ignorance in betraying me.—The villain has
220 defrauded me of seven thousand Pounds a year. Farewel.— (*Going.*)

IV. i. 218 Pillory'd] O2; Pillor'd

Enter Midnight *out of the Closet, runs to*
Young Wou'dbe *and kneels.*

Midnight. My Lord, my dear Lord *Wou'dbe*, I beg you ten thousand Pardons.

Young Wou'dbe. What Offence hast thou done to me?

Midnight. An Offence the most injurious.—I have hitherto conceal'd a Secret in my Breast to the Offence of Justice, and the defrauding your Lordship of your true Right and Title. You *Benjamin Wou'dbe* with the crooked Back, art the Eldest-born, and true Heir to the Estate and Dignity.

Omnes. How!

Teague. Arah, how?   230

Midnight. None, my Lord, can tell better than I, who brought you both into the world.—My deceas'd Lord, upon the sight of your Deformity, engag'd me by a considerable Reward, to say you were the last born, that the beautiful Twin, likely to be the greater Ornament to the Family, might succeed him in his Honour.—This Secret my Conscience has long struggled with,—upon the News that you were left Heir to the Estate: I thought Justice was satisfied, and I was resolv'd to keep it a Secret still: but by strange Chance over-hearing what past just now, my poor Conscience was rack'd, 240 and I was forc'd to declare the Truth.

Young Wou'dbe. By all my forward Hopes I cou'd have sworn it: I found the Spirit of Eldership in my Blood: my Pulses beat, and swell'd for Seniority.—Mr. *Hermes Wou'dbe*,—I'm your most humble Servant. (*Foppishly.*)

Elder Wou'dbe. Hermes is my Name, my *Christian* Name; of which I am prouder, than of all Titles that Honour gives, or Flattery bestows.—But thou, vain Bubble; puft up with the empty Breath of that more empty Woman; to let thee see how I despise thy Pride, I'll call thee Lord, dress thee up in Titles 250 like a King at Arms: You shall be blazon'd round like any Church in *Holland*; thy Pageantry shall exceed the Lord Mayor's; and yet this *Hermes*, plain *Hermes*, shall despise thee.

Subtleman. Well, well, this is nothing to the purpose.—Mrs. will you make an Affidavit of what you have said, before a Master in *Chancery?*

Midnight. That I can, tho' I were to die the next minute after it.

Teague. Den, dear Joy, you wou'd be dam the nex minute
260 after dat.

Elder Wou'dbe. All this is trifling; I must purge my House of
this Nest of Villainy at once.—Here *Teague* (*Whispers* Teague.)
Go, make haste.

Teague. Dat I can—(*As he runs out*, Young Wou'dbe *stops
him.*)

Young Wou'dbe. Where are you going, Sir?

Teague. Only for a Pot of Ale, dear Joy, for you and my
Maishter to drink Friends.

Young Wou'dbe. You lye, Sirrah. (*Pushes him back.*)

Teague. Fet, I do so.

270 *Elder Wou'dbe.* What! Violence to my Servant! Nay, then I'll
force him a Passage. (*Draws.*)

Subtleman. An Assault, an Assault upon the Body of a Peer,
within there.

> Enter three or four Constables, one of 'em with
> a black Patch on his Eye. They disarm
> Elder Wou'dbe *and secure* Teague.

Elder Wou'dbe. This Plot was laid for my Reception.
Unhand me, *Constable.*

Young Wou'dbe. Have a care, Mr. *Constable*; the Man is mad;
he's possest with an odd Frensie, that he's my Brother, and
my elder too: So because I wou'd not very willingly resign my
House and Estate, he attempted to murder me.

280 *Subtleman.* Gentlemen, take care of that Fellow. He made an
Assault upon my body, *vi & armis.*

Teague. Arah, fat is dat *wy at armish?*

Subtleman. No matter, Sirrah; I shall have you hang'd.

Teague. Hang'd! Dat is nothing, dear Joy;—we are us'd to't.

Elder Wou'dbe. Unhand me, Villains, or by all—

Teague. Have a caar, dear Maishter; don't swear: we shall
be had in the Croon-Offish: You know dere ish Sharpers
about us. (*Looking about on them that hold him.*)

Young Wou'dbe. Mr. *Constable*, you know your Directions:
290 away with em.

Elder Wou'dbe. Hold—

Constable. No, no; force him away—

> They all hurry off.
> *Manent* Young Wou'dbe, *and* Midnight.

Young Wou'dbe. Now, my dear Prophetess, my Sibyl: By all my dear Desires and Ambitions, I do believe you have spoken the Truth.—I am the Elder.

Midnight. No, no, Sir, the Devil a Word on't is true.—I wou'd not wrong my Conscience neither: For, faith and troth, as I am an honest Woman, you were born above three quarters of an hour after him;—but I don't much care if I do swear that you are the eldest.—What a Blessing it was, that I 300 was in the Closet at that pinch. Had I not come out that moment, you wou'd have sneakt off; your Brother had been in possession, and then we had lost all; but now you are established: Possession gets you Money, that gets you Law, and Law, you know.—Down on your Knees, Sirrah, and ask me Blessing.

Young Wou'dbe. No, my dear Mother, I'll give thee a Blessing, a Rent-charge of five hundred pound a Year, upon what part of the Estate you will, during your Life.

Midnight. Thank you, my Lord: That five hundred a Year 310 will afford me a leisurely Life, and a handsome Retirement in the Countrey, where I mean to repent me of my Sins, and die a good *Christian*: For Heaven knows, I am old, and ought to bethink me of another Life.—Have you none of the Cordial left that we had in the morning?

Young Wou'dbe. Yes, yes, we'll go to the Fountain-head.

Exeunt.

[ACT IV. Scene ii.]

SCENE, *The Street.*

Enter Teague.

Teague. Deel tauke me but dish ish a most shweet Business indeed; Maishters play the fool, and Shervants must shuffer for it. I am Prishoner in the *Constable*'s House be me Shoule, and shent abrode to fetch some Bail for my Maishter; but foo shall bail poor *Teague* agra.

Enter Constance.

IV. ii. 5 bail] O2; fail

Oh, dere ish my Maishter's old Love. Indeed, I fear dish Bishness will spoil his Fortune.

Constance. Who's here? *Teague!* (*He turns from her.*)

Teague. Deel tauke her, I did tought she cou'd not know me
10 agen now I am a Prishoner. (Constance *goes about to look him in the Face. He turns from her.*) Dish ish not shivil, be me Shoul, to know a Shentleman fither he will or no.

Constance. Why this, *Teague*? What's the matter? are you asham'd of me or your self, *Teague*?

Teague. Of bote, be me Shoule.

Constance. How does your Master, Sir?

Teague. Very well, dear Joy, and in prishon.

Constance. In prison! how, where?

Teague. Why, in the little *Bashtile* yonder at the end of the
20 Street.

Constance. Shew me the way immediately.

Teague. Fet, I can shew you the Hoose yonder: Shee yonder; be me Shoul I she his Faace yonder, peeping troo the Iron Glash Window.

Constance. I'll see him tho' a Dungeon were his Confinement.

Runs out.

Teague. Ah—auld kindnesh, be me Shoul, cannot be forgotten. Now if my Maishter had but Grash enough to get her wit child, her word wou'd go for two; and she wou'd bail him and I bote.

Exit.

[ACT IV. Scene iii.]

SCENE, *A Room miserably furnished*, Elder Wou'dbe *sitting and writing.*

Elder Wou'dbe.	The Tow'r confines the Great,
	The Spunging-house the Poor:
	Thus there are degrees of State
	That ev'n the Wretched must endure.

> Virgil, *tho' cherished in Courts,*
> *Relates but a spleenatick Tale,*
> Cervantes, *Revels, and Sports,*
> *Altho' he writ in a Jayl.*

Then hang Reflections (*Starts up.*) I'll go write a Comedy. Ho, within there: Tell the Lieutenant of the Tower that I would speak with him.

Enter Constable.

Constable. Ay, ay the Man is mad: Lieutenant o'th' Tower! Ha, ha, ha; wou'd you could make your Words good, Master.

Elder Wou'dbe. Why? am not I a Prisoner here? I know it by the stately Apartments.—What is that, pray, that hangs streaming down upon the Wall yonder?

Constable. Yonder? 'Tis Cobweb, Sir.

Elder Wou'dbe. 'Tis false, Sir; 'tis as fine Tapestry as any in *Europe.*

Constable. The Devil it is.

Elder Wou'dbe. Then your Damask Bed, here; the Flowers are so bold, I took 'em for Embroidery; and then the Headwork! Point *de Venice* I protest.

Constable. As good *Kidderminster* as any in *England,* I must confess; and tho' the Sheets be a little soiled, yet I can assure you, Sir, that many an honest Gentleman has lain in them.

Elder Wou'dbe. Pray Sir, what did those two *Indian* Pieces cost that are fixt up in the Corner of the Room?

Constable. Indian Pieces? What the Devil, Sir, they are my old Jack-Boots, my Militia Boots.

Elder Wou'dbe. I took 'em for two *China* Jarrs, upon my word: But hearkee, Friend, art thou content that these things shou'd be as they are?

Constable. Content! ay, Sir.

Elder Wou'dbe. Why then shou'd I complain? (*One calls within.*)

(*Within.*) Mr. *Constable,* here's a Woman will force her way uppon us: we can't stop her.

Constable. Knock her down then, knock her down; let no Woman come up, the Man's mad enough already.

Enter Constance.

40   *Constance.* Who dares oppose me? (*Throws him a handful of Money.*)

Constable. Not I truly Madam. (*Gathers up the Money.*)

Elder Wou'dbe. My *Constance*! My Guardian-Angel here! Then nought can hurt me.

Constable. Hearkee, Sir, you may suppose the Bed to be a Damask Bed for half an hour if you please.—

Constance. No, no, Sir, your Prisoner must along with me.

Constable. Ay? Faith the Woman's madder than the Man.

                    Enter Trueman *and* Teague.

Elder Wou'dbe. Ha! *Trueman* too! I'm proud to think that many a Prince has not so many true Friends in his Palace, as I
50 have here in Prison;—two such—

Teague. Tree, be me Shoule.

Trueman. My Lord, just as I heard of your Confinement, I was going to make my self a Prisoner. Behold the Fetters: I had just bought the Wedding-Ring.

Constable. I hope they are golden Fetters, Captain!

Trueman. They weigh four thousand Pound, Madam, besides the Purse, which is worth a Million.—My Lord, this very Evening was I to be marry'd; but the News of your Misfortune has stopt me: I wou'd not gather Roses in a wet Hour.

60   *Elder Wou'dbe.* Come, the Weather shall be clear; the Thoughts of your good Fortune will make me easy, more than my own can do, if purchased by your Disappointment.

Trueman. Do you think, my Lord, that I can go to the Bed of Pleasure whilst you lie in a Hovel—here, where is this Constable, how dare you do this, insolent Rascal?

Constable. Insolent Rascal! do you know who you speak to, Sir?

Trueman. Yes, Sirrah, don't I call you by your proper Name? how dare you confine a Peer of the Realm?

70   *Constable.* Peer of the Realm! you may give good Words tho, I hope.

Elder Wou'dbe. Ay, ay, Mr. *Constable* is in the right, he did but his Duty; I suppose he had twenty Guineas for his Pains.

Constable. No, I had but ten.

Elder Wou'dbe. Hearkee *Trueman*, this Fellow must be sooth'd, he'll be of Use to us, I must employ you too in this Affair with my Brother.

Trueman. Say no more, my Lord, I'll cut his Throat, 'tis but flying the Kingdom.

Elder Wou'dbe. No, no, 'twill be more Revenge to worst him 80 at his own Weapons. Cou'd I but force him out of his Garrison, that I might get into Possession, his Claim would vanish immediately—Do's my Brother know you?

Trueman. Very little, if at all.

Elder Wou'dbe. Hearkee. (*Whispers.*)

Trueman. It shall be done—Lookee *Constable*, you're drawn into a wrong Cause, and it may prove your Destruction if you don't change sides immediately—we desire no Favour but the Use of your Coat, Wig, and Staff, for half an hour.

Constance. Why truly Sir, I understand now, by this 90 Gentlewoman that I know to be our Neighbour, that he is a Lord, and I heartily beg his Worship's Pardon, and if I can do your Honour any Service, your Grace may command me.

Elder Wou'dbe. I'll reward you, but we must have the black Patch for the Eye too.

Teague. I can give your Lorship wan, here fet, 'tis a Plaishter for a shore Finger, and I have worn it but twice.

Constance. —But, pray, Captain, what was your Quarrel at *Aurelia* to day.

Trueman. With your permission, Madam, we'll mind my 100 Lord's Business at present; when that's done, we'll mind the Lady's—my Lord, I shall make an excellent Constable, I never had the Honour of a Civil Employment before; we'll equip our selves in another place; here you *Prince of Darkness*, have you ne'er a better room in your House, these Iron Grates frighten the Lady.

Constable. I have a handsome neat Parlour below, Sir.

Trueman. Come along then, you must conduct us—we don't intend to be out of your Sight; that you may'nt be out of ours—(*Aside.*)   110

                                        Exeunt.

---

94 we] The 1728 edition introduces an error by revising to 'you'.

[ACT IV. Scene iv.]

SCENE *changes to an Apartment.*

Enter Aurelia *in a Passion,* Richmore *following.*

Aurelia. Follow me not,—Age and Deformity with Quiet were preferable to this vexatious Persecution; for Heaven's sake, Mr. *Richmore,* what have I ever shewn to vindicate this Presumption of yours.

Richmore. You shew it now Madam, your Face, your Wit, your Shape, are all Temptations to undergo even the Rigour of your Disdain, for the bewitching Pleasure of your Company.

Aurelia. Then be assur'd, Sir, you shall reap no other Benefit by my Company, and if you think it a Pleasure to be
10 constantly slighted, ridicul'd, and affronted, you shall have admittance to such Entertainment whenever you will.

Richmore. I take you at your word, Madam, I am arm'd with Submission against all the Attacks of your Severity, and your Ladiship shall find that my Resignation can bear much longer than your Rigour can inflict.

Aurelia. That is in plain Terms, your Sufficiency will presume much longer than my Honour can resist—Sir, you might have spar'd the unmannerly Declaration to my Face, having already taken care to let me know your Opinion of my
20 Vertue, by your impudent Settlement, propos'd by Mrs. *Midnight.*

Richmore. By those fair Eyes I'll double the Proposal; this soft, this white, this powerful Hand (*Takes her Hand.*) shall write its own Conditions.

Aurelia. Then it shall write this—(*Strikes him.*) and if you like the Terms you shall have more another time.

Exit.

Richmore. Death and Madness! a Blow!—Twenty thousand Pound Sterling for one Night's Revenge upon her dear proud disdainful Person!—Am I rich as many a Sovereign Prince,
30 wallow in Wealth, yet can't command my Pleasure?—Woman! —If there be Power in Gold, I yet shall triumph o'er thy Pride.

Enter Midnight.

Midnight. O my troth, and so you shall, if I can help it.

Richmore. Madam, Madam, here, here, here's Money, Gold, Silver, take, take, all, all, my Rings too; all shall be yours, make me but happy in this presumptuous Beauty, I'll make thee rich as Avarice can crave, if not, I'll murder thee, and my self too.

Midnight. Your Bounty is too large, too large indeed Sir.

Richmore. Too large! no, 'tis Beggery without her,—Lord- 40 ships, Mannors, Acres, Rents, Tythes, and Trees, all all shall fly for my dear sweet Revenge.

Midnight. Say no more, this Night I'll put you in a way.

Richmore. This Night!

Midnight. The Lady's Aunt is very near her time—she goes abroad this Evening a visiting; in the mean time I send to your Mistress, that her Aunt is fallen in Labour at my House: she comes in a hurry, and then—

Richmore. Shall I be there to meet her?

Midnight. Perhaps.   50

Richmore. In a private Room?

Midnight. Mum.

Richmore. No Creature to disturb us?

Midnight. Mum, I say, but you must give me your Word not to ravish her; nay, I can tell you, she won't be ravish'd.

Richmore. Ravish! let me see, I'm worth five thousand Pound a year, twenty thousand Guineas in my Pocket, and may not I force a Toy that's scarce worth fifteen hundred Pound, I'll do't.

> *Her Beauty sets my Heart on Fire, beside*   60
> *The Injurious Blow has set on Fire my Pride;*
> *The bare Fruition were not worth my Pain,*
> *The Joy will be to humble her Disdain;*
> *Beyond Enjoyment will the Transport last*
> *In Triumph when the Extasy is past.*

Exeunt.

[*The End of the Fourth Act.*]

ACT V. [Scene i.]

SCENE, *Lord* Woud'dbe*'s House.*

Young Wou'dbe, solus.

Young Wou'dbe. Show me that proud Stoick that can bear
Success and Champaign, Philosophy can support us in hard
Fortune, but who can have patience in Prosperity? The
Learned may talk what they will of human Bodies, but I am
sure there is not one Atom in mine, but what is truly
Epicurean. My Brother is secur'd, I guarded with my Friends,
my lewd and honest midnight Friends—holla, who waits
there?

Enter Servant.

Servant. My Lord?

10 *Young Wou'dbe.* A fresh Battalion of Bottles to reinforce the
Cestern, are the Ladies come?

Servant. Half an hour ago, my Lord,—they're below in the
Bathing Chamber.

Young Wou'dbe. Where did you light on 'em?

Servant. One in the Passage at the old Playhouse, my
Lord,—I found another very melancholly paring her Nails by
Rosamond's Pond,—and a couple I got at the *Chequer* Ale-house
in *Holbourn*; the two last came to Town yesterday in a West-
Country Waggon.

20 *Young Wou'dbe.* Very well, order *Baconface* to hasten Supper,
—and d'y' hear? and bid the *Swiss* admit no Stranger without
acquainting me—

Exit Servant.

Now Fortune I defy thee, this Night's my own at least.

Re-enter Servant.

Servant. My Lord, here's the Constable below with the
black Eye, and he wants to speak with your Lordship in all
hast.

Young Wou'dbe. Ha! the Constable! shou'd Fortune jilt me
now?—bid him come up, I fear some cursed Chance to thwart
me.

Enter Trueman *in the* Constable*'s Clothes.*

Trueman. Ah, my Lord, here is sad News—your Brother 30
is—

Young Wou'dbe. Got away, made his Escape, I warrant you.

Trueman. Worse, worse, my Lord.

Young Wou'dbe. Worse, worse! what can be worse?

Trueman. I dare not speak it.

Young Wou'dbe. Death and Hell Fellow, don't distract me.

Trueman. He's dead.

Young Wou'dbe. Dead!

Trueman. Positively.

Young Wou'dbe. Coup de Grace, Ciel gramercy.   40

Trueman. Villain, I understand you. (*Aside.*)

Young Wou'dbe. But how, how, Mr. *Constable*? speak it aloud,
kill me with the Relation.

Trueman. I don't know how, the poor Gentleman was very
melancholly upon his Confinement, and so he desir'd me to
send for a Gentlewoman that lives hard by here, may-hap
your Worship may know her.

Young Wou'dbe. At the guilt Balcony in the Square.

Trueman. The very same, a smart Woman truly—I went for
her my self, but she was otherwise engag'd, not she truly, she 50
wou'd not come—Wou'd you believe it, my Lord, at hearing
of this the poor Man was like to drop down dead.

Young Wou'dbe. Then he was but likely to drop dead.

Trueman. Wou'd it were no more. Then I left him, and
coming about two Hours after, I found him hang'd in his
Sword Belt.

Young Wou'dbe. Hang'd!

Trueman. Dangling.

Young Wou'dbe. Le Coup declat! done like the noblest *Roman* of
'em all; but are you sure he's past all Recovery? Did you send 60
for no Surgeon to bleed him?

Trueman. No, my Lord, I forgot that—but I'll send immediately.

Young Wou'dbe. No, no, Mr. *Constable*, 'tis too late now, too
late—and the Lady wou'd not come, you say.

Trueman. Not a Step wou'd she stir.

Young Wou'dbe. Inhumane, barbarous,—dear, delicious
Woman, thou now art mine [*Aside.*]—where is the Body, Mr.
Constable, I must see it.

70　*Trueman.* By all means, my Lord, it lies in my Parlour; there's a power of Company come in, and among the rest one, one, one, *Trueman* I think they call him, a divellish hot Fellow, he had like to have pull'd the House down about our Ears, and swears—I told him he should pay for his swearing—he gave me a Slap in the Face, said he was in the Army, and had a Commission for't.

Young Wou'dbe. Capt. *Trueman*! a blustering kind of Rake-helly Officer.

Trueman. Ay, my Lord, one of those Scoundrels that we pay
80　wages to for being knockt o'th' head for us.

Young Wou'dbe. Ay, ay, one of those Fools that have only Brains to be knockt out.

Trueman. Son of a Whore (*Aside.*) He's a plaguy impudent Fellow, my Lord; he swore that you were the greatest Villain upon the Earth.

Young Wou'dbe. Ay, ay; but he durst not say that to my face, Mr. *Constable.*

Trueman. No, no, hang him, he said it behind your back, to be sure—and he swore moreover.—Have a care, my Lord,—
90　he swore that he wou'd cut your Throat whenever he met you.

Young Wou'dbe. Will you swear that you heard him say so?

Trueman. Heard him! ay, as plainly as you hear me: He spoke the very Words that I speak to your Lordship.

Young Wou'dbe. Well, well, I'll manage him.—But now I think on't, I won't go see the Body; It will but encrease my Grief.—Mr. *Constable*, do you send for the Coroner: They must find him *non Compos*. He was mad before, you know. Here—something for your Trouble. (*Gives Money.*)

Trueman. Thank your Honour.—But pray, my Lord, have a
100　care of that *Trueman*; he swears that he'll cut your Throat; and he will do't, my Lord, he will do't.

Young Wou'dbe. Never fear, never fear.

Trueman. But he swore it, my Lord, and he will certainly do't. Pray have a care.

　　　　　　　　　　　　　　　　　　　　　　　　Exit.

Young Wou'dbe. Well, well,—so,—the Devil's in't if I ben't the eldest now. What a pack of civil Relations have I had here? My Father takes a Fit of the Apoplexy, makes a Face, and goes off one way, my Brother takes a Fit of the Spleen,

makes a Face, and goes off t'other way.—Well, I must own he
has found the way to molifie me, and I do love him now with 110
all my heart, since he was so very civil to justle into the World
before me, I think he did very civilly to justle out of it before
me.—But now my Joys! Without there—hollo—take off the
Inquisition of the Gate; the Heir may now enter unsuspected.
>   *The Wolf is dead, the Shepherds may go play:*
>   *Ease follows Care; so rowls the world away.*

'Tis a question whether Adversity or Prosperity makes the
most Poets.

Enter Servant.

Servant. My Lord, a Footman brought this Letter, and waits
for an Answer.   120

Young Wou'dbe. Nothing from the *Elisian Fields*, I hope.
(*Opening the Letter.*) What do I see, CONSTANCE? Spells and
Magick in every Letter of the Name.—Now for the sweet
Contents.

>   *My Lord, I'm pleas'd to hear of your happy Change of Fortune,*
>   *and shall be glad to see your Lordship this Evening to wish you*
>   *Joy.*

CONSTANCE.

Now the Devil's in this *Midnight*; she told me this Afternoon
that the Wind was chopping about; and has it got into the 130
warm Corner already? Here, my Coach and six to the Door:
I'll visit my *Sultana* in state.—As for the *Seraglio* below stairs,
you, my *Bashaws*, may possess 'em.

Exit.

[ACT V. Scene ii.]

SCENE, *the Street.*

Teague *with a Lanthorn*, Trueman *in the*
Constable's *Habit following.*

Trueman. Blockhead, thou hast led us out of the way; we
have certainly past the *Constable*'s House.

Teague. Be me Shoule, dear Joy, I am never oot of my ways;

for poor *Teague* has been a Vanderer ever since he vas borned.

Trueman. Hold up the Lanthorn:—what Sign is that? The St. *Albans* Tavern! why, you blundering Fool, you have led me directly to St. *James*'s *Square*, when you shou'd have gone towards *Sohoe*. (*Shrieking within.*) Hark! what noise is that over the way? a Woman's Cry!

10   *Teague.* Fet is it—shome Daumsel in distress I believe, that has no mind to be reliev'd.

Trueman. I'll use the privilege of my Office to know what the matter is.

Teague. Hol, hold, Maishter Captain, be me fet, dat ish not the way home.

Within. —Help, help, Murder, help.

Trueman. Ha! here must be mischief.—Within there, open the Door in the King's Name, or I'll force it open.—Here, *Teague*, break down the Door. (*Teague takes the Staff, thumps at the Door.*)

20   *Teague.* Deel tauke him, I have knock so long as I am able. Arah, Maishter, get a great long Ladder to get in the window of the firsht Room, and sho open the door, and let in your shelf.

Within. Help, help, help.

Trueman. Knock harder; let's raise the Mob.

Teague. O Maishter, I have tink just now of a brave Invention to maake dem come out; and be St. *Patrick*, dat very Bushiness did maake my nown shelf and my Fader run like de Devil out of mine nown Hoofe in my nown Countrey:—Be me Shoule, set the Hoose a fire.

Enter the Mob.

30   *Mob.* What's the matter, Master Constable.

Trueman. Gentlemen, I command your Assistance in the King's name, to break into the House: There is Murder cry'd within.

Mob. Ay, ay, break open the door.

Midnight at the Balcony.

Midnight. What noise is that below?

Teague. Arah, vat noise ish dat above?

Midnight. Only a poor Gentlewoman in Labour;—'twill be over presently.—Here, Mr. *Constable*, there's something for you to drink. (*Throws down a Purse*, Teague *takes it up.*)

40   *Teague.* Come Maishter, we have no more to shay, be me

Shoule, (*Going.*) Arah, if you vill play de Constable right now,
fet you vill come away.

    Trueman. No, no, there must be Villany by this Bribe: who
lives in this House?

    Mob. A Midwife, a Midwife; 'tis none of our business: let us
be gone.

Aurelia at the Window.

    Aurelia. Gentlemen, dear Gentlemen, help; a Rape, a Rape,
Villany.

    Trueman. Ha! That Voice I know.—Give me the Staff; I'll
make a Breach, I warrant you.   50

Breaks open the door, and all go in.

[ACT V. Scene iii.]

SCENE changes to the Inside of the House.

Re-enter Trueman and Mob.

    Trueman. Gentlemen, search all about the House; let not a
Soul escape.

Enter Aurelia running, with her Hair about her Ears,
and out of breath.

    Aurelia. Dear Mr. *Constable,*—had you—staid—but a
Moment longer, I had been ruined.

    Trueman. Aurelia! [*Aside.*] Are you safe, Madam?

    Aurelia. Yes, yes, I am safe—I think—but with enough ado:
He's a devillish strong Fellow.

    Trueman. Where is the Villain that attempted it.

    Aurelia. Pshaw—never mind the Villain;—look out the
Woman of the House, the Devil, the Monster, that decoy'd me   10
hither.

Enter Teague, haling in Midnight by the Hair.

    Teague. Be me Shoul I have taaken my shaare of the
Plunder. Let me she fat I have gotten (*Takes her to the Light.*)
Ububboo, a Witch, a Witch; the very saam Witch dat would
swaar my Maishter was de youngest.

    Trueman. How! *Midnight!* This was the luckiest Disguise.—
Come, my dear *Proserpine*, I'll take care of you.

Midnight. Pray, Sir, let me speak with you.

Trueman. No, no, I'll talk with you before a Magistrate.—A
20 Cart, *Bridewel,*—you understand me,—*Teague*; let her be your
Prisoner, I'll wait on this Lady.

Aurelia. Mr. *Constable*, I'll reward you.

Teague. It ish convenient noo by the Law of Armsh, that I
search my Prishoner, for fear she may have some Pocket-
Pishtols: Dere ish a Joak for you. (*Searches her Pockets.*)

Midnight. Ah! don't use an old Woman so barbarously.

Teague. Dear Joy, den fy vere you an old Woman? Dat is
your falt, not mine, Joy! Uboo, here ish nothing but scribble
scrabble Papers, I tink. (*Pulls out a handful of Letters.*)

30 *Trueman.* Let me see 'em; they may be of use—(*Looks over the
Letters.*) For Mr. Richmore. Ay! does he traffick hereabouts?

Aurelia. That is the Villain that would have abus'd me.

Trueman. Ha! then he has abus'd you; Villain indeed!—was
his Name *Richmore*, Mistriss? a lusty handsome Man?

Aurelia. Ay, ay, the very same; a lusty ugly Fellow.

Trueman. Let me see—whose Scrawl is this? (*Opens a Letter.*)
Death and Confusion to my sight; *Clelia*! my bride!—His
Whore—I've past a Precipice unseen, which, to look back
upon, shivers me with Terrour.—This Night, this very
40 moment, had not my Friend been in confinement, had not I
worn this dress, had not *Aurelia* been in danger, had not *Teague*
found this Letter, had the least minutest Circumstance been
omitted, what a Monster had I been? [*Aside.*] Mistriss, is this
same *Richmore* in the House still thinkee?

Aurelia. 'Tis very probable he may.—

Trueman. Very well.—*Teague*, take these Ladies over to the
Tavern and stay there till I come to you.—Madam, (*To*
Aurelia.) Fear no Injury,—your Friends are near you.

Aurelia. What does he mean!

50 *Teague.* Come, dear Joy, I vil give you a Pot of Wine, out of
your own Briberies here. (*Hales out* Midnight.)

                                        Exit Aurelia *and* Mob.
                          Manet Trueman.
                          Enter Richmore.

Richmore. Since my Money wont prevail on this cross
Fellow, I'll try what my Authority can do.—What's the
meaning of this Riot, Constable? I have the Commission of the

Peace, and can command you. Go about your Business, and
leave your Prisoners with me.

Trueman. No Sir, the Prisoners shall go about their Business,
and I'll be left with you.—Lookee, Master, we don't use to
make up these matters before Company: So you and I must be
in private a little.—You say Sir, that you are a Justice of 60
Peace.

Richmore. Yes Sir, I have my Commission in my Pocket.

Trueman. I believe it.—Now Sir, one good turn deserves
another: And if you will promise to do me a Kindness, why
you shall have as good as you bring.

Richmore. What is it?

Trueman. You must know Sir, there is a Neighbour's
Daughter that I had a woundy Kindness for: she had a very
good Repute all over the Parish, and might have married very
handsomely, that I must say; but I don't know how; we came 70
together after a very kindly natural manner; and I swore (that
I must say) I did swear confoundedly, that I would marry her:
But, I don't know how, I never car'd for marrying of her since.

Richmore. How so?

Trueman. Why, because I did my business without it: that
was the best way, I thought.—The Truth is, she has some
foolish reasons to say she's with child, and threatens mainly to
have me taken up with a Warrant, and brought before a
Justice of Peace. Now Sir, I intend to come before you, and I
hope your Worship will bring me off.   80

Richmore. Lookee Sir, if the Woman prove with child, and
you swore to marry her, you must do't.

Trueman. Ay Master; but I am for Liberty and Property. I
vote for Parliament-Men: I pay Taxes, and truly I don't think
Matrimony consistent with the Liberty of the Subject.

Richmore. But in this Case, Sir, both Law and Justice will
oblige you.

Trueman. Why if it be the Law of the Land—I found a
Letter here.—I think it is for your Worship.

Richmore. Ay Sir; how came you by it?   90

Trueman. By a very strange Accident truly.—*Clelia*—she
says here you swore to marry her. Eh!—Now Sir, I suppose
that what is Law for a Petty-Constable, may be Law for a
Justice of Peace.

Richmore. This is the oddest Fellow—[*Aside.*]

Trueman. Here was the t'other Lady that cry'd out so.—I warrant now, if I were brought before you for ravishing a Woman,—the Gallows wou'd ravish me for't.

Richmore. But I did not ravish her.

100 *Trueman.* That I'm glad to hear: I wanted to be sure of that. (*Aside.*)

Richmore. I don't like this Fellow: [*Aside.*] come Sir, give me my Letter, and go about your Business; I have no more to say to you.

Trueman. But I have something to say to you. (*Coming up to him.*)

Richmore. What!

Trueman. Dog. (*Strikes him.*)

Richmore. Ha! struck by a Peasant! (*Draws.*) Slave, thy death is certain. (*Runs at* Trueman.)

Trueman. O brave Don *John*, Rape and Murder in one 110 Night! (*Disarms him.*)

Richmore. Rascal, return my Sword, and acquit your Prisoners, else will I prosecute thee to Beggary. I'll give some Pettyfogger a thousand pound to starve thee and thy Family according to Law.

Trueman. I'll lay you a thousand pound you won't. (*Discovering himself.*)

Richmore. Ghosts and Apparitions! *Trueman!*

Trueman. Words are needless to upbraid you: my very Looks are sufficient, and if you have the least sense of Shame, this Sword wou'd be less painful in your Heart, than my 120 Appearance is in your Eye.

Richmore. Truth, by Heavens.

Trueman. Think on the Contents of this, (*Shewing the* Letter.) Think next on me; reflect upon your villainy to *Aurelia*; then view thy self.

Richmore. Trueman, canst thou forgive me?

Trueman. Forgive thee! (*A long Pause.*) Do one thing, and I will.

Richmore. Any thing.—I'll beg thy pardon.

Trueman. The Blow excuses that.

130 *Richmore.* I'll give thee half my Estate.

Trueman. Mercenary.

Richmore. I'll make thee my sole Heir.

Trueman. I despise it.

Richmore. What shall I do?

Trueman. You shall—marry *Clelia*.

Richmore. How! That's too hard.

Trueman. Too hard! why was it then impos'd on me? If you marry her your self, I shall believe you intended me no injury; so your Behaviour will be justified, my Resentment appeas'd, and the Lady's Honour repair'd.   140

Richmore. 'Tis infamous.

Trueman. No, by heavens, 'tis Justice, and what is just is honourable; if Promises from Man to Man have Force, why not from Man to Woman—their very Weakness is the Charter of their Power, and they shou'd not be injur'd, because they can't return it.

Richmore. Return my Sword.

Trueman. In my Hand 'tis the Sword of Justice, and I shou'd not part with it.

Richmore. Then sheath it here, I'll die before I consent so 150 basely.

Trueman. Consider, Sir, the Sword is worn for a distinguishing mark of Honour—promise me one, and receive t'other.

Richmore. I'll promise nothing, till I have that in my Power.

Trueman. Take it. (*Throws him his Sword.*)

Richmore. I scorn to be compell'd even to Justice, and now that I may resist, I yield—*Trueman*, I have injur'd thee, and *Clelia* I have severely wrong'd.

Trueman. Wrong'd indeed Sir,—and to aggravate the Crime, 160 the fair afflicted loves you; mark'd you with what Confusion she receiv'd me? she wept, the injur'd Innocence wept, and with a strange reluctance gave consent; her moving softness pierc'd my Heart, tho' I mistook the cause.

Richmore. Your youthful Vertue warms my Breast, and melts it into Tenderness.

Trueman. Indulge it Sir, Justice is noble in any Form; think of the Joys and Raptures will possess her, when she finds you instead of me; you the dear Dissembler, the Man she loves, the Man she gave for lost, to find him true, return'd, and in her 170 Arms.

Richmore. No new Possession can give equal Joy—it shall be done, the Priest that waits for you shall tie the Knot this moment, in the Morning I'll expect you'l give me Joy.

Exit.

Trueman. So, is not this better now than cutting of Throats, I have got my Revenge, and the Lady will have hers without Blood-shed.

Exit.

[ACT V. Scene iv.]

SCENE *changes to an Apartment,*

Constance *and* Servant.

Servant. He's just a coming up, Madam.

Constance. My Civility to this Man will be as great a Constraint upon me as Rudeness wou'd be to his Brother; but I must bear it a little, because our Designs require it,

Enter Young Wou'dbe.

his Appearance shocks me—My Lord, I wish you Joy.

Young Wou'dbe. Madam, 'tis only in your Power to give it, and wou'd you honour me with a Title to be really proud of, it shou'd be that of your humblest Servant.

Constance. I never admitted any Body to the Title of an 10 humble Servant, that I did not intend should command me, if your Lordship will bear with the Slavery, you shall begin when you please, provided you take upon you the Authority when I have a mind.

Young Wou'dbe. Our Sex, Madam, make much better Lovers than Husbands, and I think it highly unreasonable, that you should put your self in my Power when you can so absolutely keep me in yours.

Constance. No, my Lord, we never truly command till we have given our Promise to obey; and we are never in more 20 danger of being made Slaves, than when we have 'em at our Feet.

Young Wou'dbe. True, Madam, the greatest Empires are in most Danger of Falling, but it is better to be absolute there, than to act by a Prerogative that's confin'd.

Constance. Well, well, my Lord, I like the Constitution we live under; I'm for a limited Power or none at all.

Young Wou'dbe. You have so much the Heart of the Subject, Madam, that you may rule as you please; but you have weak Pretences to a limited Sway, where your Eyes have already play'd the Tyrant,—I think one Priviledge of the People is to kiss their Sovereign's Hand. (*Taking her hand.*) 30

Constance. Not, till they have taken the Oaths, my Lord; and he that refuses them in the Form the Law prescribes, is, I think, no better than a Rebel.

Young Wou'dbe. By Shrines and Altars, (*Kneeling.*) by all that you think just, and I hold good, by this (*Taking her hand.*) the fairest, and the dearest Vow,—(*Kissing her hand.*)

Constance. Fie my Lord. (*Seemingly yielding.*)

Young Wou'dbe. Your Eyes are mine, they bring me Tidings from your Heart, that this Night I shall be happy. 40

Constance. Wou'd not you dispise a Conquest so easily gain'd?

Young Wou'dbe. Yours will be the Conquest, and I shall dispise all the World but you.

Constance. But will you promise to make no Attempts upon my Honour.

Young Wou'dbe. That's foolish (*Aside.*) Not Angels sent on Messages to Earth, shall visit with more Innocence.

Constance. Ay, ay, to be sure—(*Aside.*) My Lord I'll send one to conduct you. 50

Exit.

Young Wou'dbe. Ha, ha, ha,—no Attempts upon her Honour! when I can find the Place where it lies, I'll tell her more of my mind—Now do I feel ten thousand *Cupids* tickling me all over with the Points of their Arrows—Where's my Deformity now? I have read somewhere these Lines:

> *Tho' Nature cast me in a rugged Mould,*
> *Since Fate has chang'd the Bullion into Gold:*
> Cupid *returns, breaks all his Shafts of Lead,*
> *And tips each Arrow with a Golden Head;*
> *Feather'd with Title, the gay lordly Dart* } 60
> *Flies proudly on, whilst every Virgin's Heart*
> *Swells with Ambition to receive the Smart.*

Enter Elder Wou'dbe *behind him.*

Elder Wou'dbe. *Thus to adorn Dramatick Story,*
    Stage-Hero struts in borrow'd Glory,
    Proud and August as ever Man saw,
    And ends his Empire in a Stanza.
    (*Slaps him on the Shoulder.*)

Young Wou'dbe. Ha! my Brother!

Elder Wou'dbe. No, perfidious Man; all Kindred and Relation
I disown; the poor Attempts upon my Fortune I cou'd pardon,
70 but thy base Designs upon my Love I never can forgive,—my
Honour, Birth-right, Riches, all I cou'd more freely spare,
than the least Thought of thy prevailing here.

Young Wou'dbe. How! my Hopes deceiv'd! curst be the fair
Delusions of her Sex; whilst only Man oppos'd my Cunning, I
stood secure, but soon as Woman interpos'd, Luck chang'd
hands, and the Divil was immediately on her side,—Well, Sir,
much good may do you with your Mistress, and may you love,
and live, and starve together. (*Going.*)

Elder Wou'dbe. Hold Sir, I was lately your Prisoner, now you
80 are mine; when the Ejectment is executed, you shall be at
liberty.

Young Wou'dbe. Ejectment!

Elder Wou'dbe. Yes, Sir, by this time, I hope, my Friends
have purg'd my Father's House of that debauch'd and riotous
Swarm that you had hiv'd together.

Young Wou'dbe. Confusion, Sir, let me pass, I am the elder
and will be obey'd. (*Draws.*)

Elder Wou'dbe. Dar'st thou dispute the Eldership so nobly?

Young Wou'dbe. I dare, and will, to the last Drop of my
90 inveterate Blood. (*They fight.*)

Enter Trueman *and* Teague. Trueman *strikes down*
their Swords.

Trueman. Hold, hold, my Lord, I have brought those shall
soon decide the Controversy.

Young Wou'dbe. If I mistake not, that is the Villain that
decoy'd me abroad. (*Runs at* Trueman, Teague *catches his Arm*
behind, and takes away his Sword.)

Teague. Ay, be me shoule, thish ish the besht Guard upon
the Rules of fighting, to catch a Man behind his Back.

Trueman. My Lord, a Word, (*Whispers* Elder Wou'dbe.)

Now, Gentlemen, please to hear this venerable Lady. (*Goes to the Door and brings in* Midnight.)

Elder Wou'dbe. Midnight in Custody!

Teague. In my Custody, fet.   100

Trueman. Now, Madam, you know what Punishment is destin'd for the Injury offer'd to *Aurelia*, if you don't immediately confess the truth.

Midnight. Then I must own, (Heaven forgive me) (*Weeping.*) I must own that *Hermes*, as he was still esteem'd, so he is the first-born.

Teague. A very honesht Woman, be me shoule.

Young Wou'dbe. That Confession is extorted by Fear, and therefore of no Force.

Trueman. Ay Sir, but here is your Letter to her, with the Ink   110 scarce dry, where you repeat your Offer of five hundred Pound a year to swear in your behalf.

Teague. Dat was *Teague*'s finding out, and I believe St. *Patrick* put it in my Toughts to pick her Pockets.

    Enter Constance *and* Aurelia.

Constance. I hope, Mr. *Wou'dbe*, you will make no Attempts upon my Person.

Young Wou'dbe. Damn your Person.

Elder Wou'dbe. But pray Madam where have you been all this Evening? (*To* Aurelia.)

Aurelia. Very busy I can assure you Sir; here's an honest   120 Constable that I could find in my Heart to marry, had the greasy Rogue but one Drop of genteel Blood in his Veins; what's become of him? (*Looking about.*)   •

Constance. Bless me Cosin, marry a Constable!

Aurelia. Why truly, Madam, if that Constable had not come in a very critical Minute, by this time I had been glad to marry any body.

Trueman. I take you at your word, Madam, you shall marry him this moment; and if you don't say that I have genteel Blood in my Veins by to morrow Morning—   130

Aurelia. And was it you Sir?

Trueman. Lookee, Madam, don't be asham'd, I found you a little in the *disabilé*, that's the truth on't, but you made a brave Defence.

Aurelia. I am oblig'd to you, and tho' you were a little

whimsical to day; this late Adventure has taught he how dangerous it is to provoke a Gentleman by ill Usage; therefore if my Lord and this Lady will shew us a good Example, I think we must follow our Leaders, Captain.

140   *Trueman.* As boldly as when Honour calls.

    Constance. My Lord, there was taken among your Brother's jovial Crew, his Friend *Subtleman,* whom we have taken care to secure.

    Elder Wou'dbe. For him the Pillory, for you, Madam—(*to* Midnight.)

    Teague. Be me shoule, she shall be married to Maishter *Fuller.*

    Elder Wou'dbe. For you Brother—

    Young Wou'dbe. Poverty and Contempt—
        To which I yield as to a milder Fate
150   *Than Obligations from the Man I hate.*

                                         Exit.

    Elder Wou'dbe. Then take thy Wish—And now I hope all Parties have receiv'd their due Rewards and Punishments.

    Teague. But what will you do for poor *Teague,* Maishter?

    Elder Wou'dbe. What shall I do for thee?

    Teague. Arah, maak me a Justice of peacsh, dear Joy.

    Elder Wou'dbe. Justice of Peace! thou art not qualify'd, Man.

    Teague. Yest, fet am I—I can take the Oats, and write my Mark—I can be an honesht Man my shelf; and keep a great Rogue for my Clark.

160   *Elder Wou'dbe.* Well, well, you shall be taken care of, and now, Captain, we set out for Happiness,—
        Let none despair whate'er their Fortunes be,
        Fortune must yield, wou'd Men but act like me.
        Chuse a brave Friend as Partner of your Breast, ⎫
        Be active when your Right is in Contest;   ⎬
        Be true to love, and Fate will do the rest.   ⎭

FINIS.

EPILOGUE.

Spoken by Mrs. *Hook*.

Our Poet open'd with a loud Warlike blast, ⎫
But now weak Woman is his safest cast   ⎬
To bring him off with Quarter at the last: ⎭
Not that he's vain to think, that I can say,
Or he can Write fine things to help the Play.
The various Scenes have drain'd his Strength and Art;
And I, you know, had a hard struggling Part:
But then he brought me off with Life and Limb;
Ah! Wou'd that I cou'd do as much for him—
Stay, Let me think—Your Favours to excite,   10
I still must Act the Part I Play'd to Night.
For whatsoe'er may be your sly pretence,
You like those best, that make the best Defence:
But this is needless—'Tis in vain to Crave it,
If you have Damn'd the Play, no Power can Save it.
Not all the Wits of Athens, and of Rome;
Not Shakespear, Johnson, could revoke it's Doom;
Nay, what is more—If once your Anger rouses,
Not all the courted Beauties of both Houses.
He wou'd have ended here—But I thought meet, ⎫   20
To tell him there was left one safe Retreat,   ⎬
Protection Sacred, at the Ladies Feet.   ⎭
To that he answer'd in Submissive Strain, ⎫
He pay'd all Homage to this Female Reign,   ⎬
And therefore turn'd his Satyr, 'gainst the Men. ⎭
From your great Queen, this Soveraign right ye draw,
To keep the Wits, as She the World in Awe;
To her bright Scepter, your bright Eyes they bow, ⎫
Such awful Splendour sits on every Brow,   ⎬
All Scandal on the Sex were Treason now.   ⎭   30
The Play can tell with what Poetick care, ⎫
He labour'd to redress the injur'd Fair,   ⎬
And if you wont Protect, the Men will Damn him there. ⎭
Then save the Muse, that flys to ye for Aid; ⎫
Perhaps my poor Request, may some perswade, ⎬
Because it is the first I ever made.   ⎭

COMMENTARY

Love and a Bottle

0.3 [motto] Ovid's *Tristia*, Book 1.1.3, Go, but go unadorned, as becomes the book of an exile (*Ovid with an English Translation*, Arthur Leslie Wheeler, Loeb Classical Library [London, 1939], p. 2).

Dedication

[Dedication] The adulatory tone of this dedication contrasts with the irony characteristic not only of some of Farquhar's later dedications but even of that in *The Adventures of Covent Garden*, which appeared a fortnight earlier.

0.2–3 PEREGRINE, Lord Marquiss of *Carmarthen*, &c,] Peregrine Osborne (1658–1729), second Duke of Leeds, third son of Thomas Osborne. He became Marquis of Carmarthen on 4 May 1694 when his father was made Duke of Leeds. His naval career, in which he demonstrated great gallantry and mixed success, earned him a rear admiralty in 1697. Farquhar, who admits that he does not know the Marquis, may have hoped to attain a commission through his dedication. Both Stonehill (i, p. xiv) and Rothstein (p. 18) draw attention to the fact that 'Peregrine' and 'Lord C__' are the amorous rivals in *The Adventures of Covent-Garden*, but neither claims an intentional connection between the characters and Carmarthen.

2 stranger] Farquhar had only recently arrived in London from Ireland.

13–14 your Lordships youthful Bravery and Courage] Osborne's naval career was noted for bravery, particularly in the unsuccessful attack on Brest in 1690.

31 one of the greatest Emperours in the World] Peter the Great visited England in 1698; during his visit the Marquis of Carmarthen became a favourite companion. The friendship arose because Carmarthen had designed a heavily armed yacht, the *Royal Transport*, which King William presented to the Czar. Carmarthen entertained the Czar on more than one occasion, and they discussed naval affairs. He also organized a mock battle involving thirty ships at Portsmouth for the Czar's amusement. Before leaving for Holland that spring, the Czar granted Carmarthen the sole privilege of importing tobacco into Russia, a lucrative benefit (which Carmarthen immediately sold to a body of English merchants). He did not, as Stonehill says (i. 381), offer Carmarthen a high command; in fact, according to Bonnet (21/31 Jan 1698) 'Ce Milord demanda au Czar la liberte de luy rendre visite, mais le Czar la lui refusa, et lui dit que par contre il le viendroit voir souvent' (Luttrell, iv. 290, 363, 372; Andrew Browning, *Thomas Osborn Earl of Danby and Duke of Leeds, 1632–1712* [3 vols. Glasgow, 1951], i. 542–4).

Prologue

o,2 *J. H.*],, Joseph Haines, the famous comedian. Haines was particularly well-known for both writing and speaking humorous prologues and epilogues, including recantation prologues, prologues spoken while riding an ass, etc.

o.2 Mr. *Powell*] The actor George Powell was a frequent speaker of prologues and epilogues. Because he was in 1698 in charge of rehearsals under Rich, he could assign them to himself; he was, however, a favourite of audiences in performing them. Powell was well known for his love of the bottle, as Vanbrugh's preface to *The Relapse* brings to mind, 'The Fine Gentleman of the Play, drinking his Mistress's Health in Nants Brandy, from six in the Morning, to the time he wadled upon the Stage in the Evening, had toasted himself up, to such a pitch of Vigor, I confess I once gave Amanda for gone. . . .' In the prologue, his frequent draughts from the wine bottle reminded the audience of his reputation for drunkenness.

15 *foot to foot*] as in close combat.

16 *our young Authur's new Commission wet*] 'To wet a commission' meant to celebrate or have a drink over a new military commission; however, in 1698 Farquhar's only commission apparently was from the playhouse, and even there no formal agreement for playwriting had been reached. The term is used metaphorically. 'Commission' was also a cant word for a shirt; perhaps a pun on spilling liquor on the author's new shirt, as one might well do while drinking 'foot to foot', is also intended.

22 *his Night*] that is, his third night or benefit performance.

Dramatis Personae

13 *Rigadoon*] a lively and somewhat complicated dance.

23a *Bullfinch*] the term had gained the connotation of a fool, stupid person.

I

1 *Thus far our Arms have with Success been Crown'd.*] Roebuck's first line is a quotation of Maximin's opening line in Dryden's *Tyrannick Love* (1. i, l. 1). Maximin, however says 'my Arms' rather than 'our Arms'.

21 Debenter] debenture.

29–30 the brave Officers are all disbanded, and must now turn Beggars] After the Peace of Ryswick was signed with France on 20 September 1697, many regiments were disbanded. William had disbanded ten regiments before Parliament met in December 1697, and by 11 December the House had resolved to disband all forces raised since 1680. The economic problems both for the officers and the government proved egregious. Arrears were owed to a total of £1,200,000; arrears of subsistence totalled a million more, and still other debts accrued. Taxation aimed at raising £3.5 million brought in £2 million, leaving a sizeable gap in treasury funds. By January 1698 attempts to rescind the resolution were introduced, but to no avail. Petitions from officers poured into Parliament for arrears and other complaints; many officers went on half-pay. The situation was desperate. For example, from 1697 clothing was to be provided for the men by the colonels and paid for from allowances deducted from the men's pay. But when many regiments were disbanded in 1697, men took their clothing with them; in April 1698 the colonels could not get money except for men still actually on the rolls and therefore could not pay what they owed for the clothing. The unemployment caused by disbanding regiments put a great economic strain on the nation (J. W. Fortescue, *A History of the British Army* [London, 1899], i. 379–92).

Farquhar keenly felt the unfairness of the officers' treatment. He referred to it in *The Adventures of Covent-Garden*, *The Constant Couple*, and *Sir Harry Wildair*. Because Carmarthen's regiment of marines had been disbanded, the commentary should have pleased the man whose patronage Farquhar sought.

39 great full Wigs] Full-bottomed wigs had reached their peak by the turn of the century. These wigs were swept high in front, and often parted in the centre to form two pointed horns; the hair flowed over the shoulders in loose curls. The great expense of these wigs provides the irony in the beaux' lack of any farthings for the crippled soldiers who had fought to protect them. Cunnington notes the purchase of one for £22 in 1705 (*Book of Nicholas Carew*, Surrey Archeol. Coll. 1891, quoted in C. Willett and Phillis Cunnington, *Handbook of English Costume in the Eighteenth Century* [London, 1957], p. 89), and Corson says that in 1700 a fine wig could cost up to £140 (Richard Corson, *Fashions in Hair. The First Five Thousand Years* [London, 1965], pp. 265, 281).

81 Pushing-Master] fencing master.

90 fat ale] new ale. 'Fat', according to the *New Dictionary of the Canting Crew*, means 'the last landed, inned or stow'd of any sort of Merchandize whatever, so called by the several Gangs of Water-side-Porters'.

91 chop Logick] exchange or barter logic (*NDCC*).

94 Concerns] This scene contains the first of the unusually heavy use of *double entendre* in the play. Mockmode's 'concerns' in the country refers to his estate, which adjoins Lucinda's. His 'concerns' in the city are his amorous affairs. Partridge lists 'concern' as referring to either male or female genitals from *c.*1840, but this meaning is also implied in Lucinda's witty answer.

104 Colours] flags.

110 boarding all Masks they meet, as lawful Prize] Masks worn in public places were associated with invitations to assignations, either by ladies or by prostitutes. To board meant to approach or accost, although of course the term continues the nautical metaphor.

112 *French* Ware under Hatches] 'French goods' referred to syphilis, the pox. The pun was particularly timely in the summer of 1698, for 'there was only one topic of conversation in the coffee-houses of London. Parliament had received an incredible report from the Committee on Trade about the extent of the traffic which had been carried on with France during the recent war . . . the nation was shocked.' English wool had been traded for Lyons silks to such an extent that it would have proved 'remarkable for peacetime had it been conducted on a tenth of the scale'; trade to that extent during

wartime was shocking. Heavy fines were imposed and other attempts made to stop the trade; the report demonstrated the ineffectiveness of government attempts to control smuggling (Neville Williams, *Contraband Cargoes* [London, 1959; rept. Hamden, Conn., 1961], pp. 87–8).

133–4 you had best send out your Pinnace] another pun. A pinnace was a small scouting ship. Stonehill says that colloquially it referred to a pimp or procuress (i. 381); the *OED* says that figuratively it meant a woman, particularly a mistress or prostitute. Ben Jonson's Overdo in *Bartholomew Fair*, for example, speaks of Ursula as 'Punke, Pinnace, and Bawd'. Farquhar here uses the term specifically to imply a procuress. Neither *NDCC* nor Partridge lists the usage.

149 Wolf-dog] Irish greyhound or wolf-hound.

152 Bull-Dogs] sheriff's officers.

154–5 scraping acquaintance] an acquaintance developed by currying favour or insinuating oneself into familiarity (*OED*).

157 Horns] that is, the horns of a cuckold.

160 high Topknots] The *fontange*, imported from France about 1680, developed into a high and elaborate structure of curls, frequently false and dressed over a wire foundation called a *commode* (Corson, pp. 228–9). On top of the high curls was worn a top knot or large bow of brightly coloured ribbons (C. Willett and Phillis Cunnington, *Handbook of English Costume in the Seventeenth Century* [London, 1955], p. 185).

167 Toads and Adders] St Patrick is often depicted in art as ridding Ireland of serpents and other reptiles.

169 Woodcoks] Because woodcocks are easily snared, the term developed the allusive meaning of fool, simpleton, dupe.

171 Springes] often used in connection with catching woodcocks, for example, in *Hamlet* (1. iii. 115), 'springes to catch woodcocks'.

190 secrets] The lines of sexual innuendo spoken by Roebuck and Pindress about his 'distinguishing particular' play on the use of 'secrets' to mean genitals.

231 Silk Manteaux and High-Head] The silks for dresses, like the *fontange* coiffure, were imported from France, the silk smuggled in with such shocking regularity that even someone with no fortune could wear it. Manteaux were open robes worn with a petticoat, the bodice unboned and the overskirt trained. Made of silks and other rich materials such as brocades, they were worn on social occasions (Cunnington, *Seventeenth*, p. 176; *Eighteenth*, p. 116).

241 Heaven was pleased to lessen my affliction] Roebuck's callousness toward his bastards was a common characteristic of earlier stage rakes, such as Philidor in Howard's *All Mistaken* and Valentine in Congreve's *Love for Love*.

264–5 innate Principle of Vertue] James says Roebuck is making a special application of John Locke's reference to 'Virtue generally approved, not because innate, but because profitable' in the *Essay Concerning Human Understanding* (Eugene Nelson James, *The Development of George Farquhar as a Comic Dramatist* [The Hague, 1972], pp. 90–2).

279 the Trade] prostitution.

296–7 in *forma pauperis*] a legal term. Those who were paupers were entitled to be represented by any barrister who happened to be in court (see Wycherley, *The Plain Dealer*, III. i).

304 the Inns] the Inns of Court.

317 recruit] get a fresh supply of money.

327 clubb'd] combined together in joint action or contributed toward a common stock (*OED*).

347 Travel] the pains of childbirth and the fatigues of the journey.

356 insinuating] ingratiating himself.

372 Pigsnye] an endearment for an especially cherished person.

373 *Smuggles*] cuddles.

390 truck'd] exchanged.

419 Clap-Surgeon] a derogatory term. 'Clap' means gonorrhoea. 'Clap Doctor' was a term frequently used for derogation of a medical man.

429–39 [Brush's speech] Brush's witty rejoinder to Lovewell is reminiscent of the witty servants in Shakespeare.

431 Tester] sixpence.

437–8 I have sweat out all my moisture of my hand] a moist palm indicated amorous desire; Brush claims to have lost his (*Othello*, III. iv. 35–9; Dryden, *Don Sebastian*, I. i. 297).

445 to make her a Miss] make her a kept mistress or concubine.

452 a ticklish point to manage] more sexual innuendo.

461 Engineer] artilleryman.

482 School of Venus] brothel.

485 kiss the Rod] accept chastisement with submission. Again Farquhar uses *double entendre*.

II. i.

14 natural parts] a pun, implying both wit and masculine genitals.

29 precise] fastidious or over-nice.

36 the *French*] a pun on French wines and the French disease, syphilis.

45 Sweet Powder] perfumed cosmetic powder.

56–7 Chocolate-house] Although the reference is not specific, Farquhar probably refers to White's Chocolate House, founded by Francis White in 1693 and moved to larger quarters in 1697, in St. James's Street. The only other chocolate house at the time was the Cocoa Tree in St. James's Street at the end of Pall Mall, later known as a Tory house. It was from White's that Steele headed his accounts of 'gallantry, pleasure, and entertainment' in the *Tatler* (Bryant Lillywhite, *London Coffee Houses* [London, 1963], p. 639; *London County Council Survey of London* [London, 1960], p. 463).

77 take a snap] have a hasty small meal or snack.

110 *Orpheus's* fate] Virgil, *Georgics*, IV. 520–2. The Ciconian women, feeling scorned by Orpheus' devotion in mourning Eurydice, in their sacred rites tore Orpheus apart and scattered his limbs around the fields.

123–4 Money is the Sinews of Love, as of War] This proverbial expression was particularly appropriate when the government was in great distress over the financial exigencies of the war.

II. ii

0.3 *Toyes*] knick-knacks.

2 Coupé] a dance step in which the dancer puts one foot either forward or backward in a kind of bow.

37 Snush] snuff. The form 'snush' was frequent *c.*1680–1700. After 1702 a large quantity of snuff captured by the English at Vigo Bay was dumped on the London market; before that time, however, snuff was very expensive. John Ashton quotes Charles Lillie, the perfumer, as saying it was 'very rare, and, indeed, little known in England; it being chiefly a luxurious habit among foreigners residing here, and a few of the English gentry who had travelled abroad' (John Ashton, *Social Life in the Reign of Queen Anne* (London, 1883], p. 158).

42–3 their Skull is a perfect Snush-box] Addison, later, was to anatomize a beau's brain in *Spectator*, no. 275.

45 *Orangere, Bourgamot,* and Plain-*Spanish*] three of many varieties of snuff, plain-Spanish being an inexpensive variety, Orangerie and Bourgamot considerably more costly.

57 shadows in the Glass] image in the mirror.

64 *Maiden-Fair*] a well-known song, beginning 'Once I loved a maiden fair'. It was reprinted many times in the seventeenth century, including the first ten editions of *The Dancing Master*, 1651–98, and *Apollo's Banquet*, 1670 (Claude M. Simpson, *The British Broadside Ballad and Its Music* [New Brunswick, NJ, 1966], p. 556).

64–5 *Alamire, Bifabemi, Cesolfa, Delsol, Ela, Effaut, Gesolreut*] Guido d'Arezzo adopted for the notes of his hexachord the syllables 'ut', 're', 'mi', 'fa', 'sol', 'la'. His system consisted of seven repititions of the six-note structure. Every singer for many centuries memorized his gamut, that is, the alphabetic letter-name of each note of the scale along with its solmization syllables in each of the hexachords to which it belonged. The uncorrupted Guidonian system ended with Ela (e''), but Renaissance and seventeenth-century extensions of it such as that found in Playford's *The Skill of Music* (1654) would have allowed Effaut and Gesolreut to follow although they usually referred to the F and G below middle C. Mockmode's skills are not perfect; for example, he combines the names for B flat and B natural into one term. But his inaccuracies stem from naming the notes of a scale whose pitch names come from an old system combined with a new. If he was singing rather than reciting, he was singing falsetto; the actor William Bullock often played comic women's roles and was noted, according to Steele in *Tatler*, no. 188, for his 'agreeable Squal'.

77–8 *Pythagoras was a Dancing-master; he shews the Creation to be a Country-Dance*] a derogatory reference to Pythagorean astronomy with its rotational system in which earth, counter-earth, moon, sun, the five planets, and the sphere of fixed stars rotate around the central fire or 'earth of the Universe'.

89 a breathing] exercise to stimulate the respiratory system. 'Breathing' also means the opening of a vein to let blood; a pun may be intended.

91–2 the Duke of *Burgundy*] Louis de France, Duke of Burgundy, was the son of the Dauphin and the grandson of Louis XIV. In 1698 he was about sixteen years old, had married a child bride on 7 September 1696, and might well be conceived by Nimblewrist as the ideal for Mockmode.

101 *Quart . . . Tierce*] two of the fencing positions. 'Quart and tierce' means practice between fencers who thrust and parry in these positions alternately.

114–6 when every body got Commissions, I put in for one, serv'd the Campaigns in *Flanders*; and when the Peace broke out, was disbanded] In October 1690 Parliament voted 70,000 men for Flanders for the next year, of whom 50,000 were British (Fortescue, i. 351). The campaigns in Flanders included Steinkirk in 1692, Landen in 1693, and Namur in 1695. The peace left Nimblewrist one of the many disbanded officers.

119 Courages] lustiness, masculine virility.

129 A very palpable crack] reminiscent of Hamlet's duel with Laertes, 'A hit, a very palpable hit' (v. ii.).

129–30 Your Skull is only crack'd] a pun on cracked brains or lost wit.

131 Honours] bows.

146 falsify] 'Falsify' is a feint in fencing. Rigadoon also suggests a falsifier or counterfeiter.

148 But of Honour] *Le but*, in French, means the mark at which one aims.

156 Corante] a dance characterized by a gliding step.

164 *Tyburn* Jig] a hanging.

168–9 die Dancing] die by hanging.

178–9 A clean and manly extension of all your parts—ha—Carrying a true point] more *double entendre*.

194 Defend Flankonade] Mockmode's own attempt at terminology for fencing. Although apparently the term 'Flankonade' was not used by the military or by fencers, a flanker was a cannon posted to flank a position.

212 Beverage] garnish-money, or more specifically drink-money demanded of anyone wearing new clothes.

215 Champaigne] Popularized in the Restoration court by Saint-Evremond, champagne was a wine for the very rich, being the most expensive of French wines (C. Anne Wilson, *Food and Drink in Britain* [London, 1973], p. 391).

218 Campaigne] Campaign wigs resemble full-bottom wigs with the hair knotted together on either side and a spiral curl in back.

229–30 We dare not have Wit there, for fear of being counted Rakes] Farquhar seems to write from experience. A tale, perhaps apocryphal, is told of his failing to write an assigned essay at Trinity College, Dublin, on Christ's walking on the waters; he asked to give an extemporary disquisition instead. He then suggested the miracle might be explained by the proverb 'He that is born to be hanged needs fear no drowning' (*Biographia Dramatica*)

239–40 they have no Fleeces; there's a great cry, but little Wooll] Fleece was a colloquial term for wealth, connected with the verb 'fleece' meaning to rob or plunder. The expression 'great cry and little wool' means more noise than substance or great talk and little result (Partridge).

248 Pocket-book] notebook or memorandum book.

250 Butter'd Ale] a favourite version of thickened ale drink made by

boiling mild beer or ale with butter, sugar, nutmeg, or other spices, and thickening it with beaten eggs or egg yolks (Wilson, pp. 389–90).

281 wrapt in the Tail of my Mothers Smock] born lucky, particularly with the ladies.

296 Straw-Doublet] a doublet trimmed with straw. 'Straw coat' was a coat trimmed with straw.

299–306 [SONG] The song, never previously printed with the play, was engraved as one of the 'Songs in the new Comedy call'd Love & a Bottle' (copies in the Folger Library, M1497 C43 Cage, and the British Library G304.[51] and I530.[52]). A manuscript copy of the song in the library of the Bodleian notes 'In Love and a Bottle. Set by Mr. Leveridge' (Bodleian MS Mus. Sch. C95 f. 119, listed in Crum, i. 211, E20).

322 *bore a bob*] a pun. The phrase means to take up the refrain or join in the chorus. Also a 'bob' is a rounded mass or knob at the end of a rod.

332 Jingling] a pun on the jingling noise of the drinks and 'jingling' meaning plays on words for the sake of sound, and also alliteration, rhymes, or other repetitive sounds in prose and verse.

343 *Will*'s Coffee-house] Will's established by William Urwin on Bow Street shortly after the Restoration, was the coffee-house of the wits, particularly known for Dryden's patronage and that of his coterie (Lillywhite, pp. 655–7).

348 *Bedlam*] Bethlehem Hospital or Bedlam, the hospital for lunatics in Moorfields. Viewing the inmates was a major sightseeing attraction.

357 tell a secret over a Groaning Cheese] a cheese provided for attendants and visitors during a lying-in. The gossip exchanged would, of course, be far from secret thereafter.

383 a Carted Bawd] a bawd who is 'Whipt publickly, and packt out of Town' (*NDCC*).

385 the *Sun*] the Sun Tavern behind the Royal Exchange, rebuilt after the Great Fire of 1666 by John Wadloe.

386 Whet] have a drink and have sexual intercourse.

388 The fellow will have his swing, tho he hang for't] To have one's (full) swing means to allow oneself every indulgence (*OED*). Here a pun is intended, for 'swing' also meant the gallows, and 'to swing' meant to hang (Partridge).

III. i

5–21 SONG] The song, never previously printed with the play, occurred in two half-sheet broadsides, one engraved by Thomas Cross (Chetham Broadside Halliwell–Phillips No. 1908 and British Library G315.[150]), the other apparently by John Walsh (Folger M1497 C43 Cage, f. 243ʳ and British Library G304.[172]). The texts of the two engravings are identical except for accidentals. A manuscript copy exists in Bodleian MS Mus. Sch. C95, f. 122.

23 blindest] a pun on two meanings of 'blind'. Leanthe's costume is misleading or deceitful, her love incapable of vision.

26 Link-boy] a boy employed to carry a torch, or link, to light the way for

people traversing dark streets.

39 prick'd my Finger with a Pin, till I made it bleed] The line opens a passage of sexual innuendo, using such terms as 'prick'd' for having sexual intercourse and 'pin' for penis (Partridge).

45 plaister] The prescribing of a 'plaster of warm guts' was a low colloquialism meaning 'What you need is a woman' (Partridge).

50 fitter] 'Fit' meant sexually suitable (Herbert Alexander Ellis, *Shakespeare's Lusty Punning in Love's Labour's Lost* [The Hague, 1973], p. 50).

64 pos'd me] placed me in a difficulty with his question.

73 Smock face] pale, smooth, effeminate face.

98 Pincushion] more *double entendre*, a low term for female genitals.

99 sing] make advances to her (Eric Partridge, *Shakespeare's Bawdy; A Literary and Psychological Essay, and a Comprehensive Glossary* [London, 1947], p. 187).

112–31 [SONG] The music for this song was published in Vaughan Richardson's *A Collection of New Songs, for One, Two and Three Voices, Accompany'd with Instruments, &c.* (London, 1701). Richardson (1670–1729) was an organist and composer. In June 1693 he was appointed organist at Winchester Cathedral; on 16 February his music composed on the Peace of Ryswick was performed at York Buildings, with Peter the Great attending. Richardson was not ordinarily a composer for the theatre as was Leveridge.

202 Stranguary] strangury, slow, painful urination or suppression of urine (*The Universal Family-Book* [London, 1703], p. 32).

204 Paper moths] moths whose larvae devour paper; thus, bookworms.

213 copious] abounding information; full of matter.

214 Jolls] a bump or blow to the head, in this case Lucinda's boxing his ear. Also, the tolling of a bell. Both meanings are used.

228 constrain'd] again two meanings are implied. Constrained verses were forced rather than natural; persons who are constrained check their spontaneous and natural impulses. Through Lucinda's pun Roebuck concludes in his next speech that she was angry because he did not first offer to kiss her.

236–7 I make Peace with Sword in hand] more sexual innuendo.

246 chock] choke.

249 Outworks] outlying parts of a fortifiction, continuing the metaphor of the battle of the sexes.

III. ii

2 Mr. Lee] Nathaniel Lee.

3 *Let there be not one Glimps, one Starry spark, But God's meet Gods, and justle in the Dark.*] Lines spoken by Oedipus in Lee and Dryden's *Oedipus*, Act IV, ll. 627–8. The quotation actually begins with 'May' rather than 'Let'. The inaccuracy of Farquhar's quotation suggests he was quoting from imperfect memory. He may have known the play from his acting career, but it had also played at Drury Lane on 26 November 1698 (*London Stage*, i. 506), very shortly before *Love and a Bottle* opened there. Since Dryden wrote the first

two acts and Lee the last three, Lyrick is accurate in assigning the lines to Lee.

20–1 ready Coin] money in hand. The term also implies sexual rewards Lyrick can offer Bullfinch.

47 Sheets] a pun on the sheets of paper printed by booksellers and Bullfinch's bedsheets.

52–4 you have spun me so fine, that you have almost crack'd my Thread of Life as may appear by my Spindle-shanks] spun means exhausted. The verb 'to spin' is also used ironically in 'to spin a fair thread' as in 'in being your own foe, you have spun a fair thread' (*OED*). 'To spin crooked spindles' meant to make one's husband a cuckold. Lyrick's complaint is obviously a spirited one.

55–6 your *Thalia*, and your *Melpomene*] the muses of Comedy and Tragedy.

57 Stone-doublet] a cant word for prison (*NDCC*).

63 Take your course] The term may mean 'take your course of medicine' or merely 'choose the way you wish to act'.

71 Poetry's a meer Drug] that is, a drug on the market.

72 Physick] a cathartic or purge (*OED*).

81 Penance in a White Sheet] 'penance' means sexual compliance (*Shakespeare's Bawdy*, p. 163). Ellis says there is a homophonic pun on 'pen' referring to the penis (p. 175). The speech leads into another passage of *double entendre*.

90–1 *Conquest with Lawrels . . . mourn'd.*] The first two lines of Lee's *Sophonisba*, spoken by Hannibal.

95–7 *Like Gods . . . Rills*] *Sophonisba*, 1. i. 3–5.

102 *Hurl'd dreadful Fire and Vinegar infus'd*] *Sophonisba*, 1. i. 8. According to Livy, Hannibal used vinegar or soured wine to break the rocks and ease passage in making his way over the Alps.

110 Paper is so excessive dear] In 1690 the 5 per cent *ad valorem* import duty was doubled on most sorts of paper, and by 1700 it had reached 15 per cent. Meanwhile, during 1696–9, an excise on paper was combined with high import duties. An additional 25 per cent on all imported paper and books, 20 per cent on home-produced paper, and 17½ per cent to be paid by dealers on stocks of paper was imposed. A further 5 per cent import duty was added from May 1697 to February 1700; a so-called 'new subsidy' of 1698 became effective in February 1700. Many pamphlets addressed the same issue during this period (D. C. Colman, *The British Paper Industry 1495–1860* [Oxford, 1958], pp. 66–7).

116 quit cost] bring enough money to pay for themselves.

118 Member of a Corporation] probably a reference to the conger or association of London bookseller-publishers that were publishing books as a kind of closed corporation during this period.

135–6 Bays the outside, and the Lining Fustian] 'Bays' meant not only a poet's triumphal garland or his fame but also baize, a fabric that was finer and lighter in texture than what is now called baize. 'Fustian' meant not only writing full of inflated, high-sounding words, but also a coarse cloth made of cotton and flax.

149–50 any man about *Pauls*] The courtyard of St. Paul's Cathedral bore a heavy concentration of booksellers.

153 we understand trap] We are alert to our own interest, are wide awake (Partridge). 'Trap' meant trickery or fraud.

162 Corn-cutter] chiropodist.

171–2 the three Volumes of the *English Rogue*] *The English Rogue described, in the life of Meriton Latroon, A Witty Extravagant. Being a compleat History of the most Eminent Cheats of Both Sexes*, a book by Richard Head, assisted by F. Kirkman, was first published in 1665 and often republished, with different abridgements. The fourth edition appeared in 1697 (Arundell Esdaile, *A List of English Tales and Prose Romances Printed Before 1740* [London, 1912], pp. 241–2; Charles C. Mish, *English Prose Fiction, 1600–1700: A Chronological Checklist* [Charlottesville, Va., 1952], pp. 81–6, 91).

175 spunge the sheet] get his money by extortion or pressure.

176 hamper] fetter or restrain by confinement.

179 Shurking] preying upon others by trickery. The noun 'shurk' means a shark or sharper (*NDCC*).

191–2 a Game at Tables] backgammon.

204 *But know that, I alone am King of Me*] Almanzor, speaking in Dryden's *The Conquest of Granada, Part I*, i. 206.

223 breaking Windows] Young men of this period who were 'Scourers' or 'Mohocks', that is, young rakehells looking for excitement, were noted for making mischief such as breaking windows, fighting bailiffs, roaming at night while drunk, and generally causing commotion. Club has apparently received Mockmode's punishment for scouring incidents.

230 *Complement*] Exchange formal courtesies (*OED*).

239 a blow!—*Essex, a blow*] John Banks's popular tragedy *The Unhappy Favourite: or the Earl of Essex* opened about May 1681 and was published with the date 1682. It may have been revived in 1698, for it was reprinted with the date 1699, the date on the imprint of the first edition of *Love and a Bottle* (*London Stage*, i. 296, 504). In Act III Essex speaks the lines:

> *Ha! Furies, Death and Hell! a Blow!*
> Has Essex *had a Blow!—Hold, stop my Arme*
> *Some God.*

250–1 [SONG] I have located no published music for Roebuck's topical drinking song.

256 *Mirmydons*] myrmidons, constable's assistants (Partridge).

276 Senior-Fellow] a term applied at Cambridge and Dublin to a select number of fellows of longest standing; in them the greater part of the college's government was vested. At Oxford it sometimes was applied to graduates as distinguished from undergraduates.

276 Air-Pump] another sexual pun. An air-pump was a machine for exhausting the air from a vessel by strokes of a piston, but 'pump' also colloquially meant the female genitals.

281 dirting] soiling.

283 Your starch'd Band] Standing bands or collars, starched and often supported by a wire frame, had been fashionable *c.*1605–30. They were completely out of date (Cunnington, *Seventeenth*, p. 37).

285 Cravat] Cravats, scarves of linen or muslin often finished in lace or fringe, tied around the neck in various ways, were entirely fashionable, the Steenkirk being the most recent cravat fashion, named after the battle of Steinkirk (Cunnington, *Seventeenth*, p. 147; Edward Phillips, *The New World of Words: Or, Universal English Dictionary*, 6th edn. [London, 1706]).

287 hanging-sleeves] long bands of material attached to the back of the shoulders of children's frocks and used to help them walk (Cunnington, *Eighteenth*, p. 127). 'To be in hanging-sleeves' denotes childhood.

353 Presto, pass] Farquhar used this conjurer's and juggler's phrase of command, meaning 'immediately, forthwith, instantly' in the prologue of *The Stage-Coach* and the epilogue of *The Grove*.

IV. i

3 sower Sauce] Leanthe puns on the proverbial 'Sweet meat will have sour sauce'.

10 I'll be private with you] Pindress introduces another scene of sexual innuendo.

23 liquorish Chaps] lickerish or lecherous mouth.

26 Cross-purposes] a parlour game, which has been assumed to be like cross questions and crooked answers, in which each player in a circle receives a whispered question from one neighbour and a whispered answer from the other. Each then states aloud both the question and answer he received (*N&Q*, 8th ser. iii (1893), 275). The game is mentioned in *Spectator*, no. 245. However, Pindress's reference to a pawn renders the definition suspicious.

27–8 *Hungary*-bottle] bottle of Hungary-water, a distillation of rosemary flowers infused in rectified spirit of wine to revive those who feel faint (Edward Phillips, *The New World of Words*. Pindress, of course, seems to be seeking a different kind of restorative.

40 Billing] caressing or kissing, as in 'billing and cooing'.

75 assertations] a rare form meaning affirmations or assertions (*OED*).

83 chopping Boy] bouncing boy.

94 Chairs] sedan chairs.

IV. ii

9 Windmill-Pate] 'Wind-mills in the head' meant empty projects (*NDCC*).

41 embalm] perfume body with balmy fragrance, as well as preserve the body from decay.

47–8 the Hero in Comedy is always the Poet's Character] Critics have assumed that Roebuck indeed displays Farquhar's character.

108–9 easie Numbers, such as of *Rochester*, and others] 'Easy' means loose or easy-virtued; Rochester's poetry was better known for its loose and pornographic qualities than its skill at metrics.

136 brisk] sprightly, lively.

144 Quinsey] tonsillitis or an inflammation of the throat.

146–63 [SONG] This is the third of the Leveridge songs, never before printed with the play. In it Trudge betrays her Irish background through her use of Gaelic words. At least three engravings exist, one by Thomas Cross (Bodl. Mus. lc. 118 [28]), one probably by Walsh published with the other two 'Songs in the new Comedy call'd Love and a Bottle' (Folger M1497 C43 Cage, f. 167ʳ and BM G304.[172]) and another edition, *c.*1710, copies in the British Library, and the Mitchell Library, Glasgow.

149 *pouge*] a bag such as a sack for corn. Pough or pouge also means a swelling of the skin.

151 *brouge*] Brogues (first spelling) were rough shoes, generally made of untanned leather, worn by the inhabitants of the wilder parts of Ireland.

151 *Oh hone*] an Irish exclamation denoting lamentation.

219 Blowze] a slatternly woman or trull (Partridge).

228–9 the last Miscellanies] perhaps *Miscellanies over Claret*, published in 1698 and therefore easily available to Farquhar after his arrival in London. No full run of the *Miscellanies* has been located.

IV. iii

1 Coney-burrough] slang for brothel.

1–2 The Trade] prostitution.

2 Empory] an Anglicized form of 'emporium' (*OED*).

3 Change] the Royal Exchange.

26 Estate in Tail] freehold estate under limitations on tenure and inheritance because of conditions established by the donor. Roebuck uses it here as a *double entendre*; the Second Masque picks up on his metaphor.

32 Case] a slang word for the female genitals, appropriate for the legal metaphor in which Roebuck and the Second Masque conduct their sexual discussion.

42–3 the Fountain in the *Middle Temple*] The fountain court of one of the inns of court seems an appropriate place for this assignation not only because of the Masque's jurist husband but also because law students in the drama of the period were frequently depicted as looking for assignations.

43 *Cook upon Littleton*] The password is one of the best-known of lawbooks, Sir Thomas Littleton's Latin treatise on tenures with a translation and commentary by Sir Edward Coke; it was the chief authority for English property law.

45 in Sheets] a pun. A book not bound was described as 'in sheets'.

48 crack'd a Pike] Pike, lance, or sword were used metaphorically for penis. 'To crack' meant to have sexual pleasure with a woman, but Farquhar seems to imply the idea of breaking or ruining in this *double entendre*.

54 enter'd in the Inns] become a law student.

61 upon tick] on credit, on the score.

64 Cruiser] Partridge gives the definition 'harlot' for the nineteenth and twentieth centuries, and 'beggar' for late seventeenth–early nineteenth Here, obviously, and elsewhere Farquhar uses the term to mean 'harlot'.

121 Goose-Cap] sign of a fool or dolt.

123 Horn-mad] stark mad, but also extremely lecherous.

141 *Moorfields*] a place for long walks and meetings. Bedlam bordered on Moorfields.

155–6 shabb'd him off] sneaked or slid away (*NDCC*).

166 purely] excellently.

IV. iv

5 Nonsuted] interrupted or balked. A pun on the legal term meaning subjected to a nonsuit, that is cessation of a suit because the plaintiff voluntarily withdraws. In this case the 'suit' is Lovewell's romantic suit to Lucinda.

21 *Night-Gown*] a loose gown, sometimes bound at the waist by a sash, and used for negligee and informal occasions. At the turn of the century it was sometimes used as a kind of dressing-gown (Cunnington, *Seventeeth*, p. 145; *Eighteenth*, p. 73). The loose gown would have hidden Leanthe's garb and helped effect a disguise.

42 Policy] prudent or politic procedure; shrewdness and artfulness.

49 sprung] exploded.

V. i

23 Soldier offers spoils of *Flanders* Lace] Military men who had fought in Flanders brought lace, for which Flanders was noted, home to their women. In *The Recruiting Officer* Farquhar elaborates: 'Ay *Flanders* Lace, is as constant a Present from Officers to their Women, as something else is from their Women to them. They every Year bring over a Cargo of Lace to cheat the Queen of her Duty, and her Subjects of their Honesty.'

39 Principles] Principles—fundamental basis of behaviour, reason for action; and principals—the two contenders in a duel, as distinguished from their seconds.

54 an Hair of the same] a hair of the dog that bit you; that is, a drink taken to counteract drunkenness or a hangover.

92 a Jewel] that is, her maidenhead.

134 blind Guide] Love.

176 turn up Trumps] turn out well.

177 shuffle] another pun, meaning to shuffle cards but also to get out of a situation through shiftiness or evasion.

178 a Match] done, agreed upon.

183 a Green Gown] 'A throwing of young Lasses on the Grass and Kissing them' (*NDCC*). Actually the term denoted tumbling in the grass in sexual play, and, especially, deflowering a young woman (Partridge).

188 Green Gooseberry] virile, lusty young fool. Green means inexperienced, simple, or gullible, but it also has the connotations of lustfulness and of freshness (a 'green goose' meant a fresh young whore, a beginner in harlotry). 'Gooseberry' means a fool or simpleton.

v. ii

32 Stone-horse] stallion.

49 right *Shropshire* breed] an old breed of long-horned cattle. Lasciviousness is suggested by the horns, which imply both masculine tumescence and the horns of cuckoldry.

52 Gramercy] Thank you.

53 clap him in the Female Pillory] involve him in the sexual act.

57 *Irish* Quagmire, you wou'd have drown'd him in] 'Drowning' is often used to refer to a man's situation when mating with a woman of large parts. The '*Irish* Quagmire' reminds one of the geographical description of the kitchen maid Nell in Shakespere's *Comedy of Errors*, III. ii. 118–21:

> *Antipholus of Syracuse*: In what part of her body stands Ireland?
> *Dromio of Syracuse*: Marry, sir, in her buttocks; I found it out by the bogs.

57–8 we have found the bottom on't] another pun.

84 *Synelepha*] the elision of a final vowel before an initial vowel, as in 'th' animal'. It is obvious which 'limb' Lovewell plans to eliminate.

v. iii

4 lap'd up in my Ladies Lavender] 'laid up in lavender' meant pawned (*NDCC*). The clothes are pawned only in the sense that they are not present. Indeed 'lap'd up in my Ladies Lavender' would suggest much the same thing. However, 'lap'd', assuming it was not a typographical error (it was never changed in later editions), gives the additional connotation of sexual intercourse.

12.1 *Enter* Roebuck] There seems little motivation for Roebuck to be wandering around an antechamber at this particular juncture. Farquhar offers no explanation.

25–6 When her soft, melting . . . folded fast] also used in *The Adventures of Covent Garden*: 'He thought her Naked, soft, and yielding Waste, | Within his pressing Arms was folded fast'. The poem in the *Adventures* reappeared as 'The Lover's Night' with the addition of six lines in *Love and Business*.

61 Seven Champions of *Christendom*] St George of England, St Denis of France, St James of Spain, St Anthony of Italy, St Andrew of Scotland, St Patrick of Ireland, and St David of Wales.

137 Crack] harlot.

137 *Sheely*] a derogatory term for a woman. According to Partridge, variants include 'she', 'shee', 'sheelah', 'sheila', 'sheele'. The term 'sheila' is still used in Australia.

156 breath a Vein] Here obviously the term carries sexual innuendo.

189 Bullfinch *dress'd like a Parson*] Although tricked marriages were very common in comedies of the period, a woman parson was unusual.

218.1 Two dances from the play are extant, one found in the British Library Add. MSD. 29371, f. 104, another in *120 Country Dances* (London, 1711). See Price, p. 190.

218.2 Fingallion] Fingal's Cave, on Staffa, an uninhabited islet of the

Inner Hebrides, is wild and remote. Farquhar seems to refer to the dress of the islanders.

193–4 espous'd . . . And . . . divorc'd] Roebuck's imagery of espousal and divorce was of moment because of the current interest in divorce aroused by the proceedings of the Earl of Macclesfield in 1698 and those of the Duke of Norfolk from 1687 to 1700.

Epilogue

1–5 *I Come not . . . and all*] The epilogue refers to the heated competition between the Royal Theatre in Drury Lane and the 'other House' at Lincoln's Inn Fields. In 1695 the leading actors of the United Company had defected from Rich's management and established a second theatre in Lincoln's Inn Fields. The few actors who remained at Drury Lane were joined by young beginners. In 1697 they had felt a surge of hope in the competition, but by 1698 the fortunes of Drury Lane sank very low again; prologues and epilogues complained petulantly over the lack of audiences.

7 Edax, Rerum] 'Tempus edax rerum', Ovid, *Metamorphoses* xv. 234, 'O Time, thou great devourer of things'.

8 Vivitur Ingenio] The motto, which appeared over the stage at Drury Lane, is taken from [Virgil], *Elegia in Maecenatem*, l. 38, 'Vivitur ingenio, cetera mortis erunt' ('One lives by wit, the rest shall belong to death').

13 *break*] go broke.

16 *strowlers*] 'Strollers' denoted gypsies, rope-dancers, jugglers, acrobats, tumblers, tricksters, and raree-show men, among other itinerant mountebanks. Curll's *Life of Wilks* describes the period: 'About this Time the English Theatre was not only pestered with Tumblers, and Rope-Dancers from France, but likewise with Dancing-Masters, Dancing-Dogs; shoals of Italian Squallers were daily imported; and the Drury-Lane Company almost broke' (p. 8). His source, however, seems to be this epilogue. Peter Motteux, in the prologue to Mary Pix's *The Innocent Mistress* (June 1697) mentions 'dancing Swans, nimble cap'ring Chairs and Stands', etc. among entertainments. Thomas Brown in a letter to George Moult, 12 September 1699, speaks of the degraded stage and its many 'Smithfield' acts, that is, acts that should be at the fair, and complains 'we have been so unmercifully over-run with an innundation of Monsieurs from Paris, that one would be almost tempted to wish that the war had still continued, as it were for no other reason but because it would have prevented the coming over of these light-heel'd gentlemen, who have been a greater plague to our theatres, than their privateers were to our merchantmen'. (Quoted in the *London Stage*, i. 515.)

17 Bona Sere's, Barba Colar's] mockery of the Italian opera stars imported at salaries outrageously high according to British standards. *Buona sera*, of course, means 'good evening', but 'Barba colar' is harder to explain. Perhaps it refers to the beards worn in performances. From mid-season 1698–9, imported singers and dancers were introduced to try to bolster ticket sales. The *Post Boy*, 13–15 April 1699, noted that both theatres were 'very industrious to Entertain the Town with several eminent Masters in Singing and Dancing, lately arrived, both from France and Italy . . .'.

19 Seignior Rampony] Although Clementine is better known as a eunuch imported to sing, Haines makes clear that Rampony, also spelled Rampny or Ramphony, was another. Rampony, 'an Italian Musician belong to the Prince of Vaudemont', gave performances at York Buildings on 28 March, 'Half a Guinea Entrance' (noted in the *London Gazette*, 24–8 March), and 15 April (announced in the *Post Boy*, 12–14 April 1698), The *Post Man*, 12–14 April, said tickets sold at 5*s*.

21 *Blot in his* Scutcheon] Haines is Farquhar's match for bawdry.

23 Don Segismondo Fideli] The singer Sigismondo Fideli was a member of Rich's Company in the 1698–9 season. He is known to have given concerts on 22 December 1698 and 28 February 1699 at Drury Lane (*London Stage*, i. 501, 507). He, like Rampony, doubtless drew a salary disproportionately large in comparison to those of English actors. Van Lennep points out that Clementine reportedly received £500 annually (*Post Boy*, 13–15 April 1699), and Francisco, another eunuch, 120 guineas for five performances (i. cxx).

29 *We've Pickt up Gypsies*] Although nothing appears in the *London Stage* about importing gypsies at this time, *A Comparison Between the Two Stages* (1702) refers to such performers:

> *Sull.* It has always been the Jest of all the Men of Sense about Town . . . that the Stage that had kept it's purity a hundred Years (at least from this Debaucher) shou'd now be prostituted to Vagabonds, to Caperers, Eunuchs, Fidlers, Tumblers and Gipsies.
>
> *Crit.* Oh what a charming Sight 'twas to see *Madam*—What a pox d'ee call her?—*the high* German *Buttock*—swim it along the Stage between her two Gipsie Daughters: they skated alone the ice so cleaverly, you might ha' sworn they were of right *Dutch* extraction.

32 Tour] that is, the Grand Tour.

34 *They went to* Ireland *to improve their* Breeding] In the fall of 1698 Thomas Ashbury attracted two able London performers from London to Smock Alley, John Boman and Joseph Trefusis, both from Lincoln's Inn Fields. In fall of 1698 Letitia Cross also appeared at Smock Alley (Clark, pp. 110, 112). Several London actors, however, had gone to Smock Alley in 1694, including Richard and Elizabeth Buckley, Charlotte Butler, Richard Estcourt, Hugh and Mary Norton, and Robert and Elizabeth Knapton Wilks (Clark, p. 102).

36 Collier] The tone of the epilogue is decidedly anti-Jeremy Collier, whose *Short View of the Immorality and Prophaneness of the English Stage* was published in 1698.

36 *Miss* C—s] The actress Letitia Cross eloped to France after the spring of 1698. Egerton reports in his biography of Anne Oldfield that she was whisked away by a baronet, and later went from France to Dublin to perform with Smock Alley from 1698 to 1704 (*Biographical Dictionary*). Haines suggests that Collier's pamphlet frightened her into abandoning the London stage.

40 Touch-hole] the vent of a firearm through which the charge is ignited. The term was a low colloquialism for a woman's genitals (Partridge).

50 Comings in] Even Stonehill notes this pun: 'Dr. Schmidt was very

much mystified by this obscene pun' (i. 385). The last four lines of the
prologue leave little doubt as to Haines's brand of education.

The Constant Couple

Title-page [motto] Ovid, *Tristia*, iv, 10. 131–2. 'But whether through
favour or by very poetry I have gained this fame, 'tis right, kind reader, that
I render thanks to thee.' (Wheeler, p. 207).

Dedication

0.2 Sir *ROGER MOSTYN*] The third Baronet was born at Leighton,
Cheshire, in 1675. Educated at Jesus College, Oxford, in December 1701 he
was returned as a member of Parliament for Flintshire and he served in
Parliament a number of years before his death in 1739. In December 1699,
however, when the dedication was published, he was a young man of scant
power. For the second time, Farquhar chose a Welshman for his dedication,
but this time one without Carmarthen's military influence. Farquhar seems
to have had 'the honour' of Mostyn's acquaintance, although he had not
known Carmarthen when he dedicated *Love and a Bottle* to him.

8 too young an Author] Farquhar was young in years (about 21) and in
authorship.

22 some noble Appearances] that is, peers have attended performances.

27 *Materia superabit Opus*] Ovid, *Metamorphoses*, ii. 5, says 'Materiam
superabat opus'. Farquhar 'transverses' Ovid to mean 'The material will be
better than the workmanship', thus pointing an elaborate if inept
compliment to Mostyn.

Preface

6 the third Night] The beauties of the third night acknowledged here are
the profits of the author's benefit.

13–14 a Party for the Play] Farquhar refers to the practice of 'papering the
House' or furnishing tickets to sympathetic auditors to assure a favourable
reception for a play.

15–16 I have not been long enough in Town to raise Enemies against me]
Ironically, the success of *The Constant Couple* raised the ire of less successful
authors, and Farquhar was soon enough beset by 'enemy' critics who
criticized his 'farce' mercilessly.

20–1 without Smut and Profaneness] The ladies and clergy were the two
groups most often cited in the warfare between Jeremy Collier and other
reformers on one hand and authors and players on the other over the
'immorality and profaneness' of the London stage. Farquhar's decrying
'Smut and Profaneness' speaks of a considerable retreat from the unchecked
bawdry of *Love and a Bottle* and the jeering attack on Collier in its epilogue.

22 the Beauties of Action] the excellence of the performance.

26 an excellent and compleat set of Comedians] Since the dissolution of
the United Company of Actors in 1695, Drury Lane had been known for its

inexperienced actors. Farquhar here, without detracting from the merits of Betterton, Barry, Bracegirdle, and their troupe at Lincoln's Inn Fields, sees in the success of his play a tribute to actors now growing in maturity and ability. The comment was a specific recognition of the achievements of the neophytes of Drury Lane, headed by Robert Wilks.

27 *Wilks's* performance] Wilks sealed his reputation in the role of Sir Harry Wildair.

32 *the Trip to the Jubilee*] There was considerable comment that the name was indeed misleading, since the play takes place in London rather than Rome.

33 greater Trips] bigger blunders or faults.

34–5 when I find that more exact Plays have had better success] *The Constant Couple* aroused heated complaints because of its great popularity despite a lack of dramatic regularity. See, for example, John Corye, Preface, *A Cure for Jealousy* (1701); Charles Gildon, Dedication, *Love's Victim* (1701); Letter, London August 10, 1700, Mr. B— to Mr. C., *Letters of Wit, Politics, and Morality*, p. 250).

Prologue

7 *great Wig*] the sign of a Beau. See note, *Love and a Bottle*, I. i. 30.

19 *Elbow-shaking Fool*] 'He lives by shaking of the Elbow; a Gamester' (*NDCC*).

21 *scours*] runs, departs rapidly.

27 *Mother*] keeper of a brothel.

28 *Bawd Regent of the Bubble-Gallery*] The middle gallery was notorius as a place of assignations, brawls, and 'lewdness', often alluded to in prologues. See, for example, Southerne's prologue to *The Disappointment* (1684); Dryden's epilogue for the opening of the theatre, 16 November 1682; *The Playhouse* (1685). 'Bubble' means a dupe or fool.

29 *our mounted Friends*] footmen and other servants in the upper gallery, mounted or elevated above the gallants in the side-boxes. In the late seventeenth century Christopher Rich had opened the upper gallery to servants at no charge.

30 *Side-box Tricks*] Archer speaks, in *The Beaux Strategem*, IV. ii. 18–20, of the distastefulness of being 'oblig'd to sneak into the side-Box, and between both Houses steal two Acts of a Play, and because we han't Money to see the other three, we come away discontented, and damn the whole five'. Doorkeepers met considerable difficulties with theatregoers who saw an act free or who moved from place to place in the theatre without paying the proper fees. Hence the beaux and gallants, not the footmen, are those who fail to pay.

32 *Poor* Dorset *Garden-house*] By the end of the century the Dorset Garden theatre, which had opened 9 November 1671, was controlled by Christopher Rich and Sir Thomas Skipwith, who used the Drury Lane house for drama. Therefore Dorset Garden was used for popular spectacles, such as the performances of William Joye, the 'Strong Man of Kent'.

35 *That strong Dog* Sampson] Luttrell records 'We have much discourse

here of a 2d Sampson, one William Joyce [i.e. Joye], aged 24, of middle stature, born in Kent, who this week out drew the strongest dray horse Mr. Cocks, the brewer in Southwark, had; easily lifts 1500 weight, and gets much money' (iv. 577; 20 October 1699). Joye performed at Dorset Garden on 25 November 1699 'where he drew against a horse, and lifted 20 hundred weight: the boxes 10s. apeice, and the pitt 5s.' (Luttrell, iv. 586; 25 November 1699. See also *Post Man*, 25–8 November 1699.) Apparently he performed there on 29 November and 1 December (*London Post*, 24–7 November 1699), as well as 3 January 1700, when he designed 'to show the same Tryals of Strength he had the honour of showing before his Majesty, the Prince and Princess of Denmark, and several Persons of Quality, viz. The lifting a weight of 2240 *l*. Holding an extraordinary large Cart-Horse; and afterwards breaking a Rope that will bear 3500 weight. There will likewise be shown the Sister, carrying 5 Bushels of Wheat, or any other grain; She being but 15 Years of Age. They will also show on Thursday, Friday, and Saturday, beginning at 3 of the Clock, and ending at 4 in the Afternoon. Boxes 3s. Pit 2s. 1st Gallery 1s. Upper gallery 6d.' (*London Post*, 1–3 January 1700).

39 *Prizes*] Prices.

I. i

0.4 *The Park*] St. James's Park.

27 *Hobbs*] Reading Hobbes, much less considering his work excellent, would have been sufficient proof of Vizard's hypocrisy.

41–2 newly arriv'd from St. *Sebastians*, laden with *Portugal* Wines] Duties on French wines were raised by William III in 1693, 1697, and 1698. As a result, the importation of French wines became prohibitively expensive and the number of casks declined to an absurdly low number. Meanwhile French wines were regularly exported from Bordeaux to San Sebastián, and from there shipped as Spanish or Portuguese goods, in Spanish casks. James Whiston claimed, in September 1699, that the smuggling trade was so extensive that all wines coming from San Sebastián should be taxed as French. Large fines were imposed on smugglers who were caught. For details, see André L. Simon, *The History of the Wine Trade in England* (3 vols., London, 1909), iii. 127–35.

44–5 Tide-waiter] customs-house official who boarded ships to prevent the evasion of customs regulations.

45 Surveyors] supervisors who oversaw collection of taxes.

46–7 another Plague of the Nation] the problem of paying military men for their services during the campaigns in Flanders was still hotly debated in 1699. See commentary, *Love and a Bottle*, 1. i. 22–3.

48 A red Coat and Feather] a commissioned Officer.

52 disbanded] According to statute, all but 7,000 men stationed in England, Wales, and Berwick-upon-Tweed were disbanded on 26 March 1699; all others were to be disbanded on or before 1 May 1699 except 12,000 in Ireland (*Statutes of the Realm*, vii. 4523).

53 broke] turned out of his commission (*NDCC*).

68 old *Acteon*] According to Greek legend Actaeon was changed into a stag and devoured by his own hounds.

69–70 to live upon free Quarter in the City] Men could be billeted locally, in inns or even homes.

72 Leading staff] a staff borne by a commanding-officer.

81 *Rummer*] a popular tavern, two doors from Locket's, between Whitehall and Charing Cross (Henry B. Wheatley, *London, Past and Present: Its History, Associations, and Traditions*, 3 vols. [London, 1891, reissued Detroit, 1968], III. 190).

83 *Hungary*] The Turks had been defeated in 1683, but had reinvaded Hungary. Prince Eugene of Savoy won a decisive victory over them at Zenta in August 1697 (John B. Wolf, The *Emergence of the Great Powers 1685–1715* [New York, 1951], pp. 50–1). However, Hungary did not disband its armies as England did.

110–1 the Loves of *Mars* and *Venus* will never fail] perhaps a pun, referring not only to the officer's need for love but also to Peter Motteux's musical afterpiece, *The Loves of Mars and Venus*, which opened with *The Anatomist* at Lincoln's Inn Fields on or about 14 November 1696. The play's popularity helped Lincoln's Inn Fields in its early competition with Drury Lane. Farquhar may have known Motteux at this time; later he collaborated with him.

25–6 Campain in *Flanders* some three or four years ago] Wildair fought in the battle of London in 1693.

133 florid] flourishing, vigorous.

141 the *Rubrick*] A reference to the directions for conducting services, as printed in red in liturgical books, hence, figuratively, ecclesiastical duties.

153 We are all so reform'd] Societies for the reformation of manners were formed at the end of the seventeenth century. The societies worked successfully toward the conviction and punishment of thousands of 'lewd and scandalous persons', such as brothel-keepers, gaming-house keepers, people who did business on Sunday, and those who cursed or got drunk. Punishment in the stocks and pillory resulted. On 21 January 1692 William and Mary issued a proclamation 'against vicious, debauched and profane persons'. William responded to a request from Commons for a new proclamation; his request for a more effective law precipitated an act 'for the more effective suppressing profaneness, immorality, and debauchery' on 26 February 1698. In 1699 he made another proclamation on profaneness and immorality. See Joseph W. Krutch, *Comedy and Conscience After the Restoration* (New York, 1924), pp. 166–7.

163 the Groomporters] The groom porter was appointed by the Lord Chamberlain to control gambling; he ran his own gaming house, which was patronized by the nobility. The *Flying Post*, 10–13 January 1699, refers to the King playing at the groom porter's 'according to custom'.

164 *New-Market*] Horse-racing for high stakes at Newmarket was then as now a popular sport. By 1705 Queen Anne had plans to rebuild her house there for the racing (Luttrell, v. 544; 26 April 1705).

165 *Doctors-Commons*] All matters of ecclesiastical law, including divorce, were taken to Doctors' Commons for settlement.

167 the noblest Ball at the *Bath*] Bath, or 'the Bath', was the most fashionable spa: 'In Winter *Bath* makes a very melancholy Appearance; but during the Months of *May, June, July,* and *August,* there is a concourse of genteel Company, that peoples, enriches, and adorns it; at that Time, Provisions and Lodgings grow dear. Thousands go thither to pass away a few Weeks, without heeding either the·Baths or the Waters, but only to direct themselves with good Company. They have Musick, Gaming, Public Walks, Balls, and a little Fair every Day' (*M. Misson's Memoirs and Observations in his Travels over England* [London, 1719], p. 14). '*A Step to the Bath with a Character of the place*' (London, 1700) describes a ball thus: 'The Ball is always kept at the Town Hall, a very spacious Room, and fitted up for that Purpose. During which, the Door, is kept by a Couple of Brawny Beadles, to keep out the Mobility, looking as fierce as the Uncouth Figures at *Guild-Hall*; there was Extraordinary Fine Dancing. . . . A Consort of Delicate Musick, Vocal and Instrumental, perform'd by good Masters; A Noble Collation of dry Sweet Meats, Rich Wine and large Attendance. The lady who was the *Donor,* wore an Extraordinary Rich Flavour, to distinguish her from the rest, which is always the Custome . . .' (quoted in Ashton, pp. 331–2).

167–8 the *Ring*] a circle in Hyde Park, in which the fashionable promenaded: 'The *Ring* in *Hyde-Park* is shaded by fine lofty Trees, and the Dust laid by Water-Carts when the Driness of the Season requires it; and here we frequently see four or five Lines of Noblemens and Gentlemens Coaches, rolling gently round the *Ring* in all their gayest Equipage, some moving this way, others that, which makes a very splendid Shew' (Thomas Cox, *Magna Britannica et Hibernum* [London, c.1725]). Misson describes it, 'In a pretty high Place, which lies very open, they have surrounded a Circumference of two or three hundred Paces Diameter with sorry Kind of Ballustrade, or rather with Poles plac'd upon Stakes, but three Foot from the Ground; and the Coaches drive round and round this. When they have turn'd for some Time round one Way, they face about and turn t'other: So rowls the World' (Misson, p. 126).

174 Stivers] The small Dutch coin indicated an insignificant amount, comparable in connotation to a penny.

174 *Landen*] a battle in July 1693 'Unmatched in its slaughter except by Malplaquet and Borodino for two hundred years'. Despite 'heroic resistance', the allies were defeated, losing nearly 20,000 men (Winston Churchill, *Marlborough: His Life and Times* [6 vols., London and New York, 1933–8], i. 416).

175 *Swiss*] that is, by a Swiss mercenary.

185 *Ruell*] the space between the bed and the wall. When ladies began to receive morning visits in their bedrooms, visitors sat in the ruelle. Will Honeycomb, in *Spectator,* no. 530, describes himself as an *homme de ruelle.* Addison's description of the dishabille of a lady in such a visit in *Spectator,* no. 45, illustrates Sir Harry's cause for enthusiasm: 'The Lady, tho' willing to appear undrest, had put on her best Looks, and painted her self for our Reception. Her Hair appeared in a very nice Disorder, as the Night-Gown which was thrown upon her Shoulders was ruffled with great Care. For my

part, I am so shocked with every thing which looks immodest in the Fair Sex, that I could not forbear taking off my Eye from her when she moved in her Bed, and was in the greatest Confusion imaginable every time she stirred a Leg or an Arm' (i. 192–3).

186 the *Jubilee*] The English showed great interest in the Jubilee celebration of the Church of Rome in 1700. Many Englishmen attended, not for the religious ceremonies but for the revelry and debauchery that accompanied the crowds to Rome, if one may judge from contemporary references. (For details, see Morton and Peterson, 'The Jubilee of 1700 and Farquhar's "The Constant Couple" ', pp. 521–5.)

200 St. *James's*] that is, in the parish of St James.

252 a *Middlesex Jury*] Since duels were illegal, duellists could be prosecuted, although they seldom were. Farquhar, who ended his acting career after wounding a man in a stage duel, consistently wrote against the practice of duelling.

267 Pipe] half-tun wine cask.

300 Shoulder-knot] a bunch of looped ribbons or cord worn on the right, or occasionally the left, shoulder. After 1710 it went out of fashion except for apprentices and use on livery (Cunnington, *Seventeenth*, pp. 136, 141; *Eighteenth*, p. 71).

301 Sword-knot] a bunch of ribbon, often brightly coloured, attached to the sword hilt (Cunnington, *Eighteenth*, p. 100).

316 die by Raking] the usual sexual pun.

317 *Leash*] a set of three.

319 Pulvil] perfumed powder.

321–2 Like *Olivia*'s Lover, he stunk of *Thames-street*.] William Wycherley, *The Plain Dealer*, ii. i. 521. Olivia says 'Foh! I hate a Lover that smells like *Thames-street*' (*The Plays of William Wycherley*, ed. Arthur Friedman [Oxford, 1979], p. 414). Thames Street was the dock area.

323 *Princesse*'s Chocolate House] Not recorded in Lillywhite or Wheatley. Ewald says it was a small establishment near the New Exchange in the Strand, and Stonehill concurs.

I. ii

17 the *Practice of Piety*] Bishop Lewis Bayly's devotional volume *The Practice of Piety, directing a Christian how to Walke, that he may please God*, was 'the most popular piece of devotional literature in the seventeenth century' (Harry Farr, 'Philip Chetwind and the Allott Copyrights', *The Library*, 4th ser. 15 [1934], 133). Several editions were published in the 1690s; by 1705 it had reached its 'forty-sixth' edition.

19 Orangery] expensive snuff. See commentary, *Love and a Bottle*, ii. ii. 45.

134–5 of all Men he's my Aversion] another echo of Olivia in *The Plain Dealer*, who hypocritically claims all the fashionable pleasures are her aversion. Eliza replies, finally, '. . . by the word Aversion, I'm sure you dissemble; for I never knew Woman yet that used it, who did not . . . And a Man no more believes a Woman, when she sayes she has an Aversion for him, than when she sayes she'll Cry out' (II. i. in Wycherley, pp. 398–401).

136 bait] cause him to be harrassed, torment him.

139–40 'tis order'd by *Act of Parliament*] By Act of Parliament, Standard was disbanded. Therefore he can no longer afford to tip or bribe Parly.

II. i.

16 five hundred Surgeons] Dicky implies that the surgeons were 'Clap doctors', i.e. those employed to cure venereal disease.

18 Velvet Scarf, and red Knots] By 1690 scarves had become deep shoulder capes with long broad ends extending to the knees in front (Cunnington, *Seventeenth*, pp. 178–9). Knots were sets of bright-coloured ribbon bows as decoration for the gown. They were worn at the bosom, sleeves, or waist, or in the hair (Cunnington, *Eighteenth*, p. 143). The prostitute Dicky identifies is fashionably dressed.

22 *Jupiter Ammon*] 'Jupiter, the Father of Gods and Men had several names, either from the Place, or occasion of his Worship or Temple: as Jupiter Ammon, in the form of a Ram; it signifies hidden, or out of the way, and in the Lybian Desartts' [*sic*] (*Universal, Historical, Geographical, Chronological and Poetical Dictionary* [London, 1703]).

45 *Squibs*] firecrackers.

46 *Rary Shows*] portable puppet shows.

II. ii

1–2 *Like light and Heat . . . Day*] Nathaniel Lee, *Sophonisba*, i. 240–1.

3 Paper-kite] Wilding refers to the letter of introduction written by Vizard. The term refers to a toy kite, i.e. the letter, but there is a pun on the bird of prey: Marvell, in *The Rehearsal Transposed*, used the line, 'He may make a great Paper-kite of his own Letter of 850 pages'.

10 Business] One meaning of 'business' was sexual intercourse; hence Lady Darling's phrase misleads Wildair.

15 Cousin] a euphemism for 'lover'.

60 Goldfinches] guineas.

II. iii

103–4 *presto, pass . . . Hey*] one of Farquhar's many references to legerdemain.

II. iv

24 take a course] hamper him. A 'course of law' meant proceedings at law; hence, Smuggler's punning misinterpretation (*NDCC*).

32–3 the Reformation of Manners] that is, the work of the Societies for the Reformation of Manners.

37–8 *I whipt . . . Parish*] Josiah Woodward wrote in 1698 that the Society for the Reformation of Manners (actually there were then nearly twenty in the city and suburbs) had been instrumental in 'suppressing some hundreds of *Houses of ill Fame*, bringing the Frequenters of them to due Shame and

Punishment. And by the Means of this *Society* alone, about 2000 *Persons* have been legally prosecuted and convicted, either as keepers of *Houses of Bawdery* and *Disorder*, or as *Whores, Night-walkers*, and the like; and the Names of these Delinquents are set down in *three black Lists* which they have printed: All which have been sentenced by the *Magistrates* as the Law directs, and have accordingly been punished, (many of them divers times) either by *Carting, Whipping, Fining, Imprisonment*, or suppressing their *Licences*' (*An Account of the Rise and Progress of the Religious Societies in the City of London* [London, 1698], pp. 78–9).

37 *Cut and Long-Tail*] all varieties. Originally used of horses or dogs. Slender uses the expression in *Merry Wives of Windsor*, III. IV. 47.

38–9 *I voted for pulling down the Play-house*] As early as 1694 the Societies for the Reformation of Manners had attacked the playhouses, in a proposal 'To supplicate their majesties, that the public play-houses may be suppressed' (*Proposal for a National Reformation of Manners*, noted in Krutch, p. 113).

56 *Buss*] kiss.

59 Cocket] a seventeenth-century spelling of 'coquette'.

91 *Marli*] Marly was the favourite retreat of Louis XIV (John B. Wolf, *Louis XIV* [New York, 1968], p. 346. In 1699 it was the centre of attention because of the new interior decorations in rococo style by Lepautre. After the arrival of the young Duchess of Bourgogne in 1697, more liveliness in court life as well as decor brought the royal household to enjoy various residences other than Versailles and Paris (Wolf, *Emergence*, p. 249–50).

106 *Namur*] The British won a striking victory at Namur in the summer of 1695, a fact frequently recalled in comedies of the period.

108 capitulate] propose terms, treat, parley.

140 *Royal Exchange*] the building and inner walk in which merchants and businessmen conducted their affairs. The second exchange, necessitated by the Great Fire of 1666, was designed by Edward Jarman or Jerman, and consisted of a quadrangular building, inner cloister, areas for sales of gloves, ribbons, etc., a series of statues of kings and queens mostly by Caius Gabriel Cibber (Wheatley, iii. 183–4).

140–1 run the Gauntlet thro a thousand brusht Beavers and formal Cravats] that is, run the gauntlet of all the fashionable beaux in towns. Beaver hats as well as cravats were fashionable.

III. i

27 plys] works steadily.

27–8 *Blew Posts*] a tavern in the Haymarket (Wheatley, i. 212), mentioned frequently in plays, for example, Otway's *The Soldier's Fortune* (1681), Pix's *The Innocent Mistress* (1697). A reference also appears in Tom Brown's *Original Letters on Several Occasions* (*The Works of Tom Brown* [London, 1707], i. 196) and *A Comparison Between the Two Stages* (Wells, p. 39; n., p. 159).

49–50 *Thus our chief Joys . . . worst.*] The lines first appeared in *The Adventures of Covent Garden*. In *The Constant Couple*, the phrase 'base Allays' supplanted 'most allays'.

62 Lace in *Flanders*] Flanders lace was considered the best, and many soldiers returned from the wars with some. Importation of lace had been prohibited in 1662, and the laws were more strictly enforced after 1698 (Max von Boehn, *Modes and Manners* [London, 1929], pp. 19–21), so Flanders lace had premium value. Norway was not a centre of the lace industry.

65 the shavings of deal Boards] Deal refers to planks, usually of fir or pine. Of course shavings were not actually used for ornamentation. Wildair is pretending he did not smuggle lace into England.

69 Cravat] The displayed ends of cravats were edged with lace or sometimes decorated with beads (Cunnington, *Seventeenth*, p. 147; *Eighteenth*, p. 75). Lace was very expensive; William III is reported to have spent £1,918 on lace in 1694 and £2,459 the following year, but this included trim for napkins and shaving towels (Von Boehn, pp. 20–1). James II reportedly paid £36 for a cravat of Venice lace for his coronation (Cunnington, *Seventeenth*, p. 147).

73 Bravo's] mercenary murderers (*NDCC*).

74 swimming Girdle] swimming aids, worn around the chest and under the arms. Cunnington and Mansfield assume they were made of corks and bladders (Phyllis Cunnington and Alan Mansfield, *English Costume for Sports and Outdoor Recreation from the Sixteenth to the Nineteenth Centuries* [London, 1969; New York, 1970], p. 271).

79 *Bona Roba*] prostitute.

80 *Siegniour Angle*] Mr Englishman.

83 *Russel*-Street] Russell Street, Covent Garden. Both Will's Coffeehouse and the Rose tavern were in Russell Street, and prostitutes plied their trade there. The tavern referred to in line 84 would be equivalent to the Rose.

86 douse of the Face] blow to the face.

88 *Bull-Dog*] pistol. Usually applied humourously to a cannon or other firearm (*OED*).

90 Train] entourage.

93 a brace of Bullets] Farquhar used this *double entendre* often.

94 shoot seven *Italians* a Week] bed an Italian girl every day. For the colloquial 'shoot between wind and water', see Partridge, i. 760.

110 *Civita Vecchia*] the main port of Rome, thirty-nine miles from the city

III. ii

104 *Burgundy*] Since French wines carried such heavy duties, Burgundy would be the privilege of the very rich—or smugglers and their clients.

111 *Piazza* of *Covent-Garden*] an open arcade on the north and east sides of Covent Garden, built by Inigo Jones *c.*1633–4 and considered very fashionable. It is frequently mentioned in the plays as a meeting place.

III. iii

44 a Black] that is, a clergyman.

73.1 Tom Errand *in* Clincher Senior's *Cloaths*] Celadon, in answer to a copy of verses Mrs. C—ll sent him, says her fine sayings and flattery do not sit easy on him: 'They become him as ill as the Jubilee Beau's Cloaths do a Porter . . .' (Letter II, Celadon to Mrs. C—ll, *A Pacquet from Will's*, p. 90).

133 *Forthoon*] forthon, onwards, forwards.

138 a Collar of Bandileers] Bandileers were little wooden cases covered with leather each containing a charge of powder for a musket. Musketeers wore twelve of them on a shoulder-belt or collar (*A Military Dictionary Explaining All Difficult Terms in Martial Discipline, Fortification, and Gunnery* [3rd edn., London, 1708]).

161 .the Noble Poet] Rochester.

162–3 *Nothing . . . Expence*] Rochester, 'A Letter from Artemisia in the Town to Chloe in the Country' (London, 1679), ll. 224–5.

188 benighted] overtaken by darkness.

214 *Cassandra*] A ten-volume romance by Gautier de Costes, Seigneur de La Calprenède (1614–53), *Cassandra* was first published in Paris in 1642–5, translated into English in 1652, 1661, 1664, 1667, and 1673, and abridged in 1703.

253 swinge] beat him.

253 precise] Puritanical.

272 hansel] inaugurate auspiciously.

IV. i

113 *Newgate*] Newgate prison.

130 *Penelope*] In the *Odyssey*, she puts off her suitors until Odysseus' return. Robert Gore-Browne suggests that this is a reference to the actress Anne Oldfield, called Penelope in *Love and Business*, because Farquhar was 'so full of his little conquest and her amazing difference from the rest of her mercenary sex, that he could not keep her off his pen' (*Gay was the Pit* [London], 1957], pp. 37–9).

135 ocular Demonstration] Othello tells Iago:
Villain, be sure thou prove my love a whore:
Be sure of it; give me the ocular proof; (III. iii. 359–60)
In D'Urfey's *Madam Fickle* Manly says, 'But, Madam, is there no ocular proof to be given' of Madam Fickle's inconstancy ([London, 1676], p. 41).

154 *Probatum est*] it has been proved, a phrase used in prescriptions. 'Probatum' was used for a remedy that had proved efficacious.

161–5 Who d'ye . . . bewitch'd sure] The conversation between Clincher Junior and Dicky humorously emphasizes the secular nature of English interest in the Jubilee. The Pope remained anathema to Englishmen, but the Jubilee proved a fashionable jaunt to see the sights of the Continent, particularly Rome.

171 Alaw!] 'Law' is an exclamation expressing astonishment.

IV. ii

18–35 [Song] Daniel Purcell composed the music. Later Richard Leveridge reset the song to sing in the theatre in Dublin. For details of published half-sheet broadsides, see Introduction, p. 120. The singer John

Freeman rather than Wilks apparently sang the song, as the broadsides state; since Freeman left Drury Lane after the 1699–1700 season, he must have been used as singer during the first run. During the same season he also sang in Vanbrugh's *The Pilgrim* and Oldmixon's *The Grove*, for which Farquhar wrote the epilogue.

80 Pleats] By this time, open gowns had overskirts closely pleated in the back and smoothly joined in front, with a gap to show the petticoat (Cunnington, *Eighteenth*, p. 112).

116 Cully-Squire] A Cully was a 'fool or silly Creature that is easily drawn in and Cheated by Whores or Rogues' (*NDCC*).

164 swinging] great.

167 cozen] trick.

189 City Liberties] areas of the city in which he could not be prosecuted.

197 Cunning-Man] conjurer or clairvoyant. Addison wrote in *Spectator*, no. 505, 'It is not to be conceived how many Wizards, Gypsies and Cunning Men are dispersed through all the Countries and Market Towns of *Great Britain*, not to mention the Fortune-Tellers and Astrologers, who live very comfortably upon the Curiosity of several well-disposed Persons in the Cities of *London* and *Westminister*'. Grose defines a cunning-man as 'A cheat, who pretends by his skill in astrology, to assist persons in recovering stolen goods' (1788. Quoted in Partridge, i. 197).

225 *Succubus*] a demon in female form.

232 as Brazen as a Bawd in the Side-Box] Side-boxes were usually occupied by 'the great people' (Pepys, 1 May 1667). Upper-class theatre-goers, particularly women, usually did not risk the pit or middle gallery where young sparks wandered to make assignations. A bawd would have been out of place, brazen to appear there.

v. i

43 Loches] loaches, small freshwater fish, perhaps eaten to induce thirst.

95 *Rival Queens*] Nathaniel Lee's *The Rival Queens, or, The Death of Alexander the Great* opened in London in 1677 and became a sturdy repertory piece both in London and in Dublin. Although there is no knowledge of Farquhar's having played in the piece at Smock Alley, his good friend Wilks did. *The Rival Queens* had run at Drury Lane 19 November 1698, when *Love and a Bottle* was in rehearsal.

97 *O my Statyra, O my Angry Dear, turn thy Eyes on me*] *The Rival Queens*, III. i. 272–3. The first edition reads 'thine', not 'thy'. Farquhar seems to quote from memory, rather than printed text.

105–18 look ye . . . Guinea's] Rothstein points out (p. 65) that this speech is based on Falstaff's speech on honour.

115 Picquet] a popular card game.

124 Basset] 'This game, amongst all those on the cards, is accounted to be the most courtly, being properly, by the understanders of it, thought only fit for Kings and Queens, great Princes, Noblemen, &c. to play at, by reason of such great losses, or advantages, as may possibly be on one side or other, during the time of play' (*The Compleat Gamester* [London, 1721], reprinted in

Games and Gamesters of the Restoration, intro. Cyril Hughes Hartman [London, 1930], p. 271).

193–4 Dear *Roxana*, and you my fair *Statyra*] the two rival queens in Lee's play.

241–2 A license from *Doctors Commons*] that is, a marriage licence.

242 *Old Baily*] the Old Bailey Sessions House or Central Criminal Court where Wildair would be tried for killing a man.

v. ii

5 an Account of my Journey . . . *Tyburn*] Farquhar mocks the contemporary English predilection for travel books, such as 'The Travels of an English Gentleman from London to Rome, on Foot', and for the biographies of criminals. The interest in the Jubilee precipitated a number of publications including 'A True and Exact Account of all the Ceremonies observed by the Church of Rome, At the . . . Jubilee', printed in 1699 and published at 2d.

6–7 *The last and dying Speech of Beau* Clincher] The Earl of Exeter died at Turin, on his way to the Jubilee, as Luttrell records on 30 December 1699 (iv. 599). Other less distinguished travellers must also have succumbed to illness during the journey. Comparable broadsides of dying speeches were not unusual.

16 Bum-Bayliff] 'A bailiff of the meanest kind, one that is employed in arrests' (Johnson's *Dictionary*).

25 Prinking] 'nicely Dressing' (*NDCC*).

39–40 an honest sober Man can't sin in private for this plaguy Stage] Farquhar implies through Smuggler that reformers were hypocrites who attacked the stage because its satire struck uncomfortably near their faults.

v. iii

71 eating Chalk, or gnawing the Sheets] Strange appetites were evidence of the Green-sickness, a malady of young girls longing for love. Eating chalk was also symptomatic of the pica, an ailment of pregnant women that caused inordinate longings to eat chalk, charcoal, or other unhealthy snacks (*The Universal Family Book*, p. 37).

77–8 Send for the Dean and Chapter] in order to lay the ghost.

93 *Bear-Garden*] Bear and bull baiting were still popular. Such sport attracted a rough, disorderly crowd of thrill-seekers and was therefore, Standard indicates, an appropriate place for Clincher Junior.

105.1 *Singing and Dancing*] There is no indication of the songs and dances performed; probably the programme changed according to the cast of each performance. One possibility is 'A Song to a Tune call'd a Trip to the Jubilee', published as a half-sheet broadside some time near the turn of the century (copies in the British Library and Folger). A drinking-song, however, it does not seem particularly appropriate for the closing festivities.

153 That Ring] Archer, p. 129 n. 1 says the plot to accuse Lurewell of taking the ring had apparently been concocted by Wildair and Standard during their absence from stage in iv. i, 'an odd example of Farquhar's

technique'. Although the audience learns that Wildair will provide Standard 'ocular Demonstration' that Lurewell favours Wildair (IV. i. 134–5), the nature of the test is not explained beforehand.

183 *Manly*] Stonehill discusses the possibility that Lurewell was modelled on Mary de la Riviere Manley. See above, p. 116–17.

205 the Peace] the Peace of Ryswick, signed in 1697.

232–3 disbanded Quarter-Master] A quartermaster was an officer whose primary concern was looking after the quarters of the soldiers. Each regiment of foot soldiers and each troop of horse had one (*Military Dictionary*). With the great reduction in the army, quartermasters, like other soldiers, were disbanded.

255 lay your Proceedings before the Parliament] In 1698 Parliament drew up articles of impeachment against eight men accused of smuggling and prepared for Parliamentary proceedings. However, the accused men confessed, and the impeachment hearings were never held. Parliament imposed large fines on the men. After that, fines rather than impeachment proceedings were imposed in smuggling cases (Williams, *Contraband Cargoes*, pp. 87–8).

Epilogue

3 Hippolito*'s*] Hippolito's Coffee House in Covent Garden, frequented by beaux in the early eighteenth century (Lillywhite, p. 269).

4 *th'* Rose] The Rose Tavern in Russell Street, Covent Garden, near the Drury Lane Theatre, must have been a favourite haunt of Farquhar, for he mentioned it often. It was a theatrical haven, frequented by players as well as theatre-goers, and, apparently, gamblers. The actor Hildebrand Horden was killed at the Rose in 1696. See Lillywhite, p. 487.

7 *tearing*] roistering.

8 *murders* Bays] condemns the playwright, murders his reputation. A reference to the character Bays in Buckingham's *The Rehearsal* (published 1672).

10 Lockets] a fashionable ordinary at Charing Cross, often mentioned in comedies of the period.

14 Monteth] A monteith is a basin notched at the brim so that glasses could hang in the water and be cooled.

23 *From Box to Stage, from Stage to Box they run,*] By moving from one area to another, young sparks could avoid paying and thus '*steal the Play*'.

26 *our Friends in* Cornhil *and* Cheapside] the merchants in the audience.

32 *gone to* Rome] i.e. for the Jubilee.

35 *But that way's old*] Epilogues begging for the ladies' approval were frequently delivered, particularly after the controversy over things considered immoral and indecent in the theatre, as specified, for instance, in Collier's attack, *A Short View of the Immorality and Prophaneness of the English Stage*.

A New Prologue

A New Prologue] For a discussion of the circumstances precipitating this prologue, see Introduction, pp. 131–2. The prologue was first spoken at Drury Lane on 13 July 1700; it was published in the third edition, 20 August 1700 (*Post-Man*, 17–20 August 1700).

0.2 my very Good Friend, Mr. *Oldmixon*] Farquhar wrote the epilogue for John Oldmixon's unsuccessful opera *The Grove*, which played on 19 February 1700, perhaps earlier. Oldmixon had an earlier failure at Drury Lane, his pastoral *Amintas*, published with the date 1698 and probably acted the same year. He showed his 'Mind to Curry-Favour' at the new house, Lincoln's Inn Fields, perhaps as early as February 1700, the same month *The Grove* opened, by writing a prologue for Charles Gildon's adaptation of *Measure for Measure*, with music by Daniel Purcell.

3–4 Crime, . . . he has Pleas'd the Town] The 'Farce' condemned by Oldmixon in the Prologue to *Measure for Measure* was *The Constant Couple*, damned for its unique popularity.

6 *No foe to* B—re, *yet a Friend to* Wills] Controversy raged between Sir Richard Blackmore, a physician as well as author of two epics, *Prince Arthur* (1695) and *King Arthur* (1697), and the wits of Will's Coffee House, headed by Dryden, Garth, Tom Brown, and others. The first salvo was fired by Blackmore in his *Satyr Against Wit*, published 23 November 1699 (advertised in the *Post-Man*, 21–3 November 1699), in which he attacked many poets, using abbreviations such as D—n for Dryden, as Farquhar uses B—re in the prologue. *Commendatory Verses, on the Author of the Two Arthurs*, published 14 March 1700 (advertised *Post-Boy*, 12–14 March 1700) and probably edited by Tom Brown, attacked not only Blackmore's medical ability (his 'Bills' or prescriptions), but his epics as well, often using the imagery of disease appropriate to his vocation. The volume contained a number of separate satires, written by authors attacked in the *Satyr*. On 18 April 1700, *Discommendatory Verses, or Those Which are Truly Commendatory, on the Author of the Two Arthurs, and the Satyr Against Wit* appeared (advertised in the *Flying-Post*, 16–18 April 1700). Oldmixon himself, like Farquhar, was not apparently directly involved in the controversy. For details see Richard C. Boys, *Sir Richard Blackmore and the Wits*, University of Michigan Contributions in Modern Philology, no. 13 (Ann Arbor, 1949).

8 Bankrupt Brisco's Fate] Samuel Briscoe was a bookseller in London, in Russell Street, Covent Garden, between 1691 and 1705, with imprints reading 'over-against Wills's Coffee House' and 'at the corner shop of Charles Street'. In 1698 he managed a flourishing business, if one may judge from the list of *Books Newly Printed (and in the PRESS) for Samuel Briscoe* (copy in Folger Shakespeare Library, shelfmarked B4758.5), including works of Dryden, Behn's novels, collections of letters, D'urfey's songs, Dennis's *Miscellaneous Works*, many plays by leading playwrights such as Congreve and Wycherley, etc. However, during the same year, he was hauled before the justices of Middlesex, along with Congreve, over the publication of *The Double Dealer* (Luttrell, iv. 379; 12 May 1698). By 1700 he was bankrupt; Marmaduke Browne, a Ludgate Hill stationer and other creditors sued out a commission of bankruptcy against him so that debts owed Briscoe would go to Browne. One of these debts was one for £30 supposedly owed by William Wycherley in connection with proposals printed to raise a

subscription for his *Miscellany Poems*. ('Owing for advertising stiching folding Portridge time Expenses paper & printing of the sd. William proposalls.' PRO C6/314. Wycherley's Bill of Complaint, 23 January 1699). Wycherley filed a bill of complaint in Chancery, and Briscoe answered that in fact Wycherley had owed him £53. 8s. for money lent, books, and the printing costs of the proposals (PRO C6/314. Joint Answer of Samuel Briscoe and Marmaduke Browne, sworn 22 February 1700). For details of the litigation see Howard P. Vincent, 'William Wycherley's *Miscellany Poems*', *PQ* 16 (1937), 145–8. Briscoe said he himself owed Browne £100. Briscoe later complained that he had 'experienced hard Usage in the World and therefore lost all'. Associates, he suggested, led him into his financial difficulties: his 'little All, if it had not fallen into dilatory, I will not say malicious Hands, might have afforded him a Retreat, if not a comfortable Support' (Dedication of Sir Charles Duncomb, sheriff of London, *Familiar and Courtly Letters*). To rescue Briscoe from bankruptcy, a group of wits, centring on Will's and led by Tom Brown, agreed to contribute to the Voiture volume, published 11 May 1700 (*Post-Boy*, 7–9 May 1700), which revived Briscoe's business so that, according to John Dunton, 'honest Sam does, at it were, thrive by his misfortunes, and I hear has the satisfaction and goodness to forgive those enemies who are now starting, as a judgment upon them, for attempting his overthrow' (pp. 292–3). Some letters by Farquhar were included in the volume designed to revive Briscoe's business.

10 *He's none of those that Broke the t'other House*] Farquhar did not help sink the theatre in Lincoln's Inn Fields, because he did not write for that house—his plays had both gone to Drury Lane.

17 *To* Write Good PLAYS, *purpose to Starve the* Players] an answer to Oldmixon's statement that despite the fact that audiences praised the plays at Lincoln's Inn Fields and damned those at Drury Lane, they went to Drury Lane so that the actors at Lincoln's Inn Fields 'almost starv'd'.

21 *Our PLAYS are* Farce, *because our* House *is Cram'd*] Farquhar again directly answers Oldmixon's complaints, ll. 5–6, 10–11, using his terminology. Many prologues at Lincoln's Inn Fields that year made the accusation that *The Constant Couple* was farce.

28 *Old* Shakespear's GHOST] The epilogue to *Measure for Measure* was 'spoken by Shakespear's Ghost', actually owed the actor Verbruggen.

Sir Harry Wildair

Dedication

0.2 Earl of *Albemarle*, &c.] Arnold Joost van Keppel (1669–1718), first Earl of Albemarle, came to England from the Netherlands with William of Orange in 1688. A close friend of King William, he was created Earl of Albemarle on 10 February 1696 and took various military commands during the next few years. In 1701 he was appointed Colonel of the First Regiment of Swiss in the Dutch service.

Farquhar had met Albemarle in Holland in 1700. The King and

presumably Albemarle returned to England on 18 October 1700 (Luttrell, iv, 698; 19 October 1700). Farquhar himself wrote from Holland on 23 October NS to a female friend in England, 'I have transcrib'd your Letter to my Lord A—le' (*Love and Business*, vol. ii, p. 361), an indication of his acquaintance with the nobleman.

Farquhar's dedication in April 1701 was followed by Steele's dedication of *The Funeral* to the Countess of Albemarle the following December. Both Farquhar and Steele may have hoped for military preferment through their literary efforts.

'A Dialogue between the Illustrious Ladies, the Countesses of Albemarle and Orkney, Soon after the King's Death', published necessarily after 8 March 1702 when the King died, complains of the two dedications:

> Perhaps you were pleas'd with the nauseous dull Praise
> Of two dirty poets in their Damnable plays,
> Where thy Spouse for his Vertue and Wisdom is fam'd,
> And thy timorous Dad is a Hero proclaim'd,
> Tho's to Valour tis known he'd as little Pretence
> As thy Lord has to Breeding, good Nature, or Sense.
>   (Quoted in Ellis, *Poems on Affairs of State*, pp. 369–70, ll. 21–6).

14 your Royal Master] King William, who made van Keppel first Earl of Albemarle.

34 *Mecænas* and *Agrippa*] Maecenas and Agrippa were the two most trusted friends and counsellors of the Emperor Augustus. Maecenas was also a great patron of poets, including Virgil, Horace, and Propertius. Farquhar likens William to Augustus; Agrippa probably denotes the Earl of Portland, another very close friend and advisor of the King; and Albemarle is portrayed as Maecenas, worthy favourite of the ruler and patron of letters.

42 *Cæsar*] William III.

43–6 he first asserted . . . Religion] William III avoided 'Popery and Thraldom' through the Glorious Revolution, fought heroically in Europe, brought peace through the treaty made at Ryswick, and brought security to the nation's religion through continuing a Protestant succession.

69 *Maro*] Virgil.

Prologue

1–2 *Our Authors . . . damning other Plays*;] Prologues of the period attacked the offerings of the competition fiercely. Recipient of perhaps the most vicious attacks, Farquhar had every reason to be aware of the practice.

5 Athenian *Rules*] Farquhar had been condemned for his lack of respect for the Rules, as expressed in *A Discourse Upon Comedy*. He believed instead that 'An *English* Play is intended for the Use and Instruction of an *English* Audience' (vol. ii, p. 378).

10 Vossius, Scaliger, Hedelin, *or* Rapin] Not only did Farquhar scoff at Aristotle's value to a modern writer in the *Discourse*, he also dismissed Horace, Vossius, Scaliger, Heinsius, Hedelin, Rapin, and 'some half a Dozen more' as more important to the scholar than to the modern dramatist.

Vossius or Gerard Johann Voss (1577–1649) was a classical scholar and professor of Rhetoric and Greek at Leiden. The *Poetics* of Julius Caesar Scaliger (1484–1558) greatly influenced neoclassical literary principles. François Hédelin (1604–76), a poet, was Abbé d'Aubignac. René Rapin (1621–87) was a French Jesuit and poet. All were revered scholars who received frequent and awed attention in England during Farquhar's time.

12 *You are the Rules by which he writes his Plays*] Farquhar's statement predates Samuel Johnson's far more famous 'The Drama's Laws the Drama's Patrons give' by forty-six years.

18 *three Stories high*] Footmen sat in the Upper Gallery. They were notoriously boisterous in expressing displeasure at a play.

19 *the Front-Boxes*] Prologues and other commentaries of the period assign ladies of quality to the front boxes. Many theatrical poems refer to the 'Bright Circle', that is, the ladies in the front boxes. The author's style in this case is appropriate to the gentility of the ladies.

23 *the Pit*] Gentlemen and wealthy citizens, as well as young men of fashion, tended to occupy the pit.

25 *every* Covent-Garden *Critick's Face*] The beaux, wits, and other young men of fashion sat in the side-boxes.

26 Action, Time, *and* Place] the three Unities of dramatic poetry. Farquhar had attacked the Unities anonymously in *The Adventures of Covent Garden*:

> You Criticks (*said* Selinda) *make a mighty sputter about exactness of Plot, unity of time, place, and I know not what, which I can never find do any Play the least good.*

In *A Discourse Upon Comedy*, he commented that Shakespeare, Jonson, and Fletcher:

> . . . have fairly dispenc'd with the greatest part of Critical Formalities; the Decorums of Time and Place, so much cry'd up of late, had no force of Decorum with them; the Æconomy of their Plays was *ad libitum*, and the Extent of their Plots only limited by the Convenience of Action.

28 Number Three] Farquhar refers on several occasions to 'Number Three' as a place for assignations. Although rooms in taverns and inns were generally given names rather than numbers, perhaps he referred to a specific address of an establishment or to a specific room in one.

29 Masques] prostitutes who plied their trade in the theatre and sometimes ladies seeking amorous adventures behind the cover of a mask.

I. i

4 News from the *Baltick*] Augustus of Saxony, Frederick IV of Denmark, and Peter of Russia, all coveting lands beyond their own borders, entered a pact to attack the empire of Charles XII of Sweden. William III had made a pact with Charles. The Danish declaration of war, therefore, brought Admiral Rooke's Anglo-Dutch fleet to the fray. In 1700 they defeated the Danes.

On 8 August 1700 Frederick signed a treaty with the Duke of Holstein-Gottorp, Charles's brother-in-law, acknowledging the independence of the duchy and agreeing to withdraw from the alliance with Saxony and Russia. At that point the Anglo-Dutch squadron sailed home. Charles, however, refused to negotiate. Instead, he transported an army of only 6,000 across the Baltic in October; they defeated a force variously estimated as 40,000 to 80,000 Russian troops. The Battle of Narva and another victory the following spring won Charles his reputation for brilliant warfare (Wolf pp. 56–9; R. W. Harris, *England in the Eighteenth Century* [London, 1963], pp. 106–7).

Fireball, supposedly one of the naval men in Rooke's fleet, describes current events he himself has witnessed and the newspapers have described to the theatre-going public.

115 *Namur*] See Commentary, *The Constant Couple*, II. iv. 106.

118 *Kid*. William Kidd (1645–1701), the notorious Captain Kidd, was commissioned as a British privateer in 1696, arrested in 1699 on grounds of piracy, and hanged in 1701.

126 *Picket*] piquet. See Commentary, *The Constant Couple*, v. i. 115.

126 *Capotted*] won all the tricks and thus scored forty.

144 *Burgundy*] Parley's malapropism refers to a *bergère*, that is, a large, flat straw hat.

150 *Pinners*] circular caps, with frills and often lace, worn flat on the crown, often with long streamers and usually with decorations of ribbons or flowers on the crown (Cunnington, *Eighteenth*, p. 156).

153 *Favourites*] 'locks dangling on the temples' (*The Ladies Dictionary* [1694], quoted in Cunnington, *Eighteenth*, p. 185).

154 *Caul*] netted back part of the cap.

156 *Lappets*] streamers attached to the head-dress.

249 *Grays-Inn* pieces] stolen money. Gray's Inn Fields, open land north of Gray's Inn garden wall, was notorious for its footpads.

286 *Louis-d'Ors*] French gold pieces.

288 *Taillés*] serves as talliere or keeper of the bank at basset. The talliere could profit handsomely by the advantages the dealer had, such as having the first and last card at his disposal (*Complete Gamester*, in Hartman, p. 271).

290 Persecution of Basset in *Paris*] King Louis issued a public edict limiting the privilege of talliere to members of the greatest families since the role of banker in the game led to the rapid development of great riches. All others were confined to a twelve-penny bank 'for fear of ruining private persons and families'. The refugees to whom Standard refers are gamblers who came to England to make their fortunes since they had 'the liberty of staking what they please' (*Complete Gamester*, in Hartman, p. 271).

301 a Master in *Chancery's* place] one of the assistants to the Lord Chancellor in the Court of Chancery. Parley sees such a marriage as possible because of her fortune, now assured by the 'comings-in' or income from her arrangement with Standard.

301–2 a poor *Templar*] Law students were often portrayed as impecunious fortune-hunters in plays of the eighteenth century.

313 Pattins] high clogs used to protect the shoes from the mud of the streets in wet weather.

316 the dear perfume of *Fleet-Ditch*] The Fleet was 'little better than an open sewer' (Wheatley, ii. 53), the stench overpowering.

372 *Cannibal* Women] A cannibal was defined as 'a cruel rigid Fellow in dealing; also Men-eaters' (*NDCC*). A pun is intended referring to the prostitutes as cannibals.

385 Hot-cockles] Hot cockles is a game in which a player covers his eyes and tries to guess who hits him. The sexual *double entendre* here, however, relies on the slang reference to the female sexual parts as cockles (Eric Partridge, *A Dictionary of Slang and Unconventional English*. 6th edn. 2 vols. [New York, 1967], i. 166).

II. i

20 *French Refugees*] After the revocation of the Edict of Nantes in 1685, the Huguenots dispersed to other countries, including England. The persecution of the Huguenots contributed to the English hatred of the French king.

20 *Smyrna*] the Smyrna coffee-house, on the north side of Pall Mall.

39–40 Iron Swords, ty'd up Wigs, and tuck'd in Crevats] A gentleman of fashion would have worn an elaborately decorated sword, perhaps adorned with gold or silver or even jewels; he might also have carried a cane. But he would not have worn the ordinary battle sword of a disbanded officer. Campaign wigs, a fashion derived from the needs of battle, were full wigs parted at the centre and drawn into one lock on each side and one in back; these were turned up and tied in a knot, and the wig was tied back. They were practical styles for riding horseback, and were used for war duty and, after they became fashionable, for other purposes. Another military fashion was the steinkirk, named after the battle in 1692 in which the English fought the French, a cravat twisted loosely in front, the ends either inserted through a button-hole or pinned to one side with a brooch. All in all, Lurewell deplores the look of the disbanded officers.

75 the Appartments] the royal rooms in which the King's birthday celebration was held.

75 the Birth-night] The King's birthday was celebrated with elegant festivities during which the highest fashions would be displayed.

159 *Locket's*] See Commentary, *The Constant Couple*, Epilogue, l. 10.

204 make a Paroli] 'having won the couch or first stake, and having a mind to go on to get a *Sept-et-le-va*, you crook the corner of your card, letting your money lie without being paid the value of it by the Talliere' (*Complete Gamester*, in Hartman, p. 272).

247 long Wig and Sword] emblems of a beau.

II. ii

6 Pistols] pistoles, Spanish gold coins valued at slightly less than a pound.

39–40 The King of *Spain* is dead] Although in the second Partition Treaty, signed in March 1700, the Spanish succession was to go to the Archduke Charles of Habsburg, when King Carlos died on 1 November 1700, he willed his throne to Philip of Anjou, the French king's son. When King Louis decided to accept the will, the stage was set for more warfare. In July 1701, a few months after *Sir Harry Wildair* opened, King William and Marlborough sailed to Holland to negotiate the Grand Alliance, which was signed in September 1701. Farquhar wrote the play after the Spanish king's death but before the Alliance was formed, a time in which the threat of the Spanish succession held hope for the disbanded officers that there would be military action in the future.

77 Mattadors] 'The *Matadors* (or killing cards) which are the Spadillo, Malillio, and Basto, are the chief cards, and when they are all in a hand the others pay for them three of the greater counters apiece; and with these three for foundation you may count as many Matadors as you have cards in an interrupted series of Trumps; for all which the others are to pay you one counter apiece' (*Complete Gamester*, in Hartman, p. 48). Spadillo is the ace of spades; Malillio, the lowest card in the trump suit; and Basto, the ace of clubs.

78–9 *Sept le Va, Quinze le Va, & Trante le Va*] If a player had made a paroli at basset, that is, crooked the corner of the card and let his money lie, and if his card turned up again, he made seven times as much as originally laid down on the card. If he then crooked the third corner of the card and if it showed up, he would win fifteen times as much as staked. He could then crook the fourth corner and if it turned up another time, he would win thirty-three times as much. (*Complete Gamester*, in Hartman, pp. 273–4).

81–2 Nine of Diamonds at Comet, three Fives at Cribbidge, and Pam in Lanteraloo] all winning cards in three popular games. Pam or the knave of clubs was the highest card in lanterloo. Depending on the stakes, card games could involve large amounts of money.

88 Singing Birds] guineas. See *The Constant Couple*, II. ii. 54–65.

III. i

131 the new Revolution in *Europe*] that is, the northern conflict.

135 The Pope's dead] Pope Innocent XII died on 27 September 1700.

156 you maul'd *Copenhagen*] The Anglo-Dutch fleet had attacked the Danes at Copenhagen in the summer of 1700.

157 that pretty, dear, sweet, pretty King of *Sweden*] Charles XII was only eighteen years old when his kingdom was threatened.

169 Ptysick] phthisic, a term for consumption, was loosely applied to asthma, severe coughs, and other pulmonary ailments.

194 *Flying-post*] a pun, referring both to the speeding post-carriers and to George Ridpath's periodical *Flying Post*, a newspaper which had begun publication in 1695 and continued until 1733.

III. ii

15–16 Dr. *Swan* in Quibbling] Swan was a notorious punster. References
to him include Dryden's *Discourse concerning Satire* (1693), Ravenscroft's
prologue to *The Italian Husband* (1697), Wycherley's poem, 'A Panegyric, on
Quibling; to the, that way Ingenious Mr. Swan (in his *Miscellany Poems*,
1704); and *Spectator* no. 61 (1711). Wildair seems to have awarded him his
doctorate.

21 slash'd Doublets] Slashed doublets were woefully outdated. Doublets
slashed to show a bright lining had been fashionable *c.*1620–31 and less so
in the next decade; by the 1670s the term was no longer even used
(Cunnington, *Seventeenth*, pp. 18, 129). 'Close-body'd' gowns had similarly
fallen into disuse by 1700, supplanted by open gowns which displayed the
petticoat.

28 *Melpomene*] the muse of tragedy.

39 Sack-Posset] a drink made of hot milk curdled with ale or wine and
seasoned with sugar or spices.

41 the naked Statue] 'I happened to go with a lady to Hyde Park Corner,
where in an open area we saw several naked statues; at which she, out of a
fond humour, or hot fit of devotion, took some offence' (*The Original Works of
William King* [London, 1698]).

IV. i

89 *Nants*] brandy.

IV. ii

56 go Snacks] be partners; share (*NDCC*).

V. iv

18–19 Quint and Quatorz] in piquet, quint is a sequence of five cards,
which scores fifteen; quatorze, a series of four aces, kings, queens, knaves, or
tens, scores fourteen.

55–6 *White, Chaves, Morris, Locket, Pawlet,* and *Pontack*] all proprietors of
fashionable establishments. White presumably owned White's Chocolate
House. Morris owned a coffee-house in Essex Street. Locket was presumably
proprietor of Locket's; Pawlett's establishment near Dowgate, Thames-
street, had a 'Great Dancing-Room' and hosted musical entertainments.
Pontack's was a noted dining spot. I have not identified Chaves, but context
suggests that he too ran a tavern or coffeehouse.

V. vi

37–8 *Oroonoko* and the *Mourning Bride*] Thomas Southerne's *Oroonoko*
opened at Drury Lane probably in November 1695 (Advertisement, *Post
Boy*, 14 December 1695). Congreve's *Mourning Bride* opened at Lincoln's Inn
Fields, probably on 20 February 1697. Although theatrical records for these
years are scanty, both plays clearly were unusually successful. Charles

Gildon claimed that *The Mourning Bride* had greater success than any play he could remember (*English Dramatick Poets*, p. 23).

40 the Musick from both Houses] Both Drury Lane and Lincoln's Inn Fields were emphasizing musical presentations during this period. In addition, some musical entertainments were performed at Dorset Garden, for example, Congreve's *The Judgment of Paris*, for which a competition for the best score was held.

41–2 *Abell*'s Voice] John Abell (1650?–1724?) was a superb singer who, in Congreve's words, 'certainly sings beyond all creatures upon the earth' (Letter to his friend Keally, 10 December 1700). A countertenor or alto, he was appointed in 1679 to the King's private music, but during the 1690s he wandered on the Continent. He returned early in 1700 and performed in concerts. According to Congreve (letter to John Drummond, 15 January 1701), he had agreed to sing at Lincoln's Inn Fields and had received £300, but failed to perform. He published two collections in 1701, *A Collection of Songs in Several Languages* and *A Collection of Songs in English*. (For greater detail, see the *Biographical Dictionary*, from which information was drawn.)

56–7 our Ambassador's Chaplain] Perhaps a mistake for the ambassador's courier. Charles Montagu, then Earl later Duke of Manchester (1660?–1722), served as ambassador at Paris from late 1699 until September 1701. His servant, a Mr Jolly, drowned at Navarre *c.*1 February 1701 while serving as a secret courier; he was carrying, sewn into the lining of his coat, letters to Montagu from the English ambassador at Madrid. The letters were uncoded because the two ambassadors did not share a cipher. The body was recovered and the letters opened and forwarded to the Spanish authorities. The English protested, and complained even more when, intercepting a letter from the Jacobite Lord Melford, they learned the correspondence had also been shared with the French. Melford's letter was published by Parliament, and the incident became a *cause célèbre* (Christian Cole, *Memoirs of Affairs of State* [London, 1733], pp. 300–26 *passim*).

119 *L'Abbé, and Balon*] Anthony l'Abbé and Jean Balon were two French dancers who came to the London stage at the turn of the century. L'Abbé probably first came in the spring of 1698 (*Biographical Dictionary*, ix. 87); he entered a three-year contract for 1700–3 with Thomas Betterton at Lincoln's Inn Fields; Balon was imported by Betterton for five weeks in the spring of 1699 at a sum reported by Luttrell as 400 guineas (Luttrell, iv. 502–3, 8 April 1699); Lord Cholmondeley reportedly gave him an additional 100 guineas (*Biographical Dictionary*, i. 239). Fireball's reference to sending both L'Abbé and Balon back indicates that Balon, as well as his countryman, was performing in London in the 1700–1 season, although the *London Stage* does not record his presence in the company that season.

136 Washes] liquid cosmetics to improve the complexion.

137 Waters] solutions used as a medicine, cosmetic, or perfume.

Epilogue

1–30 [Epilogue] Cibber, still in character as the Marquis, doubtless spoke the prologue.

22 *short Muff*] In *Spectator* no. 129 (28 July 1711), Addison wrote of 'last Year's little Muffs' (ii. 13), but the fashion had obviously arrived in London by 1701. The Cunningtons say muffs were large until *c.*1710; however, Addison's sense of style cannot be taken quite so chronologically (Cunnington, *Eighteenth*, p. 177).

23 *large Muff*] The Cunningtons report that men wore muffs off and on throughout the period, medium or small until *c.*1730, very large from then until the 1750s. Scented muffs for beaux, 'either carried or attached by a loop to a coat button, or hung from a waistbelt, or slung from a cord or ribbon round the neck' were created of feathers, furs, velvet, chenille, and ribbon trimmings (Cunnington, *Eighteenth*, p. 99). Obviously the affectation of very large muffs long predated 1730.

23 *his sleeve down dere*] probably a reference to the frill or ruffle attached to the wristband of shirt sleeves.

25 *Furbalo*] A Furbelow is the pleated or ruched border of a petticoat or scarf.

The Stage-Coach

4–5 the *Rose-Tavern* after Play, the *Sun-Tavern* after Change, or the *Devil-Tavern* after Church] The Rose Tavern in Russell Street, Covent Garden, adjoining the Drury Lane theatre, a favourite haunt of theatrical performers and audiences, was mentioned by Farquhar in several of his plays (*Love and a Bottle*, *The Constant Couple*, *The Recruiting Officer*). The Sun Tavern, also mentioned in *Love and a Bottle*, was located by the Royal Exchange. The St Dunstan Tavern stood between Temple Bar and Middle Temple Gate, just opposite St Dunstan's Church. Because the painted sign pictured St Dunstan pulling the Devil by the nose, it was nicknamed the Devil or Old Devil Tavern (Wheatley, *passim*).

23–5 *Dolly*. Are your Pistols Charg'd. *Fetch*. Yes, yes, we always go Charg'd Child; A Brace of Bullets I'll assure you.] A *double entendre* condemned by Arthur Bedford (*The Evil and Danger of Stage-Plays* [London, 1706], p. 133.) this pun also appears in *The Constant Couple*, iii. i. 93).

37 *Teague*] A nickname for an Irishman, from the Irish name Tadhg. Howard had created a famous antecedent of Macahone named Teague in *The Committee*, and Farquhar later used the name in *The Twin-Rivals*.

50 *Blossoms-Inn*] Blossom Inn, earlier known as Bosoms Inn, was in Lawrence Lane, Cheapside.

85 *Strowler*] vagabond, used also as a term for itinerant actors.

86 *Vinegar-Yard*] an infamous area near Play House Passage, the main entrance to the Drury Lane Theatre. Vinegar Yard teemed with prostitutes plying their trade.

90 Honest *Jenny* the Player] Conceivably this is a reference to the ostentatiously chaste actress Jane Rogers, who had spurned the attentions of Farquhar's friend Wilks. The reading in Q2 is '*Jenny* the Orange-wench'. Selling oranges at the theatre was a notorious guise for prostitution. The

moralistic Richard Burridge in *A Scourge for the Play-Houses* (London, 1702) described the trade thus:

> *Orange*-Wenches . . . allow so much per Night, for the Priviledge of selling that for a Shilling in the House, which cost not Two-pence, besides the Benefit of letting out their *C—dities* in Fee-tail after Play is over. . . .

Although the term 'strowler' often applied to itinerant actors, 'Orange-wench' seems a better reading in the light of the notoriety of these women unless in fact a lampoon was intended.

90 snapt] taken, caught.

91 make a Hand of him] turn him to account, make money from him.

116 Cogue] small cup or dram.

212 to send us the way of all Flesh] Bedford complained that the phrase ridiculously applied David's text when near death, 'I go the way of all the earth', to the act of copulation.

216 Tit] a derogatory term for a young woman, suggesting a hussy.

222 Wimbled] insinuated.

231 Serve under him] one of Farquhar's many martial–sexual puns.

231–2 Broke of all sides] that is, both disbanded and penniless.

237–8 a poor Insignificant Ring-leader of Fifty Rogues] A troop or company contained approximately forty soldiers in peace, sixty in war. Each troop of foot soldiers or grenadiers had a captain and two other officers. (See R. E. Scouller, *The Armies of Queen Anne* [Oxford, 1966], p. 99).

248–82 Softly . . . *Micher.*] The scene in which Basil and Isabella talk over the head of Nicodemus is reminiscent of the scene in Wycherley's *Country Wife* in which Harcourt courts Alithea in front of Sparkish (III. ii, in *Wycherley*, pp. 293–6). Isabella, however, is a willing participant in the verbal deception.

281 watch your Waters] keep a close watch on you.

287–8 the *French* in *Spittle-Fields*] French refugees who colonized Spital-fields after the Edict of Nantes was revoked in 1685. Stonehill notes (ii. 432) they 'were so numerous that thirty churches had to be erected to care for their spiritual welfare'.

290 *Harts-horn*] used as a cure for the vapours.

296 Club this Matter] divide up the bill.

297 the Kings-Evil] scrofula, which could be cured supposedly by the King's touch.

304–41 [SONG] This song, set by John Eccles, was, according to the four half-sheet broadside engravings, sung by Doggett. The song continued in the text of the operatic version to which sixteen other airs were added.

355 Calash] a light carriage with a folding hood.

384 *Saracen's-Head*] a tavern and coach stop on the north side of Snow Hill outside Newgate (Wheatley, iii. 210).

421 *Hockley the Hole*] the site of bear- and bull-baiting.

439 *Covent-Garden*] The loose morality of the inhabitants of Covent Garden was often mentioned in the plays of the period.

464 quit scores] even the score.

515 Spatterdashes] gaiters that extended from ankle to knee, shaped like

boots, to protect the wearer from water or mud. They were worn by soldiers and sometimes civilians for horseback riding (Cunnington, *Eighteenth*, p. 82).

515 Gambadoes] leather boots attached to the saddle and used in place of stirrups, in order to protect the rider from dirt (Cunnington, *Eighteenth*, pp. 81–2).

515 Sashoons] an interlining, often made of leather, to be bound around the leg to prevent the boot from sagging (Cunnington, *Seventeenth*, p. 158).

534 Pump him] drench him with water.

534 Souse] soak or prepare with marinade for cooking.

535 Flea] flay.

535 Carbonade] cut, slash, score like a piece of meat before grilling. All in all, the Squire's revenge is vividly culinary.

549–50 Ministers Chamber] the fat country parson from the stage-coach company apparently married and accommodated the couple.

Appendix A

Dedication

0.4 *Samuel Bagshaw*] See Introduction, p. 321.

3 Silken Wits of the Time] In *Cynthia's Revells* Jonson refers to 'the silken disposition of courtiers'.

15 Lord *Verulam*] Francis Bacon, in the *Essay of Envy*, says 'A man that hath no virtue in himself ever envieth virtue in others.'

Prologue

1–6 *Poets . . . Ass.*] These lines closely echo ll. 1–4 and 7–8 of Farquhar's Epilogue to Oldmixon's *The Grove*, which opened in February or March 1700. The following changes occur:

    1. *Poets in former Days*] Time was when Poets rul'd

    2. *the*] their

    3. *but with this*] with mighty

    4. *the Gods*] their Gods

    5. *'Tis but a Word with them,*] No more than this

    6. *Jove's made*] Great *Jupiter's*

    6. *an Alderman*] Great Beaux's

Epilogue

EPILOGUE] This epilogue was taken almost verbatim from the prologue of Thomas Goffe's *The Careless Shepherdess*, published in 1656 (Lawrence, p. 392). The seemingly contemporary references did not come from Farquhar's pen.

1 *Praise a fair Day at Night*] don't commend something until it has reached its full effect.

7 *snarling Sect*] Bedford says this refers to the reformers or 'Criticks of the Age' (pp. 184–5 and n. (g)).

25 *Country Putt*] a silly, shallow fellow.

Appendix B

Prologue

1 *Like some abandon'd Mistress of the Town*] The metaphor of the foresaken woman was often reiterated at Lincoln's Inn Fields in the season of 1703–4. The prologue to Susanna Centlivre's *The Gamester*, for example, written by Nicholas Rowe for a February opening complained:

> When first you took us from our Father's House,
> And Lovingly our Interest did Espouse,
> You kept us fine, Carest, and Lodg'd us here . . .
> At length, for Pleasures known do seldom last;
> Frequent Enjoyment pall'd your Sprightly Taste,
> And tho' at first you did not quite neglect,
> We found your Love was dwindled to Respect. . . .

15 *We ransack'd the whole Globe to find out new*] In the 1702–3 season, Lincoln's Inn Fields scheduled performances by imported singers like Margarita de l'Epine and Maria Margarita Gallia, as well as the dancer l'Abbé. The intense competition between the theatres is well reflected in Philips's prologue.

19 Monimia] The failure of a revival of Otway's *The Orphan* must have proved a shocking disappointment, for it was also lamented in the prologue to Mary Pix's *The Different Widows*, which opened probably in November 1703 and was published 4 December.

30–1 *Your once-lov'd Stage its drooping Head shall raise, / And from its* Rival *boldly snatch the Bays.*] The company at Lincoln's Inn Fields was clearly feeling defeat in the competition for audiences. Farquhar himself was considered largely to blame for the decline of audiences, for *The Constant Couple* at Drury Lane had proved so popular that prologists such as Charles Boyle were still deriding it in 1703. The prologue to *The Different Widows*, which mourned Monimia's failure, also condemned the *Trip to the Jubilee*. The lapsed popularity of Betterton's company, expressed in these lines, was often mentioned in prologues and epilogues of the period.

Appendix C

Air VIII.

Dutch Skipper] a dance frequently performed in the theatres.

Air IX.

O ponder well] The same tune accompanied Polly's song 'O ponder well', Air XII in *The Beggar's Opera*.

AIR XIV.

An old woman clothed in Grey] The same tune was used for Air I in *The Beggar's Opera*, 'Through all the employments of life', sung by Peachum.

The Inconstant

Title-page

[motto] *Metamorphoses*, i. 1 'My mind is bent to tell of bodies changed into new forms', (trans. Frank Justus Miller, Loeb Classical Library, 3rd edn. [Cambridge, Mass. 1977], p. 1, 2). Perhaps Farquhar chose the motto to answer charges of plagiarism by suggesting he had transformed the original.

Dedication

0.2 Richard Tighe] Farquhar knew Tighe at Trinity College, Dublin, when both were students. Tighe matriculated on 21 March 1693 at the age of 15 as a scholar-commoner, a class of undergraduates who ate with the scholars but who had the privileges of fellow-commoners, including completion of the course of study within three years. Farquhar matriculated on 17 July 1694 as a sizar, that is, a student allowed education for performing certain tasks. Tighe received his BA in the spring term 1696; in 1703 he took a seat in Parliament (*Alumni Dublinenses*, ed. George Dames Burtchaell and Thomas Wick Saleir [Dublin, 1935]). Both men were quite young, about twenty-four, at the time Farquhar wrote his dedication. The *Biographia Britannica* suggests Tighe was the model for Mirabel. Wilkes, apparently not realizing they were contemporaries, claims that Tighe's character was drawn in Old Mirabel (i. viii).

8–9 another Character] Sir Harry Wildair.

49 the place of my Pupilage] Trinity College.

Preface

3 took the hint from *Fletcher's Wild Goose Chase*] Some critics claimed that Farquhar not only took the hint from Fletcher's play, published posthumously in 1652, but plagiarized it, and did a poor job at that. In fact, Farquhar ranged quite freely from the earlier play although there are a few passages of rather specific borrowings. These passages are noted in the Commentary below.

6–7 a kind of *Cremona* business] Luttrell recorded on 7 February 1702; 'Yesterdays Paris Gazet says, that prince Eugene thro' an aqueduct got 600 men in the night into Cremona, the head quarters of the French, and seizing upon a gate, let in 7000 Germans, who took Villeroy prisoner and carried him off; but in the morning, being overpowred by the French, were forc'd out again with great losse.' On 10 February he noted that the Germans had killed from 1,500 to 2,000 Frenchmen, taken 90 officers, 400 soldiers, and 500 horse, but had lost 400 men (v. 139–41).

8 the charms of *Gallick* Heels] Farquhar probably refers to the French dancer Marie-Thérèse Perdou de Subligny (1666–*c*.1735). Betterton had imported her in the 1701–2 season to increase attendance. The author of the *Comparison* noted that she danced on the bill with *The Way of the World* at Lincoln's Inn Fields when Bevil Higgons's *The Generous Conqueror* ran at Drury Lane, probably in December 1701 (p. 67). There are no extant

theatrical records to indicate that she did in fact bring 'some fifty Audiences in five Months', as Farquhar claims in the Preface.

14–15 Elephants that were taught to dance on the Ropes] In his *Natural History*, Book viii. 4–5, Pliny describes elephants exhibited by Germanicus Caesar. They did amazing tricks, such as flinging weapons, performing a kind of dance, dancing on tightropes, and carrying a litter bearing an elephant dressed as a lady lying in, all within a hall full of dining guests.

17 the great *Mogul*] an elephant on display at the White Horse in Fleet Street (George Walte Thornbury, *Old and New London* [6 vols., London, *c*.1875], i. 34). According to Cibber, Rich attempted to book the animal for display at Dorset Garden:

> . . . the Patentee of *Drury-Lane* went on in his usual Method of paying extraordinary Prices to Singers, Dancers, and other exotic Performers, which were as constantly deducted out of the sinking Sallaries of his Actors . . . his Sense of every thing to be shewn there, was much upon a Level, with the Taste of the Multitude, whose Opinion, and whose Mony weigh'd with him full as much, as that of the best Judges. His Point was to please the Majority, who, could more easily comprehend any thing they *saw*, than the daintiest things, that could be said to them. But in this Notion he kept no medium; for in my Memory, he carry'd it so far, that he was . . . actually dealing for an extraordinary large Elephant, at a certain Sum, for every Day he might think fit to shew the tractable Genius of that vast quiet Creature, in any Play, or Farce, in the Theatre (then standing) in *Dorset-Garden*. But from the Jealousy, which so formidable a Rival had rais'd in his Dancers, and by his Bricklayer's assuring him, that if the Walls were to be open'd wide enough for its Entrance, it might endanger the Fall of the House, he gave up his Project, and with it, so hopeful a Prospect of making the Receipts of the Stage run higher than all the Wit, and Force of the best Writers had ever yet rais'd them to.
>
> About the same time of his being under this Disappointment, he put in Practice another Project of as new, though not of so bold a Nature; which was his introducing a Set of Rope-dancers, into the same Theatre . . . (*Apology*, pp. 184–5).

19–20 a Gentleman from *France*] Sir Harry Wildair.

21–2 a *French* Lady] probably Mme Subligny.

34 some Gentlemen in the Pit] Farquhar's reference is the only evidence of the noisily antagonistic first-night audience. During the season in which the play opened, prologists at Lincoln's Inn Fields were still condemning Farquhar for inferior playwriting.

38 the Changling] that is, *The Inconstant*, metamorphosed from *The Wild Goose Chase*.

48–55 The *New House* . . . t'other.] Farquhar may have made a veiled reference here to the opening of *The Stage-Coach* at Lincoln's Inn Fields, the 'new house'. The enigmatic statement seems to suggest that Farquhar's farce ran at Lincoln's Inn Fields on the sixth night of *The Inconstant* at Drury Lane. See p. 323 above.

62–3 our devotion to *Lent* and our Lady] that is, after Lent and Lady

Day. The death of King William on 8 March, three days after *The Inconstant*
was published, however, closed the theatres until after the coronation of
Queen Anne on 23 April; there is no indication of whether *The Inconstant*
played again that season after the theatres reopened.

68 Mr *Wilks*] Robert Wilks, who played Mirabel.

71 an Adventure of *Chevalier de Chastillon* in *Paris*] Stonehill (i. 395)
identifies Alexis-Henri, Chevalier (afterwards Marquis) de Châtillon
(1650–1737). The *Biographia Dramatica* claims that the original was 'an affair
of the like nature, in which the author had himself some concern when on
military duty abroad', a notion repeated by later scholars. Unless Farquhar
served with General Schomberg at the Boyne, he did not in fact perform
military duty abroad.

Prologue

10 *balderdash and brew*] adulterate or dilute. Balderdash means to mix
liquors with inferior ingredients; brew means to dilute liquors with water.
The wit in plays, then, is adulterated and diluted.

16 hogoes] a high or piquant flavour or an offensive taste or smell.

18 *your nice* Squeaker, *or* Italian *Capon*] Signor Clementine, the famous
eunuch, servant to the Elector of Bavaria, was hired by Drury Lane in the
spring of 1699 at a reported annual salary of £500.

19 *your* French *Virgin-Pullet*] a reference to Mme Subligny.

21 *Olio*] a highly spiced dish of various meats and vegetables stewed
together.

24 *dispense with*] put up with; make do.

24 *slender Stage-Coach Fare*] a punning reference to *The Stage-Coach*. The
farce is 'slender' in two ways, both slight in size and slight in value; when no
better theatrical nourishment is available, audiences can make do with it.

29 *Wild Fowl*] another pun, referring both to the theatrical bill of fare and
Mirabel, the 'Wild Goose'.

33 *up let the Musick strike:*] The first and second music were performed
before the Prologue was delivered in front of the curtain. Then, either before
or while the curtain was raised, the overture or 'curtain tune' was played
(Price, p. 55). The instrumental music or 'act tunes' for *The Inconstant* were
written by Daniel Purcell.

Dramatis Personæ

The names Mirabel and Oriana were directly borrowed from *The Wild
Goose Chase*, and Dugard is based on de Gard. The other names, however,
are new in Farquhar's version.

I. i

1–148 *Dugard . . .* happiness;] Farquhar echoes Fletcher only in the bare
outlines of the scene: the arrival of Dugard (de Gard) and his servant Petit
(Boy), the plans for dinner, the meeting with Oriana and Old Mirabel (La
Castre), Old Mirabel's inquiries about his son, Dugard's questioning

Oriana's physical, financial, and amatory situation. Specific verbal echoes
are noted below.

81–2 *Prester John*] an alleged Christian priest and king who supposedly
reigned in the Orient. After the fifteenth century he was identified with the
king of Abyssinia.

97–8 upon Sundays go first to Church and then to the Play] In London
the theatres were dark on Sunday. The play is, of course, set in Paris.

109–112 *Oriana. Pshaw, . . . Claret:*] *The Wild Goose Chase* reads:

> *Or.* Now I say hang the people: He that dares
> Believe what they say, dares be mad, and give
> His Mother, nay his own Wife up to Rumor;
> All grounds of truth they build on, is a Tavern,
> And their best censure's Sack, Sack in abundance:

113 Loches] small fish eaten to increase thirst while drinking.

116–18 *Dugard. Ay, but . . . thing,*] *The Wild-Goose Chase* reads:

> *de G.* Well, there is something, Sister.
> *Or.* If there be Brother,
> 'Tis none of their things, tis not yet so monstrous;
> My thing is Marriage:

119–20 young *Mirabel* Marry! he'll build Churches sooner;] an interesting
adaptation of the original occurs in this line. The original reads:

> *de G.* . . . He mary? he'll be hang'd first: he knows no more
> What the conditions and the ties of Love are,
> The honest purposes and grounds of Mariage,
> Nor will know, nor be ever brought t'endeavour,
> Than I do how to build a Church;

123 Converse] conversation.

159 hatching as warmly over a Tub of Ice] brooding over the ice in which
their drinks were cooling.

166 Guineas] Although the play is set in Paris, British denominations of
money are frequently mentioned.

166 Drugget] coarse woollen cloth.

166–7 Puff Wig] a wig with the back section queued and the side hair
rolled into puffs over foundations of frizzled hair.

167 Gentleman Usher] a gentleman acting as an attendant to a person of
superior rank, an officer at court or in a dignitary's household.

1. ii

[tavern scene] The tavern scene in 1. ii broadly imitates that in 1. ii of the
Wild-Goose Chase. Mirabel converses with Duretete instead of Pinac and
Belleur. The praise of Italy and its pleasures includes some verbal echoes
noted below. The section on Dutch and English women is entirely new.
Duretete's bashfulness, based on Belleur's, is discussed in similar terms. 1.
iii of the earlier play, in which La Castre, Nantolet, and the tutor Lugien
discuss the girls Rosalura and Lillia-Bianca and the girls talk to Mirabel, is
not included in Farquhar's version.

1–8 *Mirabel*. Welcome . . . Liquor.] *The Wild-Goose Chase*, i. ii, reads:
Mir. Welcom to *Paris* once more, Gentlemen:
  We have had a merry and a lusty Ord'nary,
  And wine, and good meat, and a bounsing Reckning;
  And let it go for once; 'Tis a good physick:
  Only the wenches are not for my dyet,
  They are too lean and thin; their embraces brawn-fall'n.
  Give me the plump *Venetian*, fat, and lusty,
  That meets me soft and supple; smiles upon me,
  As if a cup of full wine leap'd to kiss me;
  These slight things I affect not.

4–5 'tis a sure sign the Army is not paid] Farquhar's attributing the tawdriness of the women to the fact the military men were not paid is an original line inserted into an imitative passage.

12 *France*! a light unseason'd Country] Fletcher's line reads: 'You talk of *France*—a slight, unseason'd Country; . . .'.

14–20 Men . . . Women!] *The Wild-Goose Chase* reads:
  Men say we are great Courtiers, men abuse us:
  We are wise, and valiant too, *non credo Signior*:
  Our women the best Linguists, they are Parrats;
  O' this side the *Alpes* they are nothing but meer Drollaries:
  Ha *Roma la Santa*, *Italie* for my money:
  Their policies, their customs, their frugalities,
  Their curtesies so open, yet so reserved too.

20–1 not pester'd with a parcel of precise old gouty fellows] Fletcher's line reads 'Not pester'd with your stubborn precise puppies'.

20 precise] puritanical; over-strict in religious observance.

33 squab] short and fat. The characterization of the Dutch as heavy and broad-bottomed like their boats was a traditional one.

53–5 *Mirabel*. Pshaw . . . upon't.] Fletcher's Mirabel says:
Mir. *Belvere*, [Belleur] ye must be bolder: Travell three years,
  And bring home such a baby to betray ye
  As bashfulness? a great fellow, and a souldier?

73–8 *Mirabel*. Come, . . . Ass.] Fletcher's lines read:
Mir. You must now put on boldness; there's no avoyding it;
  And stand all hazards; fly at all games bravely;
  They'll say you went out like an Ox, and return'd like an Ass else.

76 Side-box Face] The side-boxes in the theatre were a good location for conducting flirtations during the course of a play.

96 souse] sou.

97 *Pistoles*] 97 See above p. 616.

103 Chiari] In the spring of 1701 Prince Eugene drove Marshal Catinat's French forces back to the River Oglio near Chiari, Italy. Entrenched at Chiari, he then repulsed an attack by Marshal Villeroi, Catinat's successor, on 1 September (Churchill, i. 536–8).

125 *Charmer*] The only usage cited in the *OED* for such a dance is this one.

125 *Morblew*] a comic oath attributed to French speakers, an alteration of

mort Dieu (*OED*).

137 two or three hundred of us stay'd behind] Luttrell recorded on 9 September 1701:

> This days Dutch post sayes, 17 batallions of the best troops of France carried on the attack upon the German camp; that only 6 of the imperialists and 4 companies of grenadeers were engaged; that the first lost 2 brigadeer generalls, 5 collonels, and 300 other officers, with 24 standards, 8 cannon, about 3000 common soldiers, and about 2000 taken prisoners (v. 88).

II. i

9–10 wear my Teeth to the stumps with Lime and Chalk] Peculiar appetites for eating chalk were attributed to young women and those who were pregnant. See *The Constant Couple*, v. iii. 71.

10 all your *Cassandra*'s and *Cleopatra*'s] *Cassandra* and *Cleopatra* were two multi-volumed French romances by Gautier de Costes, Seigneur de La Calprenède (1614–53). *Cassandra* contained the adventures of the Scythian prince Oroondates. *Cleopatra*, published in Paris in 1647–56 and in English frequently, recounted the tale of the supposed daughter of Antony and Cleopatra.

13 Fourbeleau'd Smocks] Bisarre's notion of applying furbelows to smocks was a jest at the absurdity of the highly fashionable, not a reference to an actual style.

20 contracted] English marriage contracts or spousals, signed by mutual consent either as a promise to marry in the future or a present acceptance of a marital relationship, were legally and morally binding documents (Alleman, p. 5).

22 broken an old *Broad-piece* between you] After the introduction of the guinea in 1663, the term broad-piece was applied to the twenty-shilling pieces of earlier reign, which were broader and thinner coins. The breaking of a broad-piece, with each partner keeping one part of the broken coin, was a traditional folk way of committing to marriage.

66 a Bull] an expression containing obvious contradiction in terms of involving an absurd inconsistency not perceived by the speaker (*OED*).

76–86 *Oriana. I hope . . . present.*] a loose imitation of part of a scene in *The Wild-Goose Chase*, II. i. The earlier play continues the discussion for a couple of pages. Farquhar returns to it in ll. 160 ff., but there are no verbal echoes.

138–9 *Barbara, Celarunt, Darii ferio, Baralipton*] The names that the medieval logicians introduced as mnemonic terms for the valid syllogisms (*The Encyclopedia of Philosophy*, ed. Paul Edwards, 8 vols. [New York and London, 1964], v. 66). The correct spelling is *Celarent*.

146–7 a Conquest above the *Alps*] a greater victory than Hannibal's conquest of the Alps.

151 Induction] an inducement.

153 *Categorimatice*] categorically.

204–22 Morals . . . Slave.] Mirabel's cynical commentary on deceit between men and women is particularly interesting in light of Farquhar's own marriage, in which, according to tradition, he was tricked into marrying a supposedly rich but actually impoverished widow with three children. The marriage has usually been dated, without the benefit of hard evidence, at about 1703, the year after *The Inconstant* opened. One of Farquhar's detractors jeered at the marriage in the facetious *Memoirs Relating to the late Famous Mr. Tho. Brown* (London, 1704): 'Bid *F—r* (tho' bit) to his Consort be just'.

273–4 A good Husband makes a good Wife at any time.] In *Sir Harry Wildair* the same sentiment is expressed when Standard asks Sir Harry how they can keep their wives 'very honest' and Angelica replies 'By being good husbands, Sir' (v. vi. 132).

284 Harts-horn] Oriana puns on Mirabel's reference to smelling salts with her own reference to a cuckold's horns.

II. ii

1–23 *Duretete.* And she's . . . fly.] a very loose imitation of part of a scene in *The Wild-Goose Chase*, II. ii, in which Pinac questions Lillia-Bianca's servant about his mistress. The details are, however, almost all changed.

6–8 But . . . Eye-brows.] Fletcher's lines read:

> Can ye sit seven hours together, and say nothing?
> Which she will do, and when she speaks speak Oracles;

12–13 *Petit.* But . . . laughing?] Fletcher's lines read:

> *Ser.* Can ye smile?
> *Pi.* Yes willingly:
>   For naturally I bear a mirth about me.
> *Ser.* She'll ne'r endure ye then; she is never merry;

14–15 she's a Critick, Sir, she hates a Jest, for fear it shou'd please her] Farquhar's contempt for critics' lack of a sense of humour is typical of the disregard in which playwrights held critics. However, Farquhar had particular reason to see critics as splenetic and unreceptive to humour, considering how they had treated his comedies.

24–117 *Bisarre. (With* . . . Dog] Bisarre taunts and teases Duretete in this scene in the same ways Lillia-Bianca puts Pinac through his dancing, singing, and drinking paces (II. ii). Specific verbal echoes are noted below.

37–40 you're very . . . come.] *The Wild-Goose Chase* reads:

> *Lil.* O ye are welcom,
>   Ye are very welcom, Sir, we want such a one;
>   Strike up again: I dare presume ye dance well:
>   Quick, quick, Sir, quick, the time steals on.
> *Pi.* I would talk with ye.
> *Lil.* Talk as ye dance.

44–50 Come . . . modest, Sir] Fletcher's lines read:

> *Lil.* Now how do ye, Sir?
> *Pi.* You have given me a shrew'd heat.
> *Lil.* I'll give ye a hundred.

> Come sing now, sing; for I know ye sing well.
> I see ye have a singing face.

Pi.   A fine Modesty!

Farquhar gives Pinac's line on modesty to Bisarre rather than Duretete.

48 a heavy dull Sonato face] Sonatas were instrumental compositions. Bisarre implies that she considers listening to concert music, as opposed to trying one's own dancing and singing, heavy and dull.

66–69 *Duretete.* Good Madam . . . us] *The Wild-Goose Chase* reads:

Pi.   Good Lady sit, for I am very weary;
>   And then I'll tell ye.

Lil.   Fie, a young man idle:
>   Up and walk; be still in action.

69–73 what . . . Madam.] The gossip, including tag-names, has all been updated by contemporary phrases and notions in Farquhar's version.

84–98 *Bisarre.* No! . . . imaginable,] Fletcher's lines read:

Lil.   Strike me another Galliard.

Pi.   By this light I cannot;
>   In troth I have sprain'd my leg, Madam.

Lil.   Now sit ye down, Sir,
>   And tell me why ye came hither, why ye chose me out?
>   What is your business? your errand? dispatch, dispatch;
>   May be ye are some Gentlemans man, and I mistook ye,
>   That have brought me a Letter, or haunch of Venison,
>   Sent me from some friend of mine.

Pi.   Do I look like a Carrier?
>   You might allow me what I am, a Gentleman.

Lil.   Cry'ye mercie, Sir, I saw ye yesterday,
>   You are new come out of Travail, I mistook ye;
>   And how do's all our impudent friends in *Italie*?

Pi.   Madam, I came with duty, and fair curtesie,
>   Service and honour to ye.

Lil.   Ye came to jeer me:

III. i

143–4 Crambo Songs] a contemptuous term for rhyming songs, such as those for which Motteux was noted, including the 'Stage-Coach Song'.

III. ii

30–1 Dutchess of *Burgundy*] The Duke of Bourgoyne or Burgundy, son of the Dauphin, grandson of Louis XIV, and presumably future king of France, had married a child-bride, Princess Marie-Adélaïde, in 1696, when he was thirteen and she was eleven. The Duchess became an arbiter of French taste. When *The Inconstant* was performed, she was only seventeen years old.

41–3 *At Regina . . . nefas.*] In quoting Virgil's *Aeneid*, Mirabel is taunting Bisarre. The quotations are not in chronological order, and they do not really make logical points. The first one comes from Book iv. 296, 305–6. H.

Rushton Fairclough translates, 'But the queen—who may deceive a lover? divined his guile . . . False one! didst thou hope also to cloak so foul a crime, . . . ?' (*Virgil*. With an English Translation by H. Rushton Fairclough [2 vols. The Loeb Classical Library, London and Cambridge, Mass., 1940], i. 415–17).

44 Pug] nasty slut or sorry jade (*NDCC*). Mirabel refers to the point in Book IV at which Aeneas abandons Dido.

48–9 the very place . . . tooth and nail] the scene in Book IV in which Aeneas confronts Dido with the news that he must leave. She has already discovered that the fleet is being armed and ready to sail. She is raging, runs raving through the city, then accosts Aeneas with the accusations quoted here.

54–5 *Nec . . . funere Dido*] Book IV, ll. 307–8. Mirabel assigns Bisarre poignant lines spoken by Dido. Fairclough translates, 'Can neither our love keep thee, nor the pledge once given, nor the doom of a cruel death for Dido?' (Fairclough, i. 417).

59–60 *quæ . . . Juno*] iv. l. 271: 'What shall I say first? What next? Now, now neither mighty Juno' (Fairclough, i. 421).

65–6 *Perfide . . . Tigres*] 366–7. 'False one! . . . but rugged Caucasus on his flinty rocks begat thee, and Hyrcanian tigresses gave thee suck' (Fairclough, i. 421). Mirabel continues to skip around; these lines precede the last quotation in Virgil.

69–70 *I sequere . . . possunt.*] iv. 381–2. 'Go, follow Italy down the winds; seek thy kingdom over the waves. Yet I trust, if the righteous gods can avail aught, that on the rocks midway . . .' (Fairclough, i. 421).

75 *Lybian*] a reference to Dido, queen of Libya.

76 the Tragedy of *Dido*] Marlowe and Nash wrote *The Tragedy of Dido* in 1594, long before Mirabel's time, but it was not performed on the Restoration stage according to extant records. However, an opera of *Dido and Aeneas*, with verse by Nahum Tate and music by Henry Purcell, was performed at Josias Priest's Boarding School in Chelsea in 1689.

77–80 the poor Lady . . . *Eneas*] iv. 388–93. Fairclough translates: 'So saying, she breaks off her speech midway and flees in anguish from the light, turning away, tearing herself from his sight, and leaving him in fear and much hesitance, though much he fain would say. Her maids support her, carry her swooning form to her marble bower, and lay her on her bed. But good Aeneas . . .' (i. 423).

80 *Pious Æneas*] The Latin passage reads 'At pius Aeneas', and Fairclough translates 'pius' as 'good'. Mirabel, however, translates *'Pious'*. 'Pius', a standing epithet for Aeneas in Virgil's epic, is one who observes all his duties to gods and men; there is no true English equivalent, but a schoolboy will render 'pious' till otherwise informed.

III. iii

7 Puss] hare.

28 Train] Trains were worn by women of rank and fashion when in full or court dress.

29–30 a front Row in the Box] a fashionable seat at the theatre.

32 *Couchee*] evening reception or assembly of company.

39 forbid the Bans] After the marriage contract was arranged, marriage banns were announced in church on three successive Sundays before the wedding ceremony took place (Alleman, p. 5). But the betrothal itself, which preceded the banns, was the important step.

40 cross-grain'd] cantankerous, irascible, and intractable.

III. iv

1–117 [Spanish marriage trick] This scene is based very loosely on *The Wild-Goose Chase*, in which de Gard disguises himself to convince Mirabel that Oriana has married a lord of Savoy.

27 *Trinidado*] a kind of tobacco from Trinidad, and probably the only 'Spanish' Old Mirabel could think of.

72 *Dulcinea*] Mirabel manages to insult Oriana as well as his father with his allusions to *Don Quixote*.

86 *Assa fœtida*] a resinous gum with a strong odour used as an antispasmodic.

87 the Mother] Fits of the mother, or hysteria, were sometimes treated by burning feathers under the nose of the patient.

87 Ratafia] 'A delicious Liquor made of Apricocks, or Cherries, with their Kernels bruis'd and steept in Brandy' (John Kersey, *Dictionary* [London, 1713]). Women were often satirized for sipping ratafia in their closets as an intoxicant.

IV. i

3 the privilege of the Grate] that is, to speak through the grate.

IV. iii

18–24 Ogle me . . . again] The passage in which Duretete gives Bisarre ogling practice is reminiscent of Steele's scene in *The Funeral*, I. ii. 54–60, in which the Widow Brumpton practices making 'a suddain Insurrection of Fine Wigs in the Pit, and Side-Boxes':

> Then with a pretty sorrow in one's Face, and a willing Blush for being Star'd at, one ventures to look round and Bow, to one of one's own Quality, Thus: (*Very Derectly.*) To a Smug Pretending Fellow of no Fortune, Thus: (*As scarce seeing him.*) To one that Writes Lampoons, Thus: (*Fearfully.*) To one one really Loves, thus: (*Looking down.*) To one's Woman Acquaintance, from Box to Box, Thus: (*With looks differently Familiar.*) (Steele, p. 31).

IV. iv

26 *con Pompos*] Petit's stab at '*non compos*'.

53.1–131 [Oriana's mad scene] This scene is, for the most part, very closely modeled on *The Wild-Goose Chase*, IV. iii, with Oriana's mad raving particularly close to the original.

56–62 *Old Mirabel.* Ay, poor . . . head is?] Fletcher's lines read:
> *De-G.*   And who am I?
> *Ori.*   You are *Amadis de Gaule*, Sir.
>   Oh, oh, my heart! were you never in love, sweet Lady?
>   And do you never dream of Flowres and Gardens;
>   I dream of walking Fires: take heed, It comes now,
>   Who's that? pray stand away; I have seen that face sure;
>   How light my head is.

57 *Amadis de Gaul*] Amadis, the title character in a fifteenth-century
Spanish or Portuguese romance first published in the sixteenth century, was
the son of the king of Gaul. As a child he was placed in an ark on the river;
as an adult he became the flower of chivalry. He loved Oriana, daughter of
the king of Great Britain. Through coming to the rescue of King Lisuarte,
he gained the hand of Oriana. The romance was translated into French in
1540 and into English in 1693.

68–71 *Oriana.* I cannot . . . Bury'd?] an almost exact imitation of the
original:
> *Ori.*   I cannot.
>   For I must be up to morrow, to go to Church:
>   And I must dress me, put my new Gown on,
>   And be as fine to meet my Love: Heigho!
>   Will not you tell me where my Love lies buried?

74–81 *Oriana.* How . . . Passing-Bell?] Again Farquhar echoes the
wording of *The Wild-Goose Chase*:
> *Ori.*   How soft you feel; how gentle?
>   Ile tell ye your fortune, Friend.
> *Mir.*   How she stares on me?
> *Ori.*   You have a flattring face; but 'tis a fine one;
>   I warrant you may have a hundred Sweet-hearts:
>   Will ye pray for me? I shall die to morrow;
>   And will ye ring the Bells?

80–1 Passing-Bell] death-bell or knell.

92–3 *Oriana.* What . . . pray.] The original reads:
> *Ori.*   Do you weep too? You have not lost your Lover?
>   You mock me: Ile go home and pray.

98–100 *Bisarre.* Let . . . you, Sir.] The parallel lines in *The Wild-Goose
Chase* are spoken by Lillia-Bianca and La-Castre:
> *Lil.*   Let her alone; she trembles.
>   Her fits will grow more strong, if ye provoke her;
> *La-Cast.*   Certain she knowes ye not, yet loves to see ye
>   How she smiles now:

103–22 *Durelete.* Where . . . Buffoon] This scene loosely paraphrases the
conversation between Mirabel and Belleur in *The Wild-Goose Chase*.

v . i

53–4 *Protestant Gentleman . . . flying for his Religion*] a Huguenot.

112 *Tages*] Tag was a word for the lowest class of people. Servants used it to mean a lower servant.

v. ii

26 *Mustapha*] the hero of *Ibrahim*, a romance by Madeleine de Scudéry, published in France in 1641 and translated into English in 1652 and 1674. A play by Roger Boyle, Earl of Orrery, called *Mustapha, The Son of Solyman the Magnificent* was first produced at Lincoln's Inn Fields on 3 April 1665, and the last recorded performance was by the United Company on 6 October 1686.

54 The New Song—*Prethee* Phillis] I have not found this song. Stonehill suggests, 'Prithee, tell me, Phillis, why so pensive now' in *Westminster Drollery*, ii. 1672 (i. 397), a song that could scarcely be considered new. Two songs called 'The Inconstant' also date from the first part of the century. One, by Leveridge, begins 'When I behold the shining Dame, / I vow eternal love' (copy in Folger M 1620 L66 copy 1 Cage, reprinted in *A Collection of Songs with the Musick by Mr. Leveridge*). The second begins 'Fair, and soft, and gay, and young, All charms she play'd, she danc'd, she Sung:' (copy in Folger M 1497 C42 v. 1 Cage; Carey is pencilled in as the author). However, there is no reason to believe that either of these songs was performed in Farquhar's play.

83 a Western Barge] The euphemistic language informs Mirabel that the First Bravo was transported for his crimes.

96 *Tompions*] Thomas Tompion (1639–1713), the renowned English clock-maker, who gained an international reputation and had his portrait painted by Godfrey Kneller.

v. iii

3 *Mirmidons*] The Myrmidons were a warlike race of ancient Thessaly who followed Achilles into the siege of Troy. The term was transferred to faithful soldiers, watchmen, bodyguards, or even sometimes servants.

9–20 tight and light, and the fitter for sailing] Bisarre uses suggestive language. Tight means neat in appearance. Both a light woman and a light frigate suggested a lewd woman or whore; her metaphor of a ship in itself has sexual overtones.

v. iv

18 Cashir'd] banned from military or other government service because of disgrace and disqualification.

38.2 *the Grand Musqueteers*] 'The Grand Musqueteers in France, are Troopers who fight sometimes on Foot, sometimes on Horseback; they are Gentlemen of good Families, and are divided into two Troops, the one called the Grey Musqueteers, because of the Colour of their Horses, the other the Black Musqueteers, for the same reason' (*Gentlemen's Dictionary* [London, 1705]).

83 a Cart] Bawds and prostitutes were punished by being whipped and

driven through the streets in a cart (see Commentary, *Love and a Bottle*, ii. ii. 383).

153–62 [SONG] According to the printed half-sheet broadside, the singer was Hughes, who is listed in the Drury Lane company for 1701–2. Mr. O—r, the lyricist, has not been identified.

Epilogue

0.4 Mr. *Wilks*] in the role of Mirabel.

14 Villeroy's *misfortune*] another reference to Cremona, where Prince Eugene's forces succeeded by sending a force through an aqueduct to open the gate for the main body of troops.

20 *the* Greek] Achilles.

21 *a ten years Seige*] the Trojan War.

The Twin-Rivals

Title-page

[motto] Thus you labour, but not for your own advantage. Virgil built a series of four lines on 'Sic vos non vobis' when Bathyllus, a rival, had claimed a couplet of his in honour of Augustus. The relationship of the motto to the play seems tenuous; Farquhar had been accused of plagiarism in *The Inconstant* and consequently perhaps did not feel he was getting proper credit for his work.

Dedication

0.4 *HENRY BRET*] Bret or Brett of Sandywell Park, Gloucestershire, has the reputation of being one of the most charming men about town at the turn of the century; Cibber describes him as having 'an uncommon Share of Social Wit, and a handsom Person, with a sanguine Bloom in his Complexion' (*Apology*, p. 201), and speaks of his wit as glowingly as Farquhar does. Brett was educated at Oxford, then came to London to enter the Temple but was never a serious law student. By 1700 he was a popular man about town with some interest in the theatre. That year he married Anne, the ex-wife of the Earl of Macclesfield, whose divorce proceedings in Parliament and whose two illegitimate children fathered by Richard Savage, Earl Rivers, scandalized and titillated the people of London. After his marriage, Brett was elected to Parliament for Bishop's Castle, Salop., three times between 1701 and 1708. In 1705 he obtained a lieutenant-colonelcy of a regiment of foot, but he did not stay with military life long. In 1707 he joined the management of Drury Lane, having got his patent from Sir Thomas Skipwith. Cibber claims him as a drinking-partner; he was also a member of Addison's circle at Will's and later Button's. Apparently the kind of personable, amusing, agreeable companion that charmed the witty, he seems to have had a particular interest in the theatre.

33–4 Decemb. 23. 1702.] The date of the dedication provides some insight into publication schedules. The play opened on 14 December. On 22

December Lintott paid Farquhar £15 for publication rights, and the
Dedication is dated 23 December. The play was published 29 December.
Although the Dedication, appearing in the prelims, would have been the
last part of the book composed, the entire printing schedule must have been
very rapid.

Preface

3 Mr. *Collier's short View*] Jeremy Collier's *A Short View of the Immorality and
Profaneness of the English Stage*, published in 1698, introduced a period of
intense pressure by reformers to cleanse the stage. Reformers harangued
seriously enough to worry companies about the morality of their performances;
actors and managers suffered not only through problems of filling the houses
but more directly through fines and jail sentences. Farquhar's first play,
Love and a Bottle, which appeared shortly after publication of Collier's
treatise, completely ignored the strictures expressed there, but in the next
few years his plays became less bawdy. *The Twin-Rivals* is strikingly different
from *Love and a Bottle* in treatment of rakishness and unwed motherhood; the
campaign of the reformers may well have affected Farquhar's playwriting as
it did the theatres' programming.

23 the Galleries were so thin] Because advertisements did not yet run
regularly in *The Daily Courant*, there is no indication of whether the first run
was successful and therefore extended. However, Farquhar's obvious
disappointment at thin houses and the rapidity with which the play went
into print suggest that the run was not long.

31 an *Odium* cast upon this Play before it appear'd] One must surmise
that the reformers attempted to suppress the play because of the portrayal of
the bawd-midwife Midnight and the pregnancy of Clelia; perhaps the
complaints are partial explanation for the fact that Clelia does not actually
appear on stage although she is central to the sub-plot.

56 *Long-Lane* Cloaths] Long Lane was a street, stretching from Smithfield
to Aldersgate Street, in which second-hand clothing dealers sold their
wares, a place 'of Note for the Sale of Apparel, Linnen, and Upholders
Goods, both second-hand and new, but chiefly for old, for which it is of
Note' (Strype, iii. 122).

96 Mr. *Longueville*] Longueville has been variously identified. The
Biographia Britannica (London, 1739) claims that Longueville was an
Irishman and a fencing-master, who laboured to produce a comedy but
never succeeded (v. 693). Archer, following the *DNB*, identifies him as
William Longueville (1639–1721), a friend of Samuel Butler and of the
Norths; later scholars have followed this tradition. Henry V. Longueville
was made a peer in 1700.

101–2 Foreign Assistance] Farquhar received criticism for plagiarism in
The Inconstant and for modelling Sir Harry Wildair in *The Constant Couple* on
Dorimant. Critics continued to condemn him as unoriginal. *Religio Poetae: or
A Satire on the Poets* (London, 1703), complained:

> His fame he built on might *D'avenant*'s wit,
> And lately own'd a play, that he ne'er writ:

and a marginal note names *The Twin-Rivals*. Farquhar's defensiveness about his originality is not surprising under the circumstances.

Prologue

0.2 *Motteux*] Having collaborated on *The Stage-Coach* and written the Prologue to *The Inconstant*, Motteux again had a hand in one of Farquhar's productions.

4 *invested*] besieged, beleaguered.

5 *Forlorn-Hope*] a select group of men, sent to the front to begin a siege; a storming party.

13 *Snip-Snap Wit*] smart repartee.

17 *Feints, Mines, and Countermines*] A feint is a military movement made to deceive the enemy concerning the real attack plans. A mine is a subterranean tunnel under the wall of a fortress to gain access or to cause the wall to fall. A countermine is a tunnel dug by the defenders to intercept the mine of the beseigers.

22 *Counterscarp*] An escarp is the steep wall or bank immediately below the rampart, usually the inner side of the ditch. a counterscarp is the outer wall or slope of the ditch which supports a covered way.

28 Venlo] The French fort at Venlo on the Meuse capitulated to the Allies on 18 September 1702 after a fierce hand-to-hand battle (Churchill, ii. 143–7). Fifteen hundred Frenchmen surrendered to a smaller British army. Luttrell (v. 217) reported that 182 cannon and 32 mortars were found in the castle.

28 Liège] Liège was an important enemy territory because it provided the only remaining passage by which the French garrisons on the Rhine could be reached by their troops. On 23 October 1702 Marlborough's men defeated the French troops at the citadel. The British casualties numbered about 500, approximately one-sixth of the total troops; more than a third of the enemy, a force of 8,000, were killed. Six days later the garrison at the Chartreuse surrendered. In all, the French lost almost ten thousand men either killed or captured (Churchill, iii. 144–52).

40 *the Third—And, if we may, the Sixth*] that is, for either one or two author's benefit performances.

I. i

25 breaking the Windows] Rakes were notorious for scouring, that is, roistering through the streets at night breaking windows, making commotion, and assaulting watchguards.

27 a Bush to a Tavern] the sign advertising the business of the establishment.

33 *Flying Post*] George Ridpath's thrice-weekly newspaper, also mentioned in *Love and a Bottle*. Presumably Richmore studied the advertisements for medicines that might cure the venereal ailments he acquired in his days of 'dirty Linnen, Pit-Masks', and other unhealthy habits. One such advertisement had been carried repeatedly in the *Daily Courant* in 1703:

A Doctor in Physick, Cures all the *Degrees, and Indispositions, in Venereal*

Persons; and by a most easie, safe, and expeditious Method: He likewise gives his Advice in all Diseases, and Prescribes a Cure. Dr. Harborough (*a Graduate* Physician) *in* Great Knight-Riders Street, *near* Doctors-Commons.

36 Pit-Masks] prostitutes that ply their trade in the pit at the theatre.

36 Hedge-Taverns] third-rate taverns: 'a Jilting, Sharping Tavern, or *Blind Ale house*' (*NDCC*).

37–8 the Ring, the Court, *Pawlet*'s and the *Park*] all fashionable spots in which to be seen. The Ring in Hyde Park is also mentioned by Farquhar in *The Constant Couple* and *Sir Harry Wildair*. Pawlet's was a fashionable and expensive entertainment spot; Isaac Reed notes on 20 June 1702 'a concert at Pawlett's Great Dancing-Room, near Dowgate. Singing by Mr. Hughes. Tickets, 1s. 6d.' (Notitia Dramatica in British Library, noted by Archer, p. 152). St. James's Park was a prominent spot to promenade.

54 Doctor *Chamberlain*] Hugh Chamberlain or Chamberlen (1664–1728) was noted for his skill in midwifery.

77–8 *Covent-Garden*, the low Suburbs of pleasure] Covent Garden was a fashionable area but was noted for 'the loose morality of those who dwelt in Covent Garden, and the libertinism of those visitors' (Wheatley, i. 462). Frequently mentioned in Restoration comedies, it is, for example, the scene of Dryden's *Sir Martin Mar-All* and John Crowne's *Sir Courtly Nice*. The epilogue to Dryden's *The Kind Keeper; or, Mr. Limberham* includes the lines:

> This town two bargains has not worth one farthing,
>
> A Smithfield horse—and wife of Covent Garden.

139 turn'd the Pad] robbed, became a footpad.

166 Chink] a colloquial expression for ready cash.

175 Whetting-Glass] a liquor glass.

238 a Covey of Pit-Partridges] Although the context here indicates the possibility that Balderdash refers to betting at the cockpit, Farquhar uses the same expression in *Love and Business*, clearly making a pun on women seated in the pit of the theatre:

> . . . I have had no Female in my Company since I left the Town, or any thing of your Sex to entertain me; for your *Essex*-Women, like your *Essex*-Calves, are only Butcher's Meat; and if I must cater for my self, commend me to a Pit Partridge, which comes pretty cheap, and where I have my Choice of a whole Covy; . . .

261 *Broad*] Jacob Broad, a famous bailiff. Archer (p. 159 n.) notes a reference in *The Comical and Tragical History of the Lives and Adventures of the most noted Bayliffs in and about London and Westminster* by Alexander Smith (London, 1723).

II. i

93–4 to make a *Vigo* Business of it, and break the Boom at once] Having suffered some ignominy by desultory operations at Cadiz, the second Duke of Ormonde and Sir George Rooke met unexpected victory over the French at Vigo Bay in October 1702, by capturing a Spanish treasure fleet laden

with millions of pounds of cargo from the Indies. To raid the harbour, they
had to break the boom and enter a long and completely landlocked harbour
under the heaviest attack from shore. Vice-Admiral Hopson in the *Torbay*,
followed by many English and Dutch battleships, broke the boom and
penetrated the inner harbour to lead the Allied troops into a battle 'fought
with indomitable fury'. The enemy fleet was entirely destroyed, and the
victors managed to capture treasure valued at a million pounds to bring
home to Britain (Churchill, iii. 162–4).

II. ii

23 *Rosa Solis*] a cordial originally made of the juice of the plant sundew,
but later a cordial of brandy with spices, sugar, and other essences (*OED*).

24 Orange-Waters] yet another cordial favoured by ladies.

25 *Nants*] Farquhar mentions Nantes brandy in *Sir Harry Wildair* and *The
Stage-Coach* as well. French brandies had become exorbitantly expensive
because of drastically increased duties in the 1690s and the resultant
decrease in the quantity imported. Clandestine shipments arrived, but the
prices were very high (Simon, iii. 130).

II. iii

12 *Jermain*-street] Jermyn Street, St. James's, runs from the Haymarket
to St James's Street, parallel with Piccadilly. Built in 1667, it was a
fashionable street with many prominent residents. Sir Isaac Newton, for
example, was one of the inhabitants at the time of the play, and
Marlborough had lived there while still Colonel Churchill (Wheatley, ii.
306–7). The Steward's Wife is expressing very high hopes about the
possibilities of profitable service.

26–7 You may easily sink it in the Charge of the Funeral] Funerals had
become outrageously expensive, the mourners paying heavily for the pomp
of a funereal procession. Charges were made for hiring mourners, for hiring
mourning clothes, for the coffin and its accoutrements, and sometimes for
embalming the corpse. Steele satirized the exorbitant charges of undertakers
in *The Funeral*, Act I.

134–5 a Cargoe of Witnesses and Usquebaugh] Subtleman relies on the
Irish for false witnesses. Usquebaugh comes from the Irish term for
'whiskey'.

II. iv

19 Standing Army] After the Treaty of Ryswick, which ended the war
with France in 1697, King William had hoped to maintain a standing army.
England had an army of 87,000 at the end of the war, and the King believed
that 30,000 troops would secure peace. However, Parliament, feeling the
heavy costs of the war, was unwilling to support more than 7,000
(Churchill, ii. 189).

44 the Reputation of Mareschal *Boufflers*] The outstanding French
Marshal Boufflers retreated repeatedly as Marlborough's troops captured

the forts on the Meuse in the late summer and autumn of 1702. The allied troops captured Kaiserwerth, Venlo, Stevensweert, Ruremonde, Maestricht, and Liège by the time Farquhar's play appeared (Churchill, iii. 141–56). Boufflers's reputation had, as a result, suffered, to the delight of the English.

46–7 our Sieges, our Capitulations, and Surrendries] a reference to the seesawing fortunes of the allied troops in the current war.

48 good Winter Quarters] In the first week of November the allied armies, except the troops assigned to take Rheinberg, dispersed into winter quarters (Churchill, iii. 156).

58 Basset-Bank] Anyone with enough cash will be able to enjoy the sport. For a description of the card-game basset, see Commentary, *The Constant Couple*, v. i. 124.

II. V

62 Foreign Evidences] the Irishmen that Subtleman uses to bear false witness.

67–80 [Young Wou'dbe's soliloquy] Rothstein finds the speech 'rather in the manner of Edmund in *King Lear*, particularly the Edmund in Nahum Tate's version of 1681' (p. 65).

III. i

22–3 Rehearsing these Three Years and a half] David Crauford or Crawford had first taken his play *Courtship A-la-Mode* to Lincoln's Inn Fields, where, he complained, it languished through many 'sham Rehearsals' but never neared production. Irritated, he brought it to Drury Lane, where it was 'cast to the best Advantage, and Plaid in less than twenty days', ornamented with a prologue by Farquhar.

However, as a rule plays were mounted hurriedly, within three or four weeks from the time rehearsal began. One suspects that the satire is aimed at Comick, who pretends to have a play ready to open, rather than at the theatres for their slowness.

28–9 You shou'd read the *Italian*, and *Spanish* Plays] The satire is not only aimed at the complexity of plotting in Italian and Spanish plays but also at the frequency with which English playwrights borrowed plots from the Continent.

35–6 Use your Interest with the General for that vacant Commission] Farquhar had some reason by 1702 and considerably more later in his career to be sceptical about military preferment. He had dedicated *Sir Harry Wildair* to the first Earl of Albemarle in 1701, probably in the hope of military preferment, but no commission resulted. Later, of course, he did manage to obtain a commission as a recruiting officer.

67 Train-Bands] groups of citizens trained as soldiers, in London and other parts of the country.

73 Buff-Coats] soldiers.

75 the *Rhine*] In the autumn and witner of 1701 the Margrave of Baden had created the Lines of Stollhofen on the Rhine, barring a French invasion down the Rhine valley. The lines proved impregnable until 1707 when

Marshal Villars defeated the troops there (Churchill, iii. 106).

83 *Round-House*] Rakehells and roisterers taken by the constables were thrown into the Round-House or Watch House in St. Martin's Lane for the night.

161 *White's*] White's Chocolate-House was established in St. James's Street in 1693 by Francis White and moved to larger quarters on the same street in 1697. In 1702 White also leased the house next door. White's became a celebrated gathering-place for fashionable gentlemen and also a rendezvous for sharpers ready to profit from the gambling that took place there (Lillywhite, p. 639). Steele in the *Tatler* addressed accounts of gallantry, pleasure, and entertainment from White's. Farquhar also alludes to White's in *Love and a Bottle* and *Sir Harry Wildair*.

III. ii

81 *Friars*] The liberty of Whitefriars, nicknamed Alsatia, in which sanctuary was extended by law to debtors, became a favourite haunt for many kinds of criminals avoiding the law, including false witnesses as well as forgers, prostitutes, highwaymen, and various kinds of cheats. Although Whitefriars' sanctuary was legally abolished in 1623–4, the tradition continued. In 1696–7, a new law was passed to compel sheriffs to arrest debtors taking refuge there; yet another such law was passed in 1727 (Sir William Holdsworth, *A History of English Law* [London, 1924; repr. 1966], iv. 523; vi. 408; John Charles Cox, *The Sanctuary Seekers of Mediaeval England* [London, 1911], p. 336).

IV. i

42 *Lombard-street*] a street 'inhabited by goldsmiths, bankers, merchants, and other eminent tradesmen' (John Strype, ed. *A Survey of the Cities of London and Westminster*. By John Stow [2 vols., London, 1720], ii. 152).

72 Manto maker] sempstress.

96 follow the Tipstaff] go to law. The tipstaff was the constable or bailiff.

104 retort] hurl back a weapon toward the striker.

124 *Clifford*'s Inn] an inn of Chancery connected with the Inner Temple.

143 President] an obsolete spelling of 'precedent'.

IV. iii

2 *Spunging-house*] a house in which bailiffs interred debtors during preliminary confinement before prison. Friends might, during that time, settle the debt.

23 Point *de Venice*] very expensive lace.

24 *Kidderminster*] The town of Kidderminster in Worcestershire was known for its manufacture of carpets.

V. i

15 the Passage at the old Playhouse] Play-House Passage, which led to the Drury Lane Theatre in which *The Twin-Rivals* played, was notorious for

prostitutes seeking clients.

17 *Rosamond*'s Pond] The pond in St. James's Park was associated with lamenting lovers and ill-starred romances. It is frequently mentioned in plays of the period, for example, in Southerne's *The Wives' Excuse*, Cibber's *Love's Last Shift*, and Congreve's *The Way of the World*.

17–8 *Chequer* Ale-house in *Holbourn*] an inn on the north side of Holborn, east of Furnival's Inn (Henry A. Harben, *A Dictionary of London* [London: 1918], p. 138).

v. ii

6 St. *Albans* Tavern] Founded in the late seventeenth century, in 1692 it was kept by the butler of the Prince of Denmark (Lillywhite, p. 496). Located in St Alban's Street, Pall Mall, during the course of the eighteenth century it became fashionable for dinners and political meetings (Wheatley, i. 12).

18 in the King's Name] It is odd that Farquhar did not write 'in the Queen's Name'.

v. iii

20 *Bridewell*] Prostitutes and vagrants were committed to Bridewell. Beating hemp was one of their occupations, often referred to in literature.

109 Don *John*] Don Juan's name was anglicized in Shadwell's *The Libertine*, which first ran in 1675.

v. iv

145–6 Maishter *Fuller*] Archer and Stonehill agree with Ewald that William Fuller, an infamous 'impostor, cheat and false accuser' was intended. Fuller had recently been pilloried three times and was in prison (Archer, p. 238).

Epilogue

7 *a hard struggling Part*] Mrs Hook played the role of Aurelia.

15 *no Power can Save it*] Farquhar's prologue to David Crauford or Crawford's *Courtship A-la-Mode*, which opened 9 July 1700, contained the lines:

> For if the Play be good it need not crave it;
> If bad, no Prologue on the Earth can save it.

24 *this Female Reign*] Queen Anne's coronation had occurred seven and a half months before the opening of the play.

EMENDATIONS OF ACCIDENTALS

LOVE AND A BOTTLE

Title Page. *Tristia*] ed.; Trist.

Prologue. 7 *arms:*] Q2; ~?   8 *Charms?*] Q2; ~.

Dramatis Personæ. [o.1] Dramatis] Q2; Drammatis   12 *Pamphlet*] Q2; Phamphlet

I. 12 friend?] Q2; ~;   81 Dancing-Master] Q2; ~-|~   82 Beau-makers] Q2; ~-|~   99 Gentleman] Q2; ~-|~   109 Broad-side] Q2; Broad-|side 122 thou'rt] Q2; thou'at   167 Adders.] Q2; ~.,   173 Wild-fowl] Q2; ~-|~   215 sure. Q2; ~^   217 drove] Q2; droye   295 understand] Q2; ~-|~   365 kinder] Q2; kiunder   372 Lips!] Q2; ~!! 382 downright] Q2; ~-|~   411 Maidenheads] Q2; ~-|~   417 I'll—] Q2; ~.—   422 Sirrah] Q2; Sarrah   463 trudg'd] Q2; trug'd 480 things] Q2 [Things]; thing [In Q1 the 's' slipped to the following line.] 482 School] Q2; Shool

II. i. 13 over-night] Q2; ~-|~   18 Peripatetick] Q2; Perigatetick 33 themselves] Q2; themselyss   46–7 Snuff-|boxes] ed.; ~-~ 57–8 Chocolate-|house] ed.; ~-~   71 Varieties] Q2; Varities   99 Petycoat] Q2 [Pettycoat]; ~-|~   108 say.] Q2; ~:   142 squawling] Q2; squalawing 148 ago] Q2; a go

II. ii. o.2 *Flute, a*] ed.; *Flutea*   3 deral—Toes] Q2; ~^~   13–14 'Squire *Mockmode*] Q2; 'Siquire ~   24 Nobleman] Q2; ~-|~   28 pronunciation] Q2; pronunciation   47 O] Q2; Of   64 *Bells*] ed.; Bells   72 Bass-Viol] Q2; Bass-Vial   272 infallibly] Q2; infalliblly   284 instantly] Q2; ~^ 337 there] Q2; their   342 by't.] Q2; ~^   344 *Tagrhime*] Q2; *Tagrhine* 397 Mistress] O1; Mistristess

III. i. 4.1 *Allison*] ed.; *Allinson*   59 with] Q2; whit   71 all:] O1; ~^ 80–1 hard-|hearted] ed.; ~-~   140 home?] O1; ~.   208 Poet] Q2; Peot   216 Gone!] Q2; ~;   240–1 Lap-|Dog] ed.; ~-~   261 with me,] Q2; ~,~^   Choice] Q2; chocie   262–3 Maiden-|head] ed.; ~-~

III. ii. 11 penn'd] Q2; penn'p   60 Dungeon] Q2; Dugeon   66 Sir.] Q2; ~,   108 something] Q2; ~-|~   147 Gentlemen] Q2; ~-|~ 153 understand] Q2; ~-|~   162 Corn-cutter] Q2; ~-|~   199 Secrets] Q2; Secreets   243 *Tyrant*] Q2; Tyant   305 C,] O1; ~.

IV. i. 2 Sweetmeats] Q2; ~-|~   18 Vain;] O1; ~.   21 again.] Q2; ~^ 27–8 Hungary-|bottle] ed.; ~-~   28–9 *Hungary-*|bottle] ed.; ~-~   62 opinion] Q2; opionion   88 methinks] Q2; ~-|~

IV. ii. 67 sometimes] Q2; ~-|~   73 Upholders] Q2; ~-|~   81 undertake]
Q2; ~-|~   138 , before] Q2; ~,   191 bantered,] Q2; ~.   213 Tongue]
Q2; Tongne

IV. iii. 13 You're] Q2; you're   22 guess] Q2; geuss   29 shrivel'd] Q2;
shrvel'd   99.2 meeting] Q2; *meetting*   137 extreamly] O1; extteamly
163 mischief] Q2; mifchief   174.1 *laughing*] Q2; *lauhging*

IV. iv. 13 Dear?] Q2; ~∧   43 proclaims] Q2; prolaims   71 Footmen]
Q2; ~-|~   75 loves] Q2; Love's   83.1 *Fourth*] Q2; *Third*

v. i. 0.1 V] Q2; IV   82 see that] Q2; seethat   110 court] Q2; couat
133-4 other-|wise] ed.; otherwise   188 little] Q2; litlte

v. ii. 5 I] Q2; l   11 *Club*, Mr.] Q2; ~, ~,   17 Gentleman] Q2;
Getleman   25 Master.] O1; ~,

v. iii. 5 ruin'd,] Q2; ~∧   57 foul.] Q2; ~,   99 tow'rds—] O1; ~∧
137 Gentlemen] Q2; ~-|~   165 Disguise] Q2; Disuise

THE CONSTANT COUPLE

Preface. 4 Virgin] Q3; Vigin

Dramatis Personæ. 0.1 Personæ] Q2; Persona

I. i. 19-23 Rooted' out . . . *Angelica*'s Scorn] 1728; [set as verse] Many subsequent
lines in the play were originally set as verse although they were not poetry. They have
been silently changed in this edition.   203 fortnight] Q4; ~-|~   209 Sir.]
Q2; ~,   312 Foxhunting] 1710; ~-|~

II. ii. 5 one.] ed.; ~∧   29 Gentleman] O1; ~-|~

II. iv. 51 so ∧] Q2; ~'

III. i. 81 says] Q2; shays

III. iii. 85 Nay] Q2; Noy   138 Shoulders.] Q2; ~∧   186-7 Gentle-|men]
ed.; Gentlemen

IV. i. 4 What∧] Q2; ~,   42 Something] Q4; ~-|~   65 Overwhelm] Q2;
~-|~   86 Gentle-|man] ed; Gentleman   141 succeeds?] Q3; ~;

IV. ii. 212 *Petty-Larceny*] Q4; *Petty-Lacenary*

v. i. 55 Blanket,] Q3; ~;   118 score] Q3; scorce   136 Women] Q3;
Wome

v. ii. 4 Bookseller] Q3; ~-|~   8 *a piece*] Q3; ~-|~ O1 reads 'apiece'.
19 Broom-staff] Q4; ~-|~

v. iii. 22–3 Me-|thinks] ed.; Methinks   27 Basilisks] Q2; Basiliksks
61–2 Door-|nail] ed.; ~-~   94 injures] Q3 [Injures]; injure
170 which∧] Q2; ~;

Appendix A. 38 upon] ed; ~-|~   47 Gentlewoman] ed.; ~-|~
107 henceforth] ed.; ~-|~

SIR HARRY WILDAIR

Dedication. 5 Habit] O1; Hahit   30 sometimes] ed.; ~-|~
37 without] ed.; ~-|~

Dramatis Personæ. 6 *Jubilee*-Beau] O1 [Jubilee-~]; Jubile-~

I. 13 Colonel] ed.; Coll.   26 Peruke.] O1; ~∧   34 and] O1; aud
117 Colonel] ed.; Coll.   120 Colonel] ed.; Coll.   153 upon] ed.; ~-|~
265 marry'd∧ her,] O1; ~, ~∧   290 Basset] ed.; *Basset*   291 Refugee] ed.;
Refugee 295 Faithful.] O1; ~∧   325 your] O1; yonr   336 us] O1; ns
337 *French*] O1; *Freneh*   341 and whining] O1; aud   370 Heretick] O1;
Hererick

II. i. 32 Colonel] ed.; Coll.   33 Colonel] ed.; Coll.   35 Colonel] ed.; Coll.
36 Colonel] ed.; Coll.   61 can't] O1; can'f   66 Madam.] O1; ~,
74 Contour] ed.; Countour   85 speak.] O1; ~∧   91 Night,] O1; ~, and
if] O1; andf   98 Colonel] ed.; Coll.   119 Gentlemen] O1; ~-|~
133 you.] O1; ~∧   137 Sea-monster] O1; ~-|~   141 Wife,] O1; ~;
173 bus'ness] ed.; bu'ness   181 something] O1; ~-|~   193 Humour] O1;
Humonr   206 Colonel] ed.; Coll.   209 *Colonel*] ed.; *Coll.*   229 next]
O1; nex   230 opportunity] O1; opporrunity   240 I] O1; l   279
Colonel] ed.; Coll.

II. ii. 39 Captain] ed.; Capt.   99 Mortgage] O1; Mortage   108 *service.*]
O1; ~∧   121 He] O1; he

III. i. 4 Bich.] O1; ~∧   34 *Lurewell*] O1 [*Lure.*]; *Eur.*   41 drawn,] O1; ~-
67 now of] O1; nowof   128 Some] O1; some   128–9 time ago] O1;
timeago   133 Colonel] ed.; Coll.   134 methinks] ed.; ~-|~   Ear,] O1;
135 Colonel] ed.; Coll.   168 Colonel] ed.; Coll.   183 Colonel] ed.; Coll.
190 of Style] O1; ofStyle   195 *Yours,*] O1;   219 Main-top-Sail-yard] O2;
~-~-~-|~

III. ii. 28 Handkerchief] O1; Handerchief   64 understands] O1; ~-|~
66–7 Gentle-|man] ed.; Gentleman

IV. i. 81 *Shark.*] O1; Shark∧

iv. ii. 124–5 Play-|house] ed.; ~-~   195 St.] O1; S.   246 and] O1; nnd
287 wonderfully] O1; wouderfully   299 *Harry,*] O1; ~.

v. iv. 29 *Beau-monde*] ed.; ~-|~

v. v. 24 *Pardonnez*∧] ed.; ~,

v. vi. 147 leave] O1; Ieave.

Epilogue. 14 Snuff-Box] O1; Suff-Box

THE STAGE-COACH

1. 14 does] Q2; dos   119–20 Coach-|men] ed.; ~-~   181 about.] Q2; ~,
187 you.] Q2; ~,   190 Block-head] ed.; ~-|~   202 Pound] ed; Ponnd
[Pounds Q2]   207 Esquire.] Q2; ~;   295 De'el] 1718; Dee'l
299 we.] Q2; ~,   327 does] Q2; dos   409 Devil, the [om.]] Q2; ~,~ the
447 *Captain*!] 1718; ~| 467 Niece] 1718; Niecc   508 Broken-back] ed; ~-|~
535 Carbonade] Q2; Carbonado

Dedication. 34 (as] ed; ~(

THE INCONSTANT

Dedication. 0.2 Richard] ed.; Rich.   18 upon] o1; up-|on

Preface. 15 be made] O1; bemade   38 over-fondness] ed.; ~-|~   46 or]
O1; ar   66–7 out-|acted] ed.; ~-~

I. i. 20 *Mirabels*] O2; Mirabel's   33 within] O1; ~-|~

I. ii. 26 understand] O1; ~-|~   83 Why∧] 1715; ~,   97 *Pistoles*] 1728;
Pistols   105 scurvy] O1; seurvy   128–9 Gun-|powder] ed.; ~-~

II. i. 23 something] O1; ~-|~   38 Gentleman] O1; ~-|~   100 Ladyship]
O1; ~-|~   112 Ladyship's] O1; ~-|~   153 *Categorimatice*.] O1; ~∧
161 humour] O1; humonr   297 are] O1; ara

II. ii. 6 without] O1; ~-|~   112 Ha] O1; ha   113 Was] O1; was

III. i. 110 Gentleman] O1; ~-|~

III. ii. 77 into] O1; ~-|~

III. iv. 68 your new] O1; yournew

III. v. 15 ff. *First Gentleman*.] ed.; 1 *Gen.*   17 ff. *Second Gentleman*.] ed.; 2 *Gen.*
33–4 Sowre-|fac'd] ed.; ~-~

IV. i. 10 come to] O1; cometo   30 into] O1; ~-|~

IV. ii. 43 Coxcomb] 1728; ~-|~   60 Pasport] 1728 [*Passport*]; ~-|~
77 already.] O1; ~∧   139 again.] O1; ~∧   153 Boy] O1; *Boy*
158 *Mirabel*] ed.; M.r.

IV. iii. 25 Proud—] O1; ~∧   38 Sir.] O1; ~,   40 ha.] O1; ~,
41 ha.] O1; ~,   47 *First Lady*] ed.; 1. *Lady*

IV. iv. 44 Your] O1; your   53 she,] O1; ~∧   149–50 Life-|long] ~-~
150 Gentlemen] O1; ~-|~   157 horrid] O1; horrrid   171 the devouring]
O1; theidevouring

v. i. 39 Partridge] O1; Patridge   49 shame,] O1; ~∧   70 Sirrah] O1;
Sarra   97 quiet.] ed.; ~∧   The] O1; the   114 Sirrah] O1; Sarrah
123 Cat,] O2; ~∧

v. ii. 1 somthing] 1728 [something]; ~-|~   21 mutual] O1; mututal
23 In] O1; in   32 Friends,] O1; ~∧   43 Ha] O1; ha   55 Certainly] O1;
certanily   74 Please] ed.; please   81 ff. *First Bravo*] ed.; 1 *Bra.*, 1*st. Bra.*
81 Yes] O1; yes   84 Gentleman] 1728; ~-|~   91 ff. *Second Bravo*] ed.;
2 *Bra.*, 2*d. Bra.*   106 Gentlemen] O1; Gentilemen   109 swôrn.] O1; ~∧
114 Looke] O1 [Look'e]; looke   116 servant.] O1; ~∧   118 him?] O1; ~.
122 health.] O1; ~;   125 Gentleman] ed.; ~-|~   127 How] O1; how
128 I] O1; *I* In the following scene, all other italic *I*'s, used in a shortage here, have
been silently changed to roman.   135 Eh] O1; eh   136 heer] ed.; hee'r
176 ff. *Third Bravo*] ed.; 3*d. Bra.*   179 have∧] O1; ~.   181 there-|fore] ed.;
therefore

v. iii. 29 The] O1; the   37 me∧] ed.; ~.   40 Now a] O1; now ~
41 Now] O1; now   43 ay.] O1; ~,

v. iv. 18 ff. *Fourth Bravo*] ed.; 4*th. Bra.*   31 mine—] ed.; ~∧   32 mine—]
ed.; ~∧   33 mine—] ed.; ~∧   37 Child? O1; ~∧   38 Sir.] O1; ~,
50 adsmylife] ed.; ads-|mylife   68 pieces alive] O1; piecesa-|live   98 Ruffians]
ed.; *Ruffians*   106 *Oriana.*] O1; ~∧   144 Behold] O1; behold   145 off.]
O1; ~∧   147 Sex.] O1; ~∧   There] O1; there   150 Happiness.]
ed.; ~,   A] ed.; a   154 *here.*] O1; ~∧

Epilogue. 28 'em] O1; e'm

THE TWIN-RIVALS

Dedication. 18 himself] O1; ~-|~

Preface. 24 Splenetick] O1 [splenetick]; *Splentaick*   75 Constitution] O1;
Censti-|on   84 overdone] ed.; ~-|~

I. i. 4 himself] O1; ~-|~

I. ii. 5 *Stillborn*] O1; ~-|~   66 Reputation] O1; Reputatioh

II. ii. 24 *Ratafia*'s] O1; *Ratifia*'s

II. v. 42–3 under-|stand] ed.; understand

III. i. 20 one.] O1; ~?   45 Gentleman] O1; ~-|~   100 it,] O2; ~;

III. ii. 4 Friends:)] O1; ~:∧   23–4 here-|abouts] ed.; hereabouts
105 Tish] O1 ['Tish]; tish   110 noo.] O1; ~∧

III. iii. 121 here.] O1; ~∧   161 elsewhere] O1; ~-|~

IV. i. 134 Lordship] O1; ~-|~   136 whenever] O1; ~-|~   160 know] O1; kuow   225 Secret] O1; Sccret   227–8 Eldest-|born] ed.; ~-~ 239–40 over-|hearing] ed.; ~-~   308 Rent-charge] O1; ~-|~

IV. iii. 22–3 Head-|work] ed.; ~-~

IV. iv. 5 You] O1; you   40–1 Lord-|ships] ed.; Lordships

V. i. 7 midnight] O1 [Midnight]; ~-|~   77–8 Rake-|helly] ed.; Rakehelly 131 already] O1; alrerdy

V. ii. 38 presently] O1: pre-|ently

V. iii. 31 For] O1; *for*

INDEX